53 SPACE-SAVING BUILT-IN FURNITURE PROJECTS

53 SPACE-SAVING BUILT-IN FURNITURE PROJECTS

BY PERCY W. BLANDFORD

FIRST EDITION

THIRD PRINTING

Printed in the United States of America

Library of Congress Cataloging in Publication Data

Blandford, Percy W.
53 space-saving, built-in furniture projects.

Includes index.
1. Built-in furniture. I. Title. II. Title: Fifty three space-saving, built-in furniture projects.
TT197.5B8B527 1983 684.1'6 83-4849
ISBN 0-8306-0504-5
ISBN 0-8306-1504-0 (pbk.)

Cover illustration by Al Cozzi.

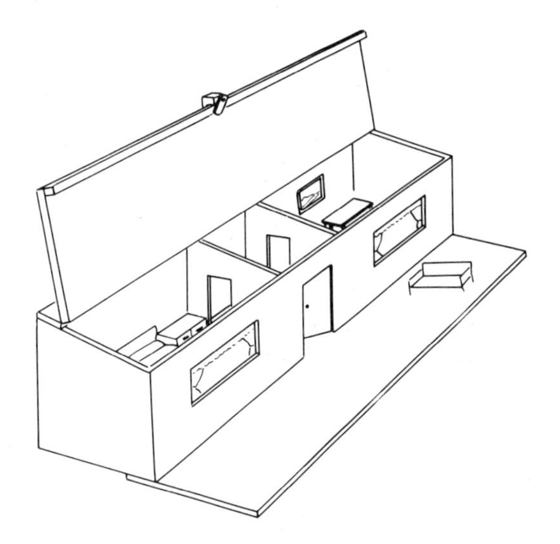

Contents

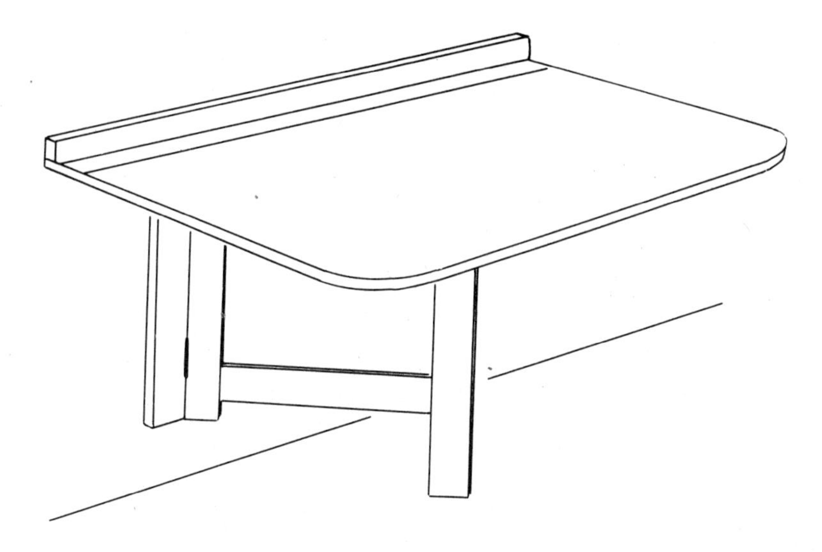

Introduction

BUILT-IN FURNITURE IS A COMPARATIVELY MODern idea. Most of our forefathers had portable furniture, and it was unusual to attach furniture to the walls or floor. There is obviously a place for freestanding furniture and we cannot do without it, but the intelligent use of built-in furniture increases comfort and convenience in the home. Usually anything built-in occupies less space than a freestanding piece that would otherwise be needed, and that may be an important consideration in a small room.

Most quantity-produced furniture that may be bought is freestanding, so anything we buy is likely to be the same as that bought by many other people. Built-in furniture usually has to be made to suit a particular position and situation. It is difficult to prefabricate built-in furniture. A few items are intended to go flat on or against a wall, but even they have to be to an estimated size. You should be able to produce an alternative piece designed for the particular place.

Although you may make portable furniture, it is rewarding when you discover that you can tailor built-in furniture to a particular place. You can exercise your skill in fitting wood exactly to its surroundings and can make the sizes that you want. You are tackling craftsmanship that cannot be matched by anything mass-produced and doing something that would be very costly if a professional craftsman was employed to do it.

When furniture is built-in, the house structure forms part of it. How much depends on what is being made, but as you build, the house gives rigidity and strength. It may take the place of some parts that would have to be made for a similar freestanding piece. This works to your advantage. Making built-in furniture is usually easier. The faces of the furniture should be a quality matching other furniture, but what comes behind uses the wall and can normally be of simpler construction, yet of more than adequate strength.

This book consists mainly of projects. Sizes are given for many of them, but these are intended more as a guide to proportions and detail dimensions. You must adapt to suit after measuring the place the furniture is to occupy. All sizes quoted are in inches unless marked otherwise. I assume that you have a basic knowledge of tool handling but offer guidance where special techniques are needed.

I hope that you will find plenty of ideas for built-in furniture in this book. Making built-in furniture grows on most do-it-yourself homeowners.

Other TAB books by the author:

No. 894 *Do-It-Yourselfer's Guide to Furniture Repair & Refinishing*
No. 937 *Modern Sailmaking*
No. 1044 *The Woodturner's Bible*
No. 1179 *The Practical Handbook of Blacksmithing & Metalworking*
No. 1188 *66 Children's Furniture Projects*
No. 1237 *Practical Knots & Ropework*
No. 1247 *The Master Handbook of Fine Woodworking Techniques and Projects*
No. 1257 *The Master Handbook of Sheetmetalwork . . . with projects*
No. 1312 *The GIANT Book of Wooden Toys*
No. 1365 *The Complete Handbook of Drafting*
No. 1424 *Constructing Tables and Chairs . . . with 55 Projects*
No. 1454 *Constructing Outdoor Furniture with 99 Projects*
No. 1574 *The Illustrated Handbook of Woodworking Joints*
No. 1634 *Rigging Sail*
No. 1644 *Maps & Compasses: A User's Handbook*
No. 1664 *Building Better Beds*

Chapter 1

Design

BUILT-IN FURNITURE IS INTENDED TO BE FAIRly permanent. With other furniture you can move it about, try different positions, revise room arrangements, or put the furniture into storage or discard it. Built-in furniture needs to be in the right place to serve a purpose and to look attractive and functional. It becomes more of the room's decoration than does a freestanding piece. Before you rush into making built-in furniture, you have to establish a need for it. There are many advantages in built-in furniture, but if you tackle the job too hastily and have to live with something that does not quite serve your purpose or is the wrong shape or proportions, correcting the mistake may be a frustrating and time-consuming task.

Built-in furniture makes the most of any room's size. For a particular purpose, it may take up less space than an equivalent piece of independent furniture. Sometimes it can provide some service that could not be managed otherwise in the available area. If built-in furniture is supported only on the wall and does not reach the floor, it can make more use of the room size, because something else can go below it. Even if nothing is put below it, it frees floor area that might otherwise be too restricted.

Built-in furniture may provide strength with lightness. If the structure of the house is taking some load, the parts of the piece of furniture do not have to be as strong individually, and some may actually be omitted. When furniture is built-in, you do not have the problem of stability. If you want to make something that will be freestanding, it has to be given proportions that will keep it from being tipped over. Sometimes that means making the piece broader than its needs warrant so it is sufficiently stable. A similar built-in item need have no bigger area than the purpose requires, as the attachments to the wall ensure absolute stability.

SIZES

Later examples show proportions and sizes for particular purposes, but there are occasions where you will have to adapt or design a piece of furniture to suit the available wall and floor area that you want to use to the best advantage. Measurements normally have to be arranged to suit people of average size. If what you are making is for a particular user, you can add or subtract to suit his or her size. This applies to children, but you have to remember that children grow—often more rapidly than we expect. Sometimes you can arrange such things as tabletops so they can be raised as a child gets taller. If you are catering for exceptionally tall people, they will appreciate sizes to suit their needs instead of having to adapt to small and cramped sizes.

Measure other furniture in the room. If it is a seat you are building in, the height can be matched to chairs that will be used with it. It may help to put a working surface at the same height as an existing table. You may find a need sometimes to bring a table alongside a working top to make a combined large table. Similarly, a built-in seat may also be used at a table when a crowd has to be seated.

Seats usually are between 15 inches and 17 inches high for use at a table. A person of average height should be able to sit with his or her thighs parallel with the floor. A lounging seat can be a few inches lower, but usually its front is within that range. The back of the seat is lower. If seating is upholstered or cushions are to be used, the height that matters is where the padding is compressed (Fig. 1-1A). Quite thick upholstery goes down to only about 1 inch when sat on.

The height of a working surface should usually be the same as a table, which is within an inch or so of 30 inches (Fig. 1-1B). If the surface will be used by a person standing, it can go up to about 36 inches. When it may also be used with a chair, you should keep the height near 30 inches. A standing person can still work on that height, but a user with an ordinary chair will find the higher surface impossible. The alternative is to make the height to suit standing, then provide taller stools, as is often done at a bar.

A working surface needs to be wide enough, but an excessive width will use up floor space. Much can be done on a width from the wall of only 12 inches, but an 18-inch width is better for a desk or similar top. If there is space available, a 24-inch width allows a student to spread books around, to use a small drawing board, or research among many papers. If what you are building will fit into an alcove, that may decide the width you use. It is always possible to bring the top out from the recess without affecting the rest of the room. Such an arrangement may look more attractive than keeping the edge flush (Fig. 1-1C).

Much built-in furniture provides storage space, either in the form of shelves for books and other things, or enclosed to provide hanging space for clothing. In a kitchen or bathroom there may be storage for the many things used in those places. You may want to store tools on racks in a shop. Consider access. Most of us do not want to bend if it is possible to get at something while standing. Also, we do not want to reach very high. The preferred positions are between table height (about 27 inches) and head height (about 70 inches). We may want to make the most use of the whole height, but it helps to put what will be wanted more between these heights. It does not make sense to put heavy things higher, so they can go below 27 inches, while light and compact things not often required can go much higher (Fig. 1-1D). A user then deals with most things at a comfortable height, but he or she may have to bend for low things (Fig. 1-1E) and stretch or use a stool for the very high things.

Another size consideration concerns how much of a wall to use. If there is a projecting fireplace or something else that produces recesses, you will almost certainly want to build in to the total size of a space and either set back, come flush with the front, or project, depending on how much of a recess there is. If it is a full wall, you may build in all over it, possibly making the back to front basic size about 8 inches to take care of books and other things. You may increase the width at some places, possibly to take care of a television set or record player. You will be reducing the size of the room's floor area by 8 inches everywhere and more in places. Can that much be allowed?

RELATING TO ROOM

A built-in fitment can be arranged to suit other furniture. In the bedroom there may be a space for the bedhead, then the new furniture can go floor to ceiling and provide about all the storage you need,

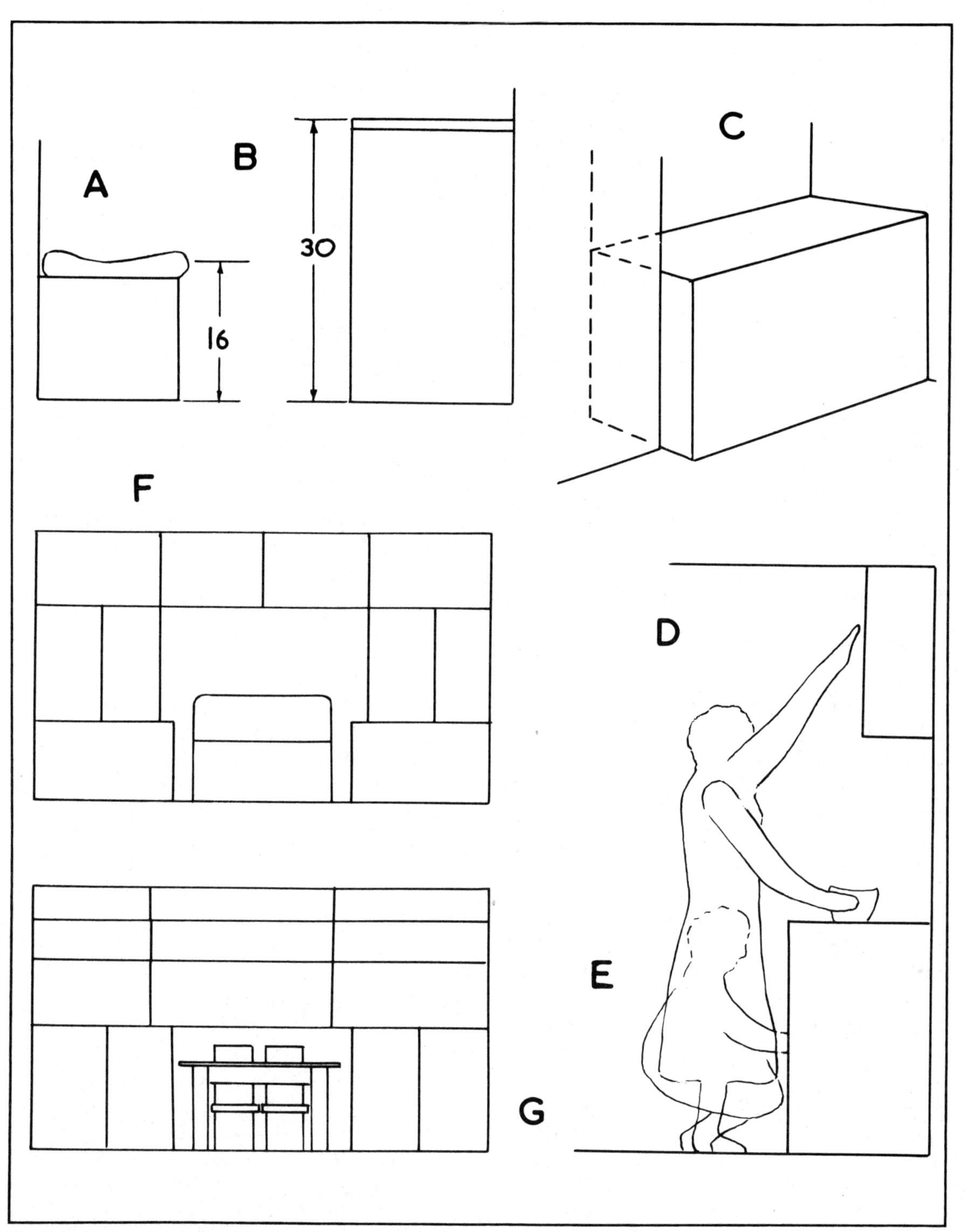

Fig. 1-1. Sizes and heights of furniture have to suit the human form.

together with bedside tables, built-in radio, and anything else (Fig. 1-1F). In a living room you may want to push a table to the wall when it is not being used, possibly with two chairs tucked under it (Fig. 1-1G). If another piece of furniture has a special place, you can stop the new built-in piece short of that position.

Think of the effect of your new construction on light and access. Don't let a built-in wall attachment obstruct light from a window. With artificial light you can always move a lamp, but a little forethought may allow you to keep an existing ceiling fitment. The new furniture may include additional lighting. If you want to build something that comes next to a doorway, how will it affect the swing of the door? Obviously, if the door swings the other way, it is no problem. If the door has to be opened into the room, make sure you do not impede it. If the door previously swung back against the wall, will your furniture reduce the swing? If so, does it matter? You may be able to reduce the width of the furniture or do something else to give the room door a better movement.

PROPORTIONS

In Victorian times furniture was made very ornate, with elaborate carving, molding, and piercing on every available bit of space. Today we prefer plainer finishes. It is not always easy to define the differences between attractive and ugly pieces of furniture.

Much of this has to do with proportions. Squares and circles are not attractive. If they are pushed out of shape to make rectangles or ellipses (Fig. 1-2A), the effect is more pleasing. In designing furniture it is best to divide areas into rectangles and make their overall shapes rectangular. This applies to flat surfaces and to the three-dimensional appearance (Fig. 1-2B). A piece of furniture should not look square if you can avoid it. If you want to give the effect of height, possibly because something is rather squat, include plenty of vertical lines (Fig. 1-2C). If you want to make a narrow thing look wider, include horizontal lines (Fig. 1-2D). Diagonal lines are a problem. They generally do not look right when most other lines are vertical or horizontal. They do not arise in most built-in assemblies. If you include diagonals, it is better to have plenty of them. Diamond-shaped panes in a glass door (Fig. 1-2E) are better than one big diagonal line across a surface.

Much of your designing will be to suit available space. Even if that settles overall sizes, you can divide up shelves and door panels to give visible lines that are artistically correct. It usually is best to let a piece of furniture look larger and heavier lower down. A few successful designs are arranged the other way, but it is better to have large compartments low, so there is a wider spacing of lines there than further up the furniture.

Even if a regular spacing will be satisfactory, possibly in a block of shelves for a bookcase, there is an optical illusion that will make that arrangement look wrong. Equal spaces tend to look closer together at the bottom than at the top (Fig. 1-2F). It is better to graduate the spaces, such as 8½ inches at the bottom, then 8¼ inches, 8 inches, and so on, even if the books are all the same height (Fig. 1-2G).

There are similar considerations in the locations of handles and hinges. Actual equal up-and-down measurements make the things look low. Drawer and door handles should come above halfway (Fig. 1-2H). Hinges look better if the bottom one is further from the door bottom than the upper one is from the top (Fig. 1-2J). It applies to door panels. The bottom rail should be obviously wider than the others (Fig. 1-2K). If it is the same width, it will look narrower.

Curves do not come into built-in furniture to a great extent. If you want to make something like a curved drop leaf, it will look better elliptical than as part of a circle. Curves more often play a minor part in relation to straight lines. If you cut away the edge of a rail, the curve can be part of a circle (Fig. 1-2L), but it will look better as part of an ellipse (Fig. 1-2M). If you use moldings that you either bought and applied or cut yourself on the edge of the wood with a suitable plane or router cutter, all the normally acceptable molding sections have elliptical rather than circular curves.

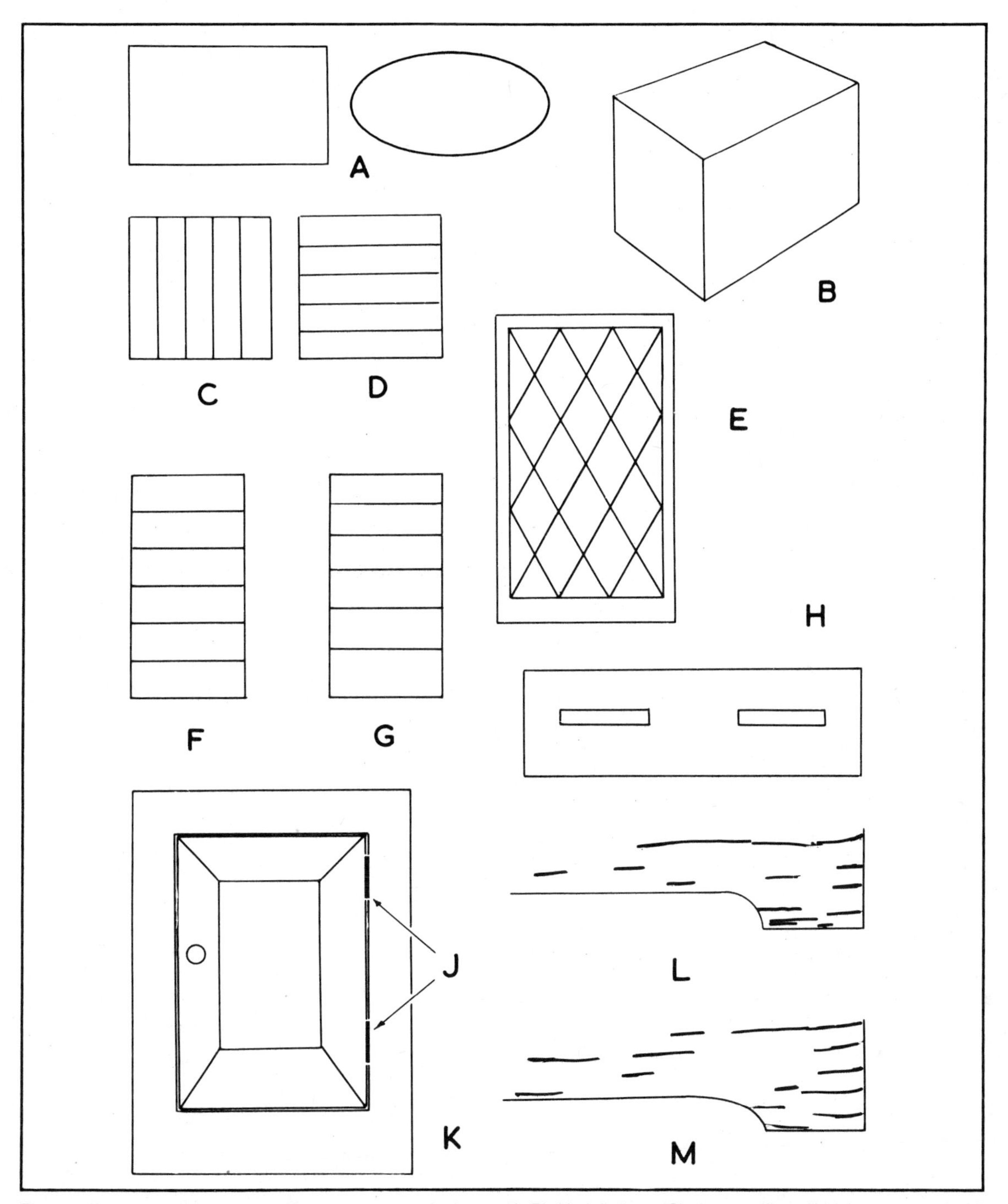

Fig. 1-2. Elongated shapes look better than symmetrical ones (A, B). Upright lines (C) give an effect of height, compared with horizontal ones indicating width (D). Diagonal lines are better avoided (E). Equal spacings (F) are not as effective as diminishing spaces (G). Greater widths below (H, J, K) look better than lesser heights. Part of a circle (L) is not as attractive as part of an ellipse (M).

MATCHING

The furniture you make has to match the part of a house that is already there. That may seem simply a matter of measuring, but you soon discover that many houses are far from square. Floors are usually level overall. When you try to build in, you may discover minor undulations that affect the part you are working on by a few degrees. The error is not apparent in normal use. Similarly, walls may be reasonably upright(plumb) overall, but locally there may be variations that are not noticed and do not matter normally. You may have to consider them when attaching furniture.

Many room corners and the corners due to a fireplace or the room being L-shaped are a long way from 90°. It is no use making a carefully squared piece of furniture and find that there are gaps you did not expect or, even worse, that part of the recess is not as wide as where you measured it.

Furniture should be made square in its general form, but you may have to do some adapting where it contacts the parts of a house. Don't make a frame that matches an inaccurate wall, then keep the wood parallel so a door opening comes out of square. The strange shape is very apparent to viewers. Instead, make the door opening square at the corners, so its sides are parallel. The frame side may have its edge to the door absolutely plumb, while its other edge follows the wall (Fig. 1-3A)., The alternative is to make the furniture square throughout, then cover the front gaps with border pieces that form a frame (Fig. 1-3B).

If the floor of the room is not level, you can make the bottom of a cabinet as part of the furniture and have it level. Raise the piece on packing or wedges during fitting, then put a cover piece at the front. If you need maximum depth inside, the furniture bottom can match the slope of the floor while keeping the front edges upright. If there is no bottom to the furniture and the room floor takes its place, you will have to make this allowance. If the wall at the back is out of plumb, you usually can make the back of the furniture plumb, but carry the top far enough over it to take care of the inaccurate wall. Fortunately, room errors are not usually enough to be very apparent. Allow for even slight discrepancies while keeping the new furniture square and true in all directions, except where it meets the wall.

MEASURING

Before you start to make a piece of built-in furniture, you need to measure where it will go. That may seem simple enough and it often is, but if there is a corner involved or the piece has to fit into an alcove, you need to know angles, any unevenness,

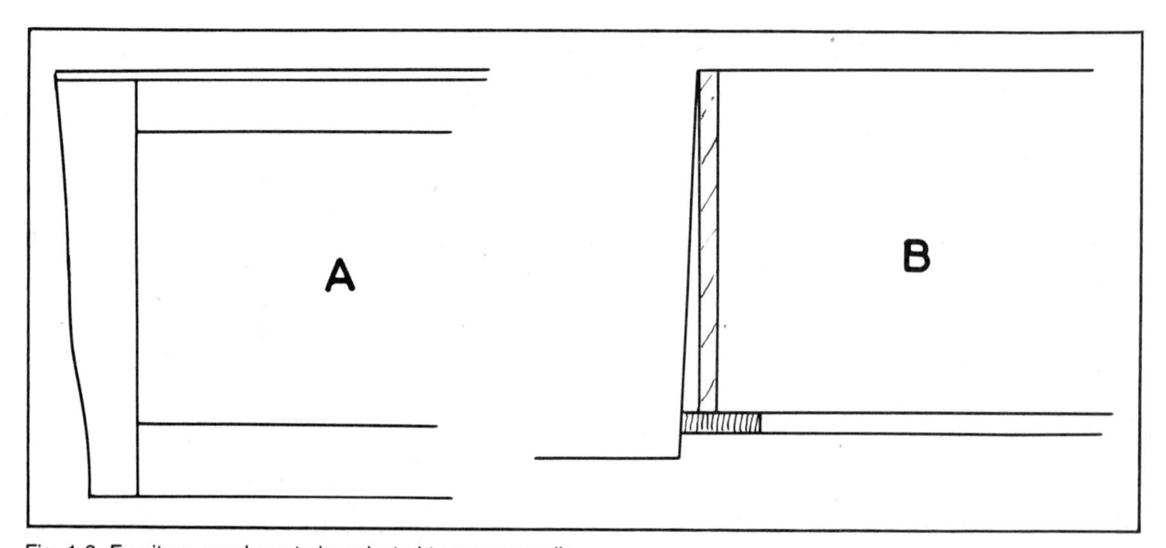

Fig. 1-3. Furniture may have to be adapted to uneven walls.

whether the floor is horizontal and the wall plumb, and measurements in relation to other parts of the immediate area.

You need a carpenter's level. A long level may be used directly. If the level is much shorter than the part where the furniture is to come, use it on a straight parallel piece of wood (Fig. 1-4A). This will bridge over any unevenness and avoid the false reading you would get at a shorter distance. If the floor is not horizontal, you will have to decide what to do about it. If the thing you are making will have a bottom, it will have to be packed to come horizontal in all directions. If you are building in shelves on supports, independent of any other framing, check the level across supports (Fig. 1-4B) rather than measure parallel to the floor, if you have doubts about it being true. If it is an assembly you are making up as you build it in, rather than one that is made on the bench and brought in almost complete, establish one horizontal surface. Use that as a datum for dealing with other parts that have to be horizontal by measuring parallel to it.

The wall you are working to is unlikely to be out of plumb enough to matter. If it is masonry or brick, you may find that it is out of plumb even if it has been plastered. if what you are making will have its edge against the wall hidden, you can cut it straight and keep it plumb and clear of the uneven wall. If it is a visible edge, the wood looks better if it makes a close fit. One method of getting the shape is called *spiling.* It is possible to mark the wood direct, but it is safer to make a template that can be adjusted to a close fit and used to mark the final piece of wood.

The template may be any scrap piece of wood as tall as the part that is to be shaped. Support it close to the wall and note the greatest distance from it. Make a block of wood to that distance (Fig. 1-4C). Run this down the wall with a pencil against it so you draw a replica of the shape on the template (Fig. 1-4D). Cut to the line and test the template in position. Draw a plumb line on the template with the plumb part of a carpenter's level.

Put the template on the wood that is to be built in, with the plumb line parallel with an edge that is to be vertical. Mark the edge to be cut (Fig. 1-4E).

If the wood has to be cut around something with much detail, as when molding has to be matched, the block of wood and a pencil cannot be used. Sometimes it may be simpler to cut away the molding if that is possible. Otherwise, the shape can be reproduced using a *spiling stick,* which is a small strip of wood cut to a wedged point (Fig. 1-4F).

Use a piece of thin scrap wood that is wide enough for the strip to lap on it at any position. Support this near the shape to be copied, then put the pointed piece against the shape at many positions and draw along one side and the end each time (Fig. 1-4G). Put the spiling piece on the wood to be shaped and return the spiling stick to each of its positions. This time pencil round its point to give a series of Vs that can be jointed to get the replica of the molding or other shape (Fig. 1-4H). Adjustable templates are obtainable for small work, but their size limits the possible applications.

CHECKING ANGLES

A carpenter's adjustable *bevel* can be used to check angles that are not square. Put it in a corner (Fig. 1-5A) and use it like a square to mark the wood that is to fit there (Fig. 1-5B). If the furniture is to be wider than the extension of the bevel, you should make something to extend at least as far as the new parts will go. Two strips tightly bolted are suitable (Fig. 1-5C). When measuring or marking, it is always best to check to a size larger than the finished size. If you use a bevel or measure at a shorter distance and extend it, there is a risk of slight errors being magnified at the further point.

If you are dealing with fairly large sizes, it is better to depend on measuring. Remember the 3:4:5 method of making a right angle. A triangle with the sides in that proportion will have its inner corner 90° (Fig. 1-6A). The units can be anything convenient. If you measured 18 inches (three times 6 inches) along one wall and 24 inches (four times 6 inches) the other way, a diagonal between your marks will be 30 inches (five times 6 inches) if the corner is square (Fig. 1-6B).

If the corner is not square, you can use any convenient distances each way to make marks, then measure between them (Fig. 1-6C). Go to the wood

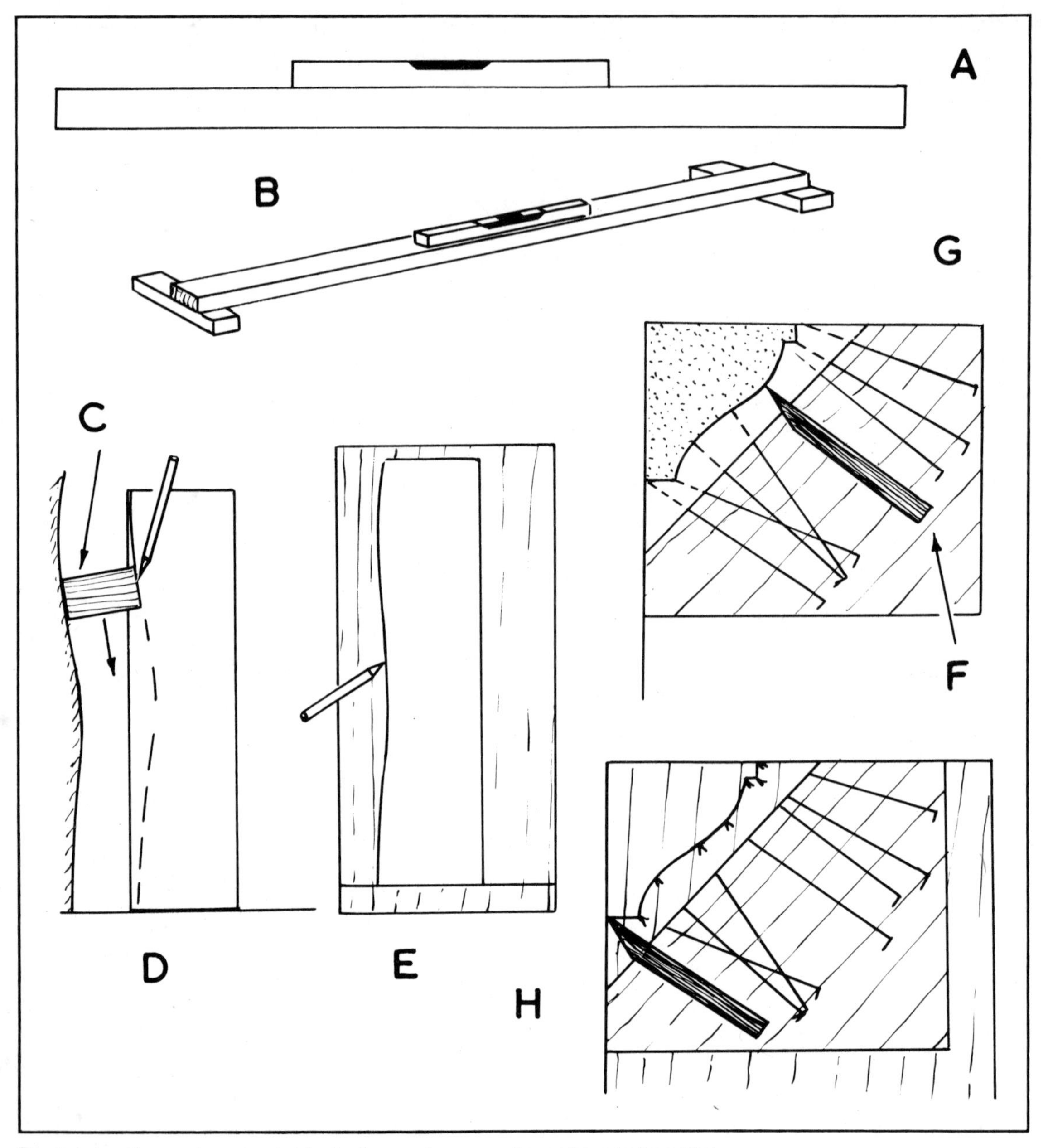

Fig. 1-4. Levels may be extended for testing, and uneven shapes have to be spiled.

to be marked and repeat the distance along an edge. Swing a short arc of one of the distances and measure to it the other way, then a line through the edge mark and that crossing will repeat the angle of the corner (Fig. 1-6D).

There is a practical difficulty in measuring the diagonal between walls. You can do it with care using an expanding tape rule, but you have to hold one end and bend the tape at the other position. It helps to use two overlapping strips of wood with

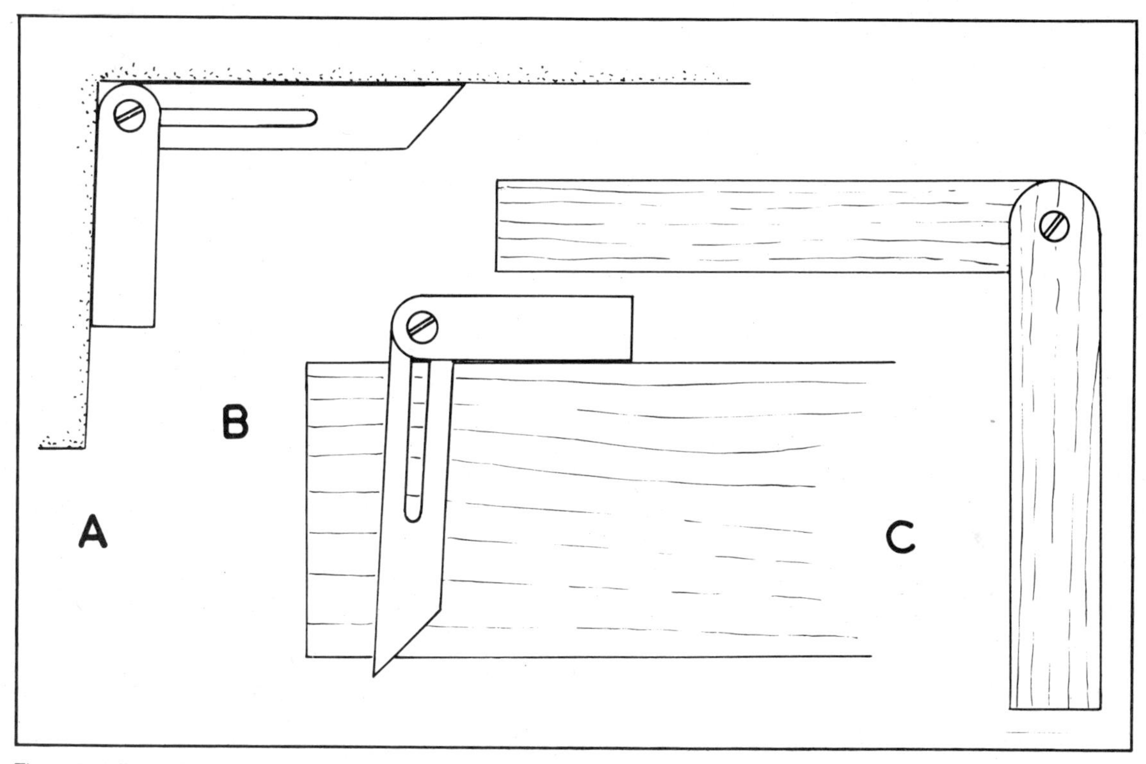

Fig. 1-5. Adjustable bevels test and transfer varying angles.

slim wedged ends (Fig. 1-6E). Extend them to the two points on the wall and mark on one where the other comes. You can then move to the wood to be marked, set the pieces correctly in relation to each other, and be certain there is no error. You can make a permanent pair of strips if you expect to need them frequently by putting sliding metal straps on their ends to hold them together (Fig. 1-6F).

If you need to get the shape of a recess, the method of checking corner angles can be used both ways. Usually you can measure from the internal corners with the overlapping strips (Fig. 1-6G). Besides doing this, measure in all directions along the walls (Fig. 1-6H) and across the opening (Fig. 1-6J). These serve as checks on each other and are particularly important if the recess is narrower at the front than the back. In that case you cannot cut approximately, taking off a little at a time until the wood fits, as you might if the front is wider than the back. It has to be right the first time. It may be worthwhile making a template if you want to get a perfect fit. Plywood cut for a template will probably have uses later for making internal parts.

Although you may want a working top or some other visible part to be a close fit, other parts are usually better cut square. Any gaps should be covered by fitted pieces at the front. If you are working against a flat wall or fitting into only one corner, make sure the parts that stand free of the walls are plumb and horizontal. Errors on an exposed edge become rather obvious when you line up a corner with the edge of a window or door in your line of sight, and the two do not match.

DETAILS

A few features are not immediately obvious if you are planning built-in furniture for the first time. Suppose the lower storage space has room for a shelf. The obvious way to get maximum storage is to make the shelf as wide as possible (Fig. 1-7A).

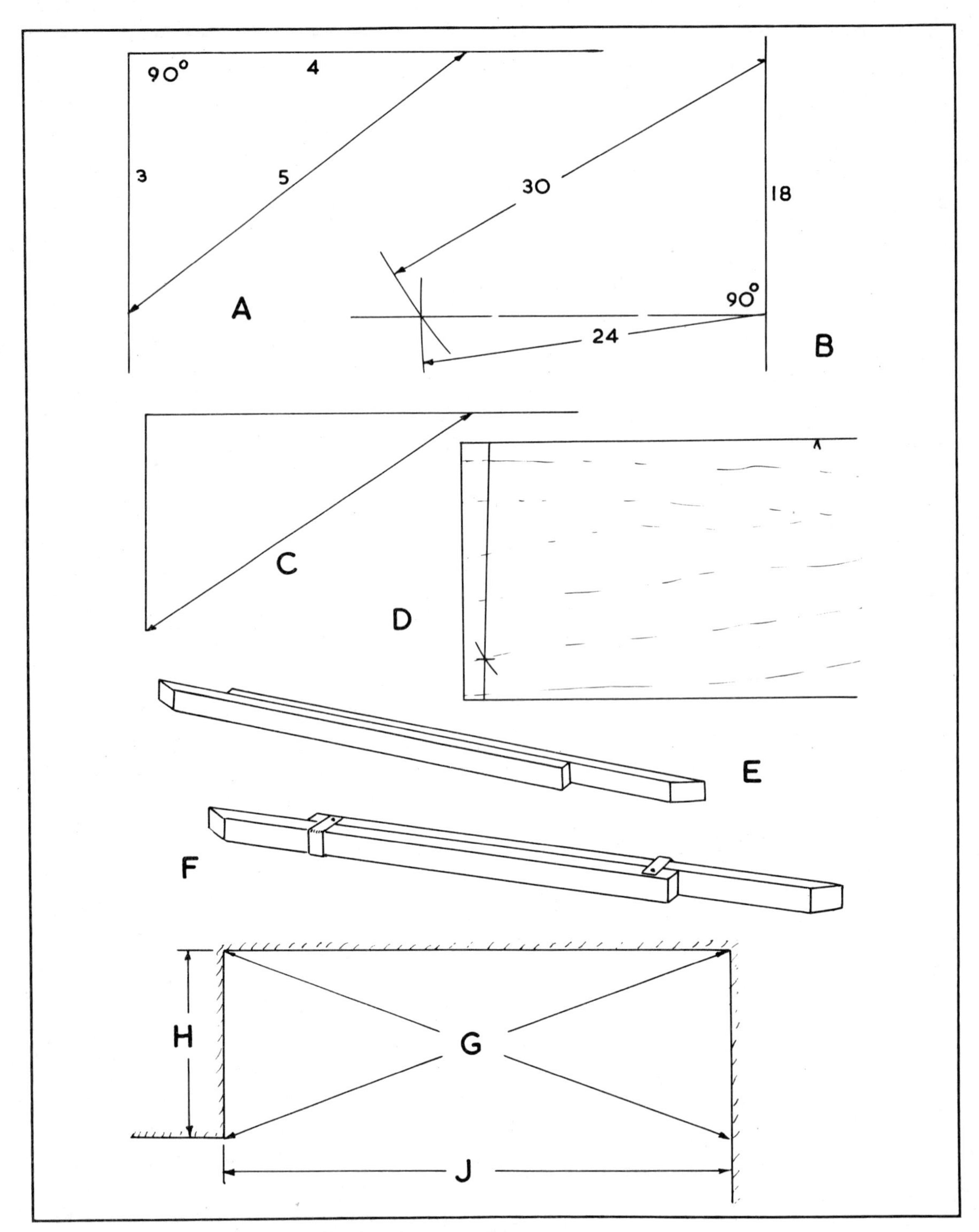

Fig. 1-6. Angles can be drawn geometrically and by triangulating.

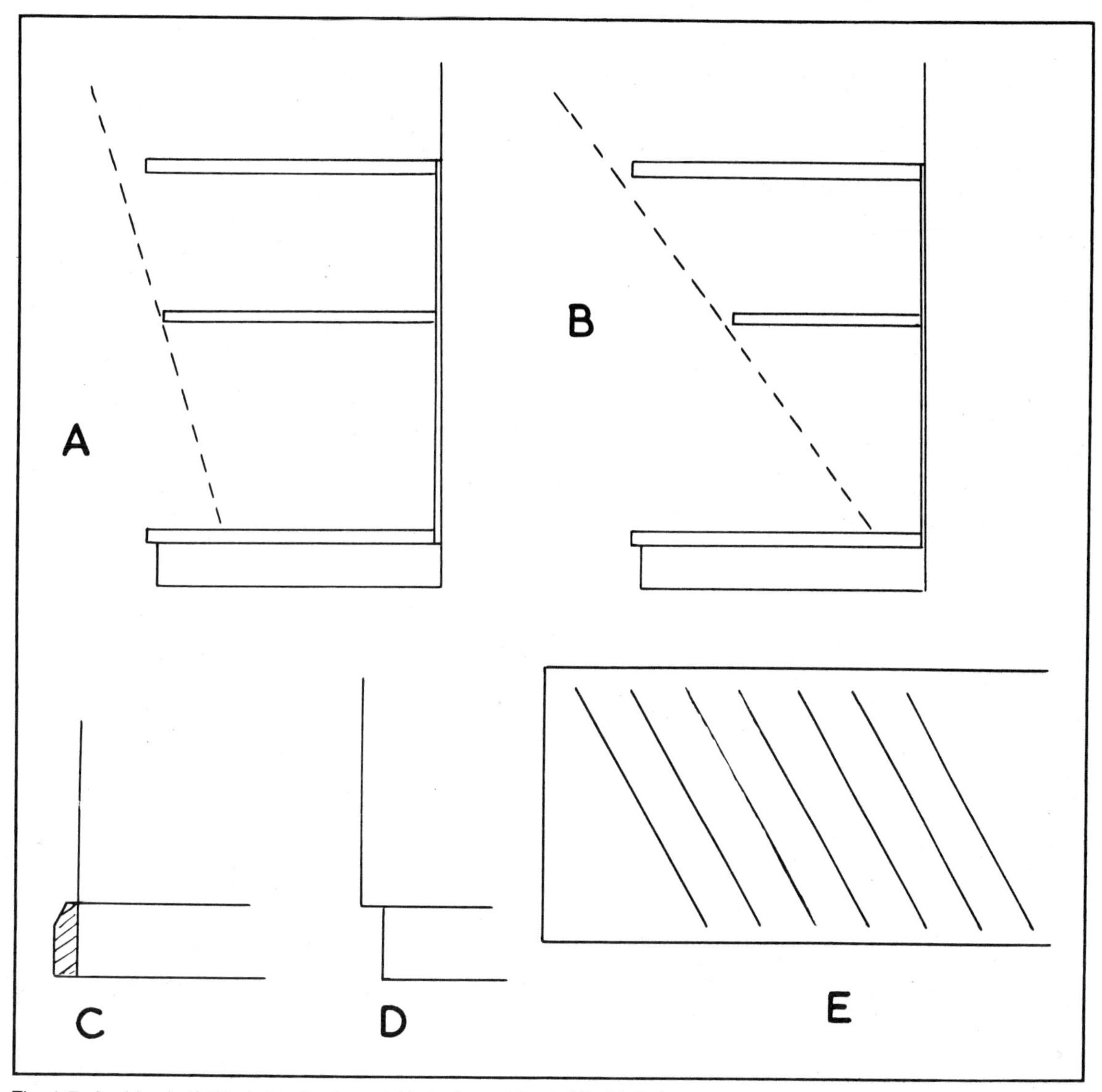

Fig. 1-7. A wide shelf (A) obstructs view and is better cut back (B). A plinth may extend (C) or be inset (D). Articles stowed diagonally (E) will go into a narrow space.

This makes it almost impossible for anyone to see and get at things below it, without crawling on the floor, so it is better to cut the shelf back (Fig. 1-7B). How far depends on the internal measurements, but think of someone standing or stooping slightly. They should be able to see toward the back.

Most furniture was made with a plinth at one time (Fig. 1-7C). This gave the appearance of weight and stability, which is desirable, and covered some constructional details. There are occasions when a plinth is the correct finish, but if someone is standing at the front of a kitchen cabinet or something similar, his or her feet are liable to kick against the plinth. They could stand closer if the bottom was inset (Fig. 1-7D) instead of projecting.

Another thing to watch is the suitability of the item for its purpose. In a clothes closet you have to allow about 22 inches for the width of a coat on a hanger. You must make the furniture about 24 inches wide if hangers are to be edgewise. If a projection of that much from a wall will take up more of the room than can be allowed, you may consider having a rail back to front or making the closet shallower. The clothing will hang diagonally (Fig. 1-7E), but the capacity will be reduced.

If there are to be doors, how should they open? Think of the direction of light. Opening a door should not put the inside into shadow. Will one door be satisfactory, or will it be better to have a pair? How does the door have to move in relation to the user? If the hanging side does not matter, do you want to pull the door with your left hand and reach inside with your right or vice versa? Will it be satisfactory for the door to swing out not much more than squarely, or do you want it to open right back? Is there clearance for that movement?

If the door comes low, you may consider hinging it on its lower edge, so it swings out to give a better view of the inside. You may then fit its inside with racks. If the door is high, you can hinge its top edge, but there will have to be a strut or catch to hold it up when open. Gravity will tend to close it, where in a low door gravity will tend to open it.

Chapter 2

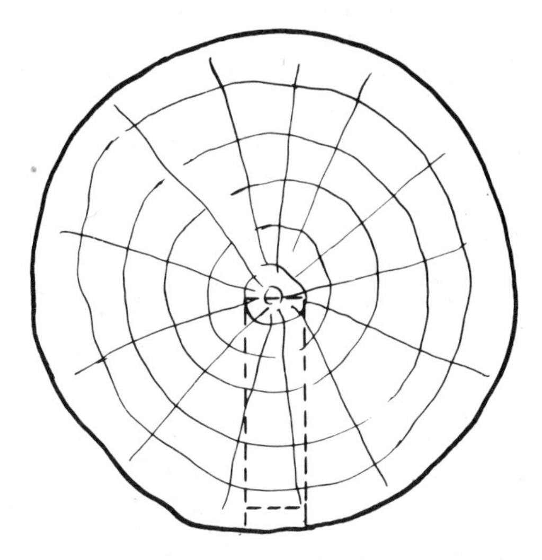

Materials

THE OBVIOUS CHOICE OF MATERIAL FOR MAKing built-in furniture is solid wood. It is the most used material for all kinds of furniture. Where wood is available and economical, it is nearly always best, but some types of solid wood have become either unavailable or very costly. There are now many manufactured forms based on wood, some of which have superior qualities, but more often their appeal is that they are cheaper. Metals and plastics have their place, but built-in furniture is usually wood. Other materials used in the furniture provide strength or decoration.

Wood comes from trees that grow prolifically all over the world. The trees are regenerating, and what you use will eventually be replaced by nature. New growth does not take the place of trees converted to boards anything like the rate of felling and conversion. Plastics, most of which are based on oil, will not be replaced. Most metals have a very long life. It is possible to use metal a second time when its first application is no longer wanted, or it can be melted and made into a different form. Corrosion takes its toll, but most of the metal survives.

WOOD

Felling your own tree and converting it into boards that become furniture may seem very attractive, but there are many problems. Most of us buy prepared wood from a lumberyard and take no part in the preparation of the wood before that stage. It helps to know something of the earlier stages, so we can visualize the probable behavior of the wood when we make it into furniture.

All woods we use are broadly divided into *hardwoods* and *softwoods*. Most are hard or soft as their names imply, but a few hardwoods are softer than some softwoods. The names are derived from other features. Hardwoods come from trees with broad leaves that are shed during the winter in temperate climates. Softwoods come from trees with needle leaves and are cone-bearing. The better furniture woods are all hardwoods, but there are uses for softwoods in internal work and less important construction. Softwoods generally are cheaper.

No two trees are identical, so the wood from them varies. If a tree only grows with a slender trunk, it cannot produce wide boards. If a tree grows in the open, it may have a twisted and bent trunk, as well as often not reaching very high. If it grows among other trees, it competes with them to reach sunlight at the top, so it will be long and straight. It will not have many branches lower down, but the tree growing away from others will have many low branches. Boards from the forest tree will have fairly straight grain. Those from the other tree will have a winding grain and many knots, because knots occur where the branches come. The straight-grained wood will be chosen for strength in large structures, but for furniture much of the beauty comes from the uneven grain pattern produced by a twisted tree and exposed when the wood is cut into boards.

Knots in hardwood trees usually do not affect the strength of the wood, although sometimes they are difficult to plane without the grain tearing out. Small knots in many softwoods will have to be accepted, but large knots weaken the wood and should be avoided. Some knots in softwood tend to fall out—not always in the new board. If a softwood knot has a dark border, it can be expected to dry and loosen even if it does not fall out.

Sap goes up and down a growing tree, and new wood is formed on the outside. As the tree ages, it produces annual rings. You can measure the age of a cross section of a tree by counting the rings. It is usually possible to discern the rings in any wood, but they are more obvious in most softwoods. The annual rings produce the grain pattern when cut through lengthwise. The wood near the center of the tree becomes compounded into strong heartwood. The softer wood near the outside is sapwood, and in some trees a board cut across sapwood will be weaker and more prone to rot than heartwood. Fortunately, in many hardwoods there is little to choose between heartwood and sapwood, providing the wood immediately inside the bark is removed.

A log from a newly felled tree contains plenty of moisture in the form of sap. If you worked with this green wood, anything made would warp and shrink. Cracks would develop. The wood must be seasoned. This is the process of drying out the moisture to an acceptable level. Bark is removed from the log, and the wood is cut into boards. In traditional seasoning the boards are stacked so air can circulate. They are left to dry for a long time, allowing usually one year for each 1 inch of thickness. Modern methods of seasoning take a few weeks.

Wood intended for furniture will be dried to something like a 10 percent moisture content. The wood will always absorb more moisture from a wet atmosphere or dry out further in a dry one. If furniture is to be made for use in the dry warm atmosphere of a centrally heated home, store the wood in these conditions for several weeks before making the furniture, so it stabilizes to the condition in which it has to be kept.

Moisture content affects the shape and size of the wood. If you reduce the moisture content, you reduce the size of the wood. You can also expect it to warp, depending on from which part of the tree it was cut. Shrinkage is in the direction of the lines of the annual rings. If a board is cut radially from the log (Fig. 2-1A), the lines of these rings will be across it. Shrinkage will make the wood thinner. Difficulties come when boards are cut from further out. Shrinkage in the direction of the rings can best be visualized as a tendency for them to try to straighten (Fig. 2-1B). Examination of the end of a board will show you the way it can be expected to cast or warp—if it does. Properly seasoned stable wood may not change whatever the arrangement of rings shown on the end.

To guard against the risk of overall warping, when you make up a width by gluing several boards together, try to get grain patterns opposite ways at the ends (Fig. 2-1C) if you do not have radially-cut boards.

Besides annual rings, there are medullary rays that go from near the center radially outward (Fig. 2-1D). In most woods you cannot see them, except under a microscope. In woods where they are more

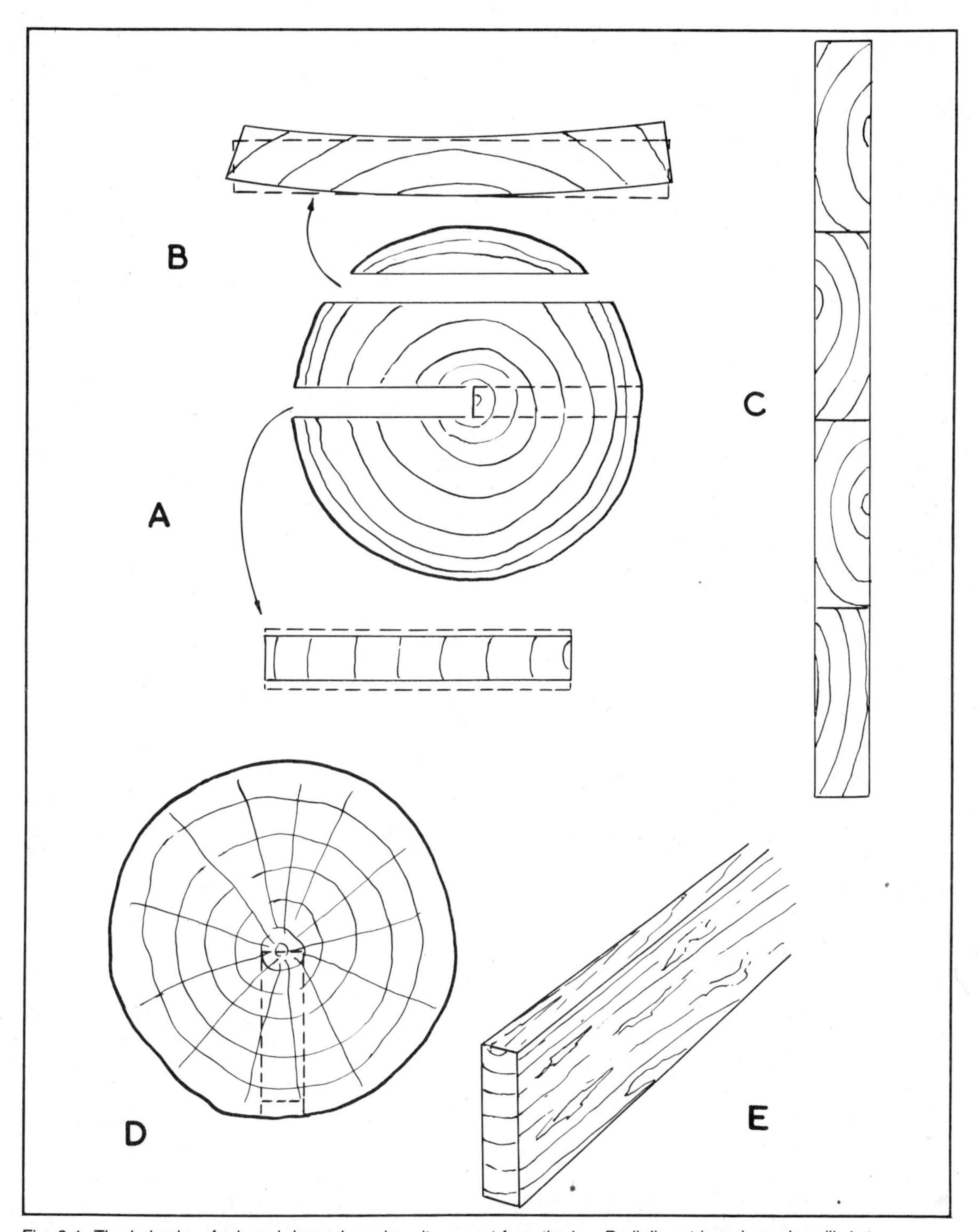

Fig. 2-1. The behavior of a board depends on how it was cut from the log. Radially-cut boards are less likely to warp.

prominent, a radial cut shows them on the surface. Oak is the best example, where the medullary rays produce the well-known figuring in quartered or quartersawn wood (Fig. 2-1E).

Besides knots, there are defects that occur in a growing tree and may not become apparent until the wood is cut into boards. Cracks that occur naturally are called *shakes.* If you use the wood in a part that is hidden, the cracks may not matter, but otherwise they must be cut around. Many softwoods are very resinous. Resin aids durability, but sometimes there is a resin pocket in the wood that will have to be cut away. The resin never dries out and will affect any applied finish. Some boring beetles will attack a tree. They may not outlive seasoning, but the holes they leave are unsightly. Other worms will attack furniture in the home—going for sapwood more than heartwood. Chemical treatments will kill them. It is unlikely that you will be offered new wood with rot in it. If you are reusing wood, beware of any that has become soft and spongy or has discolored. Rot is a fungal attack that will be much more widely spread than the obviously affected wood. If you don't burn rotten wood, the spores may attack other sound wood.

The range of wood species runs into thousands. It is difficult to be specific about woods for purposes. Oak and mahogany are traditional furniture woods, but each can be divided into many species. We often come across imported wood with a name we have never heard before. The only accurate way to identify wood is in a laboratory and then to use a scientific name. We have to use other names for everyday use, but then one name may not mean the same wood in every part of the world.

There are no specifications of wood for the projects described in this book. Most are better made throughout of hardwood, but softwood may be satisfactory if what you are making is for a playroom or laundry. Pine and other softwoods look nice in their natural color, but they must be protected with a good clear finish and even then will suffer more than hardwoods from knocks. If the built-in furniture is to match other furniture in the room, that will be your guide to the choice of wood. A visit to a local supplier will let you see what is available and there you will probably get advice on what is most likely to serve your purpose. A wood available in one place may be attractively priced, yet it may be very expensive someplace else.

PLYWOOD

Plywood is the best-known of the manufactured forms of wood. Although Douglas fir is what we are all familiar with, plywood is made from many woods. Fir plywood does not have a surface that is right for most exposed parts of furniture. It can be veneered, either in manufacture or by the craftsman using it. Other woods have better surface finishes and are more suitable for furniture.

The great advantage of plywood is in its large areas of flat stable pieces. There is no risk of shrinkage or expansion. Some thin plywood may twist if unsupported, but it can be held by a frame. Unless you are making reproduction furniture that needs solid wood for panels, plywood is the choice for paneled work. For backs of cabinets and bottoms of drawers, plywood is much better than thin pieces of solid wood joined together.

Plywood is made from veneers of wood cut on a lathelike machine from a rotating log. Surface veneers do not have a normal grain pattern due to the circular way of cutting. The pattern repeats at intervals across a sheet, depending on the diameter of the log at the stage the veneers were cut. Veneer thickness varies depending on the wood, as they will not all pare equally thinly, and on the intended construction of the plywood.

Veneers are laid with their grains square to each other in alternate layers. There is always an odd number, so the grain on the outside faces is the same both sides. There are never less than three layers (Fig. 2-2A). Veneers of the same thickness can be added to make up greater sheet thicknesses (Fig. 2-2B), or there can be thicker veneers to get the same total thickness (Fig. 2-2C). In a given sheet thickness a greater number of veneers should produce a stiffer sheet than a smaller number.

Alternate veneers of the same thickness may be used to make up quite thick sheets, but solid wood may be substituted inside to make solid core plywood (Fig. 2-2D). There are usually two

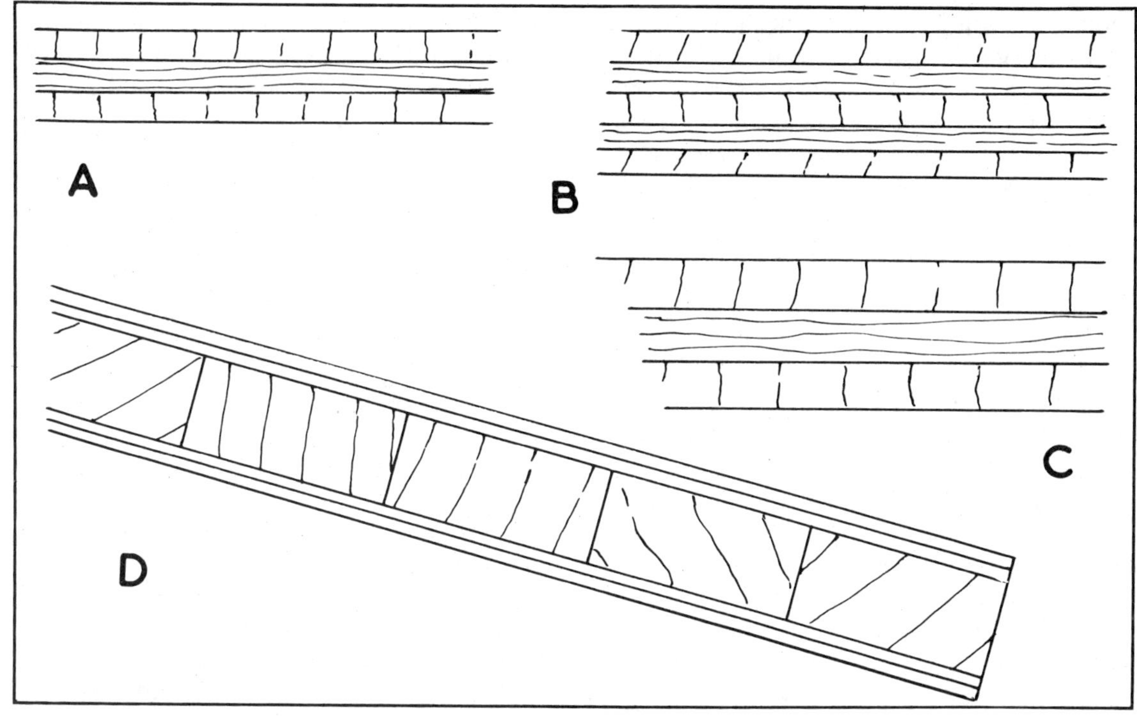

Fig. 2-2. Plywood is made in layers with the grain crossing (A). Many plies (B) make a stiffer sheet than one with fewer plies (C) in the same thickness. Thicker boards have solid wood cores (D).

thicknesses of veneer the same way on each face to give stiffness.

Plywood can be bought with decorative veneers on the faces. These veneers are quite thin compared with those in the plywood. There may only be a decorative veneer on one face. Where there is a risk of the plywood base warping, there is a veneer of similar thickness on the other face, but not always a decorative one.

Plywood is made in many thicknesses. Some aircraft birch plywood has three veneers, all within a total thickness of 1/25 inch, but most plywood has veneers nearer 1/16 inch or even thicker. Total thicknesses may be in fractions of an inch or in millimeters. The thinnest plywood needed for furniture will usually be ¼ inch (6 mm), but where it has to take a load, ⅜ inch (9 mm) or ½ inch (12 mm) is more suitable. Solid wood is more suitable than thick plywood for thicker parts of furniture, although many areas can be built up from plywood of ½ inch or less inside a thicker solid wood frame to give the wood an overall effect of being more solid than it actually is.

Plywood sheets are available in many sizes. The largest size that can be conveniently moved by one man is 48 inches by 96 inches. There are larger sizes, but if you want to buy plywood for stock, that size sheet will probably be your most economical purchase. Other smaller stock sizes are made for door panels and similar things. You can look around a yard for offcuts, which should be cheaper than asking for a particular size to be cut. The supplier will then have to make allowance for the waste, which he otherwise may not be able to sell. If you hope to make several pieces of furniture, it is always worthwhile building up a stock of plywood by buying more than you actually need for the job in hand.

PARTICLE BOARD

One of the more modern boards made from wood is described as *particle board* or chipboard. It is made from the waste from sawmills. The pieces are broken down into chips that are then embedded in a synthetic resin to make a hard, flat, and rather heavy board. In the better boards the wood chips are packed tightly. The result is mostly wood fiber with resin bonding everything together. The edge of this board can be planed, but a more loosely bonded board is not as suitable for furniture.

Particle board is rather unattractive, but it can be bought faced with wood veneer or plastic that looks like wood or is patterned to suit kitchen working tops or other purposes. The facing is on both sides. The edges are also supplied veneered in long pieces intended for shelves and similar constructions. There usually is little choice of thickness. You have to take the stock sizes of a particular manufacturer, which will not be much under ⅝ inch and can be up to 1 inch. The boards are usually available already veneered in widths from 6 inches up to about 36 inches, and they are in several stock lengths sufficient for any furniture needs. Large sheets are made, but they are usually not veneered and are intended for floors and other house construction.

Particle board can be cut to size with woodworking tools. The resin content is rather harsh on edge tools, so frequent sharpening is necessary. A cut exposes the unattractive core, but strips of the same materials used for facing are available to apply to new edges. In most cases these strips are self-adhesive and can be attached by smoothing down with a domestic iron used over paper. Normal joints are unsuitable for particle board, and it does not take nails satisfactorily. Ordinary wood screws can be driven into prepared holes, but there are special screws for the material.

Particle board is heavier than solid wood or any of the other prepared boards. Allow for this when building particle board into furniture. If it is to be used as shelves, supports should be at 24-inch intervals or closer. Sags may develop after some time under a sustained load.

HARDBOARD

Many manufactured boards compress wood fibers to varying degrees. Where the compression is slight and fibers are only just holding together, the board may be intended for insulation. It is not a structural material. Other boards may be more tightly compressed, but they are of no use in furniture. *Hardboard* is compressed more tightly than other boards. Nearly all of it is ⅛ inch thick, with one smooth glazed surface and the other side patterned. Quality varies. Some is soft and little better than cardboard, but the hardest type is very smooth and strong. The toughest type is described as oil-tempered or in some other way that indicates an oil treatment. Oil gives the hardboard water resistance and toughness.

The smooth surface of hardboard is its face. The other side has to be hidden. Some boards are available where two pieces are joined to give two face sides, but for general use you have to accept that one side is not meant to be visible. The smooth surface must not be sanded or otherwise penetrated; it depends on remaining intact to provide smoothness and strength. You may find the brown surface suitable to go with some solid wood surrounding it, but usually exposed hardboard is more suited to a painted finish. For inside work, such as backs of cabinets or bottoms of drawers, hardboard is an alternative to plywood.

Hardboard generally is not considered a furniture material, but it has uses where economy is important or you are making something where utility is more important than a fine finish. Hardboard is a stable material that will usually remain flat. If you have to make templates to get the shape of a part before fitting it to a wall or into a recess, hardboard is a very convenient material.

SALVAGED MATERIALS

You do not have to use new materials for all parts of a new piece of furniture. A surprising amount of wood can be recovered from discarded furniture and even packing cases. A machine from Malaya may come in a mahogany crate, because that is the easily obtained wood there. If wood is with a sawed surface, plane a bit of it or take a slice with a knife. That will show you the grain and give you an idea what the wood is and if it is worthwhile salvaging and putting through a jointer.

Old furniture, doors, and window frames from a house that does not have any future may yield wood that can be used again. One attraction of this old wood is that it will be fully seasoned. If you are able to use it, there should be little fear of it shrinking or warping later. You are never certain with new wood if a change in moisture content may affect it.

Do not worry about old finishes on the wood or even shallow dents or torn grain. You may be able to use the wood so the surfaces that were outside come inside in the new construction. It is always possible to cut off a stained or worn surface on a table saw and plane a new one. Be careful of any metal that may be in the wood. Withdraw screws and nails carefully. If there are broken pieces that will not come out, punch them far enough below the surface to be out of the way of tool edges.

Old hardwood from any source is worth keeping. Plywood panels may also be retrieved. Even if the panels are not good enough for face use, they may find a use inside as backs or shelves, possibly edged with solid wood.

METALS

Metal is in fasteners, hinges, handles, and similar things. You may want to make part of the structure from metal. Shelves and other assemblies may have metal legs or other framing. You may want to make rails from metal. Sheet metal may be needed in some assemblies.

The general-purpose metal is often described as iron, but today it is actually mild steel, which is iron with some carbon, but not in the proportion that makes it into tool steel that can be hardened and tempered. Mild steel has adequate strength and does not have to be in very large sections. The main problem with steel is its tendency to corrode or rust. Any steel used should be protected in some way. Steel can be obtained plated, but for most furniture purposes it can be painted. Painted metal goes well with polished wood.

Mild steel is available in many sections and sheets. Strip is described by its width and thickness, round rods go by their diameter, and tubes are known by their diameter and the thickness of their walls. Sheets are known by a gauge thickness, with the lower numbers being thicker. Remember that 16 gauge is not far off 1/16 inch thick.

Mild steel is easily cut with a hacksaw, then filed and drilled with the usual electric drill up to about ⅜-inch holes. Smaller sections can be bent cold by hammering in a vise. Cutting a thread in a hole with a tap is simple, so bolted construction is possible.

Old-time cabinetmakers regarded brass as the metal particularly suited to their needs. It is more correctly called an *alloy,* which means a mixture of two or more metals—in this case copper and zinc. In normal indoor conditions brass resists corrosion well, and its yellow/gold color has a rich appearance. Brass is now more costly, but it makes good screws and hardware. It can be polished and lacquered to hold its appearance and occasionally needs polishing. If you want to make things from brass, it is obtainable in strips, sheets, rods, tubes, and all the forms available in mild steel. The ease of working it depends on the proportions of the two metals in the alloy, but the grades normally available can be cut, drilled, and bent easily.

An alloy that looks like brass but has a deeper golden tone is bronze or gilding metal, which is an alloy of copper and tin. In salty atmospheres bronze resists corrosion better than brass, so it is used for marine applications.

Pure aluminum is very soft, but the quality normally available is an alloy including fairly large proportions of other metals that make it harder. The silvery color of aluminum makes it suitable without special treatment alongside wood. Characteristics vary according to the parts of the alloy, but most of the material available can be worked like the other metals. Aluminum is the lightest of the common metals. Soft versions are needed for elaborate bends, but they do not drill or machine easily.

Most metals may be obtained plated. You expose the base metal if you cut them, so plating is more applicable to hardware bought ready-made.

Lead is the heaviest of the common metals. It is also soft and has a low melting point. Its dull gray color makes it unsuitable for most display positions, but it is useful where weight is needed. If you make a tall lamp standard, lead can be included in the standard's base to make it less likely to be knocked over. Lead can be melted with common heat sources, so it is possible to melt it with a torch or other flame and pour it into a mold to get a particular shape or weight. Scrap lead can be used up in this way. If you buy it new, it is mainly obtainable in several thicknesses of sheet.

PLASTICS

The term *plastics* actually covers a range of materials with more widely different characteristics than available woods. The plastics that interest us for use with built-in furniture are mostly those obtainable in sheet form, to be worked with tools, or those used like veneers on other surfaces. People tend to use trademarks for plastics.

For a hard working surface as required in a kitchen, Formica laminated plastic is usually the material used. This glues to a plywood or other wood backing, and its surface can be bought patterned in many ways. It can be cut and drilled with woodworking tools and may be attached to wood and cut to size with it. Other surface plastics that are not so hard may be applied for decorative purposes. Some surface plastics are obtainable already attached to particle board or other backing.

Plexiglas acrylic plastic is available in sheet form in various thicknesses. It may be opaque or transparent. It is easily cut to shape and drilled. Some grades can be curved with moderate heat. This makes plexiglas acrylic plastic an alternative to glass where shaping is required and allows for special effects that are impossible with glass.

Other plastics are used to make hardware that once would have been metal. Many strong plastics may be molded or otherwise formed into handles and similar things—in some cases to look like metal.

Some plastics have been finished to look like wood, either with surface graining or colored and shaped to look like wooded molding. You will have to decide whether or not to accept these things in your work. No plastic can be so disguised that it can be mistaken for wood. If the beauty of real wood is what attracts you in making furniture, the plastic substitutes may not seem right to incorporate. If you do not feel strongly about it, plastics resembling wood are appropriate to such situations as a working surface that may frequently become wet. The plastic does not suffer, but a wood surface might—no matter what finish is applied. Even if you do not accept plastics that imitate wood, a plastic surface with other decoration that is unashamedly plastic may be appropriate and welcomed.

Chapter 3

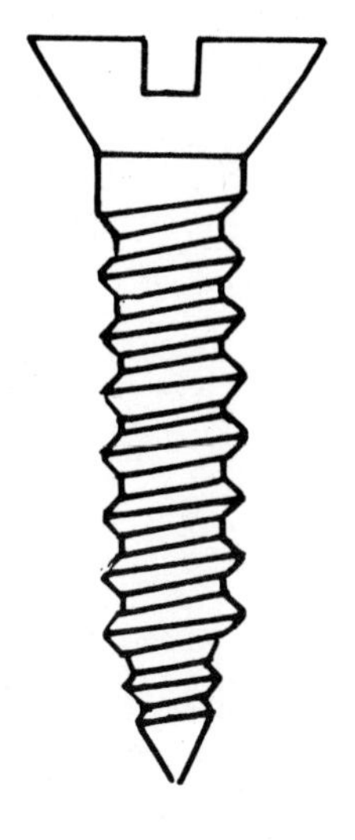

Hardware

THE FURNITURE MAKER HAS USES FOR NAILS, screws, and other fasteners. Hinges, handles, and other hardware may be needed. When you make built-in furniture, you have the additional problem of attaching to walls. Hardware that would not normally be required in freestanding furniture may be used. While some attachments to walls use fasteners that are already familiar, some fasteners made specifically for this work may not be as well known. This is particularly so where strength is required, as when the piece of furniture hangs from the wall or can be subject to loads pulling from the fastener.

Much of the work of making built-in furniture involves building up an assembly in position. You must be familiar with fasteners and know how to use them so you can select the appropriate one to suit circumstances, which may not always be simple. Some fasteners may be prefabricated on the bench, where work is more straightforward. Fitting to the walls is necessary, which can mean careful work in position, particularly if the furniture is going in a recess where corners are not square and the walls are not exactly plumb.

NAILS

Many types of *nails* are available. One method of specifying sizes can be confusing to a newcomer. This is the *penny* system that came over with early settlers from England, where it fell from use a long time ago. The size is indicated by d, which stands for the Roman *denarius,* and was still in use in England until fairly recently for their penny, so 2d is a recognized size of nail. For instance, 2d is actually a nail 1 inch long and weighing about 850 to 1 pound weight. Lengths increase at first by ¼ inch between these sizes. You can always order your nails by length, but the salesman may talk about penny sizes.

The thickness of a nail is indicated by a gauge number. There is only one thickness with each length, but where there is a choice or you may change to another type, the lower the gauge number, the thicker the nail. Nail points vary, but usually there is no choice in a particular nail type. Some nails have diamond points of varying steepness, while others are round needle ends.

The nail is described as *common* for general

use (Fig. 3-1A). The head is flat and of a moderate size. An almost identical nail, but thinner in most lengths, is a *box* nail. Both are suitable for general nailing in furniture construction or any woodworking done in the home. It is possible to get both types grooved in their length, with ridges on the high parts, to give increased grip. *Ring-shanked* or *barbed-ring* nails are available (Fig. 3-1B). The rings resist pulling out and provide strength comparable to a screw. They are difficult to withdraw, as they will tear the fibers of the wood.

Most nails you need are often described as iron, but they are actually mild steel. They can be zinc-plated or protected in other ways from corrosion. Nails are also made in other metals, usually for better protection against dampness. Steel will do for most indoor work. If you are attaching metal fittings that will be exposed to the weather or damp conditions, choose nails or screws of the same metal, if they are available, to reduce the risk of electrolysis causing corrosion.

The usual flat head provides a good grip, but it will be ugly on some surfaces. To allow for punching or setting a nailhead below the surface, there are nails with very small, deeply countersunk heads (Fig. 3-1C). The general name is *casing* for nails between 1½ inches and 3½ inches. Similar nails intended for flooring may be called *flooring* nails in the size suitable for floorboards. Where something finer is needed, there are *finishing* nails that have brad heads (Fig. 3-1D) and are available in lengths up to 3 inches. Some smaller and finer nails of very similar form are described by the material they are to be used with, such as *insulation building board* and *fiberboard.*

Where these nails are to be sunk below the surface, you drive them level, or nearly so, then use a nail punch or set. Some have hollow ends that reduce the risk of slipping off the nailhead. The end of the punch should only be slightly larger than the nailhead, so the hole in the wood is kept small (Fig. 3-1E). Use a stopping in the hole. A prepared stopping in a tube is simplest to use, but others are described in Chapter 5.

Nails for attaching to concrete or masonry are available. They may be hardened steel and are thicker than common nails. Whether they are of use to you or not depends on the wall. Usually you have to drill a hole and then plug it to take an ordinary fastener.

There may be occasions when you want a nail with a larger head to prevent fabric or soft materials from pulling off. It is always possible to put a washer under a standard head, but nails up to about 2 inches with large heads are described as *roofing* nails (Fig. 3-1F). Nails with in-between head sizes are *wood shingle* nails.

A nail with two points may be described as *double-pointed* or as a *staple* (Fig. 3-1G). They are made in many sizes, but smaller ones have limited uses in upholstered furniture. One with a small second leg is an electrician's *staple nail* (Fig. 3-1H).

Nails with small heads are called *tacks* and are used mostly for attaching cloth to wood in upholstery. They may have a full taper (Fig. 3-1J) or be parallel for a short distance before a long point (Fig. 3-1K). The alternative in modern production upholstery work is a wire staple similar to those used in office stapling machines. It is driven directly into the wood with a special tool. You can use an office stapler with its base turned back.

Most craftsmen accumulate many nails. Many of them can be used for internal work on furniture, even if that was not their original intention. Any serviceable nails are worth keeping even those salvaged from broken furniture or other woodwork.

NAILING

In most woods it is possible to drive nails without any preparation. It is wiser to drill first near ends and corners where there may be a risk of splitting. The size hole you drill depends on the wood and the nail, but usually a slightly undersize hole that is not as deep as the nail will do (Fig. 3-2A). A nail grips by squeezing the top piece of wood between its head and the lower piece of wood. No strength comes from the grip in the top thickness, so in hardwood you may find driving easier and just as strong if you drill the same size as the nail in the top piece (Fig. 3-2B).

The size and spacing of nails is largely a matter of experience. There must be enough of each nail in

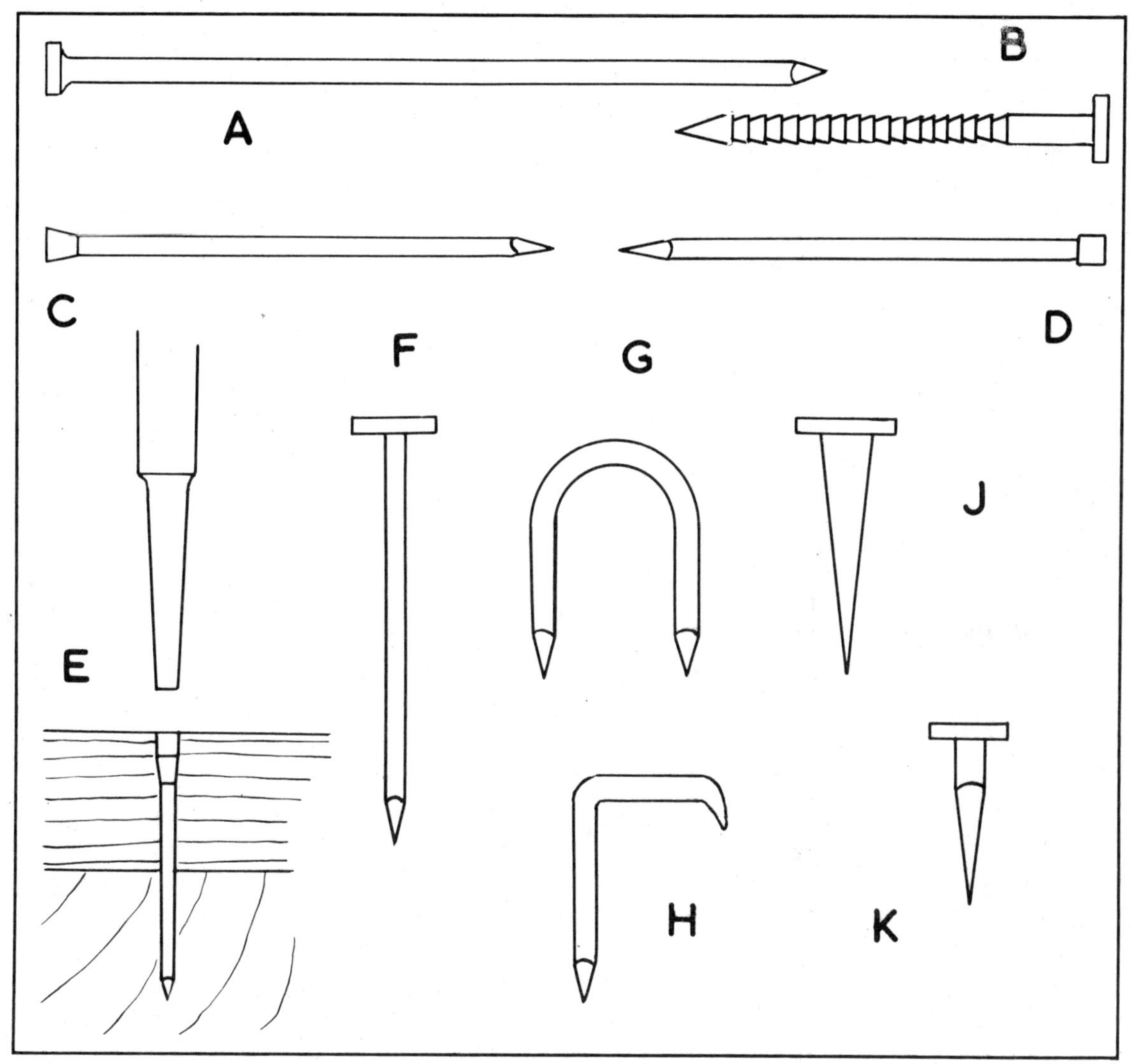

Fig. 3-1. Nails are made in many forms (A to F). Those with small heads may be set below the surface (E). Staples are double-ended nails (G, H). Tacks (J, K) are small and tapered.

the lower wood to provide strength. A nail should go through the upper part(s) and have maybe a further 1 inch in the lower part. Much depends on the wood thickness below; usually three-fourths of the thickness will do. You may want to use a fairly large number of thin or short nails, or it may be better to use fewer stouter nails to get a comparable strength.

Notice grain lines. Nails close together in one line of grain may develop a split between them. It is better to stagger nails, even if only slightly, to get into different grain lines (Fig. 3-2C). You can increase the hold of a row of nails by driving them at slight angles in opposite directions. This is known as dovetail nailing (Fig. 3-2D). The angle does not have to be excessive.

There are not many places in built-in furniture where you have to join very thin pieces of wood. If you do, it is worthwhile taking nails through and clenching them. It is neatest to hammer the end

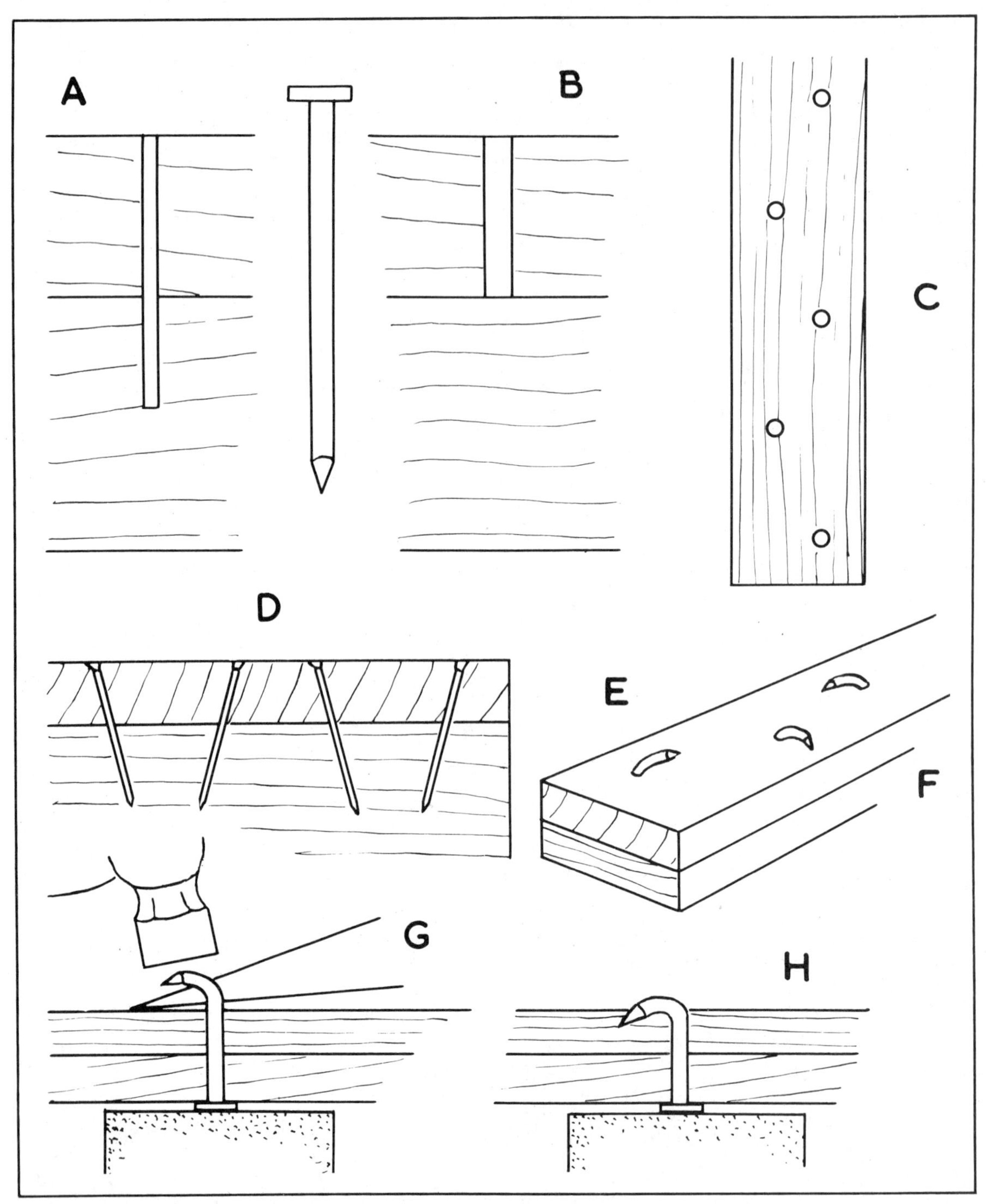

Fig. 3-2. Holes (A,B) are needed for nails in some woods. Staggering nail positions reduces the risk of splitting (C). Dovetail nailing gives strength (D). Nails may be clenched (E,F) for strength in this wood. The point is bent over an awl or even a thick nail (G) before it is driven into the wood (H).

along the grain (Fig. 3-2E), but that may cause splitting and is not the strongest way. It is better to go across or diagonal to the grain (Fig. 3-2F). If the points come somewhere out of the way, it does not matter if they are above the surface. Otherwise, it is better to bury them. Support the nailhead on another hammer or an iron block, then first bend the point over an awl or even a thick nail (Fig. 3-2G) before driving it into the wood (Fig. 3-2H).

SCREWS

A cabinetmaker or finish carpenter generally prefers screws to nails as being more craftsmanlike fasteners. When a screw is driven, it pulls parts together. A nail does not always do so; the action of hammering a nail in one place may loosen one elsewhere. There are many uses for nails in furniture. If you have any doubts about which to use, though, screws probably are better.

To an engineer, a *screw* is a type of bolt with threads almost to the head. To distinguish what we use on wood, it is safer to talk of *wood screws.*

Wood screws are made in several metals. For general use the steel ones are satisfactory and cheapest, but in cabinetwork any screws that will be visible are better made of brass. They can also be plated, and that may be worthwhile if they are required to match plated handles or hinges. Brass screws are not as strong as steel, but they should have ample strength for furniture. There is a tendency for very thin screws to shear off when being driven. You should not use brass screws less than 4 gauge, except in the smallest sizes. A steel screw of a similar size can be driven first, then withdrawn and replaced with a brass one, but that is obviously tedious.

Screws are described by their length and diameter and are indicated by a gauge number. Several thicknesses are available within each length. Screw lengths may be from ¼ inch up to sizes you are unlikely to need. Some typical general-purpose sizes are: 4, 5, and 6 gauge by ½ inch; 6 and 8 gauge by ¾ inch; 6, 8 and 10 gauge by 1 inch; 8, 10, and 12 gauge by 1¼ inch; 8, 10, and 12 gauge by 1½ inch; and 8, 10, 12, and 14 gauge by 2 inch. The gauge size refers to the diameter of the unscrewed shank below the head. The threaded part is usually about two-thirds the length of the screw.

Flathead screws are countersunk to pull into softwood or fit into prepared countersinks in hardwood (Fig. 3-3A). A roundhead screw stands above the surface (Fig. 3-3B), but its length is quoted as from the surface of the wood. An oval or raised head is like a flat head with a curved top (Fig. 3-3C). Its particular use is for attaching hinges that will show on surface, where it looks better than a flathead screw. Several other heads are used on wood screws, but they are not applicable to furniture construction. If you have to use very large screws for attaching to a wall, the head may be square for use with a wrench (Fig. 3-3D). That is a *lag screw* or *coach screw.*

The majority of wood screws have had slotted heads to take wedge-shaped screwdrivers (Fig. 3-3E). Other heads have been designed mainly for power driving in quantity-production work, but they are found in hand assembly work. There may be a square socket (Fig. 3-3F) or a Phillips head (Fig. 3-3G). There are special hand screwdrivers for both types. The screwdriver should have an end that matches the screwhead for the best work. You should have several screwdrivers in your kit. The end for a slot head should not have worn rounded, either on the surface or the corners (Fig. 3-3H). There are three sizes to suit the usual range of screws for Phillips heads.

Screwdriving

Pump action and ratchet screwdrivers are attractive and may have interchangable points, but several plain screwdrivers may be of more use than these special ones. It is easier to drive with a long screwdriver, but there are many places in furniture construction where space is limited and you need short drivers. For very large screws, you should have a screwdriver but in the chuck of a woodworking brace to help get sufficient leverage. There is no need for power screwdrivers when building in furniture. A countersink bit to fit the woodworking brace is more useful than one in a power drill. The slower speed suits the bit and allows better control.

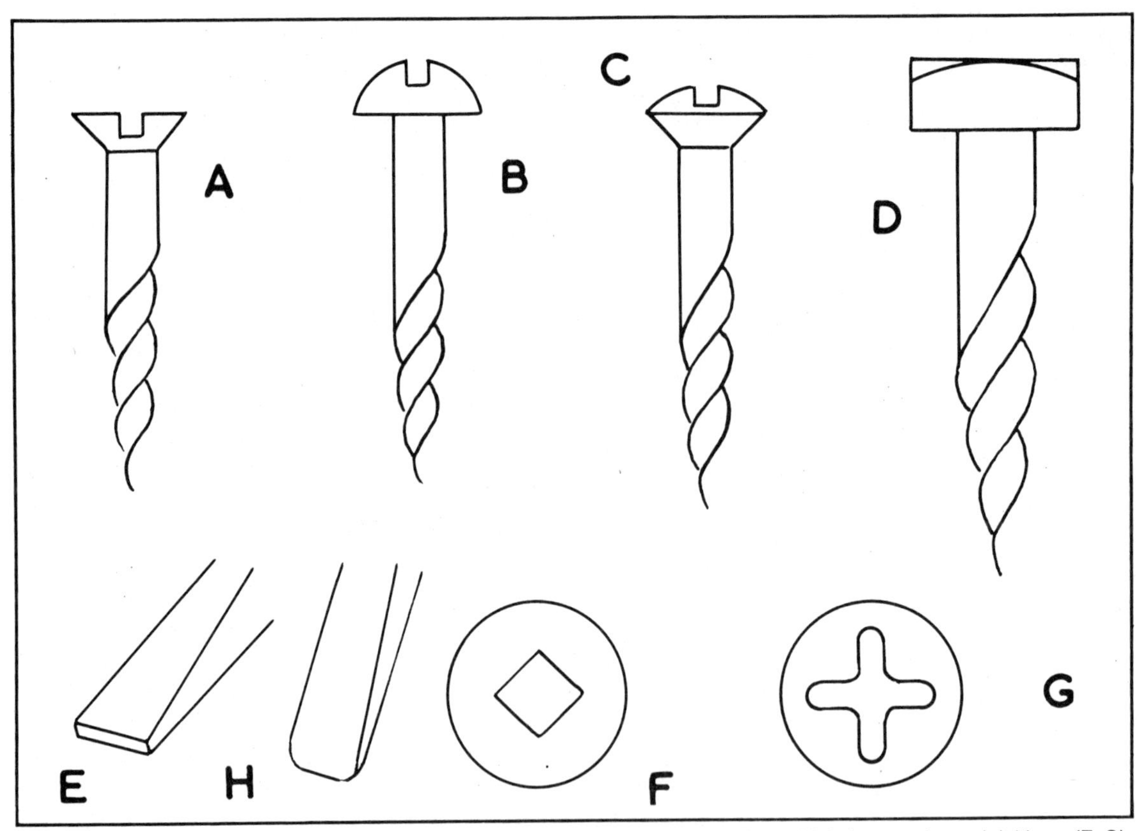

Fig. 3-3. Screws have many heads (A to D) and may be slotted for a screwdriver (E) or with holes to suit special drivers (F, G). The end for a slot head should not have worn rounded (H).

Usually the amount of countersinking does not have to be as much as the size of the screwhead. You must allow for some compression of the wood as the head pulls in.

A screw draws two pieces of wood together by squeezing the top piece between the head and the threads pulling into the lower piece. The screw should not be tight or threaded into the top piece, so always drill a clearance hole there (Fig. 3-4A). Countersink the top if necessary. The size hole to drill into the lower piece depends on the wood. You may be able to put a small screw through the top hole in softwood and give it a light tap with a hammer to start it. Let it cut its own way into the bottom piece as you turn it. For a larger screw in softwood, there may have to be an undersize hole taken a short way to start the screw (Fig. 3-4B). In hardwood you may need to use a larger pilot hole and take it deeper (Fig. 3-4C). It is often advisable to experiment. A screw holds more strongly with the minimum of wood removed by drilling, but you have to compromise to make driving possible. Similarly, do not countersink excessively. See how far a screwhead will pull in first. A head that has pulled below the surface looks bad.

The sizes and spacing of screws depend on experience. They normally will not need to be as close as nails in a similar joint. Make sure there is enough screw into the lower part to provide strength. Thicker screws should be stronger than thinner ones, but you may get all the strength you require with a neater effect by using slightly more thinner screws in a particular joint.

When making an assembly with screws, it will often help to work progressively and tighten various parts so as to get an even pressure. If the joint is also glued, you can see this happening as the glue oozes out all around.

Other Screws

Common wood screws will do what you want in wood construction, but with the coming of other materials and manufactured boards there have been accompanying new fasteners. The thread on an ordinary wood screw is what is called *single-start;* one thread twists around. Some screws are made *double-start* with two threads around the screw. Such screws can be used on wood, but they are particularly suitable for particle board.

There are special self-tapping screws made of hardened steel for sheet metalwork, with threads to the head, that can be driven into holes and cut a thread as they progress. Their particular use is in the automobile industry, but they have many other applications. Similar-looking screws are made for driving into particle board (Fig. 3-5A). The threads have a better grip in the resin and wood chip mixture than ordinary wood screws. Undersize holes must always be drilled for the full depth of any screw in particle board.

Screw hooks (Fig. 3-5B) and *screw eyes* (Fig. 3-5C) have wood screw threads so they can be driven into undersize holes. Gauges vary with sizes. Whenever possible, these should be driven until the curved part touches the wood. Otherwise, there is a risk of breaking or bending at the neck.

There is sometimes a need for a double-ended screw (Fig. 3-5D) that can be driven with the aid of pliers into one piece. Another part with a suitable hole already drilled in it is turned on to the projecting thread. This can only be done with a single screw, but it is a way of attaching a knob or other item of small section.

A hanger or table screw (Fig. 3-5E) has metal threads at one end to take a nut. The best way to drive into wood is to jam two nuts against each other on their threads so you can turn into a hole in the wood with a wrench, then remove the nuts. These screws are useful where you want to bolt something in place, but you can't get at the far side to insert ordinary bolts.

BOLTS

A *bolt* or machine screw differs from a wood screw

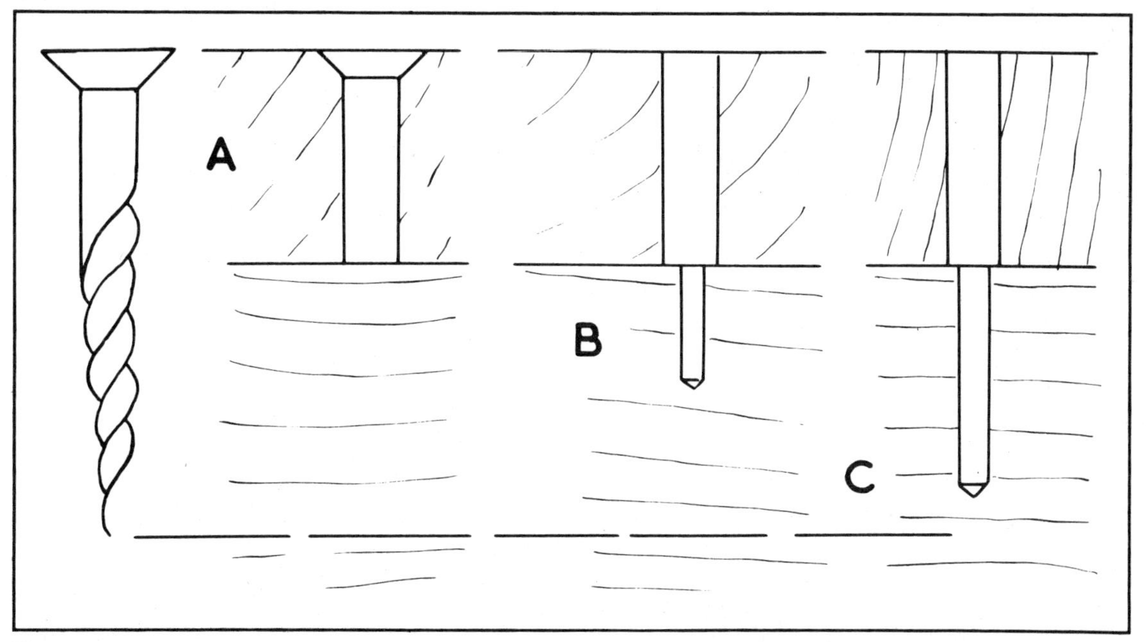

Fig. 3-4. Holes for screws should give clearance in the top piece (A) and may be drilled to suit the hardness of the other piece (B, C).

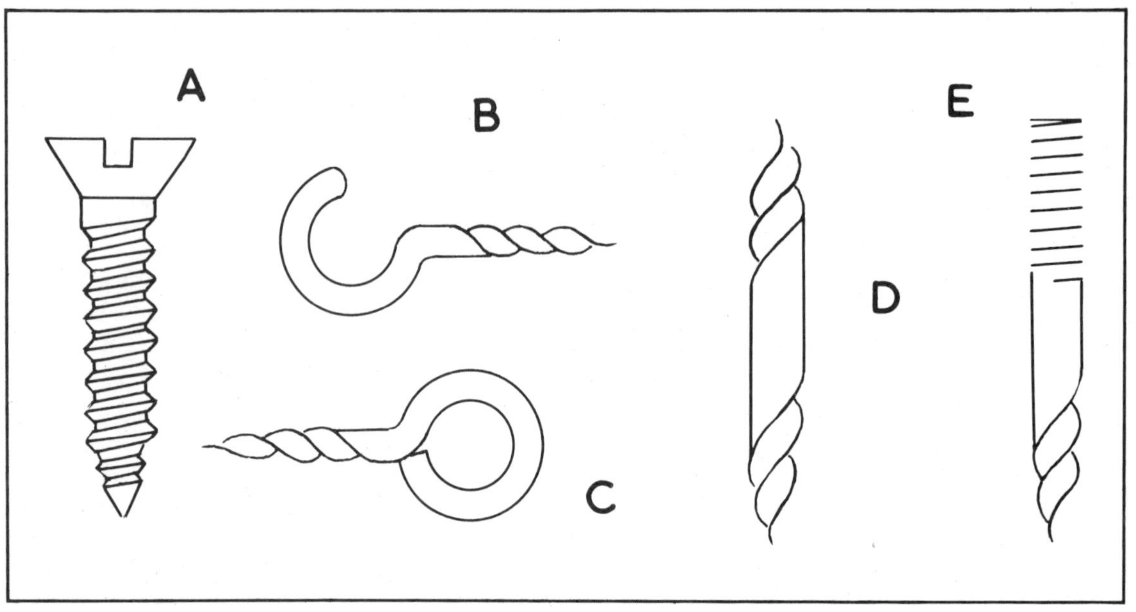

Fig. 3-5. A screw for particle board or to cut into sheet metal is threaded to the head (A). Hooks and eyes (B, C) have wood screw ends. A double-ended screw (D) pulls two pieces of wood together, another screw (E) draws metal to wood.

in that it has threads on a parallel cylindrical part. The threads usually have to mate with a nut or a thread cut in a metal part. There are many of these screwed fasteners, and not many of them are needed in the construction of built-in furniture. There are places where bolts are more appropriate than nails or wood screws.

A bolt has a threaded end extending only partially along its length (Fig. 3-6A). A *machine bolt* has a hexagonal head and a nut that matches. Some bolts that are usually intended for rough work have coarser threads and square heads and nuts. The name screw is more often given to a similar fastener that has threads to the head, but there are exceptions.

A useful bolt or screw for use in wood is a *carriage bolt* (Fig. 3-6B), which has a shallow oval head and a square neck below it. The square pulls into the wood and prevents the bolt from turning. Some variations might be employed as alternatives if you have them available. A *roundheaded bumper bolt* is fully threaded and generally shorter. A *Norway* or *elevator bolt* has a much wider flat head and is intended for holding soft materials. A *reliance bolt* also has a wide flat head with a screwdriver slot, but there are ribs under the head to press into wood or soft materials instead of a square neck.

There are stove bolts, for more slender nut and bolt fastenings, which have heads like flat wood screws and threads full length (Fig. 3-6C). Similar bolts can be had with round, oval, and other heads. Stove bolts can be obtained up to 6 inches long and in diameters from 5/32 inch on up, so they are suitable for passing through many thicknesses of wood.

For most woodwork construction, the nuts can be the common square or hexagonal ones used over a washer to resist pulling into the wood. Standard washers are not much bigger than the nuts, but you can get larger ones with the same size hole for wood or soft materials.

For situations where the screwed end has to be driven and you can't get at the far side to use a wrench, nuts can be secured to the wood. Some require one or more pins through tabs, but a *tee nut* (Fig. 3-6D) has prongs that sink into the material as the bolt is tightened. The nut will stay there after the bolt has been removed, so it is useful where the furniture you make has to be removed from a board permanently attached to the wall.

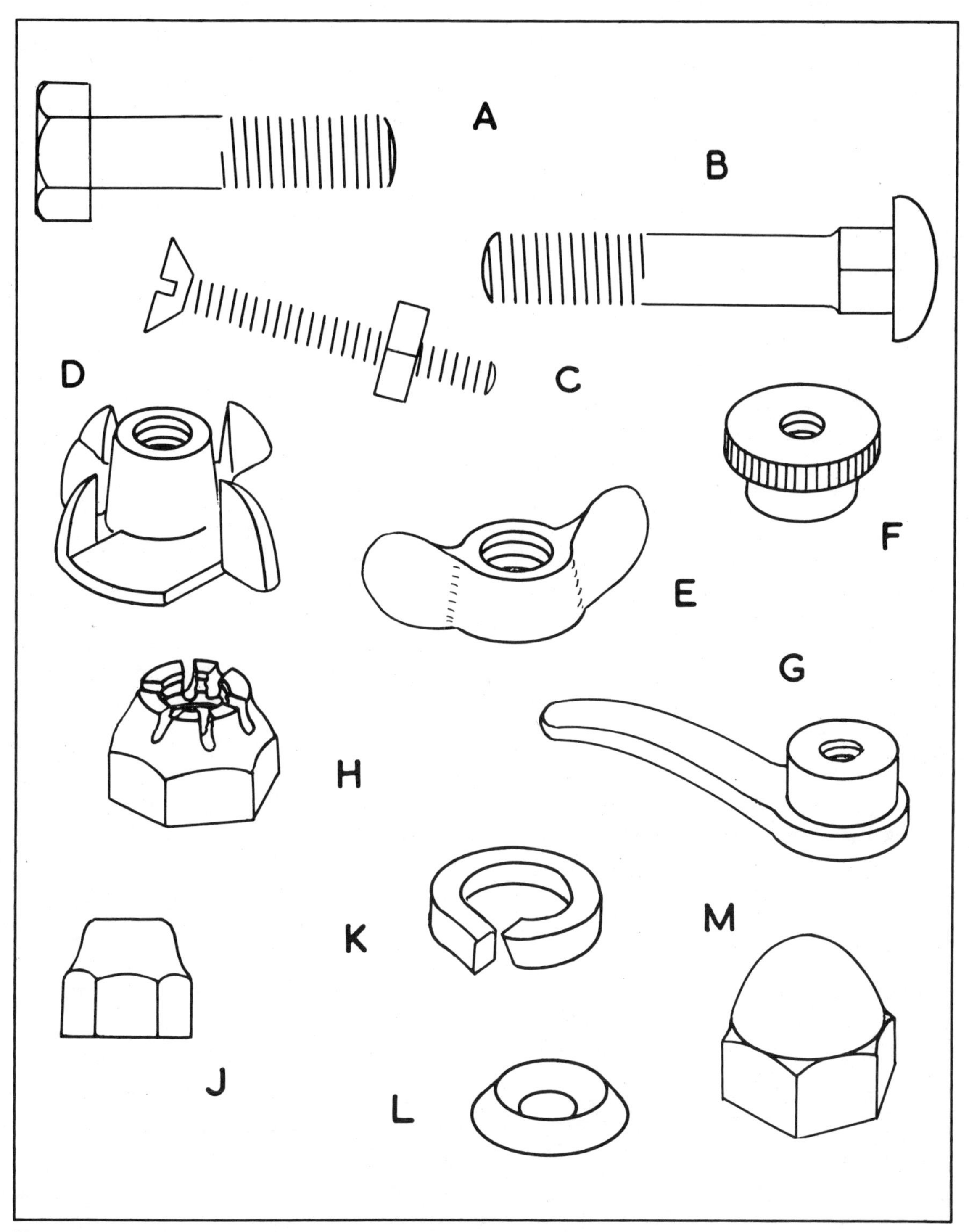

Fig. 3-6. Metal-thread screws have a variety of heads and nuts.

The other way of dealing with this problem is to have the bolt ends projecting, with the other side held with square necks. The removable part can be held to each bolt with a nut and washer. If you want the nut to be removable without the use of a wrench, it can be a *butterfly* or *wing nut* (Fig. 3-6E) or, for a smaller fastener, a *knurled nut* (Fig. 3-6F). A *handle nut* (Fig. 3-6G) may be used for more leverage.

You can use one plain nut over a washer in most furniture construction. If the joined parts will have to move over each other, they must be locked. The traditional way of locking is with a second thinner nut, and the two are forced against each other with two wrenches. That is satisfactory, but there are alternatives. Castle and slotted nuts are made with slots so a *cotter pin* can be put through a hole drilled across the bolt (Fig. 3-6H). There are several versions of stiff nuts, usually with a part extending above the wrench part (Fig. 3-6J). There may be a sprung or distorted part of the thread in the nut to provide a grip, or there can be fiber or plastic that the bolt end passes through. In these cases there is enough resistance to vibrating loose, but the nuts can be unscrewed with a wrench. Two-part epoxy adhesives are used for locking nuts. They glue the nut and bolt together, but a wrench will separate them.

Another way of securing is to use a *locking washer*. There are several versions. A common type is a *spiral split washer* (Fig. 3-6K). It is made of hardened steel. When used between a plain washer and a nut, its ends dig into the nut and washer to resist unscrewing. Other washers have many teeth to dig in all around. Some washers are sprung and are intended to take up play where the fastener is not fully tightened, rather than to prevent unscrewing.

Nut and bolt fasteners will be away from any exposed finished surfaces in most built-in furniture. If you can't avoid a head or nut showing, there are ways of making the part more attractive. A plated head will look better than a plain one. *Cup* or *finishing washers* (Fig. 3-6L) may be used under a countersunk or oval head. Besides improving appearance, these washers prevent wear on the wood if it is a fastener that has to be removed and replaced occasionally. If it is the bolt end that comes on the surface, you can use an *acorn* or *cap nut* (Fig. 3-6M). That hides the bolt end, which will have to be sawed off if there is too much projecting to be enclosed in the nut.

WALL FASTENERS

Built-in furniture has to be secured in place; it would not be built-in if it was not attached to the wall or floor. How it is attached depends on into what you have to drive fasteners. If it is wood, the attachments will be nails or screws driven as already described. You have to deal with other materials in most cases, although there may be wood studding and other framing behind a fairly thin facing material. If it is brick or masonry, you have the extra problems that come with the hardness of the material.

If you can locate the studs and use screws long enough to pass through the covering material and go far enough into the wood, that should be your usual fastening choice. This depends on being able to space the holes for fasteners at places in the furniture that will provide the necessary strength and rigidity. You may have to use different fasteners away from the studs.

The most common fastener for a hollow wall is a *screw anchor* (Fig. 3-7A). The hole in the wall is slightly larger than the screw. The body part is pushed in, and the screw is driven into it. The effect is to pull back the far end of the body, so its cut parts spread against the back of the wallboard or other material.

There is a *toggle bolt* for a similar situation (Fig. 3-7B). There may be one offset toggle or a pair. The hole has to be large enough to push the folded toggles through. At the other side they open and are drawn back against the other side of the sheet by tightening the bolt. Other metal and plastic anchors depend on a screw being tightened to expand their far end and grip the other side, where that is inaccessible. Some of these have strengths comparable with the other fasteners, but others are only intended for light duties such as hanging a picture. Be careful that the anchoring devices you get are suitable for the loads to be applied.

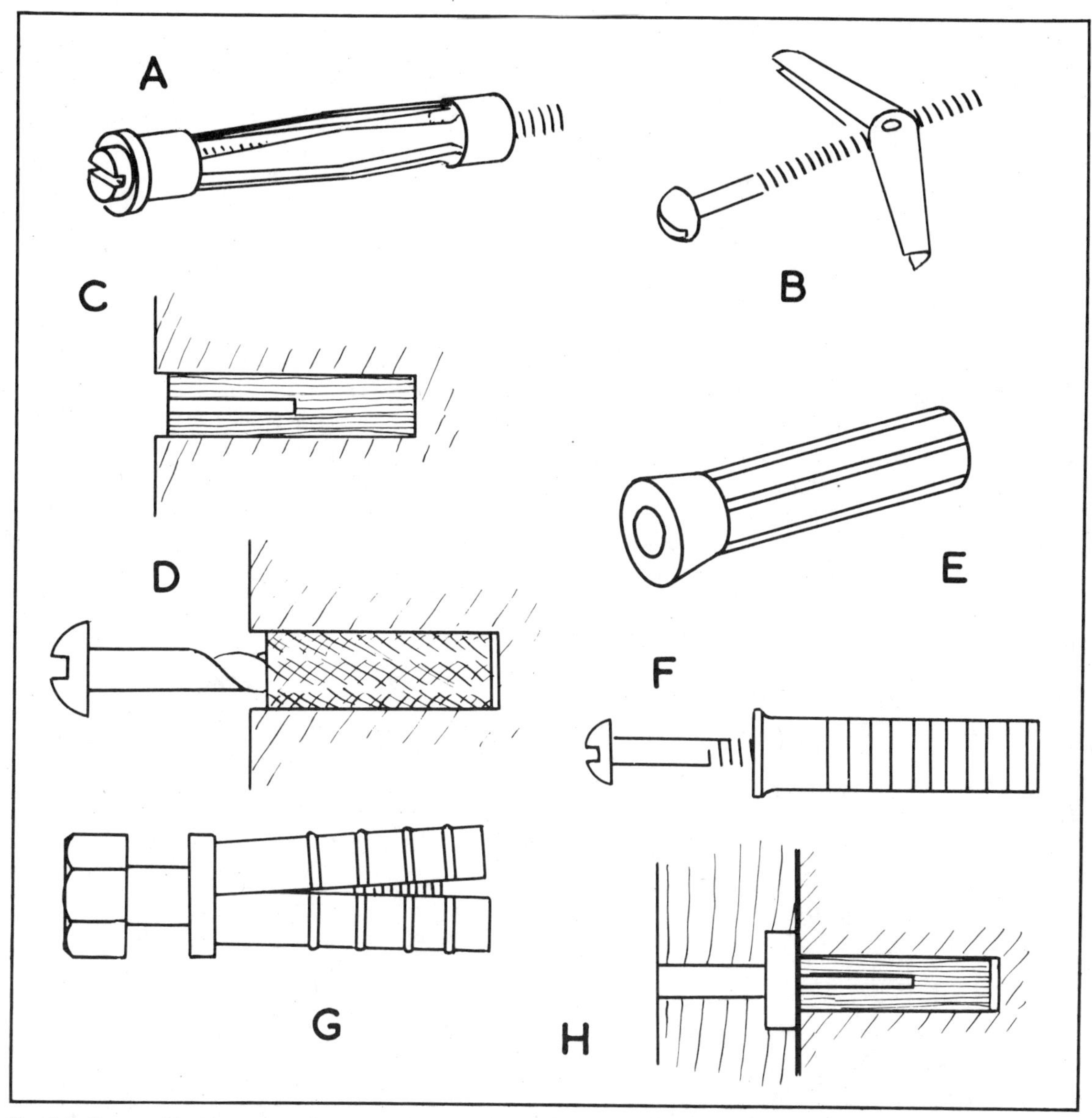

Fig. 3-7. Screwed fasteners to walls depend mostly on expansion as they tighten into a plug or their own body.

If you want to attach to brick or masonry, you have to drill holes first. If the fastener can come at a joint, though, it may be possible to chop out for a wood plug to be driven in. This is generally less satisfactory than a hole drilled in the solid material, as the plug may loosen. Drills for brick, masonry, and other hard materials look like metalworking drills, but the tips have hard inserts to cut when driven by an ordinary electric drill or one with a jump action. If you have to make a hole without a drill, there are tools to hit. They are slower and do not produce as good a hole.

The simplest plug is wood, and it should be satisfactory. The wood need not be cut exactly round, but it should be fairly tight in the hole as you drive it. You may have to make it too long and cut off the surplus with a chisel. If it is possible to sink its end with a punch (Fig. 3-7C), this removes the risk of wood spreading above the surface as a screw is driven and allows what is being attached to come close to the wall. Drill only a small pilot hole into the plug, so the screw will expand the wood and make it grip the surrounding masonry or brick.

Rawlplug screw anchors are fibrous and used in the same way as wood plugs (Fig. 3-7D). They are in several diameters and lengths to suit a variety of wood screws. Plastic anchors are similar (Fig. 3-7E), but they are not suited to such heavy duties. Another plastic anchor is provided with a screw (Fig. 3-7F). The screw expands the plug as it is tightened, either in a hole or a hollow wall, but this is only intended for light duty.

Those fasteners should satisfy most furniture attachment needs. Other more massive fasteners are better suited for attaching machinery to masonry, but you should be aware of them in case you have to deal with a heavily loaded situation. Most of these anchors use a shield or cylinder that will go into a prepared hole. The tightening of a bolt expands and grips the hole (Fig. 3-7G). The head is usually shaped to tighten with a wrench.

Some anchors tend to lift on the surface or raise the surrounding surface slightly as they are tightened. Some have a rim that is not intended to pull into the wall. These characteristics may prevent you from tightening the furniture as closely to the wall as you would like to get a closer fit, either countersink the back of a hole or counterbore it (Fig. 3-7H) to give clearance for a rim or raised edge, or chips or dust that come out as you tighten.

The number of attachments required depends on many factors. A few fasteners spread as widely as possible are more effective than more fasteners put close together. If all the weight has to be taken by the wall attachments, they will have to be more numerous and stronger than if the furniture stands on the floor and the wall fasteners only have to prevent movement. If you expect to remove the furniture if you move from the house, attachments will have to be more inconspicuous in the wall than if the furniture is to stay in place.

If you want to build in without actually making holes anywhere, it may be possible to fit a thing closely in a recess, so it can be prevented from movement with wedges that may be hidden by removable facing pieces (Fig. 3-8A). You can lock the furniture in place with a screw through a tee nut—pressed against a strip of sheet metal and tightened from inside the cabinet (Fig. 3-8B).

You can't avoid drilling the wall for something that hangs on a flat surface, unless there is already a curtain rail or other support from which it might hang. If you can arrange supports from floor to ceiling, they may have wedged ends (Fig. 3-8C). Even a single piece arranged in this way might be strong enough for bookshelves or similar things that otherwise would have been hung. Even with large assemblies that occupy a whole wall, it may be possible to use wedges above or below and hide them with front parts. Such furniture should be given full backs so the wall does not show through at any place, and a perfectly tight fit at the rear is unnecessary.

BRACKETS AND BRACES

Several stock types of metal hardware have more uses in built-in furniture than in freestanding items. Some may be needed to attach to a wall. They may have to form joints when parts are assembled in position, and it is impossible to make the more usual wood-to-wood joints or to insert screws or nails between parts directly.

Shelf brackets can provide intermediate supports where the distant ends have more conventional joints. They can also share the weight of a wall cabinet or similar item.

Some shelf brackets have a strut built in and the screw holes arranged so the screwdriver can be used from opposite sides of it (Fig. 3-9A). The strut puts strength where it is needed, but there are places where it can interfere with something else and restrict stowage or limit what can be put on a shelf below. Brackets with a rib pressed into the center (Fig. 3-9B) give enough strength without limiting very much what goes below. The brackets are pressed from comparatively thin sheet steel, but the method of construction gives adequate stiffness.

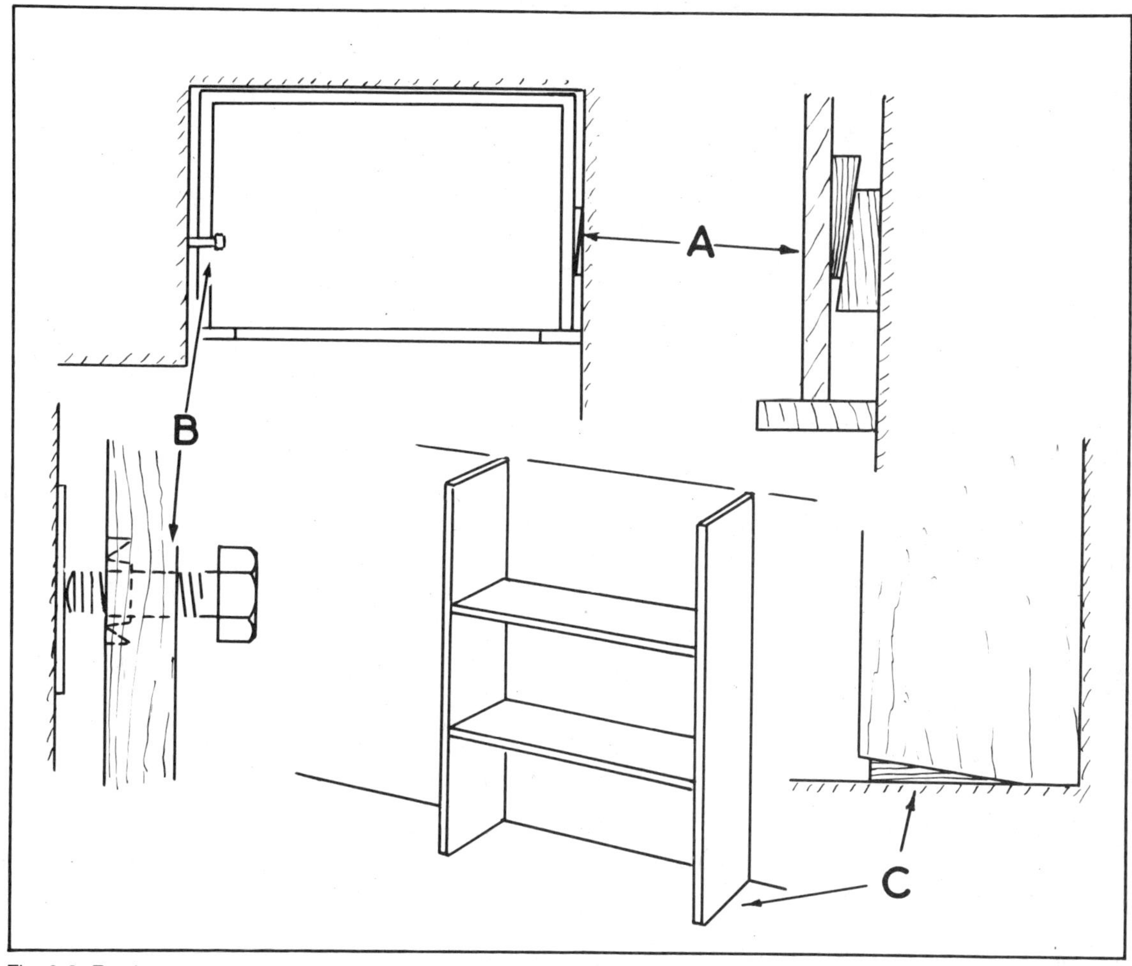

Fig. 3-8. Furniture may be tightened in place with wedges (A, C) or pressure from a bolt (B).

If any shelf bracket is checked with a square, it will be found to be 1° or so more than 90°. That allows for any slight sag, so the shelf does not finish tilting forward. Shelf brackets range from 3 inches by 4 inches up to at least 10 inches by 12 inches.

A *corner brace* (Fig. 3-9C) may be mistaken for a shelf bracket, but it is flat strip metal without stiffening. Screw holes are countersunk inside so the brace can be used inside two meeting boards, such as the corner of a box, to strengthen a weak joint or to take the place of any other jointing. If you want to put a brace outside a corner, you will have to countersink the other side or drill and countersink new holes. Normal corner braces are made of light strip steel, with its section varying according to size. A variant made of stouter strip may be called a *corner iron,* but it is otherwise similar. Lengths of legs can be anywhere between 1 inch and 10 inches.

Straight and angled plates may be described as mending plates (Figs. 3-9D and 3-9E). They come in many sizes from 2 inches up to 12 inches and in varying widths. They are intended for repairs to cracked or broken furniture, but they can be used for attaching a part to another that is already screwed to the wall.

Although brackets and braces may be bought, they are simple things to make—at least in the smaller sizes—if you have facilities for sawing,

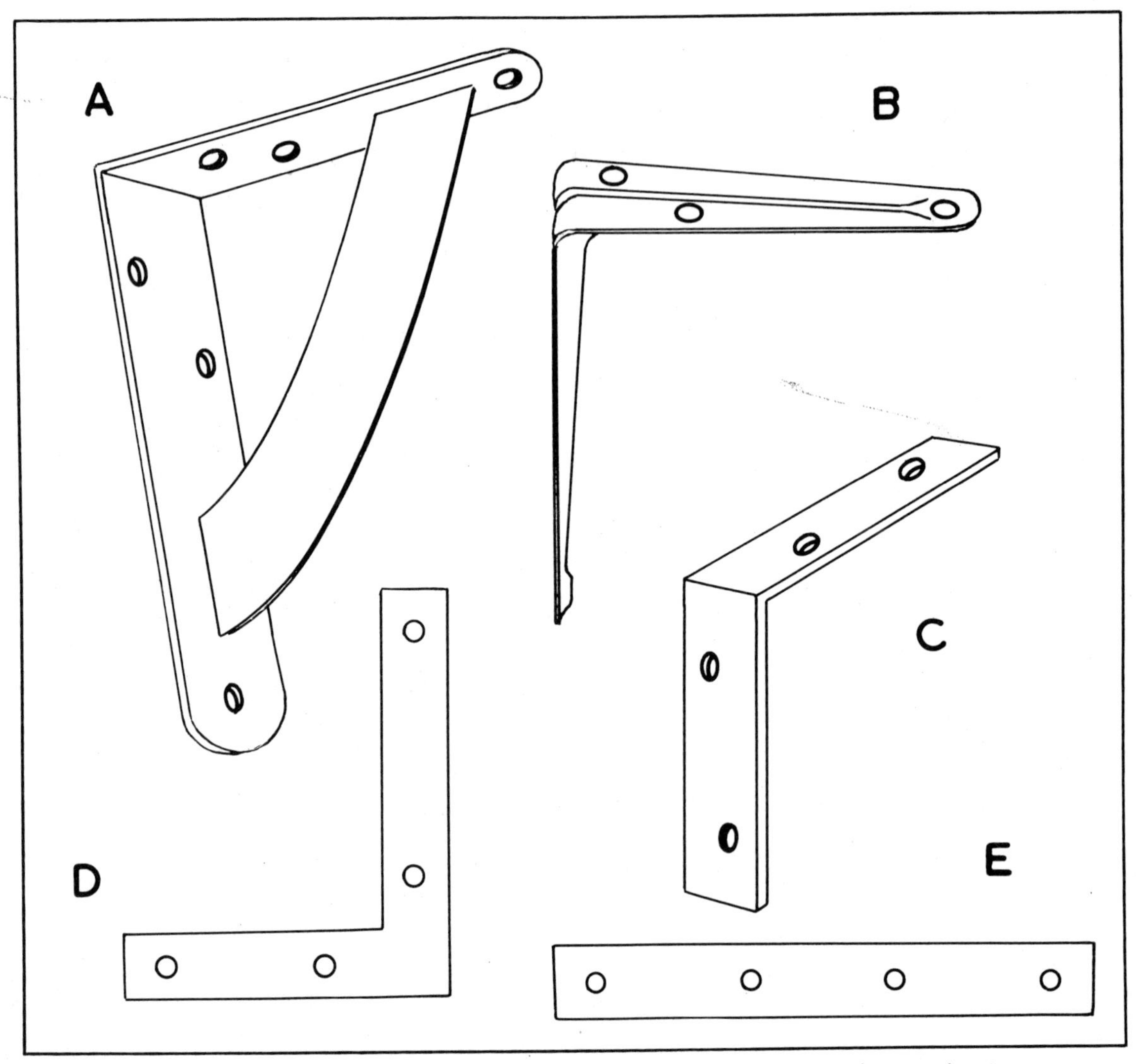

Fig. 3-9. Metal brackets (A, B) and shaped plates (C, D, E) are used to support and strengthen wood parts.

filing, and drilling metal. Bending is simply done by hammering over in a vise. Strip steel from ½ inch wide and in thicknesses from 1/16 inch upward makes useful stock from which to make braces and other things. You can use other metals, but for most purposes steel has the strength, although brass and aluminum will resist corrosion.

HINGES

Hinges are made for all kinds of situations. The traditional types are generally most suitable for most furniture but there are ingenious hidden hinges and others with double actions or for mounting at edges of doors. Some are intended for use with particle board. If all you want is to mount a door in a piece of furniture, the well-established type of hinge will do, unless you want to provide a special action or the door or its frame are unusual. Only the common hinges are described in this chapter, with notes on some others, but particular applications are described later in projects where they occur.

A *butt hinge* (Fig. 3-10A) is the basic type made of iron or brass for furniture. It is described by its length and widths increase for longer hinges. Screw holes also vary according to the length. The flaps of the hinge are arranged to swing on the knuckle and come parallel without actually meeting (Fig. 3-10B) to give clearance between a door and its frame. Unless it is an exceptionally tall door, two hinges are used. You must get the knuckles in line for the door to swing smoothly.

If the door surface is flush with its frame, the flaps may be let into both surfaces (Fig. 3-10C). The hinge is arranged so its knuckle is clear of the surface (Fig. 3-10D), then the door will swing without binding. If you let the hinge only into the door edge, the pivot center is moved slightly. The door will swing with a greater gap in the open position, but the flap of the hinge that is not let in will look ugly.

A butt hinge extended to a considerable length is called a *piano hinge* because of its application in pianos, but it can be cut to make short hinges. A writing flap or similar thing then needs a strut or chain to hold it level; several versions are available. For small lightly loaded flaps, there are hinges with stops that prevent them from going more than 90° open, but they cannot take much strain.

Thin hinges are made where one flap fits into the other as it closes (Fig. 3-10E). The thickness matches the clearance the door needs, so there is no need to let in the hinge. These hinges were produced for use with particle board, but they can be used with solid wood.

A butt hinge fitted between the parts is fairly inconspicuous. Don't put butt hinges on the surface, except in the roughest work. Hinges cut to decorative outlines and possibly with ornamented surfaces go on the front of a door (Fig. 3-10F). They may be matched to handles or catches, so the assembly presents an attractive overall appearance. Screws are often sold with the hinges so their heads match.

Door fronts are not always level with their frames. In a kitchen cabinet the door may have a rabbet over the frame. Hinges are made with double bends to allow for this (Fig. 3-10G). A hinge of rather similar appearance may be used where more strength is needed at the edge of a thin door when the flap can go behind to take extra screws (Fig. 3-10H).

Some hinges are made wider than butt hinges, particularly for use where the hinge cannot be very long and extra screw holes are needed further from the knuckle (Fig. 3-10J). One hinge that looks like this at first glance is actually a *backflap hinge*. It is designed to suit a rule joint in a table or other edge, where a flap can drop and leave what looks like a molded edge. The hinge is used with its knuckle upward, and it swings back further than a normal hinge (Fig. 3-10K).

If a hinge has to extend some way onto one surface to provide strength or sufficient grip, it can be a tee hinge (Fig. 3-10L) obtainable in sizes up to much larger than you will use on furniture. If the hinge has to extend in both directions it is a *strap hinge* (Fig. 3-10M).

A pivot hinge (Fig. 3-10N) comes at the end of a door. There are many variations designed for use with bathroom and kitchen furniture. The hinge has legs with enough screw holes and may be arranged to lap over edges for additional fasteners. The pivot is arranged to clear both surfaces, so the door swings to leave a gap as it opens.

HANDLES

Handles to drawers and doors serve decorative and, practical purposes. They are available in many types, and you can choose them to match your needs. Make sure the chosen handle is large enough to provide a grip, even if it is only for a couple of fingers on a light drawer. A handle may provide part of the whole decorative effect, with hinges and other hardware arranged as part of a matching set. Handles may be wood, which you may make yourself, but they are more often metal or plastic.

Here we are concerned with the attachment methods and not with the design features that affect appearance. In the simplest examples you can provide a grip in the thing itself, so there is no need for an applied handle. In a simple door where utility is the only concern, you can drill one or two holes large enough to put fingers through (Fig. 3-11A).

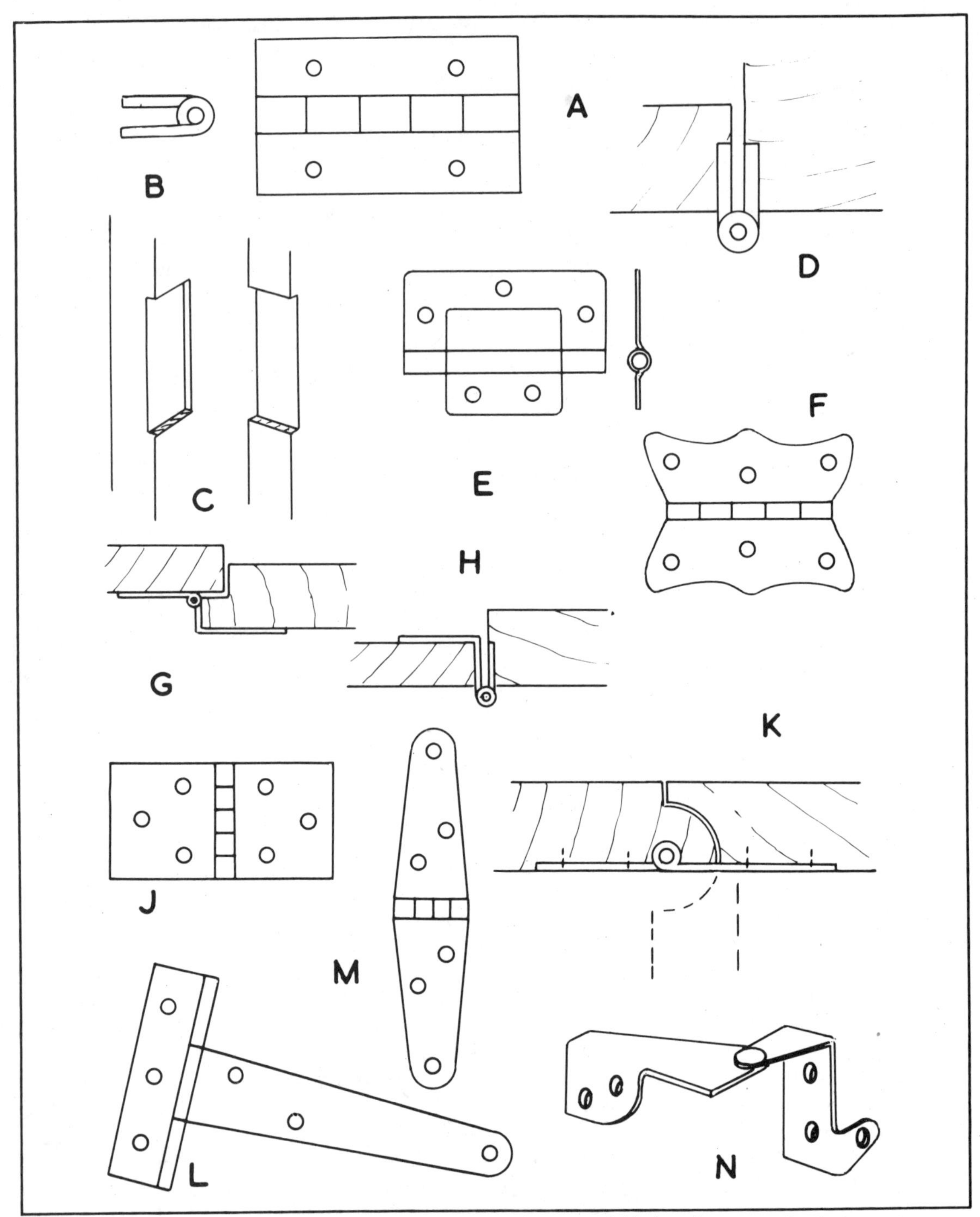

Fig. 3-10. A hinge pivots on a knuckle pin, but there are many shapes available to suit many applications.

You can drill a pair of smaller holes and put a loop of rope through to provide something to pull. Another way is to cut away the edge of the drawer or door, so you can put fingers through (Fig. 3-11B). If this is neatly rounded, it may be better than projecting handles in a compact kitchen, where a person may knock against them. In a block of drawers the notch in one drawer allows your fingers to go under the one above.

Flush-mounting handles require a piece cutting out of the wood (Fig. 3-11C). They are more appropriate to drawers than doors, other than sliding ones.

When you pull a door or drawer by a handle, all the load comes on the attachment to the wood. If this is by wood screws, the pull is in the direction of withdrawal. You must choose screws large enough and long enough to withstand these loads. For a large door or a drawer that may be heavily loaded, it is better to have some sort of through fastening.

In early Colonial furniture most handles were turned wooden knobs, probably because there was no nearby hardware store and everything had to be made by the carpenter. A knob turned with a dowel on it makes a secure attachment when glued in place (Fig. 3-11D), and it is even stronger if its end is cut and wedged (Fig. 3-11E). A knob without the dowel can have a screw from the back (Fig. 3-11F). An even stronger fastening is with a metal-thread screw into a metal or plastic knob (Fig. 3-11G). Loop handles of many types use a pair of screws in this way. Some have a plate with two holes to spread the load inside (Fig. 3-11H). If not, put the washers under the screwheads. In some handles there is a plate on the screws at the front. The wood tends to get soiled round a handle. Provide a piece of plastic or metal there, even if it is not provided with the handle. Black Plexiglas acrylic plastic or something similar sets off the handle and protects the wood (Fig. 3-11J).

Special handles for faced particle board cover edges and are available to suit drawers or doors (Fig. 3-11K). There are metal and plastic inserts to fit in flush for sliding doors, or you can merely use finger holes.

CATCHES

Catches are available in various patterns. In most furniture the catch has to hold a door shut, so it does not swing open unintentionally. It can be easily opened when needed, either by a simple action or merely by pulling the handle. A definite action may be preferable when a child might open a door that he shouldn't. You may want to shut a door or drawer more securely, then a lock has to be fitted. Usually that means having a key, although some locks can be released by pressing a knob or other action that will not be obvious.

A turn button was the first closure (Fig. 3-12A). It still has uses, either as a simple piece of wood on a screw or as a decorative metal piece on a backing plate. If you want to secure a drawer or a drop flap, a single-sided turn button will fall down into place due to gravity (Fig. 3-12B). A fairly similar idea has the turn button inside and a knob outside connected to it (Fig. 3-12C). This is effective and gives you a handle and catch in one thing. It is particularly appropriate if you are aiming at a reproduction effect to match Colonial or other older furniture.

Where you want to use a catch that will release with a pull, you can choose between a friction type depending on a spring and a magnetic type.

A *ball catch* in its simplest form has a sprung ball in a tube that can be let into a drilled hole. The ball engages with a plate having a hole in it and screwed to the other surface (Fig. 3-12D). Larger versions have the ball part with lips for screws, and there are other variations for mounting to the insides of doors. The simplest type can be used on a door edge. There can be two—at top and bottom. Arrange clearance between the parts to allow the ball to engage with just enough movement.

Another sprung catch is made in several versions, but the holding arrangement is a pair of sprung jaws that engage with a shaped piece or a knob (Fig. 3-12E). The part with the spring is given slots for the screws so it can be adjusted to get just the right tension, with the jaws closing over the other part without slackness. Roller arrangements are more suitable for sliding doors, where a sprung

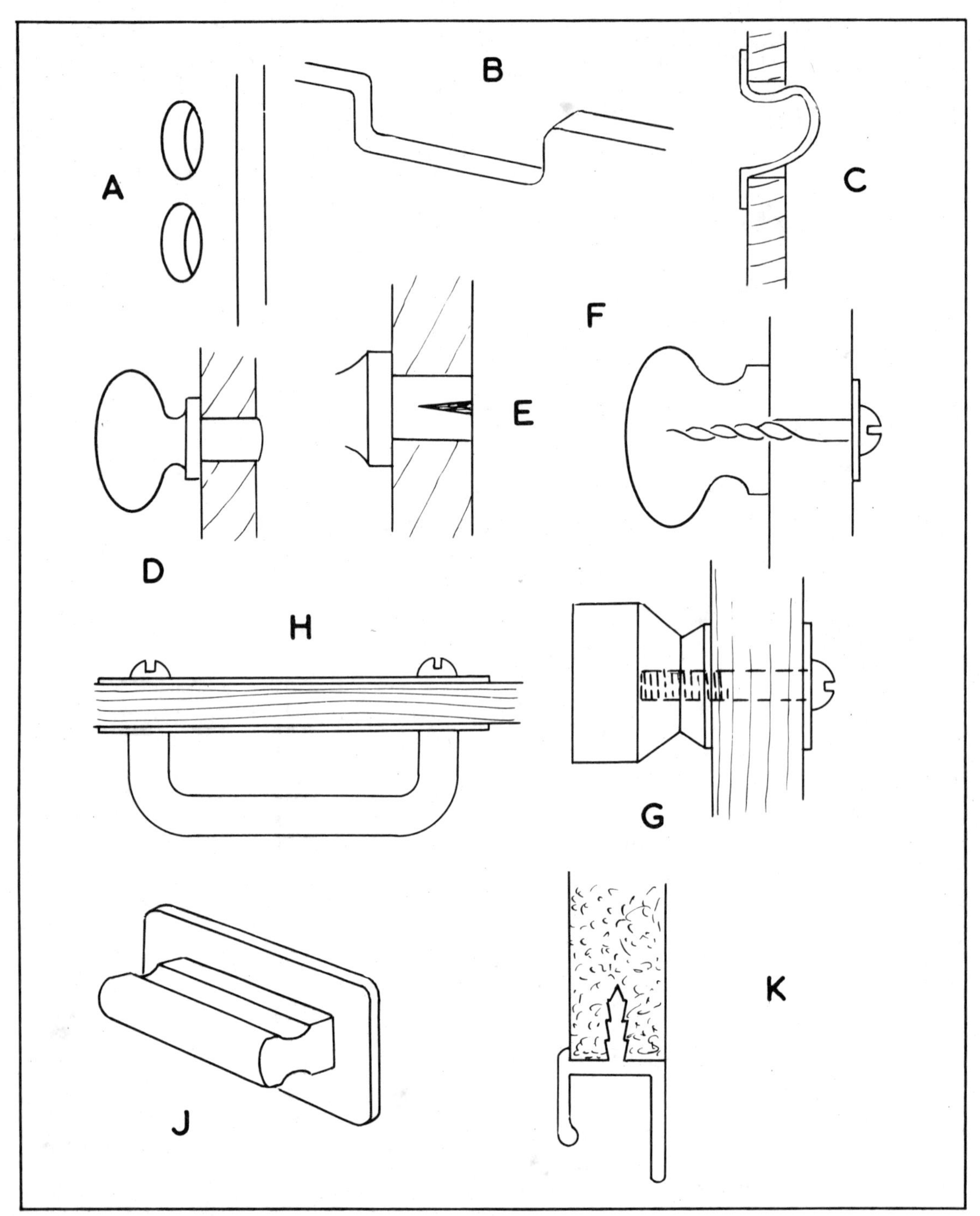

Fig. 3-11. Holes (A) or notches (B) provide a hand grip. Handles may be let in (C) or held with dowel ends or screws (D to J). A handle for particle board (K) has a toothed piece to fit into a groove.

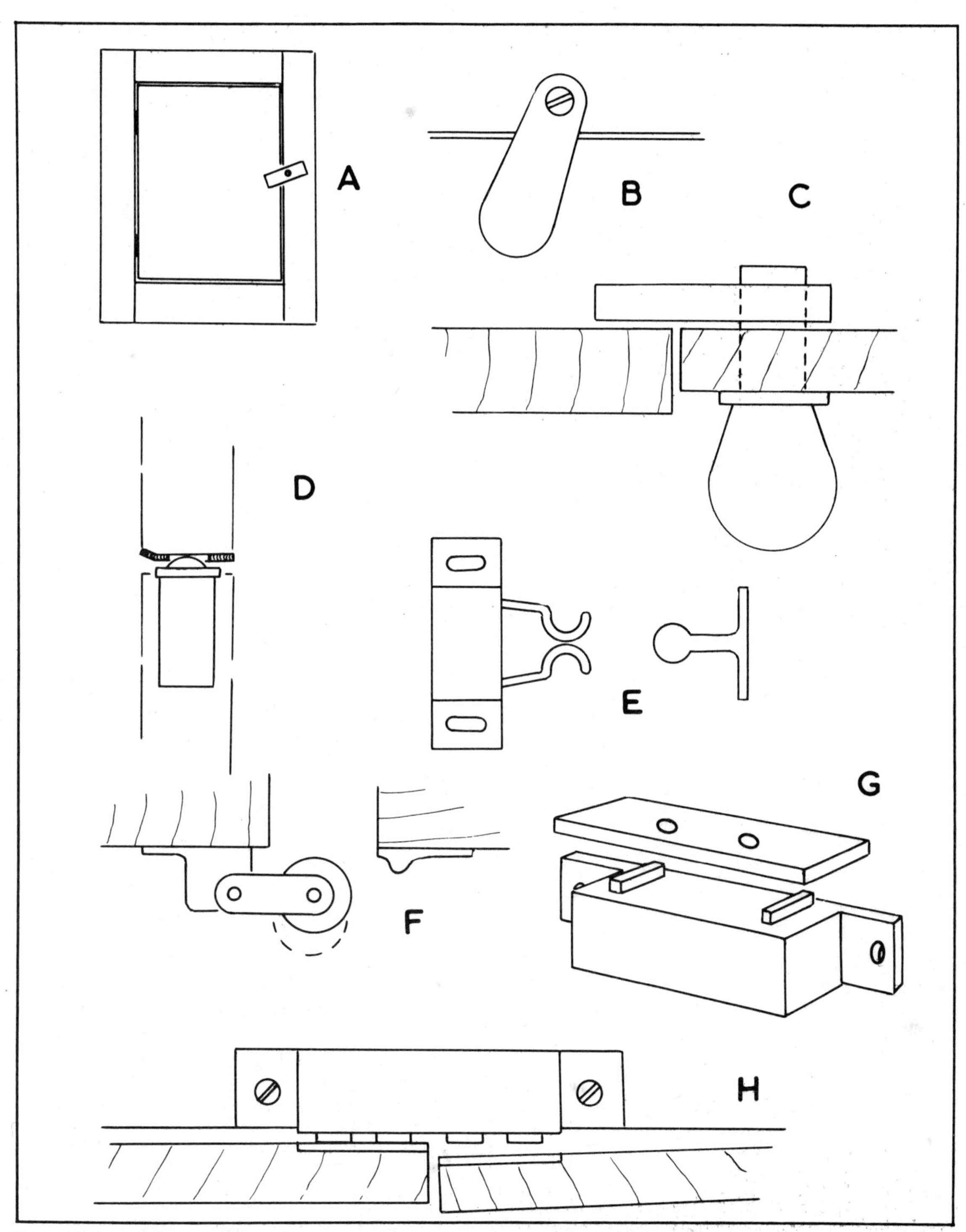

Fig. 3-12. A catch may turn (A to C), be sprung (D to F), or be magnetic (G, H).

arm with a roller goes over a projection on the other part (Fig. 3-12F).

A magnet needs two jaws to engage with a flat piece of iron for it to work. Magnetic catches use this principle. For a simple door catch, the magnet is in a piece with slots for adjusting on its screws. A flat plate is screwed to the other surface (Fig. 3-12G). This catch can be at the center edge of a door, or it can be arranged under the top of a cabinet or on a shelf edge. There may be catches at top and bottom on a large door. There can be two on a shelf edge for a pair of doors. Combined ones are available (Fig. 3-12H).

Magnetic or spring catches also act as doorstops. Otherwise, you have to provide a separate stop. There are metal angle pieces for this purpose, but usually a strip of wood makes a better independent stop.

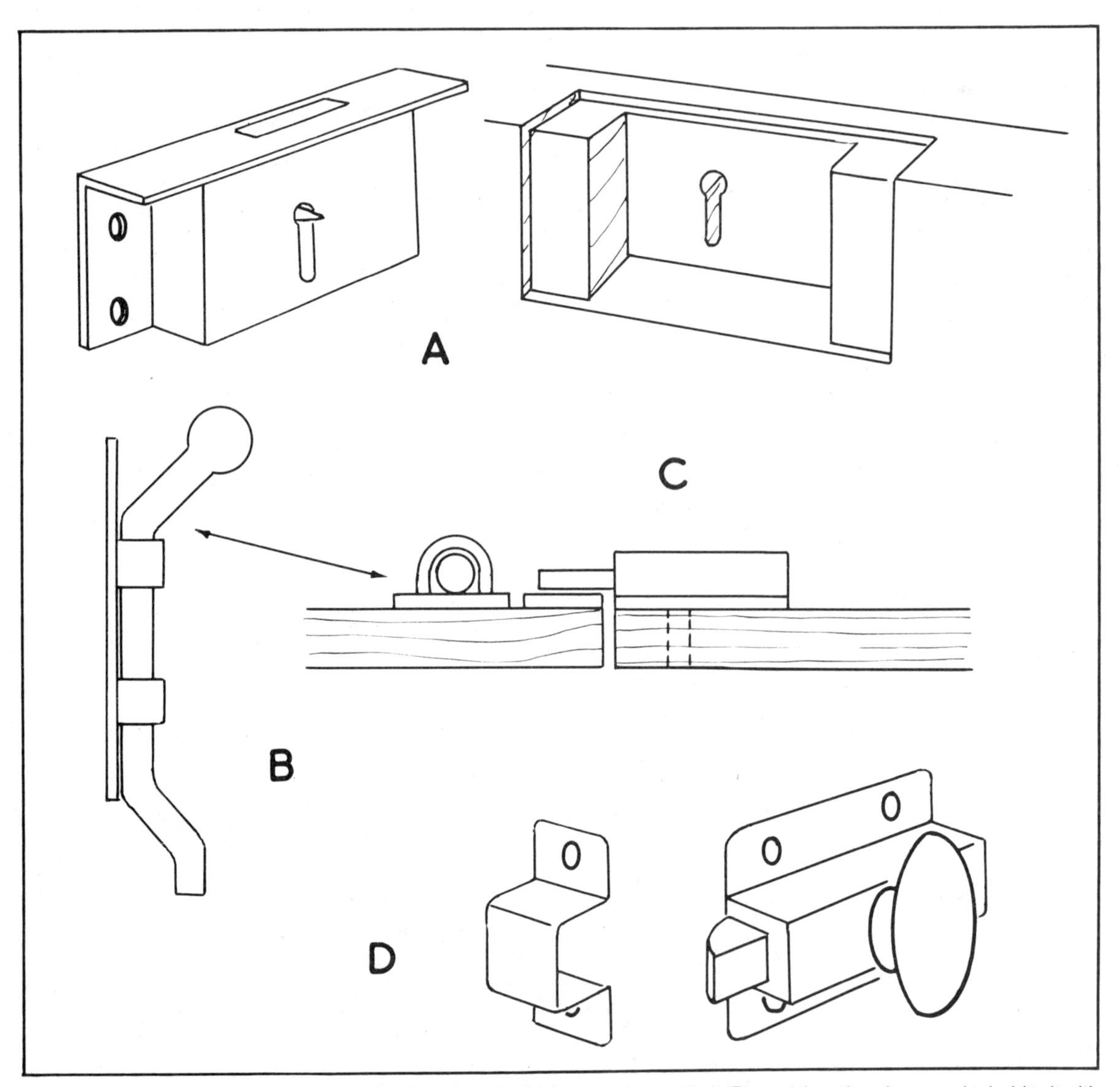

Fig. 3-13. A lock may be let into a recess (A). One of a pair of doors may have a bolt (B), and the other door may be held to it with a lock (C) or catch (D).

The usual type of lock with key for a drawer or door fits into the edge of the wood inside. The key enters through a hole, then the lock bolt engages with a plate on the other part. If a lifting lid is to be secured, there are hook arrangements that can be substituted for plain bolts. The lock is fitted in the same way. Some careful recessing of the wood must be done to take the lock and the escutcheon hole, as the key must have a neat finish at the front (Fig. 3-13A). Metal escutcheon plates are made in designs to match handles and can be screwed or nailed over the keyhole. Matching fine pins are provided as even the smallest screws will be ugly.

When a pair of swinging doors have to be locked, it is common to secure one with a bolt inside and lock the other to it. A small drop bolt (Fig. 3-13B) goes inside into a hole in a shelf if possible, but otherwise it may be better to have bolts at the top and bottom of the door. The lock on the other part can mount on the inner surface, so its bolt goes behind a plate on the bolted door (Fig. 3-13C). The key goes through a hole in the usual way.

Except for use inside double doors, bolts have little use in furniture. They are more appropriate in larger sizes for such things as garage doors. A smaller surface-mounted door catch that works on the bolt principle may be suitable for some applications. The sprung bolt part goes on the door and engages with a keeper on the framing (Fig. 3-13D). The knob also acts as the door handle.

Chapter 4

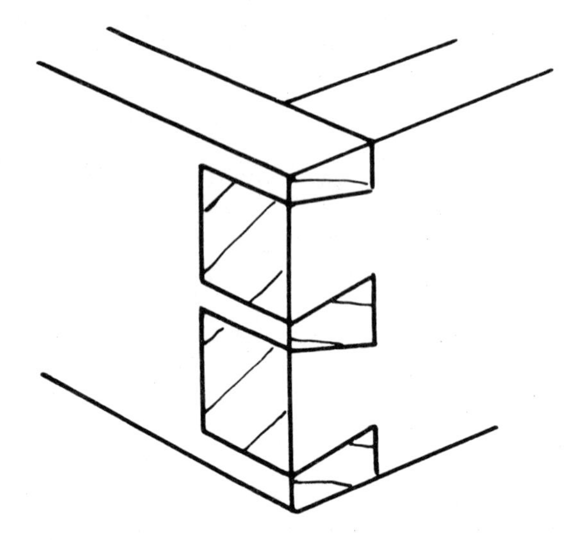

Special Techniques

THIS IS NOT A BOOK ON WOODWORKING SKILLS and techniques. I assume that you are reasonably proficient in handling tools, but advice is offered here on those techniques related to the making of built-in furniture, the choice of joints, and the making of drawers, doors, and special parts that occur frequently in this furniture. Consult *The Master Handbook of Fine Woodworking Techniques & Projects* (TAB Book No. 1247) and *The Complete Handbook of Woodworking Tools and Hardware* (TAB Book No. 1484) for information on woodworking techniques and tools.

RODS

When you are making freestanding furniture, you have a self-contained project. All measurements and constructional details are related to other parts within whatever you are making. When you make built-in furniture, you have to relate it to a wall or other part of the house. Even if you will be attaching to just a plain wall, you have to consider if it is flat and upright. You also have to consider height, particularly if what you are making goes from the floor to near the ceiling. If you are building into a corner, there are shape considerations. You also need to think about furniture in relation to doors, windows, and other furniture. When the work has been finished, the furniture will be, in effect, part of the house. If it projects too far or has some other snag that you had not anticipated, alterations can be a nuisance or impossible.

It is helpful at the planning stage and later for marking out to have some strips of wood, which a cabinetmaker calls *rods*. They can be pieces cut to the dimensions the furniture is expected to be in the main directions (Fig. 4-1A). You can try them in position. On them you can mark the locations of major parts. The upright rod can have the intended positions of shelves and other divisions (Fig. 4-1B). The rod projecting from the wall may show how far different levels may extend (Fig. 4-1C). The rod parallel to the wall can show door widths and other dividing parts (Fig. 4-1D).

You can make a mock-up of an end view from scrap hardboard or even cardboard if that seems a better way to show others the final projection of the

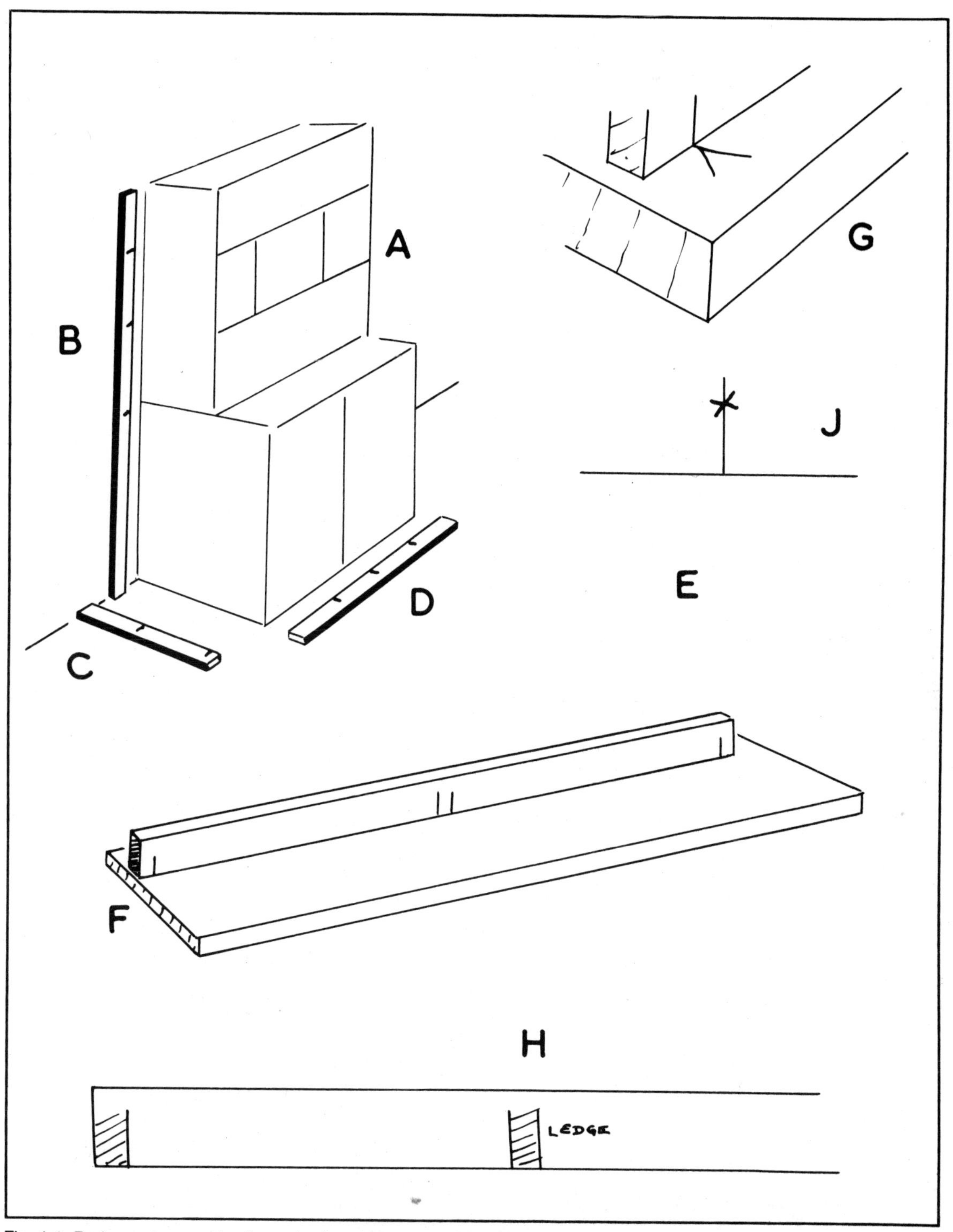

Fig. 4-1. Rods can be used for the main dimensions to transfer sizes to the wood so comparable parts will match exactly.

furniture when it is in position. Any such demonstration will be justified if it prevents someone saying after the work is done that the finished work is not what they expected. Holding rods in position to show where various parts will extend should indicate to you and other people the size of the finished piece of furniture before you start cutting wood.

When you have used the rods for visualizing the project in position, they can be used for marking wood. This is much better than always referring to measurements on a rule or tape. Human error may come in, particularly if you have to measure to fractional divisions. A rod marked with all main dimensions in a particular direction can be used to transfer sizes to all parts (Fig. 4-1E), with the knowledge that they will match exactly their partners. You needn't worry about checking that you used the correct division on a rule each time.

When marking from a rod or a rule, stand it on edge, so the mark you want is actually in contact with the surface (Fig. 4-1F). This avoids *errors of parallax* or faults due to your line of sight being askew when there is a gap between the marks. You should *peck* marks, with the actual position being at the point of the V (Fig. 4-1G). This gives a more positive position, particularly when you put a try square through to draw a line later.

A rod should be reasonably straight, but it can be scrap wood or something that will later be cut to form internal parts of the furniture after it has served its purpose as a rod. It may be 1 inches by 2 inches for floor to ceiling, but for shorter parts it can be a lighter section. Put on all the marks you need, but make sure you know what they are. Write against a line if you wish. Shade or color to indicate wood thickness (Fig. 4-1H). If you make a mistake or change your mind, you can always plane off the wrong marks. It helps to start with the working surface and edge of a rod planed smooth. For utmost precision, cut the marks in with a knife. As the cuts may not be easily seen, you can draw attention to them with pencil marks (Fig. 4-1J). Fine pencil marks will do for most work.

JOINTS IN WOOD

One of the simplest fitted joints to cut is a *halving*, either at a corner (Fig. 4-2A), a crossing (Fig. 4-2B), or at a T meeting (Fig. 4-2C). If the parts are the same thickness, cut half from each. If one is thicker, cut more from that one.

The halving joint does not offer much resistance to pulling apart. Supplement glue with screws or dowels for further strength (Fig. 4-2D). Resistance to sliding apart can be given by dovetailing one or both sides (Fig. 4-2E) of a T halving joint.

The *housing* or *dado joint* is related to the halving joint (Fig. 4-3A). A groove across one board takes the end of a shelf or similar part. Cut the groove deep enough to provide support, but not enough to weaken the wood.

If the joint is not to show at the front, it should be stopped (Fig. 4-3B) and the shelf notched. If the groove is cut by hand, drill and chisel the closed end, so a saw can work to cut the sides (Fig. 4-3C). Cutting with a dado head is simple as only the rounded end has to be chiseled. A screw through the outside of a dado joint is ugly, but strength can be provided by screws or nails driven diagonally from below (Fig. 4-3D). A further resistance to pulling apart comes from dovetailing the groove (Fig. 4-3E).

The most commonly used joint in good quality built-in cabinetry is the *mortise and tenon* in its many versions. If the parts are the same thickness, you can make the tenon one-third of the thickness (Fig. 4-4A). If the mortised part is thicker, the joint will be stronger with a tenon more than one-third of the other part's thickness (Fig. 4-4B). If the tenon does not go through, it is blind or stopped or stub (Fig. 4-4C), where its end will spoil the appearance of the mortised piece or that piece is very thick.

If a mortise and tenon joint comes at a corner, it can go right through. That is a *bridle joint* (Fig. 4-4D). Screws or dowels across are needed for strength. A better joint has a stub tenon either cut back (Fig. 4-4E) or with a short piece (Fig. 4-4F) that can be sloped where the edge shows (Fig. 4-4G).

If a tenon has to be very deep, the mortised part will be weakened by one hole. It is better to divide the tenon with a short shallow piece between (Fig. 4-4H).

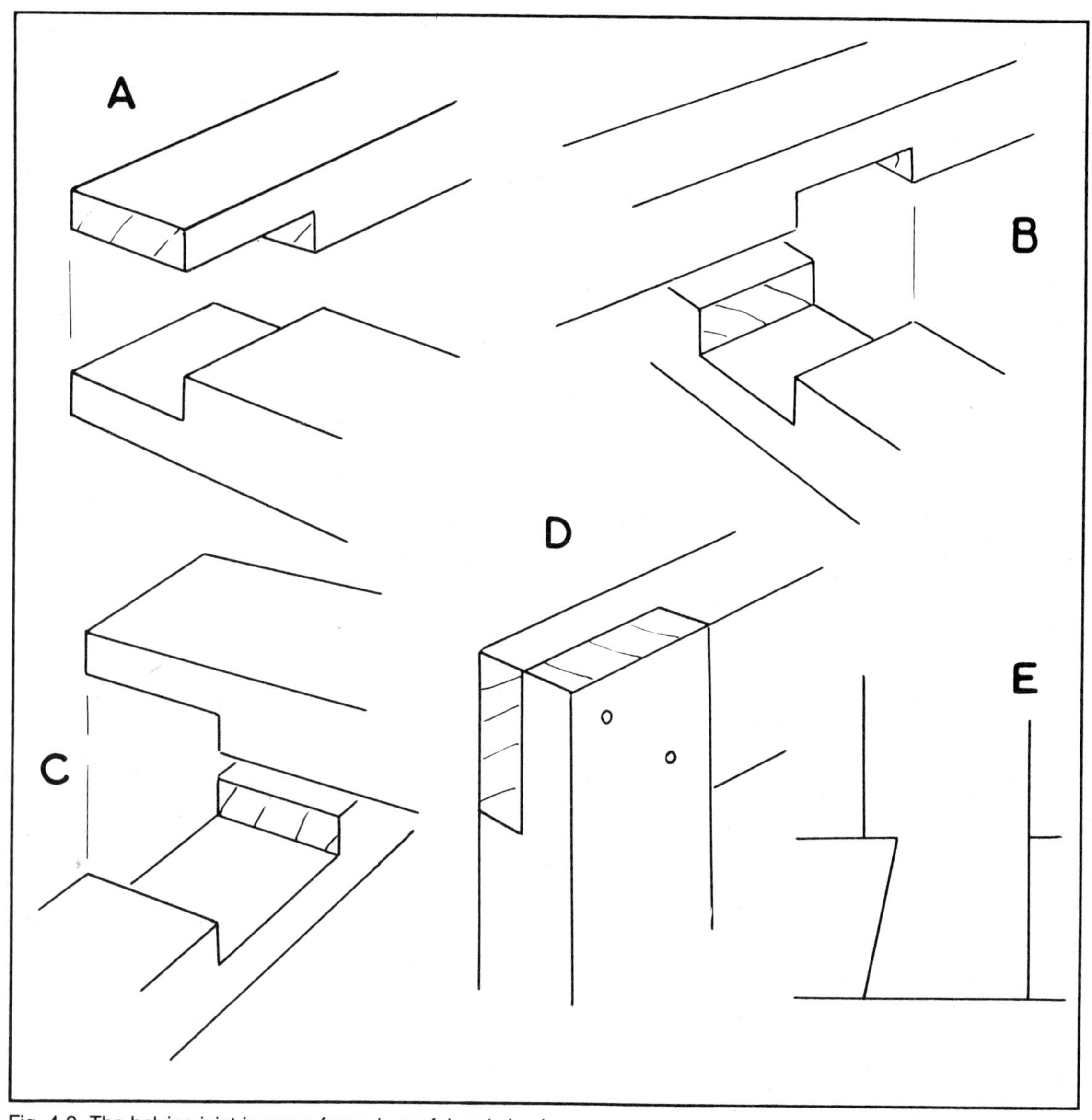

Fig. 4-2. The halving joint in many forms is useful and simple.

The strong corner joint, particularly for drawers, is a *dovetail* (Fig. 4-5A). A guide for a special tool driven by an electric drill will make a joint with tails and pins the same width (Fig. 4-5B). The tails should be much wider than the pins (Fig. 4-5C). Such stopped dovetails are needed more than through dovetails. Make the slope about 1 in 8, although it may be slightly more for softwoods.

An alternative to a dovetail may be a *comb joint* (Fig. 4-5D). If this is cut and fitted accurately, there are good glue surfaces for a strong joint. With strong modern glues there is not quite such a need for joints with an inbuilt resistance to separating. No glue holds well on end grain, so the best joints are those with good meeting areas of side grain.

Several joint forms are particularly intended

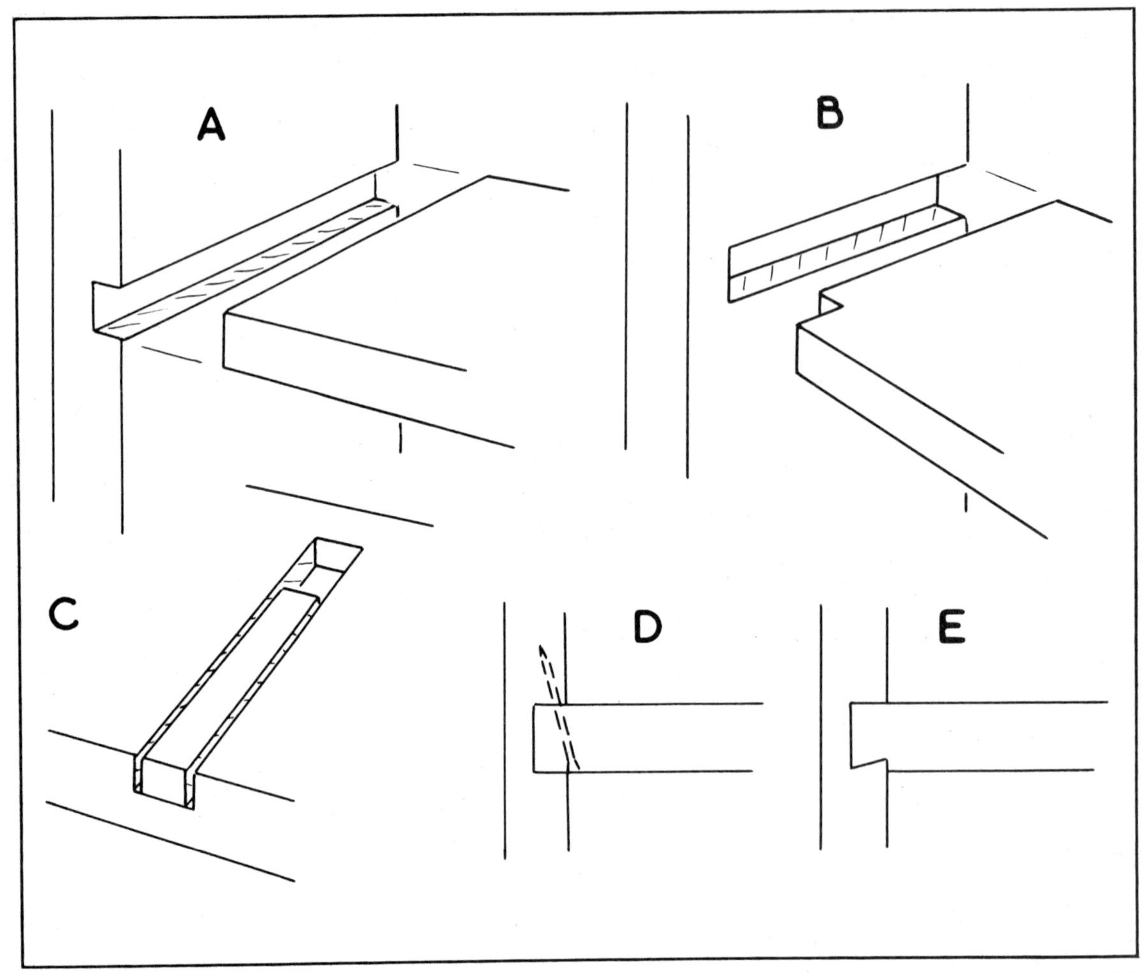

Fig. 4-3. Dado or housing joints take shelf ends (A, B). Hand cutting needs a cut hollow (C). Diagonal nails (D) or dovetails (E) increase strength.

for machine cutting, but they usually involve short grain (Fig. 4-5E) that can break out. For a nailed or screwed joint, there is an advantage in notching one piece over the other, so fastenings can be driven both ways (Fig. 4-5F).

JOINTS IN PARTICLE BOARD

Most woodworking joints are unsuitable for particle board. It is unwise to attempt to cut slots or notches for joints like mortise and tenon or dovetail. Nailing is not impossible, but holes have to be drilled carefully. The nail grip may not be very good. It is better to use screws or dowels.

You may use ordinary wood screws, but it is better to obtain special screws, which look like one type intended for self-tapping in sheet metal and may have double threads. They are available in all the usual sizes. Unlike wood, holes for screws should be taken as deep as the screw or a little deeper. Do not leave any depth for the screw to cut its own way, as it will in wood.

The length of screw to use depends on the length of joint and the number of screws. There is considerable strength at each screw with holes of the correct size. As an approximate guide, let the screw go into the lower part between 1 and 1½

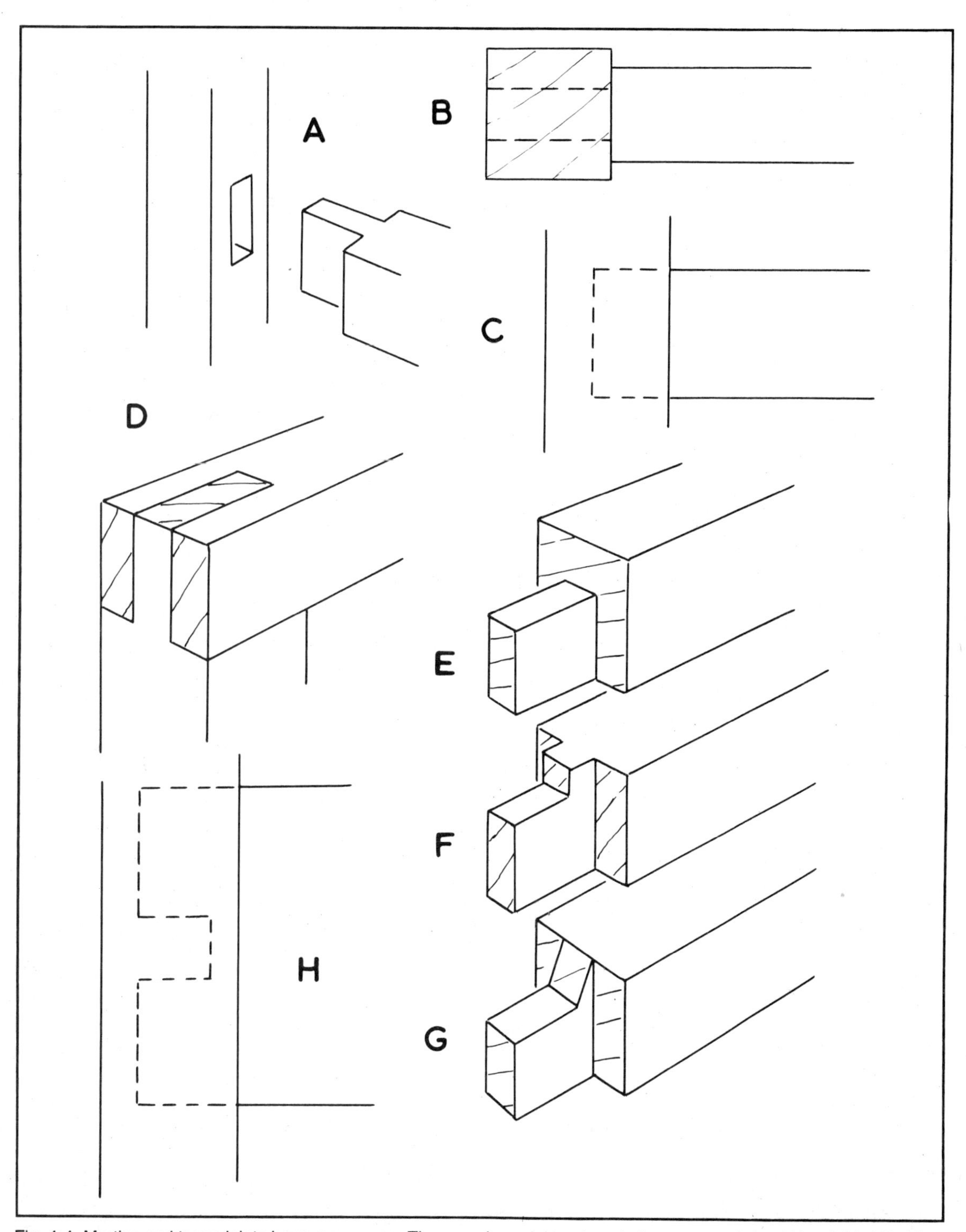

Fig. 4-4. Mortise and tenon joints have many uses. They need special treatment at corners and should be divided if wide.

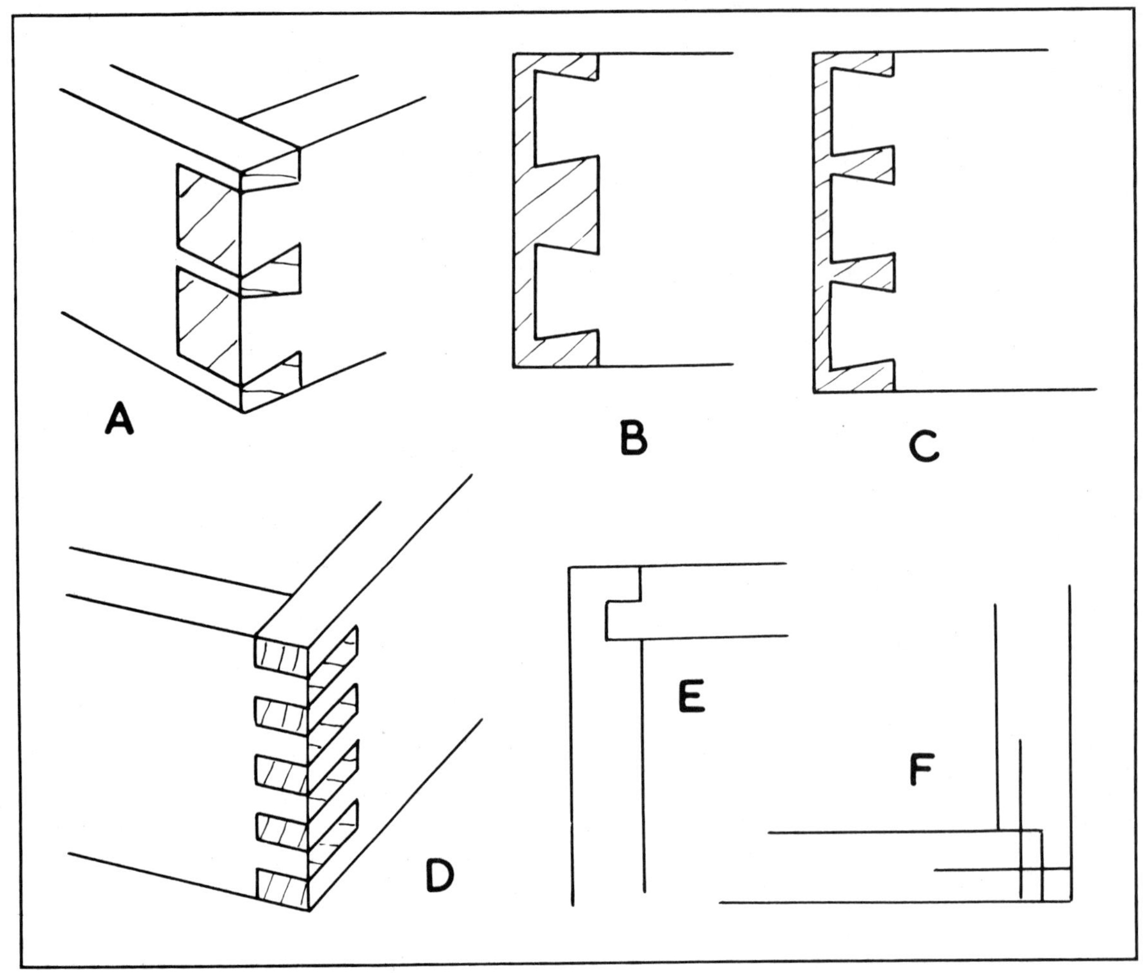

Fig. 4-5. Dovetails make strong corner joints (A). A machine-made joint (B) has equal spacing compared with a hand-cut joint (C). A comb joint (D) may be cut by hand or machine. Other corner joints are notched (E) or double-nailed (F).

times the thickness of the particle board (Fig. 4-6A). The hole in the top piece should be a clearance size. The hole in the lower part should be about the diameter at the bottom of the screw thread (Fig. 4-6B). If the screwhead is to finish on the surface, countersink the hole (Fig. 4-6C). The head will only pull in a negligible amount, so countersink fully.

The screw may be counterbored and a wood or plastic plug glued in (Fig. 4-6D). It can be in a matching or contrasting color and regarded as a decorative feature. Plastic plugs available with shallow domed tops (Fig. 4-6E) can be used where their raised tops are acceptable. They may attractively break up an otherwise flat area.

Another way of screwing is from inside. A strip of wood may be used with screws driven both ways (Fig. 4-7A). Where one piece meets another at a corner, you can screw the strip a short distance back from the end of the covered piece (Fig. 4-7B). The action of screwing the other way will draw the joint close.

Plastic blocks are available in pairs already drilled for screws into the particle board and with metal-thread screws to join them (Fig. 4-7C). They are of more use for take-down or manufactured

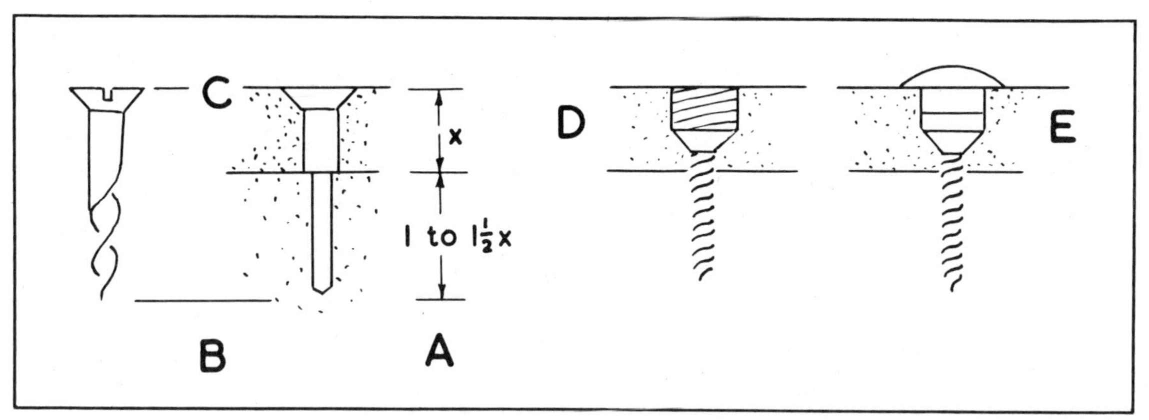

Fig.4-6. Screws need good penetration in the bottom piece (A to C). A head may be sunk and covered with wood (D) or plastic (E).

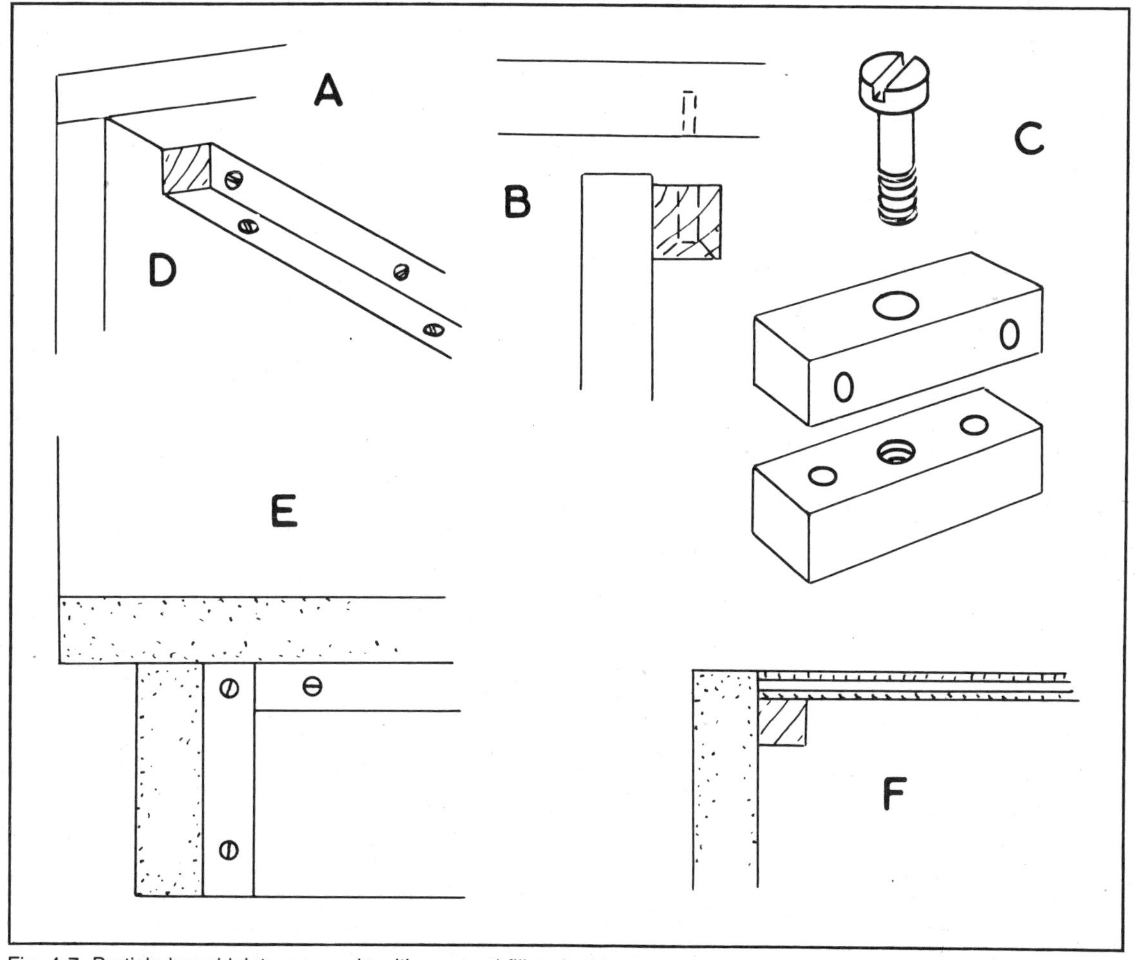

Fig. 4-7. Particle board joints are made with screwed fillets inside.

ready-to-assemble furniture, but they can be used for joining parts of built-in furniture, especially if you plan to disassemble the furniture at some time.

Particle board furniture can be designed to allow for wood strips screwed inside. A strip under a top may also serve as a drawer guide and stop (Fig. 4-7D). A base may be set back between the sides and a shelf (Fig. 4-7E). If there is to be a plywood or hardboard back, it may come inside the other parts and be screwed or nailed to wood strips (Fig. 4-7F). The section of wood to use for inside strips depends on the size of furniture, but ⅜ inch or ½ inch square will usually be large enough.

Careful arranging of the screws can make them inconspicuous. For a joint where the method of attachment cannot be seen, dowels are a better choice. When screws are used, the action of driving them pulls the parts together. That does not happen with dowels. Joints have to be drawn tight and held close until the glue has set. You may be able to push the parts together so they will stay in place, but usually clamps or weights are needed. Always spread pressure and protect surfaces from damage with wood strips under the clamp jaws.

Dowels should usually be about half the thickness of the particle board (Fig. 4-8A) and then taken as deeply into the overlapping part as you can safely drill. Go as much or slightly deeper in the other direction. Drill slightly too deep in that piece, so there is no risk of the dowel touching the bottoms of the holes before the surfaces are drawn tight (Fig. 4-8B).

Prepared dowels may have their ends beveled and grooves cut spirally around them to release air and surplus glue (Fig. 4-8C). If you cut dowels from long rods, take the sharpness off the end and saw a groove lengthwise (Fig. 4-8D). Without an escape for air and glue, the dowel acts like a piston and can burst the chipboard.

Dowels should be arranged fairly close to edges, then at intervals across a joint. Three inches apart will usually be satisfactory (Fig. 4-8E). You can arrange the spacing by careful measuring. Mark each center with an awl or other point (Fig. 4-8F). Dowel jigs can be adjusted so the parts match and spacing is uniform. Use a depth gauge on the drill. If a hole breaks through or cracks the surface, there is no way of disguising the damage. Use ample glue on the dowels. A line of glue along the joint will help, but it is the dowels that provide strength.

You can make a good corner joint with screws or dowels, but be careful that the covered piece does not project (Fig. 4-9A). The error is less obvious if the other piece overhangs slightly (Fig. 4-9B). A definite overhang can be used in many designs (Fig. 4-9C), so a slightly misplaced joint will not be apparent. This can be arranged vertically in some furniture (Fig. 4-9D). If the particle board is bought with veneered surfaces and edges, but you have to apply veneer to a cut end, allow for this small extra thickness when preparing joints.

Parts may be joined with metal angle brackets, or you may want to screw on handles or other metal or plastic parts. None of these things are very thick. Guard against the surface of the particle board rising or breaking out when a screw is driven. If you use a screw with a thread to its head, countersink each hole (Fig. 4-10A), so there is no surface to raise. If you use an ordinary wood screw, drill a clearance hole as deep as the unthreaded part will go (Fig. 4-10B). An alternative for either type of screw is to plug the hole and screw into that. The plug may be wood, plastic, or one of the fiber plugs used in masonry. Punch the plug below the surface (Fig. 4-10C). Drill the plug to the tapping size for the screw. An undersize hole may cause the plug to expand too much and burst the particle board.

DRAWER CONSTRUCTION

A *drawer* is a sliding tray or box. In traditional cabinetry the craftsman was very proud of the fit and construction of the drawers he made. They were usually flush, and the gaps around were kept as narrow as possible. You can make similar drawers, particularly if you are making reproduction furniture. In much modern construction it is better and simpler to have the drawer front overlap the carcass, so the closeness of the drawer's fit is not apparent.

In a traditional drawer the sides slide on runners (Fig. 4-11A) and are prevented from tilting as they are withdrawn by similar strips above. These

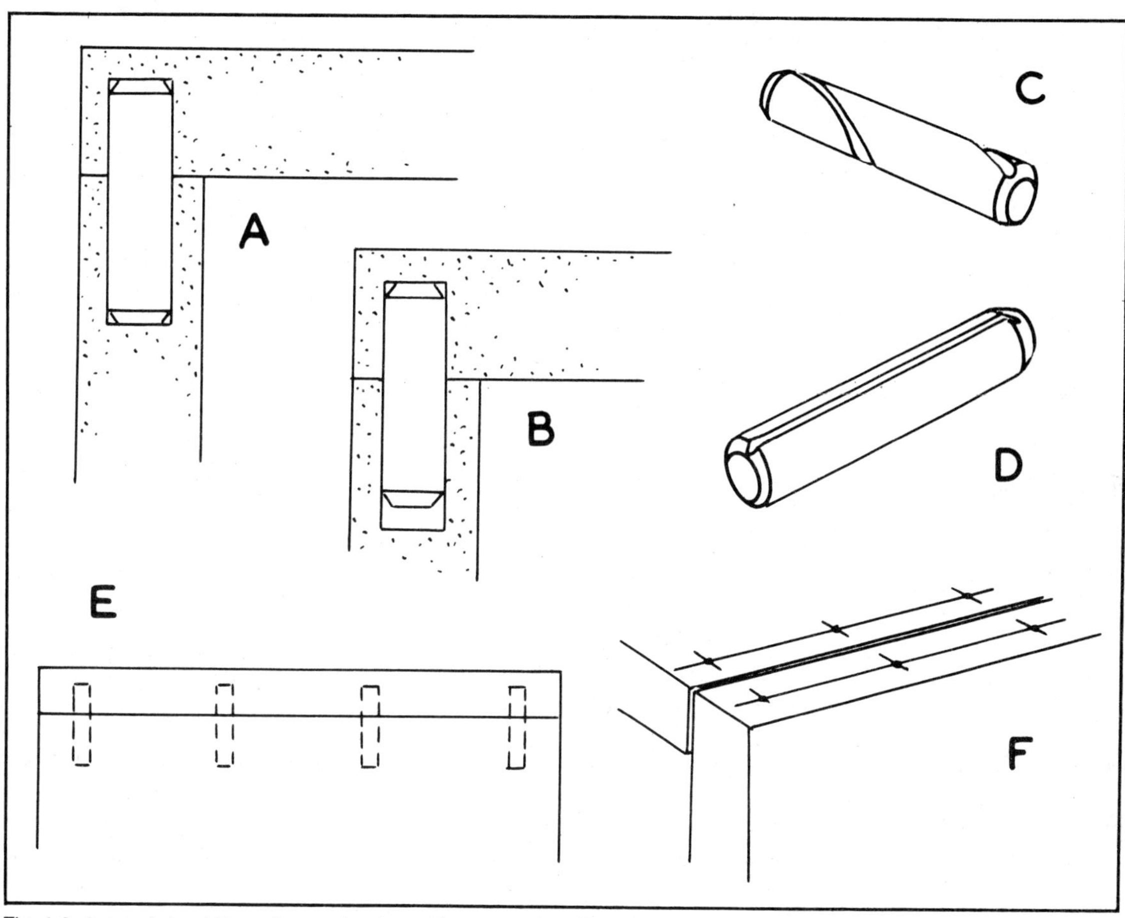

Fig. 4-8. A dowel should have tapered ends and be grooved to allow air to escape (A to D). Exact spacing is important (E, F).

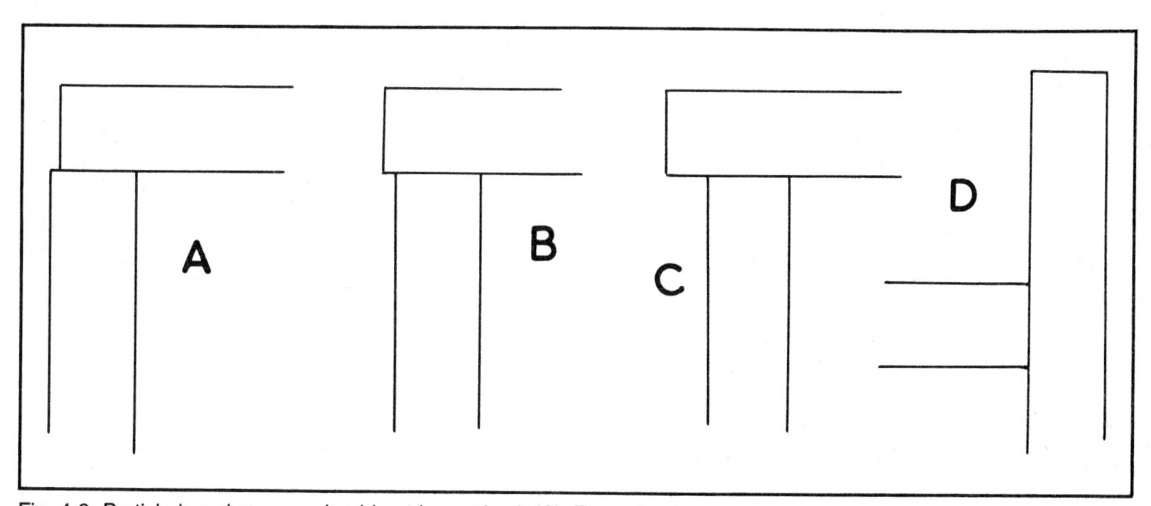

Fig. 4-9. Particle board corners should not be set back (A). They should overlap (B, C, D).

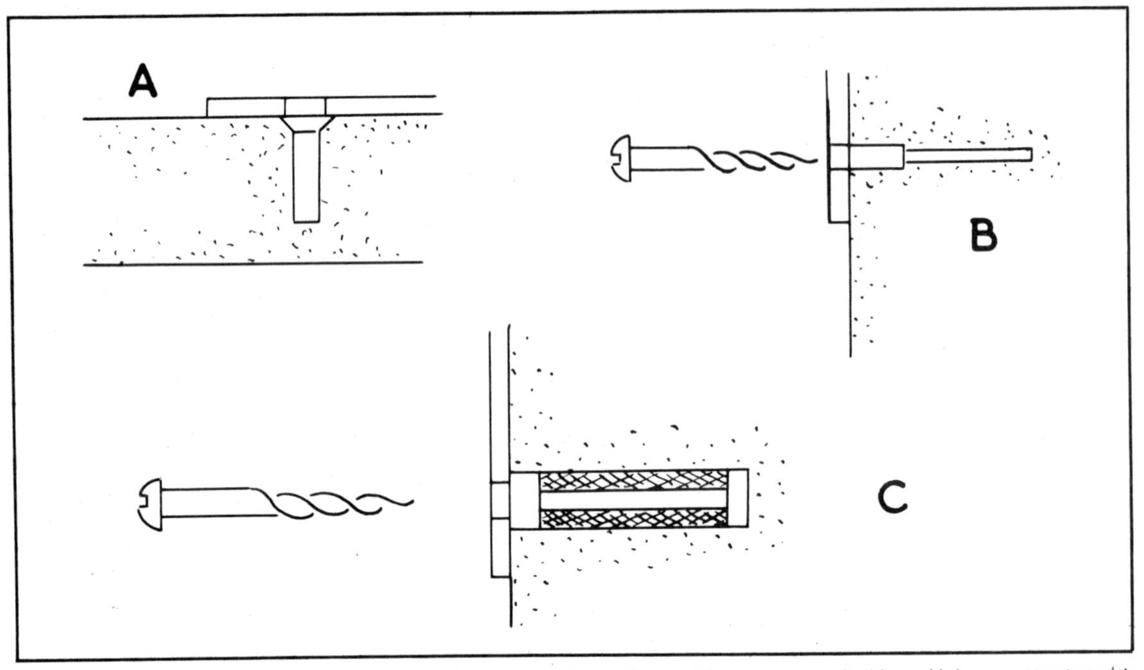

Fig. 4-10. The surface below a metal fitting should be recessed so it does not rise as a screw is driven. Holes are countersunk (A). A clearance hole is drilled as deep as the unthreaded part will go (B). The plug is punched below the surface (C).

strips are called *kickers* (Fig. 4-11B). If the drawer does not rub against the sides of the carcass, there may be guides against the runners (Fig. 4-11C).

Sometimes a drawer is hung, then the guides and runners are at the top (Fig. 4-11D). Another way of supporting a drawer is to groove the sides to slide on runners (Fig. 4-11E). Metal and plastic drawer runners may be simple slides or can incorporate rollers and extensions for easy movement of heavily loaded drawers. To include these runners, you should usually allow about a ½-inch gap at each side of the drawer. Runners should be obtained and measured before making the drawers. Similar runners can go under the center of a drawer. They ease and guide the drawer, relieving the side supports of some of the load.

A drawer that is narrow across the front in relation to its depth back to front will always slide easier than a wide drawer (Fig. 4-12A), even if it is not very accurately fitted. The wide drawer tends to pull slightly askew and become jammed. Metal slides and guides help wide drawers move easier. Waxing the bearing surfaces also helps. Two narrow drawers will be better than one very wide one (Fig. 4-12B).

There is an optical illusion to consider if you are fitting several drawers. In a block of three or more, if you make them all the same height, the bottom one will seem narrower than the top one (Fig. 4-12C). Make the heights progressively more from the top down (Fig. 4-12D). This is required anyway in many cases, so the lower drawers can hold larger and heavier things.

The drawer bottom is commonly plywood or hardboard notched into each side (Fig. 4-13A). To increase the bearing surface that the sides slide on, there may be pieces inside (Fig. 4-13B). The bottom is notched into the drawer front in a similar way, but at the back the wood is kept above the bottom (Fig. 4-13C). This avoids the edge of the back catching when the drawer is pulled out. Its top edge may be kept low for a similar reason (Fig. 4-13D). The bottom can be slid in from the back during assembly, then it is screwed up into the back.

In a traditional drawer the sides are joined to

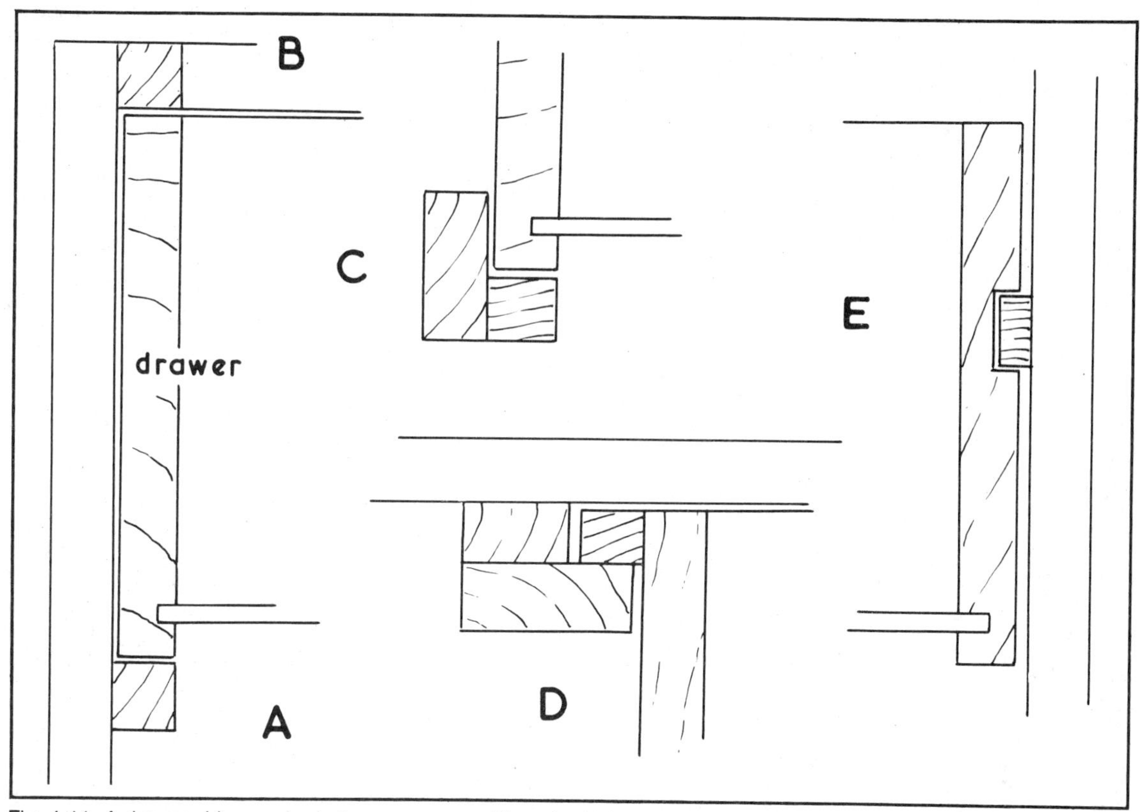

Fig. 4-11. A drawer side may be between a runner (A) and a kicker (B) or be supported on other strips (C, D, E).

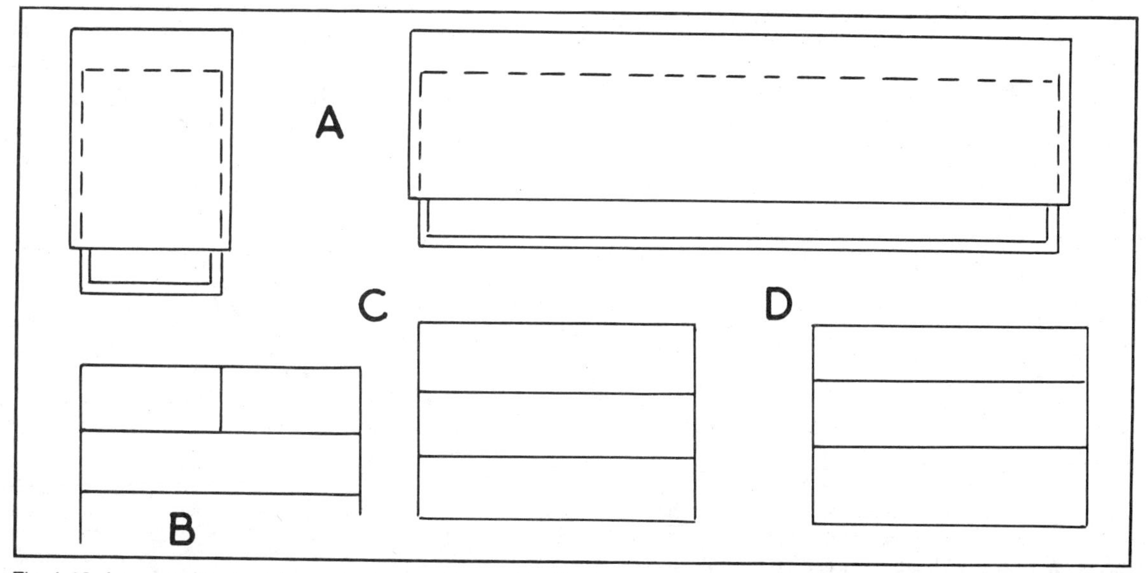

Fig. 4-12. A narrow drawer slides easier than a wide one (A). Width may be divided (B). Equal depths (C) do not look as good as graduated ones (D).

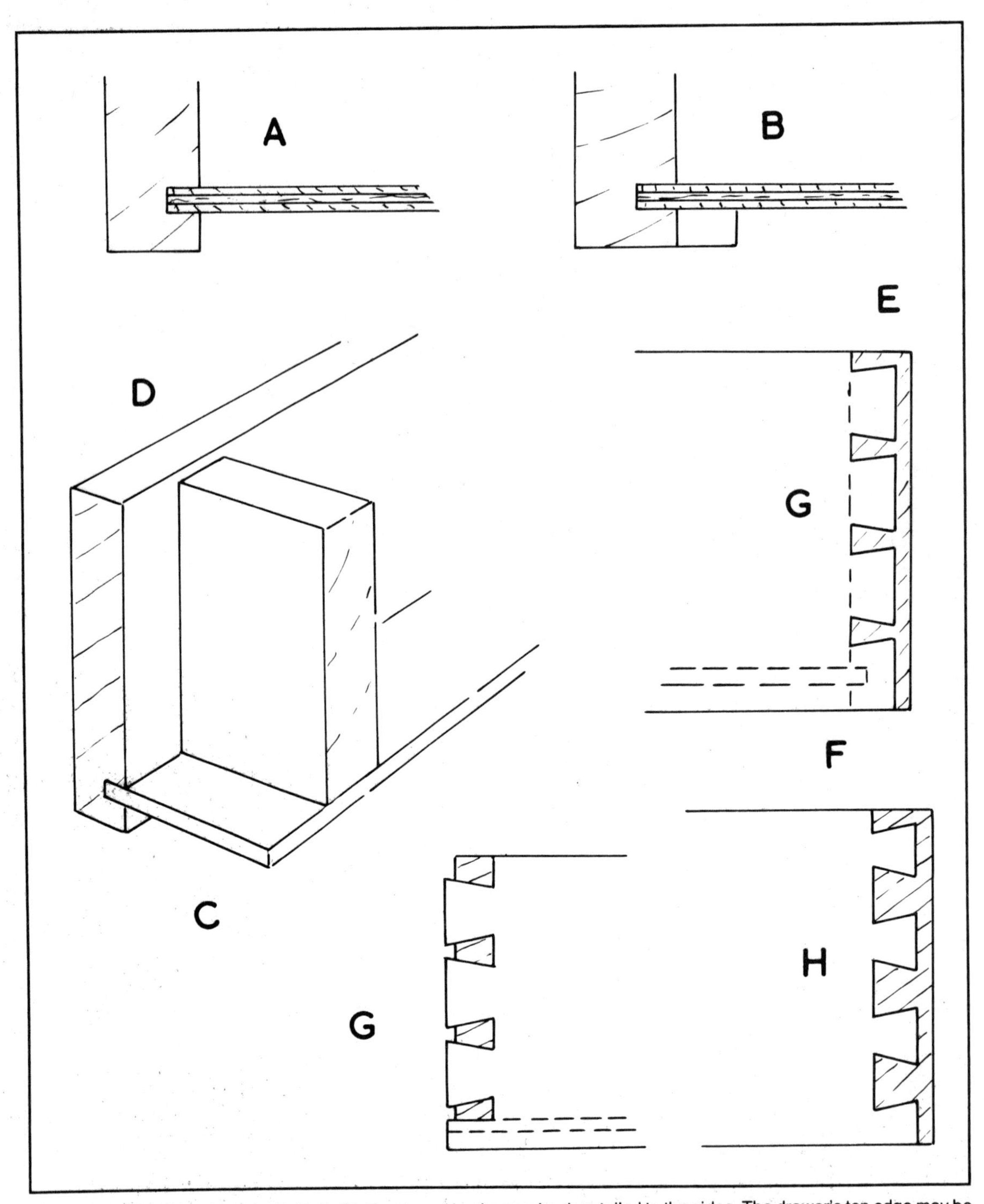

Fig. 4-13. A plywood button is let in (A, B, C). Fronts and backs may be dovetailed to the sides. The drawer's top edge may be kept low (D). Sides are joined to the front with dovetails (E). The bottom tail is arranged to hide the slot (F). Hand-cut dovetails have pins narrower than the tails (G). Machine-made dovetails have them the same width (H).

the front with dovetails (Fig. 4-13E). The bottom tail is arranged to hide the slot (Fig. 4-13F). With hand-cut dovetails the pins are always narrower than the tails (Fig. 4-13G). Machine-made dovetails have them the same width (Fig. 4-13H). The old-time cabinetmaker made the pins extremely narrow. There is no virtue in this, except as a test of skill.

There may be through dovetails at the back (Fig. 4-13J). The tails usually extend slightly, so the back is set in. The sides can be planed over the tails if they are to act as stops when the drawer is pushed in.

The drawer back can fit into dadoes (Fig. 4-14A). A dovetail bevel (Fig. 4-14B) will give strength, but it may be sufficient to nail or screw through the sides.

If the drawer front is to overlap, there can be a false piece (Fig. 4-14C). Otherwise, it is necessary to cut rabbets (Fig. 4-14D). One way of avoiding this is to dado the sides into the front (Fig. 4-14E). The load comes in the direction that tries to break the joint, which would be better with a dovetail bevel and the sides slid in from below (Fig. 4-14F). It is possible to dowel the sides to the front, but there is a similar problem with a breaking pull.

When there is a false front, the sides may have through dovetails (Fig. 4-14G) or be merely screwed (Fig. 4-14H). A comb joint (Fig. 4-14J) or any other box corner joints will enclose the drawer bottom slot and be hidden by the false front.

A drawer must stop at the correct position when it is pushed in. A false or rabbeted front acts as a stop. If the front fits into the carcass opening, the sides may be adjusted in length so they hit the back of the carcass when the front is level. If the drawer does not go fully back, there can be stops on the runners or kickers (Fig. 4-15A). It may be possible to put thin stops on the rail under the drawer bottom to stop its front. Locate one toward each side on a wide drawer (Fig. 4-15B).

You have to prevent a drawer from falling out if it is pulled too far inadvertently. A strip under the top rail may act as a stop to prevent the drawer front from going in too far. As the drawer is pulled out, its back will come against the strip and be prevented from coming out further. If the drawer is tilted upward, it can be freed (Fig. 4-15C).

You may want to make it difficult for a child to open a drawer. That can be done without using a lock by notching the sides behind the front (Fig. 4-15D). There must be as much clearance above the sides as the depth of the notches. To open the drawer, it is first lifted.

You can provide a lip on a drawer to serve as a handle, but that is more suitable for quantity production. A drawer front may project below, so you can get fingers under (Fig. 4-16A). The top edge can be notched enough for fingers (Fig. 4-16B). Two holes in the front may be enough for fingers to open a light drawer (Fig. 4-16C).

Various wooden handles and an even greater variety of metal and plastic handles can be bought. A narrow drawer may have a single handle, but otherwise it is better to have two handles widely spaced for an even pull with two hands. As a guide, consider the drawer width divided equally into four. Put the handle centers one-fourth in from each side (Fig. 4-16D). Put the handles above the center of the front (Fig. 4-16E). If you put them exactly halfway, they will appear to be below the center, which is not as pleasing.

The pulling of handles can put a considerable strain on their attachments. Through fastening from inside the drawer front is better than wood screws driven into the surface. Much depends on the chosen handles. Consider whether projections will be acceptable or if people are likely to knock on a handle. If so, you may have to notch the drawer front for a handle with a bail or other grip to fold out of the way.

DOORS

Most doors swing on hinges and are held closed by catches at the opposite side to the hinges, with a knob or handle for pulling open. In some cases the knob also operates the catch, but in many modern constructions the catch is sprung or magnetic. The handle only has to provide a grip for pulling. Sliding doors can have special tracks or be arranged to work in grooves in the wood. Sometimes it is convenient to have a door to lift out. A removable door

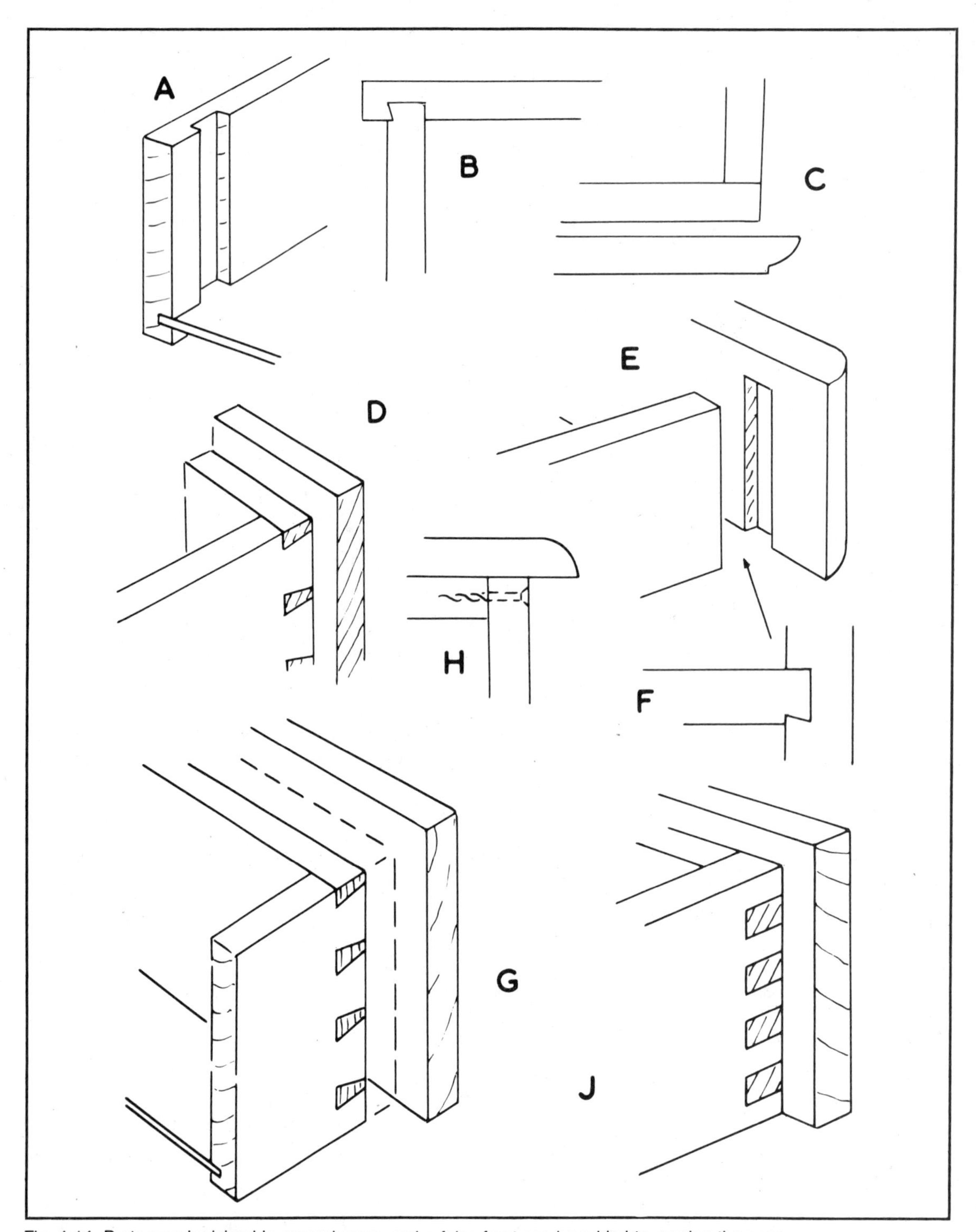

Fig. 4-14. Parts may be joined in several ways, and a false front can be added to overlap the gaps.

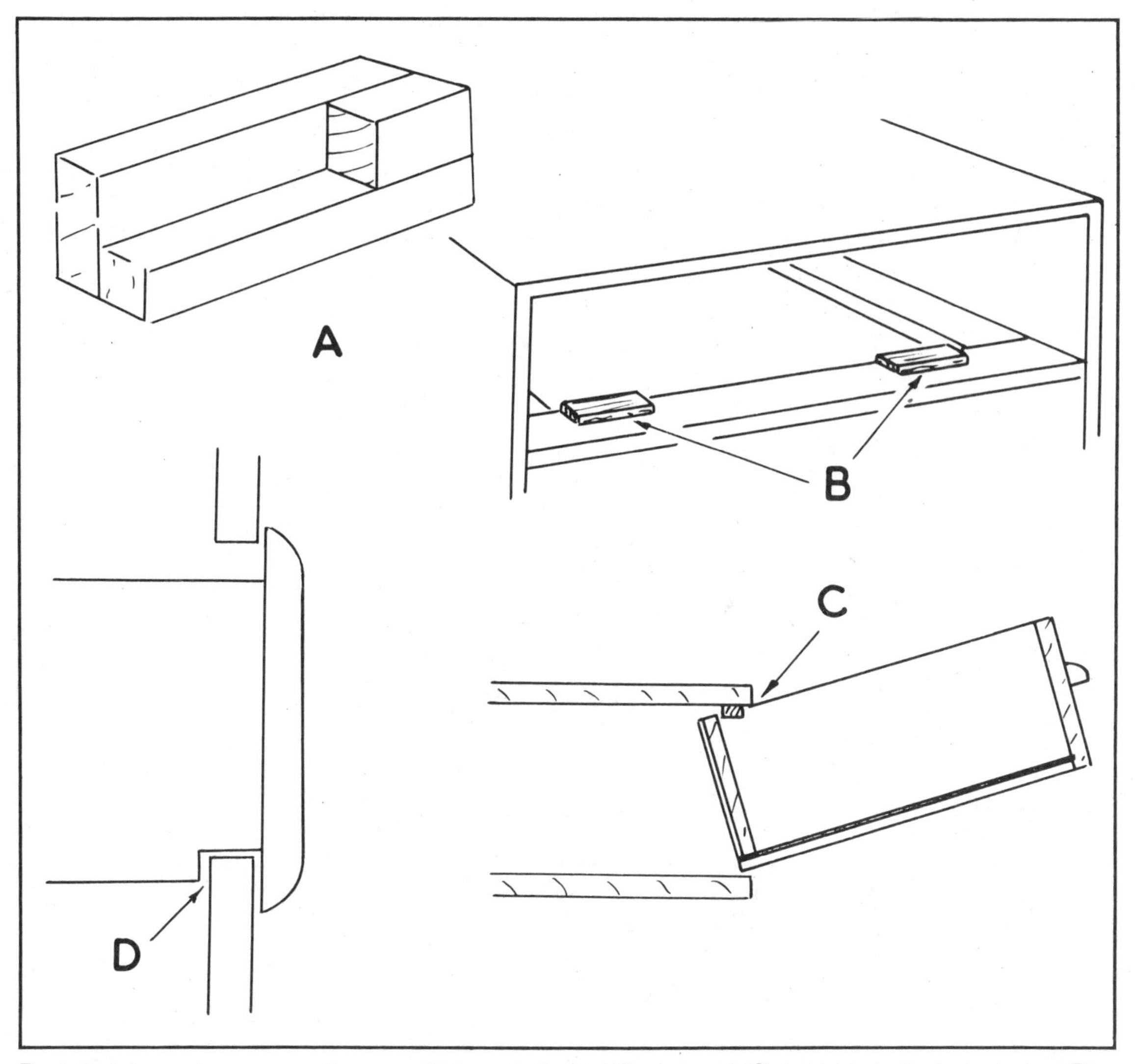

Fig. 4-15. A drawer stop may go on the runner (A), be under the front (B), or above it (C). A notch locks the drawer in place (D).

gives the clearest access to the interior, but it has to be put somewhere when removed. A hinged door gives almost as clear access, but there must be enough room for it to swing. Sliding doors are usually in pairs. Only about half the width can be reached at a time. The doors have to slide the other way to allow access to the other half, but the doors do not project when open. This may be an overriding advantage. Sliding doors can be glass panels without framing.

In most situations swinging doors should be regarded as normal, unless there is a particular reason for choosing sliding or lifting doors. A swung door is always best with the greater dimension along the line of the hinges (Fig. 4-17A). Sometimes a door has to be greater the other way (Fig. 4-17B), but that puts more load on the hinges, with only slight slackness there causing the further part of the door to sag and possibly touch the framing so it will not shut. If you have to put doors on a wide opening, it is better to use a pair (Fig. 4-17C). This looks better and is better practically. Less space is

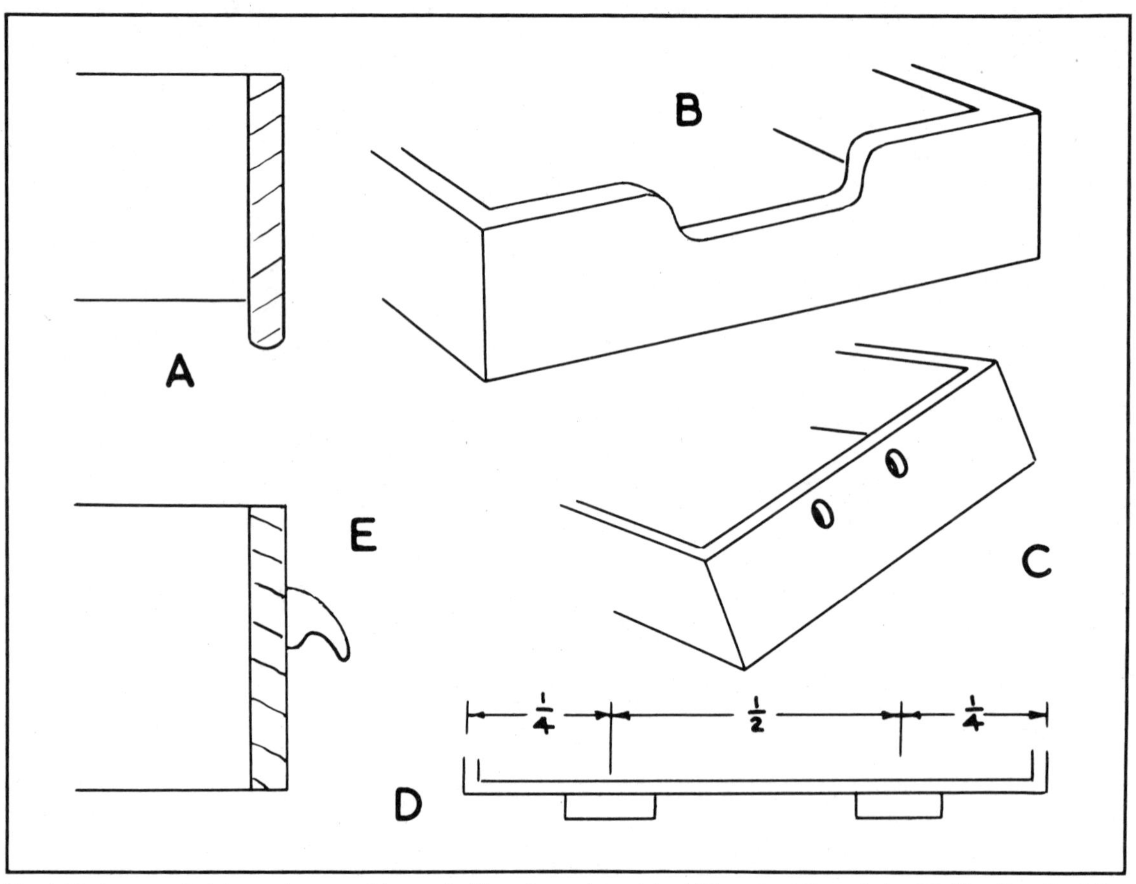

Fig. 4-16. An extended drawer front provides a grip (A), or it may be notched (B) or given finger holes (C). Handles should be symmetrically spaced (D) and usually above the center (E).

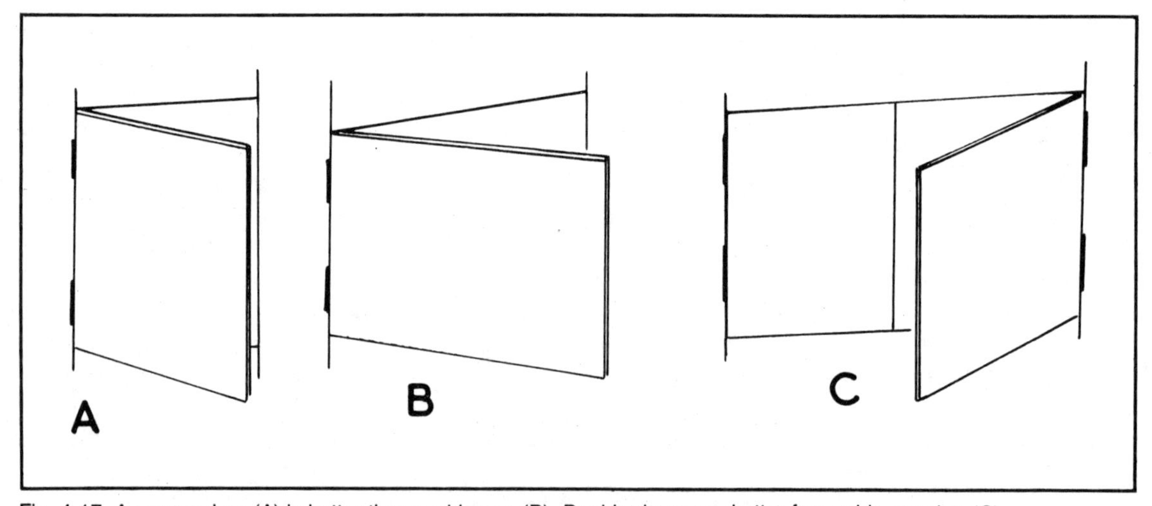

Fig. 4-17. A narrow door (A) is better than a wide one (B). Double doors are better for a wide opening (C).

needed in front of the furniture for the doors to open.

A door may be just a single piece of wood, but this can bring problems. It may swell or contract, so its width alters across the grain. It may warp or twist, but that will be minimized if wood is properly seasoned and a piece is chosen that has been radially cut, and the grain lines on the end run across the thickness. Variations can also be reduced by gluing several pieces to make up the width and arranging them so the grain of their ends curves in alternate ways. It is generally better to avoid using a plain piece of wood for a door, except sometimes for quite a small one.

Particle board does not have the problems of solid wood. Normally it should remain stable, with no tendency to warp or alter its size. A panel of particle board may form a door. It will be veneered on both sides and all edges, so there is a wood-grained surface visible all around. It may have a plain white surface for some situations. There should be hinges and hardware intended for particle board, using screws as described earlier.

Veneered particle board doors are satisfactory for kitchen cabinets and many other assemblies. If you have made a piece of furniture mainly of solid wood, such doors will not match. It is better to assemble doors with solid wood and plywood.

Sometimes it is possible to make a plywood door without framing or stiffening. Thick plywood may be sufficiently stable to keep its shape, but most plywood doors made in this way tend to warp. Very slight warping is enough to spoil appearance. Unsupported plywood can be used for doors sliding in grooves, but the grooves keep it flat. If you use plywood and veneer the front, put more veneer on the back. Otherwise, there will be an unequal strain due to the glue, and the panel may pull out of shape. Use framing with plywood, even if it is quite thick.

One way of preventing a plain thick plywood door from warping is to put racks inside to serve as battens (Fig. 4-18A). There can be plain battens, but in most built-in furniture you can use racks, bins, or some other internal structure that will also provide stiffening. There may be quite wide shelves or bins attached to the door, probably with curved edges to clear the door frame as the door swings open. For the sake of stiffening, make sure there are parts going across the door and securely attached to it to keep the wood flat.

Don't make a door by putting framing behind a single piece of plywood or hardboard (Fig. 4-18B). This puts an uneven strain on the plywood, and the door will probably twist or pull hollow. Such a door is better made with panels on each side of solid wood framing (Fig. 4-18C). An attractive door can be made with a lip put around the edge to cover the plywood (Fig. 4-18D).

For the size doors needed in furniture, it may be sufficient to frame around the edges only, but strips can be put across in the thickness, too. Usually a door is best made by first cutting one panel to size and gluing strips to it. With modern glues it should be possible to assemble a door without metal fasteners, but you may have to use a few inconspicuous pins. When the glue has set, trim the surfaces of the battens level if necessary, then glue on the other panel. If it is slightly oversize, it is easier to position. Its edges can be planed level after the glue has set. The lip strips go around the outside, preferably with mitered corners.

It is possible to include racks for papers or books in the thickness of the door by cutting away the inside panel and including suitable framing (Fig. 4-18E). Do not cut away too much, or you will lose the stiffening value of the inner panel.

At one time all doors were made to fit into their frames. A craftsman was proud of his ability to make a door to swing with the minimum gaps all around. Such doors are still used, but much furniture is made with the doors overlapping their openings. A precision fit is not needed, as the gaps are hidden when the door is closed. The appearance may also be more in keeping with modern trends, but that may be because of the familiarity with mass-produced furniture. A door built with plywood each side of the solid wood framing can have its front extended (Fig. 4-18F), but be careful how you cut and finish the plywood edges. Splintering or loose chips will spoil appearance.

Traditionally, doors were made as frames to the outline needed. The space was filled with panels

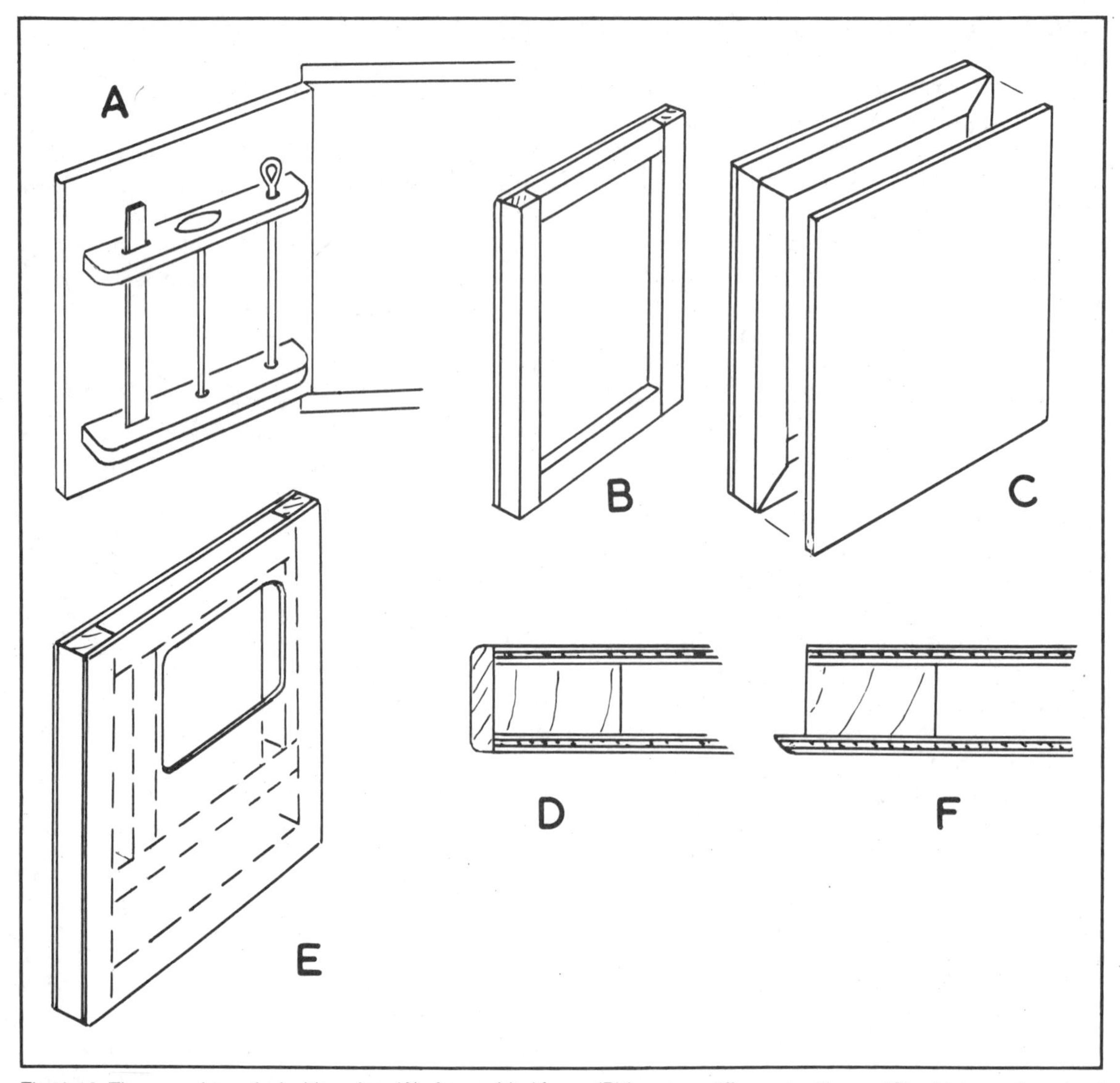

Fig. 4-18. There can be racks inside a door (A). A one-sided frame (B) is not as stiff as a double one (C), which may be cut out for storage (E). Ply edges may be covered with a strip (D). One side can make an overlapping front (F).

of thin solid wood taken even thinner at the edges and fitted into grooves. The panels were not glued into the grooves. They were allowed to move as they expanded and contracted, with differences in moisture content. As the width of available wood for the panels was limited, a door might have to be made with one or more extra upright pieces of framing to accommodate whatever panel widths could be used. That type of construction presented an attractive appearance and something like it is often used today, but the panels are plywood. As the size of plywood should remain constant, it can be glued into the grooves so it contributes strength to the door, which the traditional panels did not. Their frames sometimes sagged out of true.

Usually a panel is thin plywood let into grooves (Fig. 4-19A). It should have a veneer to match the surrounding wood, preferably on both sides. To avoid difficulty in tightening corner joints, cut the plywood so it does not quite reach the bottoms of the grooves. The inner edges of the framing may be left square, given a chamfer (Fig. 4-19B), or be molded (Fig. 4-19C). Molding can be worked on the solid wood, or it may be small strip molding glued and pinned in place after assembly. Molding has to be cut back and mitered at the corners.

Normally the plywood is arranged centrally in the framing. It need not be if it will be better nearer one surface. If you intend to put racks inside, it may be better to have the panel nearer the front. Another strong construction uses thicker plywood, which is rabbeted around the edges so it comes flush at the front (Fig. 4-19D). There can be a decorative chamfer at the front (Fig. 4-19E), or a strip of half-round molding can cover the joint (Fig. 4-19F).

The framing needs secure joints at the corner of a paneled door. In most furniture construction it is common to carry through the uprights and joint the top and bottom into them. It is unusual to fully miter frames for doors, because such joints are difficult to make sufficiently rigid. Only very slight movement in a door frame joint will affect the fit of a door.

Corners may be made with mortise and tenon joints or dowels. Mortise and tenon joints are traditional and probably stronger if properly cut and fitted. Dowels, fitted with the aid of jigs to get the holes true and matching, should have adequate strength. If the inner edges of the framing are left square, the uprights can go through the full width. If there is molding or a chamfer, there has to be a miter to the depth of the molding, which is most conveniently the same as the depth of the grooves.

For a tenon joint, cut back to the depth of the groove on a horizontal tenoned part. On the other, mark out the mortise to cut away the width of the groove (Fig. 4-20A). If you are mitering, the joint is very similar. Even if the molding is cut in the solid wood, you should visualize a joint as if the mitered molding is imposed on the solid wood when marking out (Fig. 4-20B). If you use dowels, they project as an alternative to the tenons (Fig. 4-20C).

If all four sides of a framed door are the same width, the bottom will appear narrower. Make the bottom rail obviously wider than the others. To get a good shape to the final assembly, leave the sides too long, so they project above and below the other rails by an appreciable amount. That prevents breaking out when cutting joints and allows you to

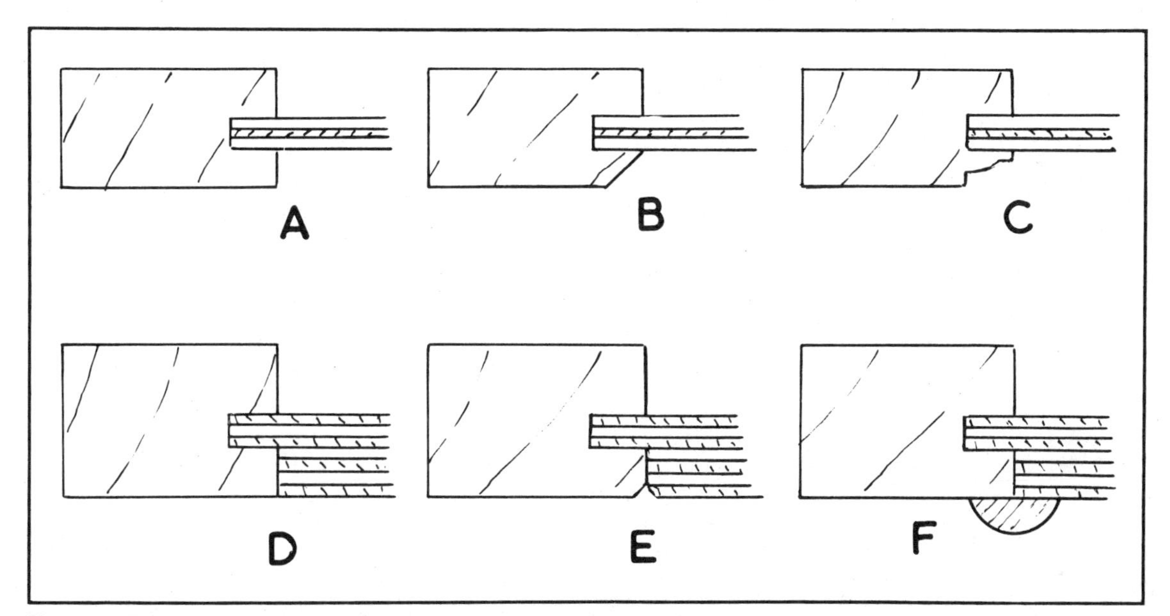

Fig. 4-19. There are several ways of letting plywood panels into door frames.

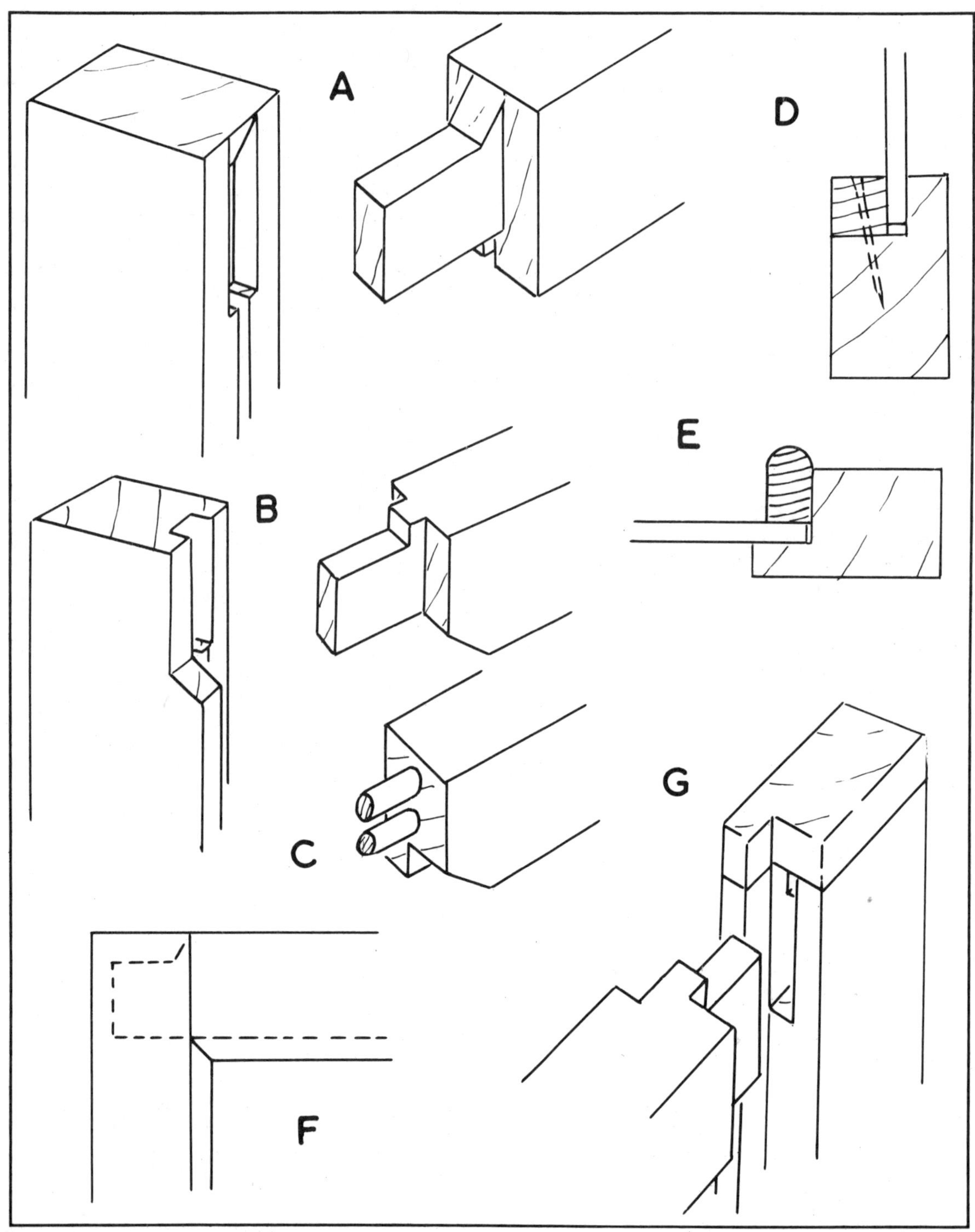

Fig. 4-20. Tenons have to be arranged to suit grooved or rabbeted frames (A, B, C). Fillets (D, E) are used to hold plywood or glass in a rabbet, which may be mitered (F) or carried through (G).

trim the ends more accurately when all the parts have been joined.

You can put a glass panel in grooves instead of the plywood one, but then you have a problem if the glass has to be replaced. There is no way of doing it. Make glass-paneled doors with the frames rabbeted instead of grooved, so the glass is held by fillets (Fig. 4-20D). The fillets are held in with screws or pins but no glue, so they can be taken out if new glass is to be fitted.

As with plywood panels, let the glass be a loose fit in the rabbets. Arrange the size of the fillet section to fit the available space, although some doors are attractively finished with fillets having projecting rounded edges inside (Fig. 4-20E). To reduce reflection inside, the surfaces of the wood coming against the glass may be stained black.

The projecting part above the rabbet may be mitered at the corner of the frame. The joint becomes a simple mortise and tenon or dowel construction (Fig. 4-20F). Alternatively, with a square edge to the frame, carry through and notch the horizontal rails over the upright ones (Fig. 4-20G) whether you use dowels or tenons.

PLASTIC WORK TOPS

Melamine laminated plastic makes good work tops for a kitchen or anywhere that a wipe-clean surface is desirable. Formica laminated plastic and similar plastic sheets are supplied in thin pieces to be attached to wood or other backing. The material does not expand and contract, so it must be attached to a surface that is equally stable. Do not use solid wood, but plywood and particle board are suitable.

One problem is fitting accurately without air bubbles. Use the adhesive recommended by the makers or one described as being suitable for the purpose. Read and follow the directions carefully. You do not get a second chance if the assembly goes wrong. Some of the strongest adhesives are *impact* types. As soon as the surfaces meet, they are there and cannot be moved. Some other adhesives allow a slight amount of adjustment, but it is unwise to count on being able to do much repositioning.

Have the base piece ready. Its top should be flat and free from blemishes. Coarse sanding may be advised by the adhesive manufacturers. Another way of providing a grip for the adhesive is to draw a saw blade sideways across the wood in several directions to produce a pattern of crossing scratches that will allow the adhesive to penetrate. Make sure no dust from this scratching is left or any raised fibers.

The base usually should be finished to size, but the plastic can be slightly oversize for trimming later. If you are dealing with a shape with square edges, it will help in positioning to lightly nail on guide strips to two edges (Fig. 4-21A). Most adhe-

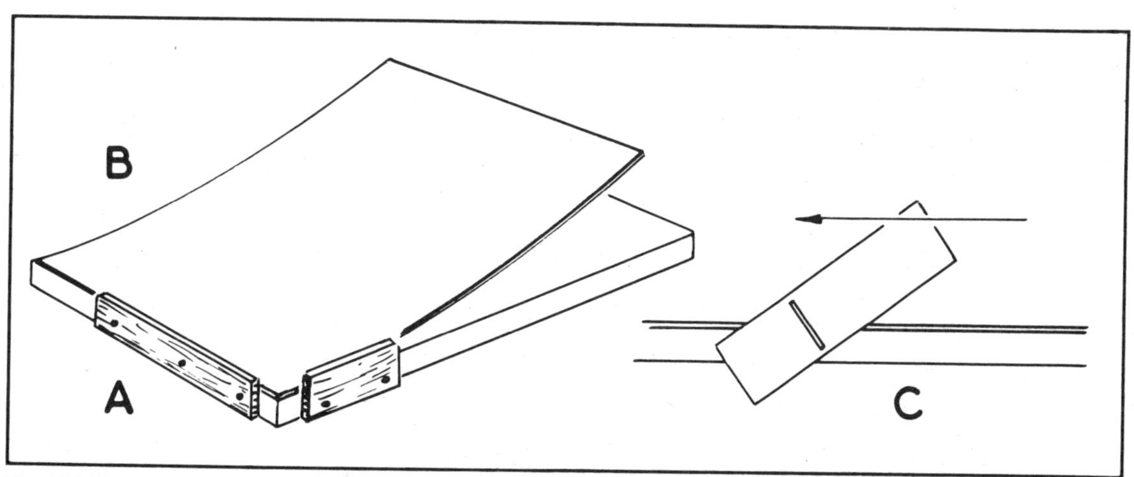

Fig. 4-21. Formica laminated plastic should be lowered onto the adhesive while controlled by guides, then its edges are planed diagonally.

sives require you to coat both surfaces evenly, usually with a spreader provided, and then wait until they are nearly dry before bringing them together.

To avoid air bubbles, position the plastic against the stops and curve it, so only one edge is in contact first (Fig. 4-21B). Lower the plastic with one hand. Use the other hand to press it in place as you progressively bring the sheet down on to the wood. Finally, rub down, working with a circular motion from the center toward the edges. Leave it for the time indicated by the adhesive suppliers before doing anything else to it.

For many purposes, it is sufficient to trim the plastic level with the wood and give it a slight chamfer. If the wood edge is stained black, that may be all the treatment needed. There are several metal and plastic moldings that can be put around Formica laminated plastic edges. The edge need not then be trimmed with quite such precision, but it should still be reasonably accurate. Special tools that work like little planes have diagonal blades that cut as they are guided along the wood and plastic. Formica laminated plastic can be trimmed with an ordinary plane. Use a sharp finely set small plane, with its mouth set narrowly if there is an adjustment. Hold the plane so it is inclined toward the wood side to give a slicing cut as you go along (Fig. 4-21C).

Chapter 5

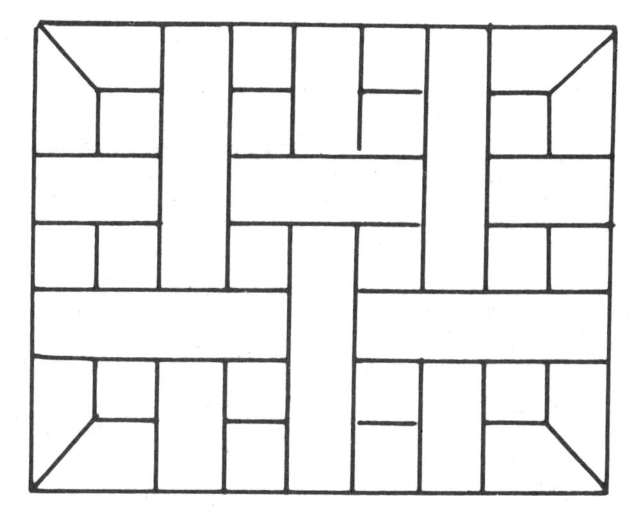

Upholstery

IF THE FURNITURE YOU BUILD IN INCLUDES seating, it may have a hard surface that can be softened by loose cushions. Alternatively, you can upholster the seat. This may just be a softening of the seat area, or you may also pad the back and arms. Much depends on the purpose of the seat. If it is to be used for fairly brief periods while eating or working at a table, a hard seat may be acceptable, or you can provide little more than token padding. If it is more of a lounging seat, much more softening will be required. This may be completely built in, or you may supplement the attached upholstery with cushions, preferably made fitted, although in some places scatter cushions may be adequate.

There has been a revolution in upholstery since World War II. Older upholstery used various fillings and springs. The main difficulty was that few of the filling materials remained soft and flexible indefinitely, and some would move and cause bumps and hard spots. Springs rusted and caused supporting webbing to break. Some Victorian furniture may appear attractively upholstered. Although the surface finish is good, the softness and comfort provided are inferior to modern comparable furniture with very different filling.

Rubber and plastic foam have revolutionized upholstery. Both materials retain their softness almost indefinitely. They are available as large pads of thicknesses varying from fractions of an inch up to many inches and in slabs up to any size likely to be needed in a seat. Having the padding in this form means that you don't have to spread fillings in the form of hair, felt, or other smaller pieces. The material should stay put once in place.

The sponginess and softness of foam rubber or plastic come from the multitude of tiny air cells in the materials. In some foam the air cells are interconnected, making the material more like natural sponge. If the foam gets wet, it soaks up water. It is difficult to dry out cushions where spilled water has penetrated the covering. The common foam today is of a closed-cell type where water can not get from one cell to another, and the risk of filling becoming staturated is avoided. The foam used today should also be flame-retardant. Some early plastic foams were very inflammable. Rubber fillings may be in pieces already molded to standard sizes with shaped tops. The rubber may be molded internally with large cavities to increase the sponginess of the seat. If you have to cut it, you may have to attach strips around the edges to cover cavities. For occasional built-in upholstered seats, it is simplest to use plastic foam filling.

Foam plastic can be cut best with a large thin-bladed knife. Wetting the blade may help it to cut. Cut a slab slightly too large, so the covering will compress it slightly. It then keeps its shape and cannot move about. If you are making a fitted cushion, the edge will be left square. If you want to finish with a rounded edge, bevel the underside and not the top (Fig. 5-1A). The covering will pull down the slab to make a neat curve (Fig. 5-1B). At a corner, it will sometimes help to have a bevel under the angle (Fig. 5-1C) if the top is to finish with a rounded appearance.

Traditional covering materials usually went on in at least two layers. An inner plain cloth was needed to pull the rather loose filling into shape before the finish material went over it.

In some work there is still a need for an inner piece, particularly if the finish material is a fairly light or loosely woven cloth. If you are using plastic-coated fabric such as leathercloth, there is no need for anything between it and the foam.

LOOSE SEAT

A simple example is a piece of plywood with a padded top. It may form a lift-out seat or be the top of a bench. A similar method can be used for a seat back. The foam may be between 2 inches and 4 inches thick for a seat. How much bigger you cut the foam depends on its size, thickness, and softness. Some foam is firmer than others. Allow about ½ inch oversize on a seat about 15 inches across, with foam 3 inches thick.

If the base is a piece of ½-inch plywood, make sure there are no rough edges or corners. Otherwise, no special preparations are needed except to drill a few holes (Fig. 5-2A). The holes are there to allow air to pass in and out of the filling as it is expanded and compressed in use.

With a decorative woven cloth covering,

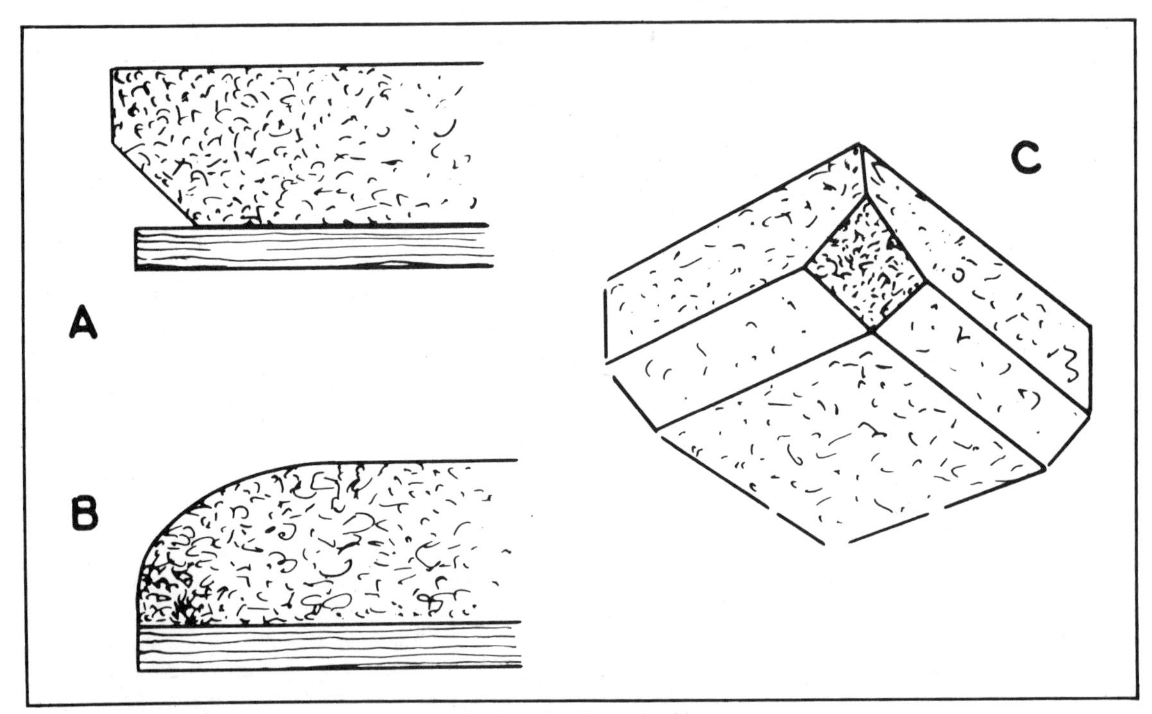

Fig. 5-1. Foam filling can be pulled to a curve after beveling its underside.

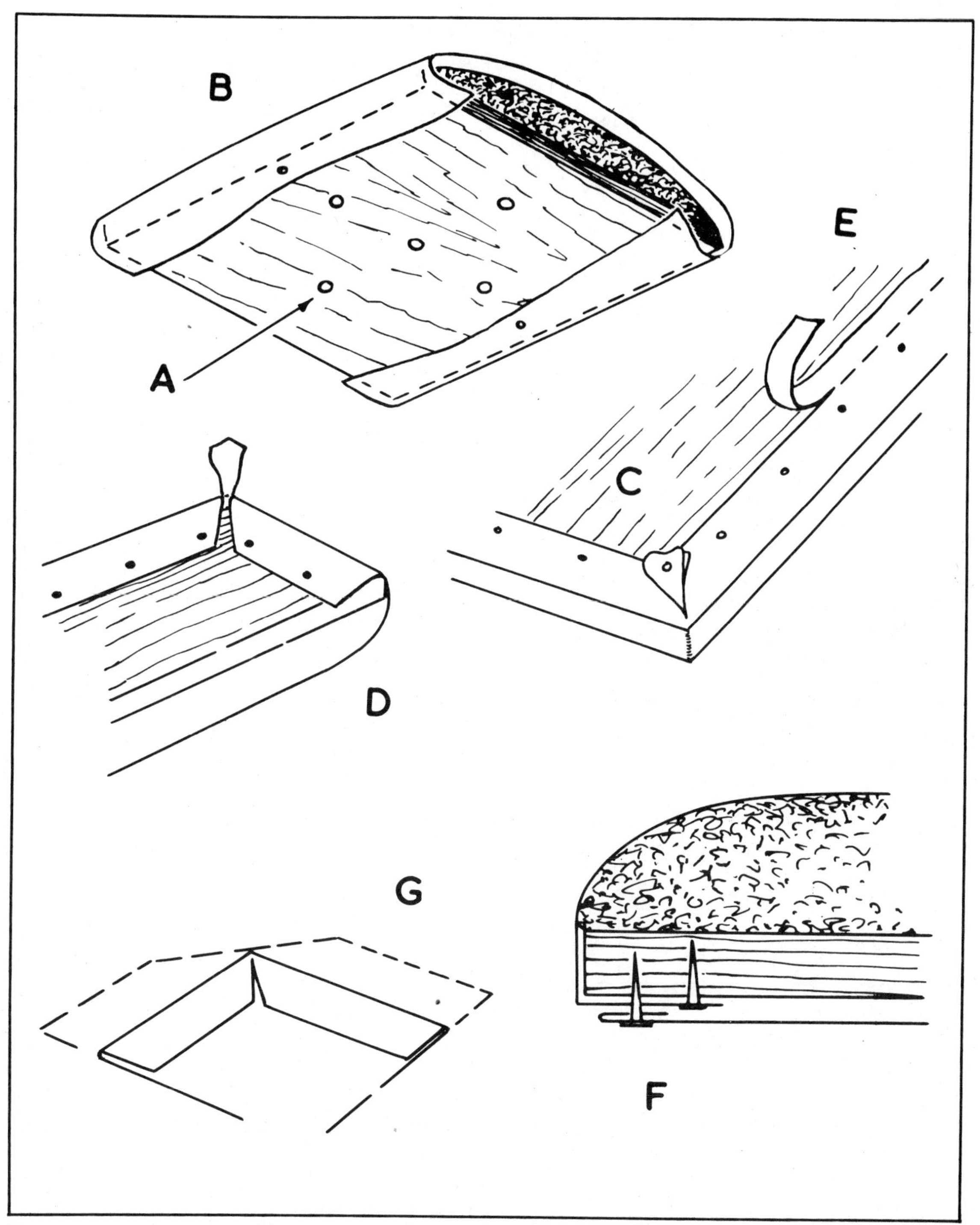

Fig. 5-2. Ventilating holes should be drilled in a wood base, then the covering is pulled over (A to E). Cloth below makes a neat finish. Turn in the edges and tack through (F). At each corner cut across to make a miter underneath (G).

choose an inner piece of light flexible cloth such as *muslin*. If you are using leathercloth, there is no need for it. The cloth is attached with tacks that should be shorter than the thickness of the plywood. You can drive staples with a trigger tacker. These tackers are used extensively in commercial upholstery. If you have one or intend to do a lot of upholstery, a tacker speeds work. Tacks are simple and satisfactory for occasional upholstery.

Pull the cloth over the foam at the centers of opposite sides and tack underneath (Fig. 5-2B). How far in you put the tacks depends on where the seat is going. If it has to fit a recessed support, have the tacks far enough from the edge to clear the support. Do the same the other way. Put on enough tension to curve the foam as you want it. Add more tacks. Work outward toward the corners and keep the same distance from the edge of the wood. How close to put the tacks depends on the materials. If the tacks are spaced too widely, the curved edge will be uneven and show as a series of bulges between the hollows due to the tacks. Spacing 1 inch to 1½ inches should be satisfactory.

Pull diagonally at first at the corners. That will shape the filling. Tack there, but you will have creases on each side of the tack to deal with. For the light inner material, you can fold over the creases and tack through (Fig. 5-2C). For heavier covering materials, it may be better to cut out V-shaped pieces to avoid creases (Fig. 5-2D). Do not cut the Vs right to the edges of the wood, leave a little to be brought into shape by stretching.

Trim the cloth inside the tacks parallel with the edges of the wood (Fig. 5-2E). If you have to put another piece of cloth over the first, arrange the tacks between the first. Get sufficient tension without pulling enough to slacken the inner cloth. Any remaining unevenness of curve due to the first tacks should be smoothed out. Trim that cloth over the first.

If you want the seat top to be curved back to front, you can put thin foam strips across under the main piece to lift it to a curve under a sitter's thighs.

A top covering usually is all that has to be applied. If the plywood is visible frequently, as it would be in the lid of a locker, you can cover the underside with another piece of cloth laid flat. Turn in the edges and tack through (Fig. 5-2F). Rub down each fold first with a flat piece of wood or the handle of a knife. At each corner cut across to make a miter underneath (Fig. 5-2G). Avoid the extra thickness due to a fold there. If the cloth is stretched as it is tacked, it should remain flat. You can put other tacks in the cloth or use glue there if it tends to sag.

COVERING OVER A RAIL

In some assemblies the top may be padded in a similar way. Because there is a rail across and the plywood is not intended to be lifted out, edges of cloth have to be dealt with in a different way. Pull the cloth over the rail and tack into it (Fig. 5-3A). How far down to take the line of tacks depends on the furniture. Going some way down on the rail gives an accompanying feeling of sumptuousness.

With two thicknesses of cloth, the inner piece may be tacked without folding the edge. The outer piece goes a little further. A flexible woven cloth can be folded under and tacked through that (Fig. 5-3B). With heavier material it can be tacked without folding under. A finish is given to this edge with *gimp*, which is a type of narrow tape produced in many colors and styles of finish to match covering materials. For plastic-coated fabrics, you can cut narrow strips of the same material to use as gimp.

Gimp is attached with gimp pins, which are fine nails with small heads. The pins are usually colored black so they are inconspicuous. Put the gimp over the edge (Fig. 5-3C) and use enough gimp pins to make it lie flat. Giving a slight stretch helps keep the gimp straight. If you are going all around a top, overlap the ends of the gimp at the back or another less obvious place.

WEBBING SUPPORTS

With a sufficient thickness of foam, you will have all the comfort required over a piece of plywood. A more flexible support may be better for some purposes. The foam usually will be thinner—2 inches instead of 3 inches.

Flexibility of support can be given with webbing. There are two types: the woven cloth type

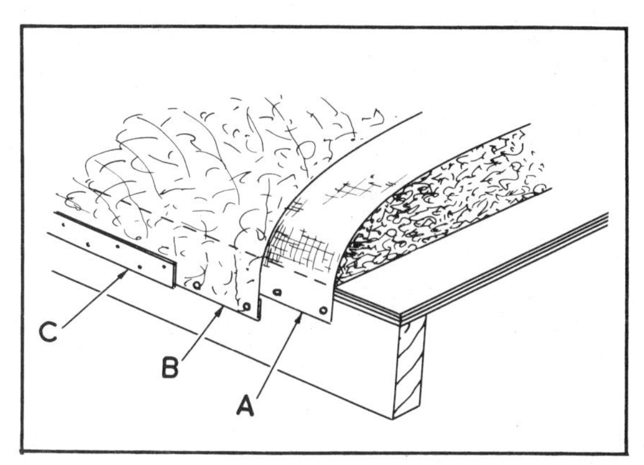

Fig. 5-3. A good finish is obtained with inner cloth pulling to shape, then the outer covering edge is hidden by gimp.

with little stretch and rubber webbing. The ordinary webbing under foam will be satisfactory for a small seat. Most of this webbing is about 2 inches wide. It is used on an open frame, which may be beveled at its outer edges and the sharpness taken off elsewhere. For the average seat, the bands of webbing are arranged with about 2-inch gaps. These will have to be adjusted to get a satisfactory arrangement, such as two one way interwoven with three the other way (Fig. 5-4A).

The webbing has to be tensioned, as it should not develop too much sag in use. The ends are tacked. At the start of a piece, it may be sufficient to drive two tacks and turn over the end to take another (Fig. 5-4B). If that does not seem strong enough, make it three and then two tacks. The other end should be tacked the same way, but with the webbing under tension. Special tools are available for straining webbing, but you can manage with a small piece of wood about ¾ inch thick, 2 inches wide, and 5 inches long. Fold the webbing over this and lever it against the frame (Fig. 5-4C). When you have enough tension, put in the first tacks and cut off the webbing with enough to turn over (Fig. 5-4D). The tension should be the same on all bands the same way. If you put a pencil mark on the untensioned webbing (Fig. 5-4E), note how far it has moved when you tension the first band. You can get the others stretched to the same amount.

If you have to fit much webbing, buy or make a tensioner. There are metal versions and some that grip the webbing in other ways, but a simple one to make puts a loop of webbing through a slot where it is held with a peg (Fig. 5-5).

Except for the webbing, upholstery can be applied in the same way as on a flat board, but there are two possible extra treatments. With most foam and reasonably close webbing bands, there should be little fear of the foam bulging downward in the spaces. That can be prevented with cloth tacked over the webbing (Fig. 5-4F). The traditional material for this is burlap, but you can use any cloth not too tightly woven. When tacking this cloth and the webbing, keep the tacks in some way from the edge. When the foam is drawn down by the covering, any unevenness will be too far in to be noticeable.

If the webbing-covered frame may be seen from below when a lid is opened, it can be improved with cloth turned in and tacked to the frame (Fig. 5-4G).

Rubber webbing is similar in size to fabric webbing, but it has some elasticity and provides more springy support. It can be fitted interwoven across a frame, but it may be sufficient to use it one way only, keeping the bands fairly close together. You can tack rubber webbing in the same way as fabric webbing. Get equal tension on the bands, so mark the first strip and pull the other the same amount.

There are other ways of dealing with the ends of rubber webbing. A metal clip with teeth can be squeezed on to the end of the webbing. There is a hole in the clip (Fig. 5-6A), so you can nail or screw it to wood, but it is better to use a groove. If you plow a groove in the wood a short distance below the top surface, the clip goes into it and a nail secures it (Fig. 5-6B). If the groove is put on the top surface and given a slight angle, the clip will stay in place without a nail (Fig. 5-6C). You can put the groove outside, so the webbing goes all over the top (Fig. 5-6D).

For most built-in seating that does not have a solid support, webbing will be the usual choice. It is unlikely that any work will justify using coil springs in the traditional way they were needed with the older stuffing materials, but there are tension springs that can be used in place of webbing. They

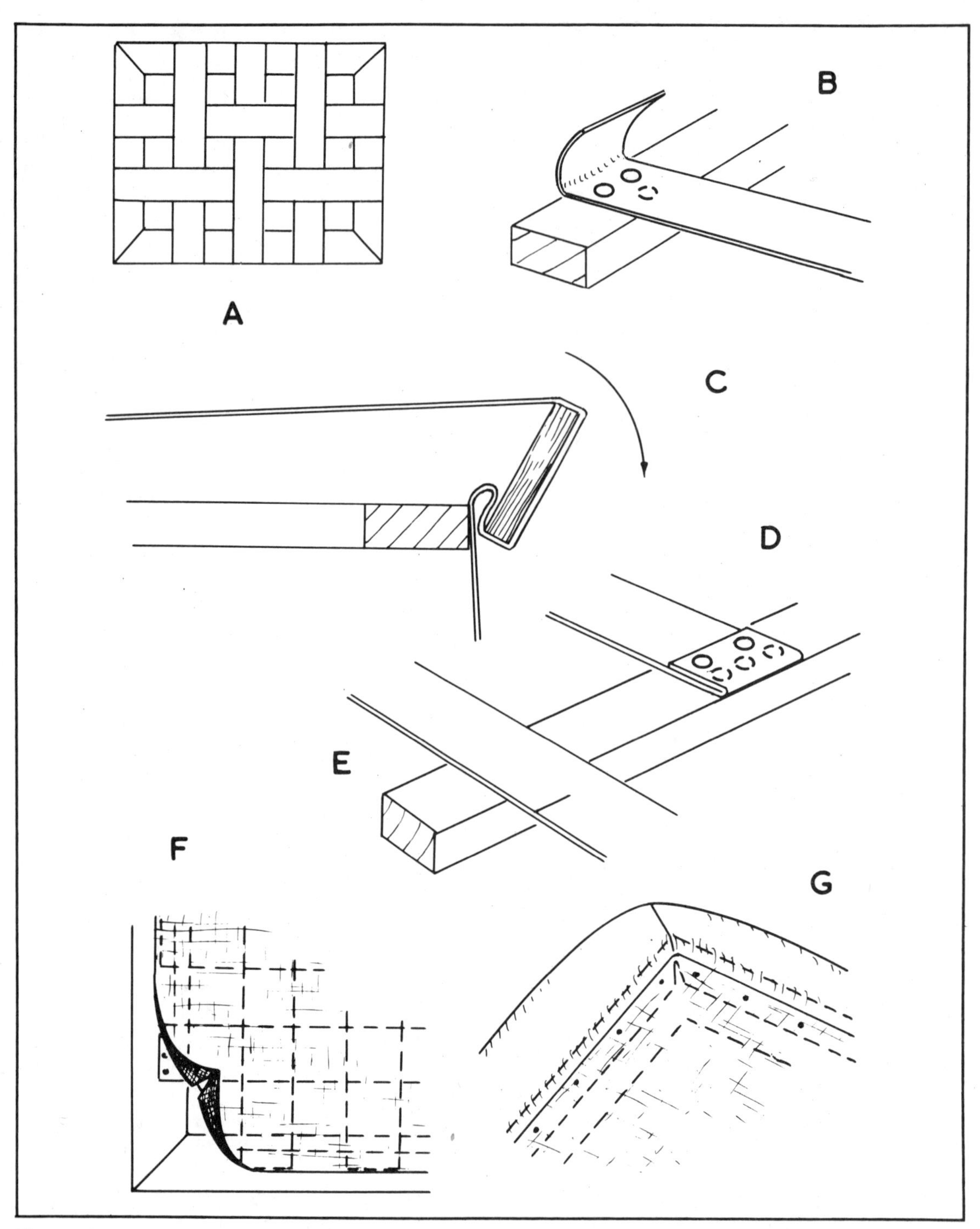

Fig. 5-4. Webbing provides support below padding. Strips are interwoven and tacked (A to E), then covering cloth is put below (F, G).

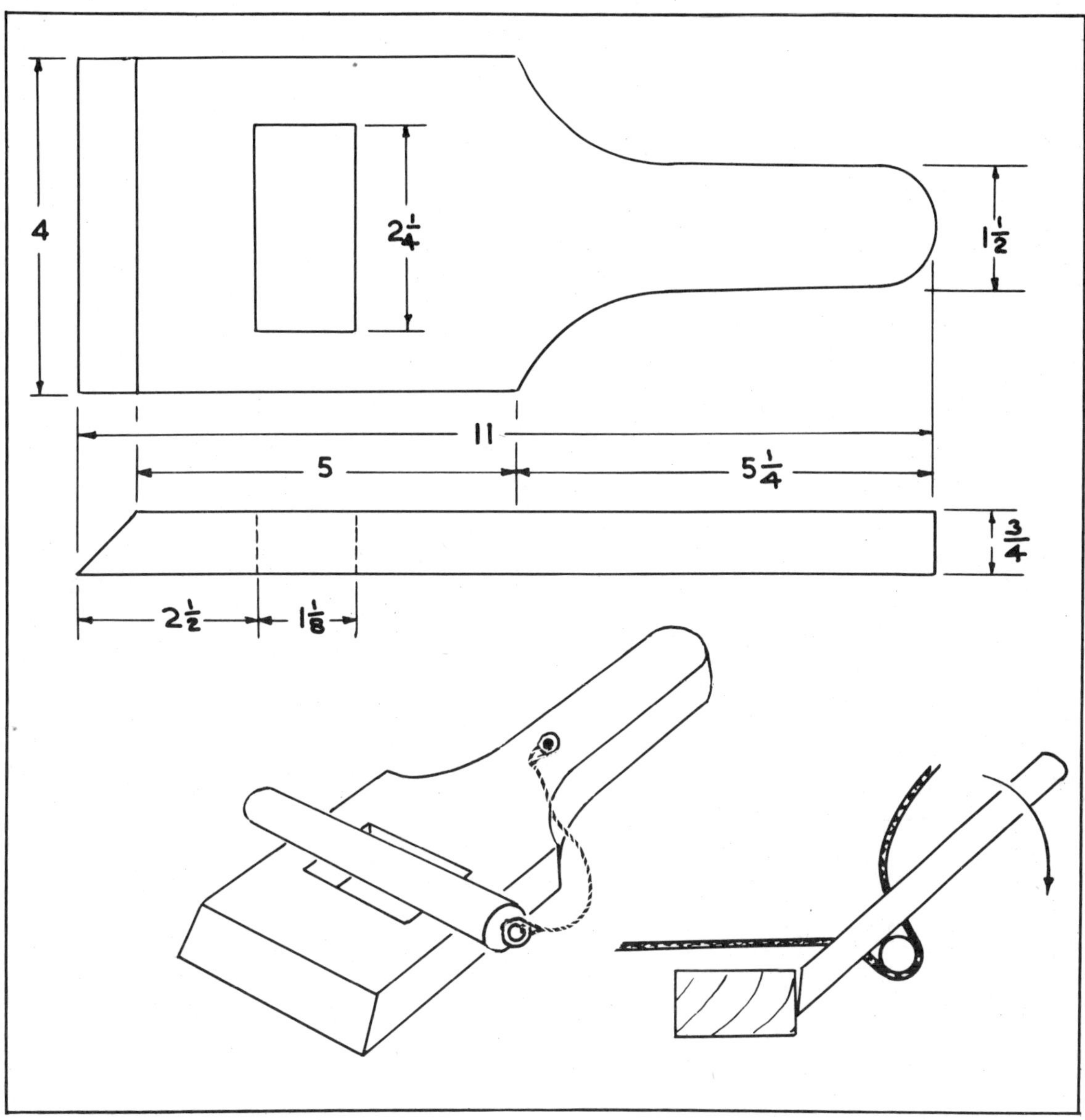

Fig. 5-5. Details of a wooden webbing strainer.

are put across in one direction only, fairly close together (1½ inches to 3 inches), possibly with cloth over to support loose fitted cushions. These springs are available in many lengths, and they should be chosen so they need a slight pull to their attachments. A cord through an end eye will allow a lever to stretch a spring.

The simplest attachment for a tension spring is a nail or screw, probably with a washer (Fig. 5-6E) on the surface. You can use a groove with a nail through (Fig. 5-6F). Metal plates can be bought or made to take the springs, either in a rabbet (Fig. 5-6G) or on a bevel (Fig. 5-6H).

BUTTONING

Much upholstery will be found with a pattern of

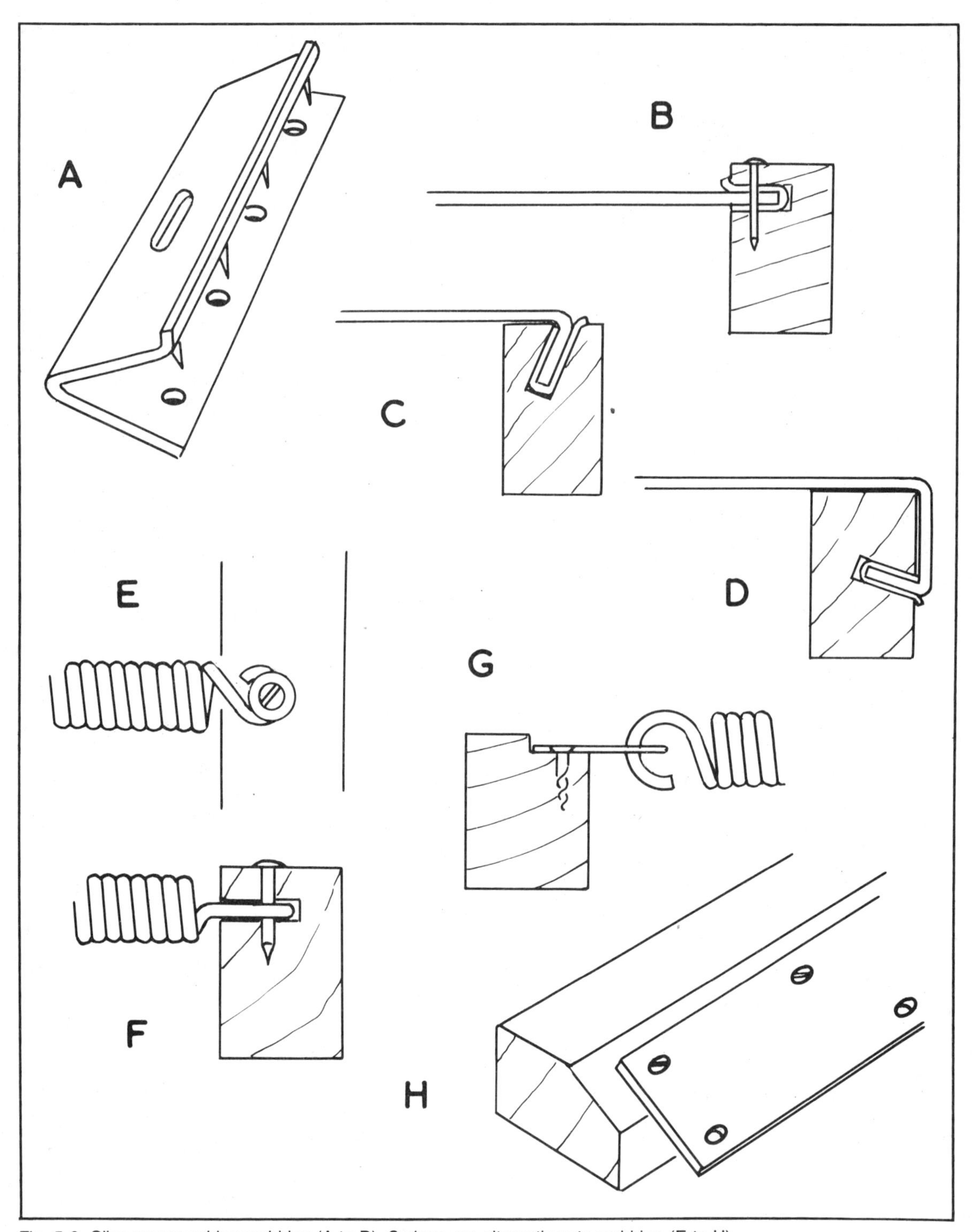

Fig. 5-6. Clips secure rubber webbing (A to D). Springs are alternatives to webbing (E to H).

buttons on the surface. These are sewn through to the back. With the older upholstery methods, the threads through were important as they limited the amount of movement of loose filling materials. They are not so important for this purpose with foam filling, but they do help to keep it in place and hold down the covering on a large area. Buttons are attractive and users have become accustomed to them, so buttoning is done on many pieces of upholstery.

Buttons can be obtained to match most covering materials. Upholstery suppliers have machines to cover buttons with cloth you supply, so you can use offcuts to get an exact match. The thread used is described as *twine* and is somewhat between thread and string thickness. With it goes a needle that must be long enough to go through the upholstery, with something to spare. These needles can be obtained with points at both ends, but for most work it is easier and safer to have one without a point at the eye end. There may be another button on the underside, or you can use a little wood rod with a hole across it. A second button is needed on a cushion that will be turned over, but the peg—which you can make—will do in other situations.

If you are working on a plywood base, mark it out and drill for the twine before covering (Fig. 5-7A). When the covering is on, measure and mark the holes on the surface. This will result in a more even pattern than relying on pushing a needle up from below.

Have the button on the twine. If possible, get both ends of the twine through the eye of the needle. Otherwise, you will have to pass the needle through twice (Fig. 5-7B). Push the needle through. Take it off the thread ends and put the other button or the peg on one end. Join the ends with a slipknot. A suitable one takes one end around the other in a figure eight (Fig. 5-7C). Notice that you arrange this so both ends stand up together. Twisting the twine the other way puts one end downward.

Draw up the slipknot until the button on the surface has pulled in as much as you want—just below the normal surface level is usual (Fig. 5-7D). Deeper buttoning looks good on some leathercloth furniture. When you have the twine adjusted, put a half hitch over the end from the figure eight to lock the knot (Fig. 5-7E). If you compress the filling to slacken the twine, you can manipulate it so the knot buries the thickness of the cushion.

In many cases it will not matter if the pegs are on the undersurface of the plywood. If you want to cover the plywood with cloth, the twine holes may be counterbored, so the pegs are drawn into them (Fig. 5-7F).

If you are buttoning a cushion, the method is the same, except that you have buttons on both sides and have to adjust tension so the buttons pull in the same amount. Have all buttons in position on the twine at the slipknot stage, then they can be adjusted and the knots locked when they all match.

SEWING

If you want to shape the covering on a seat, some seams will have to be sewn. A domestic sewing machine will deal with most upholstery materials. The machine ideally will have a special foot to allow it to stitch close into an angle, but seams sewn with a normal foot should be satisfactory. There may have to be some hand sewing, but that need not be much if the work is carefully planned.

If the seat or a loose cushion is to keep its thickness to the edges instead of being drawn down to a curve, the covering has to be boxed over it. For a built-in seat with the upholstery attached, the covering has to be cut at the corners (Fig. 5-8A) to get a square appearance. Make the covering inside out and sew down the seam (Fig. 5-8B). Cut off surplus cloth a short distance inside the stitching. Make sure the stitching goes into and slightly over the inner end of the cut, so it will not pull open. The covering can then be brought down to be tacked under or outside the woodwork (Fig. 5-8C). As with other upholstery, have the foam filling slightly too big.

If you are making a loose fitted cushion, have the sides (walling) separate from the top and bottom, particularly if the shape is not a simple rectangle or you have to shape around a part. It is then best to cut the foam to size and pin the covering material inside out over it (Fig. 5-9A). Use a pencil to make register marks on adjoining pieces,

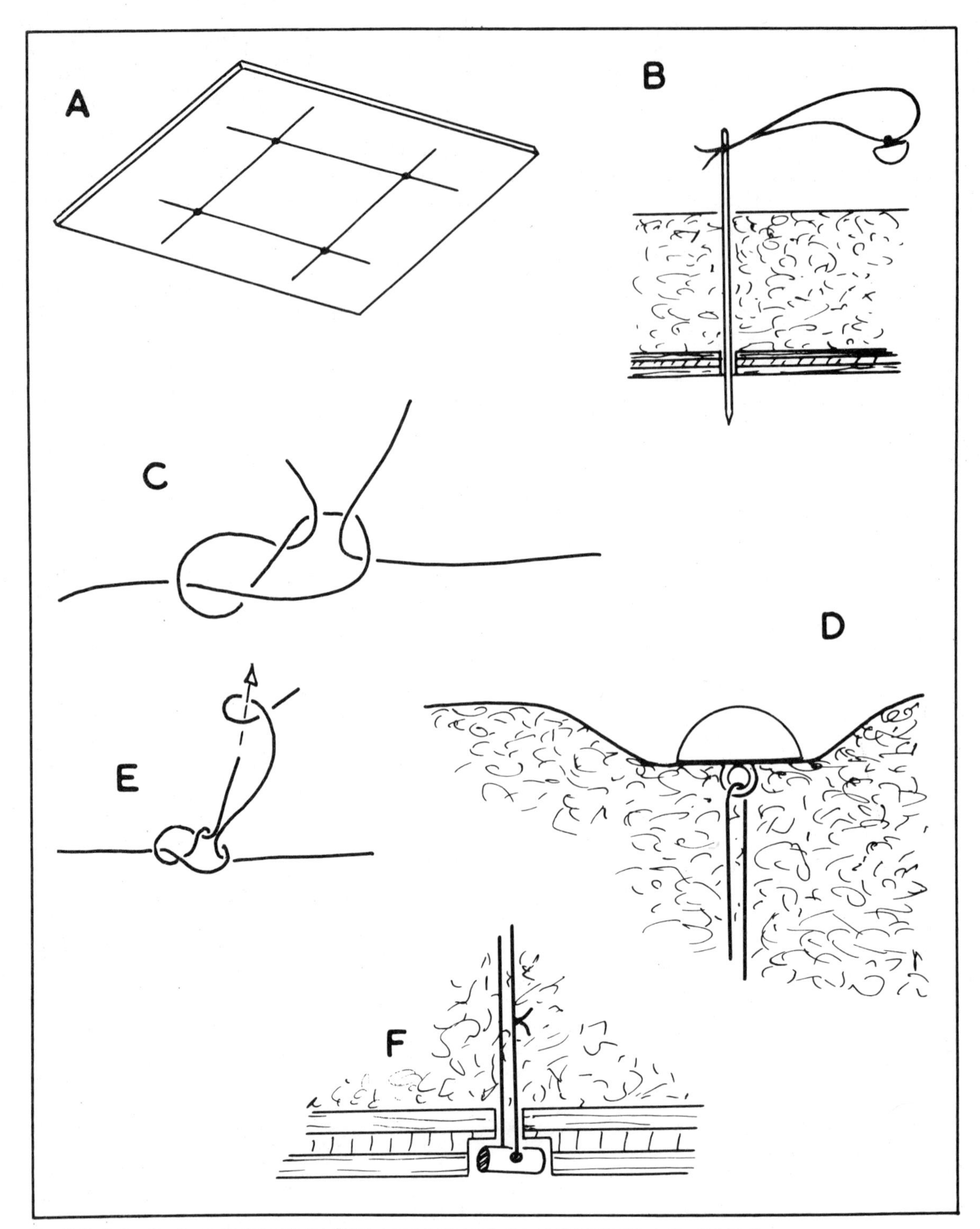

Fig. 5-7. Buttoning is sewn through the filling and baseboard, then adjusted with a special knot.

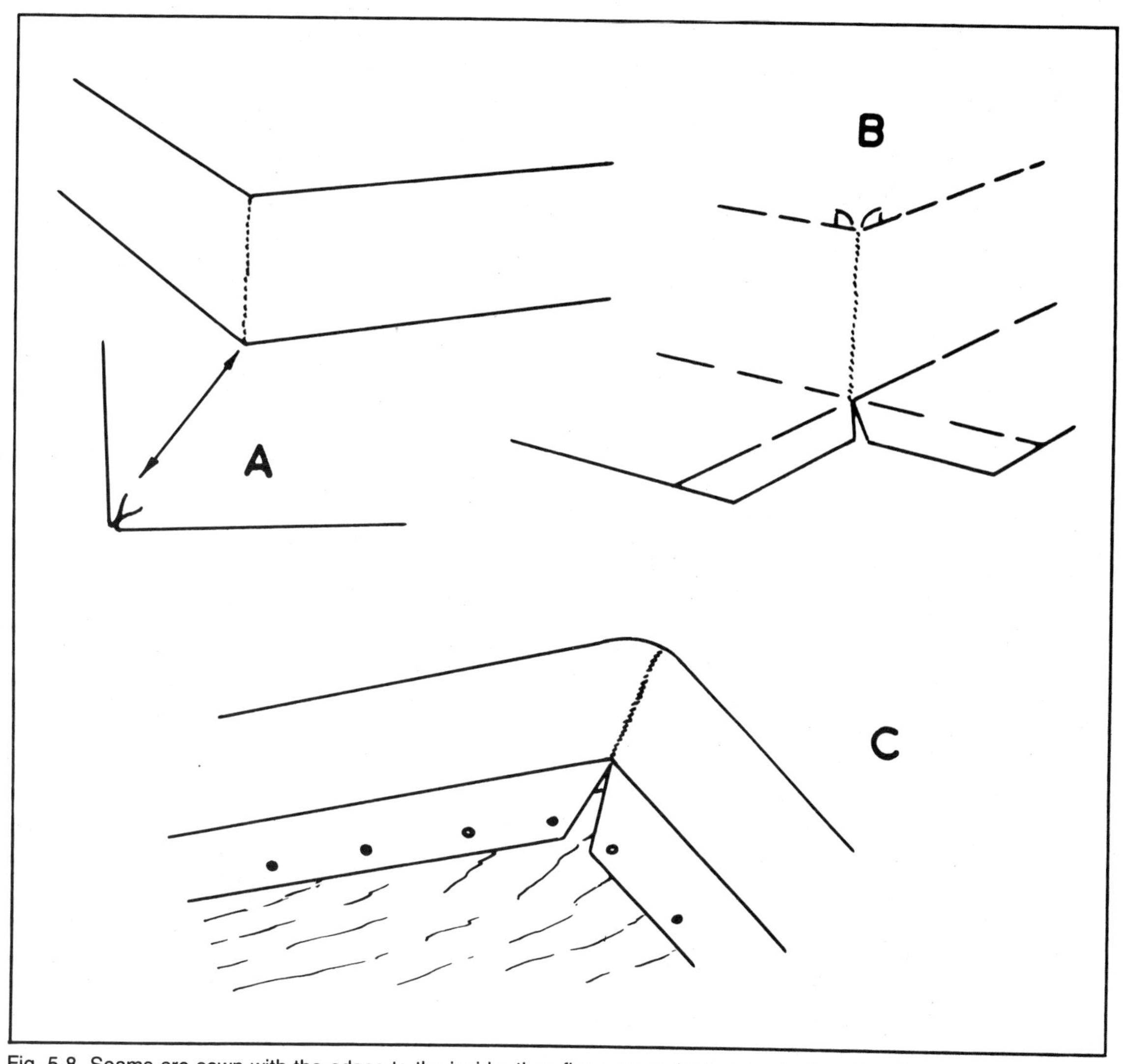

Fig. 5-8. Seams are sewn with the edges to the inside, then flaps are tacked under the baseboard with a boxed filling.

so you keep them correctly related as you remove pins and sew seams. Make the covering slightly smaller than the block of foam filling. If you are making a cover that may be turned over, use the same material everywhere. If it only goes one way, there can be cheaper plain cloth underneath.

The walling does not have to be in one piece. Short pieces can be used up. Seams can be arranged inconspicuously at corners or at the back. The filling has to be taken out, if only to allow the sewn covering to be turned the right way, so there should be a space for it to pass through. One way is to sew a zipper at the back, either its full width or around one or both corners (Fig. 5-9B). The foam will compress, so the opening can be much smaller than the overall width of the expanded foam.

A zipper will allow the foam to be removed easily later if the covering has to be washed or dry-cleaned. If that is not required, the foam can be inserted through one back seam, which is sewn up. You can machine sew all the seams and a short distance each side of the opening, so there is a

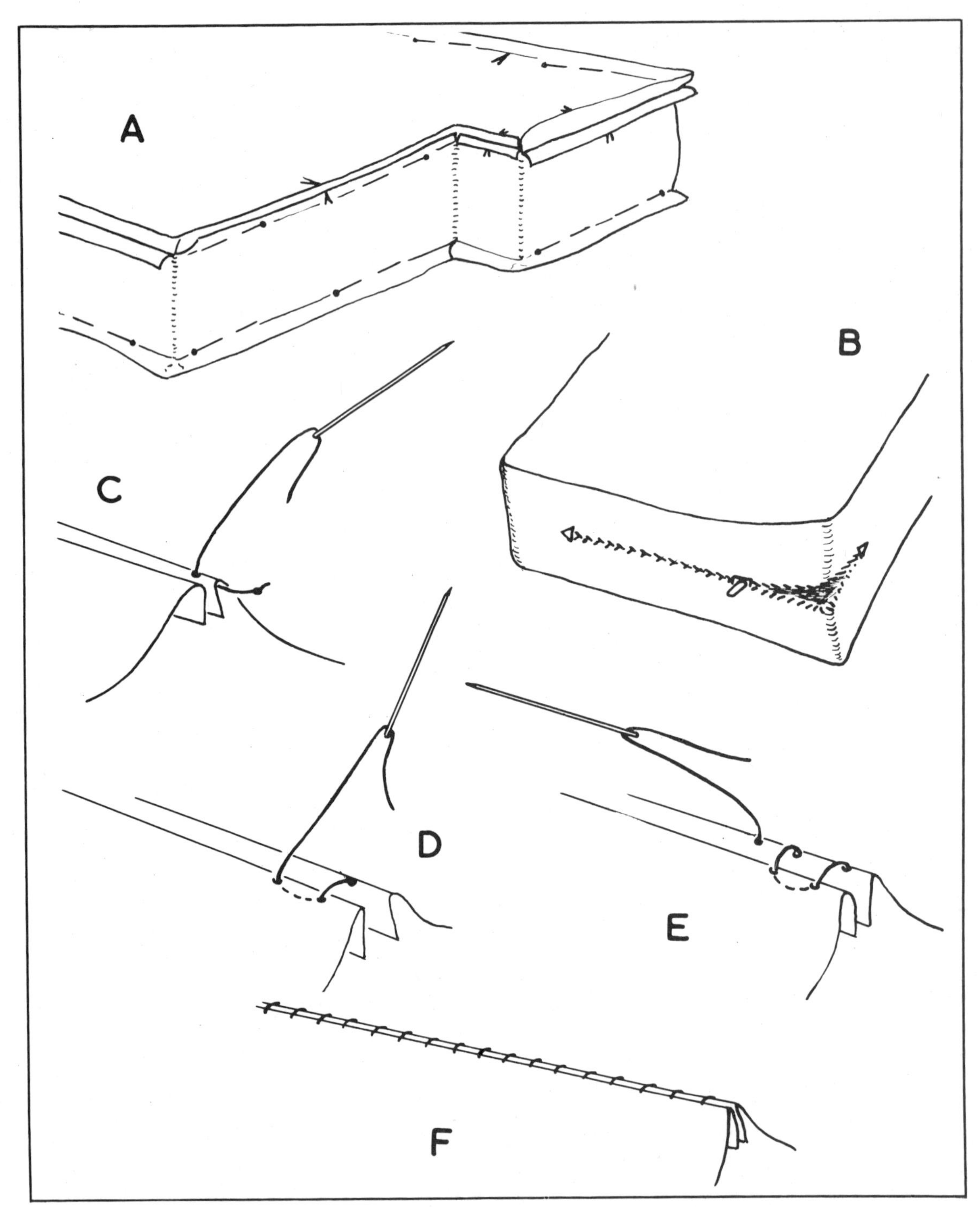

Fig. 5-9. Covering is marked, tacked, and sewn inside out. The open side is closed with a zipper or hand stitching after inserting the padding.

minimum amount of hand sewing to be done. You may compress the filling enough to machine sew the seam outside if it will come in a place that will be hidden. Hand sewing is not difficult and uses a slip stitch that finishes with little of the thread visible outside.

Have single or double thread on a small straight or curved needle. Turn in the edges while the foam is pushed out of the way. Start with a knot inside one of the folds (Fig. 5-9C). Take the needle straight across into the other fold, then inside to come out a short distance along (Fig. 5-9D). Go straight across to the first side and along the fold (Fig. 5-9E). Continue in that way along the seam. When it is pulled tight, only the crossing threads will show (Fig. 5-9F). The distance you go between crossings depends on the material. A soft material will need closer stitches than a stiff cloth or plastic covering. Stitches ¼ inch long may be regarded as maximum.

If you are faced with the problem of pulling edges together with hand stitching, a herringbone stitch draws and locks the edges with each stitch. Have doubled thread in the needle and knot the ends together. Go up through the far side at the left of the seam (Fig. 5-10A). Take the needle down through the near side and up on the left of the stitch (Fig. 5-10B). Pull tight and go up through the far side again (Fig. 5-10C). The crossing action will lock the first stitch. Cross to the near side and make another tight stitch in the same way (Fig. 5-10D). Continue along the seam in the same way, with about five stitches per inch. Pull each stitch tight as you make it. The seam is shown open for clarity (Fig. 5-10E). Finish by knotting the thread into the last stitch before cutting off.

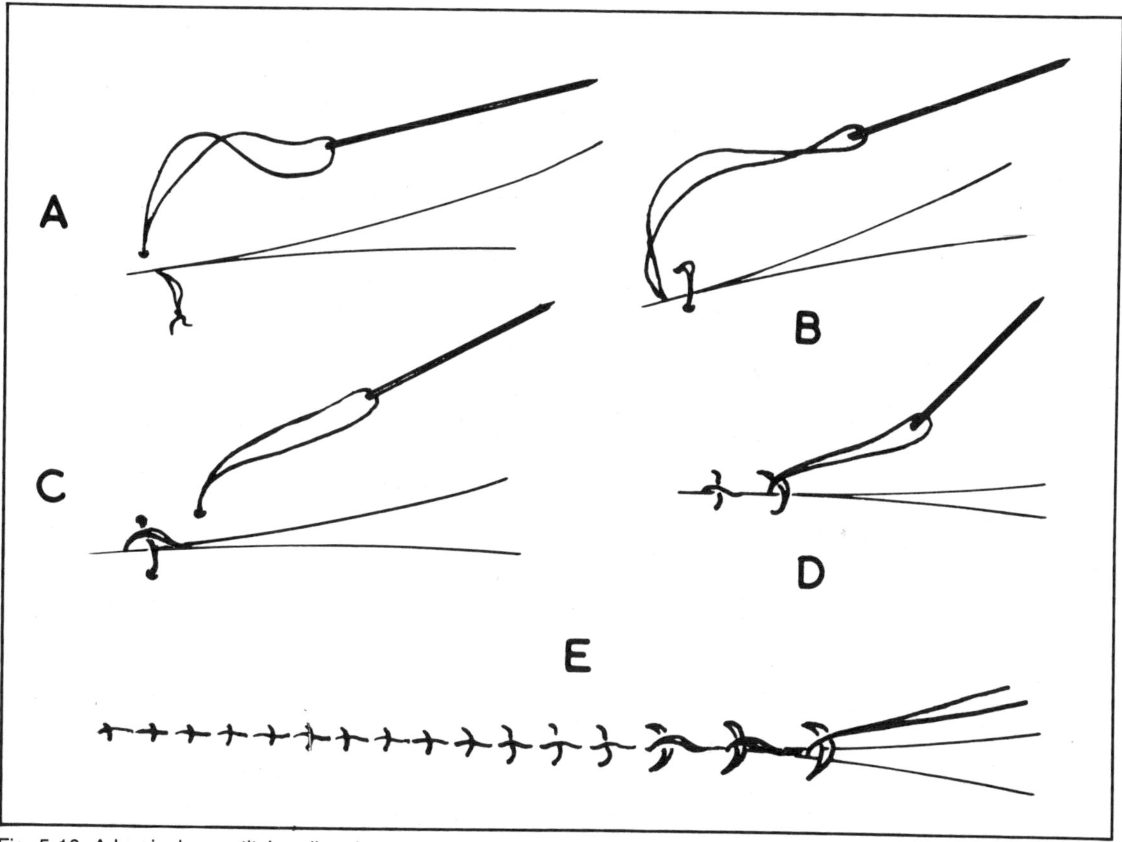

Fig. 5-10. A herringbone stitch pulls edges together as it progresses.

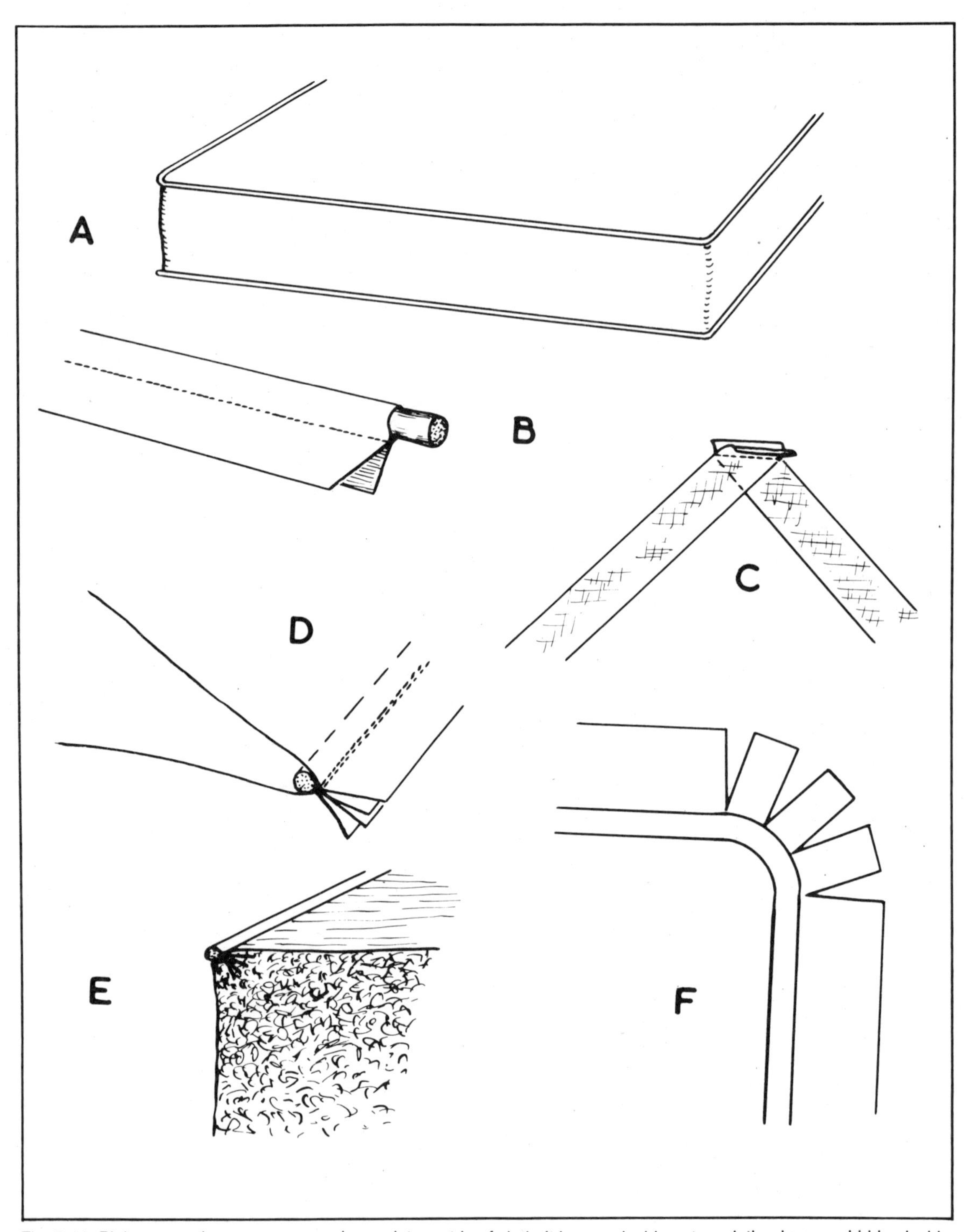

Fig. 5-11. Piping around a seam uses cord sewn into a strip of cloth. It is sewn inside out so cloth edges are hidden inside.

PIPING

Much upholstery has *piping* along the visible seams (Fig. 5-11A). It may be in the same material as the covering or in a contrasting color. This applies to woven cloth and plastic-coated fabrics. The latter sometimes has piping color very different from the main color, such as white piping on a blue main color. Piping makes a neater line at a seam than just stitches.

Piping is cord enclosed in a strip of fabric (Fig. 5-11B). It can be bought ready for sewing in, or you can make it from offcuts of covering material, preferably cut diagonal to the weave (on the bias). Pieces to make up the lengths are best sewn at 45° (Fig. 5-11C). They are then used with the cut edges inward so the joint is almost invisible outside. There are special piping cords, but you can use any light line about ⅛ inch thick. Sew close to the cord and leave ½ inch or more of the cloth extending. Usually on built-in furniture you will be concerned only with front seams. If you want to take piping all around, you can hide the meeting ends by cutting the cord back in one part. The other end may extend and go into its space, with the two parts of cloth overlapping.

When you sew a seam inside out, include the piping with its tabs outward (Fig. 5-11D) between the cloths. Make the seam as close in to the piping cord as possible. That is where a special foot on the sewing machine is an advantage. Include a second line of stitching if you wish. When the cover is brought the right way, the piping will settle close into the seam (Fig. 5-11E).

A problem comes at corners as piping is fitted. The tabs will pull into the bend when being sewn inside out. To prevent that, make several cuts toward the corner (Fig. 5-11F).

When planning built-in furniture that includes upholstery, treat the job as a whole, even if you will only do the woodwork and your wife, or someone else, will handle the upholstery. Prepare the woodwork to take springs or webbing. Allow for the thickness of cloth on a lift-out seat edge or provide clearance for a hinged padded top. It is no use doing the woodwork as one project without considering the problems of finishing it with upholstery.

Chapter 6

Finishes

A FURNITURE PIECE'S FINISH MAKES IT ATTRACTIVE. You may get the furniture accurately made with good joints, but a poor finish will spoil the effect. There are some situations where wood may be left untreated. A work surface for using tools on may be better in its natural state. A place for preparing meat or other food may be better left plain so it can be scrubbed occasionally. A few woods look their best untreated, but nearly all the wood made into furniture must have a surface treatment to provide protection and enhance appearance.

If you are making furniture to be built in where there is plenty of freestanding furniture, consider the room scheme as a whole. Adopt a finish for the new work that is the same as or complementary to the finish on other furniture. The bulk of the material in built-in furniture will be wood. If you use plastics, they will usually be left in their manufactured state. Metal will usually play a secondary role in the decorative scheme, so it may be painted black or a color that is unobtrusive among the wood parts. Exceptions may be aluminum or plated metal, where the polished silvery color may form decorative features. If the metal parts are iron or steel, there is a risk of corrosion, so it is common to paint them.

PREPARATION

The quality of a finish applied to wood depends to a great extent on the way the wood has been prepared. Furniture finishes cannot be regarded as means of covering poor construction and surface damage. Remember this when you are preparing the wood. Ragged grain due to planing the wrong way cannot be disguised at the finishing stage. Get surfaces as smooth as you can while the furniture is in pieces. Do not damage the wood during construction. If you have to hit to make joints come together, use smooth scrap wood to cushion the hammer blow and spread the load. If you need to use clamps, put scrap wood under the jaws. If you put a piece of wood down to work on one side, think of the other side, too. Beware of nails or other items on the bench that may mark the undersurface.

Keep your tools sharp; this applies to hand and machine cutting tools. Using a blunt tool will cause poor surfaces or edges. The surface from a sharp tool needs less treatment later. It is always better to cut than to abrade. Sanding is a final treatment on surfaces that come against other parts where smoothing to their ends will be difficult then, yet easy before making joints.

Machine-planed wood saves plenty of labor and should get surfaces reasonably true, whether you buy wood already planed or prepare it with your own jointer. Do not leave a machine-planed surface on wood that forms faces of the furniture. The action of machine planing leaves a pattern of ridges across the wood. They may be minute, but there is a risk that they will show through the finish applied later, even after thorough sanding. It is better to hand plane a machine-planed surface. There is another purpose besides removing the ridges. The cutters of a planer are at varying degrees of bluntness. The pounding of rotating cutters that are not perfectly sharp tends to compress the surface fibers. Applying a liquid finish may raise some of the bent fibers and give you trouble in getting the result you want. Such a surface becomes *case-hardened* due to pounding. This does not allow glue to penetrate readily and reduces the strength of a glued joint.

Some attractive grain is difficult to plane in any direction without causing fibers to tear. Use a scraper. There are handled scrapers, but the traditional type is a flat piece of steel with its edge turned over. Both scrapers can be used over bad grain, and the very fine shavings removed will leave a better surface than any plane.

Excess glue can interfere with a finish as it prevents stain soaking in evenly and may affect the appearance of any liquid finish put over it. If the glue used is a type that is soluble in water before it sets, wipe off any surplus around a joint with a damp cloth. Do not make it excessively wet. Be careful not to smear glue over other parts and leave it. If the glue has to be dealt with after it has set, you may be able to chip it away with a chisel or scrape it off. Be careful not to scrape away wood fibers, particularly across the grain, as the difference in surface texture may cause a variation in the final finish.

Although some surfaces have to be dealt with after the furniture has been assembled, there may be some parts that are better worked on while they are loose. It is always easier to work on a piece of wood on the bench than to try to do the same things to it after it has been connected to other parts. Plane, scrape, and sand individual pieces before assembly. If you expect that you may have to take off a few shavings after assembly, it will be a waste of time finishing that surface. There are many inner surfaces that come against other parts where smoothing to their ends will be difficult then, yet easy before making joints.

Much furniture-quality plywood has good sanded surfaces. Check all pieces before building them into a frame or otherwise enclosing them so work on the surface is difficult. Look across toward a light. That may show up high spots and irregularities. There is not much thickness of surface veneer, but you may be able to scrape and sand to get a better appearance.

SANDING

Power sanders have their uses, but they are not alternatives to planes. They tend to bend fibers instead of cut them. Sanding is an important final process before applying a finish, but the procedures leading up to it should ensure that it does not take much effort or time.

The term *sanding* is a carry-over from much earlier days when the abrasive was sand glued to paper. This was followed with powdered glass, which is still obtainable and makes a good abrasive for wood. A cheaper grit is *flint*, which wears quickly and soon clogs with dust. A good grit for general sanding is *garnet*. There are many other grits, but some are more suitable for plastics or metal. Be careful that any abrasive paper you get is intended for wood.

Silicon carbide is a grit used on plastics or wood. One version is described as wet-and-dry, meaning that it can be used with water. That keeps down dust. In woodworking the only time you may need it is if you apply a hard synthetic finish, which has to be smoothed between coats.

Nearly all abrasive sheets available today have

the grit held to the backing paper or cloth with waterproof adhesive. If you doubt the waterproofness of the glue, warm the paper before use to drive off any moisture. Otherwise, the glue will allow the grit to pull away. A cloth backing will last longer than paper, but paper is satisfactory for most purposes. Cloth backing is better for dealing with awkward shapes or for work rotating in a lathe.

There have been many ways of indicating the coarseness of the grit on abrasive paper. Your supplier may talk of *cabinet* papers for use on bare wood and *finishing* papers for rubbing down an applied finish. Most grits are now graded by numbers; the higher the number, the finer the grit. The roughest you are likely to need after planing is 60 grit. The finest you are likely to use directly on wood is 180 grit. Others between are mostly in steps of 20 such as 80, 100, and 120. For light rubbing of finishes, the numbers continue getting finer to 400 grit, which is further than you will probably go.

Paper for hand sanding is mostly in sheets about 9 inches by 11 inches. If folded and used freehand, it may not last long. Tear the paper into four pieces and wrap it around a block of wood thick enough to grip and with a face about 3 inches by 5 inches. You can buy cork blocks or wood sanding blocks faced with hard rubber. Surface sanding by hand need not be arduous. You can use an electric orbital oscillating sander, which gives a surface treatment comparable with hand sanding. Do not use a belt sander or a disk sander for surface finishing.

Hand sand a flat surface with the abrasive paper on a block. Sand with the grain. If you have to sand diagonally to the grain to remove an imperfection, sand over it with the grain sufficiently to remove any diagonal scratches. Scratches across the grain may not show much at this stage, but they may become obvious when polished.

Leave all sanding until you have finished using planes or other cutting tools. Particles of sanding grit embedded in the wood will blunt a cutter. You may get the finish you want with only one grade of grit. If you follow one grit with a finer one, be careful that there are no particles of the coarser grit left to be picked up with the finer paper, or they will travel with the fine grit and cause scoring of the surface. Use a soft brush to clear the wood before moving to the finer grit. A *tack rag* can be wiped over the surface to pick up grit.

For moldings you may manage with the abrasive paper used freehand and folded into the shape, or you can use a piece of wood behind it to approximate to the shape. Turned work is sanded in the lathe, but that makes grit scratches across the grain. If you finish with fine paper and are certain that scratches from coarser grit have been removed, it is unlikely that fine cross-grained scratches will mar the final finish. If there are long sweeping curves in the length, it will help if you rub them lengthwise with fine abrasive paper after the work has been removed from the lathe.

Steel wool is an alternative to abrasive paper. Do not use the type sold for domestic scouring. Steel wool comes in grades from 000 (finest) to 3 (coarsest) for use on wood. You will not need coarser than grade 1, and 00 and 000 are the grades to use for finishing wood. Steel wool may be more suitable than paper for shaped parts. Some woods can be discolored by steel wool. Make sure you remove all particles, as they can rust and affect appearance if left embedded in the grain. A damp cloth should lift out steel wool particles.

STOPPING

Wood is a natural material, and that accounts for much of its beauty. Wood is not of uniform texture, though, and you may have to deal with a flaw or blemish in an otherwise perfect surface. There is also the need to fill or obscure any damage you have done yourself, such as a sunk nailhead or a joint that does not fit as closely as it should. Plan construction so any shakes (natural cracks) in the surface come where they will not show or can be cut out, but you may still have to deal with some exposed surfaces.

Materials for filling cracks and holes are collectively called *stoppings*. They may be referred to as *fillers*, which are the more liquid compounds used to fill the pores of grain before applying a finish. In some cases the mixtures are the same, but they are of different consistencies.

You should buy prepared stoppings. The stopping should be as inconspicuous in the finished work as possible. This means that it should finish the same color as the wood. Some stoppings are supplied in different colors. Others are a neutral shade and will accept stain. If the wood is to be stained, it may be better to use a colored stopping after staining. If the stopping accepts stain, it may absorb it differently from the surrounding wood and finish a different shade. You may have to experiment with stoppings.

Stick shellac or plastic stoppings (sometimes called *beaumontage*) are good for covering sunken nailheads or filling small cracks. These stoppings do not take stain, so they must be bought correctly colored and used after staining the wood. Older workers used oil putty (a mixture of whiting and linseed oil), but it is not recommended as it takes a long time to set. Also, oil absorbs into the surrounding wood, causing discoloration.

Plastic water putty is effective. It comes as a powder and is mixed with water to form a thick paste. It can be pressed into cracks or holes with a putty knife, screwdriver, or chisel. Any excess should be cleaned off quickly, because it sets rapidly. Do not mix more than you need at one time, as it cannot be softened again with water. Sand the area after stopping. Make sure there are no stray particles of putty left in the grain, as they may affect the appearance of the finish. Wood compound is the name of another stopping paste used in the same way as wood putty, but it takes longer to set.

Wood plastic (or plastic wood) is a thick paste in cans or tubes, and it is the nearest thing to wood in its characteristics. It can be pressed into holes, with a little left above the surface for sanding level. It does not contract as it dries. If you have to remedy slight damage, such as a piece splintered off a molding, it is possible to build up with wood plastic, then bring it to shape with tools and sanding. It is the only stopping compound strong enough to allow this work.

Glue should not be regarded as a stopping. It does its job by uniting surfaces that fit fairly closely. There is little strength in the glue itself, so it cannot be expected to fill a gap and hold the parts securely. When most glues have set, a thick deposit will *craze*—become a network of tiny cracks—and that is where the weakness is.

If you want to fill a gap and provide strength, you can use a mixture of glue and sawdust. Then the glue bonds to the sawdust and does not craze. Mix sawdust from the wood you are using to a fairly thick paste and press it into the gap. This mixture will not take stain.

If you paint the furniture, the color of the stopping does not matter, but you still need to get surfaces level. If you use a resinous softwood, resin may come through the paint long after it has been applied, particularly from end grain or the vicinity of knots. There has to be a barrier over these places before you start painting. This can be two coats of shellac dissolved in alcohol, such as a shellac varnish or French polish.

FILLERS

On many woods you can apply a finish without any preparation after sanding, but the woods with more open grain are better filled. Any wood under a microscope will show a mass of pores. If the pores are very small, they will dry smooth. If the pores are large, the dried finish will show dents over them. There may also be tiny natural cracks lengthwise along the grain. If they are large enough to be seen, as in most oaks, the wood requires filling if you are to get a smooth finish. Most of the furniture-quality hardwoods benefit from the application of a filler. Fillers are divided into *paste fillers* for open-grained woods and *liquid fillers* for close-grained woods.

Fillers can be bought ready for use, which is preferable to mixing your own. Some fillers can be used before staining, but others may resist stain penetration. It is better to stain before filling. The filler color obviously must match the stained wood. In most newer fillers the material is a finely ground crystal called *silex*, or it may be some other fine powder. This is formed into a paste with linseed oil or other binder, then it can be thinned for a more liquid filler.

Prepared fillers come in many wood colors. A filler should be slightly darker than the stain, because fillers tend to dry lighter. If paste fillers are being mixed, prepare enough for the whole job in one mix. Make sure there are no streaks or unmixed powder in a batch. It is difficult to get exactly the same color again in a fresh mix.

Spread plenty of paste filler evenly and thoroughly. Leave it long enough for the surface to dull, then rub with a piece of coarse cloth across the grain until all excess filler has been removed. Do not rub too hard, or you may lift out filler that has entered spaces. You have to get filler everywhere, but be careful of leaving any on the surface, particularly in shaped parts or corners. You can use a short-haired stiff brush in awkward places. If excess filler becomes to hard to wipe off, it can be softened with *benzene*. Leave a filled surface for a day before applying anything over it.

Liquid fillers for close-grained wood are similar to the pastes, but they are thinned. You can convert most pastes by thinning with turpentine or benzene. Brush it on and wipe it smooth when the surface has dulled. Shellac in alcohol can be used as a liquid filler. Apply it and sand it lightly, then repeat. Shellac may be white or orange, and the latter can be used over darker stains. Shellac also makes a filler for hardboard that otherwise will absorb a considerable amount of finish. If the final wood finish will be varnish, a thinned first coat will act as its own liquid filler on appropriate woods. Do not use varnish as a filler if the finish is to be by another method.

Woods that have grain open enough to need paste fillers include oak, ash, chestnut, elm, and teak. Woods that need no filler include aspen, cypress, ebony, gaboon, magnolia, and most of the spruce and pine families. Woods that are better with medium and liquid fillers are butternut, mahogany, rosewood, walnut, beech, birch, maple, and sycamore.

STAINS

Many woods are quite attractive with a clear finish over their natural color. Many woods are often stained to what has been accepted as their normal furniture finish color. The brownness of oak and walnut may be intensified. Mahogany usually has its redness increased. It is generally good policy to make more of the existing color than to try to change it. You may have to try to make the built-in furniture match the other furniture in the room, although it is not made of the same wood. Do not try to get a red effect on a brown wood. You may bring one wood to the same color as another, but the grain differences will show that it is another wood. If you mix woods, you will have to try to get them all the same color by staining. Plywood panels will have to be stained to match the surrounding wood. *Stain* may give an inferior wood an appearance of quality. Some rather drab woods with little grain marking may be quite good in construction, but stain will be needed to give them an acceptable furniture finish.

Stain differs from paint in coloring wood without obscuring its appearance. The details of grain should show through. Stain penetrates the surface layer of the wood. Paint and some other surface finishes have little penetration. They hide what is below if built up in sufficient thickness, even if it is a mixture of wood, metal, and plastic.

One problem is getting the stain to color the wood evenly. This is dependent on the solvent. A quick-drying stain has some uses, but it may not be as easy to get into the wood evenly as a slow-drying stain. Stains consist of a pigment in a solvent to provide the color. Different solvents have different penetrating qualities. A reasonable penetration is desirable, as it tends to look better and is proof against knocks. If the finish becomes damaged, a thin stain cover will come away and leave wood in its original color, where a deep stain will hold its color. A good range of colors is obtainable with each type of solvent, and it is the choice of solvent that mainly concerns the finisher.

Oil Stains

These popular stains have a light oil solvent such as *benzene, naphtha*, or *turpentine*. Ready-made stains are available in all quantities and in colors usually described by the name of the wood they are intended to be used on or to represent. The actual colors include a variety of browns, reds, yellows, and oranges, as well as deep black.

Oil stains penetrate quickly. Brush them on

plentifully along the grain. Get the whole surface covered quickly and evenly. The intensity of the stain depends on how long it is given to penetrate. Use a cloth to wipe off surplus stain when you judge the color to be right. It will finish lighter as it dries and is covered with a clear finish. Oil stain is very tolerant and it will usually dry evenly, despite rather erratic brushing and wiping.

It is usually best to do the least important parts first with oil stains, leaving the most prominent part (usually the top) until last. Move the work about if possible, so the surface you are working on is near horizontal. Work in a cross light so you can see how the staining is progressing.

End grain will soak up more stain than the other surfaces and finish much darker. Quick wiping of the end grain will minimize this, but even then you may not reduce darkening very much. A better way is to partially seal the end grain. Put on a coat of thin shellac and let it soak in and dry before staining. Be careful not to get shellac on any adjoining side grain. This will limit penetration of the end grain by the stain and should result in a more even overall cover.

Although oil stain appears to dry rapidly, leave the work at least a day before applying a finish over it. The solvents are flammable, so take the obvious precautions while working. Destroy rags used for wiping.

Water Stain

Water stains are cheap and easy to use. They come as powders to mix with water. The suppliers will indicate proportions, but you can vary the intensity of the color by using different strengths. Dissolve in hot water, but use the stain cold. Dissolved stain can be bottled and kept almost indefinitely. You can mix powders for special effects. Concentrated stain can be kept and diluted when needed, but make sure of a consistent color by diluting sufficiently for the whole job at one time.

Water stain does not penetrate as deeply as oil stain, but it is adequate. Drying time depends on temperature and humidity. One problem is the way water raises the grain. Wet wood with clear water first. Allow this to dry and sand down any raised grain before applying the stain.

Use plenty of water stain and apply it with a brush along the grain. For an even effect, it is easier to apply two coats of a lighter shade than to use one coat of a darker stain. Stain a piece of furniture fairly quickly. It is not common to wipe water stain with a cloth, but excess stain can be lifted with the edge of a dry cloth.

Spirit Stain

A large range of colored pigments can be dissolved in alcohol (*spirit*). These include all the wood colors and blue, green, and yellow, which may be needed for special effects. You can buy powders that dissolve easily. Concentrated mixtures can be stored, stoppered tightly to prevent evaporation, and thinned for use.

Penetration is quick and not always very deep. Drying is almost instantaneous. Spirit stains thus cannot be put on smoothly over a large surface. Use the brush rapidly. Keep it moving with sweeps. Refill the brush quickly as needed and try to follow a wet edge rather than a dry one. An exception is spraying, where a more even effect can be obtained.

Spirit stain is not the choice for first staining of furniture because of the difficulty of applying it smoothly. It has uses on moldings where the narrow parts should finish evenly. It is useful for touching up. You can use it over other stains, and it will penetrate some finishes to correct color on a damaged part.

Other Stains

There are other solvents, but oil and water are best for furniture. Pigmented oil stain is really thinned paint and is not to be used on furniture. Penetration is slight, and you are really applying translucent paint.

Some finishes are sold as varnish stains or with a similar name. These are varnishes with stain added. They generally are not advisable for quality furniture. The idea is to apply coloring and gloss at the same time, but the stain is in the finish and does not enter the wood. In later wear, any rubbing away of the gloss finish also removes the color. This would not happen if the stain was applied as a separate first treatment.

There are chemical ways of altering the color of wood. Some are inappropriate to furniture already built in, and most are unsuitable for the one-off furniture made in the home shop. One safe way of chemically getting a brown color on many woods uses permaganate of potash bought as crystals and dissolved in water. Paint it on like water stain.

VARNISHES

Furniture makers used to consider *varnish* as unsuitable for their products, and they preferred one of the rubbed finishes. Modern synthetic varnishes are a different quality. Most are waterproof and resist heat well. They can be applied to give a smooth hard surface. Usually the final surface has a high gloss, but it is possible to get varnish with little or no gloss. Besides the uses of varnish throughout, it is possible to build up a base with varnish. It is then sanded, and another treatment is used for the outer surface.

There are many varnishes. Household varnish may be described as quick-drying. Some of the best varnishes are made for boats, but they are equally suitable for furniture. Varnish may be thought of as a paint without color. Many have a slightly golden shade, but that is not apparent over most woods.

Precautions had to be observed when applying traditional varnishes made from natural lacs. Synthetic varnishes are much more tolerant. A varnished surface becomes dustproof in about two hours. The work area should be kept as dustfree as possible, and the wood surface should be cleaned of dust from sanding or other causes. Vacuum cleaning is better than brushing dust. Be careful of drafts.

Varnish is affected by temperature. It gets sluggish at less than 65°F. It may be too liquid over 85°F. In cold conditions it helps to have the wood warm and stand the varnish can in warm water.

Use a clean soft brush. Do not use it for anything besides varnish. Do not stir modern varnish. That causes tiny air bubbles that will transfer to the wood where they will burst and cause blemishes. Flow varnish on with little attempt to brush it out. Brush with the grain. Make final strokes back toward the work previously done and lift the brush as it goes over its edge. Do not go back over a surface for a further smoothing, as that may lift the varnish. You cannot put the damaged surface right until it has dried, and you sand it for the next coat.

A first coat may be thinned using the solvent recommended by the makers. This penetrates and acts as a grain filler. Other coats are full strength. Never use shellac as a filler under varnish. When the first coat is dry, rub it down lightly with a paper of a fine grit such as 300 or 400. Clean off dust before applying the next coat. Three coats may give an acceptable finish, but you can apply four or five. Make sure each coat is absolutely dry before rubbing down and applying the next coat. Read the maker's instructions. There is a maximum and a minimum recommended time between coats with some synthetic varnishes.

SHELLAC

Shellac has been used as a wood finish for a long time. Much older furniture was finished by *French polishing*, which is one method of applying shellac. Shellac dissolves readily in denatured alcohol (methyl alcohol or methylated spirits). It can be bought in liquid form in various concentrations. Normal shellac is a golden color. Bleached shellac is a clearer type, but that does not keep very long.

Except for filling the grain, brushed shellac does not have much use on furniture. It does not wear very well and can be damaged with moisture and heat. It is a rather inferior varnish.

Traditional French polishing is a way of applying shellac to build up a surface with a smooth even gloss. It was one of the best ways of getting this effect a century or so ago. Shellac applied in this way suffers from the same problems of dampness and heat as brushed shellac. Many old pianos show how a rich finish can be obtained by French polishing.

French polishing is not recommended for modern furniture that gets normal usage. If you want to use the process, instructions are given in my book *Do-it-Yourselfer's Guide to Furniture Re-*

pair & Refinishing (TAB Book No. 894).

SPRAY FINISHES

Spraying is the finishing process of most mass-production furniture. The maker of individual built-in pieces of furniture may prefer to avoid it. If spraying is used, the furniture has to be treated before it is built in. The usual finish applied with a spray gun is lacquer, which is formulated to give a quick finish that is highly resilient. If the wood requires sealing or filling, there is an appropriate lacquer. Although most lacquers produce a high gloss, there are flat and less glossy finishes.

Spraying puts the finish on without the risk of brush marks. There are many other possible flaws, mostly due to putting on too much in one place. Practice is needed to finish furniture evenly.

Although actual spraying does not take long, much time is used afterward in preparing and cleaning equipment. This work is about the same for a one-off job and for working all day on many items.

If you want to use a spray finish, familiarize yourself with the spray gun and the associated equipment. Practice with suitable lacquers so you can get the desired effect before starting on the actual furniture.

OIL AND WAX POLISHES

Some furniture that has survived for hundreds of years still has a fine polish. Age has enhanced its patina and sheen. Such beauty is the result of expert craftsmanship and either wax or oil polishes.

Oil is probably the older of the two polishes. It takes a long time to use, although it produces beautiful results. Many oils can be used, but the most common is *linseed oil.* Oil is spread on, then polished by vigorous rubbing with cloth. Because most of the oil applied is rubbed off and only a thin film is left in the pores of the wood, the building up of sheen takes many applications at long intervals. Warming the oil by standing its container in hot water aids penetration.

Polishing at each stage may be started with a coarse cloth. Rubbing has to be hard and kept up for as much as 20 minutes. You can use a stiff brush instead of a cloth. Cloth wrapped around a brick can be used on a flat surface. The heat developed by friction causes the shine, so there is some advantage in using a power polisher.

Using those traditional methods is time-consuming. One way of speeding results is to add a little varnish and turpentine to the linseed oil. One or two applications of this mixture may be brushed on, but later applications should be friction-polished with a cloth. Some oil polishes contain other ingredients to hasten the production of a good finish.

Wax also has a long history as a polishing material. The finish it produces lasts longer than oil. Many kinds of wax are used for polishing, but beeswax, produced by the honey bee, is most popular. Turpentine is used with most waxes to make a paste or liquid polish. *Carnauba wax* is hard and is made into a polish with turpentine and other waxes such as ceresin, paraffin, and beeswax.

Dissolving waxes to make your own polish can take some time. It may be better to buy prepared wax polishes. Usually the wax is in its natural color, but it can be darkened with oil stain.

As with oil, using wax directly on bare wood can take time to build up a good finish. Where oil tends to sink into the grain, wax tends to build up on the surface. Wax can be applied over other finishes, and this makes it suitable for individually-made furniture.

You can treat your new wood with shellac, lacquer, or varnish sufficiently to seal the wood and make a coat on the surface. Rub that down with sandpaper, steel wool, or a mild abrasive powder such as pumice on a damp cloth. Remove any dust from the work.

Wax has to be applied all over the surface. You may need a brush in corners or moldings, but application is mainly with a cloth. Get the wax on without any attempt at first to polish it. Leave it for 10 minutes or so. Rub it briskly with another cloth, first polishing in all directions, then along the grain. If it is a hard wax polish, the first rubbing will require considerable friction. A stiff brush or a cloth around a brick will help. Do all the first polishing by hand, but you can use power polishing in later stages.

It is not essential to go all over in one action with wax polishing. You can concentrate on a part. When you have done all other parts, a final all-over polish will get an even effect.

Wax polish can follow an existing finish when the furniture has been in use some time. Prepared furniture polishes contain wax. Some modern versions require very little rubbing. Spray polishes leave a good surface without rubbing.

PAINTING

Most furniture is finished by one of the methods already described. Painting is unusual, except it may be the choice for a child's room or for special effect. If you build in something made from a variety of woods, possibly salvaged from other furniture, paint will obscure the wood grain and color. You must apply a good finish to the wood surface. Blemishes will show through. Paint cannot be expected to hide bad workmanship or a surface with flaws. Stopping and filling may be needed with many woods, although the color may not matter.

Like varnish, there has been something of a revolution in the production of paint. You should get the whole paint system from one maker. Products of some manufacturers are not compatible with those of others. The choice and sequence of paint coats are not always the same.

The first coat is a primer in a normal paint system. Its purpose is to soak into the grain to provide a grip and base for further coats. The recommended primer is not always the same color as later coats. Primer is followed by an undercoat. This is a flat-finish paint that has a color compatible with the final coat. In some systems the primer is thinned undercoat. Two applications of undercoat may be needed if the first does not cover very well. If necessary, rub it down to form a smooth base for the topcoat. Read the directions for the topcoat. It may be like synthetic varnishes in not having to be stirred, due to bubbles, and having to be applied with minimal brushing out. Usually it is inadvisable to apply more than one layer of a topcoat. If you need to build up the coating of paint, do it at the undercoat stage.

Chapter 7

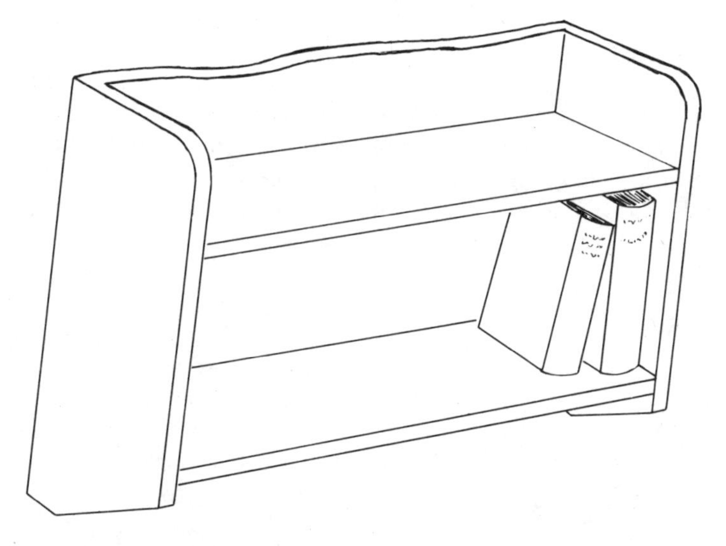

Simple Wall-Supported Items

Many things can be made to hang on a wall, and most of them are of quite simple construction. In most cases they provide useful storage and decoration. They usually fill a wall space that would otherwise be vacant. Unless the items are very large, they do not make any appreciable difference regarding floor space and usage. Quite often they can be arranged above another piece of furniture, so they serve a purpose without taking up room that would otherwise be needed.

The obvious wall-hung items are shelves, but there are many other things such as mirrors, small cabinets, and book racks. The common thing among them is the need to be securely attached to the wall, because that provides the entire support. In much other built-in furniture there are parts to the floor, and sometimes the ceiling, that share support with the wall. There must be sufficient attachments of the right type to share the load. High attachments take the most load. Lower ones take a share. If you arranged screws only low down, though, the weight of the object would tend to fall forward and put more of a withdrawal load on the fasteners. Spread the attachments as much as possible. Screws near the limits of the article's width resist better any tendency to twist on the hanging than similar fasteners arranged closer together. A few widely spaced fasteners may be more secure than a larger number located nearer the center of the object being hung.

It is the grip of the screw or other fastener in the wall that takes the load. If you are dealing with wood and can get at least some screws into studding, a few long screws will take a considerable load. If it is a hollow wall, you may need more suitable fasteners. It is better to have a lesser load at each fastener. If it is a brick or stone wall, much depends on how well you are able to drill and plug it. Good plugs in strong stone or brick will take an enormous load. If there is a tendency for the stone to powder or the blocks to be loosely compounded, you may have to use many fasteners so the load on any one of them is not too great.

Before deciding on the layout of the item you plan to make, check over the wall. You may find that by increasing or decreasing a size slightly, it will become easier to pick up studs or other strong points for fasteners. Make sure that what you want to do is possible on the particular wall. If you want to use shelf brackets, can you safely screw enough of them directly to the wall, or must you first attach battens and join the brackets to them? If you are using something else with screw holes in definite places, will you be able to use them all? Check that what you intend to hang will not interfere with anything else, be liable to knocking by passing heads, or otherwise be unacceptable. Check with other users that the item will serve their needs and not be a nuisance to them.

SHELVES

The obvious material for a shelf is a piece of planed wood of the right size. If possible, choose a piece with the end grain markings through the thickness of the wood. There will be little risk of warping. If the shelf is going in a recess, the supporting pieces at the ends will prevent warping if the shelf is screwed securely to them. If the shelf is going against a flat wall, battens at the bracket positions will serve the same purpose (Fig. 7-1A). If the shelf is given a rim to prevent things from falling off, the end pieces of that will also act to resist warping (Fig. 7-1B), whether the corners are closed or open for ease in cleaning.

Many shelves made from plain boards are too thin. If they have to carry a load such as a row of books, they will develop a sag between supports many months after being put into use. Sizes depend on circumstances, but a shelf 6 inches wide and 36 inches between supports should be at least ¾ inch thick. It should be thicker for a greater distance between supports. Closer supports may allow slightly thinner wood, but do not reduce it much.

An alternative to solid wood is plywood. It can be as thick as the solid wood, but the edge of plywood is unattractive. It is better edged with solid wood, either a strip held with glue and thin nails with their heads sunk and stopped (Fig. 7-1C) or with a tongue and groove joint (Fig. 7-1D). Another plywood shelf uses much thinner material framed underneath (Fig. 7-1E). There can be a front piece with a rabbet to enclose the plywood (Fig. 7-1F), or a piece standing up will hide the edge without the need of a rabbet (Fig. 7-1G). Allow for thickening where the brackets come.

Shelves can also be made from faced particle board. It can be bought with wood veneer attached to match other furniture. There may be a plastic surface—plain white for kitchen or laundry use or patterned elsewhere. Exposed cut ends can be covered with the self-adhesive matching material available for applying with heat. Screws can be driven directly into the particle board for brackets, or you may fit battens.

As you do not usually have much choice regarding thickness of particle board, you have to guard against it sagging under a sustained load. One way is to keep supports reasonably close. For particle board about ⅝ inch thick used to support books or other heavy loads, brackets should not be much more than 24 inches apart. It may be possible to support a greater length between brackets with a rail below the front (Fig. 7-1H) and another at the back—above or below (Fig. 7-1J). If you put a back rail below, the brackets will have to be packed out (Fig. 7-1K).

If one end of the shelf goes into a corner or both ends are enclosed in a recess, the support may be a strip of wood screwed to the wall (Fig. 7-2A). A wide spacing gives better support than having the screws closer together. If the front of the support will show, bevel or round it (Fig. 7-2B). If you are putting a stiffening rail under the front (Fig. 7-2C) or extending it above to retain things on the shelf (Fig. 7-2D), that can hide the end support.

A shelf must be level. Otherwise, any error will be very obvious to viewers. It is usually best to make up the shelf assembly with its brackets and any battens attached, then bring this to the wall and check it by measuring parallel with the floor at the height you want it. Use a level. Drill for one high fastener into the wall. Drive that while the rest of the assembly is temporarily held up. Have the level in place as you pivot the shelf on the one screw to find the correct position. Mark the place and drill so you can drive another screw some way from the first. If the shelf can still be checked level after these two fasteners have been driven, you can go ahead and drive the others tightly.

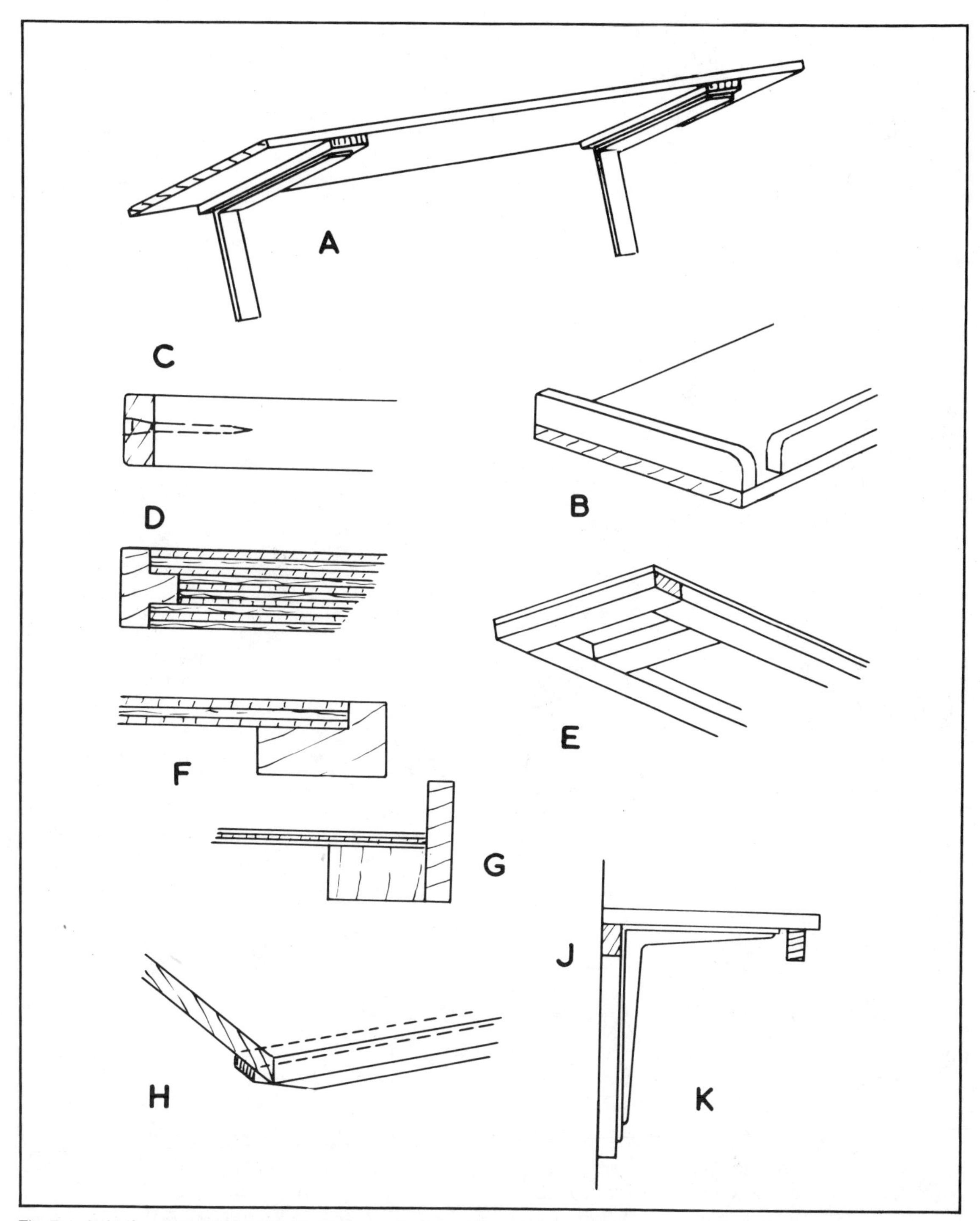

Fig. 7-1. A shelf may be solid wood with edging (A, B, C) or stiffened plywood (D to G). Lengthwise stiffening may be needed (H, J, K).

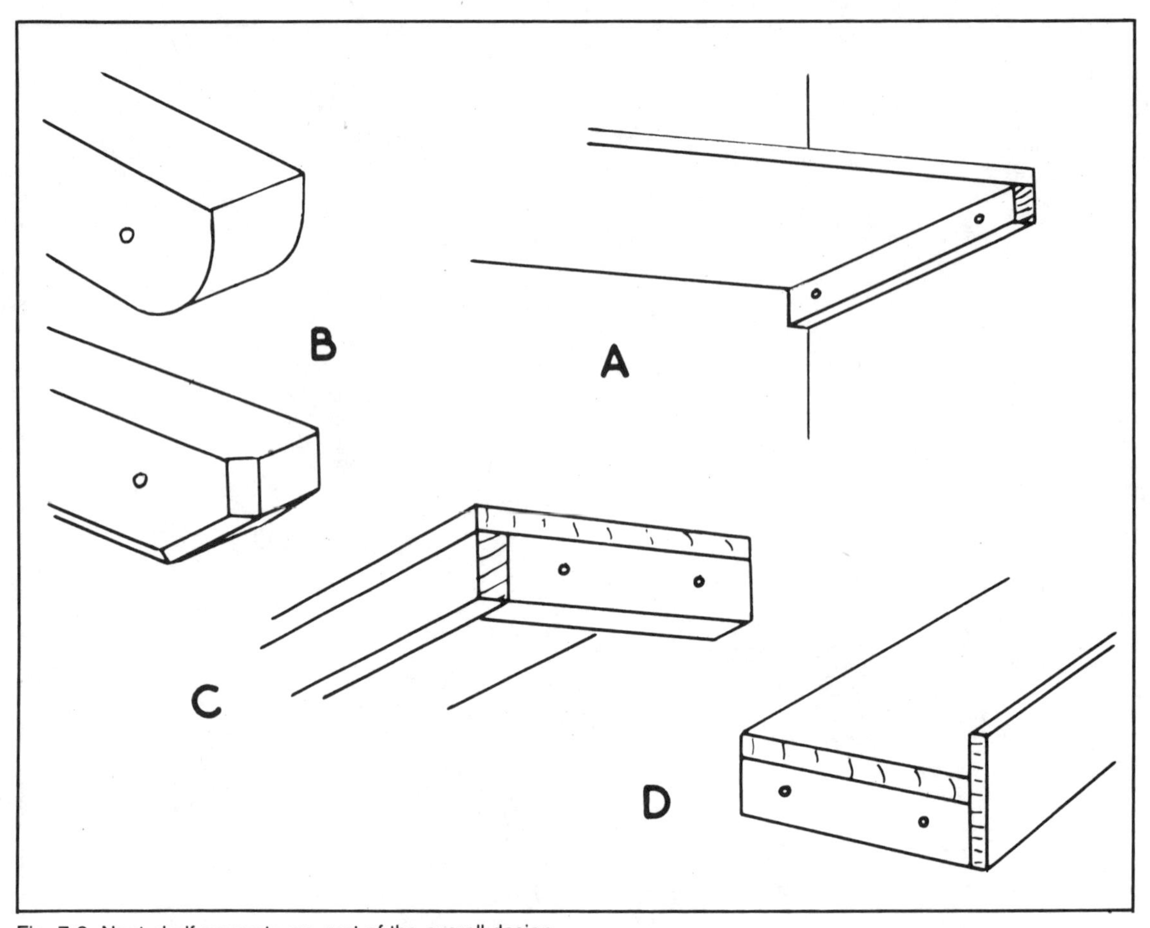

Fig. 7-2. Neat shelf supports are part of the overall design.

When one end of the shelf is in a corner, start by fitting the supporting cleat there first. Check its level back to front. Rest the shelf on it and move it up and down to get the top level. Drill so you can drive another screw near the far end. If it is still level after that, drive the other fasteners.

If both ends are to be supported on cleats, fit one, as before, then move the shelf to a level position while resting on it. From that, pencil on the wall where the other cleat has to come.

WOOD BRACKETS

Metal shelf brackets are probably the best choice in many places, but you can make wooden brackets. If it is a large broad shelf, a wooden bracket should give better support than a metal one.

The example is for a broad shelf (Fig. 7-3A). Join the two main parts with a dovetail. Notice that it is arranged so the pull under load on the top part is resisted by the dovetail shape (Fig. 7-3B). Mark where the diagonal is to come on both pieces. Set out 90° on a piece of plywood, then alter one line to come slightly wide of that—maybe ¼ inch at the end of 12 inches. That is to allow for the bracket still holding up to a right angle, even when the load is trying to force it down.

Set the two meeting parts to the lines, then put the diagonal piece across and mark on both crossings where each part comes on the other. Separate them and mark and cut the diagonal ends. Use them to mark the notches to cut in the other parts (Fig. 7-3C). Assemble with glue and screws into the

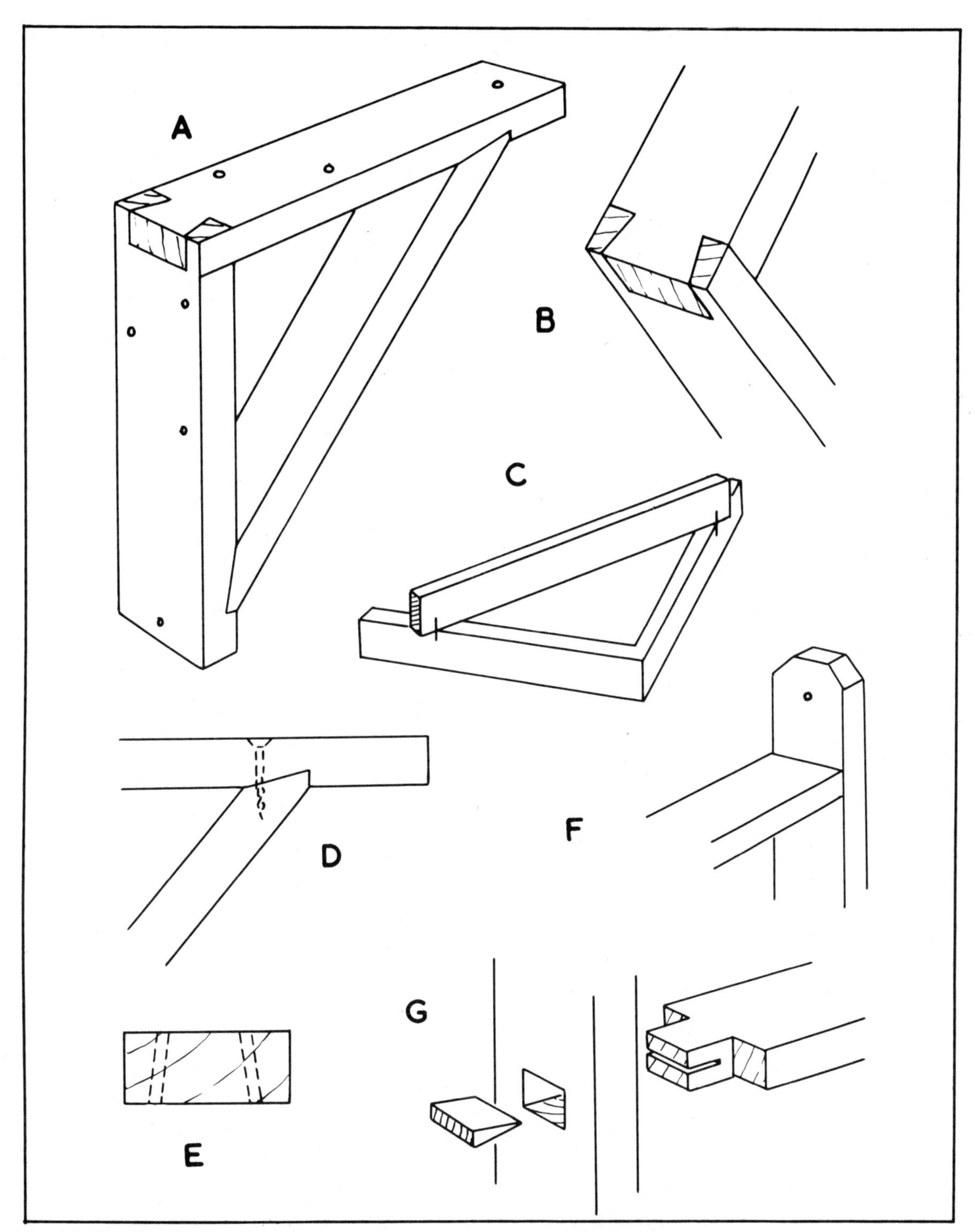

Fig. 7-3. Wood brackets can be built up with notched, dovetailed, and tenoned joints.

diagonal ends (Fig. 7-3D). Holes for screws into the wall should be slightly angled for ease in driving (Fig. 7-3E).

If a projection above the shelf is acceptable, the back of each bracket may continue upward. The advantage is that a screw is in the best position for taking a load (Fig. 7-3F). You cannot use a dovetail between the parts, but a tenon can be taken through and wedged (Fig. 7-3G).

You can use a shaped block between the main parts for a smaller wooden bracket. It can be narrower to allow for screws (Fig. 7-4A). The outer edge may be profiled as you wish, or the whole block may be carved. It need not go fully into the corner, but it can be cut as a scroll (Fig. 7-4B) or other shape. You can carve a stylized leaf or even a cherub's head if you are skilled with carving tools.

Shelf brackets are usually under the shelf, and that is the best place for ease of support. Sometimes it may be better to have the supports above the shelf or projecting both up and down. Metal shelf brackets can be put above the shelf so it hangs from them. Loads on the screws into the shelf will then be in the direction of withdrawal. In thick wood they should have adequate strength. Otherwise, you can use small nuts and bolts through the shelf and its brackets for greater strength.

If wood brackets come above a shelf, they can serve as bookends, either a short distance in from the ends (Fig. 7-5A) or at the end, where there can be a cleat below and a rail hiding it at the front (Fig. 7-5B). You can have the bracket extending below as well as above, then you can do some decorative shaping (Fig. 7-5C). In this case the bracket is best made with cleats to the wall (Fig. 7-5D). They can come inside if that will not interfere with what goes on the shelf, or they can be outside and continue the decorative outline.

DOUBLE SHELVES

If there are two or more shelves in a block, you can hang them without brackets. They essentially form

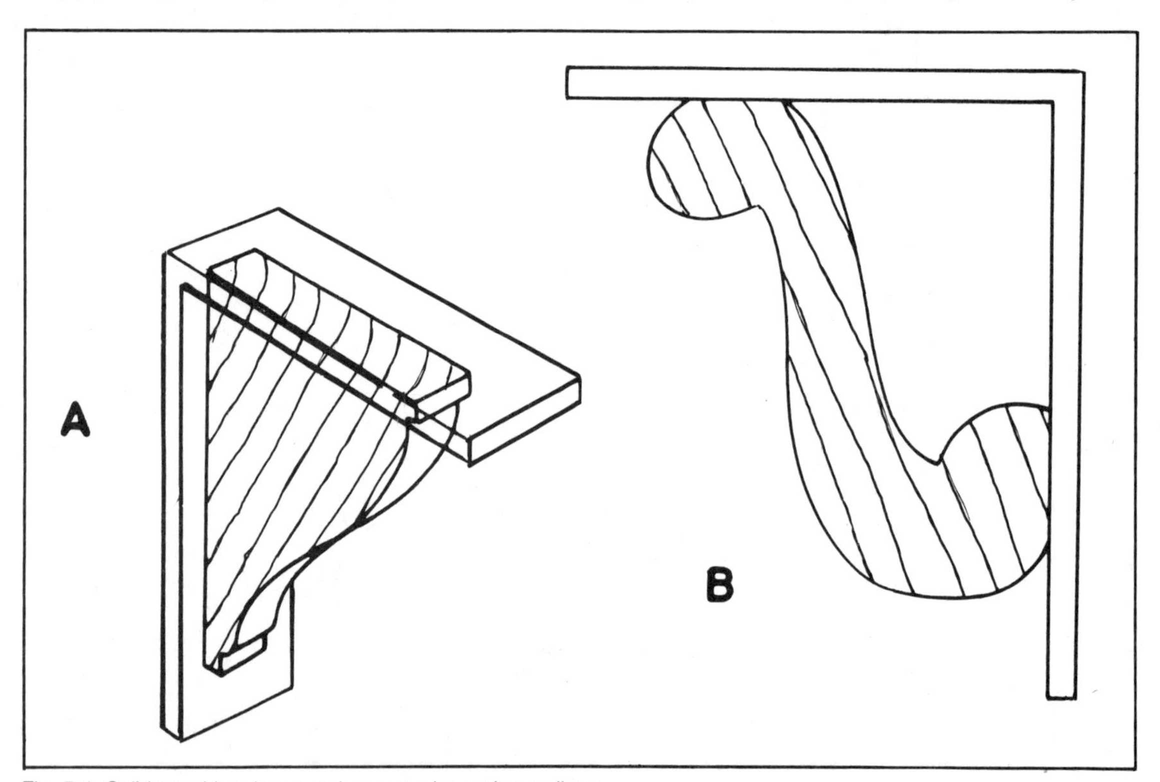

Fig. 7-4. Solid wood brackets can be cut to decorative outlines.

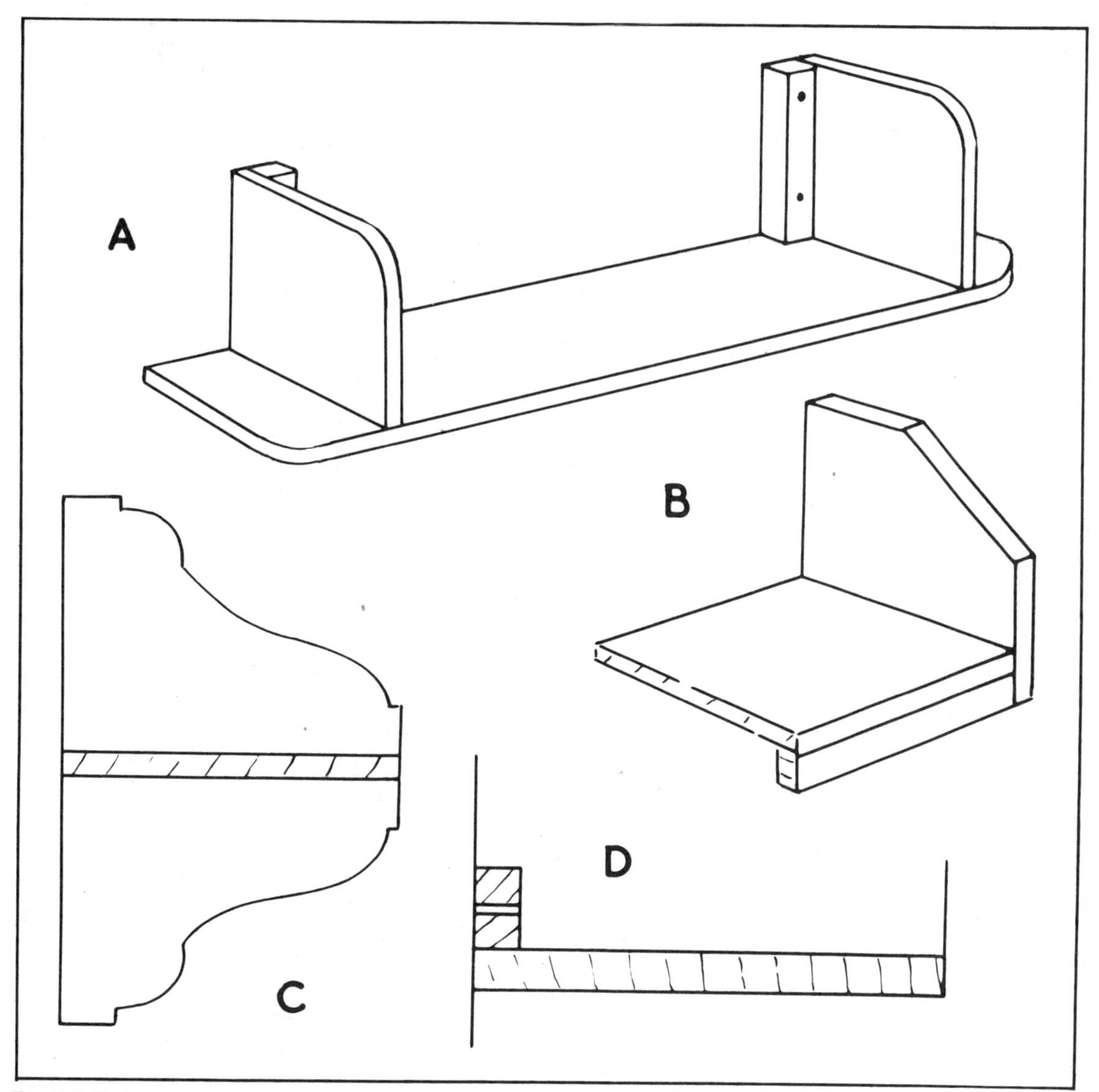

Fig. 7-5. Ends mounted on shelves may double as supports.

their own brackets. In some circumstances you may want to put brackets below, but it is neater to omit them.

End pieces can extend above and below the two shelves (Fig. 7-6A), or they may be cut off level. The shelves can merely be screwed through the ends, but dado joints (Fig. 7-6B) are better. Stop them at the front (Fig. 7-6C) for the neatest finish. If the ends do not extend, the strongest joint is a dovetail (Fig. 7-6D), or you can notch one piece so nails or screws can be driven both ways (Fig. 7-6E).

There can be a rail under the top shelf to hang the double shelves (Fig. 7-6F). If it is a large assembly or has to carry a heavy weight, there can be pieces inside the ends and at the bottom shelf for screws into the wall. When the double shelves go into a corner, you can screw through one of the ends into the wall. For a very light double shelf arrange-

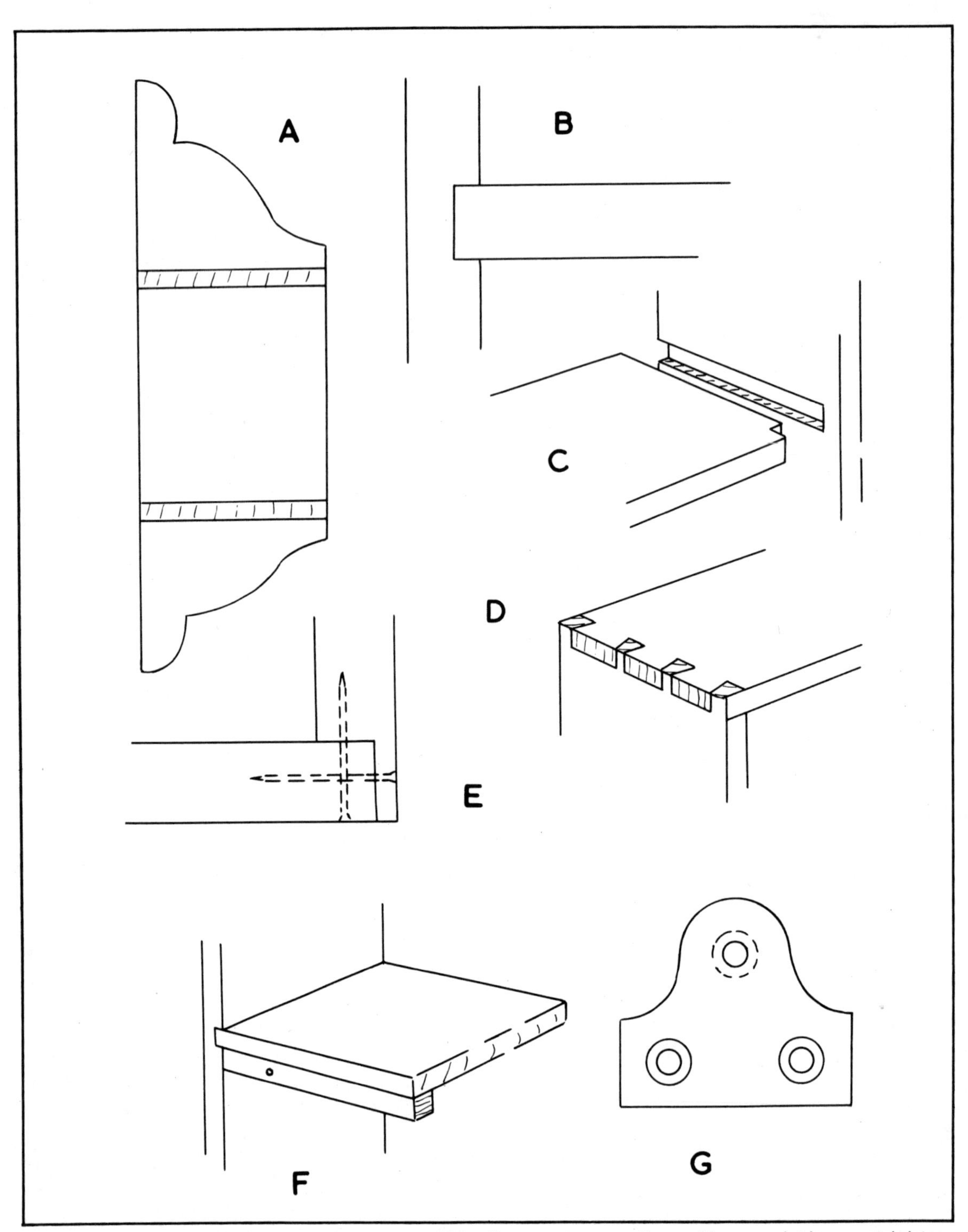

Fig. 7-6. Double shelves have mutual support and may be joined in several ways and hung with screwed strips or metal plates.

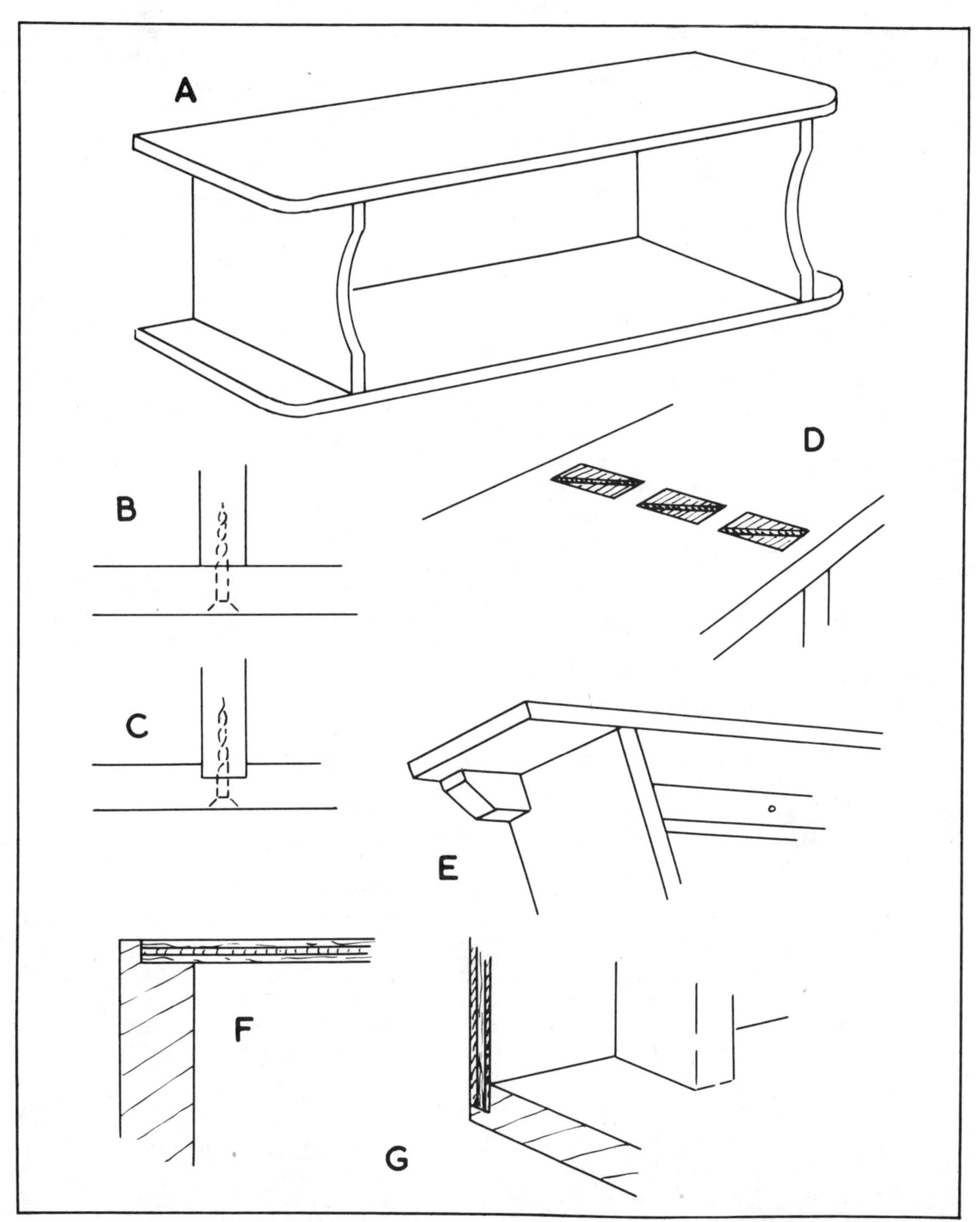

Fig. 7-7. Double shelves may have the dividers screwed or tenoned (A to D). The back can be open (E) or closed with plywood (F, G).

ment, it may be sufficient to use two or more metal plates behind the top shelf (Fig. 7-6G), so the assembly hangs from there without any attachment lower down.

In another double shelf arrangement the upright parts come a short distance in from the ends of the shelves (Fig. 7-7A). The ends of the shelves may be rounded or otherwise decorated, and you can shape the fronts of the uprights to match.

The joints can be screwed for a light assembly (Fig. 7-7B), possibly with the screws sunk slightly and covered with stopping or plugs if you do not want the heads to show. The uprights can go into dadoes in the shelves, but you still need screws (Fig. 7-7C). If there is expected to be much load on the shelves, use multiple mortise and tenon joints taken through and wedged (Fig. 7-7D). The number of tenons depends on the width in relation to the wood thickness, but usually a tenon no more than three times the thickness of the wood should suit. Have one fairly near the front where the greatest breaking load will come. Any rail at the back will also strengthen the joints, particularly if it can go through (Fig. 7-7E).

The back can be open to show the wall, or you can fit a piece of plywood or hardboard. Besides giving a more closed appearance, this helps in squaring the assembly and adds to strength. It may be sufficient to glue and nail or screw back on. If you want to hide the edges, the ends may be rabbeted (Fig. 7-7F), leaving the edges overlapping the shelves. If you want to hide those edges, the shelves may be rabbeted, too. You have to miter where the parts meet at corners. If the shelves extend, the back may go into rabbets in the shelves (Fig. 7-7G), and the other parts may be brought forward of it.

HANGING BOOKCASE

This is shown as a bookcase suitable for one row of books and a top shelf for other things or more books (Fig. 7-8). The sizes suggested in Table 7-1 make a rack of reasonable size, but obviously sizes can be adapted to suit needs. The design can be extended to take in more shelves. There is space for a row of books of average hardback sizes (Fig. 7-9). If you have particular books in mind, measure them and make the rack accordingly. Allow a little shelf width in front of the books and at least 1 inch above the books for ease in removing them.

The bookcase has a solid top behind the shelf there, but it is open behind the books. You can add a plywood back, make suitable rabbets in the sides, and cut the shelves narrower than the sides.

Start by setting out a side (Fig. 7-10A) and marking its partner at the same time. Allow for the shelves going into stopped dadoes (Fig. 7-10B). Both shelves fit in the same way, but above the top cut away for the back (Fig. 7-10C), which is glued and screwed to the sides. Two or more screws are driven upward into it through the shelf (Fig. 7-10D). This assembly gives the case rigidity and keeps it in shape. Make sure parts are cut squarely, as they control the whole bookcase.

Something has to be done to take away the angular appearance. The sides above the top shelf may be left mostly square but with rounded front corners (Fig. 7-10E), so they can keep a row of books upright. The bottom may have a simple bevel (Fig. 7-10F) or be given more shaping (Fig. 7-10G). If you do not plan to put books on top, you can use matching shaping there.

If the shelves make tight fits in their dadoes, you may be able to rely on glue there. It is safer to use a few thin screws diagonally upward in the joints (Fig. 7-10J), particularly near the fronts of the shelves.

The back can be shaped if it is not to be hidden by a row of books (Fig. 7-10H). The fronts of the ends may be left straight, or they can be hollowed between the shelves.

Hanging may be by two screws through the back. They should be sufficient, unless you make a deep bookcase with more shelves. Then you can put a strip under the bottom shelf to take screws or fit metal plates behind the sides, projecting inward, so the screws through them are hidden by books.

Table 7-1. Materials List for Hanging Bookcase.

2 sides	7 × 19 × 5/8
2 shelves	7 × 22 × 5/8
1 back	4 × 22 × 5/8

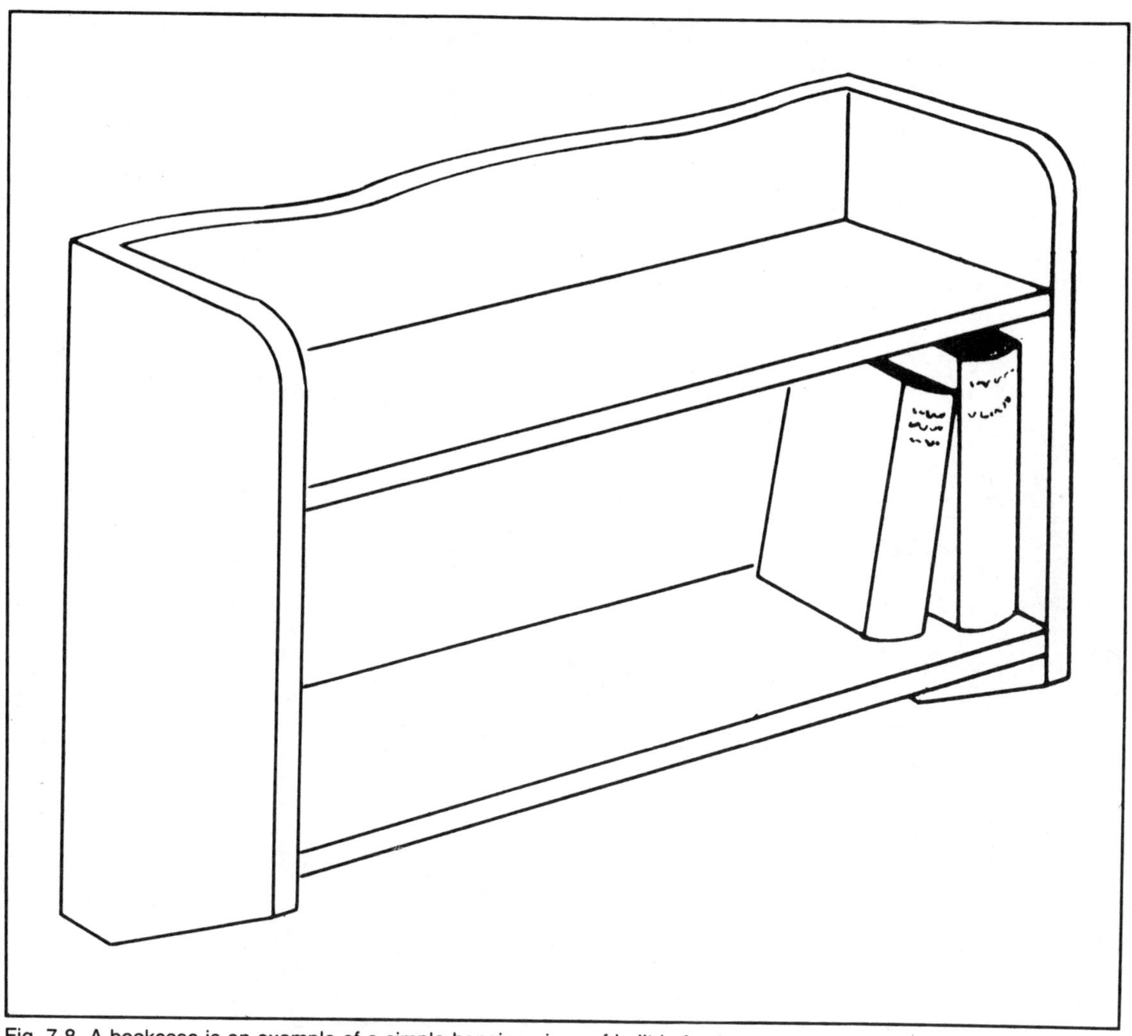

Fig. 7-8. A bookcase is an example of a simple hanging piece of built-in furniture.

DISPLAY RACK

This rack is very similar in form to the hanging bookcase, but it is of lighter construction and will display a collection of small items such as souvenirs collected during travels, small pottery, or models. The rack will look best in an attractive hardwood with decorated edges (Fig. 7-11). Whether you fret or pierce the wood, too, depends on having suitable equipment. At one time this type of display rack was heavily fretted in complicated designs, but in a modern home a less fancy treatment is more acceptable.

Suggested sizes (Fig. 7-12 and Table 7-2) may be modified. The shelves should not be too narrow, even if the items to be displayed do not have much width. Do not bring the shelves too close together, even if what is to be put on them is rather low. You need space for viewing. Too close an arrangement

Table 7-2. Materials List for Display Rack.

Part	Size
2 sides	4 × 21 × ½
2 shelves	3½ × 18 × ½
1 shelf	3 × 18 × ½
3 stiffeners	1¼ × 18 × ½

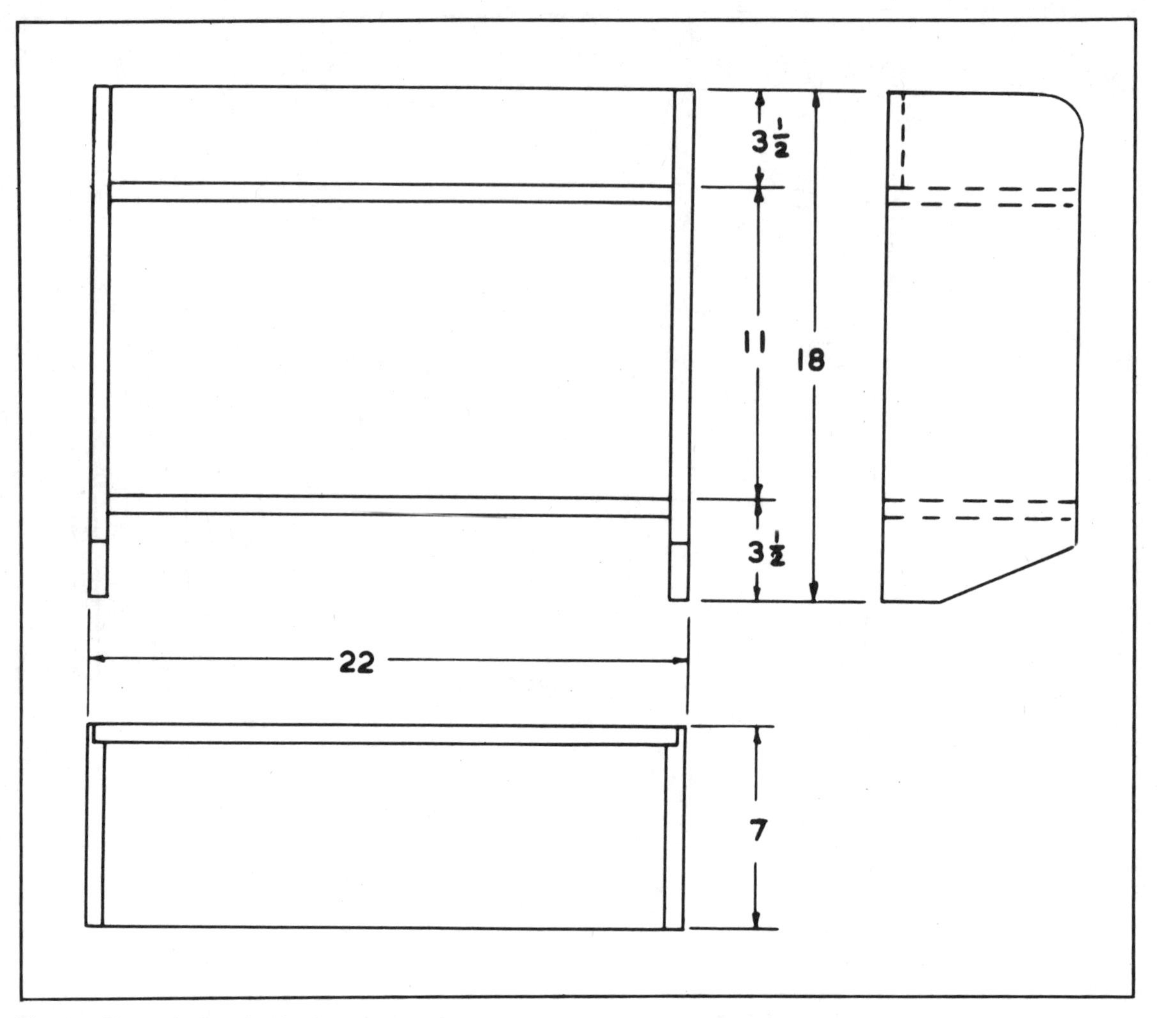

Fig. 7-9. Sizes of a hanging bookcase.

seems to box the items, and they cannot be seen to best advantage.

Mark out the sides (Fig. 7-13A). The shelves go into dadoes. Because of the thin wood, they cannot go very deeply (Fig. 7-13B). Screws from below are needed. Unless the shelves are very wide, one screw near the front of each joint should be sufficient as back edges are held by the stiffeners. The back stiffener at each shelf is screwed into the shelf edge and into recesses in the sides (Fig. 7-13C). Glue all parts, too.

Do all joint cutting and drilling of screw holes before tackling shaping. It is easier to handle square-cut pieces than to try and cut joints in shaped wood. Apart from awkwardness of holding, you may damage shaped edges.

Round all exposed edges. Keep the front edges of the shelves and stiffeners square where they go into the sides, but round the parts between. Be careful that no saw marks are left on shaped edges. They will show more when a finish is applied. Sand inside any piercing and make sure no ragged edges are left.

Hanging can be by screws through stiffeners. It will probably be sufficient to put two widely spread screws through the top one and one through the

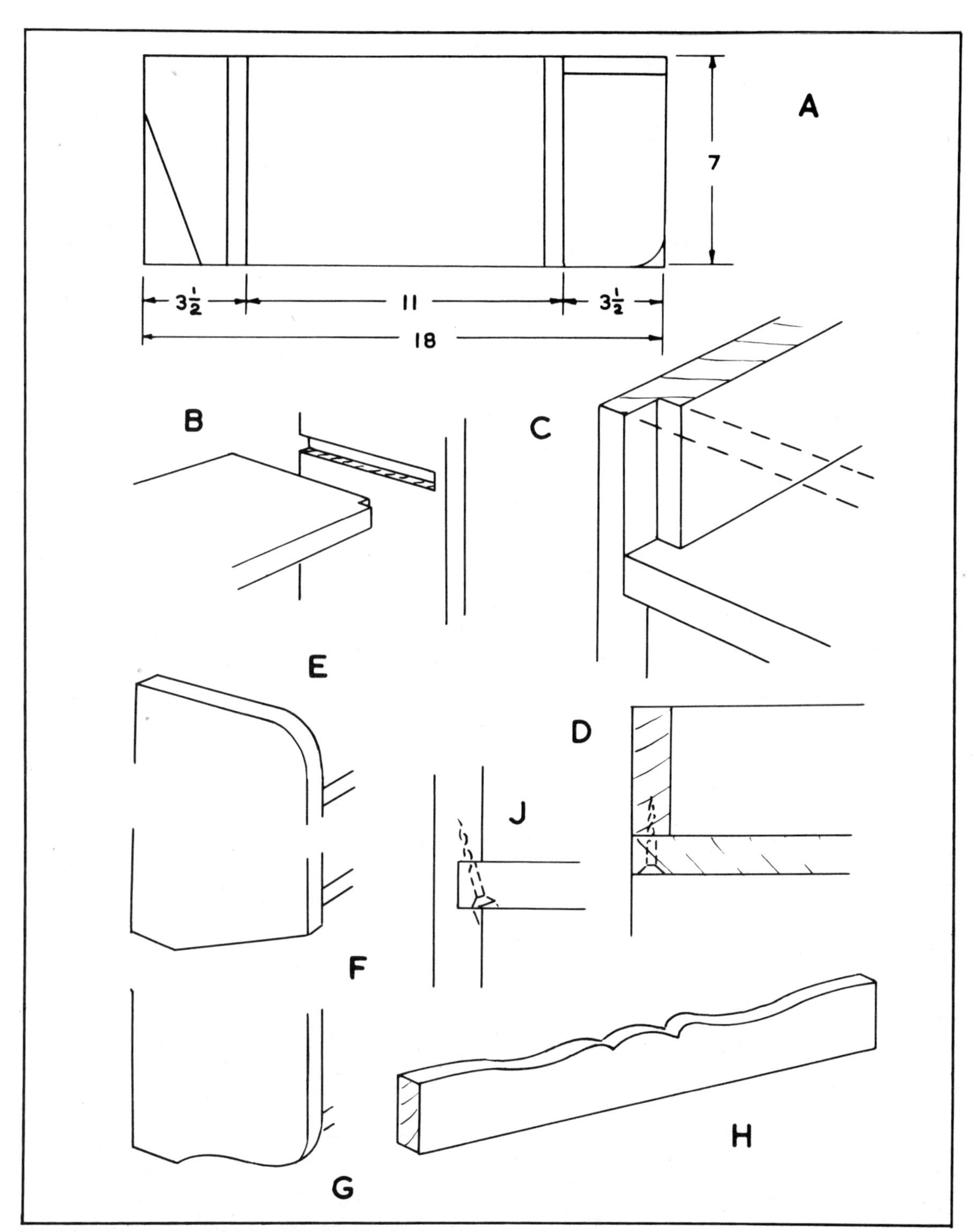

Fig. 7-10. Constructional details of the hanging bookcase.

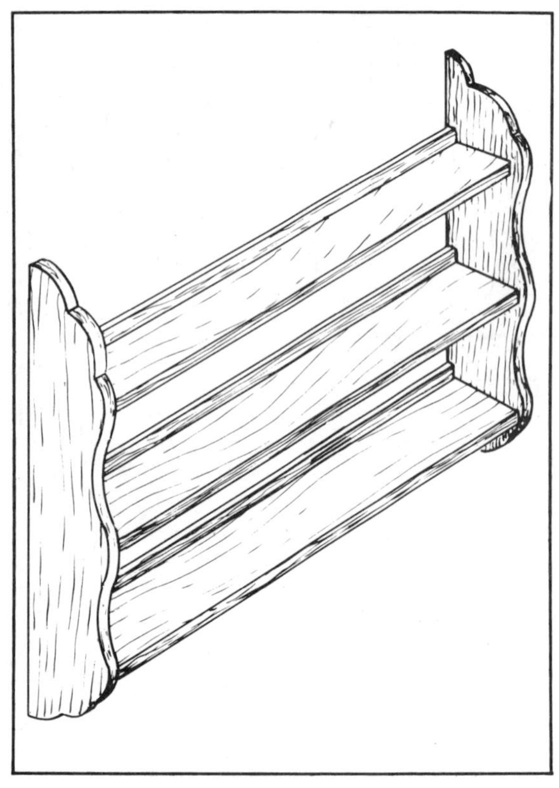

Fig. 7-11. A display rack is made like a hanging bookcase.

center of the bottom one, unless the contents will be very heavy.

KNICKKNACK RACK

This rack is of very light construction. It can hold various small items that can be arranged on the extensions and in the openings. The same idea can be used for a larger rack, but the interlocking joints will not have sufficient strength for wood of large section.

The rack shown (Fig. 7-14) is small enough to go anywhere. With a colorful collection of small items on it, it will break up the plainness of an otherwise blank wall.

The general construction may look complicated at first (Fig. 7-15A), but it is actually very simple. Careful workmanship is needed to get accurate fits in the joints. The parts are almost identical. They are 22 inches by 2 inches by ¼ inch, with two notches (Fig. 7-15B) and four the same size, but with three notches (Fig. 7-15C). The widths of the notches must match the thickness of the wood and go halfway across the width. The finished thickness of the wood is only ¼ inch, so choose closer-grained hardwood that will not tend to break out as the notches are cut or assembled. Mark all the parts together across their edges while they are gripped in a vise. Check accuracy by turning a piece end-for-end to see that spacings are the same, then square over on to the surfaces for cutting.

Although the rack can be left with the front edges straight and square, it looks better with slight hollows between joints (Fig. 7-15D) and the exposed edges rounded. After a trial partial assembly (do not force the joints tight), mark all the back edges so you do not shape them by mistake.

If you think you may want to take the rack apart, it can be assembled without glue providing the joints are reasonably tight. Otherwise, glue the joints and check squareness before the glue sets.

One way of hanging the rack is to put two small screw eyes into the top or second piece (Fig. 7-15E) and hang these on screws in the wall. You can put small metal plates on the back edge of a piece and screw through that, or there can be a strip of wood above the top piece, so you can drive screws through it into the wall.

When you finish the wood, be careful of making it too slippery or small items may slide off. Avoid a high gloss. Settle for mat or semimat.

TWO-PART OPEN BOOKCASE

This basic floor-to-ceiling open case for books of all sizes is made in two parts. The lower part can be used alone. The two sections are joined to each other and to the wall. A full load of books can be very heavy, so secure attachment to the wall, particularly near the top, is important. The height is assumed to be 96 inches, and this will have to be modified to suit the actual room (Figs. 7-16 and 7-17). The sides do not have to reach the ceiling, but the bookcase looks better closely fitted. See Table 7-3.

The shelf spacing is shown graduated. Besides suiting books of many sizes, this looks better than having equal spaces. The extra depth back-to-front

Table 7-3. Materials List for Two-Part Open Bookcase.

2 sides	7 × 61 × ¾
2 sides	12 × 37 × ¾
5 shelves	6¾ × 36 × ¾
2 shelves	11¾ × 36 × ¾
1 shelf	13 × 39 × ¾
1 plinth	3¼ × 36 × ¾
2 fronts	2 × 36 × ¾
1 back	36 × 60 × ¼ plywood
1 back	36 × 33 × ¼ plywood

of the lower part should take such things as atlases and "coffee table" books.

The framework can be left open to allow the room wall to form a back, but the construction described allows for a plywood back. Hardboard can be used. The assembly is all of solid wood, preferably hardwood. The 36-inch width is the maximum advisable for ¾-inch wood. If you want to make the bookcase wider, make the shelves thicker. Otherwise, they may start to sag under the weight of books after a few months. Veneered particle board

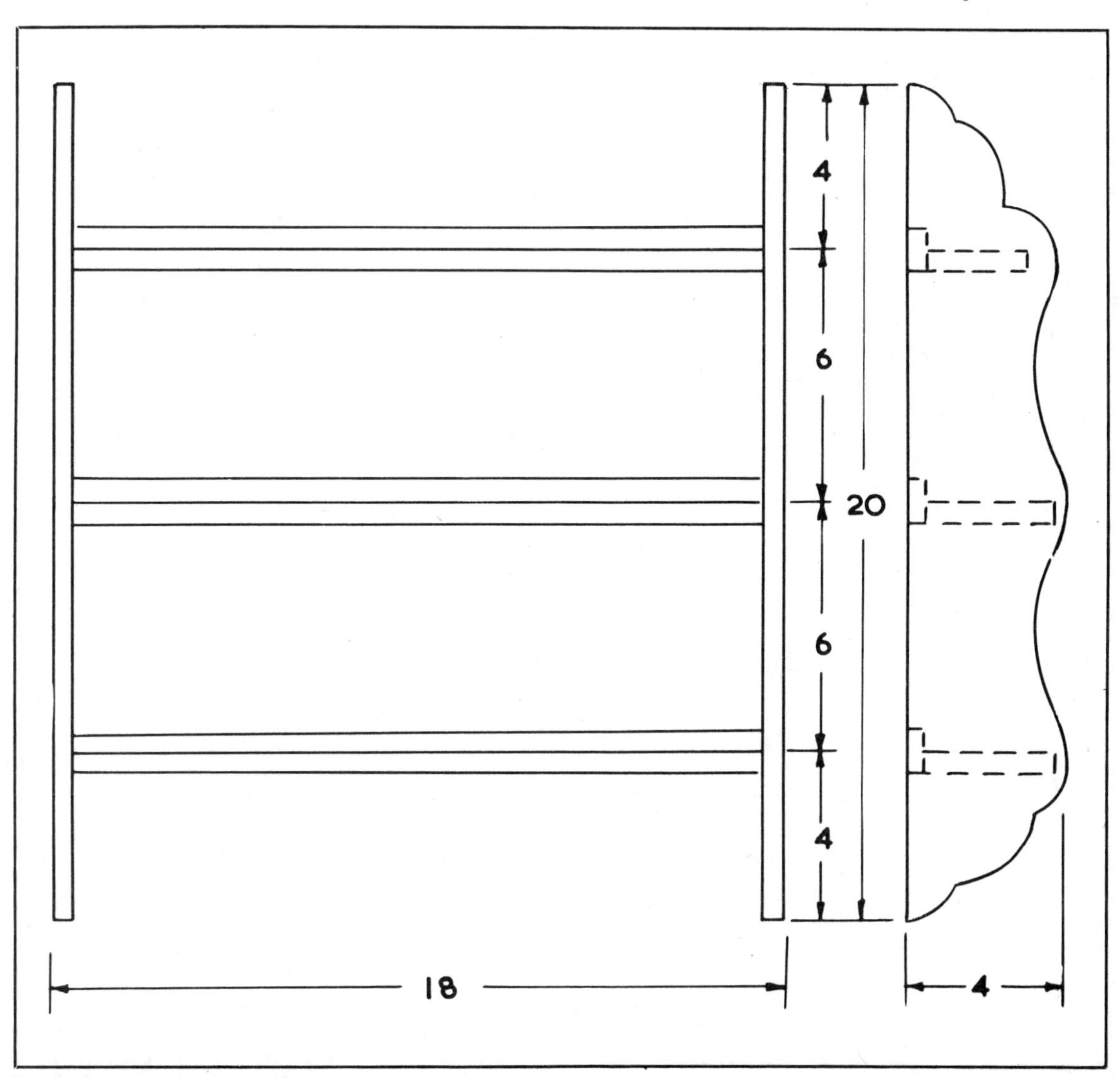

Fig. 7-12. Sizes of a display rack.

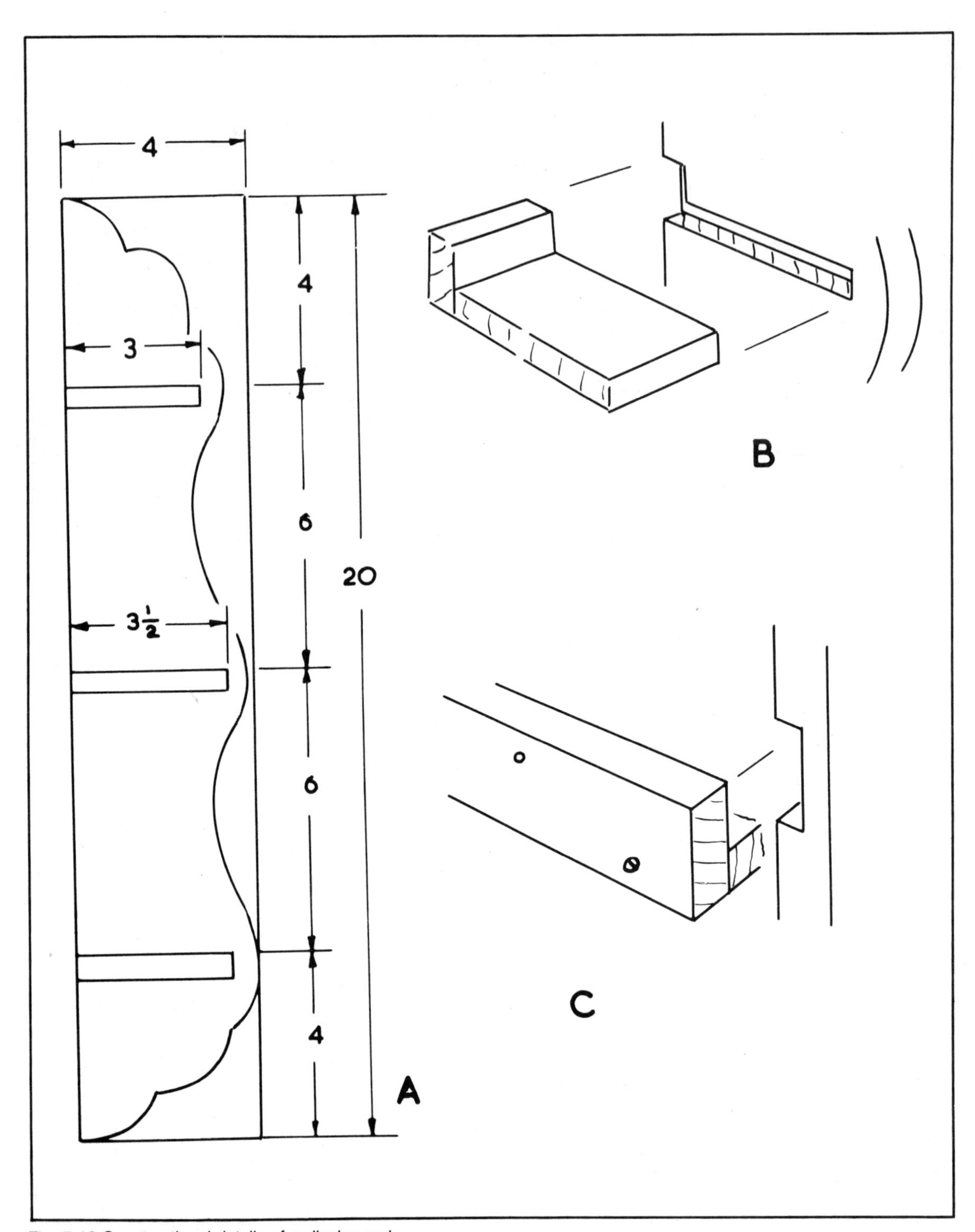

Fig. 7-13.Constructional details of a display rack.

Fig. 7-14. A knickknack rack is a place for displaying small souvenirs and similar things.

can be used throughout, but that will have similar sagging problems.

Prepare the wood for the sides by cutting rabbets to sink the plywood backs (Fig. 7-18A). Mark the lengths and shelf positions where there should be stopped dado joints (Fig. 7-18B). The bottom of the top section may fit into a similar rabbet, with screw upward (Fig. 7-18C). The front against the ceiling is cut back for most of its length, leaving the full width at the ends. It then can be doweled to the sides (Fig. 7-18D).

Carefully square the plywood back, so it holds the whole assembly true. Check squareness by measuring diagonals. The pieces across at top and bottom will pull the parts close, but drive screws or nails upward under the shelf fronts to keep the dado joints tight (Fig. 7-18E). Use nails or small screws and glue to hold the plywood back tightly in place.

The bottom part is assembled in a generally similar way. Use dadoes for the lower shelves, but the shelf that forms the top is intended to overhang at sides and front, so the uprights can dowel into it (Fig. 7-19A). The front piece, made to match that against the ceiling, may be doweled to the shelf and uprights (Fig. 7-19B). The overhanging edges may be left square or molded to suit your choice and available equipment (Fig. 7-19C).

There is a plinth set back under the bottom shelf (Fig. 7-19D), with a few dowels into the shelf and two at its ends into the sides. At the back there is no need for the plywood to be taken to the floor. It can be cut off below the bottom shelf.

When attaching to the wall, two screws between the bottom of the top section and the other part should be enough to keep them together. Drive them upward if you do not want them to show.

DISPLAY BOARDS

Most of us have collected items that should be displayed. They will look better on permanent display than in a box or drawer to be brought out only occasionally. Some may require supports, while others can be attached permanently to a backing. Modern two-part epoxy adhesives have made permanent mounting of most things very easy, as they will strongly join such unlikely things as metal and wood, stone and metal, or most plastics to almost anything else. You can use epoxy adhesive to mount stones, arrowheads, sharks' teeth and other small items in patterns on wood.

The shape of a display board can be anything you wish. It may have to fit into a particular place on the wall, and that decides its shape and size. You may shape the board to relate to what it displays. A collection of scout merit badges will look well on an arrowhead outline (Fig. 7-20A). Use a half template to turn over on the center line. Sharks' teeth may go on a board cut to a shark outline (Fig. 7-20B). Remember that you are making a base for displaying things and not necessarily an exact replica of a badge or fish, so you can thicken some parts if that gives you more space, while retaining a recognizable outline. Avoid fine detail in the outline. It may break, and it will be difficult to clean up to remove saw marks.

A shield shape is a good one if there is no special shape suggested by what you want to mount. Many shields can be drawn freehand. Examine some coats of arms for ideas. A geometric way of drawing a shield can be used as a starting point.

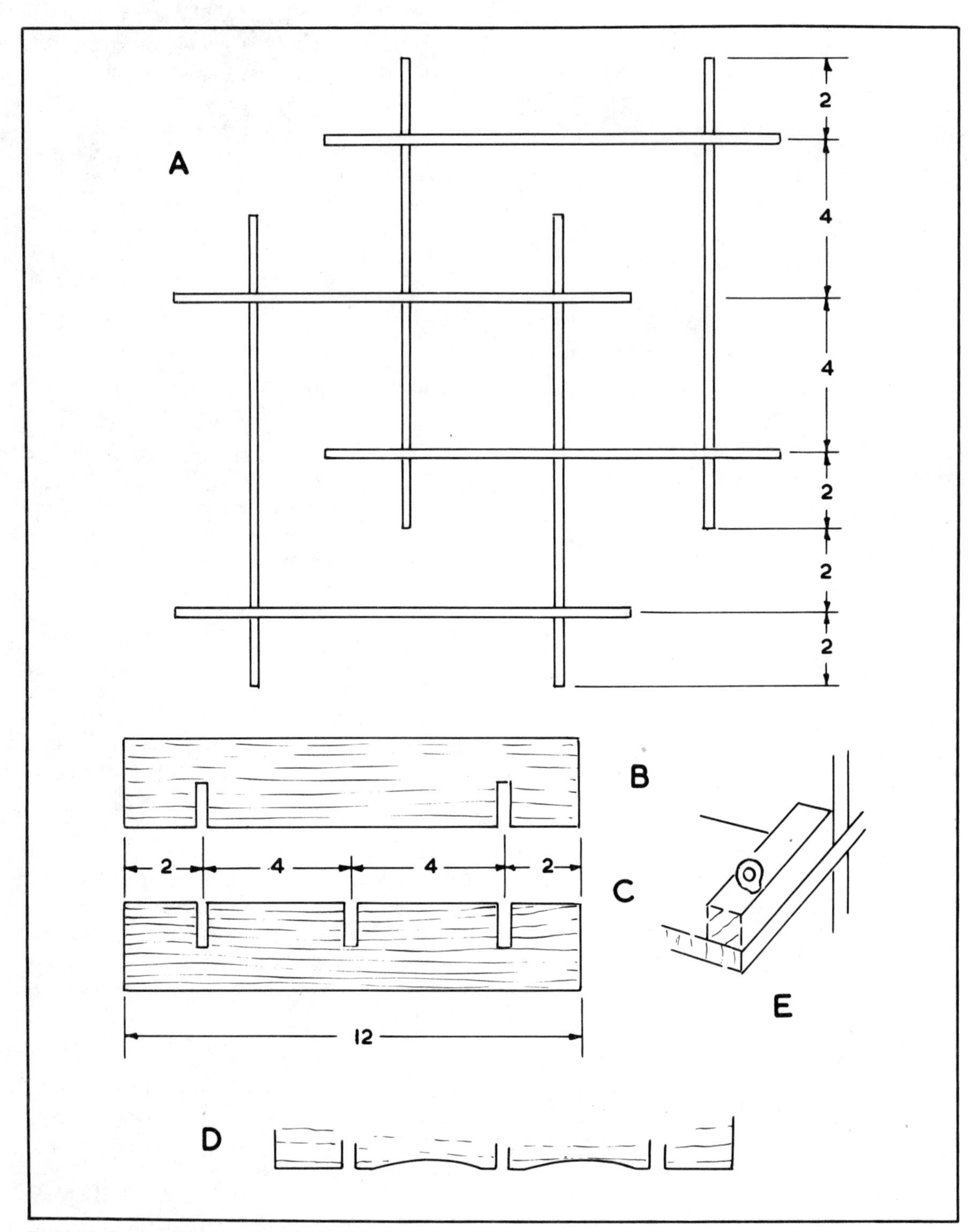

Fig. 7-15. Sizes and construction of a knickknack rack.

Fig. 7-16. This bookcase is made in two parts.

Divide a circle into six by stepping off the radius around the circumference (Fig. 7-21A). With two alternate points as centers, draw curves through the opposite points (Fig. 7-21B). The top can be a straight line (Fig. 7-21C), or you can draw two curves (Fig. 7-21D). Maybe that shape does not appeal to you. Try deepening the side curves (Fig. 7-21E) and raising the center point (Fig. 7-21F). When you have a shape that satisfies you, make a half template so you get a symmetrical outline to cut.

While one shield may take all the items you want, remember that this sort of thing always looks better in pairs. You may even have enough items to warrant several shields arranged in a pattern on the wall.

Whether the board is a shield or other outline, its purpose is to display your collection. It should be unobtrusive. A simple molding or rounding of the edges will be enough. Finish the wood without a high gloss in a color that will give prominence to the collected items.

If the item to be displayed is too bulky to glue in place or you want to be able to take it down, supports will be needed. An antique gun or replica is a common example.

If the gun is a pioneer weapon, it will look better on an apparently old mount than on an obviously new piece of polished mahogany. You can use a weathered piece of wood from an old barn. It need not be parallel, and you may trim the ends to an uneven outline (Fig. 7-22A). If you have to use new wood, it can be made to look old by leaving a sawed surface and treating it with gray stain.

For anything round, like the barrel of a gun, a spring clip can be used (Fig. 7-22B). You will have to make racks and hooks for other parts. A wood projection can be shaped to match what it has to hold, then be given a tenon to go through the backboard (Fig. 7-22C). Try to arrange for there to be no short grain where grain lines run off both ways (Fig. 7-22D). If they run through (Fig. 7-22E), the part will be stronger. Rounded internal corners (Fig. 7-22F) are always stronger than angular ones (Fig. 7-22G).

An alternative to a shaped hook is a turned peg with a dowel end to go into the backboard (Fig. 7-22H), but that will have a more prominent end than you may wish in some places. The rounded end can be carved to make a hook (Fig. 7-22J). Spend some time rounding all the visible parts of all hooked supports. This gives them an authentic hand-worked appearance, which is better than a more angular outline.

The support for some parts is better shaped to fit in all directions. You can make a piece to go under a part to locate and hold it. Much of the work has to be careful whittling and sanding, but you can start with a sawn outline (Fig. 7-23A) and round the parts in all directions (Fig. 7-23B) to produce the supporting hollow and a lip to keep the article from

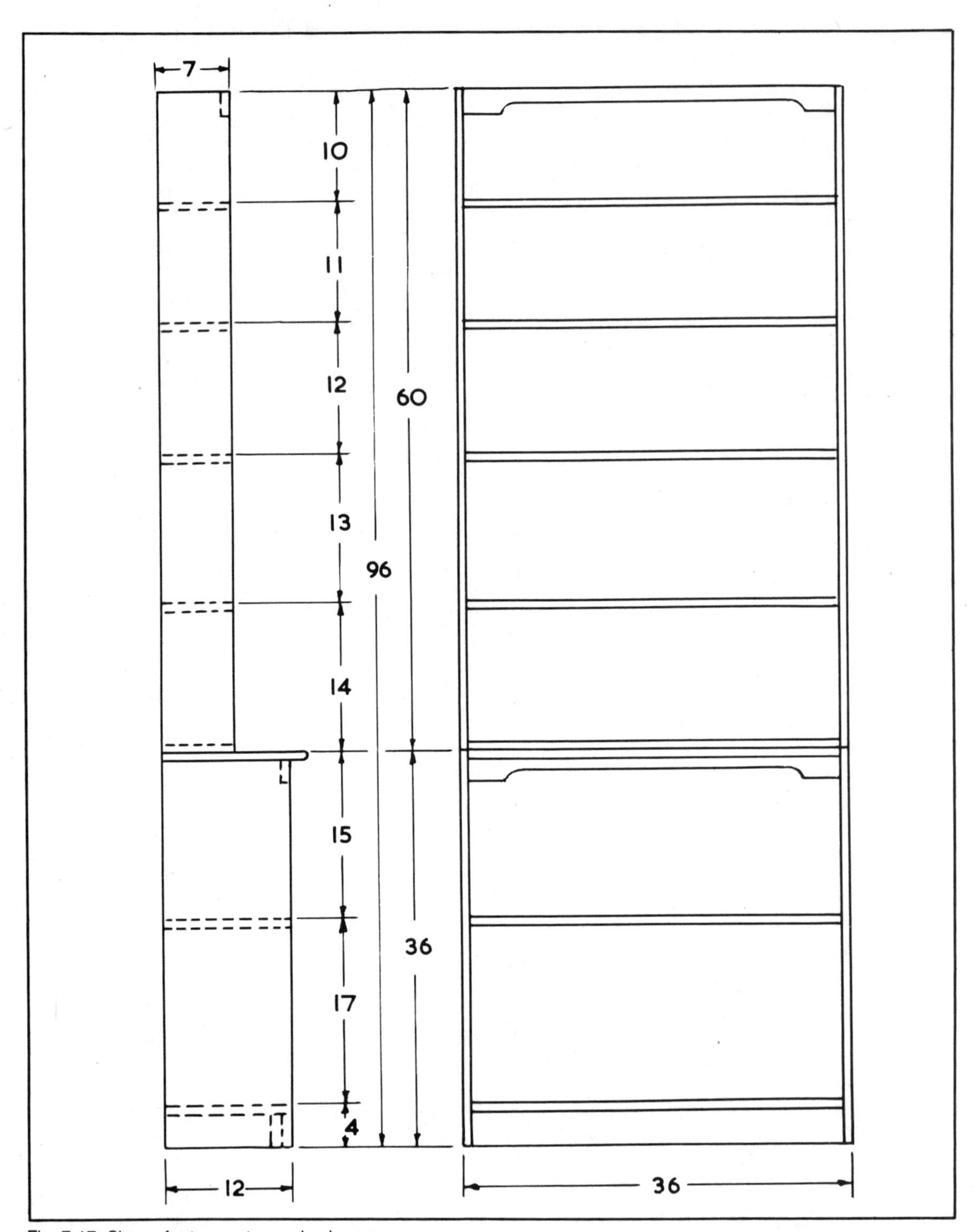

Fig. 7-17. Sizes of a two-part open bookcase.

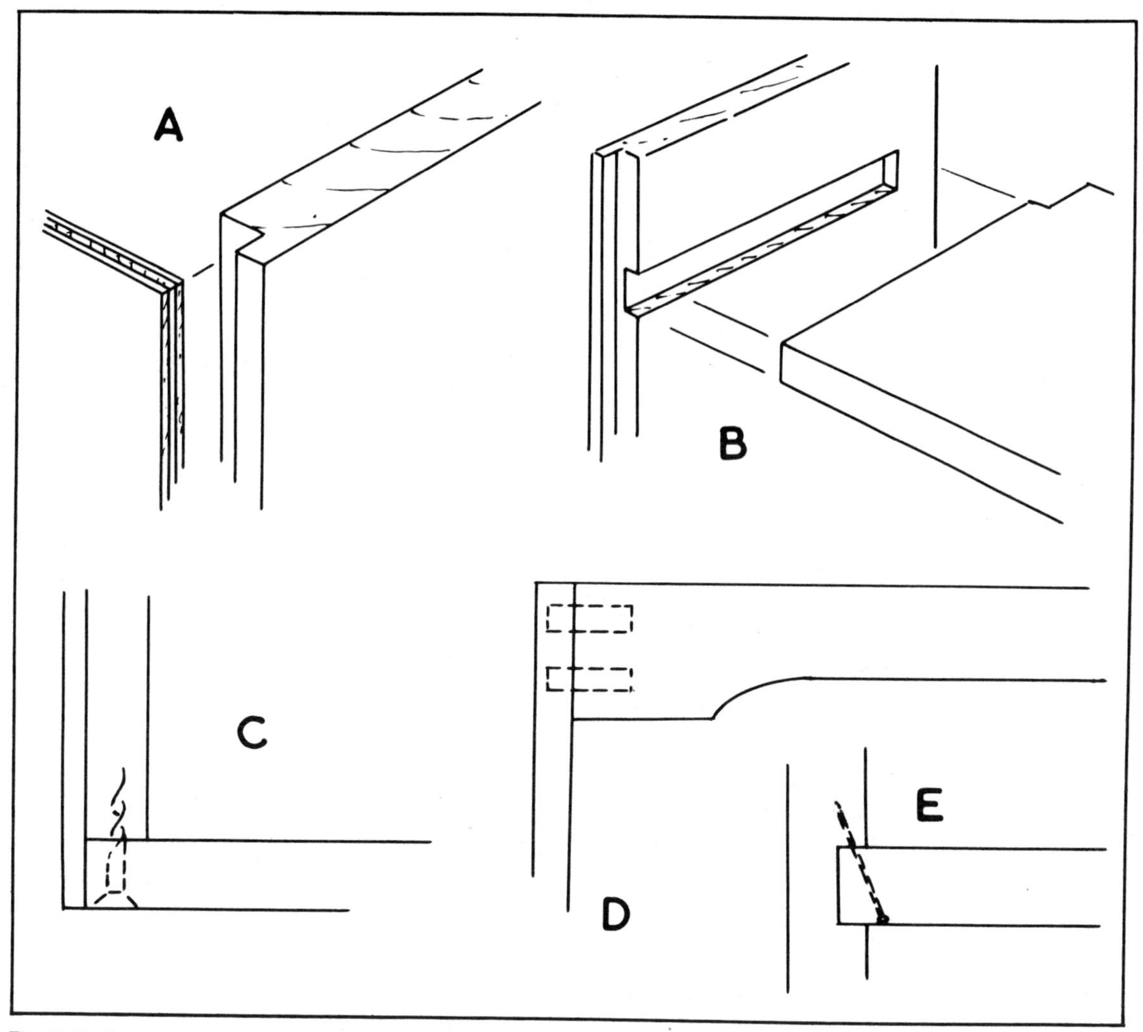

Fig. 7-18. Constructional details of the two-part open bookcase.

falling forward. Such a block is best fitted with screws from the back (Fig. 7-23C).

Some things that are better held a short distance forward on their mount. The resulting shadow behind gives prominence, particularly if the article is shiny, such as a knife or sword. You can give the hooks ledges to prevent the sword from going too far back (Fig. 7-23D). The point (which should be protected in any case) may go into a block that keeps the sword parallel (Fig. 7-23E). Anything long may be mounted on a variety of shaped boards (Fig. 7-23F). The article does not have to be upright or symmetrically mounted. Sometimes it looks better askew.

SPOON RACK

If you collect souvenir spoons with badges or emblems on their handles or bowls, you will want to display them. This rack (Fig. 7-24) will hold 24 spoons with their bowls downward. It should suit any small souvenir spoons, but you should check your collection. You may find it necessary to increase spacing for a row of larger spoons. Unless the spoons have very large bowls, the spacing along

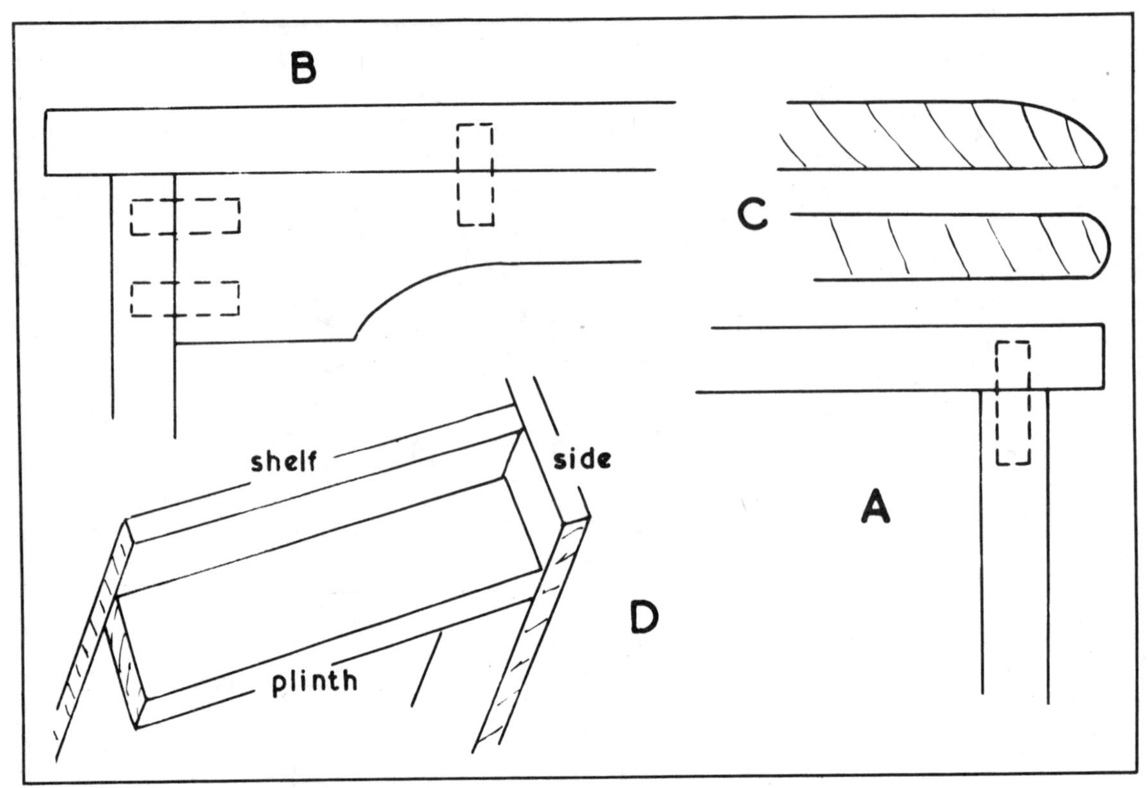

Fig. 7-19. Assembly and edge details of the two-part open bookcase.

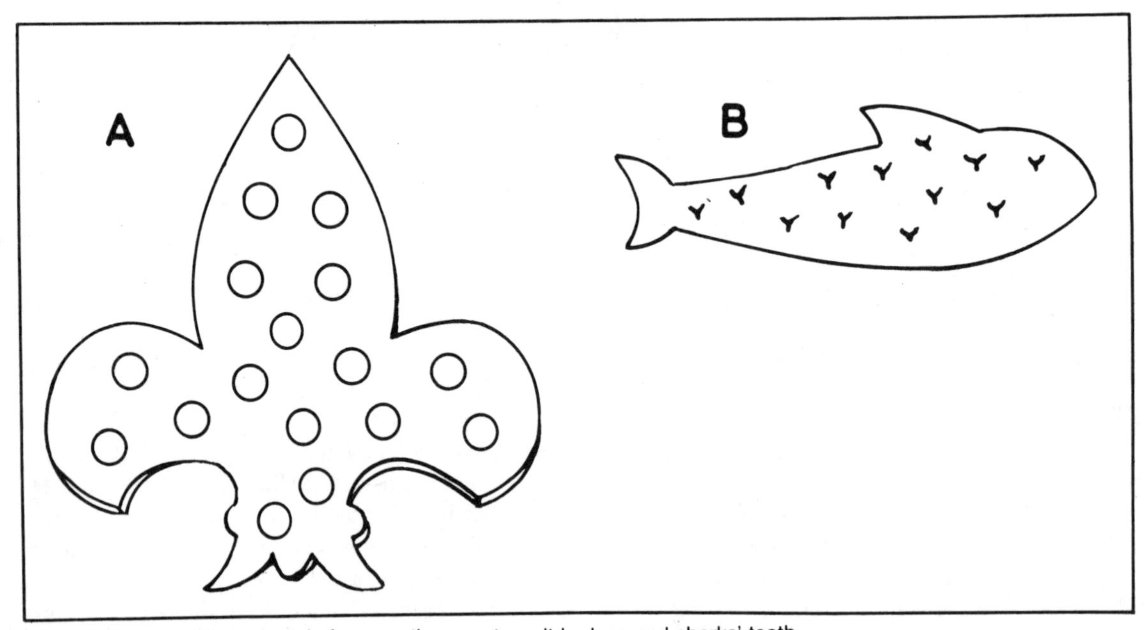

Fig. 7-20. Typical display boards for mounting scout merit badges and sharks' teeth.

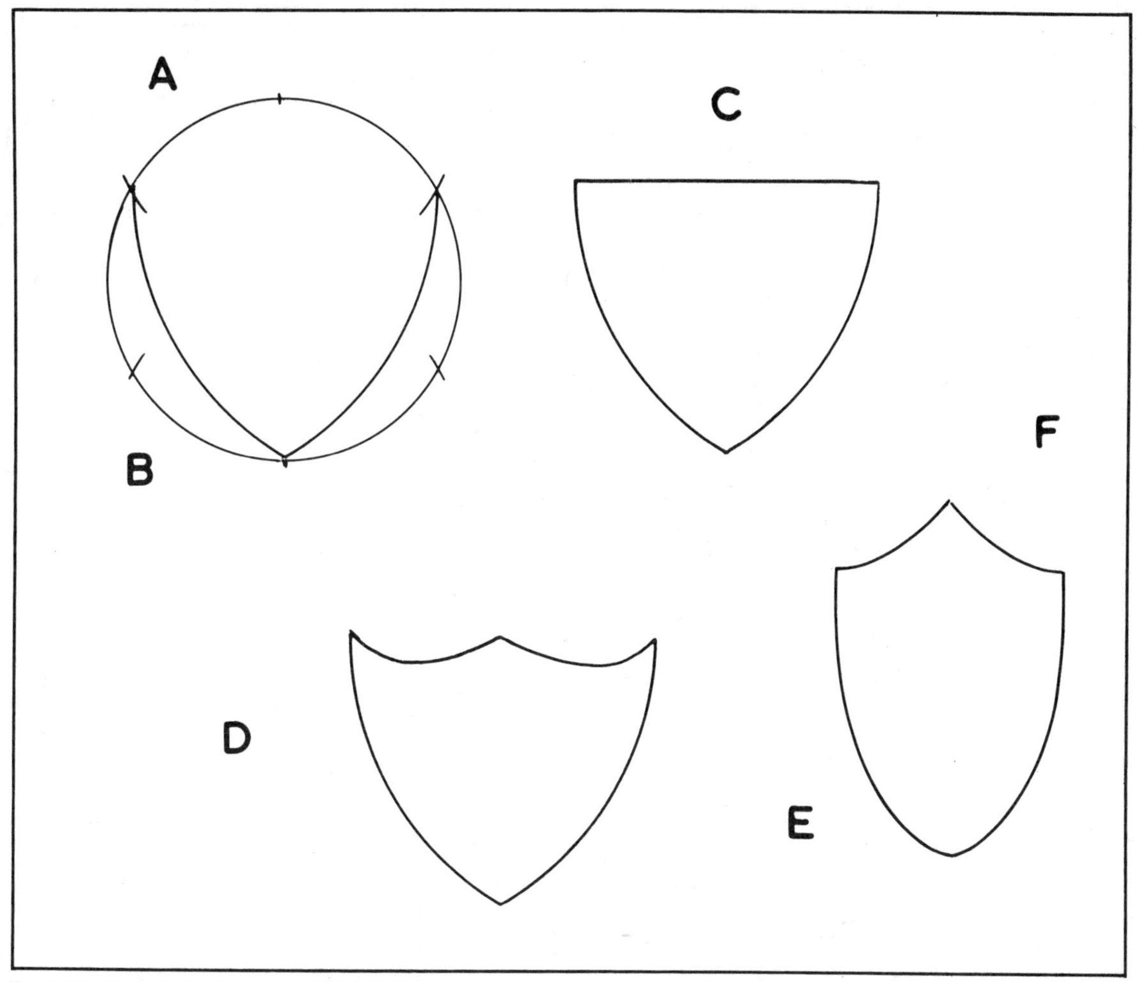

Fig. 7-21. Steps in laying out a shield design.

the shelves should be sufficient (Fig. 7-25).

Use a close-grained hardwood for the sides and shelves. The back can be thinner than ¼-inch plywood, preferably faced with a veneer to match the other wood. See Table 7-4.

Mark out a side with the positions of the shelves and draw the curved front (Fig. 7-26A). You may have to nail the back directly to the sides. If you are able to make rabbets in the thin wood, the sides will look better. To positively locate the shelves, cut shallow dadoes for them. Fine brads will be needed through the sides for strength (Fig. 7-26B). Cut a pair of matching sides and round the front edges.

Mark out the three shelves together, so the centers of the slots match. Measure each side of the centers and draw lines from the front edge. Where these lines cross the line the other way, drill ¼-inch holes (Fig. 7-26C). Saw into them to make the slot. Cut away the waste wood between the holes to get the outline of the shaped slot (Fig. 7-26D).

Table 7-4. Materials List for Spoon Rack.

2 sides	2 × 22 × ¼
3 shelves	1¼× 16 × ¼
1 back	16 × 22 × ¼ plywood

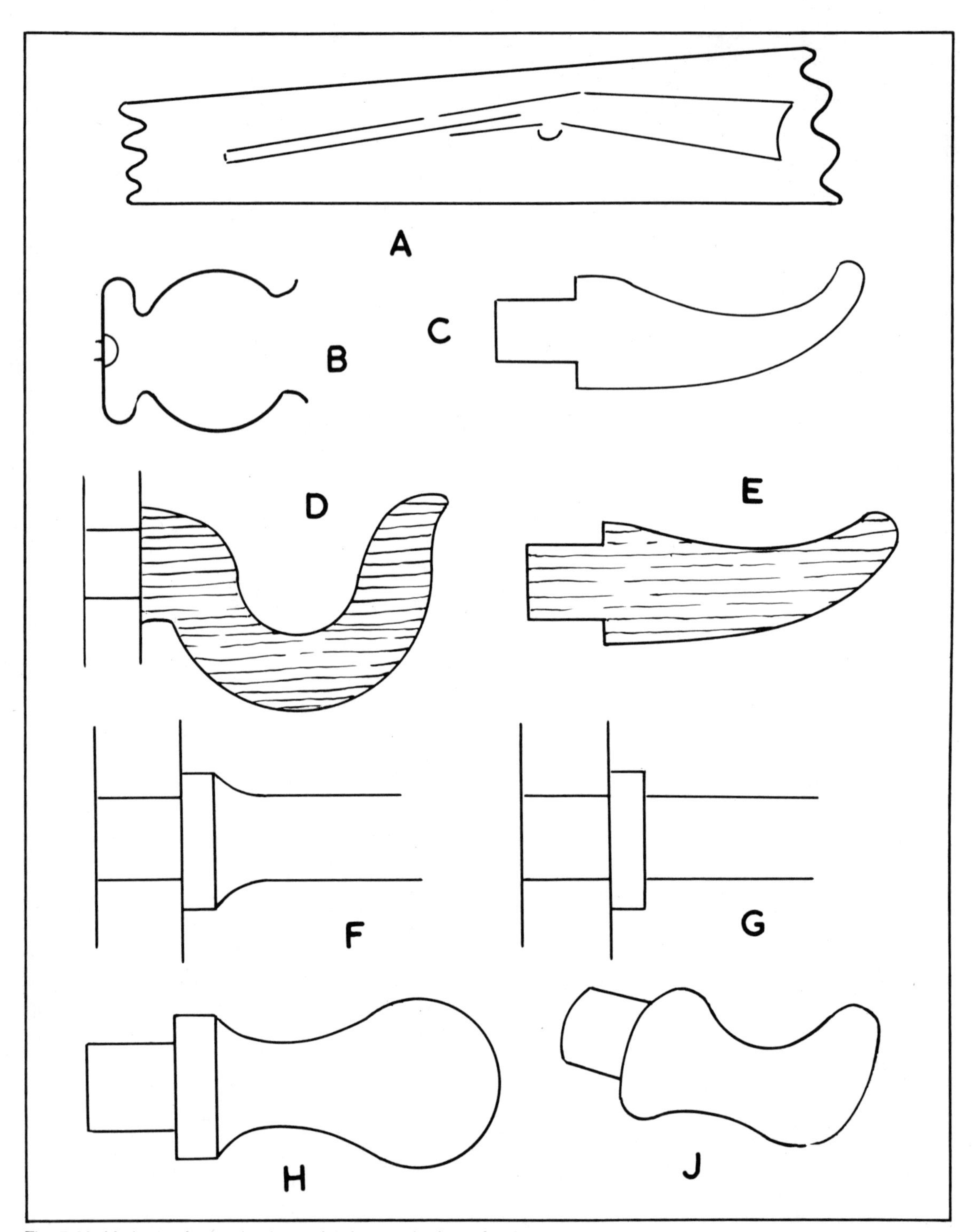

Fig. 7-22. Methods of mounting items that have to be hung for display.

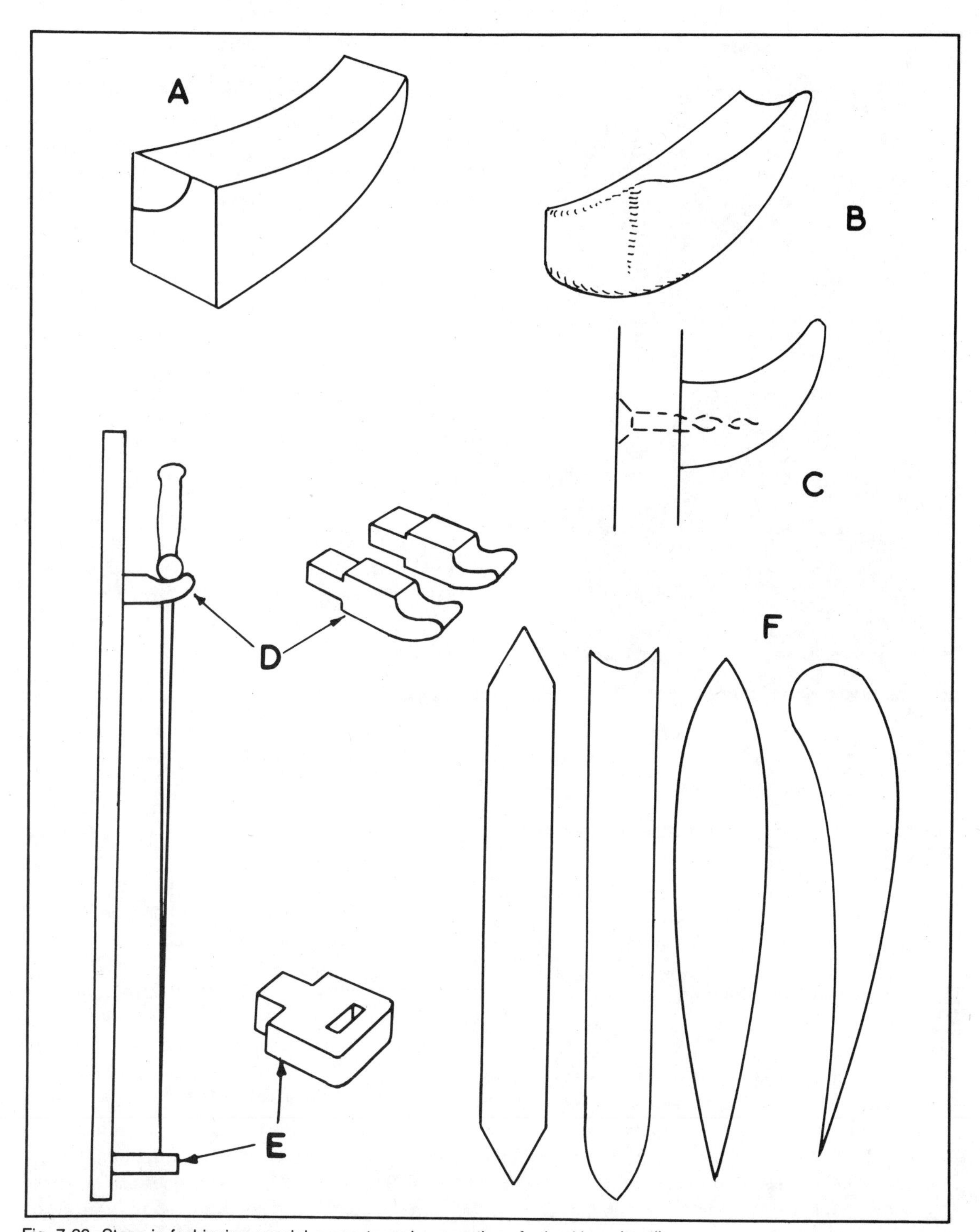

Fig. 7-23. Steps in fashioning special supports and suggestions for backboard outlines.

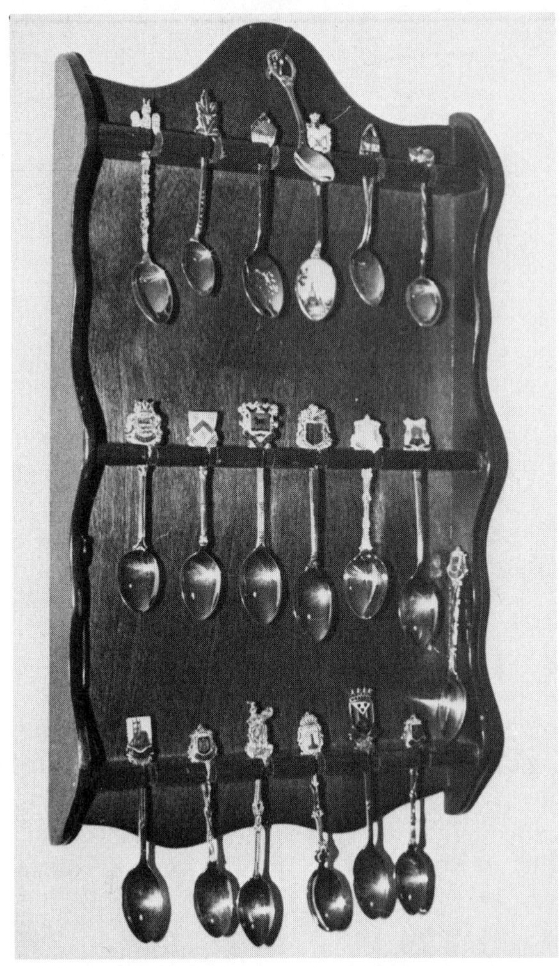

Fig. 7-24. A spoon rack will display the spoons collected during your travels.

Do each stage of the work to each of the 24 slots in turns, so you make them as uniform as possible. Use sharp tools and either drill partly from each side or have scrap wood held close to prevent the wood from splintering on the underside. When all the slot outlines have been cut, round their edges slightly.

Assemble the ends to the shelves and mark the back from this. Top and bottom edges are symmetrical and the same. Make a template of half the shape, so the curves are all made the same. Glue and thin nails or brads into the sides will keep the rack in shape, but drive a few into the shelves as well. If screws into the wall are put close under shelves, they will be inconspicuous.

DISPLAY PLATE RACK

If you have a single decorative plate to hang on the wall, wire clips are probably best. You may prefer to make a wooden rack if there is a set of two or more to hang. The example (Fig. 7-27) is intended for three 7-inch plates. You will have to adjust sizes to suit the actual plates. Arrange the racks close enough to allow for putting in the plates and no more. It will probably be best to have the wood for the back too long and lay out the support positions with the aid of the actual plates, particularly if they are graduated in size. Plates vary in the amount they are dished and in their diameters, so check what extension to allow on the supports.

For the 7-inch plates the back is 4 inches wide, and the supports are ½-inch square strips near its edges (Fig. 7-28A). They are notched at the front and shaped plywood pieces are screwed on (Fig. 7-28B). With just one screw at back and front, the supports can be turned to exactly match the plate edge (Fig. 7-28C).

If possible, make the shaped plywood pieces with wood to match the back. They also can be stained to a color that will show up the plate pattern.

To prevent a plate from being knocked out, you can make small turn buttons to close over the top of it. Its size will depend on the amount the plate is dished. Let it turn on a screw, and you can cushion it with thin rubber (Fig. 7-28D). Except for the top one, the turn buttons will be hidden by the supports.

Shape the ends of the back in any way you wish, but these are where you will put the screws into the wall and the design should allow for that (Fig. 7-28E). The edges of the back's exposed parts may be beveled or molded, but most of its length will be hidden. You can extend the bottom to include a rack for a few spoons.

MAGAZINE RACK

Although described as a magazine rack, this can be used for other papers, envelopes, and similar things behind a desk or telephone. The sizes can be modified. See Table 7-5. The rack should hold most magazines, including those of pocket size (Fig.

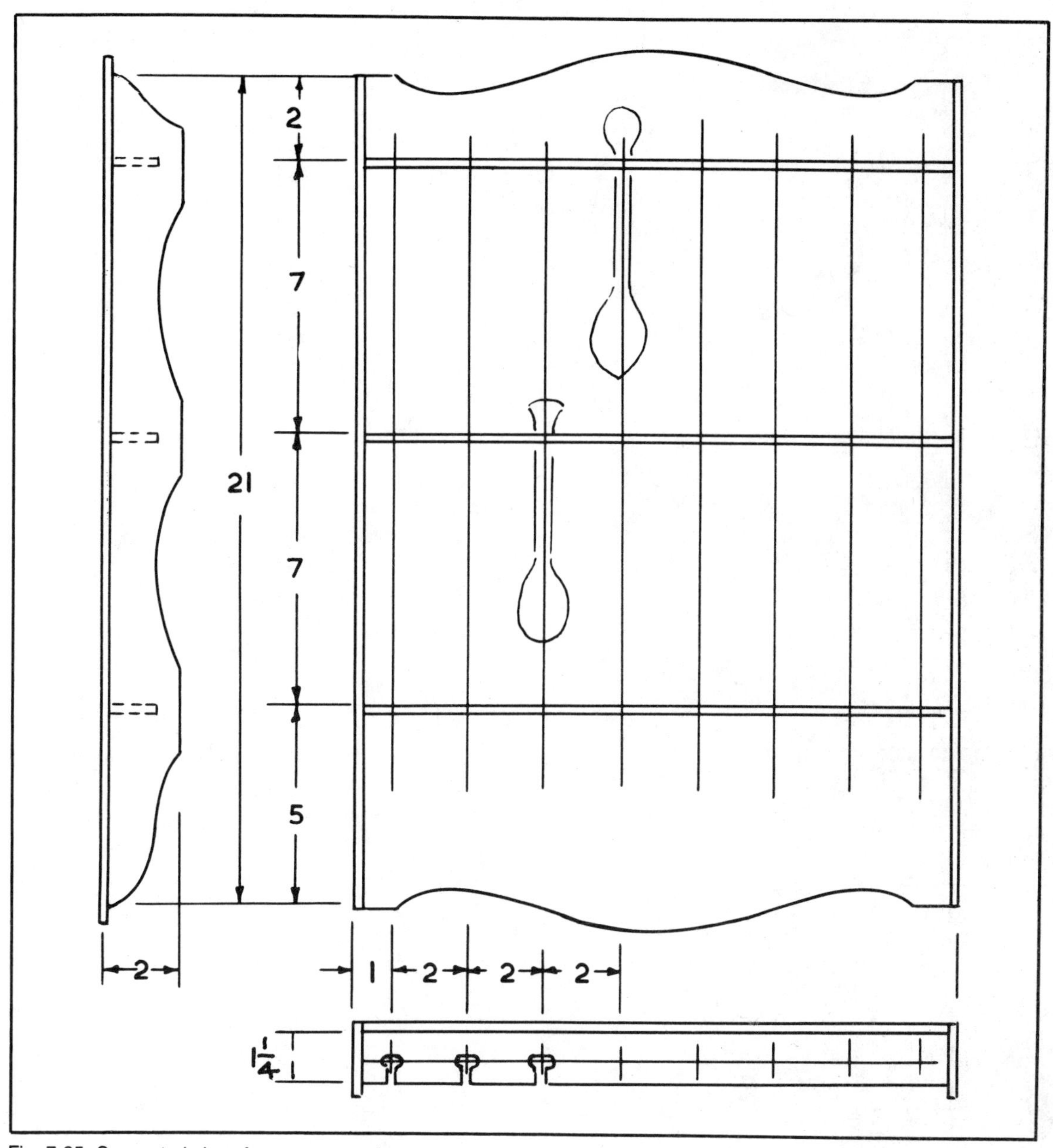

Fig. 7-25. Suggested sizes for a spoon rack.

7-29). The rack looks well in two colors of wood, with the main parts one color and the crosspieces another. The surroundings determine which parts are light and which are dark.

Make a full-size drawing of an end view showing both heights (Fig. 7-30A). Assembly is by screwing, but for neatness the plywood back can be let into the ends (Fig. 7-30B). The central piece must be that much narrower. Cut these three pieces to size. If roundhead brass screws are used for visible parts of the assembly, their heads can be regarded as a decorative feature. The bottom is

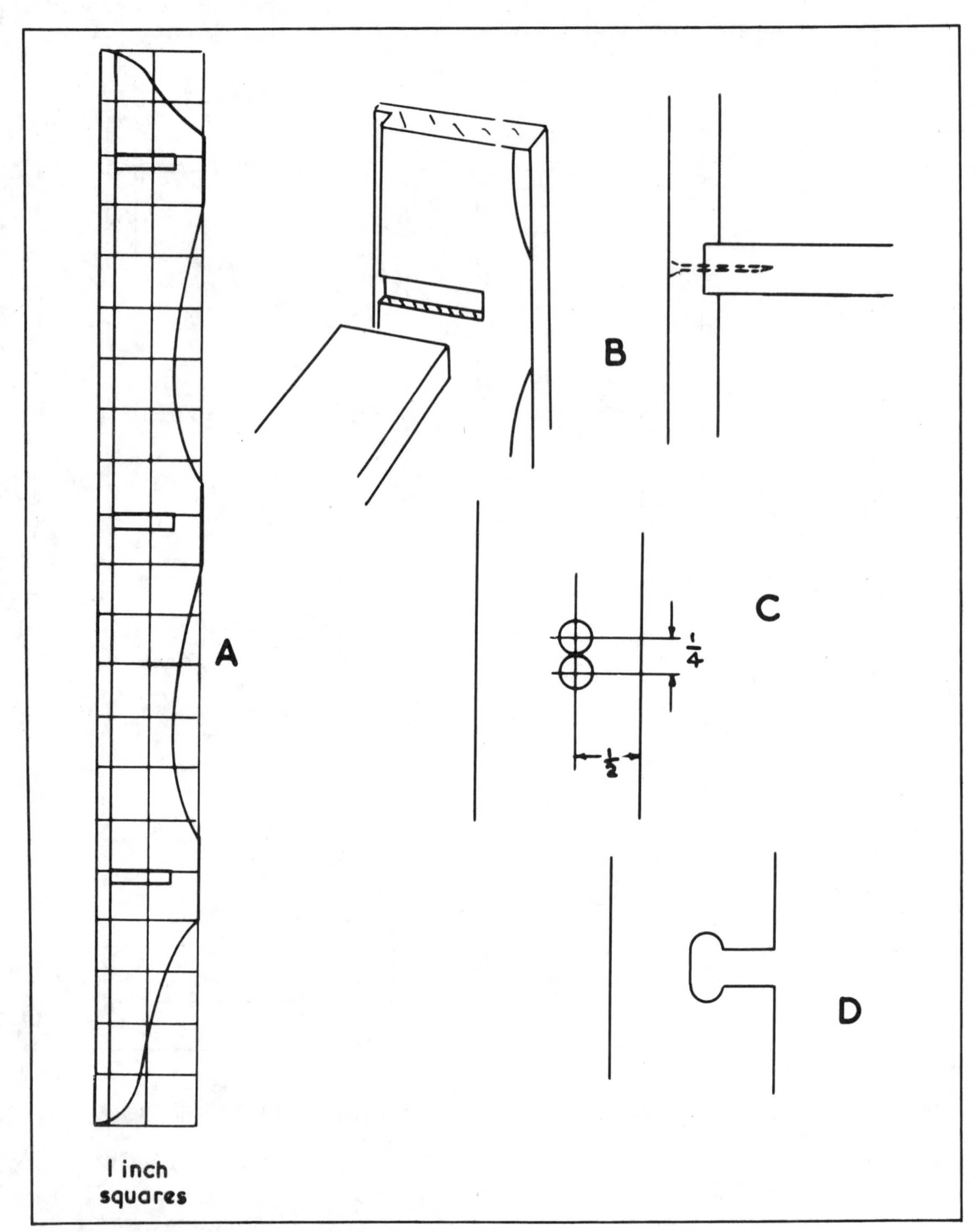

Fig. 7-26. The side shape and shelf details of a spoon rack.

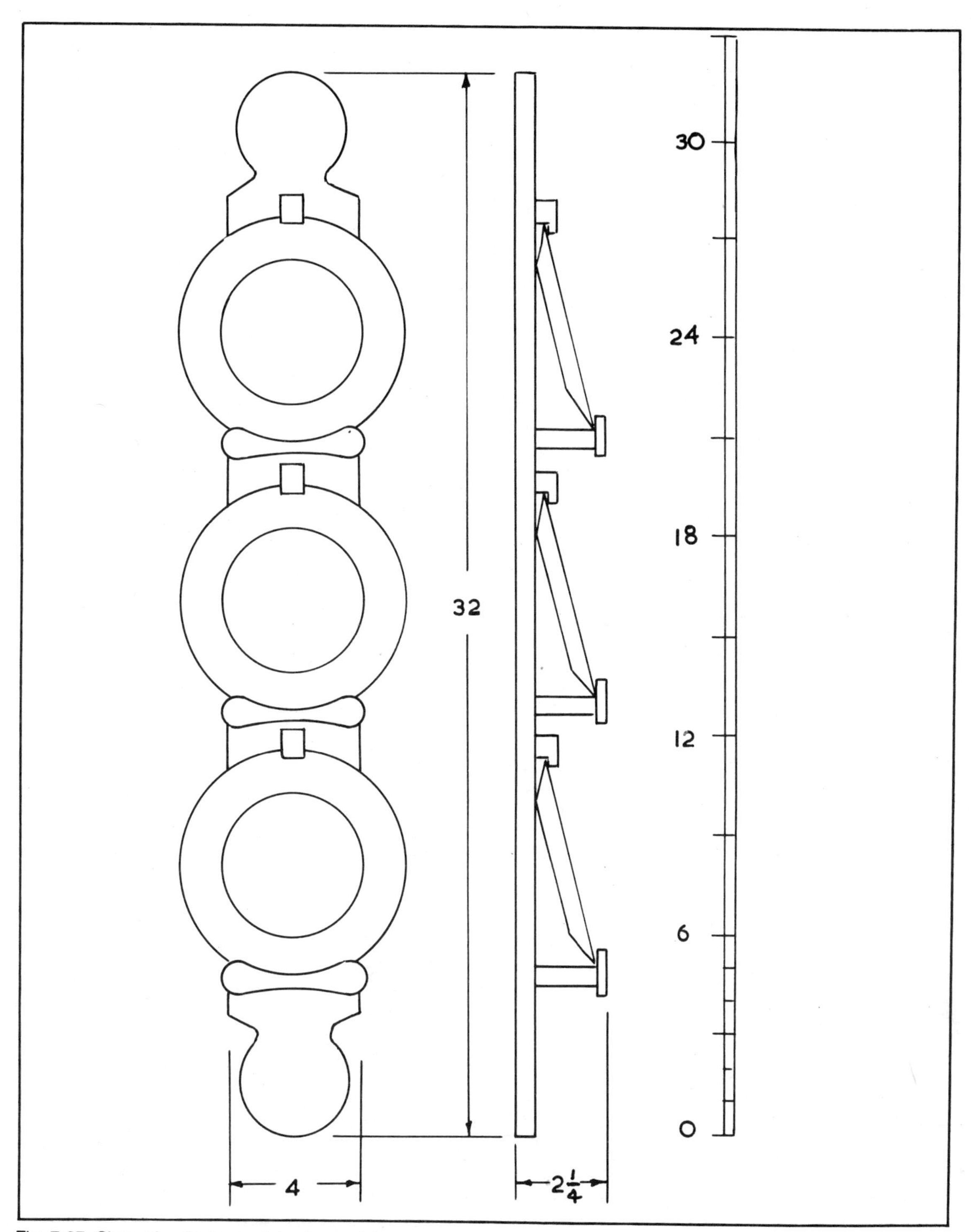

Fig. 7-27. Sizes of a display rack for three plates.

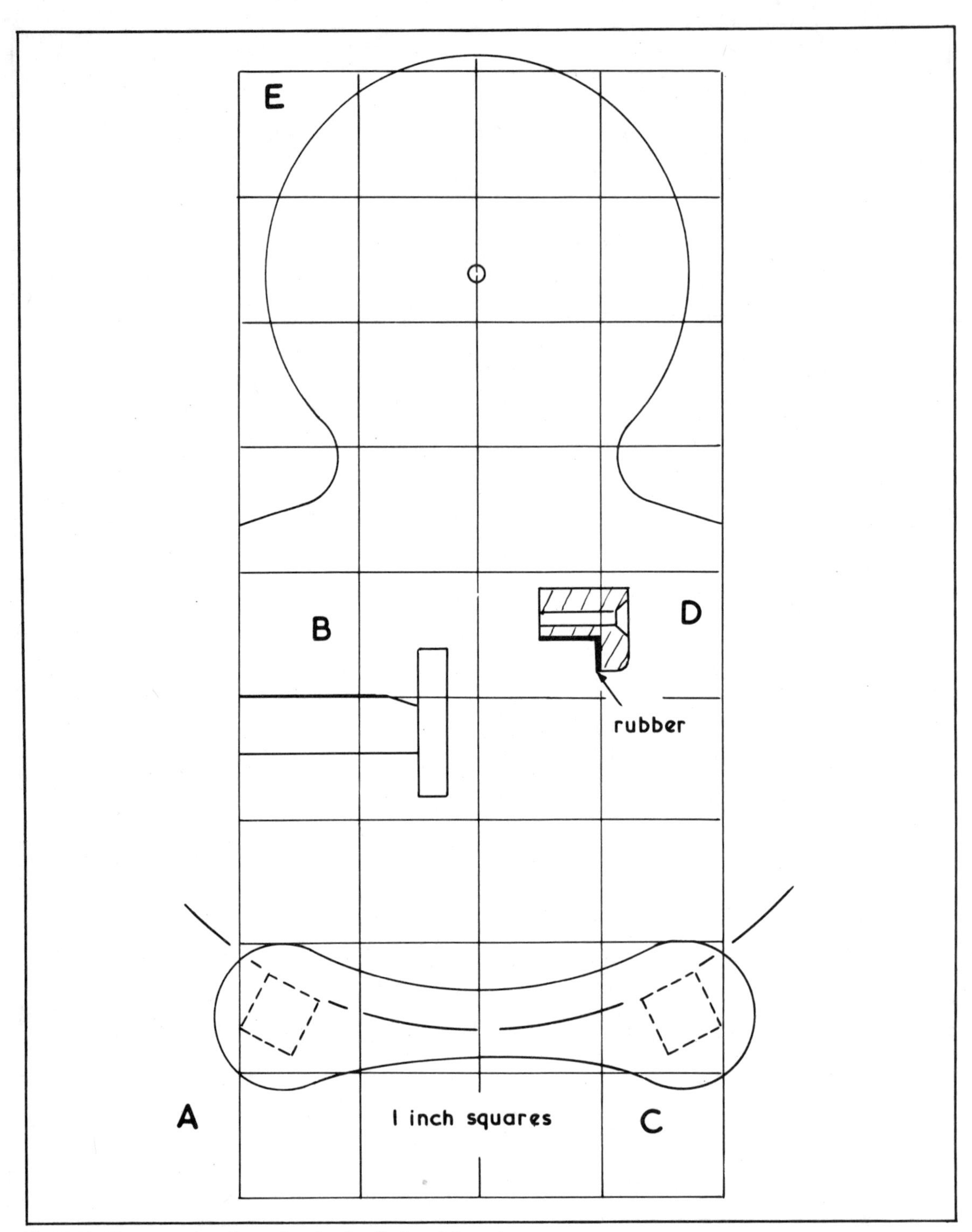

Fig. 7-28. Shapes and sections of parts of a display plate rack.

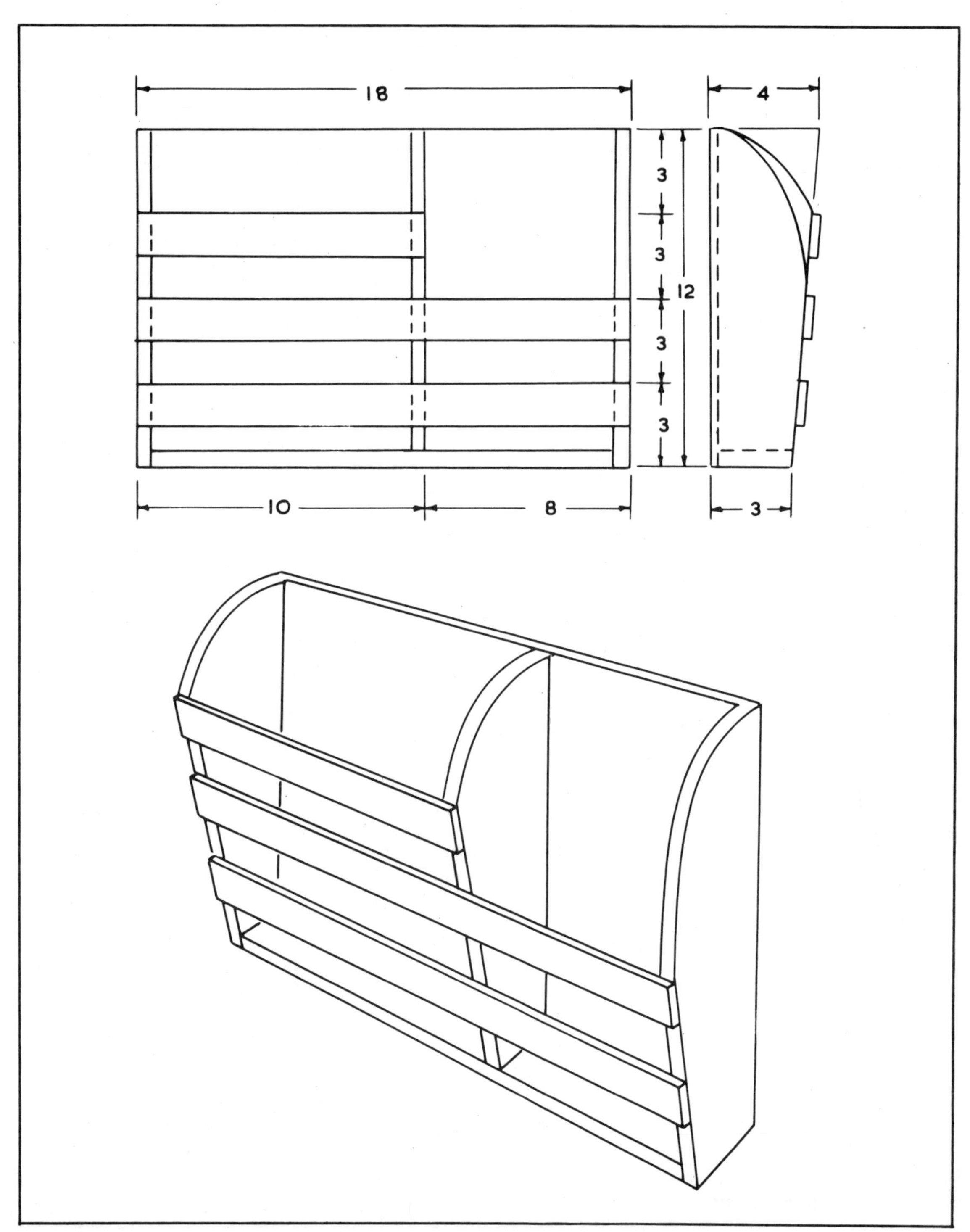

Fig. 7-29. A two-part magazine rack.

Table 7-5. Materials List for Magazine Rack.

3 ends	4	× 13 × ½
1 bottom	3	× 13 × ½
2 rails	1½	× 13 × ¼
1 rail	1½	× 11 × ¼
1 back	12	× 18 × ¼ plywood

screwed between the ends (Fig. 7-30C) and up into the central piece. Dovetails will look craftsmanlike at the ends (Fig. 7-30D).

Assemble these parts to the plywood back. Add the crosspieces, which should have their edges rounded (Fig. 7-30E) and their ends rounded on the exposed corners. A single screw at each crossing

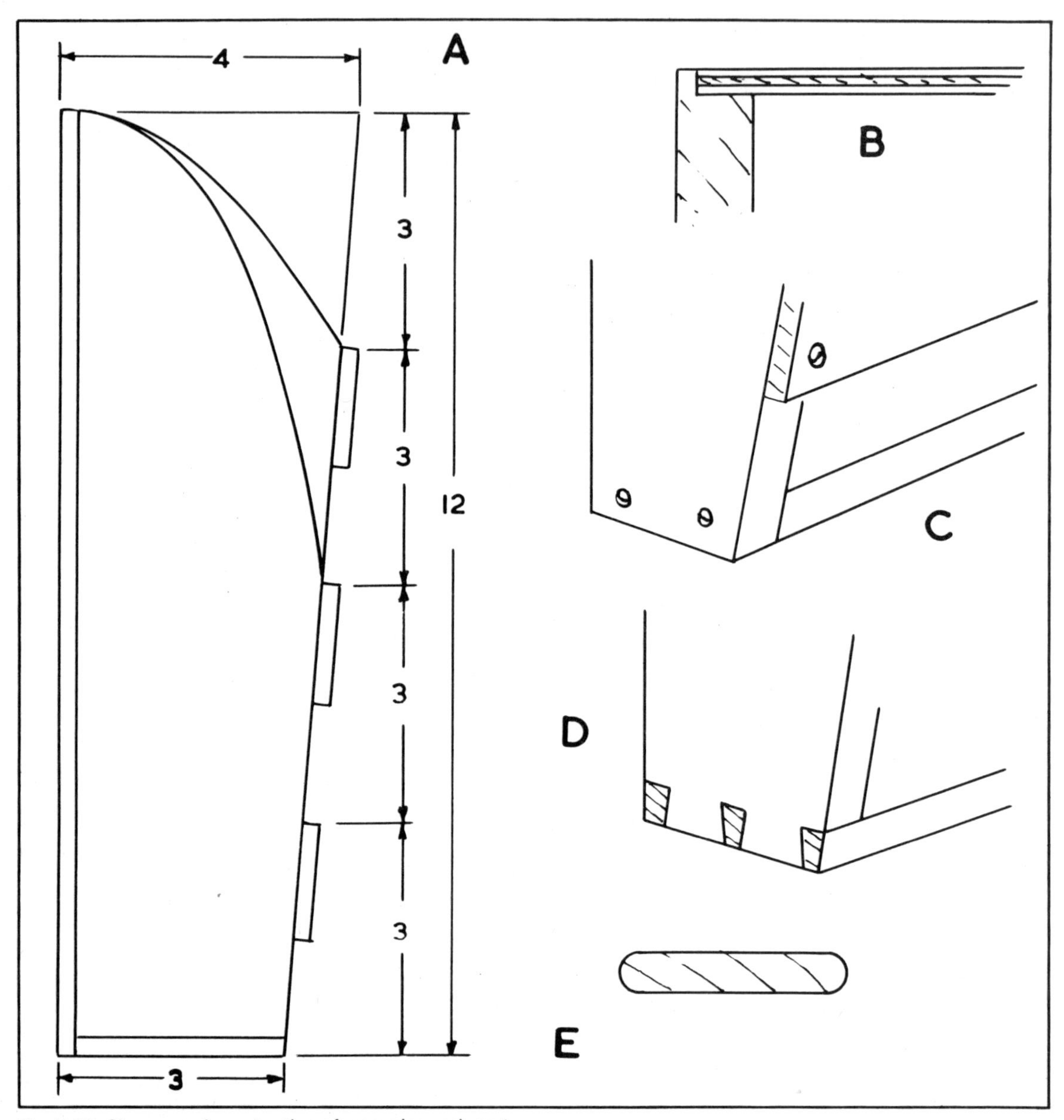

Fig. 7-30. Shapes and construction of magazine rack parts.

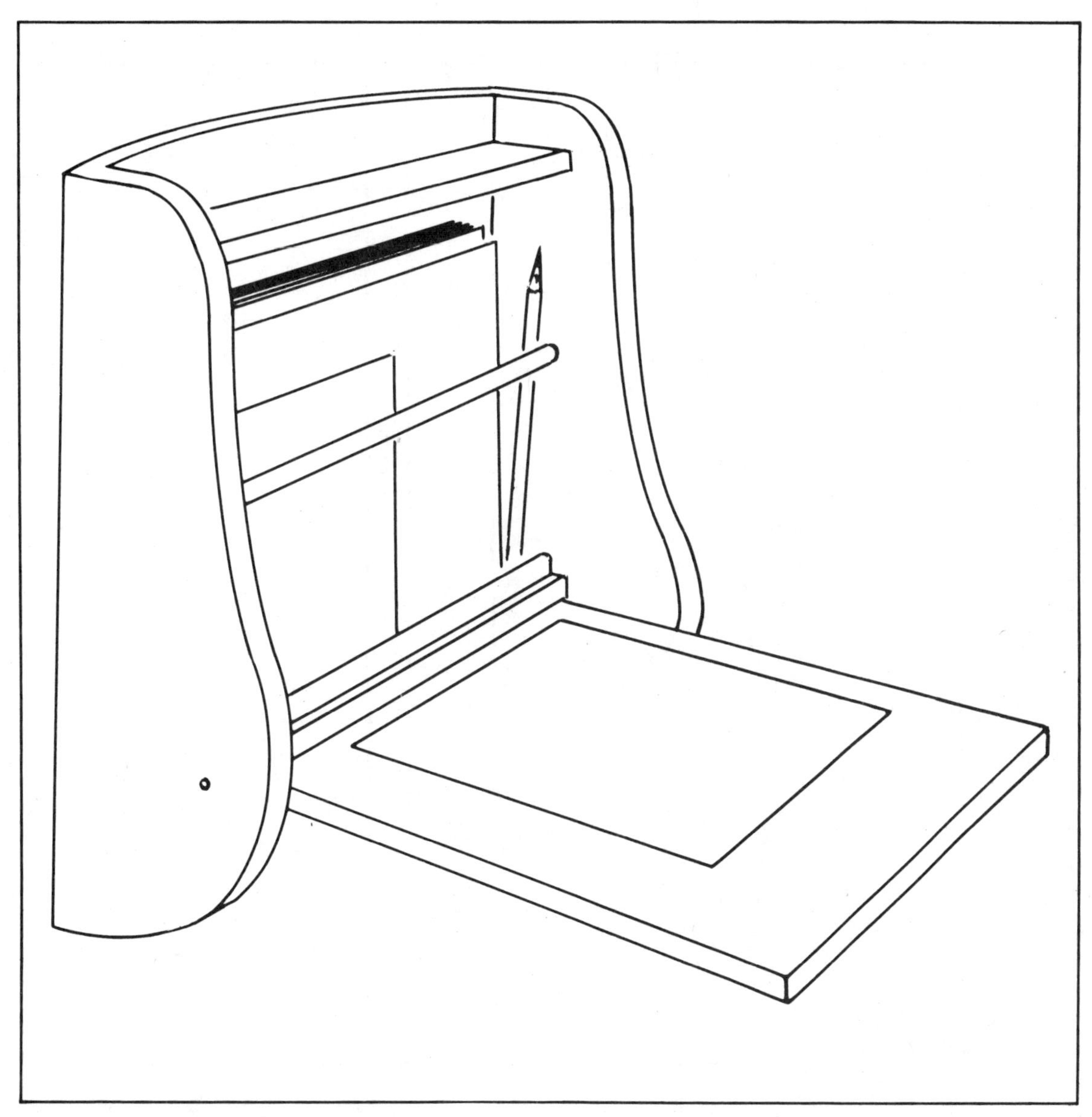

Fig. 7-31. A note holder with a swinging flap.

should be enough. Drill clearance holes to prevent the short grain from breaking out.

After a trial assembly, the rails can be removed for ease in applying varnish or other finish.

NOTE HOLDER

This is an enclosed holder for a note pad or loose pieces of paper and a pencil or pen. When the flap is lowered by pushing its bottom, it becomes a small desk on which to write (Fig. 7-31). The sizes given (Fig. 7-32 and Table 7-6) will take most sizes of pad and paper. If the holder is needed for brochures or questionnaires, its size will have to be modified to allow them to be moved in and out easily.

The shape that governs most other parts is a side. Draw this full-size (Fig. 7-33A) directly on one

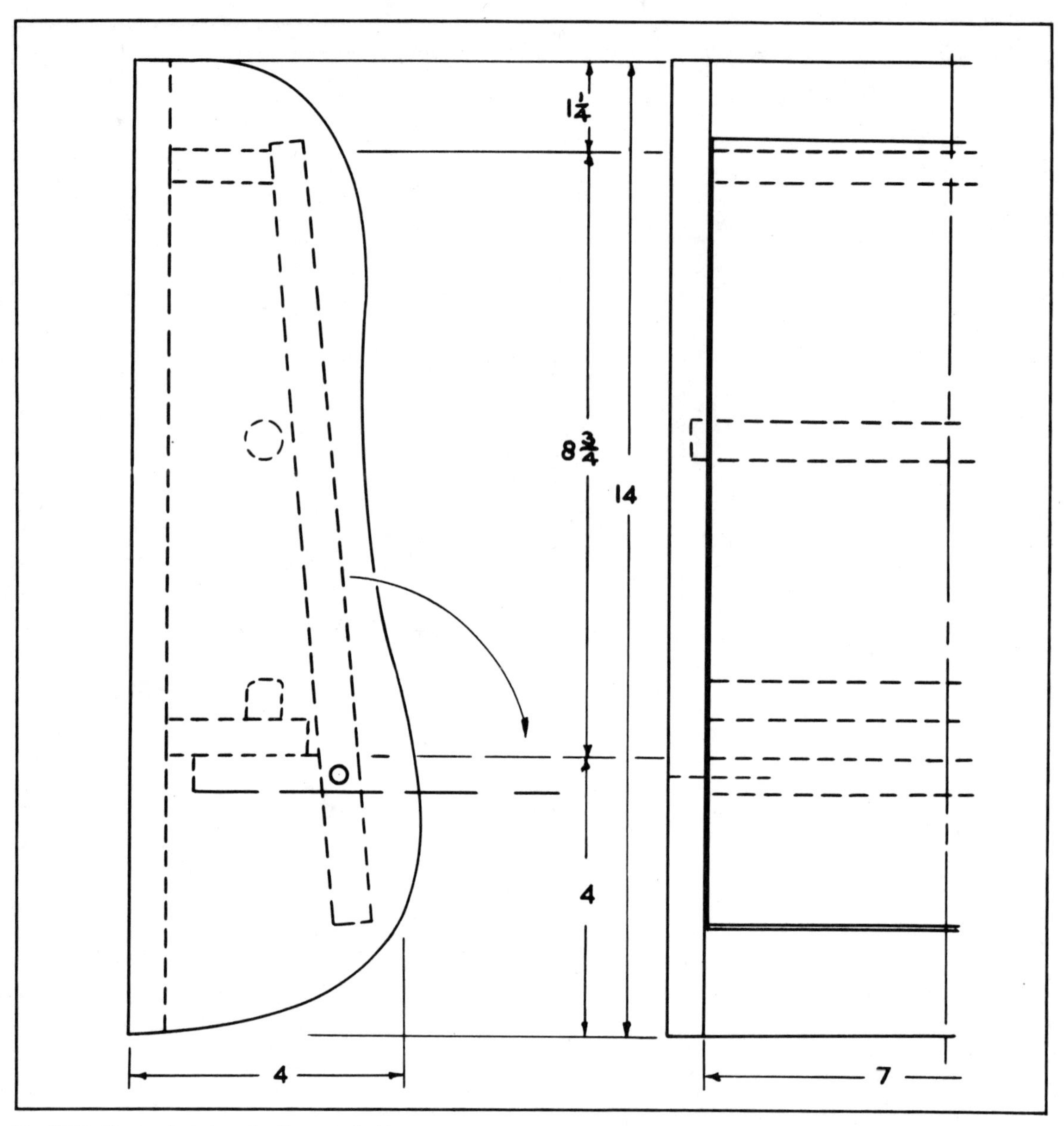

Fig. 7-32. Suggested sizes for the note holder.

Table 7-6. Materials List for Note Holder.

1 back	7 × 14 × ½
2 sides	4 × 13 × ½
1 shelf	4 × 8 × ½
1 shelf	4 × 8 × ½
1 front	7 × 11 × ½
1 rod	⅜ diameter × 8

piece of wood. All the parts are ½-inch thick and can be plywood, although the holder will look better if made of solid hardwood. Assembly can be with nails punched and covered with stopping, or brass screws with their heads exposed may be decorative.

Make the back (Fig. 7-33B) to go between the

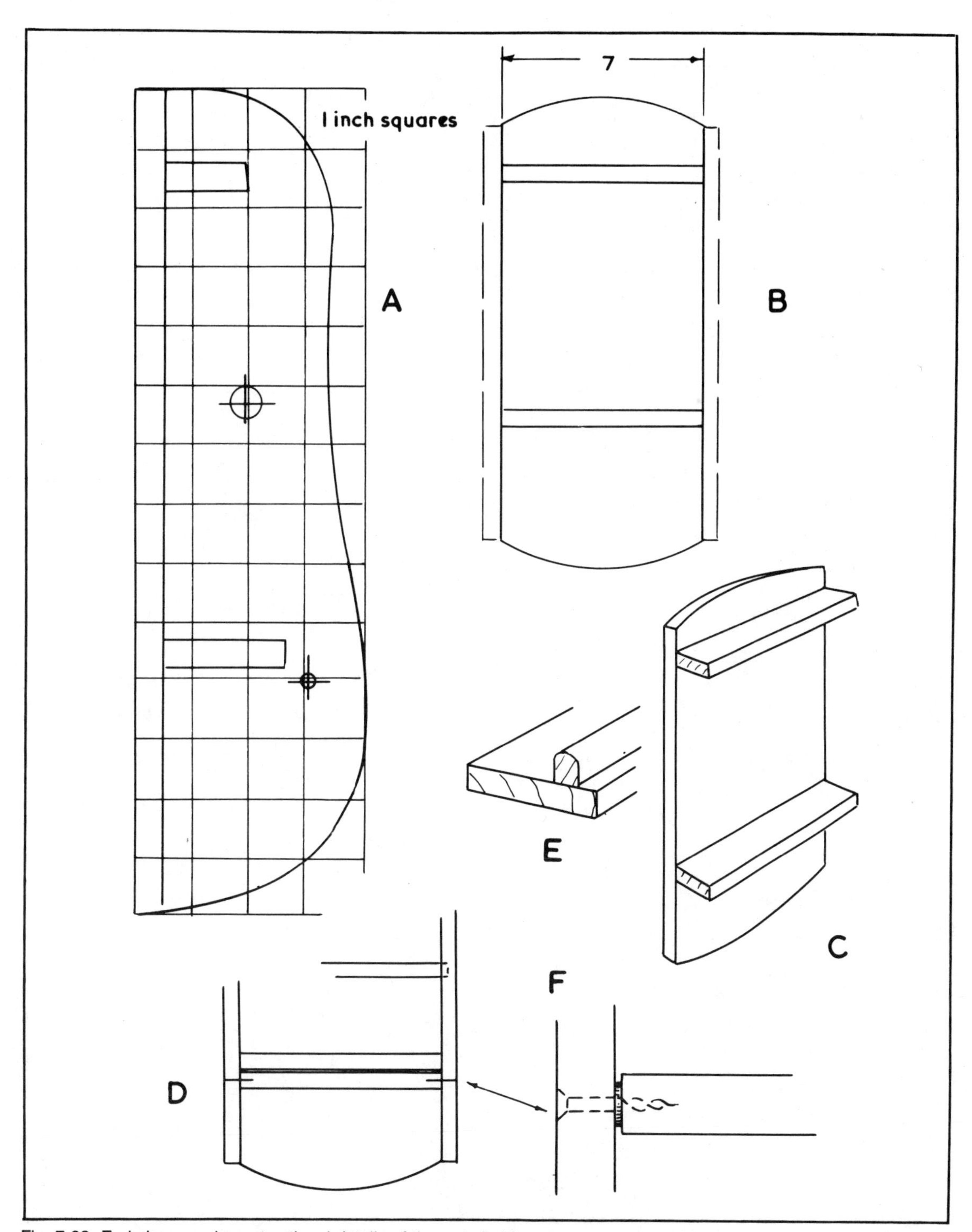

Fig. 7-33. End shape and constructional details of the note holder.

sides and the shelves to match (Fig. 7-33C). The rod that retains the papers is dowel rod taken into shallow holes each side (Fig. 7-33D). Put a strip across the lower shelf to hold back the bottoms of the papers (Fig. 7-33E). Shape the front of the top shelf to match the angle of the closed front.

Assemble the parts made so far. Make the front to fit easily between the sides. Its pivots are two screws. There can be thin washers in the joints (Fig. 7-33F). Take the sharpness off the top and bottom of the front, but otherwise leave the ends square.

If the holder is given a gloss finish, leave the inside of the front bare wood or rub off any gloss to leave a mat surface, so paper does not slip when you are writing on it.

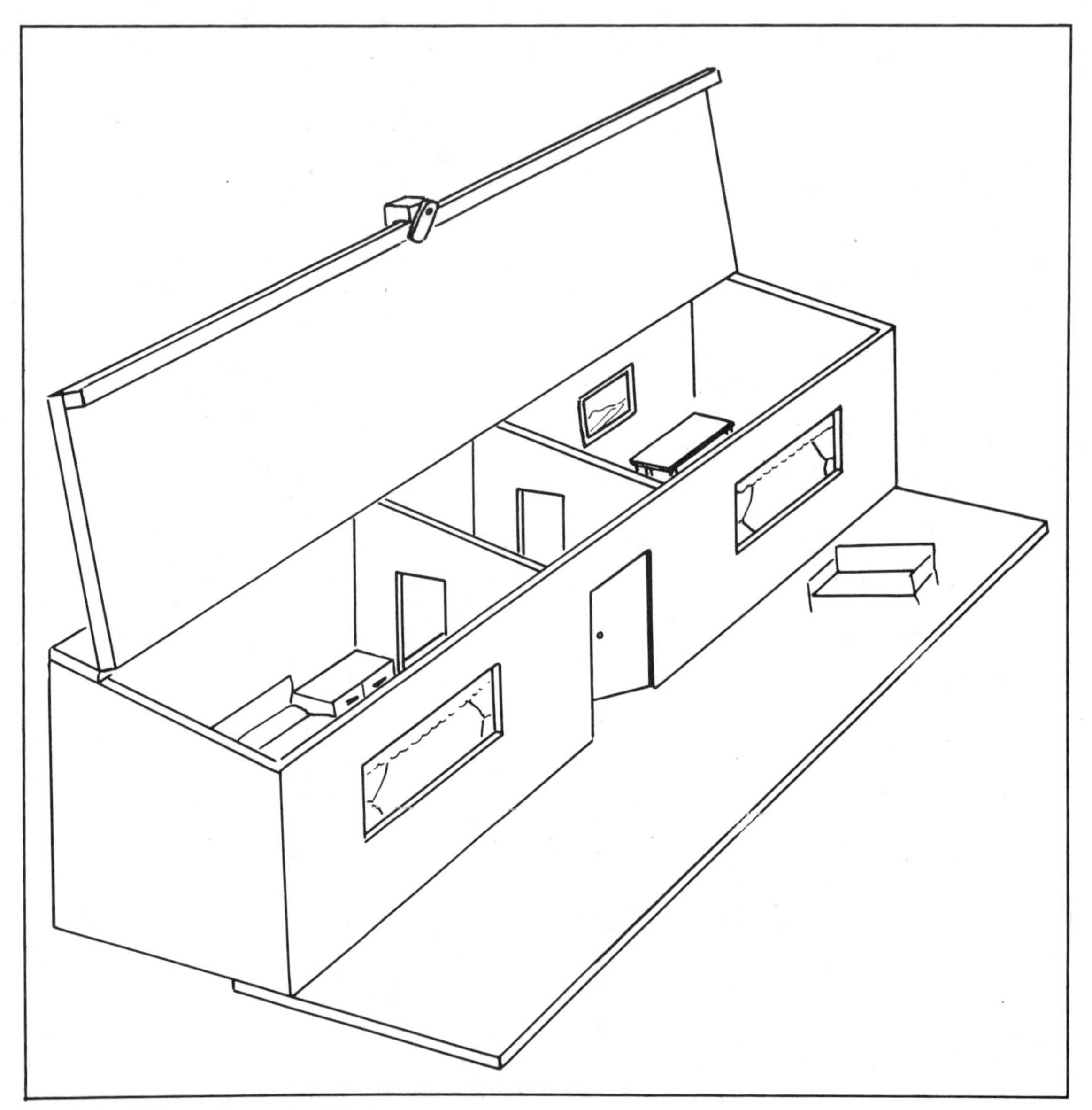

Fig. 7-34. A folding wall-mounted dollhouse.

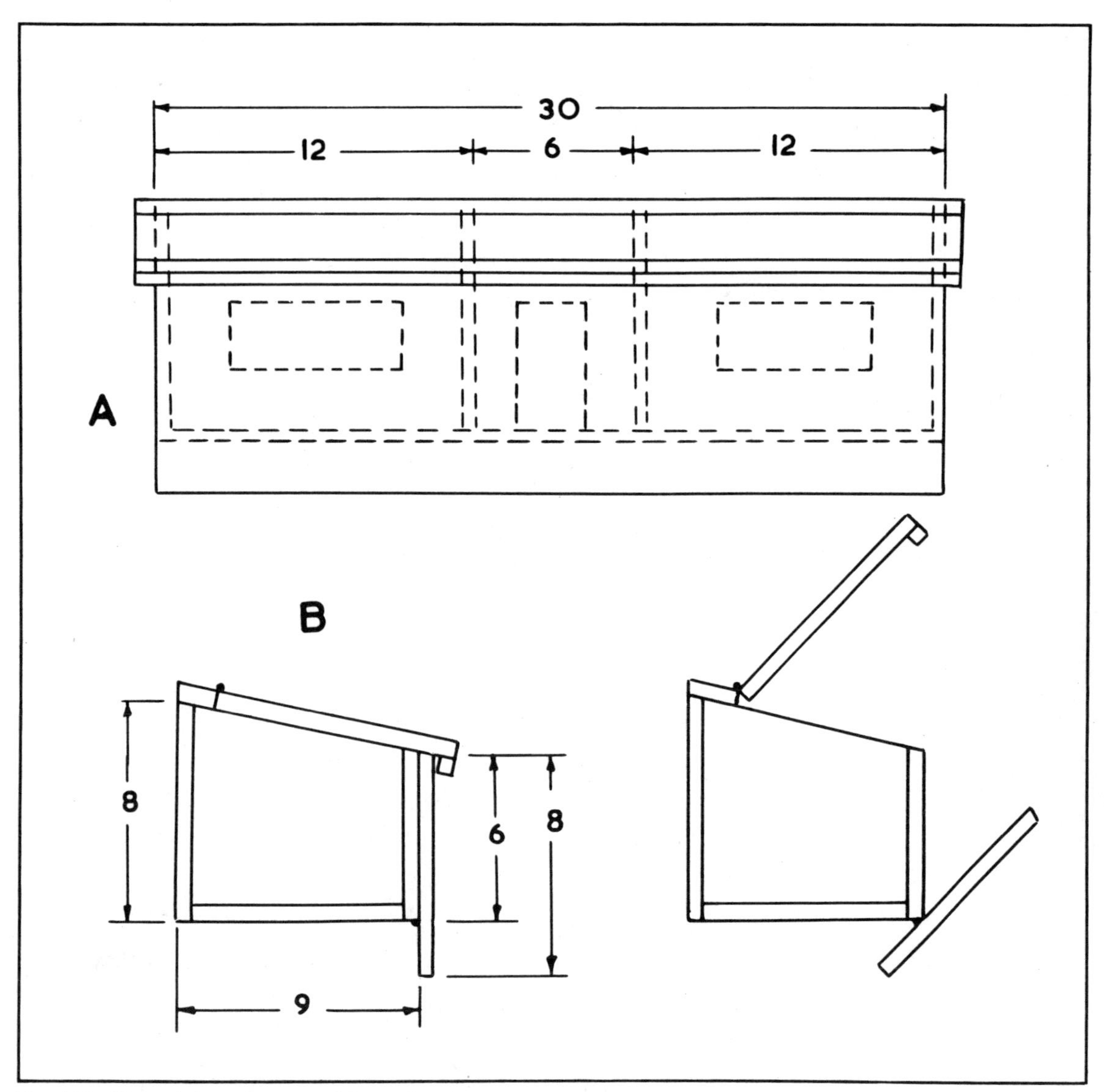

Fig. 7-35. Sizes of the main parts of the wall dollhouse.

WALL DOLLHOUSE

There may be little space in a small bedroom or playroom to spare for a girl to have an ordinary dollhouse. This compact one can be mounted on a wall at a height where the child can reach over the front to arrange furniture and dolls inside. The front flap can be painted as a patio or front yard, which provides space for many things while the inside is being rearranged. The roof lifts and can be held to

Table 7-7. Materials List for Wall Dollhouse.

Part	Size
2 ends	9 × 9 × ½
1 back	9 × 31 × ½
1 front	6 × 31 × ½
2 divisions	9 × 9 × ½
1 flap	8 × 31 × ½
1 roof	9 × 31 × ½
1 roof	1 × 31 × ½
1 roof	½ × 31 × ½

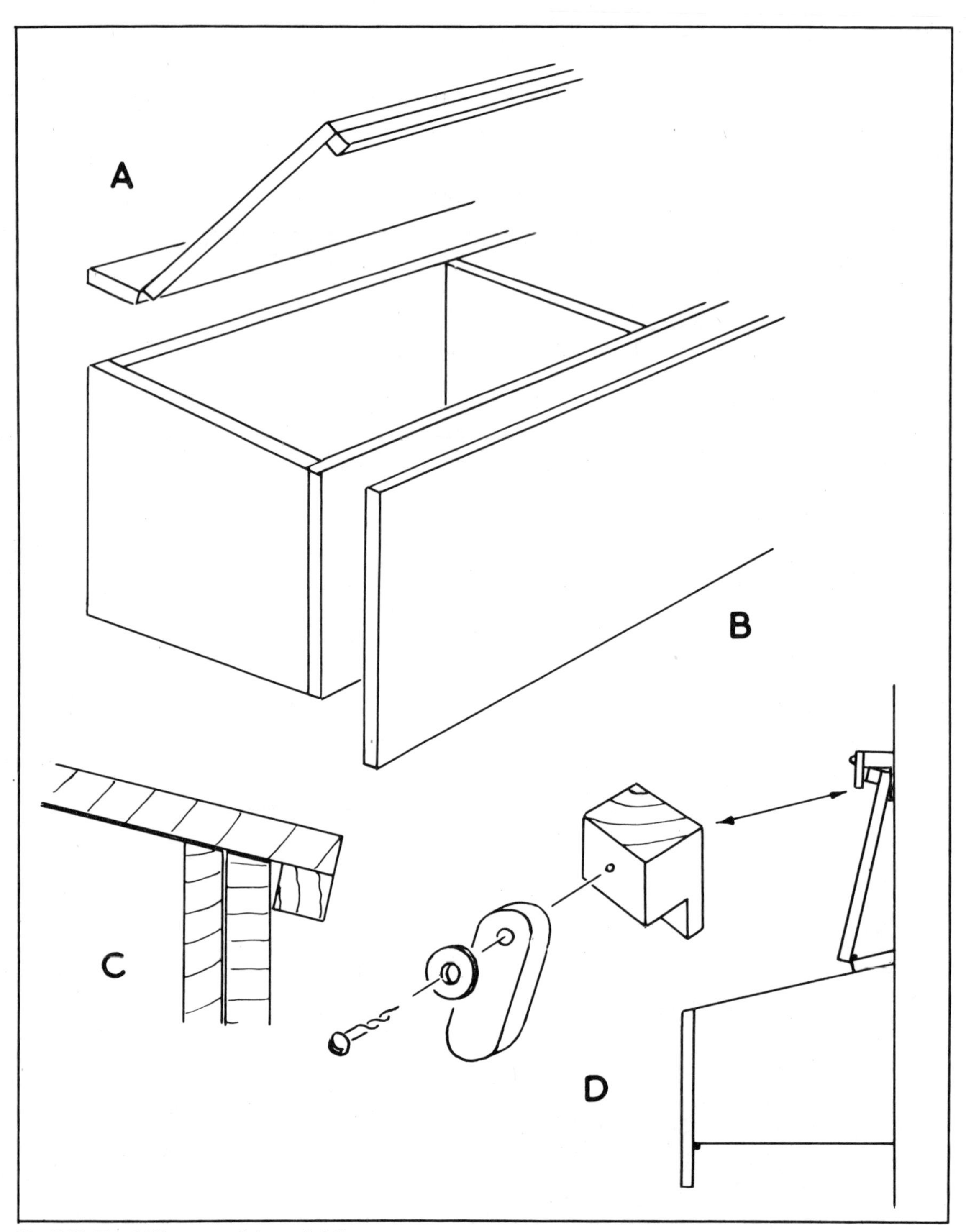

Fig. 7-36. The folding parts of the wall dollhouse.

the wall for access to the inside. When the dollhouse is not being used, the front flap can be swung up and held by the lowered roof (Fig. 7-34).

This construction benefits from plenty of decoration. Door and windows may be bought and fitted together with other fittings and model wallpapers and furniture. You also can make many things and provide effects with paint. A yound child may be just as happy with simple things as with those elaborate things more pleasing to an adult's eyes.

The dollhouse can be made of ½-inch plywood, except that the narrow strips can be solid wood. Assembly may be with glue and nails, although screws are better at the points of greatest load.

The sizes shown (Fig. 7-35A and Table 7-7) will make a house that is large enough to provide plenty of play opportunities, yet not take up too much room. If you use bought doors and windows, get them first and modify sizes to suit.

Set out an end (Fig. 7-35B). Use that as a guide for the shapes of the divisions and the widths of the lengthwise parts. The ends overlap the back, front, and bottom, but the roof overlaps the ends (Fig. 7-36A). Cut the door and window openings, then make up the house.

The flap is a plain rectangle, with its top beveled to match the slope of the roof (Fig. 7-36B). Join it to the bottom with four hinges, so it closes with the top edge level and opens with its extension under the bottom.

Make and fit the narrow part of the roof, then make the main part with a strip over the raised flap

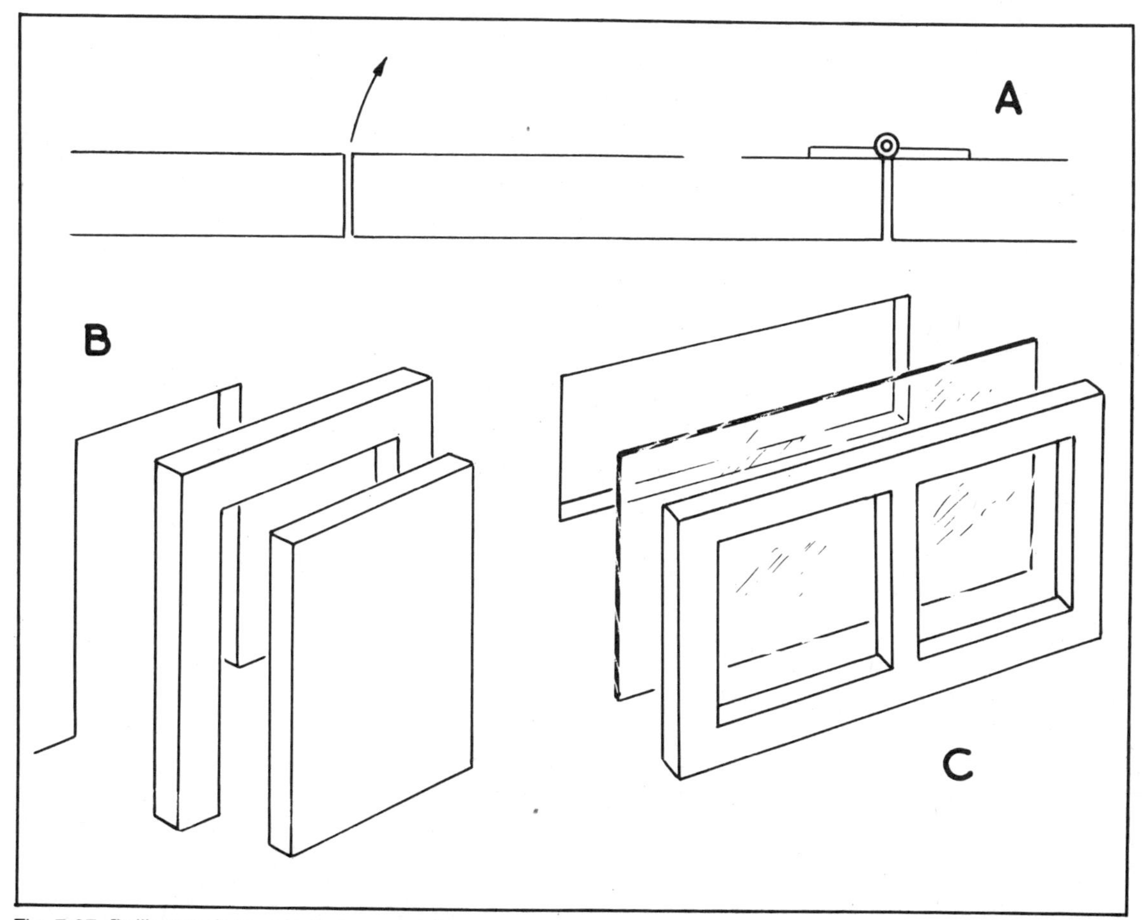

Fig. 7-37. Dollhouse door and window assembly.

(Fig. 7-36C). Hinge the roof parts together. Arrange a catch higher on the wall to hold the raised roof (Fig. 7-36D).

Do not put anything on the face of the house front, as it will prevent the flap from closing completely. The door can be arranged in the thickness with hinges inside (Fig. 7-37A), or there may be an extra frame for it inside (Fig. 7-37B). A window can be a piece of thin transparent plastic held with a frame inside (Fig. 7-37C). The appearance of windowsills and door frames will then be painted in. You can paint shingles or tiles on the roof and siding or bricks on the walls. Inside you can paint the floor and walls.

Chapter 8

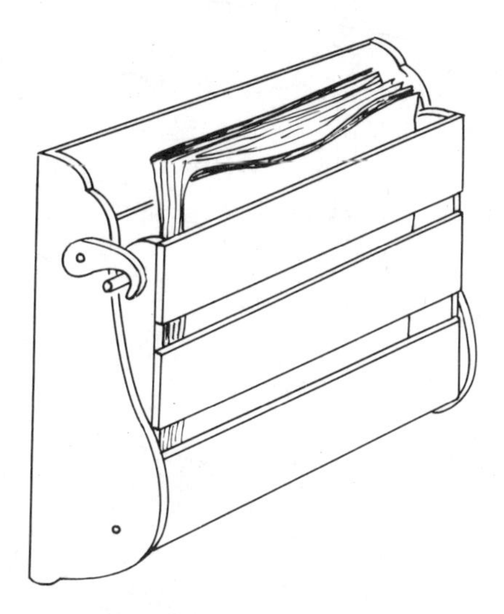

More Advanced Wall-Supported Items

THE DIVIDING LINE BETWEEN SIMPLE AND MORE advanced projects will not be the same for everyone. Much depends on the degree of skill possessed and the available tools and other equipment. The furniture pieces in this chapter all require more skill to make than those items in Chapter 7. Most of the work is only basic tool handling, but some projects have slight complications or some detail that requires more skill or experience. No item is likely to be beyond your capabilities if you work carefully and slowly.

The furniture described in this chapter and the previous one may be regarded as introductory. If you are new to this type of woodwork, you should tackle at least one of these items before moving on to the larger and more completely built-in pieces of furniture.

HANGING RACK WITH TURNED POSTS

If you have a small lathe, you can use it for this project. This hanging rack relies on the turned posts as the main decorative feature. The posts' sizes should be within the capacity of any wood turning lathe. The shelves may be solid wood or veneered plywood or particle board. The sizes should suit many situations, but they can be modified (Figs. 8-1 and 8-2 and Table 8-1). Two supports are provided to screw to the wall. The front corners of the shelves are rounded. If the rack is to go into a corner, that end of each shelf should be left square.

Mark out and shape the shelves. Make the supports that will be glued and screwed under two of them (Fig. 8-3A). All the holes can be ½ inch, except upper and lower posts go into the same hole at the rear corner of the center shelf. For the strongest joint there, one post should fit into the other (Fig. 8-3B). Drill a ¾-inch hole at that position. Round the front edges and the corners of the shelves.

Cut the pieces for the posts slightly too long. Turn one post for each position (Fig. 8-4A and 8-4B). Use a hole drilled in a scrap piece of wood as a gauge for the dowel sizes. Use these turned pieces as patterns for making the other posts. Mark a rod (Fig. 8-4C) as a guide for marking the important spacings. Make one lower post with an over-

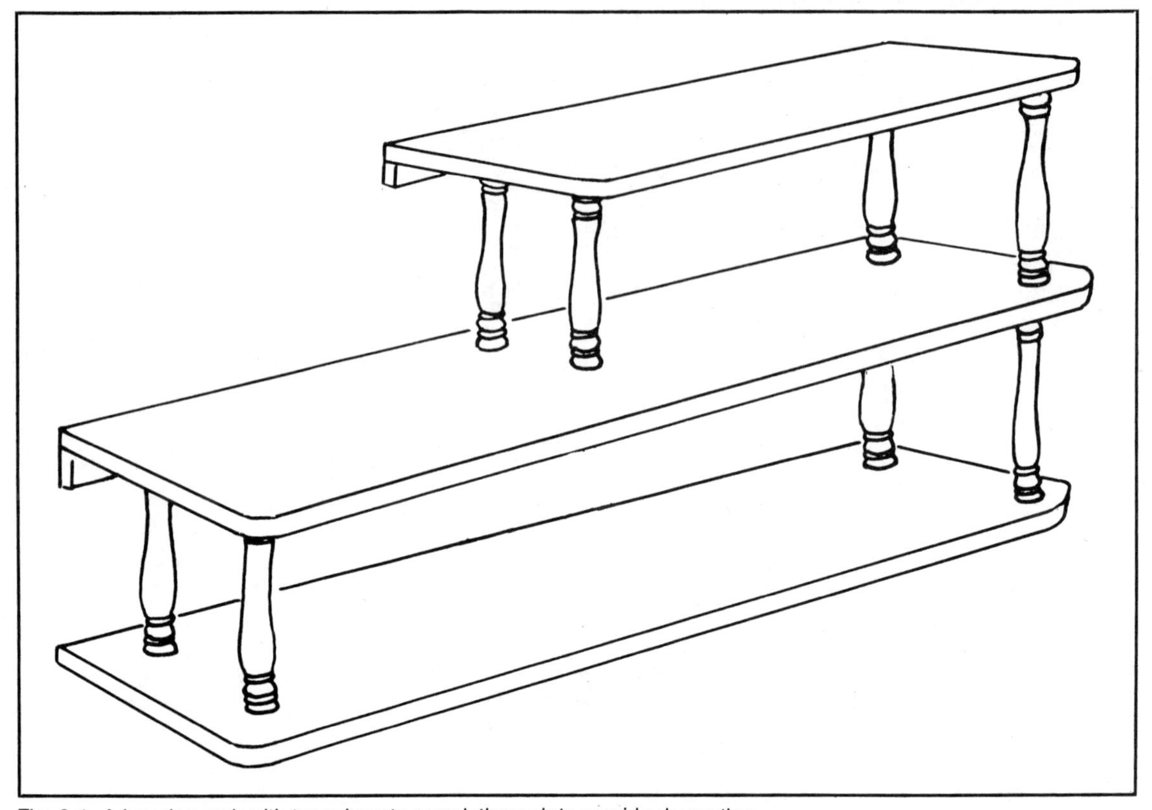

Fig. 8-1. A hanging rack with turned posts uses lathework to provide decoration.

size dowel for the rear corner position. Use the mark from the lathe center as the location for drilling to take the end of the other posts.

The dowel ends may go through and be planed level after gluing. For extra strength, make a saw cut across each end before driving it. Arrange this to be across the direction of grain in the shelf. Drive in a wedge and plane it level (Fig. 8-3C). These exposed post ends may be a decorative feature, but if you don't want them to show, the post dowels can be made shorter to go into blind holes (Fig. 8-3D).

Table 8-1. Materials List for Hanging Rack with Turned Posts.

2 shelves	7 × 31 × 3/4
1 shelf	5 × 21 × 3/4
1 support	1 1/2 × 31 × 1/2
1 support	1 1/2 × 21 × 1/2
4 posts	1 1/4 × 9 × 1 1/4
4 posts	1 1/4 × 7 × 1 1/4

You can wedge them by *foxtail wedging.* Make the saw cuts and use little wedges that will hit the bottoms of the holes and expand the dowels. You have to estimate what size to make each wedge, but this can produce an extremely strong joint.

Be careful to assemble squarely. Make sure all the rear edges will come flat on the wall.

HIGH STORAGE

In most rooms the part of the volume that gets least use is the angle between ceiling and wall. If no furniture goes to ceiling height, that is waste space if you are thinking of storage capacity. High storage projecting from all four walls may have an overpowering effect, so too much should be avoided. There are many places where high storage is welcomed.

In a workshop high racks will take care of short pieces of wood or metal that may otherwise clutter the floor area. In a bedroom you can arrange storage

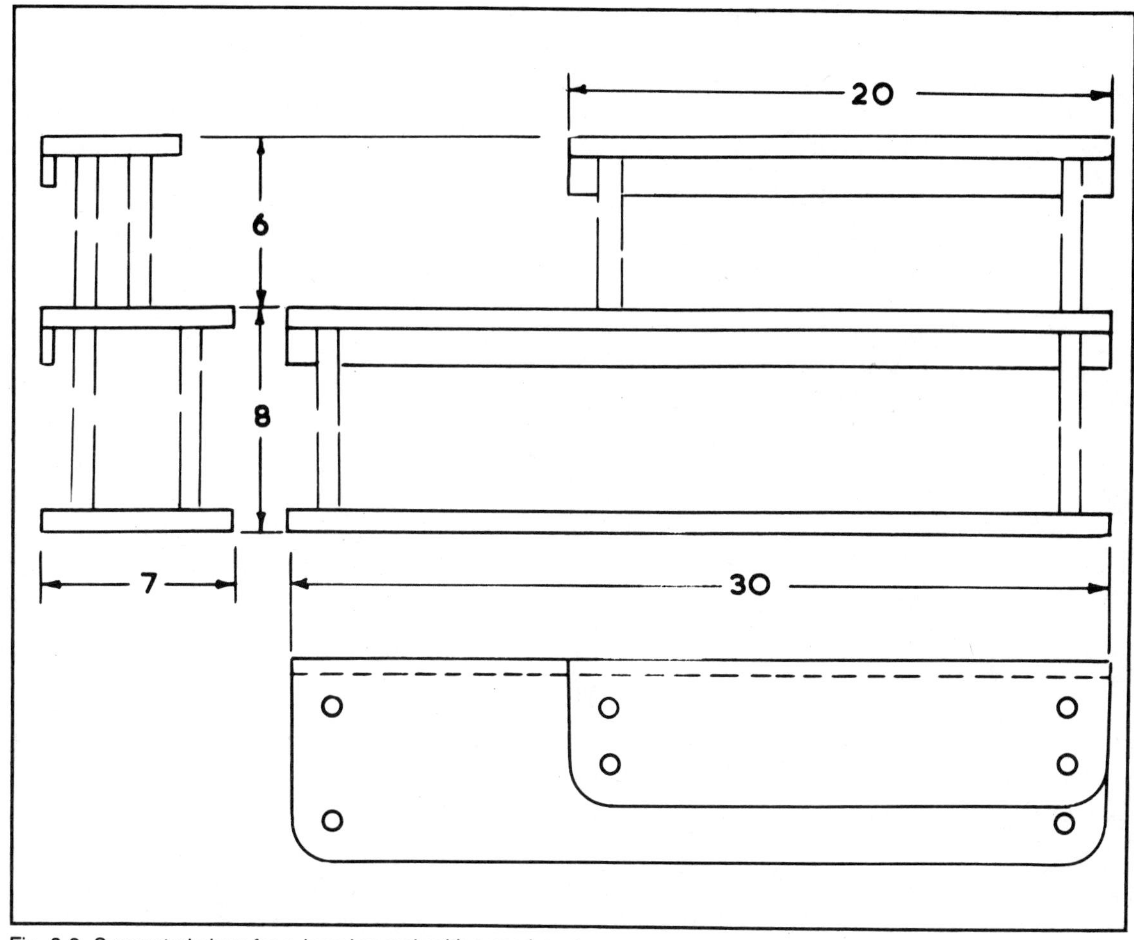

Fig. 8-2. Suggested sizes for a hanging rack with turned posts.

for stacks of clothing and bedding that are rarely used. You will usually need to stand on something to reach the high storage, so do not use this sort of accommodation for things that are used frequently.

The storage can take at least two forms. You can make an open rack (Fig. 8-5) where most of the contents are visible, and this may be best in a shop or den. It makes good storage for sports and games equipment. A closed rack (Fig. 8-6) keeps things out of sight and looks neater. It is more suitable for a living room or bedroom where the finish can match other furniture.

High storage must hang, so all the load is taken by the fasteners and to what they are attached. If you are dealing with a very light structure, it may be unwise to use high storage. In most places you can locate studding and ceiling joists to receive the fastenings.

If you consider the section of a high storage rack (Fig. 8-7A), loads on it try to make it fall and tilt forward (Fig. 8-7B). The greatest strength is needed near the angle between wall and ceiling (Fig. 8-7C). If the rack had enough internal strength, a good fastener there would be the only thing needed. More fasteners upward (Fig. 8-7D) will share the load. Any fasteners into the wall (Fig. 8-7E) may help to resist sliding down the wall. Any tendency of the rack to tilt forces that part back—not out.

For a shop or other place where the rack is

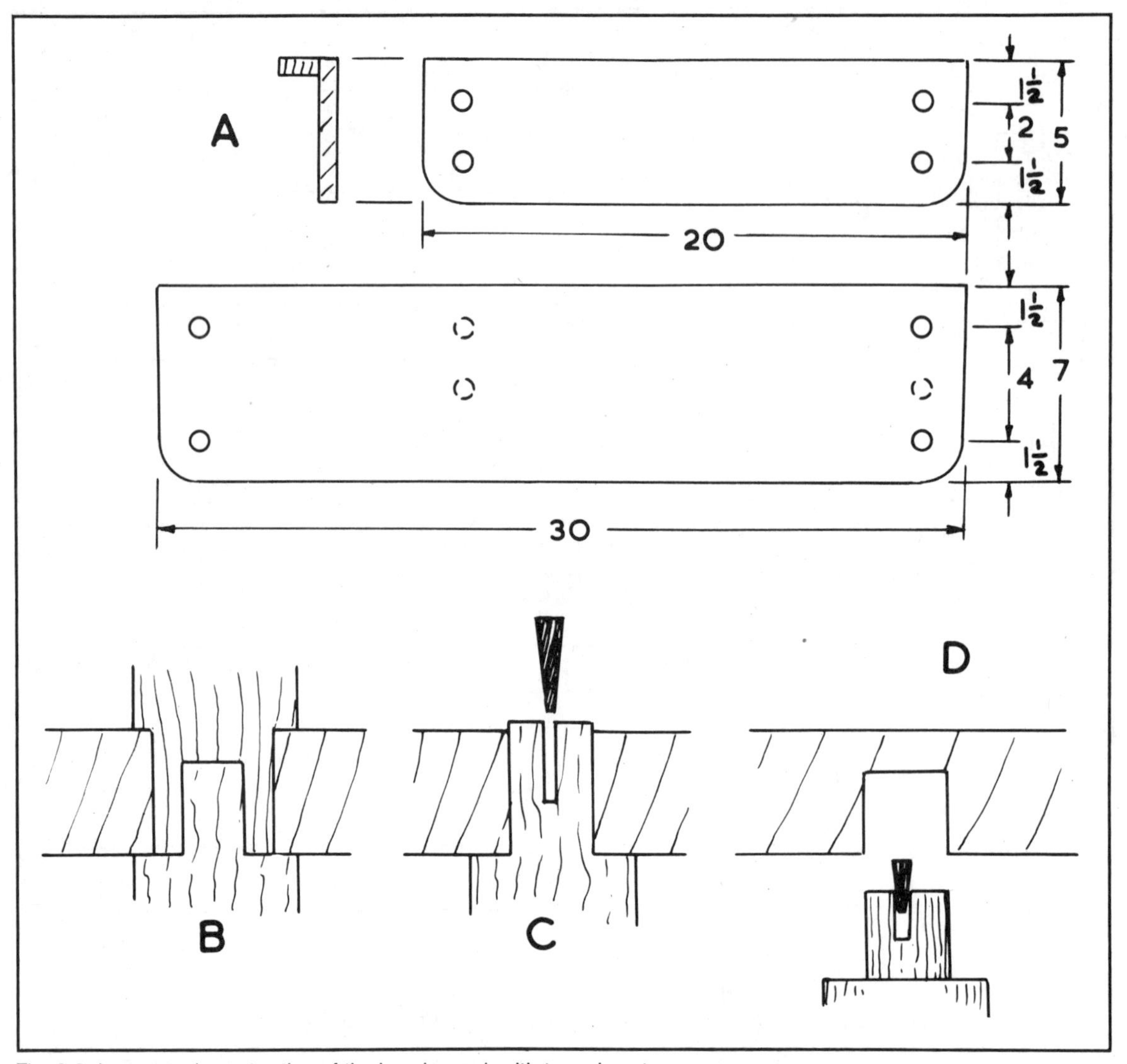

Fig. 8-3. Layout and construction of the hanging rack with turned posts.

functional and appearance is not important, you can make up several frames and arrange strips between them (Fig. 8-8A). Dovetails resist pulling apart (Fig. 8-8B). In the example all the parts are 1-inch-by-2-inch strips, but you can use wider boards for the shelf.

Make up the frames completely and drill them for screws to the wall and ceiling. The battens can be screwed to them, or they may be assembled with cross battens to come against the supports (Fig. 8-8C). It is then possible to lift them off for cleaning.

For similar type storage in a position where it must be better looking, the battens are better made up into a platform first (Fig. 8-9). Halving joints can be used (Fig. 8-10A). Let the lengthwise parts go right through as viewed from below. At the front hide the ends of the crosspieces by cutting them short (Fig. 8-10B). At the ends you can let the long pieces be on top and cut back (Fig. 8-10C). If you must avoid exposing laps at the corners, use mortise and tenon joints (Fig. 8-10D). Round the corners and visible edges of the platform.

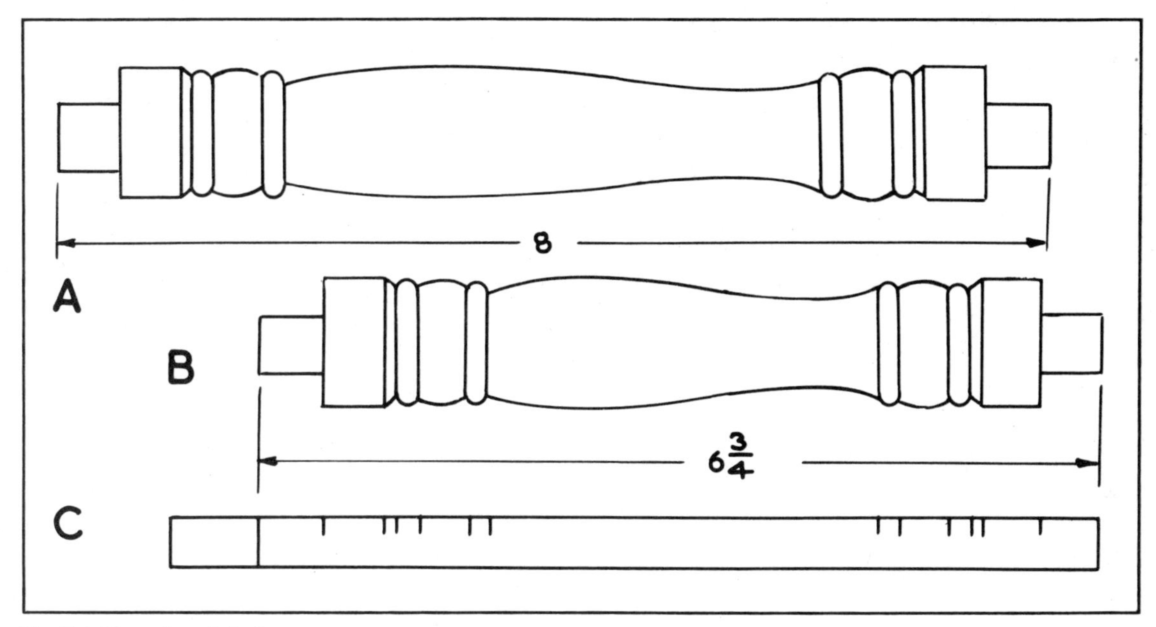

Fig. 8-4. Turned post design.

At the back dovetail the upright supports into the rear piece of the platform (Fig. 8-10E), but at the front it will be better to make the joint on the inside of the front batten (Fig. 8-10F). Carry a top piece across the ceiling with dovetailed ends (Fig. 8-10G).

Sizes and spacings for open racks will depend on circumstances. A rack may extend about 18 inches from the wall, hang down about 15 inches, and need supports at about 30-inch spacing.

Design a cabinet for closed storage so you have a reasonable number of doors. If the doors are to be hinged at their sides, they should not be much wider than they are high. You can't swing a wide shallow

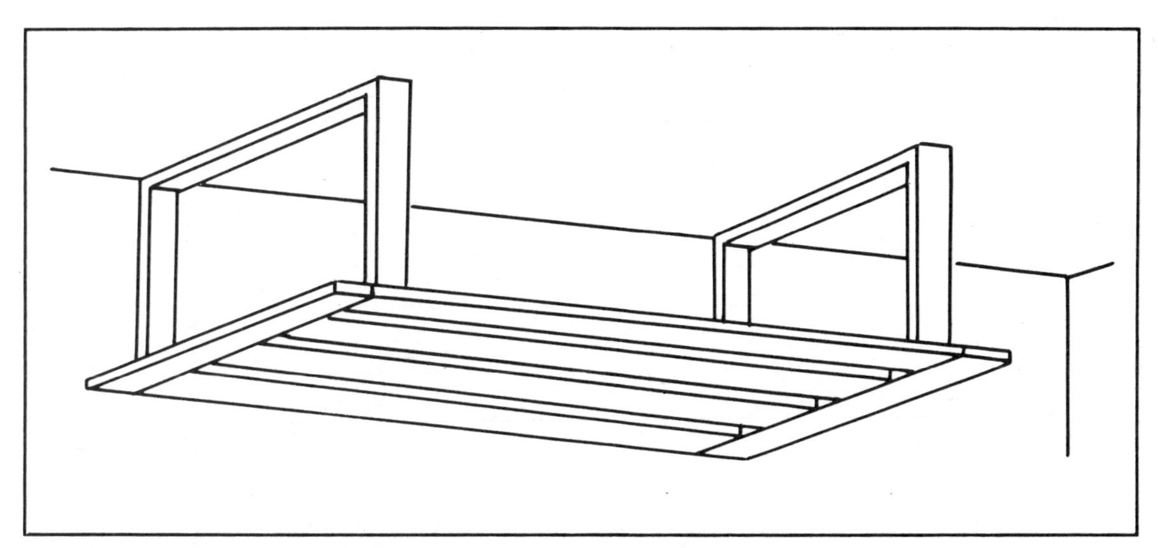

Fig. 8-5. An open high storage rack allows you to see what is put on it.

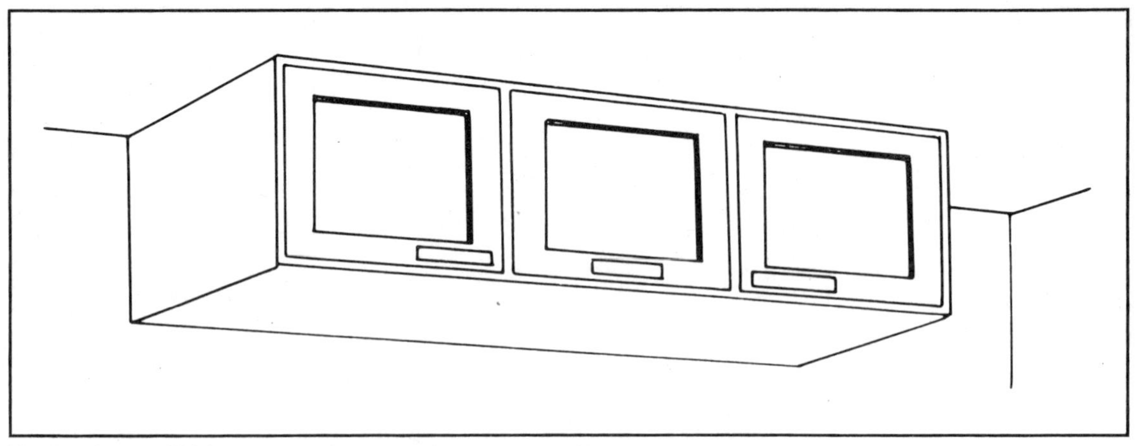
Fig. 8-6. A closed high storage rack protects the contents and has a neat appearance.

door. You can hinge a wide door at the top, so it has to be lifted. Either you hold it open or arrange a catch on the ceiling to hold it up.

The load-bearing supports should be very similar to those for a simple open rack (Fig. 8-8B). Arrange one frame at each end and one at each space between doors, but not more than 30 inches apart. The plywood base is strongly screwed and glued to the frames (Fig. 8-11A). Lengthwise strips go in front of this and against the ceiling (Fig. 8-11B), with more upright strips to bring the front level (Fig. 8-11C) for the doors. Close the ends with plywood. In some situations one end may come against a corner wall. Fasteners into it will provide good resistance to tilting under load.

Many types of doors can be used. For a smaller cabinet you can use single pieces of thick plywood, possibly lipped with strips around the edge to hide the plies. Two pieces of thinner plywood will make an overlapping door (Fig. 8-11D), but they need cranked hinges so the knuckles come outside.

Doors can be framed with thin plywood panels in solid strips (Fig. 8-11E), or you can put thin plywood or hardboard on each side of a solid frame (Fig. 8-11F). If you make a door with a flat surface, its plainness can be covered with half-round molding (Fig. 8-11G). You can use similar molding at the end of the cabinet if there is edge plywood to hide.

If you decide to have one or more lifting doors and do not want to hold them up, you can put a turn button on the ceiling (Fig. 8-11H). It needs to be packed out and angled to suit the door.

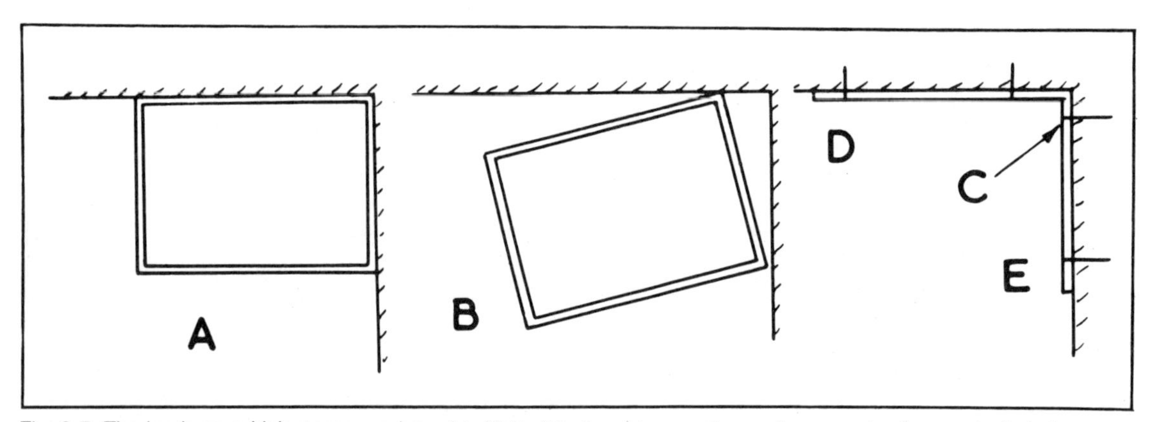

Fig. 8-7. The loads on a high storage rack tend to tilt it. Attachments near the angle are under the greatest strain.

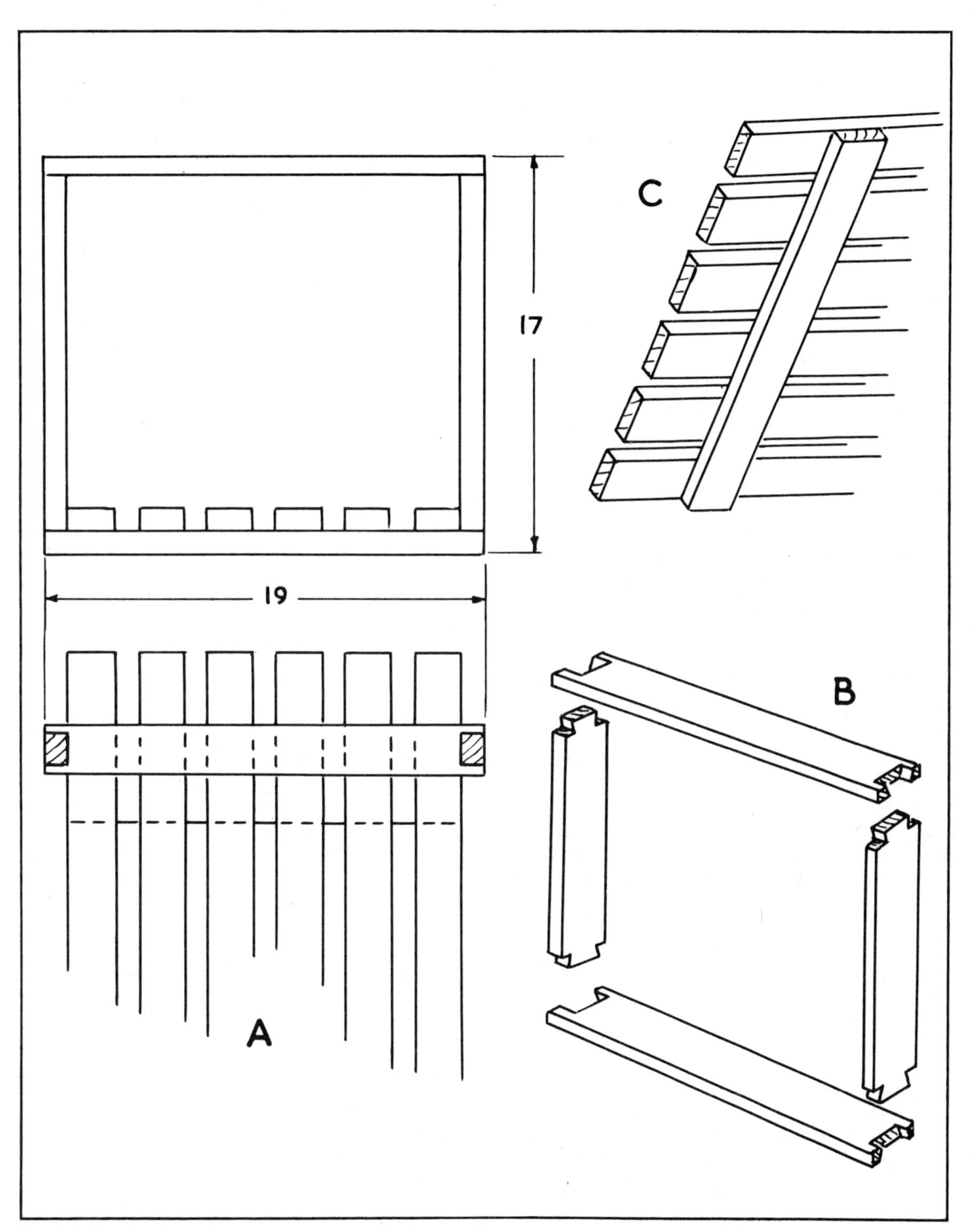

Fig. 8-8. Details of a high open storage rack with open battens.

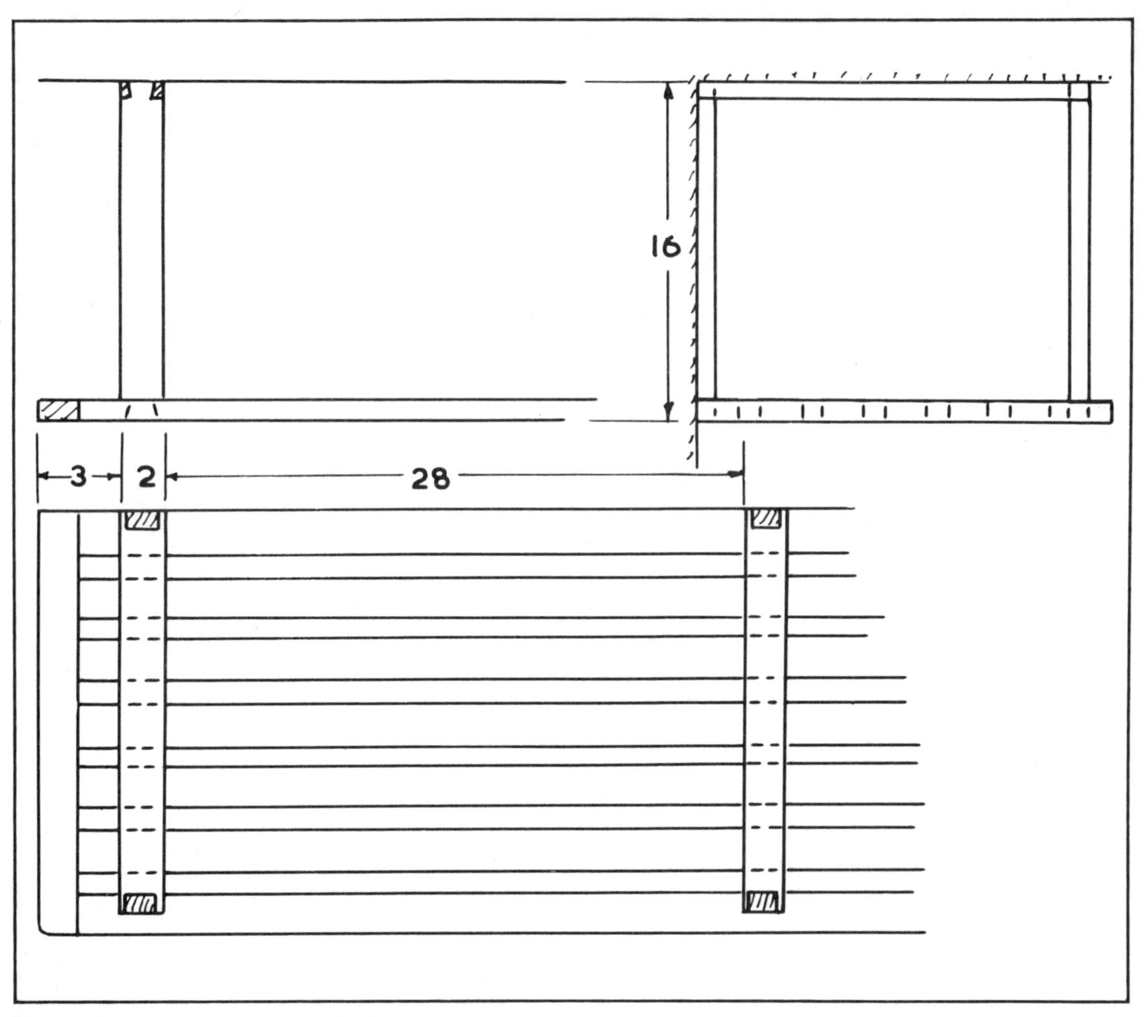

Fig. 8-9. Details of a level open high storage rack.

TILTING MAGAZINE RACK

The usual wall-mounted rack for magazines and loose papers serves a purpose. It suffers from having all the papers packed tightly and vertically. It is difficult to sort out those in the center, and there has to be space above the rack to lift out magazines vertically.

This rack (Fig. 8-12) stores the magazines parallel with the wall, but they can be tilted forward and the tightness of the pack relaxed so you can select something without pulling out anything else. Put the magazines in a container with a hinged back that pivots on screws, but is in a frame attached to the wall where it is kept upright by hooks. The sizes (Fig. 8-13 and Table 8-2) should suit most purposes, but if you have magazines of unusual sizes or want to store special papers, adjust the sizes accordingly. Design starts from the center outward. Allow for the magazine size and a little to spare. Draw the inner container around that and the outside part around that.

Draw a full-size end view (Fig. 8-14A) to get the sizes of the main parts. Make the two inner rack ends from this view. Joint the ends with a block at the bottom and slats across the front (Fig. 8-14B). Its back is in two parts. The lower narrow piece is

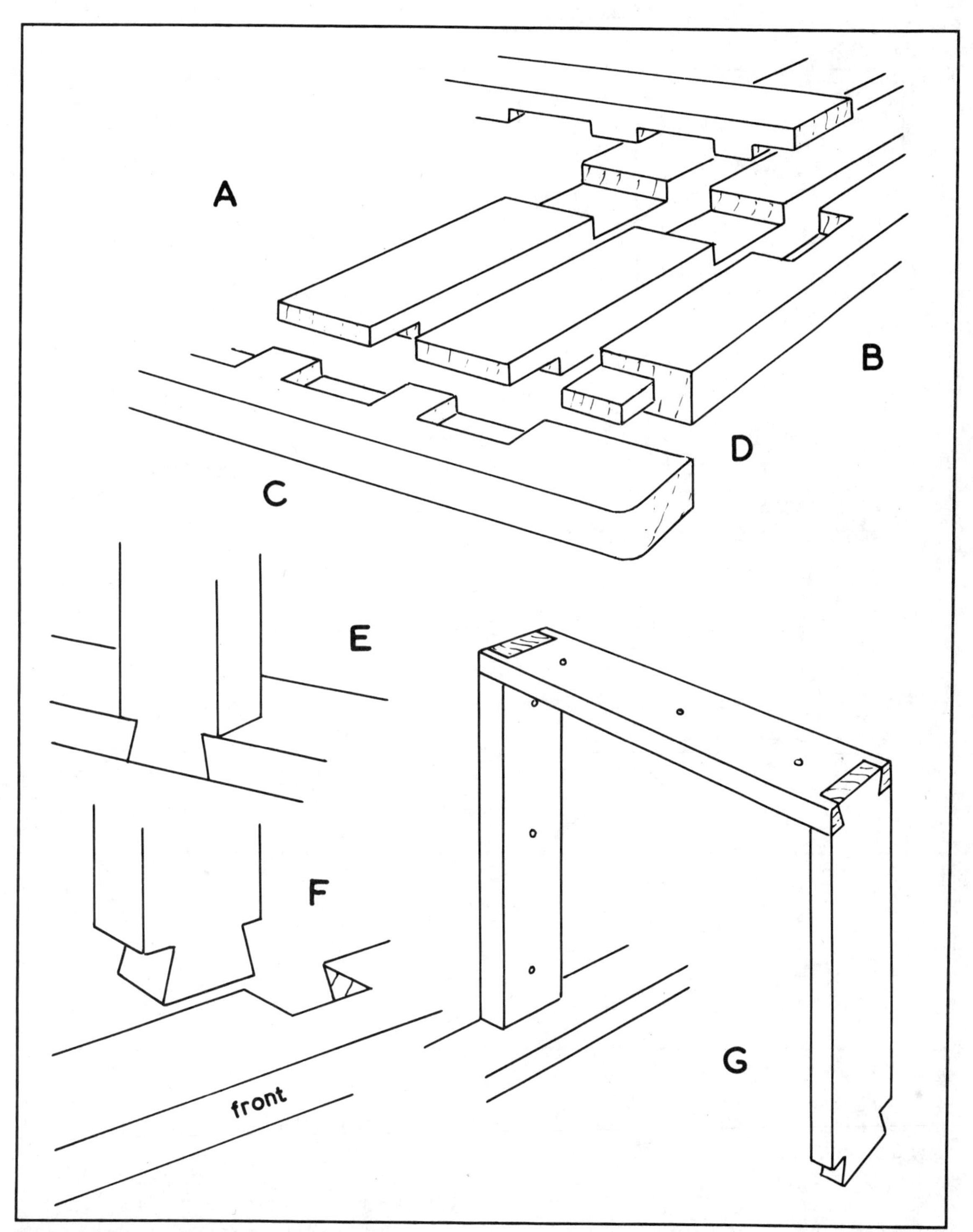

Fig. 8-10. Joints for a level open storage rack.

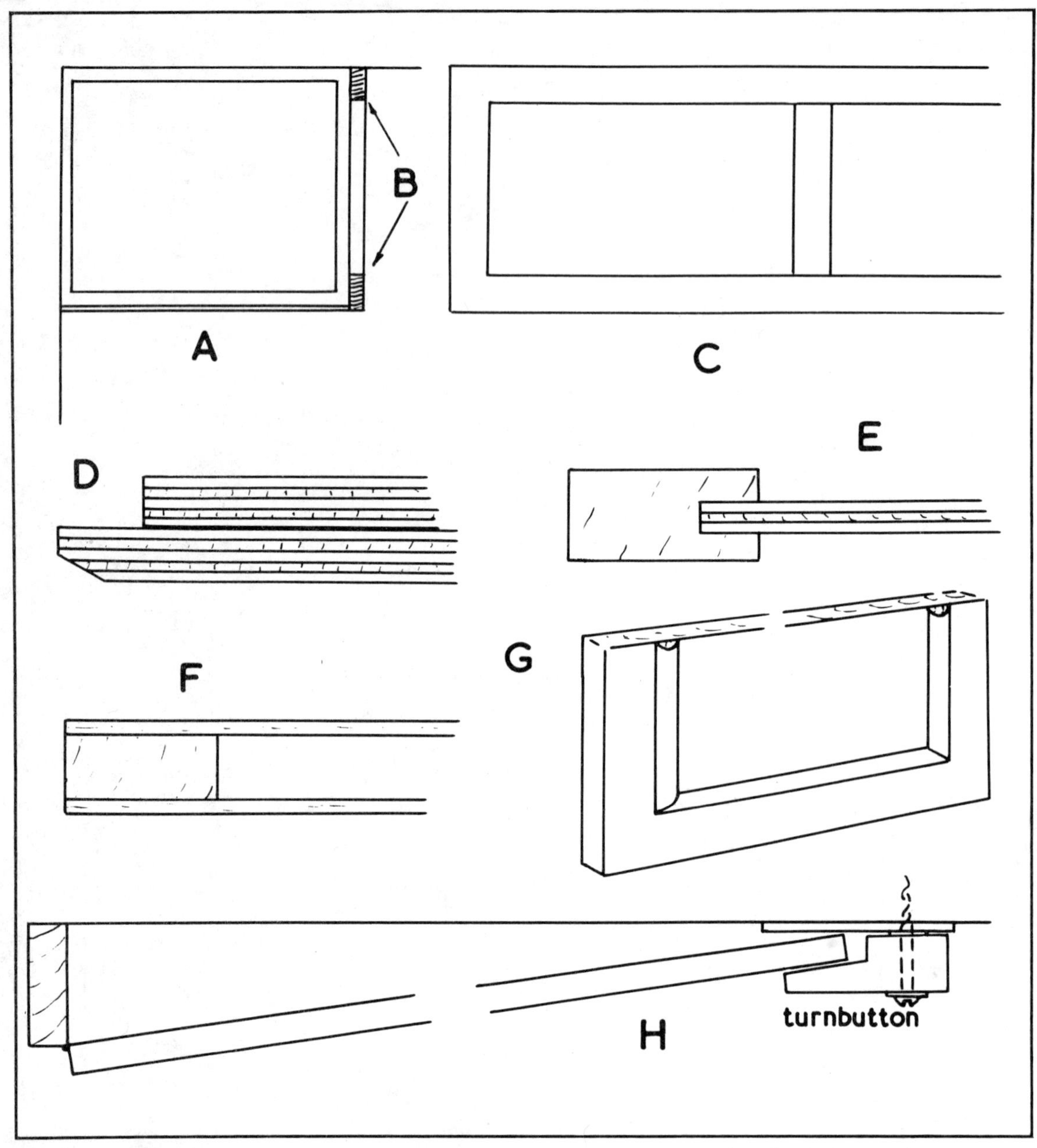

Fig. 8-11. Arrangement of a high closed storage cabinet (A, B, C) and door details (D to G), including a lifting door (H).

attached to the block, but the other piece is hinged to it. You can use small metal hinges, but there will not be much clearance behind. A strip of cloth glued on may be better (Fig. 8-14C). Fit ¼-inch dowels into the ends, projecting far enough to take the hooks. You may prefer to drill the dowel holes and not insert the dowels until the parts are assembled.

Rabbet the outer sides for the back for the best result. Otherwise, screw it on with its edges exposed. Cut the pair of sides to match. They are the

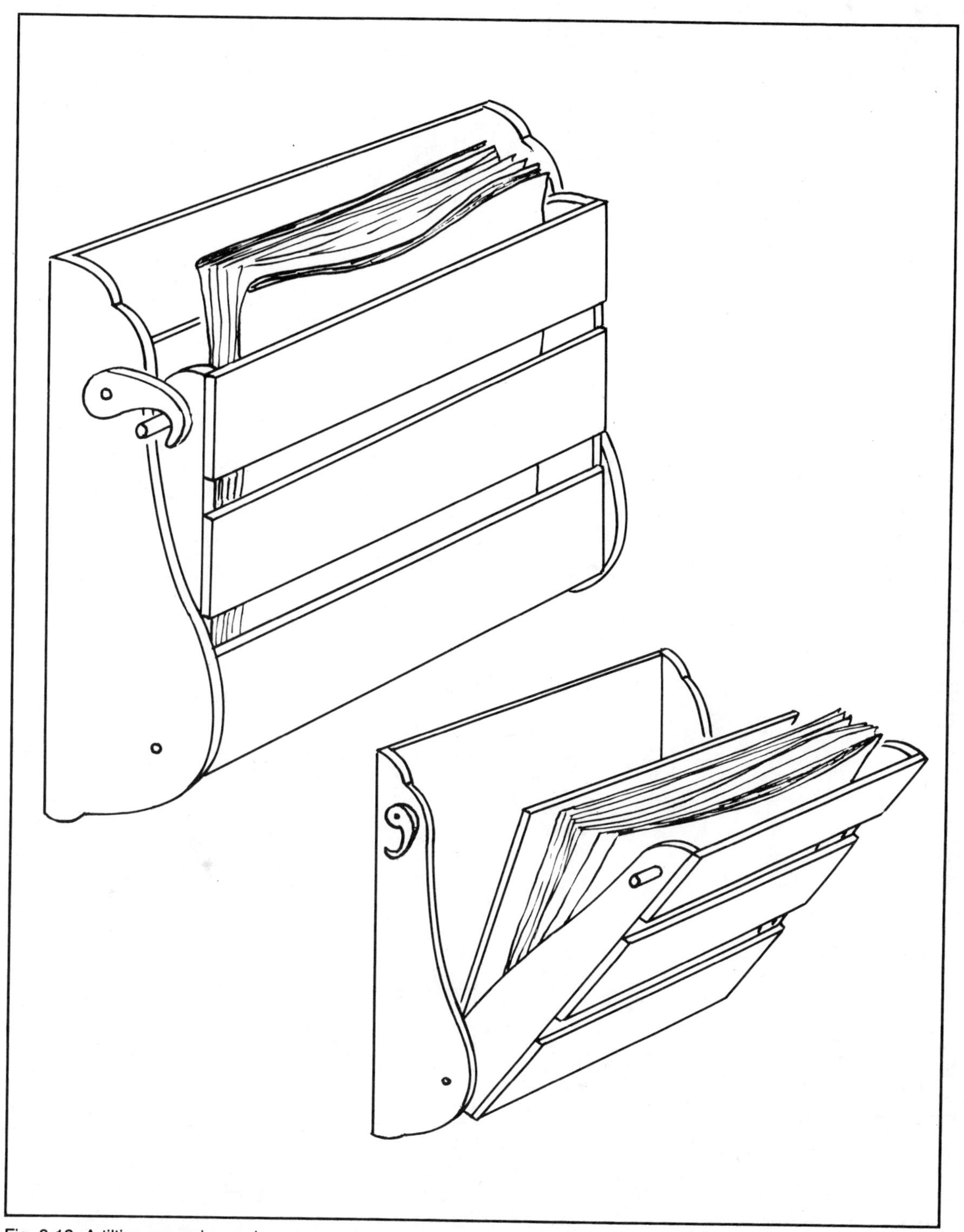

Fig. 8-12. A tilting magazine rack.

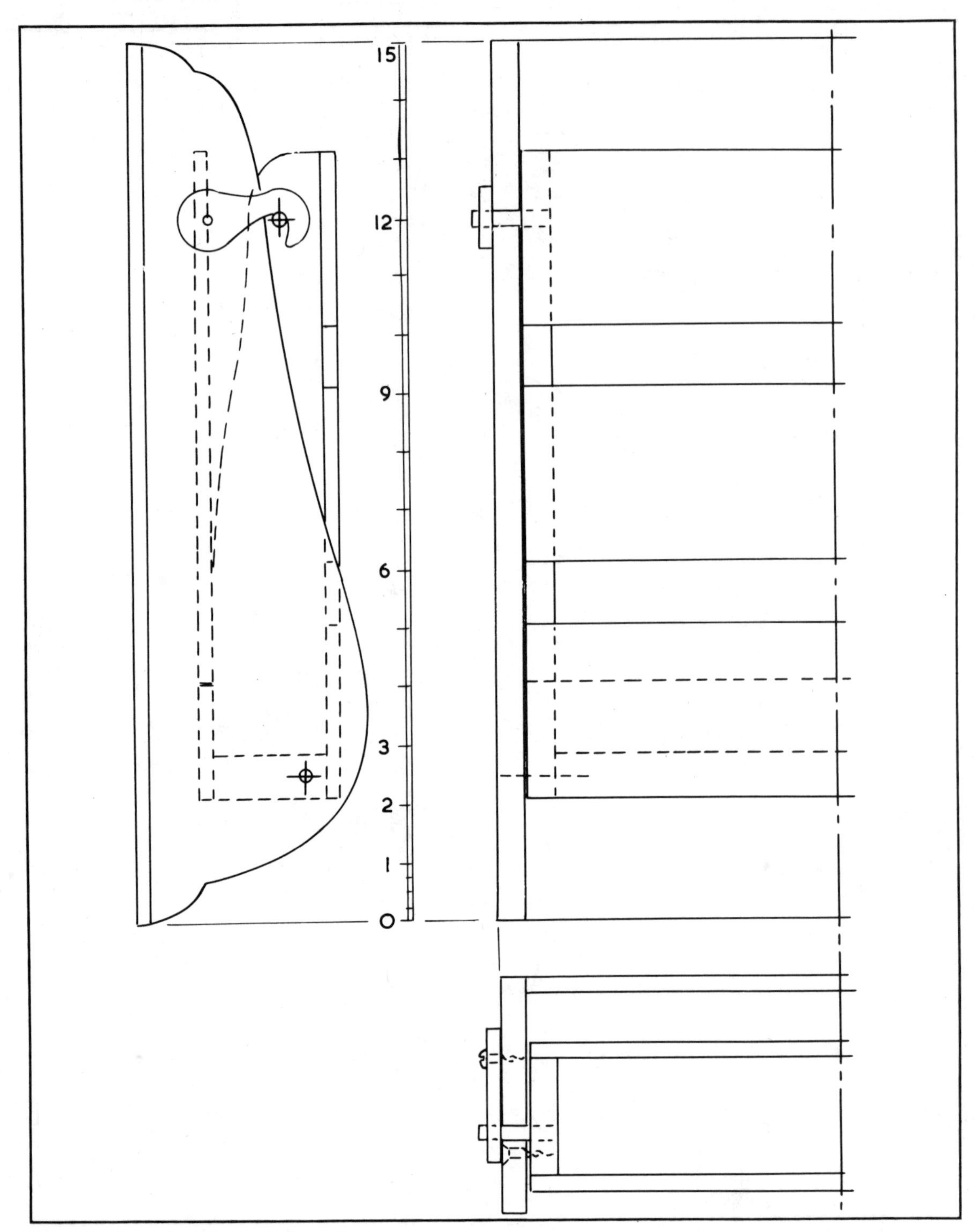

Fig. 8-13. Sizes of a tilting magazine rack.

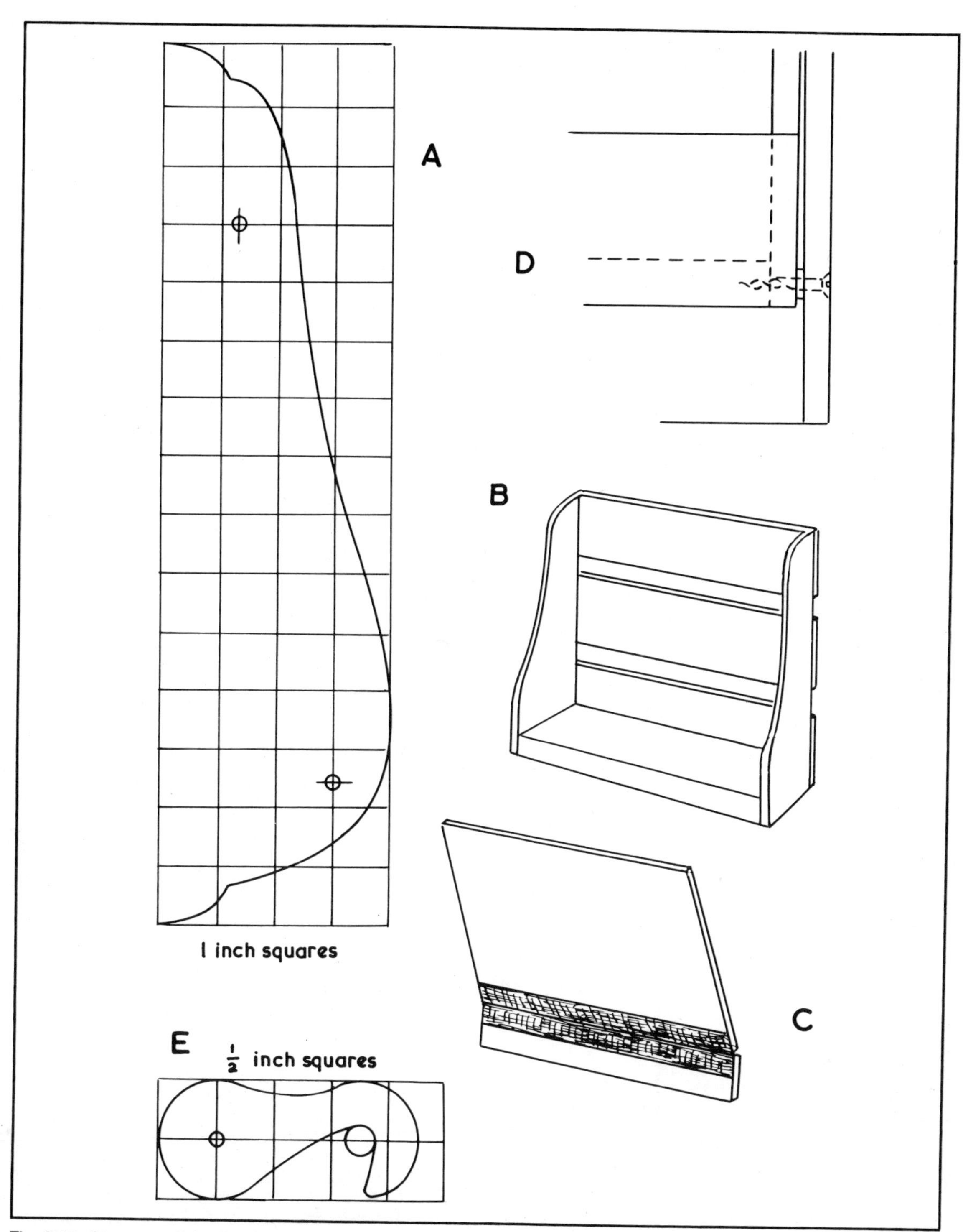

Fig. 8-14. Shapes and details of tilting magazine rack parts.

Table 8-2. Materials List for Tilting Magazine Rack.

2 sides	4 × 16 × ½
1 back	12 × 16 × ¼ plywood
1 rack back	11 × 13 × ¼ plywood
2 rack ends	3 × 11 × ½
1 rack bottom	2 × 11 × ¾
3 rack fronts	3 × 11 × ¼

most prominent parts, so see that they match and their edges have all saw marks removed and are rounded in section.

Keep the width of the outer frame enough to allow the inner rack to swing easily, preferably with washers on the screws (Fig. 8-14D).

The hooks that hold the rack upright can be metal ones engaging with dowels or screw eyes, but those shown (Fig. 8-14E) are cut from ¼-inch solid wood or plywood. Let them swing easily on screws with washers, so they fall upright when disengaged. Round the ends of the dowels and let them project for the hooks to engage.

TILTING BINS

There are storage problems where drawers or cupboards do not quite fill the need. It is useful to be able to remove a container and take it and its contents to where they are needed instead of having to transfer the contents to another container. This may happen in a kitchen where certain foodstuffs can be taken from storage and placed on a table. If

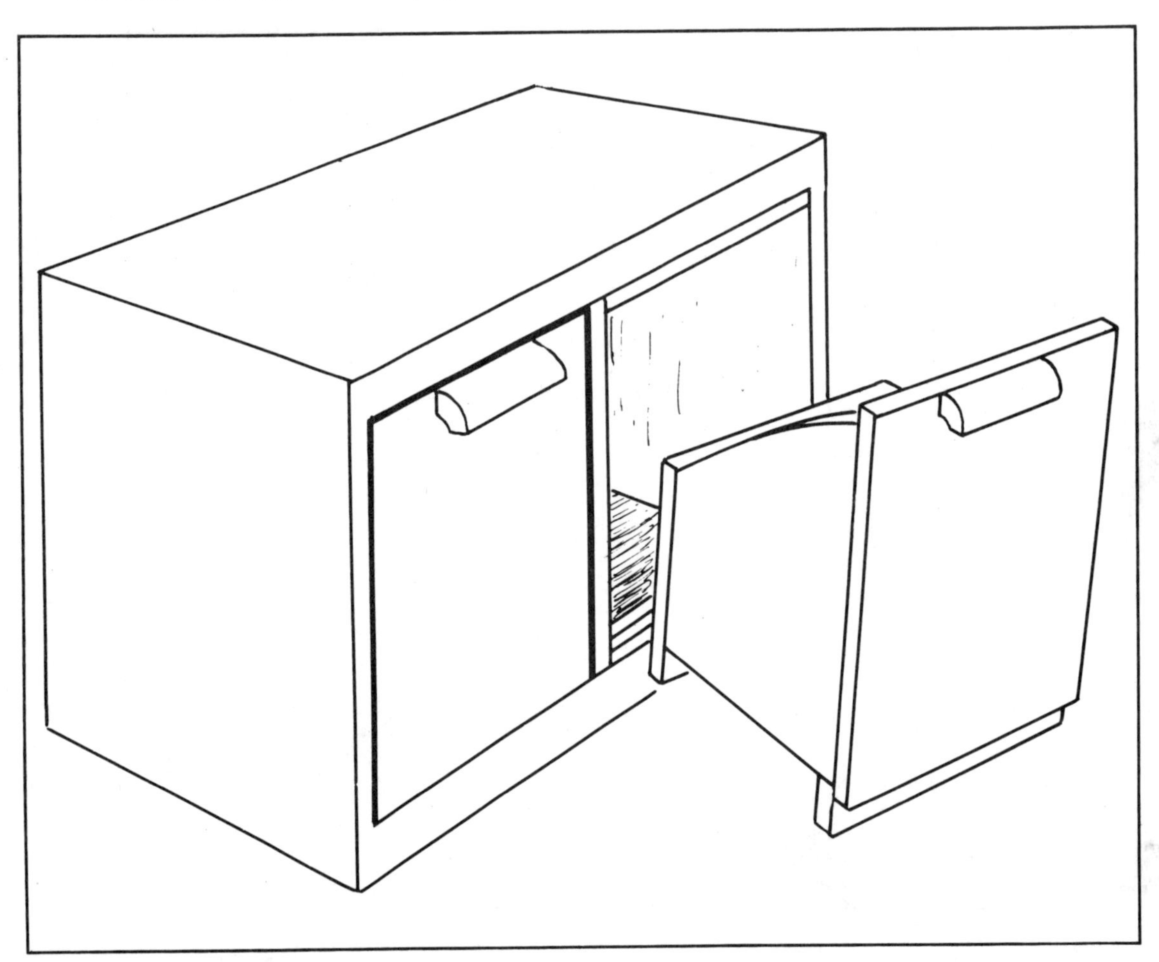

Fig. 8-15. Tilting bins can be arranged to lift out.

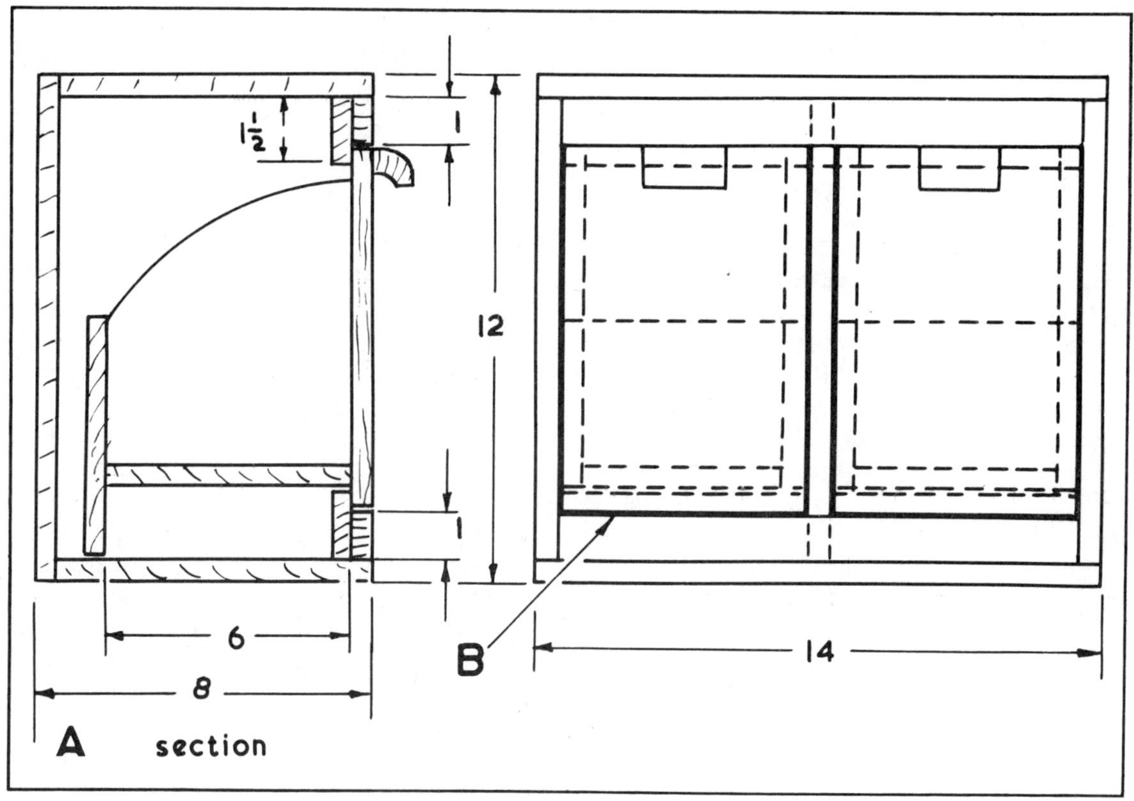

Fig. 8-16. Suggested sizes for a pair of tilting bins.

you keep poultry or animals, their feed can be treated in the same way. It may happen with nails and similar things in your shop. The answer is a storage bin that tilts for access to the inside and can be lifted out and taken away (Fig. 8-15). You can make a single bin, extend the case to take in several alongside each other, or have a second tier, with any number up to a multiple assembly covering a wall. The bins may be any size, but the example is a double case with contents in each bin about 6 inches each way (Fig. 8-16 and Table 8-3).

Table 8-3. Materials List for Tilting Bins.

Part	Size
1 back	12 × 14 × ½
2 ends	8 × 12 × ½
1 top	8 × 14 × ½
1 bottom	8 × 14 × ½
2 fronts	1 × 14 × ½
2 top stops	1½ × 7 × ½
2 bin fronts	7 × 10 × ½
2 bin backs	7 × 7 × ½
4 bin ends	7 × 9 × ½
2 bin bottoms	6 × 7 × ½
2 bin ledges	7 × 1½ × ½
2 handles	¾ × 4 × ¾
1 divider	8 × 12 × ½

The twin bins are purely functional and are intended for use where appearance is not important. If they are to go with other furniture, they can be made more decorative. The back may be extended up and down, so it can be given a curved outline. The parts can be ½-inch plywood, and the joints can be glued and nailed or screwed. Nails set below the surface and stopped will be neat and satisfactory.

The important drawing is the sectional end view (Fig. 8-16A). Draw this full-size on a scrap piece of plywood. Start by drawing the bin. When the bin tilts, it swings on the lower front edge (Fig. 8-16B). Use that as the center for a compass when drawing the top edge of an end. The curve gives you the height of the back. The bin back and the ledge under the bin front should be level to form feet to stand the bin on when it is removed. They do not rest on the inside of the case. Draw the case around the bin. There must be a small amount of clearance between the back of the case and the back of the bin, so the bottom of the bin does not rub as it swings up.

Make the case as a box, with the top and bottom overlapping the ends and the back edges hidden by being enclosed in them. Notch the divider so you can fit the front pieces across (Fig. 8-17A). Fit the top stops inside (Fig. 8-17B). You now have the case squared and ready for the bins. Try to get the sizes the same so the bins will go into either side.

Make the bin fronts an easy fit in their openings. Cut the four bin sides so they come behind the fronts. Have the backs overlapping, but enclose the bottoms (Fig. 8-17C). Round the top edges of the bin backs and ends. Assemble these parts and put ledges under the fronts (Fig. 8-17D). Try the bins in position. They should hang inside, with gravity keeping them in place.

The handles are shown as strips of wood beveled under and located at the tops of the fronts (Fig. 8-17E). When a bin has been drawn forward a short distance, you can put your hand over the top edge to pull it further or lift it completely. An even simpler handle is a pair of ¾-inch finger holes (Fig. 8-17F).

If you do not plan to lift the bin out, but it will serve your purpose by just tilting forward, it can be hinged at the bottom and the ledge omitted (Fig. 8-17G). To prevent the bin swinging too far forward, you can make the bin back higher so it catches against the top stop (Fig. 8-17H).

CORNER CUPBOARD

The corner of a room is the least used part. It is unusual for anyone to walk completely into a corner. Any piece of furniture built into the corner of a room will do less to restrict the room area than furniture built in elsewhere. The example (Fig. 8-18) is a small storage closet that makes use of this otherwise unwanted area. It can serve as storage for medicines, small office items, or valuables. See Table 8-4.

The simplest corner cupboard has a triangular plan (Fig. 8-19A), but that does not provide much useful area. It is better to project squarely from each wall (Fig. 8-19B) before angling across. If the door is to be hinged there, the acute angle makes strong screwing of the hinges difficult (Fig. 8-19C). It is better to include more uprights beside the door (Fig. 8-19D).

The example is set out in this way (Fig. 8-20). The door is paneled, and the design follows a Colonial pattern.

Check the angle of the corner of the room at the position the cupboard will be. It should be square, but it may not be exactly. You may have to cut your wood to match. Draw the top view full-size (Fig. 8-21) to show the widths you have to prepare the upright parts. One side overlaps the other at the rear corner. Prepare the wood for the upright parts slightly too long at this stage. Miter the meeting surfaces at the front. Make the top and bottom with the grain parallel with the front edges. Be careful of breaking out the short grain at the back when planing the edges.

Cut the upright parts to length. Glue the mitered front and sides. The backs may be screwed together and to the sides, as the screwheads will be hidden when the cupboard is in position on the wall.

Check the sizes of the top and bottom on the assembly. Make sure that the door opening will have parallel sides and square corners. Round the exposed edges of the top and bottom. Join them to the other parts with glue and screws, preferably sunk, so there can be stopping to hide their heads.

The door (Fig. 8-22A) is made with the bottom rail wider for the sake of appearance. Plow grooves for the plywood in all four pieces. The joints are mortises and tenons. With ¼-inch plywood in ¾-inch wood, the tenons are the same thickness as the grooves. If a thinner panel is used, keep the tenons ¼ inch thick.

Cut back the tenons and stop them at about half the thickness of the sides (Fig. 8-22B). When you cut the panel, keep it slightly too small to press on the bottoms of the grooves. It will not prevent the corner joints from being pulled tight.

Leave the sides overlong until after the joints

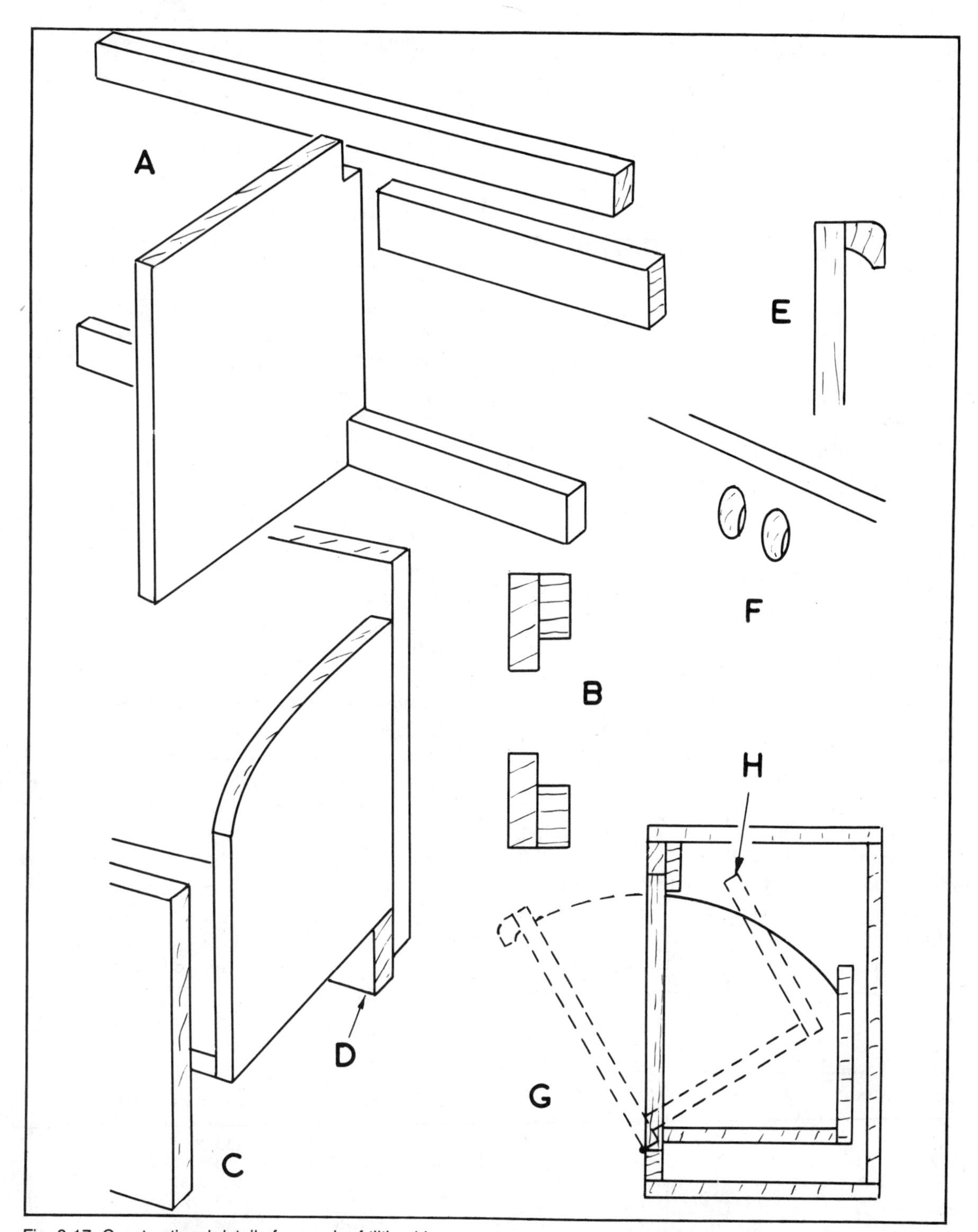

Fig. 8-17. Constructional details for a pair of tilting bins.

Fig. 8-18. A small corner cupboard.

have been glued. Plane the door to fit its opening. Use two hinges—set half into the door and front. There can be a catch at the other side that also acts as a stop. Put small blocks at the top and bottom as stops (Fig. 8-22C).

To complete the Colonial theme, there should be a round knob (Fig. 8-22D). Some other type of handle can be used.

There can be a shelf inside. If it is the full width, it will also act as a doorstop, but it will have to be fitted before the top or bottom. A narrower shelf may pass through the doorway and rest on side supports (Fig. 8-22E).

Table 8-4. Materials List for Corner Cupboard.

2 top and bottom	11 × 18 × 3/4
2 sides	2 1/2 × 20 × 3/4
2 fronts	1 × 20 × 3/4
2 backs	12 × 20 × 1/2
2 door sides	1 1/2 × 20 × 3/4
1 door top	1 1/2 × 10 × 3/4
1 door bottom	2 × 10 × 3/4
1 door panel	8 × 18 × 1/4 plywood

FLAP TABLE

A tabletop or broad shelf that can be swung down when not needed is useful in a confined space. It ideally reduces to a minimum thickness from the wall when folded, yet it must be rigid and of a useful size when opened. Arrange for the supporting bracket to go flat to the wall as the top comes down, and there must be room for it to swing without obstruction as the top is lifted. The tabletop has to be designed wider than its depth from the wall if the bracket is to be central (Figs. 8-23 and 8-24).

The tabletop does not have to be horizontal. If it is, make the bracket a degree or so more than 90° to allow for any slight sag. The top can be given a slope, if it is required as a desk, by making the bracket to the required angle (75° or 80° will probably do).

Suggested sizes are given (Figs. 8-23, 8-24, and Table 8-5). If they are modified, allow for a top length near twice its width. If the top is to be longer or extra strength is desirable, have two brackets arranged near the ends, but with enough space to fold inward (Fig. 8-25A). In the design shown there is a strip under the back for screwing to the wall (Fig. 8-25B) and a total folded depth of about 4 inches. This can be reduced by having the strip above the back piece (Fig. 8-25C), then the bracket can be hinged on its other edge to fold against the wall (Fig. 8-25D).

It will help in making the flap table as drawn to set out a side view full-size (Fig. 8-26A). Notice

Table 8-5. Materials List for Flap Table.

1 top	15 × 37 × 1
1 back	3 × 37 × 1
1 strip	2 × 37 × 1
1 support	2 × 20 × 1
3 brackets	2 × 21 × 1

that the bracket is kept a short distance down from the top so it will clear the hinge knuckles as it swings. It then engages with a block of a matching thickness in the open position.

The tabletop may be solid wood, solid-core plywood, or particle board. If you want to guard against warping, there can be battens across under the ends arranged far enough out to clear the bracket. In a table with two brackets the battens will also act as stops for the opened brackets.

Have the back the same thickness as the top and screw the wall strip to it. The number of hinges depends on the stiffness of the top; two may be enough. They can be butt hinges, but T hinges are stronger (Fig. 8-26B).

The support on which the bracket pivots need not be joined to the wall strip, providing both parts are securely attached to the wall. The support is shown taken just below the bracket, but it can reach the floor.

Join the main parts of the bracket with a bridle or open mortise and tenon joint (Fig. 8-26C). Besides glue, put dowels or screws through the parts, as this is the corner that takes the most load.

Mark the diagonal and its joints against each bracket side. Cut notches and screw through the joints (Fig. 8-26D). Round all exposed corners and edges. Attach the bracket to its support with two hinges.

You should mount the table on the wall in its final position before putting a packing under the top where the opened bracket will come. You then can

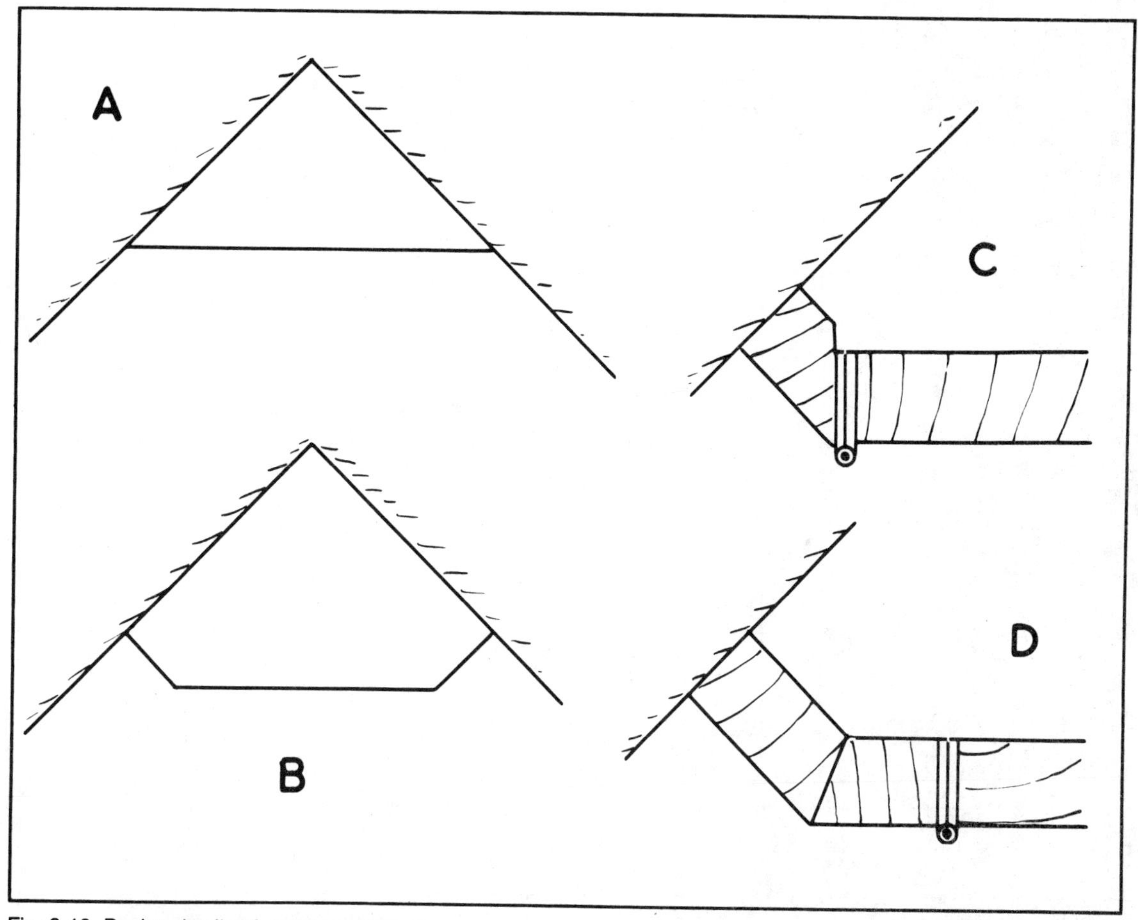

Fig. 8-19. Design details of corner cupboards.

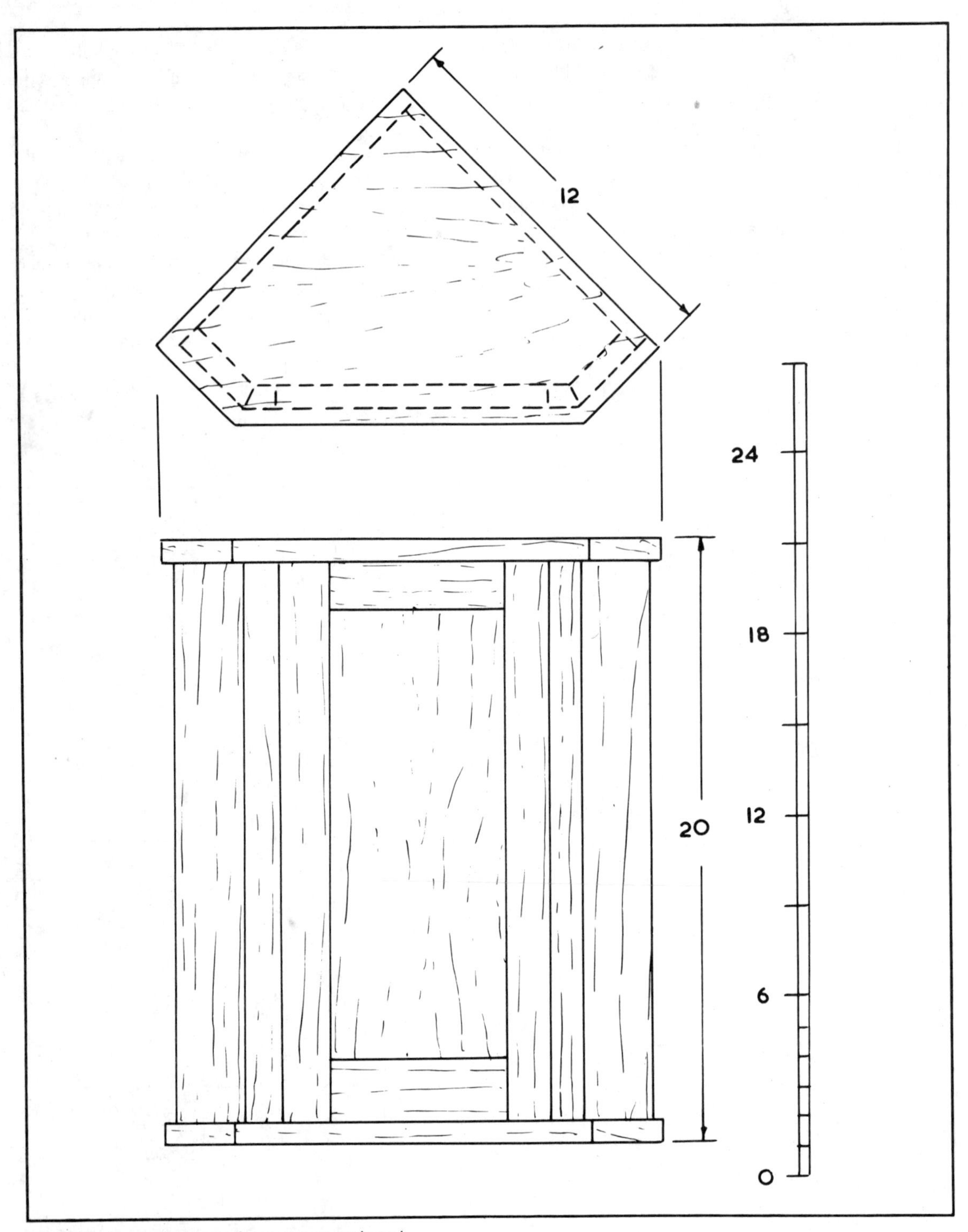

Fig. 8-20. Suggested sizes for a corner cupboard.

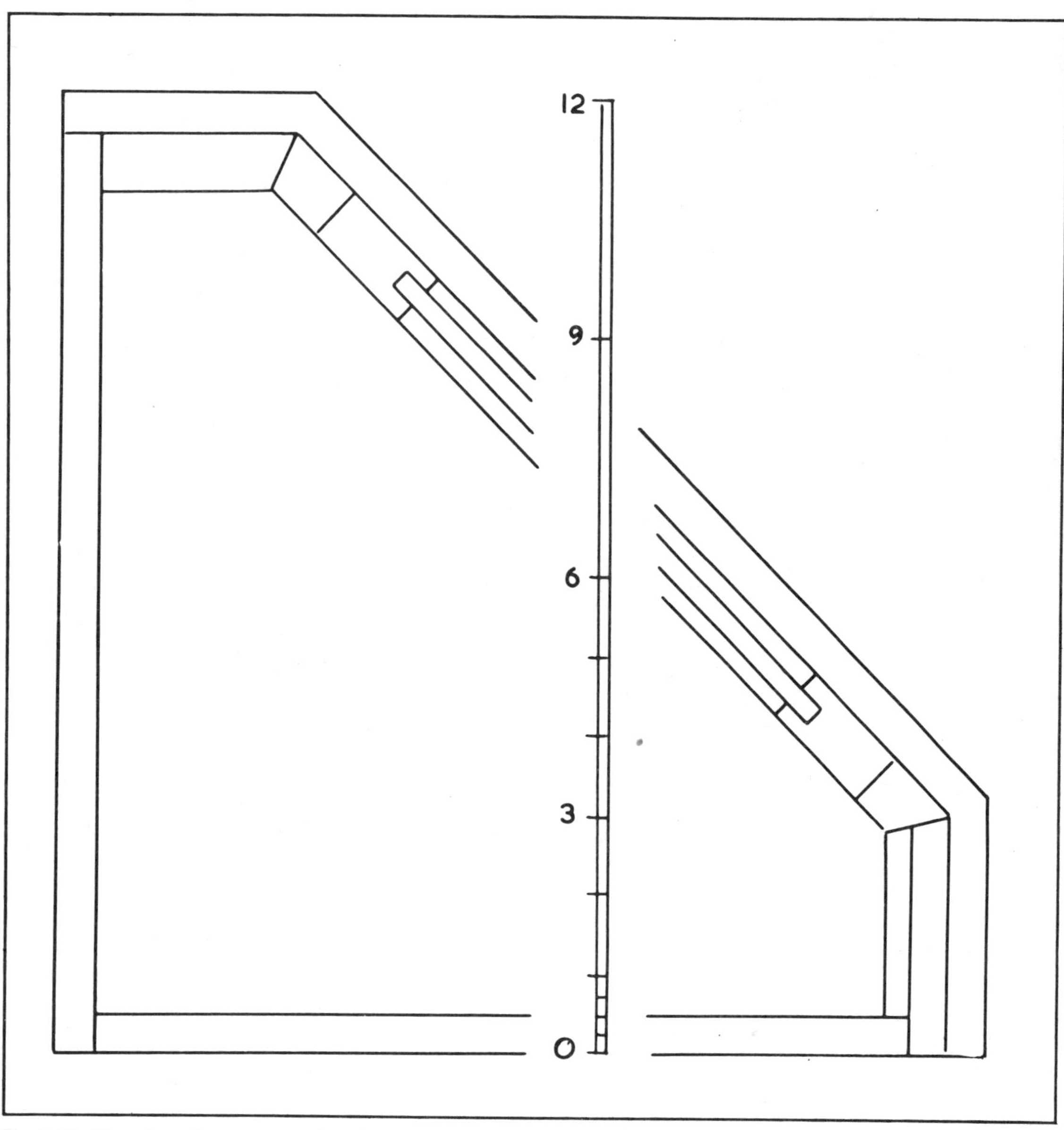

Fig. 8-21. Plan view of a corner cupboard.

measure the exact thickness needed to bring the top level. Make a packing with a flat area and a taper leading up to it, then a stop to prevent the bracket from going too far (Fig. 8-26E). Do not make the stop very thick, or it may hit the bracket support when down if you are making a table that folds to minimum thickness.

FOLD-FLAT SEAT AND TABLE

Furniture that will fold flat against a wall when not needed is attractive, but there are design limitations due to the folding problems. If the supporting leg is to fold under the top when that is hanging downward, the extension from the wall must be little more than the height. You cannot plan a long

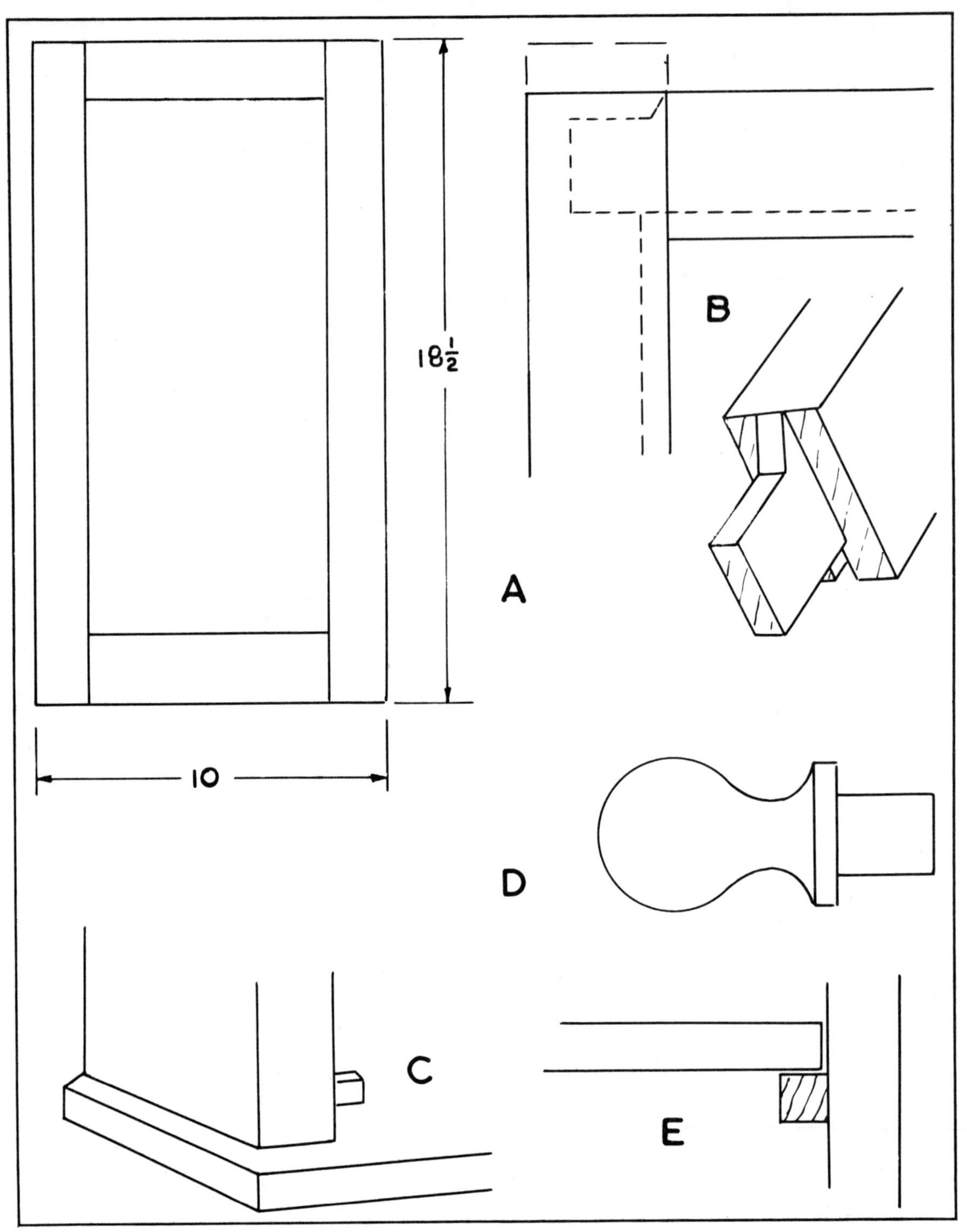

Fig. 8-22. Door details (A, B), a doorstop (C), a handle (D), and a shelf (E) for the corner cupboard.

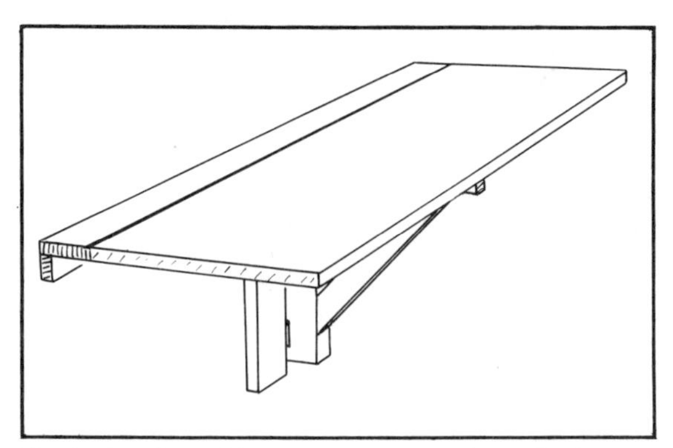

Fig. 8-23. A flap table can hang close to the wall when not being used.

seat or table, and a seat cannot be made to extend as far as the higher table. If these restrictions are accepted, you can make simple seats and tables attached to a wall that do not project more than 2 inches when folded. This makes them suitable for occasional use indoors, or they may be useful on a patio or at a place where someone has to sit and collect tickets or otherwise check passersby.

The table is square, and the seat projects far enough for one person (Fig. 8-27). In both cases the leg folds under and up as the top folds down. See Table 8-6 and 8-7.

The seat (Fig. 8-28A) has a solid top, although it and the leg can be framed plywood. The thickness of the top is necessary to add to the leg length in the erected position and allow for the leg going underneath (Fig. 8-28B). The block behind the top should be thick enough to give clearance to the folded leg, but there is no need for more than that.

Three screws into the wall should be enough; the screws can be counterbored if that results in a better grip (Fig. 8-28C). The screws for the hinges have to go into the end grain of the seat. To improve their grip, put dowels into holes drilled in the underside (Fig. 8-28D).

Arrange the leg to be flush with the edge at the outer end of the seat (Fig. 8-28E). If the seat parts are to fold, there is no room for a strut or other means of holding the leg upright. A folding strut can be put on the outer edges opposite to the usual way of sitting, though, if that will not be in the way. You can put some thin pieces of wood on the floor for the leg to fit between. With careful use, the leg should stay upright without assistance. Another way of keeping it upright is to use a flush bolt like that sold for sliding doors (Fig. 8-28F). Make a hole in the floor for this to engage with when the leg is down.

The table folds in a similar way to the seat. The parts are arranged in the same way in the folded side view (Fig. 8-29A), but the top is made of ½-inch plywood with stiffening. The leg is built up in a T shape. To get your sizes, lay out the underside of the tabletop (Fig. 8-29B).

Table 8-6. Materials List for Fold-Flat Seat.

1 top	7 × 15 × 1
1 leg	7 × 15 × 1
1 block	1¼ × 8 × 1¼

Table 8-7. Materials List for Fold-Flat Table.

1 top	30 × 30 × ½ plywood
1 top framing	3 × 26 × ½
2 top framing	3 × 30 × ½
1 leg top	3 × 12 × 1
1 leg	7 × 30 × 1
1 block	1¼ × 31 × 1¼

Square the piece of plywood and round the outer corners. Attach one ½-inch strip across the back to take the hinges, then the other three pieces with the further one level with the outer edge (Fig. 8-29C).

The leg is shown with a tape from the cross member (Fig. 8-29D). Dowels will probably not be strong enough in this joint. Use tenons (Fig. 8-29E), or you can halve and screw as well as glue the parts (Fig. 8-29F).

Hinge the parts in a similar way to the seat, strengthening with dowels along the rear table edge, if necessary. Three or four 3-inch hinges will be needed there, but two should be enough on the leg. Arrange a bolt or retaining strips for keeping the leg upright, as suggested for the seat.

ADD-ON DRAWERS

Where there is already a shelf or tabletop built in, it is often convenient to add one or more drawers

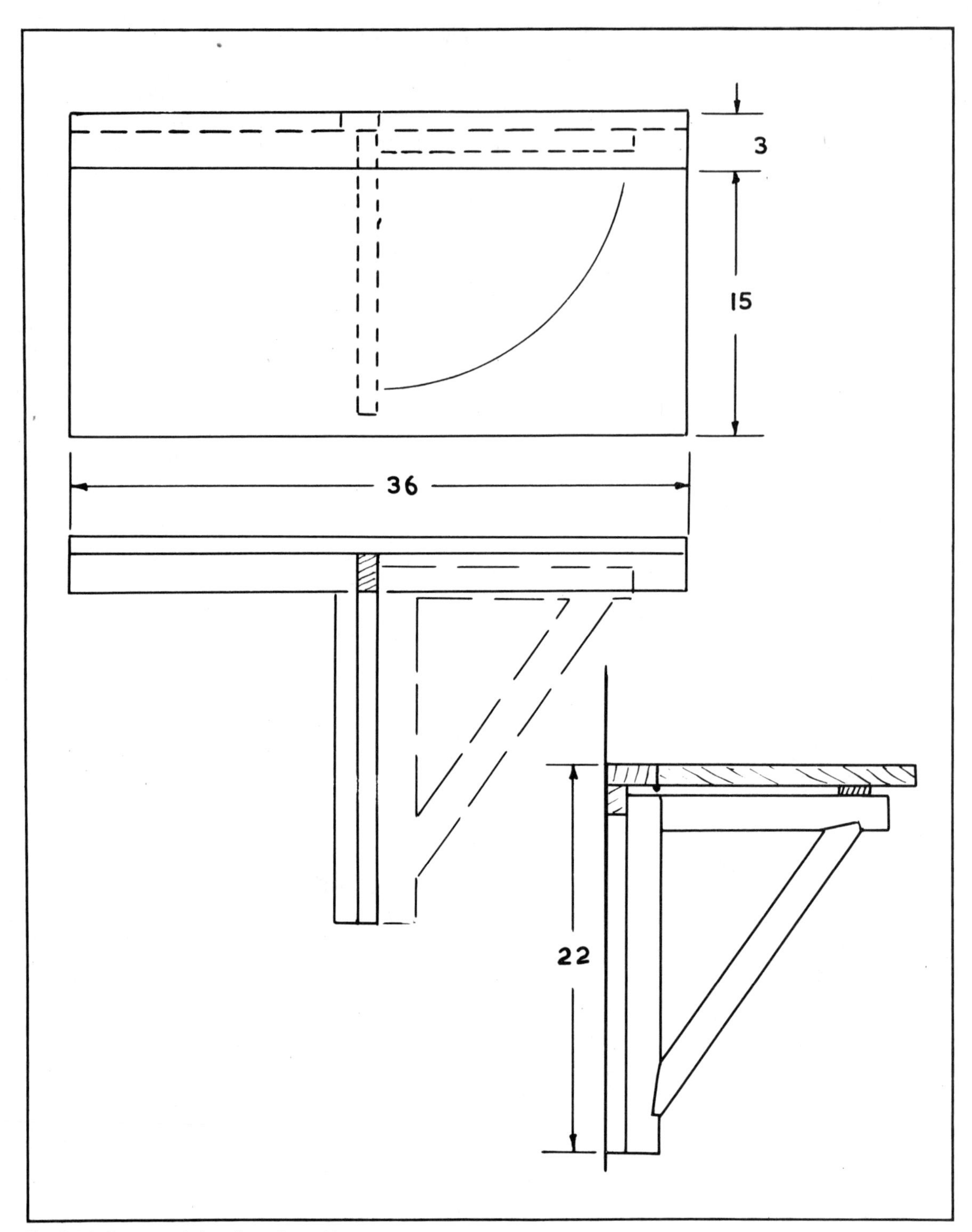

Fig. 8-24. Suggested sizes for a flap table.

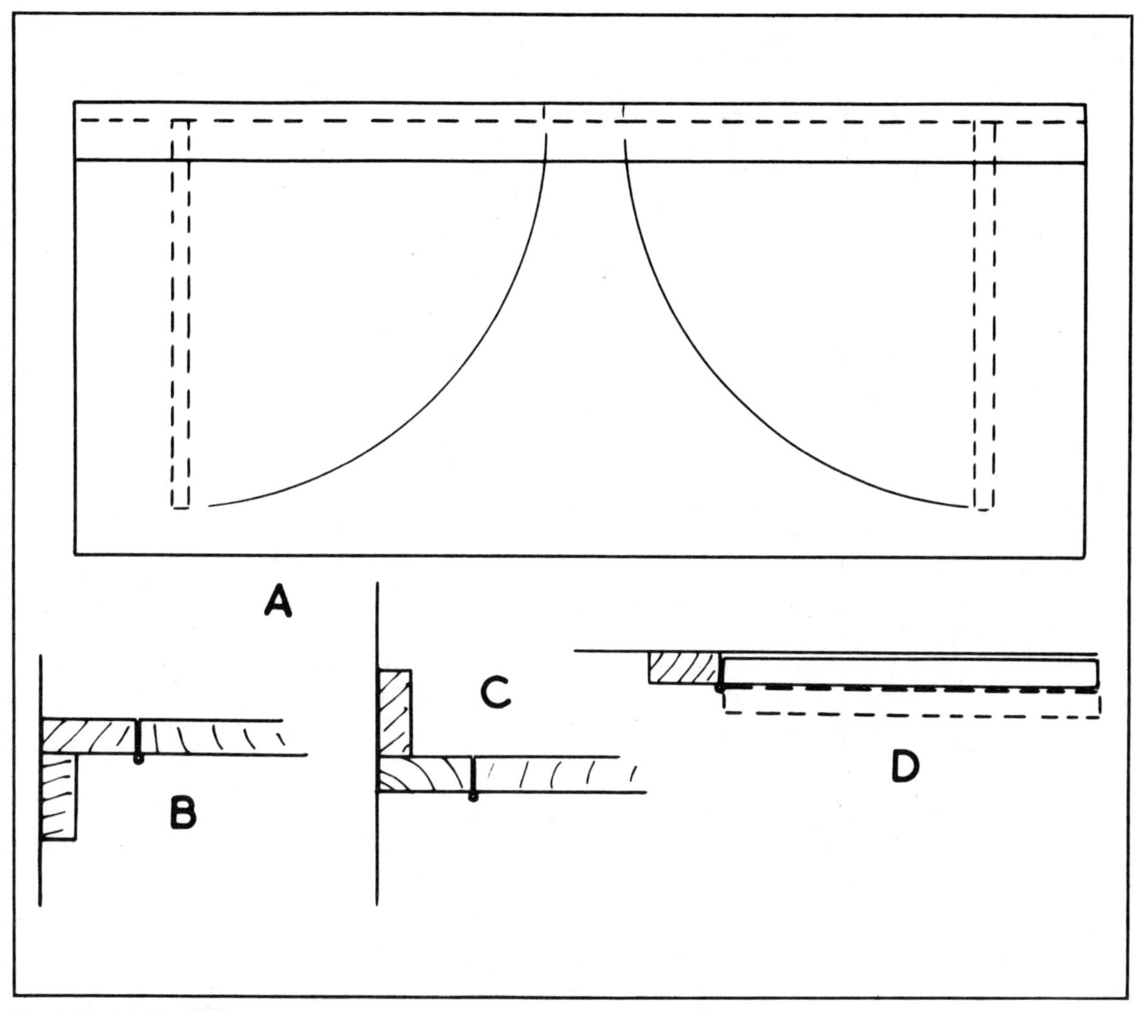

Fig. 8-25. A table with two supports.

slung below it. In that way you can provide storage for small items that will be used on top. Writing equipment can go below the top on which it is used. All the small items needed by a cook can be left just below the working surface.

A simple thing to stow is a plain board, which may be a piece of plywood used for drawing on or a chopping board needed by the cook. Two guides include bearers. You can rabbet solid wood (Fig. 8-30A) or build up with strips (Fig. 8-30B). Allow enough width for driving screws upward through a bearing surface that will not twist under load (Fig. 8-30C).

A drawer may be hung in a similar way, using strips on its sides (Fig. 8-30D). Check that the underside of the shelf is flat. If it is framed with a thinner center part, make up the thickness above the drawer sides to act as kickers and prevent the drawer from tilting as it is pulled out (Fig. 8-30E).

You can make the drawer with a plywood bottom in grooves. There can be a handle on the front (Fig. 8-30F), but extending the front downward will provide a grip without any projection (Fig. 8-30G). Sometimes it is useful to be able to lift the drawer out and have it on top or elsewhere when you are using its contents. Make it as a tray or box in that

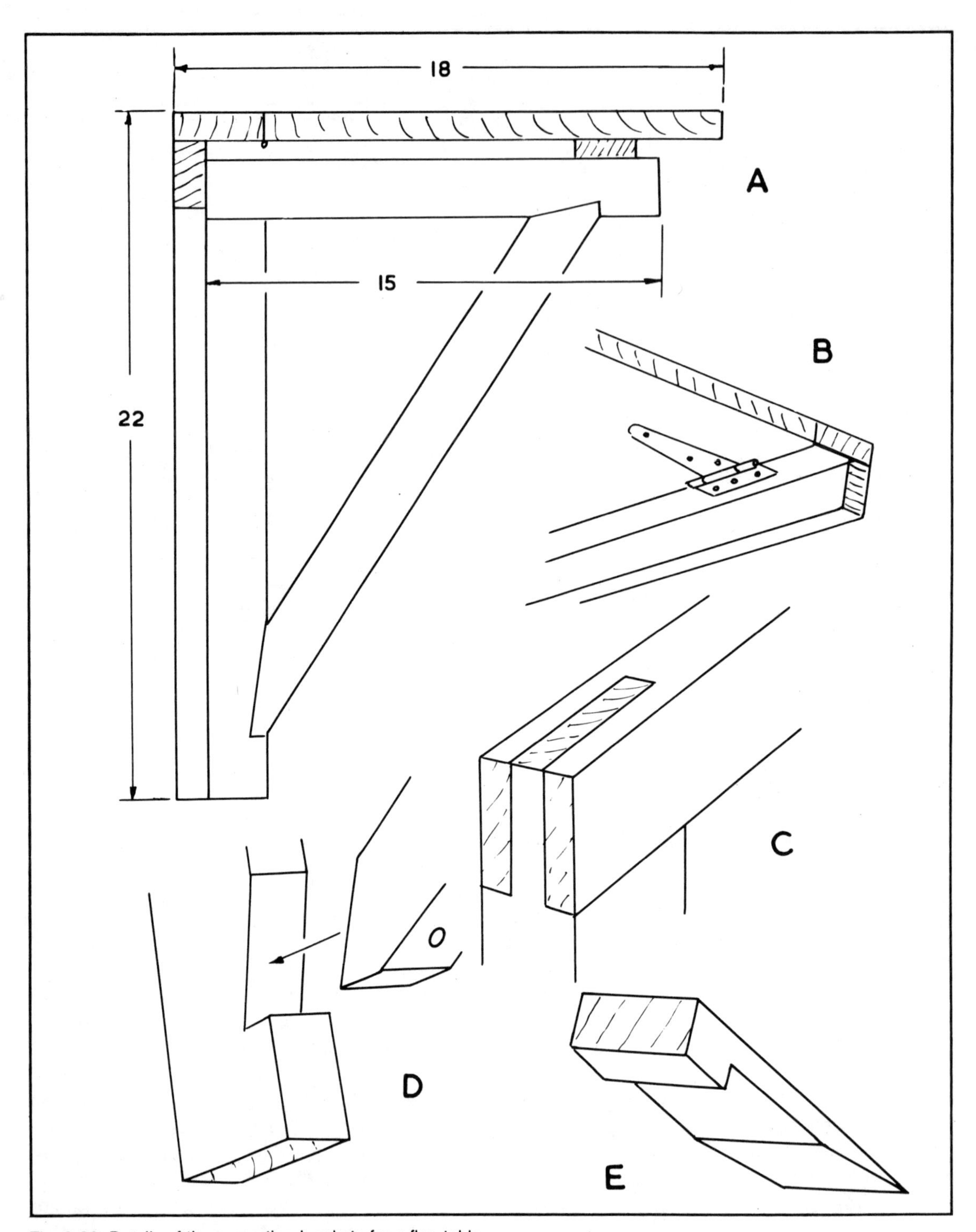

Fig. 8-26. Details of the supporting brackets for a flap table.

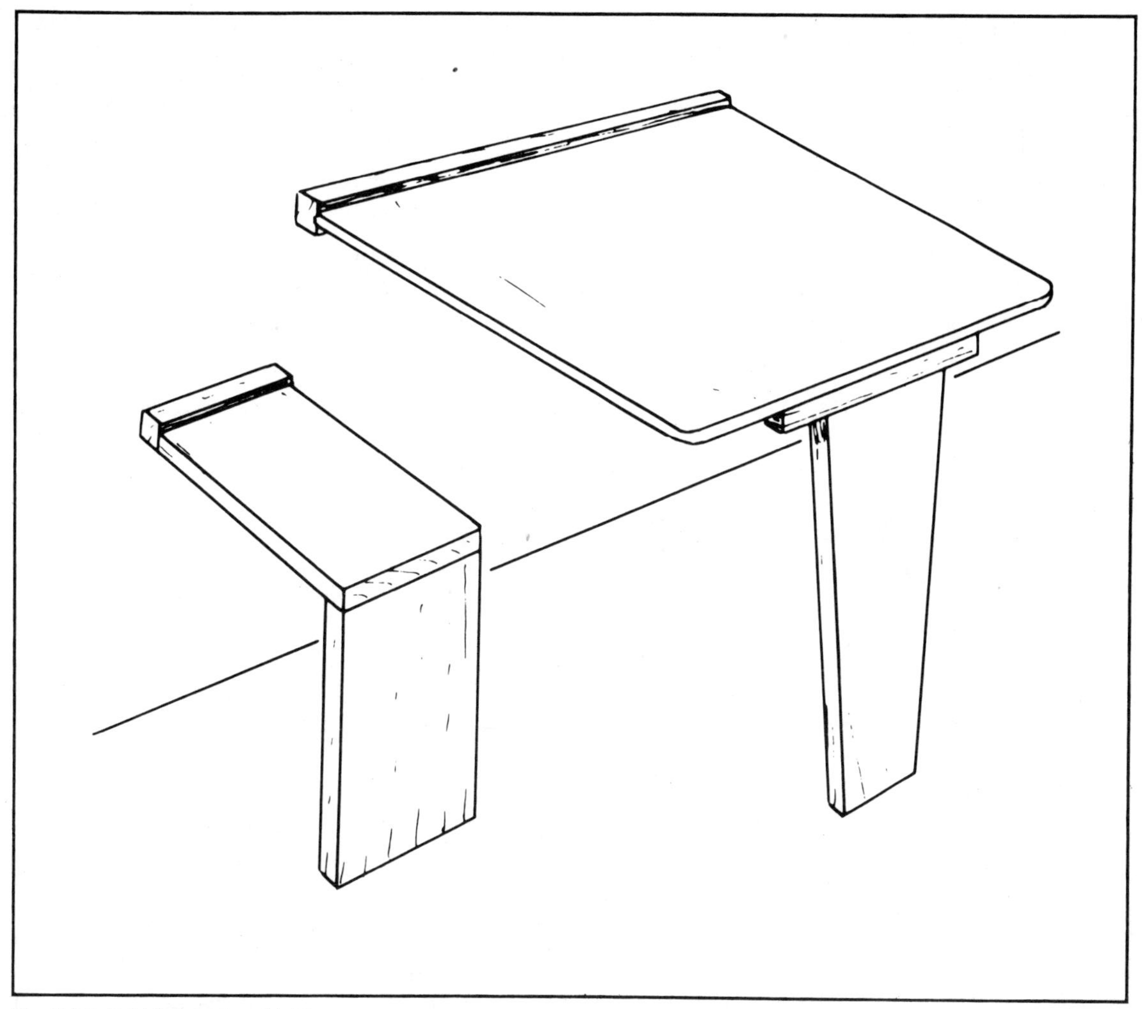

Fig. 8-27. Fold-flat seat and table.

case. Projecting the front below will prevent it from standing level, so an alternative handle is just a hollowed edge (Fig. 8-30H).

With all the drawer arrangements described so far, the ends of the guides show at the front. That may not matter in some situations. If you want to hide them, they can be set back and the drawer extended over them—either the single front (Fig. 8-31A) or a false one (Fig. 8-31B). It need not be rectangular, but its outline can be decorative with a rounded grip (Fig. 8-31C).

If you want to hang more than one drawer, the guide between may be double-sided (Fig. 8-31D). The overlapping drawer fronts can almost meet (Fig. 8-31E). The drawers need not be the same depth or go back the same distance. Overlapping fronts will act as stops, but for other types you can put stop blocks on the guides if the drawers are not stopped by the wall or other obstruction.

If you want to use spare depth below a table or shelf, you can make quite a deep drawer and fit it with a tray that slides and can be lifted out (Fig. 8-32A). If you put a division across the center of the tray, it can have finger holes (Fig. 8-32B). A drawer with a tray is particularly useful for sewing and knitting items.

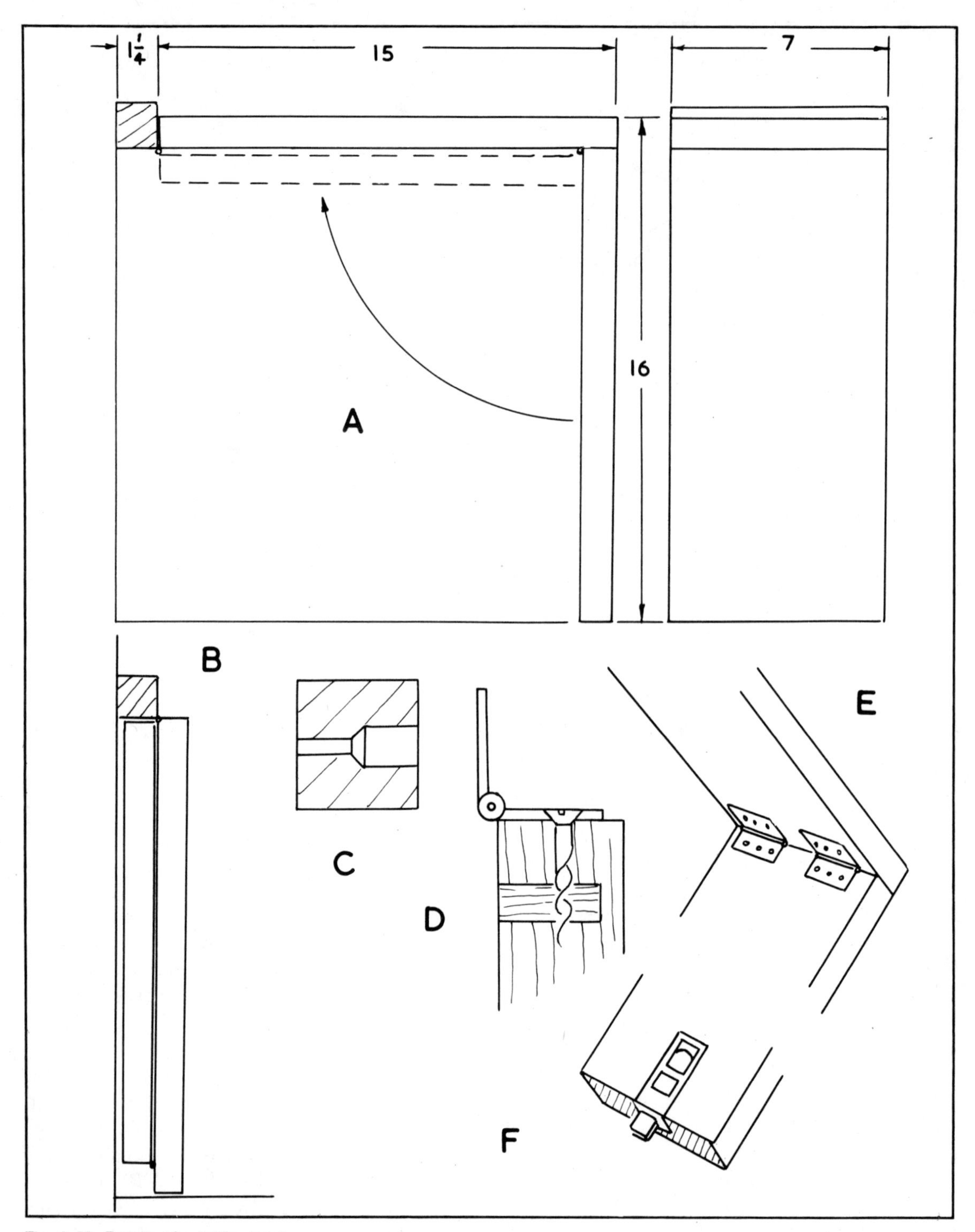

Fig. 8-28. Details of a folding seat.

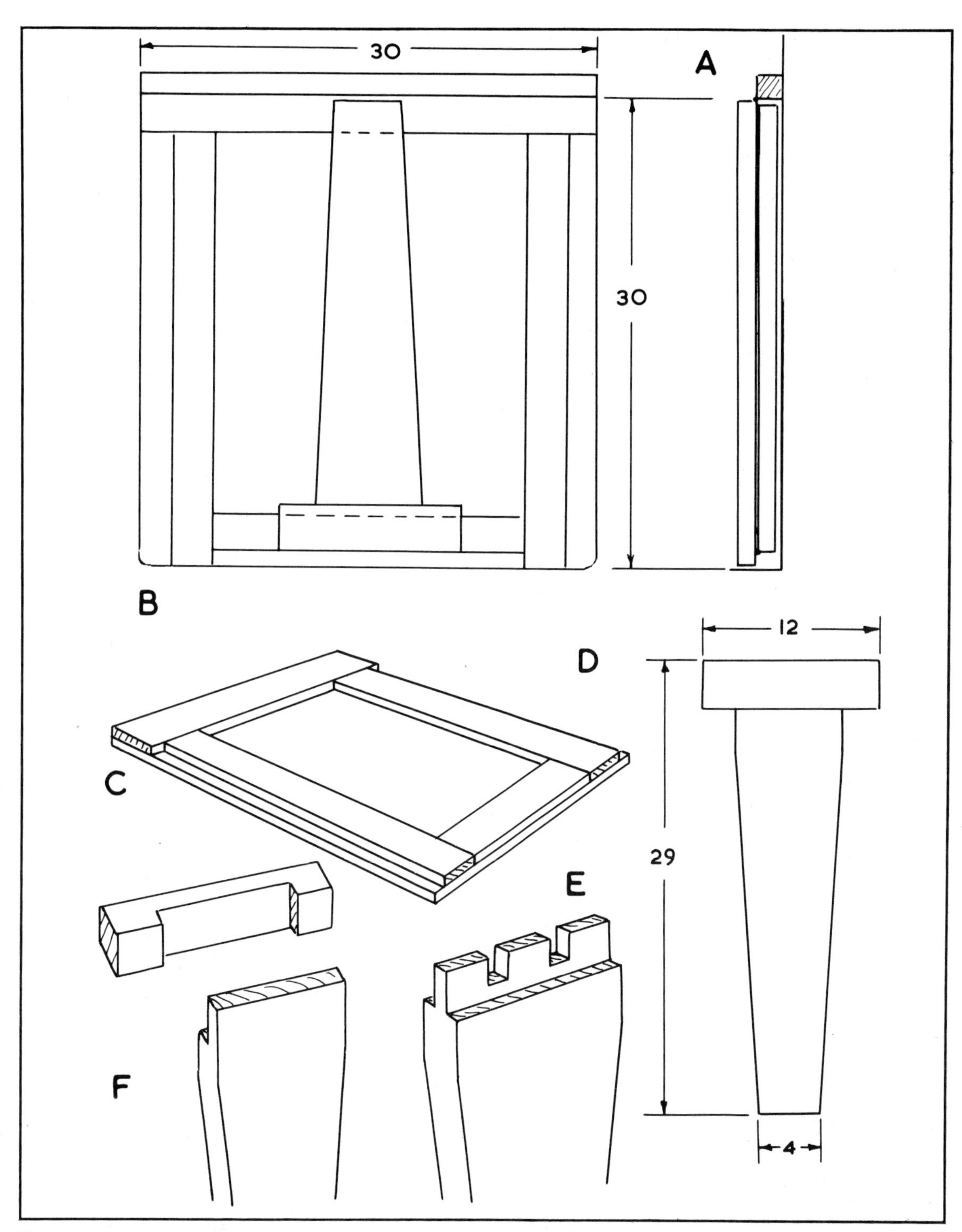

Fig. 8-29. Details of a folding table.

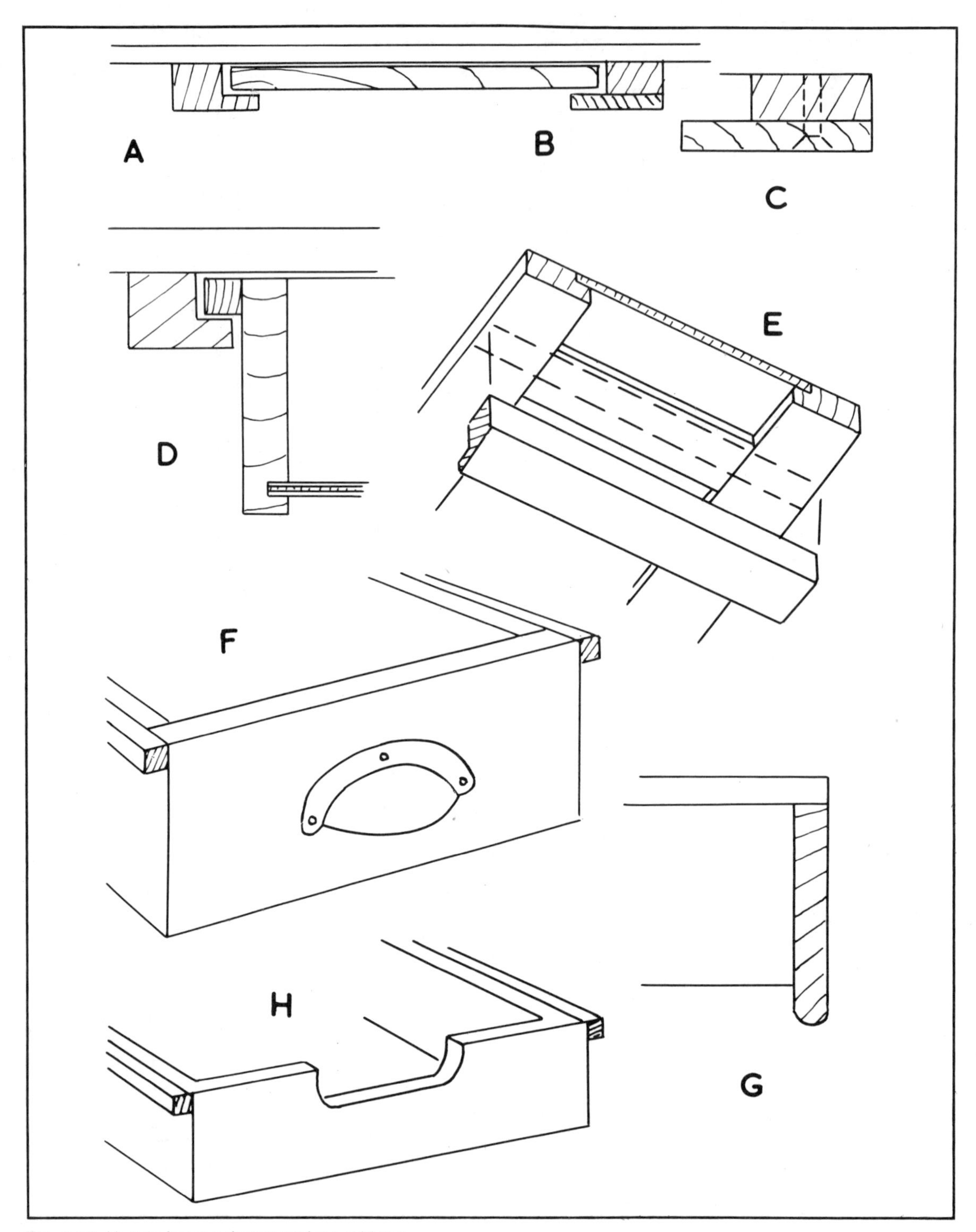

Fig. 8-30. How to hang a drawer under a tabletop.

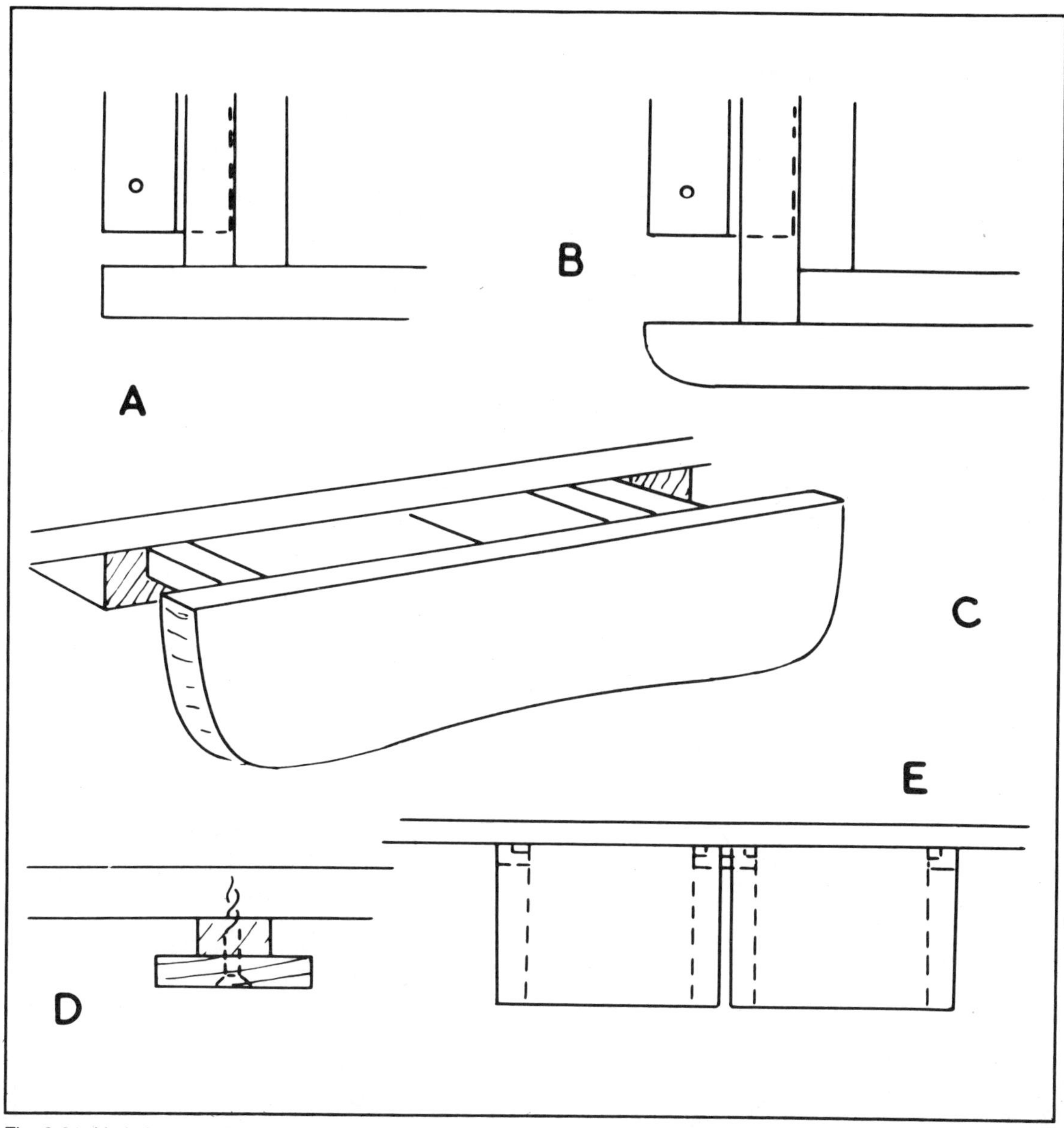

Fig. 8-31. Variations on single and double hanging drawers.

If two or more drawers are to be arranged vertically, you will have to extend the top guides far enough down to take the lower drawer. To keep the extensions true, arrange crosspieces at the front and at or near the back. The drawer fronts can meet and overlap the guides.

Although these hanging drawers have obvious uses under open shelves, they can be used inside some closed things. If you open the door of a closet or cupboard and find that the contents do not reach the top or underside of an internal shelf, you can use that space by hanging a drawer there. Make sure you set its width so it can be pulled out when the door is opened. You may have to keep the guide

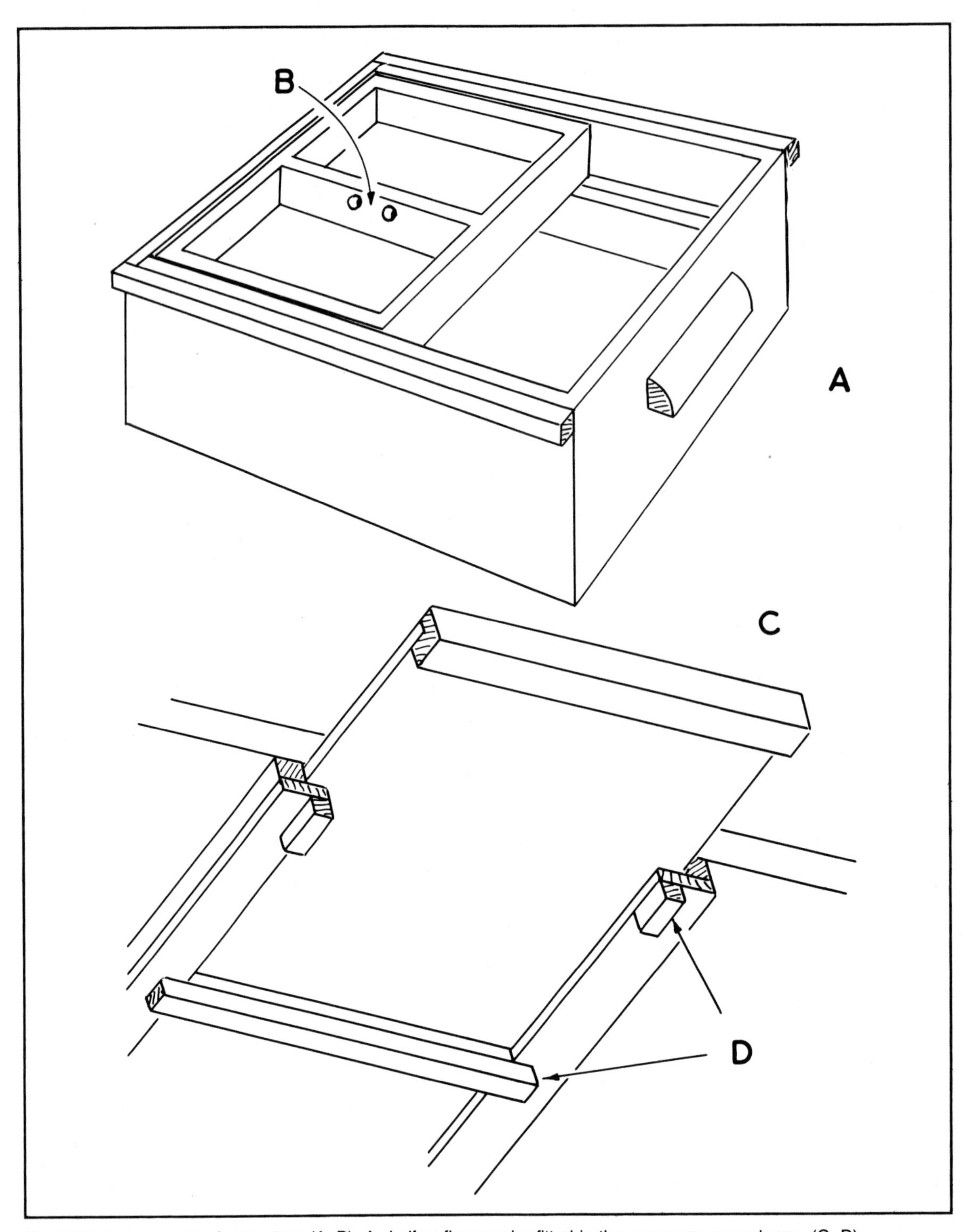

Fig. 8-32. A drawer may have a tray (A, B). A shelf or flap can be fitted in the same way as a drawer (C, D).

away from the hinge side or make an extra wide guide there.

The same idea can make an extended working surface. A flap may be pulled out of a telephone table or at the side of a desk to give space for extra papers.

The flap is a piece of plywood between guides, with a front that acts as a handle (Fig. 8-32C). To keep the flap from being pulled right out, put a strip across under its back and arrange stops on the guide (Fig. 8-32D) that will hold it.

Chapter 9

Built-In Examples

FURNITURE MAY BE BUILT IN FLAT AGAINST a wall. It may rest on the floor, extend to the ceiling, go along a wall to a corner, and be made diagonally in a corner. If there is a recess, it can be made to fit into all or part of it. The house walls, floor, and ceiling may actually make parts of the furniture, or it may be built in unit form with its own back and sides to fit closely to the house parts.

This chapter is mainly concerned with examples of general types of furniture to illustrate the applications of various techniques. The projects described can be put to good use. They are useful pieces of furniture for many parts of the home. Even if some of the projects in this chapter are of no use to you, it is worthwhile reading the instructions in relation to the drawings to follow the construction methods.

RECESS SHELF

If a shelf is to be fitted into a recess such as may occur beside a fireplace (Fig. 9-1), you must get a true shape. If all angles are square, there is no problem, but usually they are not.

Start with a piece of wood that is slightly too big. If it is to be made the same width as the depth of the recess, start by drawing a line at the height you want the top surface to be on the back of the recess and projecting from it (Fig. 9-2A). This should be parallel with the floor, but you should check with a level.

Mark the wood to width, but do not cut it yet. Measure on it the length of the back of the recess (Fig. 9-2B). Measure a diagonal in the recess (Fig. 9-2C) and transfer this to the wood (Fig. 9-2D). A line through the points should be at the angle of that corner of the recess, but do not cut it yet. Do the same the other way (Fig. 9-2E). Before you cut the ends, check the distance across the front of the recess (Fig. 9-2F) and compare it with the distance between the marks on your board (Fig. 9-2G). If this is wrong, go back over your measurements before cutting. An adjustable bevel tried in the corners is a further check.

If the shelf is fairly wide, it can be made of plywood or particle board. Something must be done to the front edge to improve appearance. It helps if

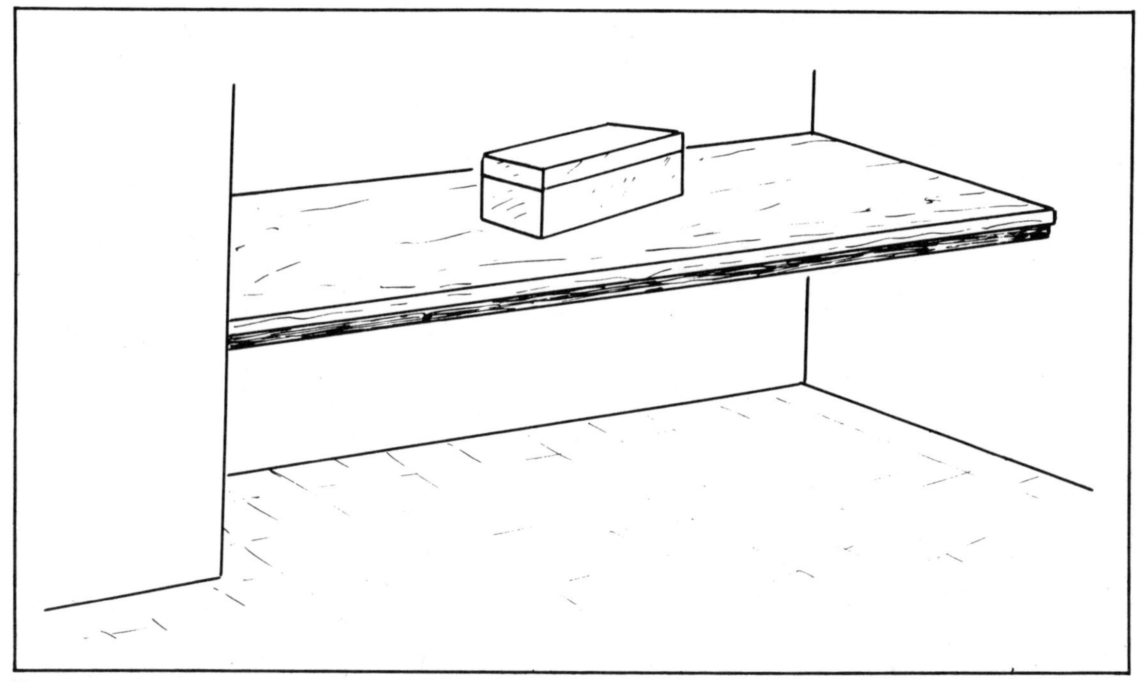

Fig. 9-1. A shelf or table is easily built into a recess or alcove.

the shelf can be made to look thicker than it is. One treatment is to put a strip under and another over it (Fig. 9-2H). There can be a rabbeted strip and another on edge under it (Fig. 9-2J).

Support the shelf on battens screwed to the wall. Notch the supports around the front thickening pieces, which can be screwed to their ends.

If the shelf is to have strips around its edges to protect the walls, there is no need for the shelf to be a precision fit. Instead, the front can be kept to the correct width, but the other edges need not touch the walls. Put the battens on the wall ready for three sides of the shelf (Fig. 9-3A). Cut each of the shelf ends to less than square, but not tapering to as much as the thickness of a batten. That should allow the shelf to be pushed in (Fig. 9-3B). If necessary, take something off the rear edge. Screw the shelf to the battens, with the front edge true. Make the strips to go around the shelf and cover the gaps at its edges (Fig. 9-3C).

CORNER SHELVES

These shelves can be made to almost any size. See Table 9-1. Triangular shelves are not very spacious, even with the end brought out square to the wall, so it is unwise to reduce the widths of the sides much. The height can be increased so the sides go from floor to ceiling. Shelves made as shown (Figs. 9-4A and 9-4B) can be attached to the wall at about eye level, where the items displayed will attract most attention.

It is the view from above which controls most other sizes, so make a full-size drawing of the first (Fig. 9-5A). Check the angle at the corners of the room where the shelves are to be. If it is not square, make your full-size drawing to the actual angle. It is better for the outer edges to touch the wall than for the corner to make an exact fit, so a slight error that way will not matter.

The two sides overlap. Mark out the narrow one (Fig. 9-4B). Make a template for the end shapes (Fig. 9-5B). Use the narrow piece to mark the other to match.

The shelves fit into stopped grooves (Fig. 9-5C). The grooves in the wide side can go through at the back, as the open ends will not show. Make

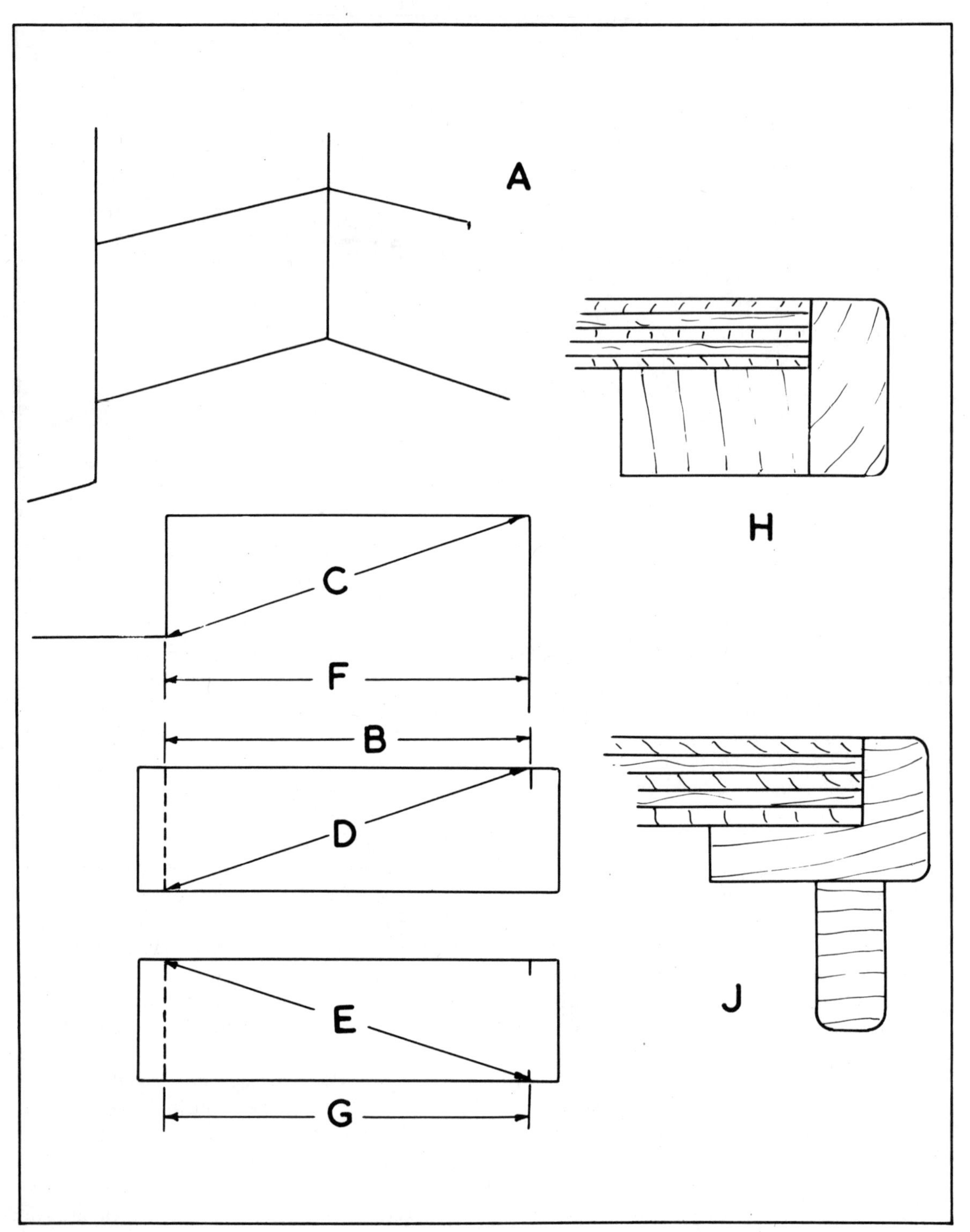

Fig. 9-2. Sizes can be found by measuring diagonals (A to G). A plywood shelf should have its front stiffened (H, J).

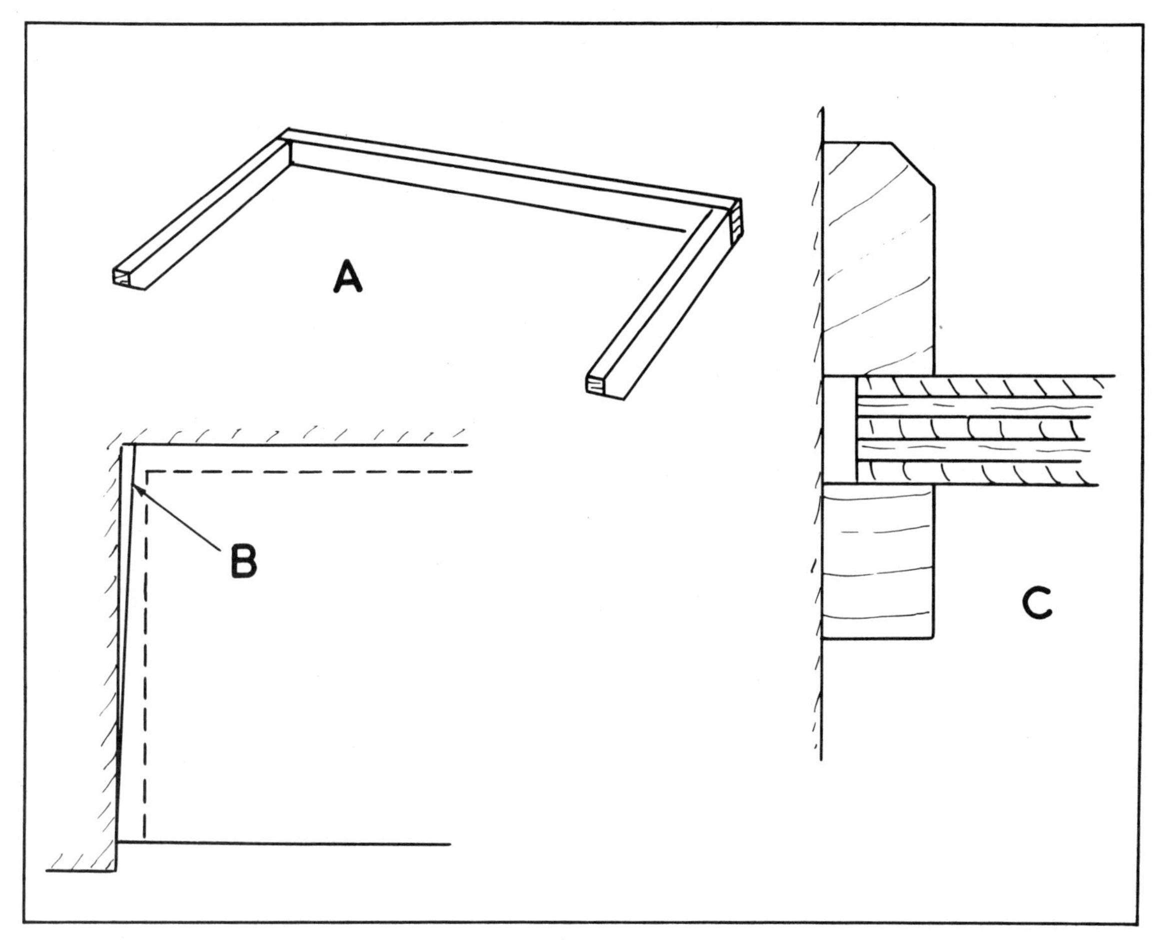

Fig. 9-3. Supports on the wall can enclose a loosely fitted shelf.

the shelves to match (Fig. 9-5D). Screws and glue can be used to hold the shelves (Fig. 9-5E), as their heads will not show. Assemble all the shelves to one side first, then bring the other side to them to get tight front joints before screwing the sides together. If the angle between the walls is not sharp, you may have to plane a bevel along the rear corner before mounting the shelves.

If you want to display plates or there are other things that may fall off, narrow strips with rounded edges can go along the fronts of the shelves (Fig. 9-5F).

Table 9-1. Materials List for Corner Shelves.

1 side	9 × 31 × 5/8
1 side	8 3/8 × 31 × 5/8
4 shelves	8 × 13 × 5/8

CORNER TABLE

A table across a corner may make use of space not otherwise occupied (Fig. 9-6). It can be made any size, but there is not much useful area, due to the shape, if it is too small. See Table 9-2. The example (Fig. 9-7A) increases the area with small projections square to the wall. The construction method makes the table look thicker than it is, yet does not involve grooves or rabbets. The table is shown with a shelf underneath and a curtain on a rail to hide anything stored below.

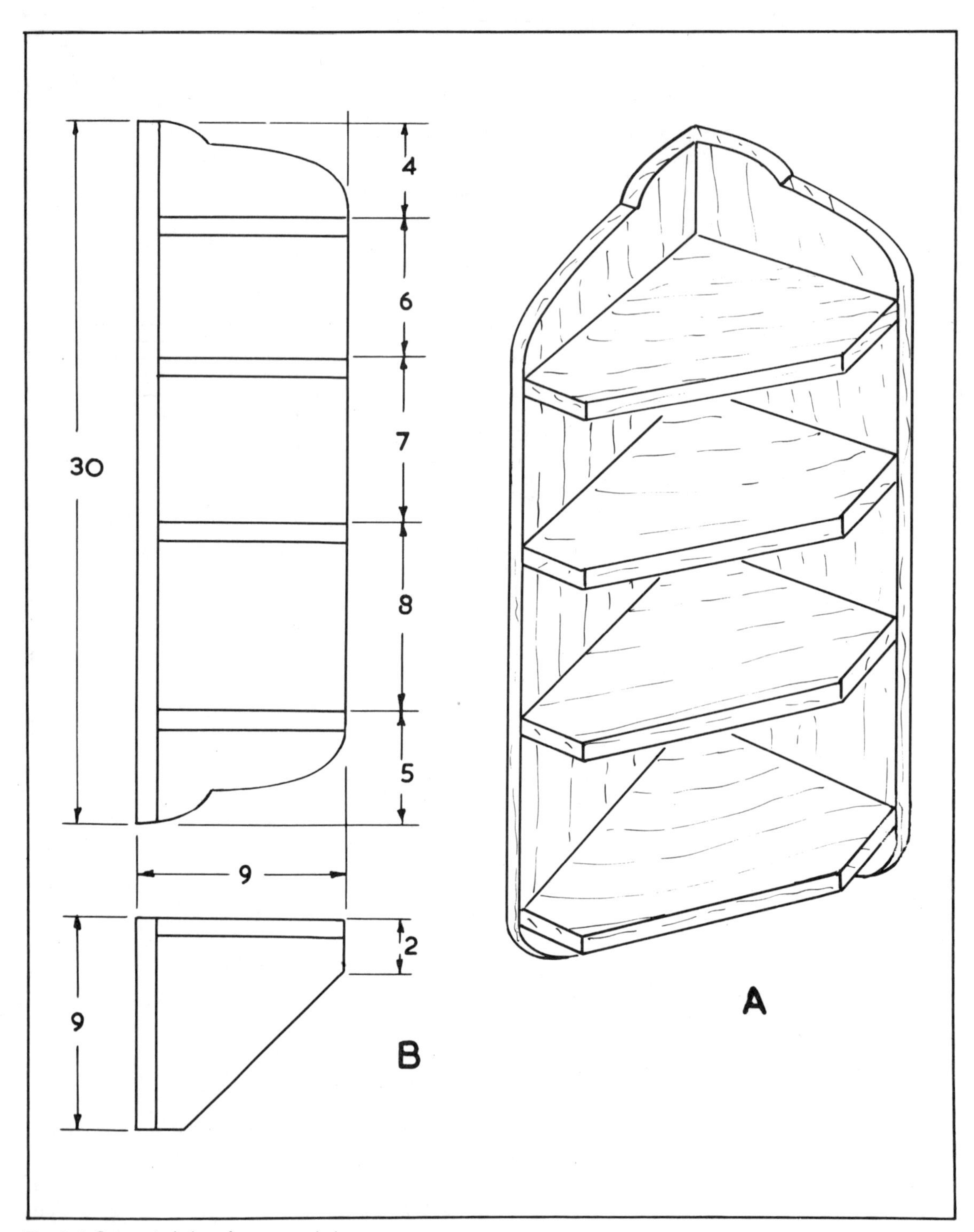

Fig. 9-4. Suggested sizes for corner shelves.

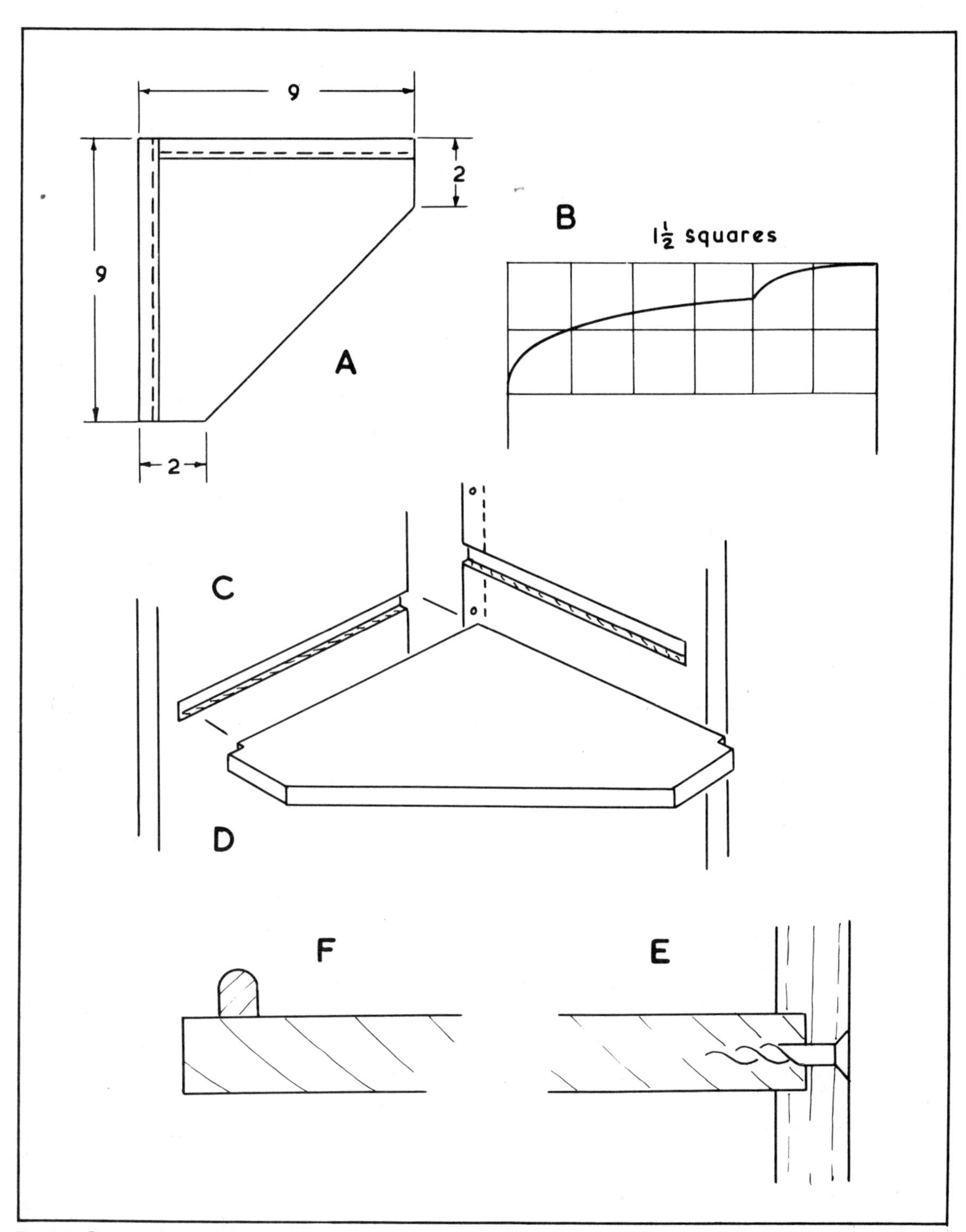

Fig. 9-5. Constructional details of corner shelves.

Fig. 9-6. A corner table can have a shelf below.

Cut plywood to shape to fit the corner, which may not be exactly square. Put strips under its outer edges (Fig. 9-7B). Face them with strips deep enough to hide the curtain track, mitering at the front angles (Fig. 9-7C). To further give the impression of bulk, put half-round or other molding around the top edge (Fig. 9-7D).

Make cleats to screw to the wall to support the tabletop, with notches under the front framing (Fig. 9-7E). See that they are mounted level and try the tabletop in position. When this fits correctly, remove it and fit the curtain track before finally screwing the table down.

If there will be a shelf, make and fit it before finally attaching the tabletop. As shown (Fig. 9-7F), this is a simple triangle stiffened across the front edge (Fig. 9-7G). The top shape can be repeated, but keep it far enough back to be clear of the curtain when it is moved to one side.

CORNER BOOKCASE/CABINET

A problem with arranging any type of built-in furniture along two meeting walls is what to do with the parts that meet in the corner. If you arrange bookshelves to meet, you cannot put books on the shelves both ways in the corner. If you fill the shelves one way, you have to leave space for removal the other way. You finish with some waste space in the corner no matter how you try to arrange storage. One way to use this space is to cut the shelves short and put a cabinet there.

Several arrangements are possible, but that suggested (Fig. 9-8) has two blocks of shelves of different lengths and a cabinet projecting above and below. Sizes can be varied to suit available space, but you should not make the cabinet less than 15 inches each way with 6-inch shelves. This gives a diagonal of about 12 inches. Anything less will have a door too narrow to be useful. The suggested sizes suit this arrangement (Fig. 9-9 and Table 9-3). The back of the cabinet should be closed with plywood, but you can choose whether to put plywood behind the shelves or let the walls show through.

Start by making the cabinet as a unit. The simplest construction is with dowels. If you use solid wood, have the grain of top and bottom diagonal to the corner (Fig. 9-10A). Use plywood or hardboard for the backs and rabbet the sides (Fig. 9-10B). Put fillet strips at top and bottom and where the backs meet (Fig. 9-10C). At the door there must be two strips with the joints beveled to the sides (Fig. 9-10D). You should not need dowels between these parts. Glue will be enough if the edges are a good fit.

When the cabinet is assembled, top and bottom can be left level with the sides, or you can add half-round molding (Fig. 9-10E). Do not assemble the cabinet until you have prepared the sides to take the shelves, as described below.

Table 9-2. Materials List for Corner Table.

1 top	18 × 18 × ½ plywood
1 thickening piece	2 × 24 × 1
2 thickening pieces	2 × 5 × 1
1 front	3 × 24 × ¾
2 fronts	3 × 5 × ¾
1 molding	1 × 24 × half round
2 moldings	1 × 5 × half round
1 shelf	15 × 15 × ½ plywood
2 shelf edges	1 × 20 × ½
2 cleats	2 × 18 × 1
2 cleats	2 × 15 × 1

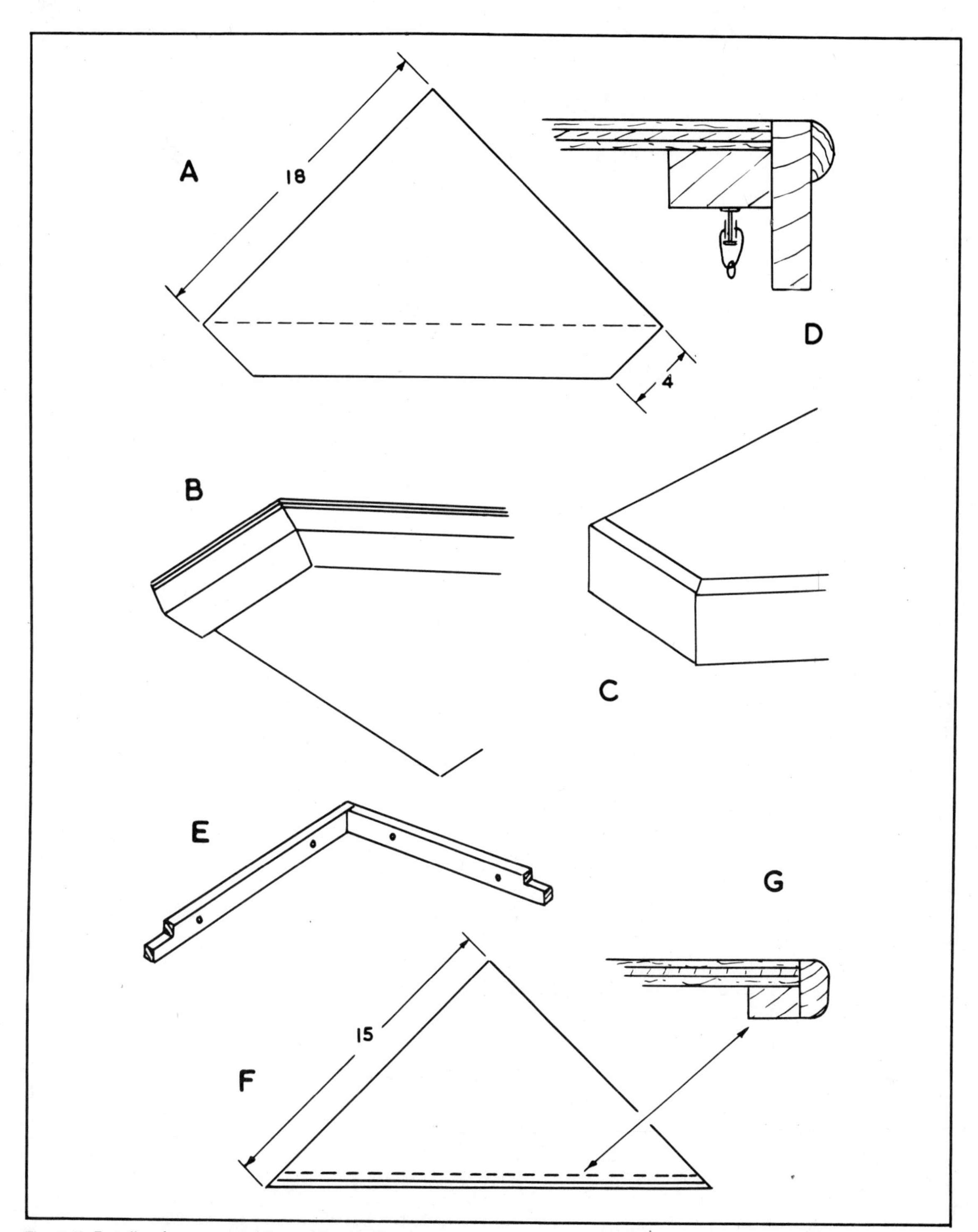

Fig. 9-7. Details of a corner table and its shelf.

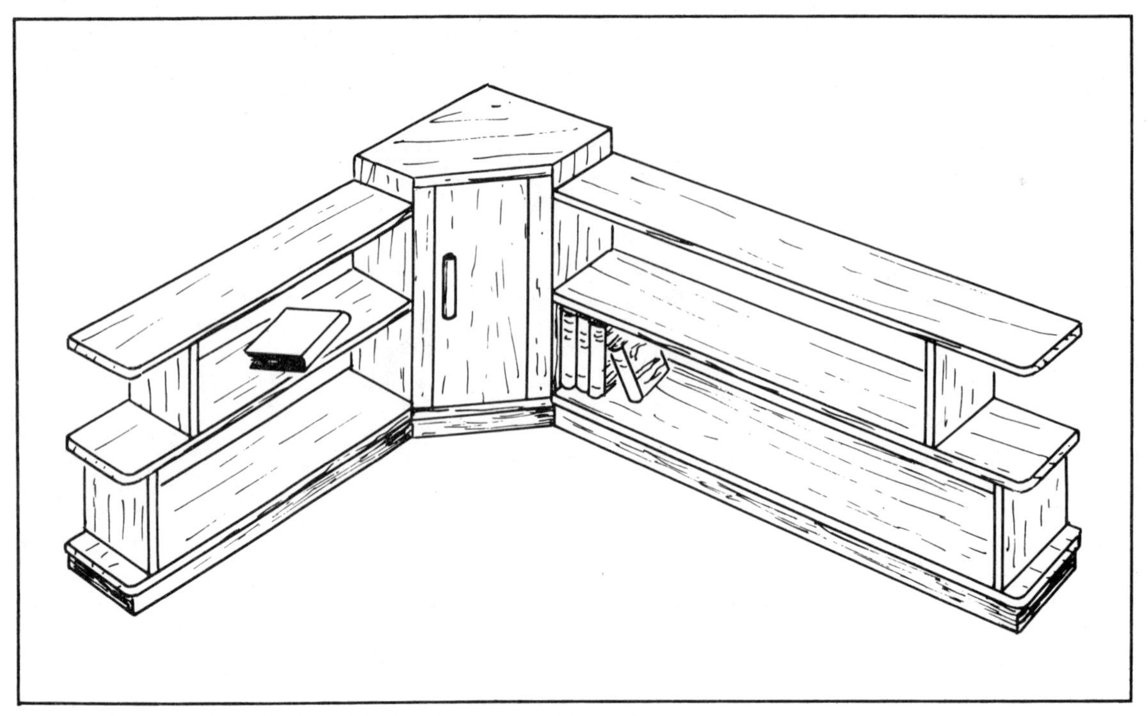

Fig. 9-8. Shelves and a cabinet provide storage along meeting walls.

The arrangement inside the cabinet depends on what you want to put in it. If there will be bottles or other tall things, you may leave it clear. There can be shelves for other things, and they must be put in during assembly as you cannot add them later in a cabinet of this shape. Put fillets as supports on the backs and make a shelf to rest on them. It may go straight across (Fig. 9-10F) or be cut close to the front pieces (Fig. 9-10G), but keep it far enough back so as not to interfere with the action of the door.

The door is most easily made from a piece of plywood or solid wood. You can use decorative hinges on the surface (Fig. 9-11A) or put plain hinges in the joints (Fig. 9-11B). The handle at the other side may be metal, plastic, or a strip of wood (Fig. 9-11C). Use a spring or magnetic catch.

You can use dowels where the shelves join the cabinet (Fig. 9-12A), or tenons can go right through (Fig. 9-12B). The traditional craftsman's method would combine a dado joint with tenons (Fig. 9-12C). If the shelves are to have plywood backs, rabbet the top and bottom ones and cut back the widths of the middle shelves (Fig. 9-12D).

There are spacers in two different positions at the outer ends (Fig. 9-12E). A row of books puts a considerable load on the shelves, so the joints should be strong. If you use dowels, they should be taken right through the shelves (Fig. 9-12F). Tenons can be taken through and wedged (Fig. 9-12G).

Table 9-3. Materials List for Corner Bookcase/Cabinet.

1 cabinet top	15 × 22 × ¾
1 cabinet bottom	15 × 22 × ¾
2 cabinet sides	6 × 28 × ¾
2 doorway sides	2 × 28 × ¾
2 backs	15 × 28 × ¼ plywood
fillets from	½ × 150 × ½
molding from	¾ × 50 half round
1 door	9 × 28 × ¾
3 shelves	6 × 36 × ¾
3 shelves	6 × 48 × ¾
2 spacers	6 × 11 × ¾
2 spacers	6 × 13 × ¾
1 back (if required)	24 × 36 × ¼ plywood
1 back (if required)	24 × 48 × ¼ plywood

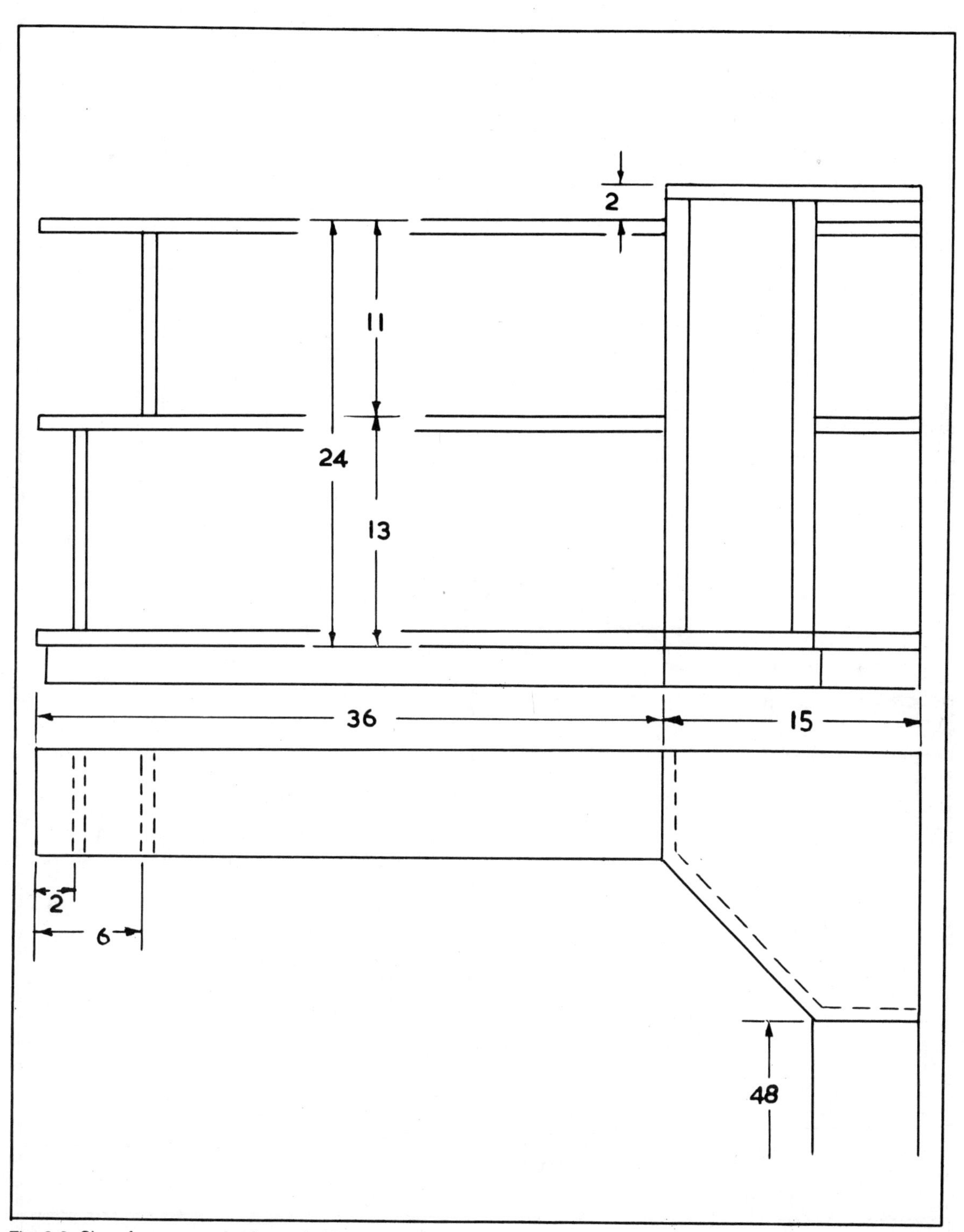

Fig. 9-9. Sizes for a corner bookcase/cabinet.

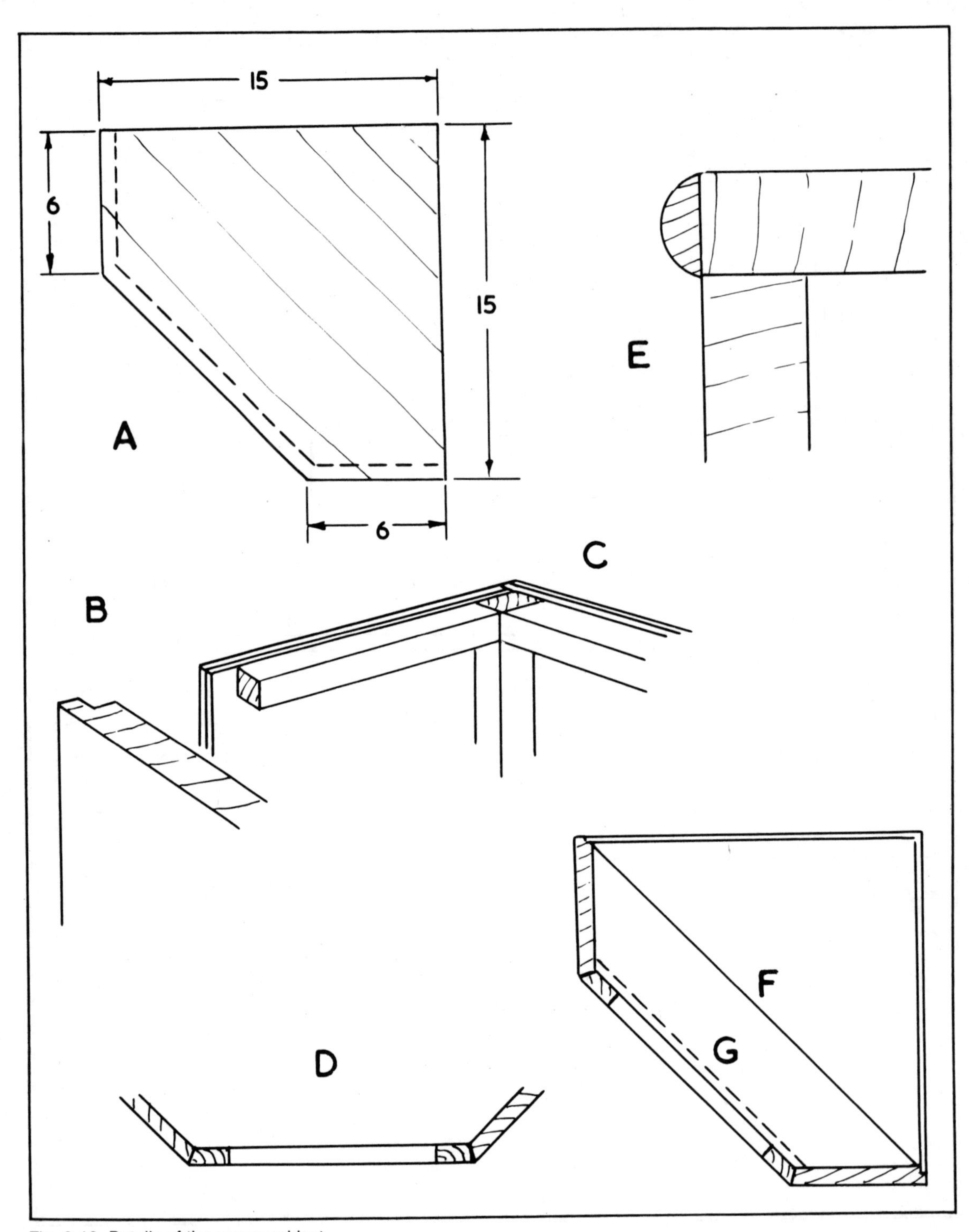

Fig. 9-10. Details of the corner cabinet.

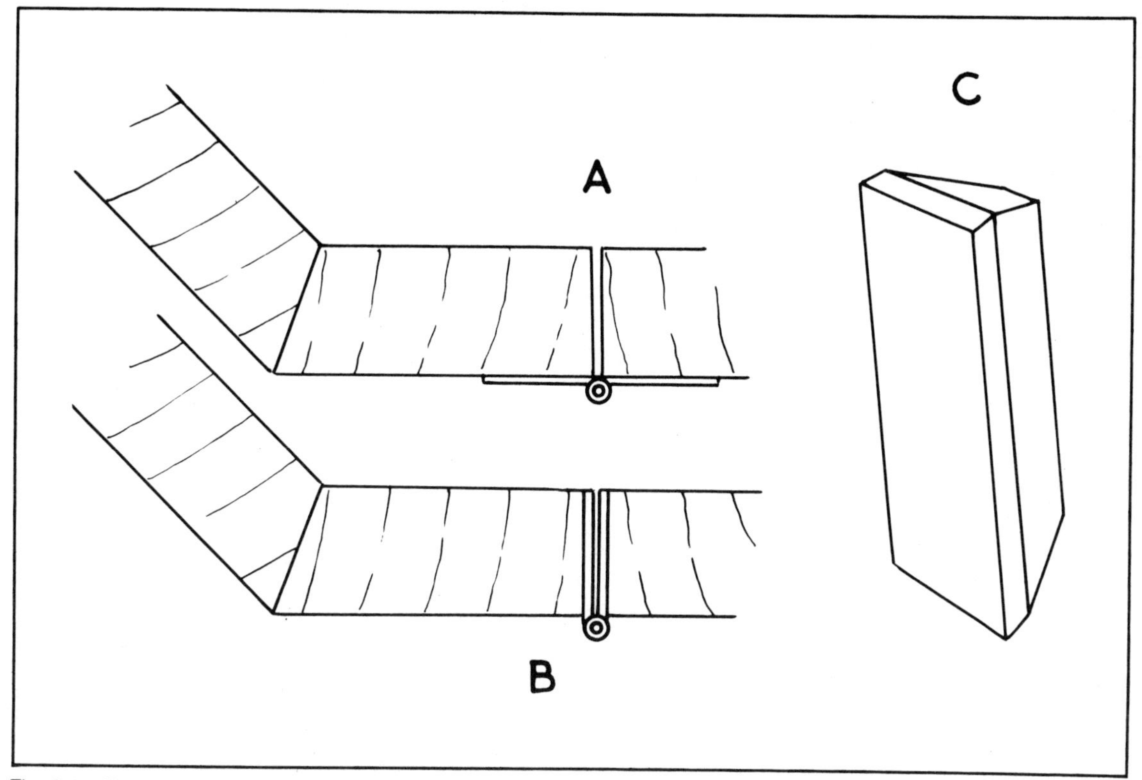

Fig. 9-11. Door and handle details for a corner cabinet.

Neatly finished joints can be regarded as decorative features in both cases. Round the exposed shelf corners.

When you finally assemble and mount the shelves and cabinet on the walls, be careful of squareness, particularly if you do not have plywood to keep the shelves in shape. Also, watch that the shelves finish horizontal and parallel with the floor. If there are plywood backs, you can screw through them. Otherwise, you can put strips under the top and middle shelves (Fig. 9-12H) for screwing without interfering with the storage of books.

FULL WALL UNIT

One of the best uses of available space is a built-in assembly that occupies all, or nearly all, of one wall. The effect is to get the maximum storage space, which can be arranged to suit things ranging from a large television set to glasses and bottles in a cocktail cabinet and small books.

The full wall assembly looks better balanced if large things are at the bottom, although some layouts can be effective with some large things high. No matter how you plan your requirements and make the shelves, some things will not fit into racks or shelves, or you may not want them visible at all times. You should enclose a part with doors for these items. It is usually best to have a wider part up to about table height. This gives increased capacity and makes a working surface at a convenient height.

You can make the whole thing in position, but that means working in the room. This may not matter if the room is empty, but the mess will be a nuisance if it is furnished. You may also have to go frequently to your shop if you want to use equipment that cannot be brought into the room. The suggested construction makes the whole thing in sections, which can be prefabricated almost completely in the shop with very little sawing, planing,

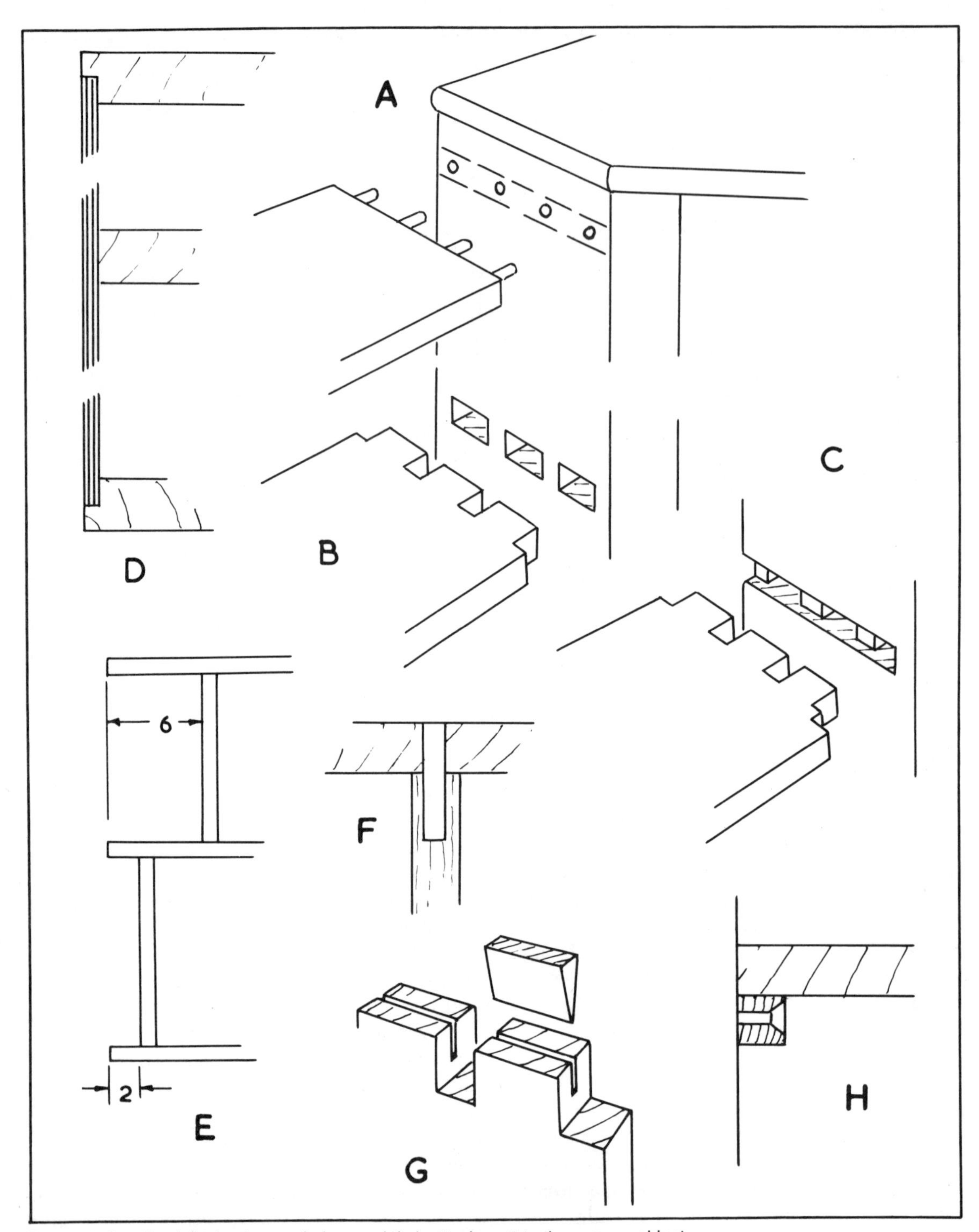

Fig. 9-12. Details of the bookcase shelves and their attachment to the corner cabinet.

or other messy work in the room. There also is the advantage of easy access. If you try to make the whole assembly in one piece elsewhere, it will be too big to pass through doorways.

The wall unit can be made of solid wood, plywood with exposed edges covered with solid wood, or veneered particle board. The suggested thickness for most parts is ¾ inch, but long shelves or other parts with heavy loads and no intermediate supports may have to be thicker. See Table 9-4. Arrange vertical dividers under shelves that may sag under load, so they provide support.

The design shows two bottom units with doors and similar sizes topped with shelf units to the ceiling. Between them come more shelves (Fig. 9-13A). The side units do not have to be the same width, and their internal arrangements may differ. The central shelves may go to the floor, or they can be stopped at a height that allows chairs or a table to be pushed under them (Fig. 9-13B).

Sizes are given on the drawings as a guide, but they will have to be modified to suit the particular situation. Make a sketch of a side view (Fig. 9-13C) and use that for key measurements when making the main parts.

The sides of a bottom section may be made by gluing pieces of solid wood to make up the width.

Table 9-4. Materials List for Full Wall Unit.

Two bottom sections	
4 sides	17 × 37 × ¾
2 bottoms	17 × 37 × ¾
2 plinths	3 × 37 × ¾
2 tops	18 × 37 × ¾
2 shelves	16 × 36 × ¾
4 shelf cleats	¾ × 16 × ¾
1 back	34 × 36 × ¼ plywood
Two top sections	
4 sides	9 × 61 × ¾
10 shelves	9 × 36 × ¾
2 tops	3 × 37 × ¾
1 back	36 × 61 × ¼ plywood
Dividers from	9 × 96 × ¾
Middle section	
6 shelves	9 × 36 × ¾
2 dividers	9 × 15 × ¾
1 back	36 × 72 × ¼ plywood

The back edge is rabbeted for a plywood or hardboard back (Fig. 9-14A). If you cannot rabbet plywood or particle board and do not want the edge of the back to show, put strips inside (Fig. 9-14B).

Whatever the material used, dowel the sides to the top (Fig. 9-14C). As the rear edge will be hidden, there is no need to allow for the back coming underneath. Nail it directly to the rear edge. Let the front edge overhang the sides by up to 1 inch. That edge can be rounded or molded. If either side of the unit will be exposed, the top can overhang there and be molded to match. Put a supporting strip under the front (Fig. 9-14D).

The bottom comes between the sides. It may have a supporting strip and dowels with the plinth set back from the front edge (Fig. 9-14E).

A shelf can be doweled in during assembly. The shelf is probably better arranged loose on side supports (Fig. 9-14F), though, so it can be removed for cleaning or if you want to alter the internal layout.

There can be swinging or sliding doors. Plywood or particle board may stay flat without framing, but strips on the inside will prevent twisting (Fig. 9-15A). One-sided framing may draw a door out of shape. It is better to frame the front and back, not necessarily at the edges (Fig. 9-15B). Better doors are made with thinner panels in grooved framing tenoned at the corners. The doors can be left square where they meet, or rabbets may be cut (Fig. 9-15C). One door can be fastened with small tower bolts and the other held to it with a catch.

If the doors are to slide, metal guides can be obtained with rollers so the doors move easily. Usually there is a piece to inset in a groove in the bottom of the door, and this travels on a rail. There is a simple guide at the top. Get the running gear before making the doors, as it will affect their sizes.

If thin plywood is used for the doors, it is possible to make wooden tracks. At the bottom is a strip with two grooves in which the plywood will slide easily (Fig. 9-15D). At the top is a similar piece with the grooves twice as deep (Fig. 9-15E). Round the edges and corners of the plywood, then wax them and the grooves. The doors will stay

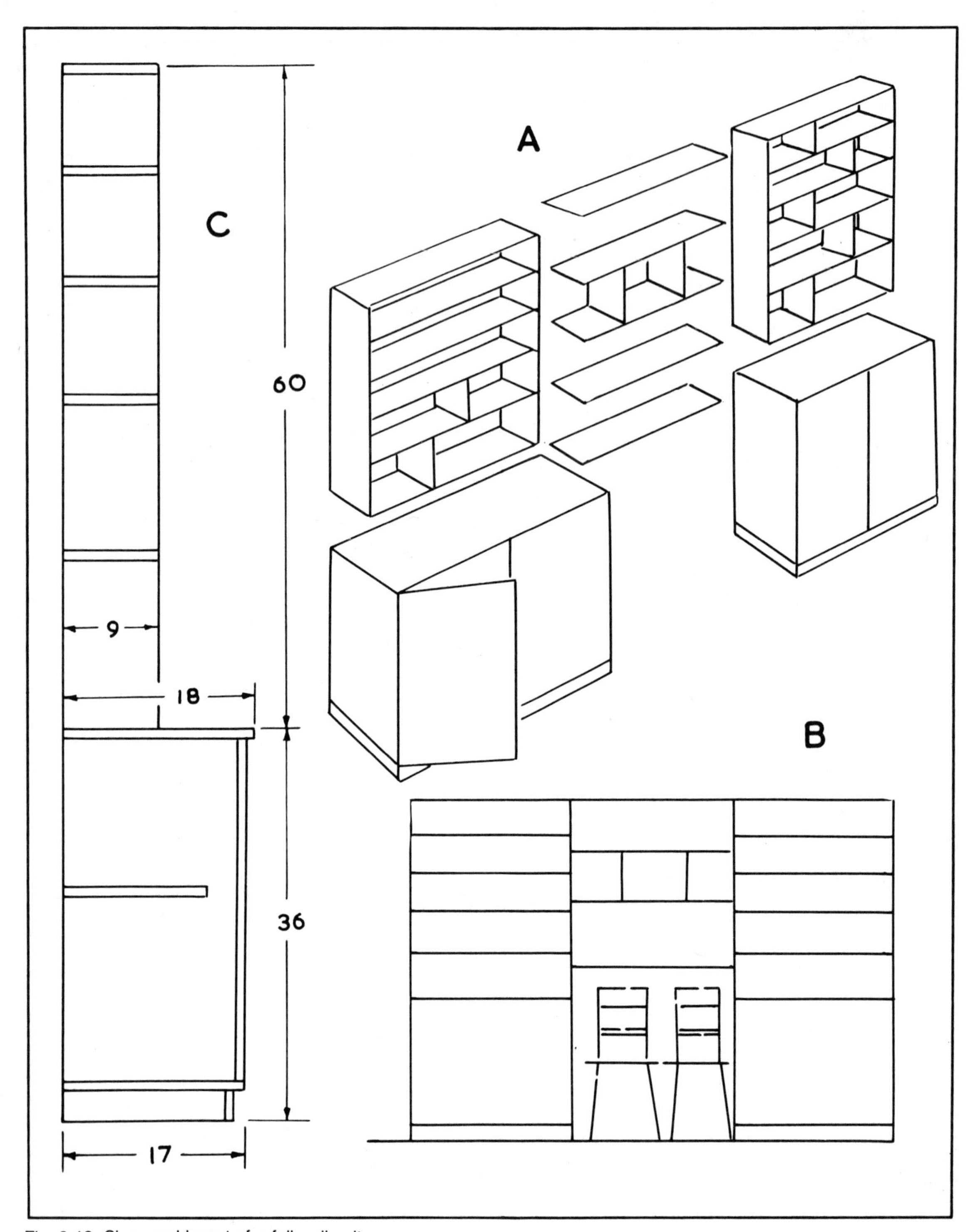

Fig. 9-13. Sizes and layout of a full wall unit.

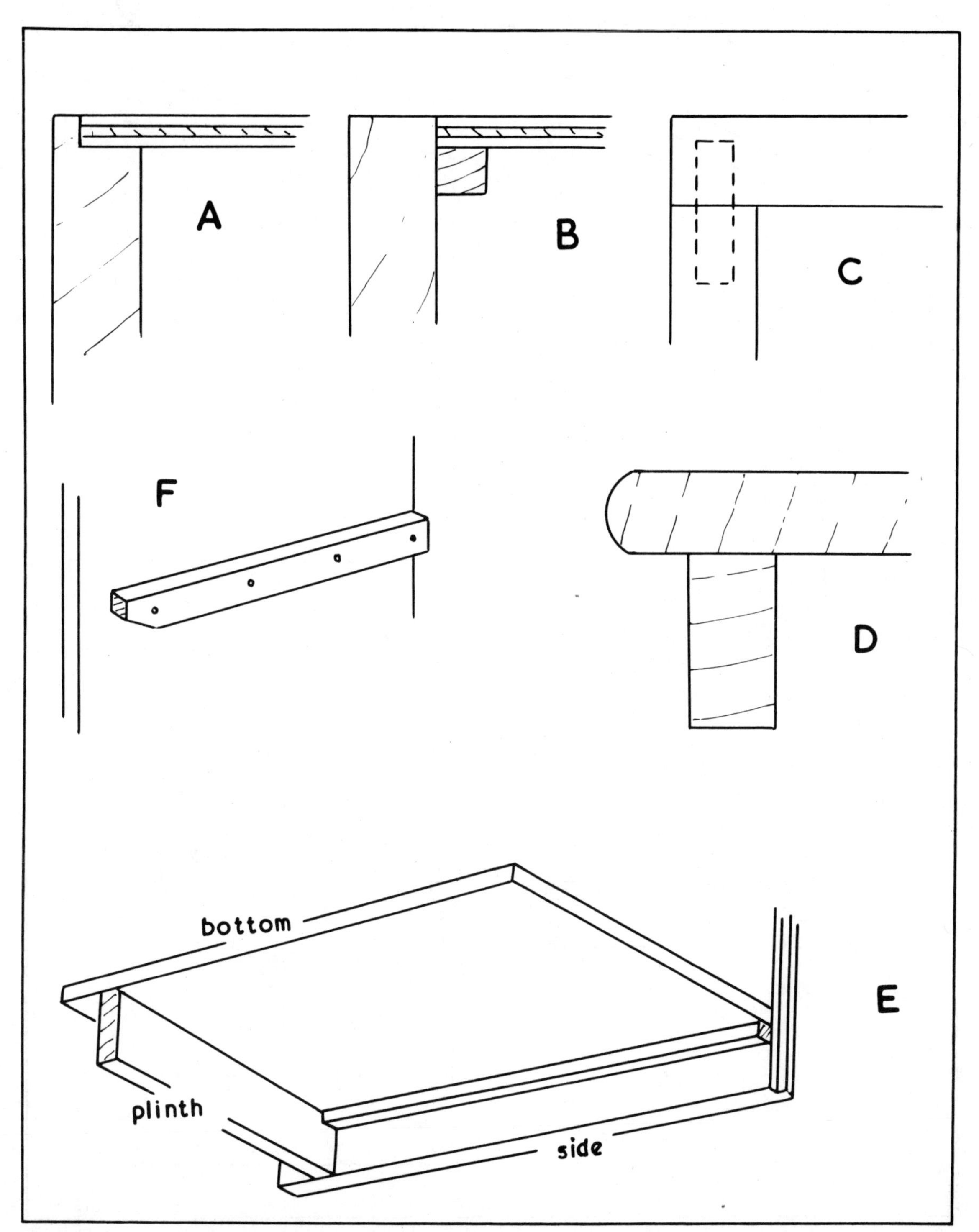

Fig. 9-14. Constructional details of parts of a full wall unit.

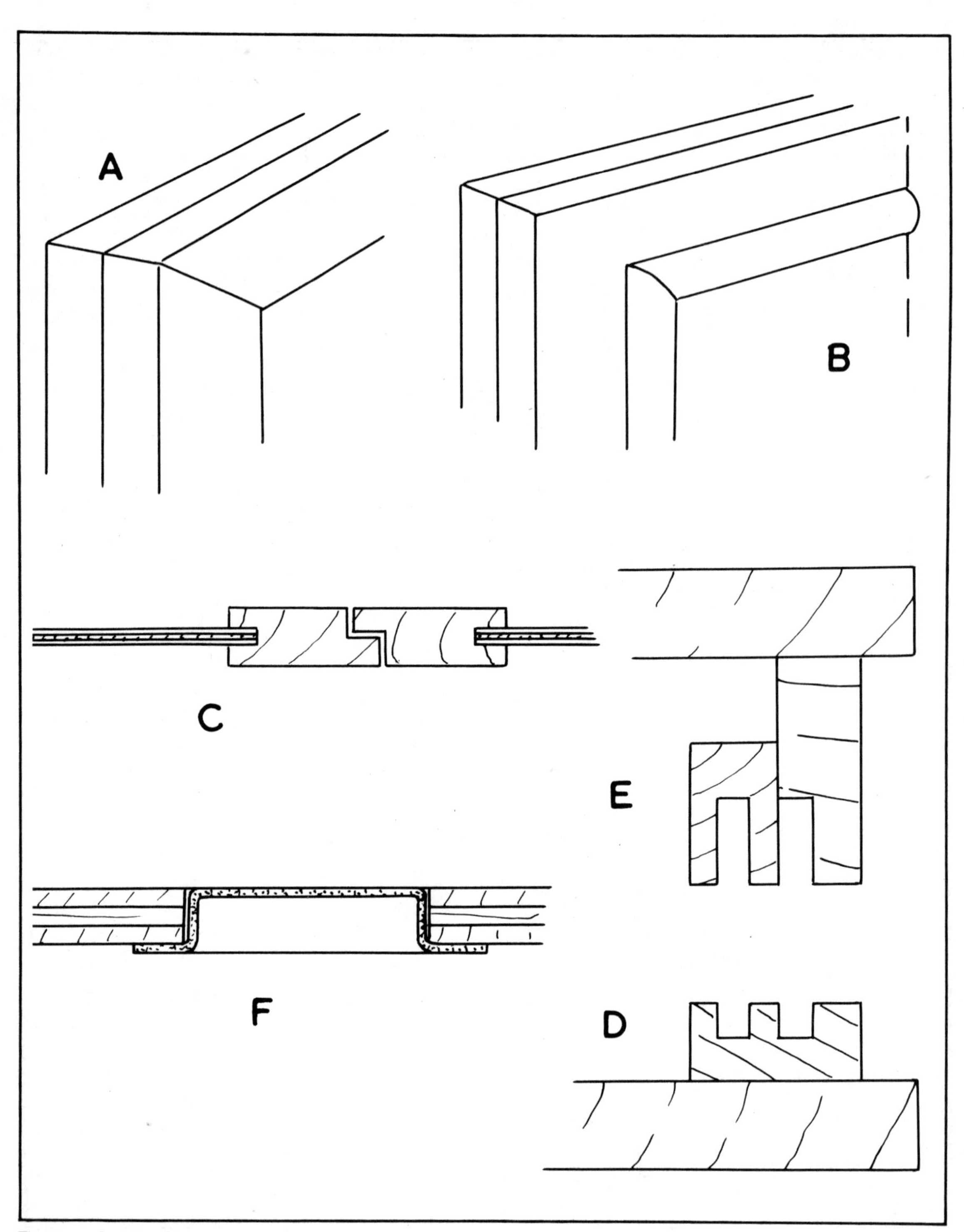

Fig. 9-15. Details of hinged and sliding doors.

down under their own weight. If you want to remove them, the clearance at the top guide allows you to lift the plywood away at the bottom. There are dished handles to let in for this type of door (Fig. 9-15F). Sliding glass doors between shelves can be arranged in a similar way.

The top sections are made like bookcases. If a top will not reach the ceiling, close it with a piece across. If the sides reach the ceiling, you can put a strip across the front (Fig. 9-16A). If the piece is molded or you add other pieces to it to give a molded effect, it is easier to disguise any unevenness in the ceiling (Fig. 9-16B).

Rabbet the sides or put strips inside to take the back in the same way as in the bottom sections. Choose between long strips to which the shelves must be notched or short strips put between the shelves (Fig. 9-16C).

The shelves can join the sides with dado joints or be doweled. For most purposes the front edges of the shelves are level with the sides, but they do not have to be. It may be better to have some shelves narrower. If you want to put a door anywhere, it may be better to set shelves back so the door overlaps them (Fig. 9-16D).

Where there are dividers, measure carefully so the shelf spacing on the sides matches and the dividers will finish square (Fig. 9-16E), both across and in front view.

The bottoms of the top sections can be made with shelves (Fig. 9-16F) screwed to the lower sections, or the sides can be doweled into the lower sections (Fig. 9-16G) without any cross member or just a strip at the back (Fig. 9-16H).

The shelves that go between the units are mostly plain pieces, except that any dividers should be positioned before the shelves are doweled to the sides of the other sections. If there is any doubt about the squareness of the wall (many walls are slightly out of true), position the upper and lower sections at each side. Get them as nearly parallel as you can, then screw the sections to the wall before trimming the shelves to go between.

If the whole unit does not completely fill the width of one wall, you can position one unit, then leave the other to bring into position as the doweled shelves are fitted into place (Fig. 9-17A). Pressure can be applied to bring the joints close with wedges against the further wall (Fig. 9-17B).

If the side sections come against other walls or it is necessary to attach them to the wall first for some other reason, dowels at one or both ends of the shelves must be taken right through (Fig. 9-17C). To position the holes accurately, put a shelf in place and pencil around it. Mark and drill for dowels (Fig. 9-17D). Drill these holes, with scrap wood against the other side to prevent the surface from breaking out. Put the shelf back in place and drill into it from the other side. Dowel ends will not be very obvious in the finished unit, but in veneered particle board you can cut them short and cover them with plastic plugs (Fig. 9-17E).

If there is to be a back to the center shelves, prepare the top and bottom ones first. Nail or screw the back to them before they are doweled in place. Bring the other shelves close to the back and put glue on them as they are doweled to the uprights.

Plan the layout so there are no shelves at the same level on opposite sides of an upright. It will then be impossible to dowel the central shelves with the side sections already in position. If putting shelves at the same level cannot be avoided, the second shelf will have to rest on cleats (Fig. 9-17F) screwed to the sides. The shelf then will be screwed to them.

UNIT GLASS-DOOR BOOKCASE

Any book lover needs plenty of shelf space if his collection of books is to be kept tidily. The library becomes an attractive part of the home's furnishing with ample shelving. It is not always easy to forecast the shelf spacing that will be required as the number of books increases, so adjustable shelving has attractions. If some of the books are valuable, sliding glass doors keep the books clean and free from dust.

The case suggested (Fig. 9-18) is not intended to be used alone, but it can be one of a set of units placed on and beside each other. See Table 9-5. Supports and top decorations may be added to decorate a set of units. Although one smaller unit may stand freely, even that will tend to fall forward. If

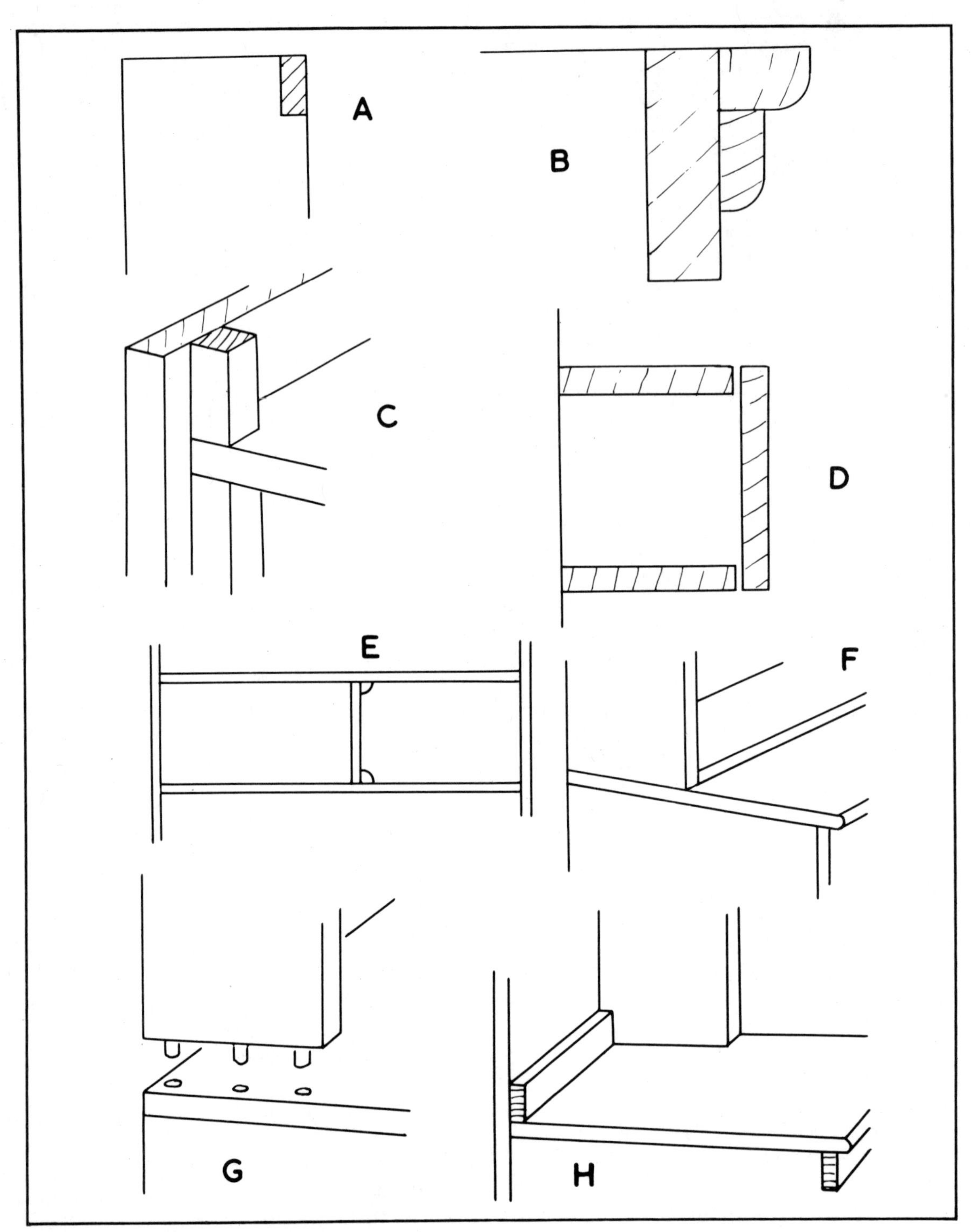

Fig. 9-16. Methods of assembling parts of a full wall unit.

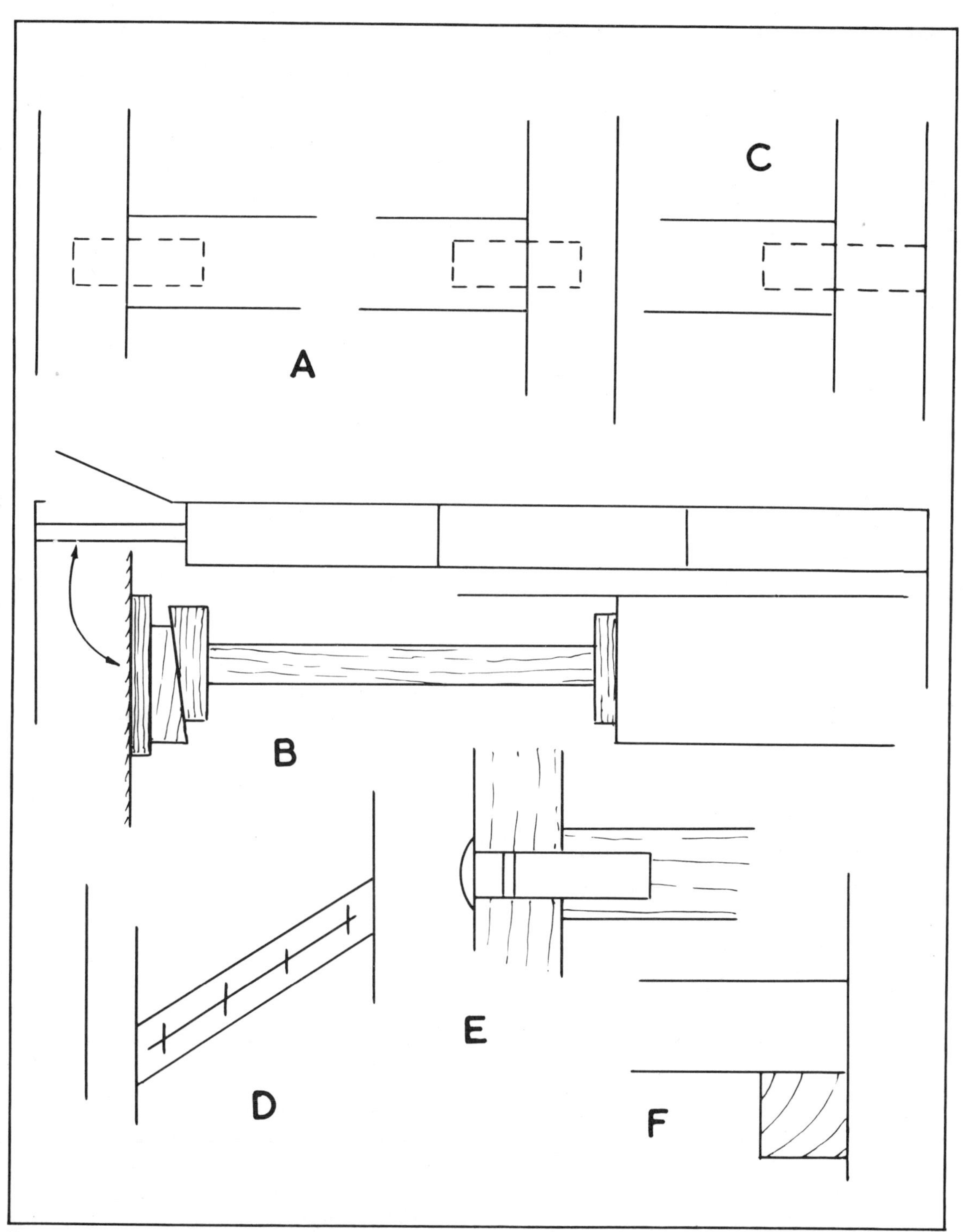

Fig. 9-17. Doweling and clamping with wedges when assembling the full wall unit.

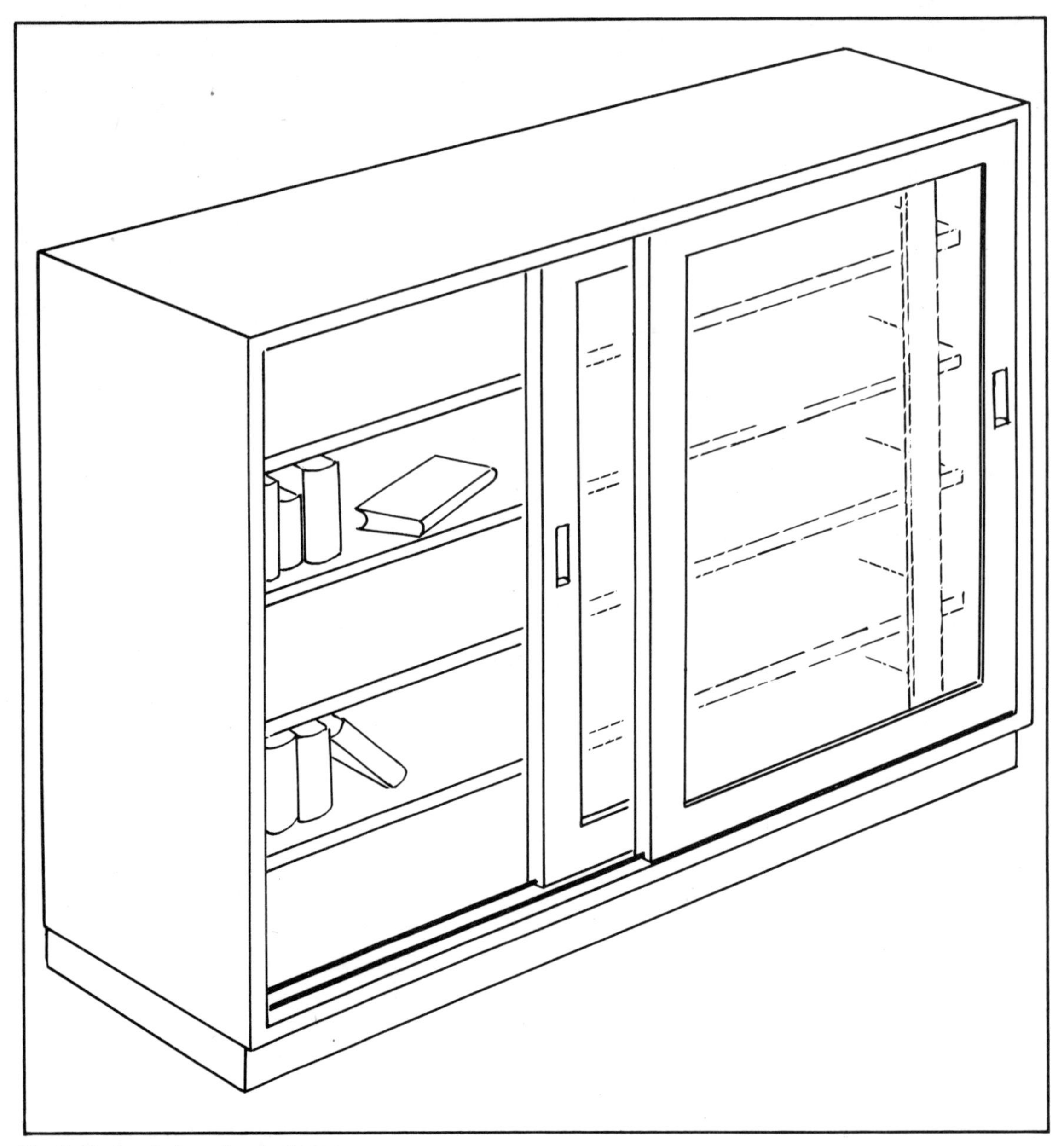

Fig. 9-18. A unit glass-door bookcase.

one unit is put on another, both should be secured to the wall.

One unit is dimensioned as a guide to detail sizes (Fig. 9-19). You can regulate sizes according to books, with a lower case with bigger books projecting further, so there is a ledge below the narrower upper unit. A case about 48 inches high gives a top convenient for use when standing, then there can be another almost as high on top of it. Allow for a plinth below the bottom case.

The key sizes are obtained from a cross section. In this case we have allowed for books up to 7

Table 9-5. Materials List for Unit Glass-Door Bookcase.

2 sides	10½ × 45 × ⅞
top and bottom	10½ × 55 × ⅞
1 back	44 × 54 × ¼ plywood
4 shelves	7½ × 54 × ⅞
4 door stiles	2 × 44 × 1
2 door rails	2 × 29 × 1
2 bottom door rails	3 × 29 × 1
4 fillets	½ × 40 × ½
4 fillets	½ × 27 × ½
1 plinth front	4 × 54 × ⅝
2 plinth ends	4 × 10 × ⅝
1 plinth back	2 × 54 × ⅝

inches wide (Fig. 9-20A). That settles the width of boards needed.

For a unit of the size suggested, the parts should be made of a strong hardwood no thinner than specified. A row of books is a considerable weight that will cause a weak shelf to sag after a few weeks of use.

The case is really a rectangular box with a plywood back. Make it square, as an error in shaping may affect the action of the sliding doors.

The best corner joints are through dovetails cut by hand (Fig. 9-20B). You can cut dovetails with the aid of a jig and a cutter driven by an electric drill (Fig. 9-20C). In a simple assembly you can lap and screw the corners or use one of the other box joints. Cut rabbets for the plywood back on all four pieces, then the top and bottom need grooves for the rails on which the doors run. These are ¼-inch-by-½-inch straight-grained hardwood strips, which will be glued in the bottom grooves. The top ones should only be a push fit, so they can be put in as the doors are fitted. They may be pulled out if you ever need to remove the doors later.

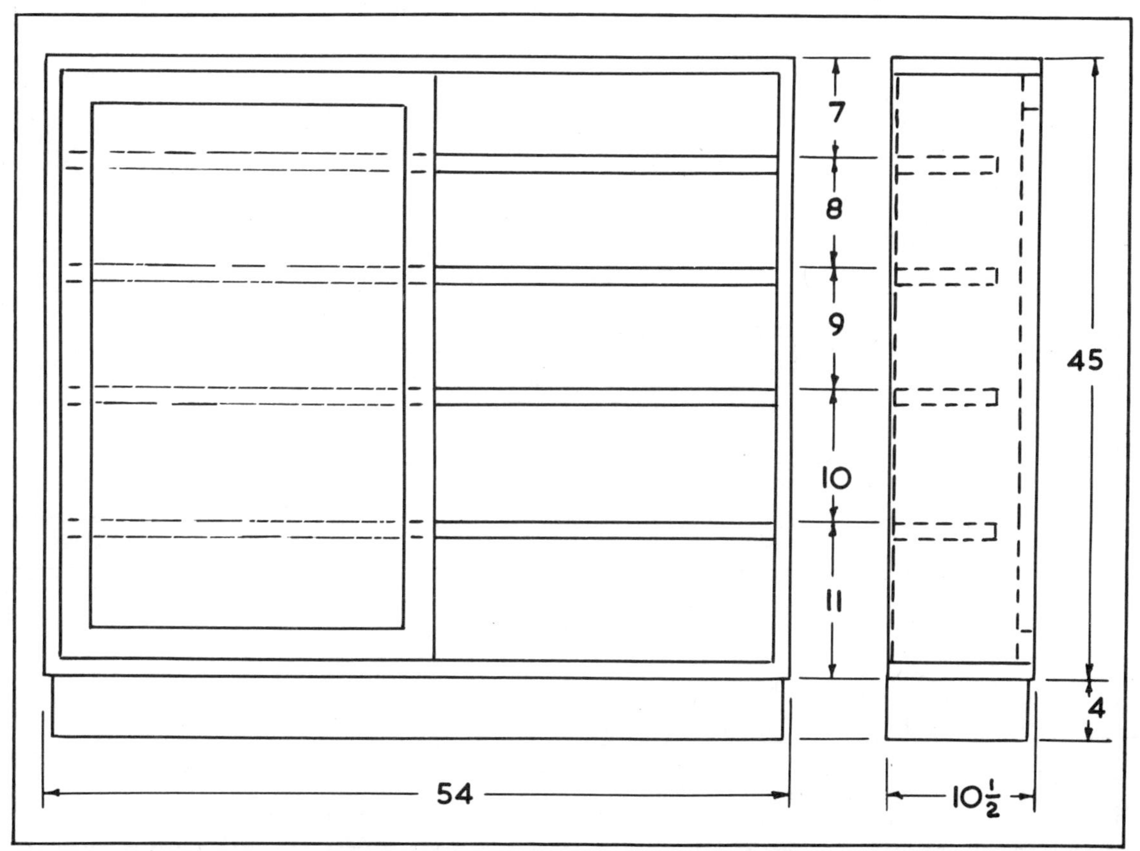

Fig. 9-19. Sizes of a glass-front bookcase.

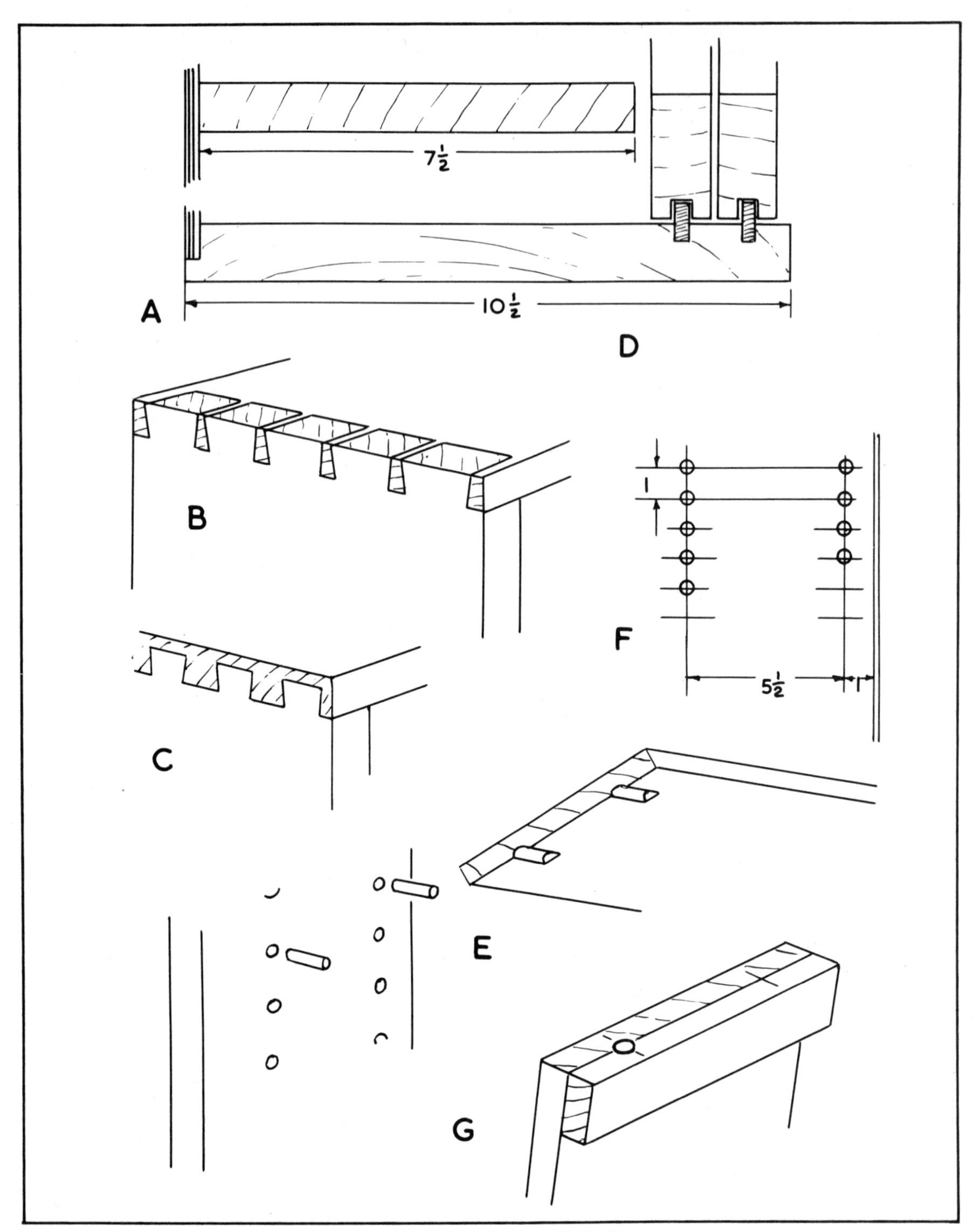

Fig. 9-20. Carcass construction (A to D) and adjustable shelf details (E, F, G).

You can buy door track, with balls or rollers to take the weight. The doors have to be made to suit. These instructions assume you will use wood tracks.

Prepare the grooves to suit the strips and position them so they will come central in the door frames (Fig. 9-20D). Let slightly less than half the depth of a strip into its groove.

Holes for pegs in each end are needed so the shelves can be adjusted. The pegs may be pieces of ½-inch dowel rods. Half holes in the ends of the shelves are for mating with the pegs (Fig. 9-20E).

Marking out and drilling must be done as precisely as possible. Have two lines of holes in each end, starting at the lowest position you expect to need the bottom shelf and finishing at the highest position that you expect to put the top one. One-inch spacing can be used (Fig. 9-20F), although a little more than that will suit most needs. Use a stop on the drill or drill press, so all holes finish the same depth. Choose a drill that allows a push fit on the dowel, so it will not be difficult moving dowels.

Mark where the half holes are to come on the undersides of the shelves. Clamp a piece of scrap wood across an end and drill where the surfaces meet (Fig. 9-20G). If you go between ⅝ inch and ¾ inch into the side and the shelf, that will be satisfactory. Cut pieces of dowel rod to lengths that allow the shelves to drop on easily. You may find it easier to be accurate if you drill the sides, then assemble the case before cutting the shelves to length and drilling them.

The doors look best if their bottom rails are wider than the others, but you can make all the frame parts the same width. In the bottom rails make grooves wide enough to slide easily, but only deep enough to run on the rails without their edges touching the bottom part of the case (Fig. 9-21A). At the top you can make the grooves deeper without affecting performance (Fig. 9-21B). Deep grooves prevent the doors from binding when they are moved, and they allow you to plane off the top of a door if you need to during fitting.

You can set the glass panels in grooves in the frames. If you break a piece of glass, though, you can not fit another and will have to make a new frame. It is better to rabbet the frames so the glass can be held in with a fillet (Fig. 9-21C), either screwed or lightly nailed, so it can be pried out if necessary.

The corners may be doweled (Fig. 9-21D) or tenoned (Fig. 9-21E). Notice that the sides go the full depth. After the doors have been assembled, you must cut the grooves across the end grain of the sides by using a fine backsaw and a narrow chisel (Fig. 9-21F).

Both doors slide the full width, and their inner stiles (upright rails) overlap. You can put a knob or handle near the center of an outer stile (Fig. 9-21G) and rely on reaching inside to move the inner door, as that cannot have a projecting handle. Another way is to put finger grooves in both doors (Fig. 9-21H).

Try the doors in position without the glass and check their action. If that is satisfactory, you may want to stain and polish all the wood before fitting the glass. Finish the insides of the rabbets and the fillet strips, as their surfaces toward the glass will show through it.

The glass should be a fairly close fit, but it should not be so tight as to need forcing in, as that will bring a risk of cracking when a door is moved. Fit the fillets closely; the glass must not rattle.

A bottom unit should be raised from the floor. This can be by a plinth (Fig. 9-22A), which is full depth at front and ends, but at the back you only need fit a strip for screwing to the wall.

If the wall has a baseboard, the plinth can be the same depth, so the bookcase unit goes flat on the wall.

You can raise the unit more with legs, made up like the frame of a table (Fig. 9-22B), to any height you wish. If you make the legs very long, lower rails will be needed. With the plinth or table frame, set it back a short distance from the case edges.

With a single unit there is a useful broad top that should be given a back rail, which may be straight (Fig. 9-22C) or shaped (Fig. 9-22D). You can provide end supports so another row of books may be put on top (Fig. 9-22E).

If one unit is put on top of another and there is space between it and the ceiling, appearance is improved with a headboard at the front. The head-

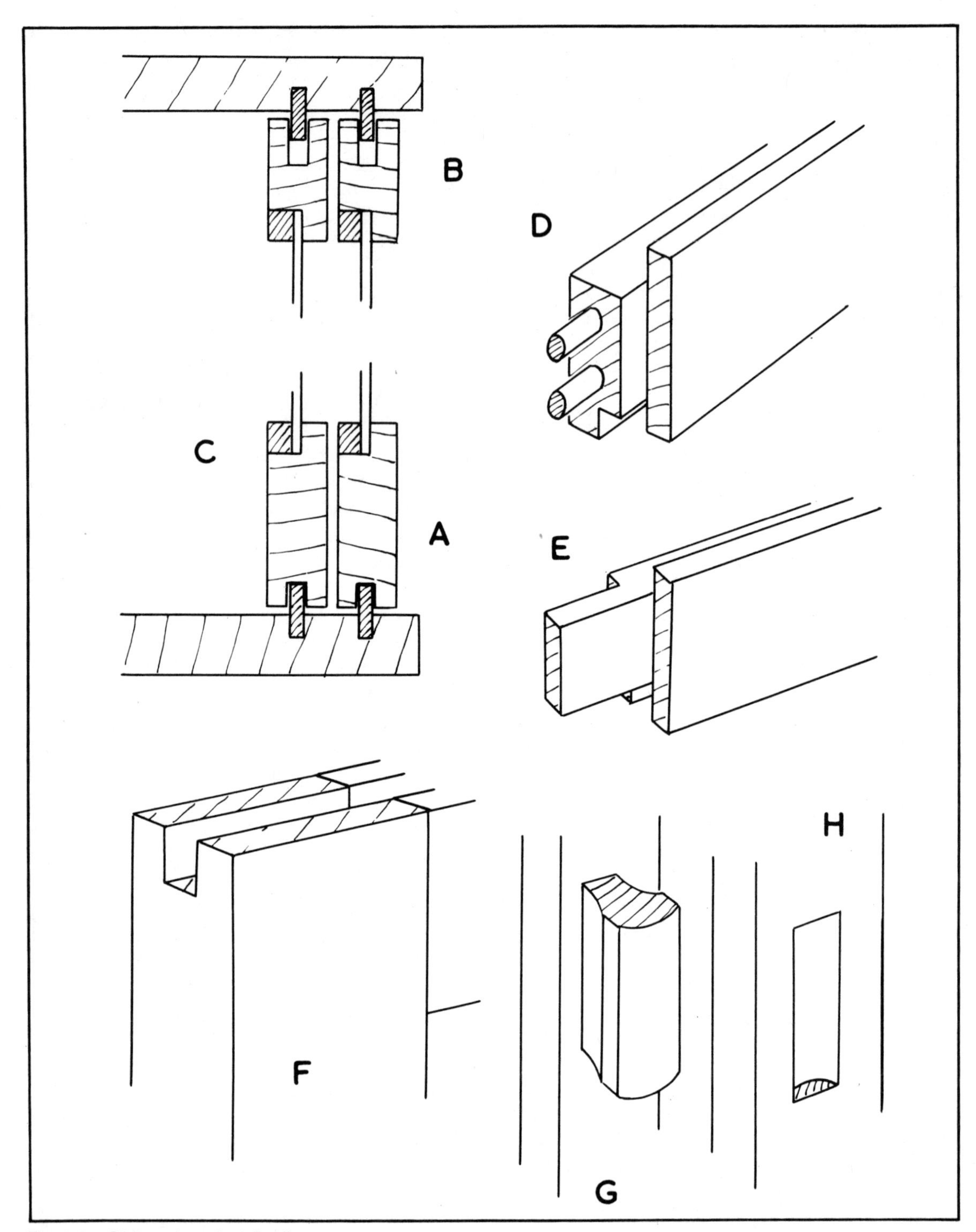

Fig. 9-21. Sliding glass door details.

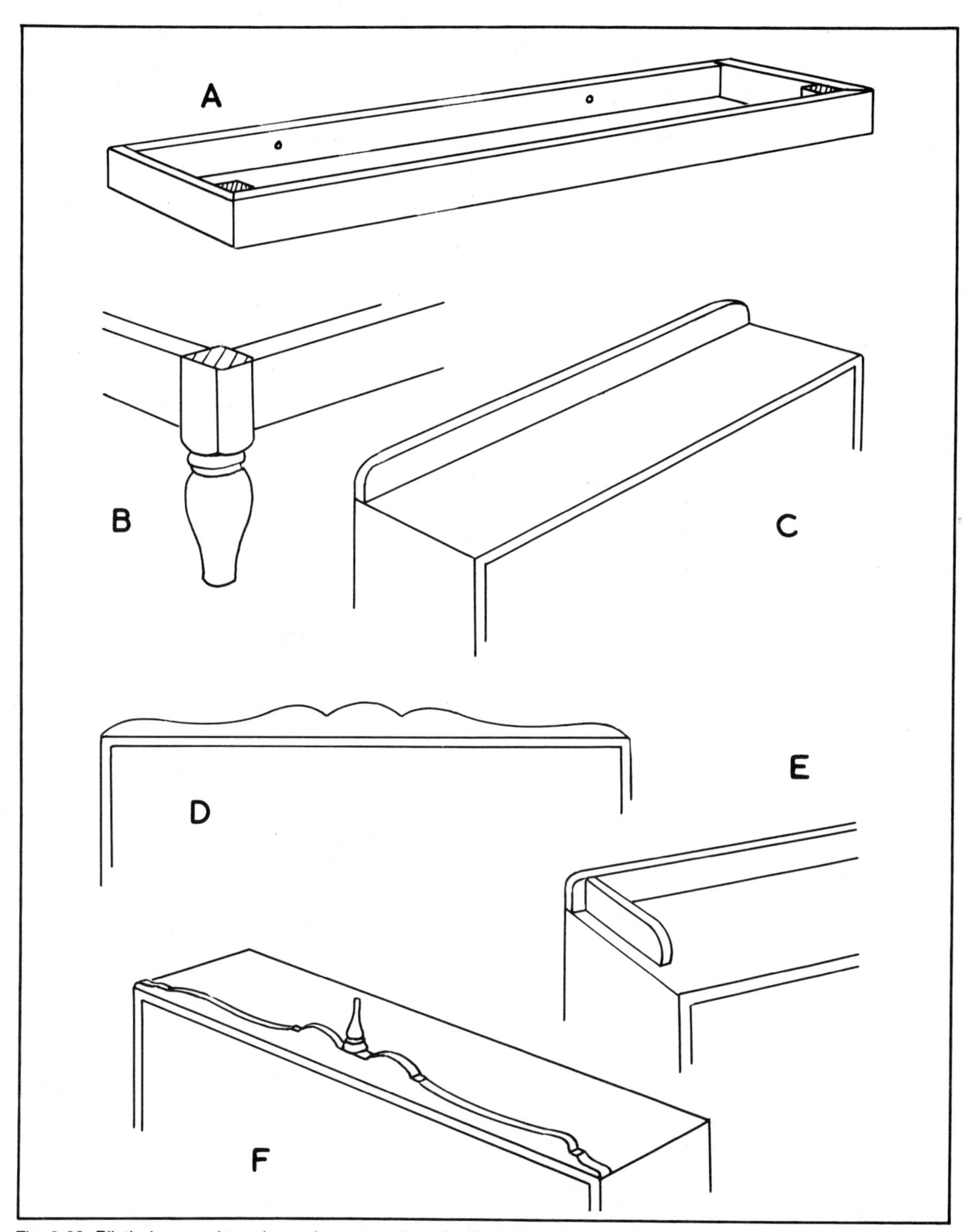

Fig. 9-22. Plinth, legs, and top decoration suggestions for the bookcase.

board should be shaped if the available space will allow it (Fig. 9-22F).

When one unit is put on another, both should be screwed to the wall. There may also be screws through the bottom of the top unit into the other. If units are put beside each other, they can be screwed together. Any plinth or stand is better made in one length under both parts. A headboard should also go right across, with the center of its shaping over the joint.

WINDOW RECESS SEAT

If a room includes a window recess where the window projects outward in a bay, that is an obvious place to provide a seat with storage underneath. The storage can be arranged with doors to open at the front of the seat. There can also be drawers, but probably the most convenient and simplest access is by treating the seat as a chest with a lifting lid (Fig. 9-23).

Sizes will have to be arranged to suit the available space, but the seat height should be between 14 inches and 16 inches. The front may be paneled, with the width divided so the panels are approximately square (Fig. 9-24). The seat should be a comfortable distance front to back, probably about 18 inches. If cushions are to be used at the back, it may be a few inches more. A wide chest will have increased capacity, but the primary use is as a seat, so comfortable proportions are important. The lifting top should not be made the full width, as it must swing up without rubbing the sides. Its hinge line should be far enough forward for the raised top to clear the windowsill or any other obstructions.

Set out the seat's outline on the walls of the recess. This can be light penciling indicating the height and width. Get the sizes to make the chest front from this penciling.

There are at least two ways to make the front. The simplest way is to cut a piece of plywood to size

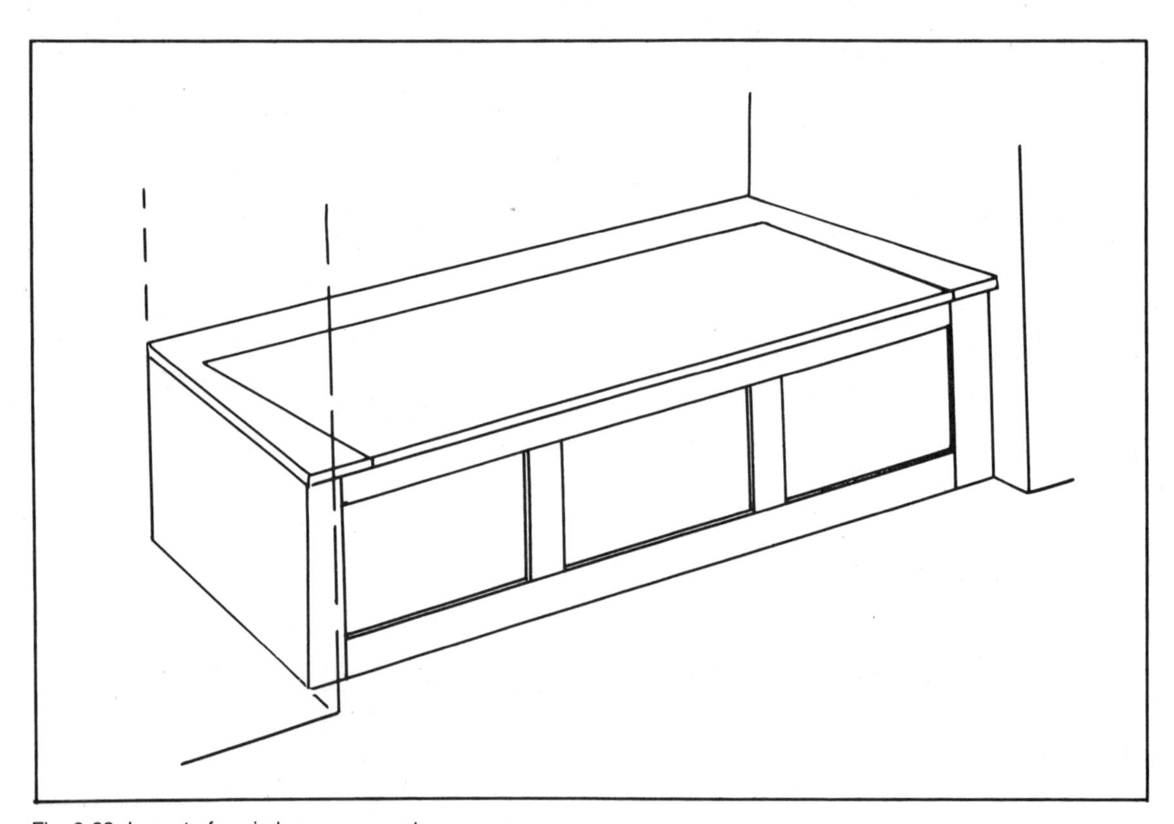

Fig. 9-23. Layout of a window recess seat.

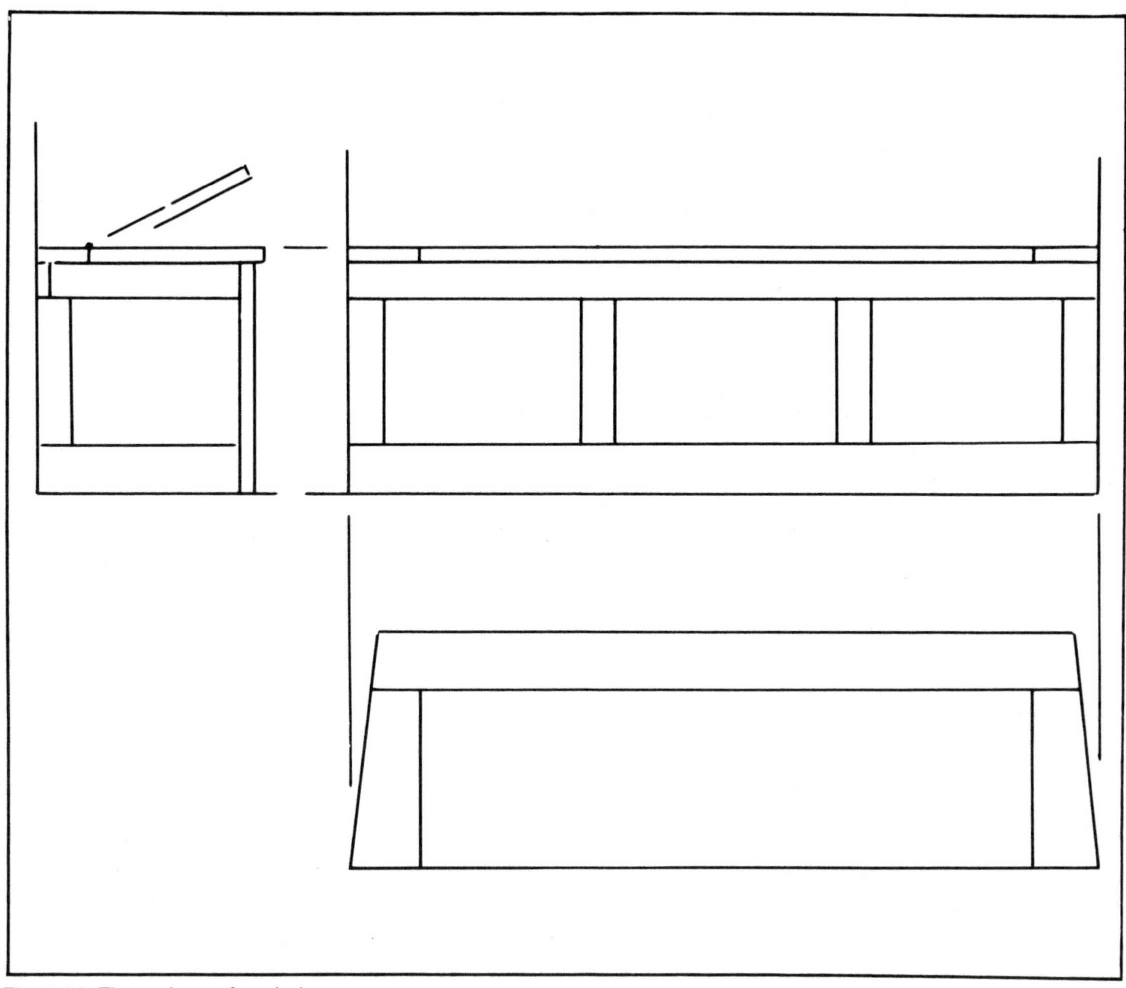

Fig. 9-24. Three views of a window recess seat.

and add the framing to its front (Fig. 9-25A). Use glue and screws or nails from inside. If the recess sides slope, bevel the end pieces to make a tight fit at the front.

The traditional construction uses grooved framing with plywood panels (Fig. 9-25B) and mortise and tenon joints (Fig. 9-25C). Whatever method of construction is used, stopped chamfers on the framing around each panel are decorative (Fig. 9-25D).

Arrange vertical strips inside the ends of the front for attaching to the wall (Fig. 9-25E). There can be a similar strip along the bottom for screws to the floor.

The rest of the framing may be fitted in position. Put a strip along the wall at the back and side pieces out to the front strips (Fig. 9-25F). Arrange the pieces that frame the top on the strip (Fig. 9-26A). It may be sufficient to screw to the supporting strips, but the tops can be kept level with shallow tenons from the sides into the back (Fig. 9-26B). Let the sides overhang the front by about 1 inch, which will also be the overhang of the lid.

In a small seat the lid can be solid wood or a piece of thick plywood. In a larger seat it may be plywood framed below (Fig. 9-26C). Arrange a strip at the front to hide the plywood edge (Fig. 9-26D) or rabbet the front frame (Fig. 9-26E).

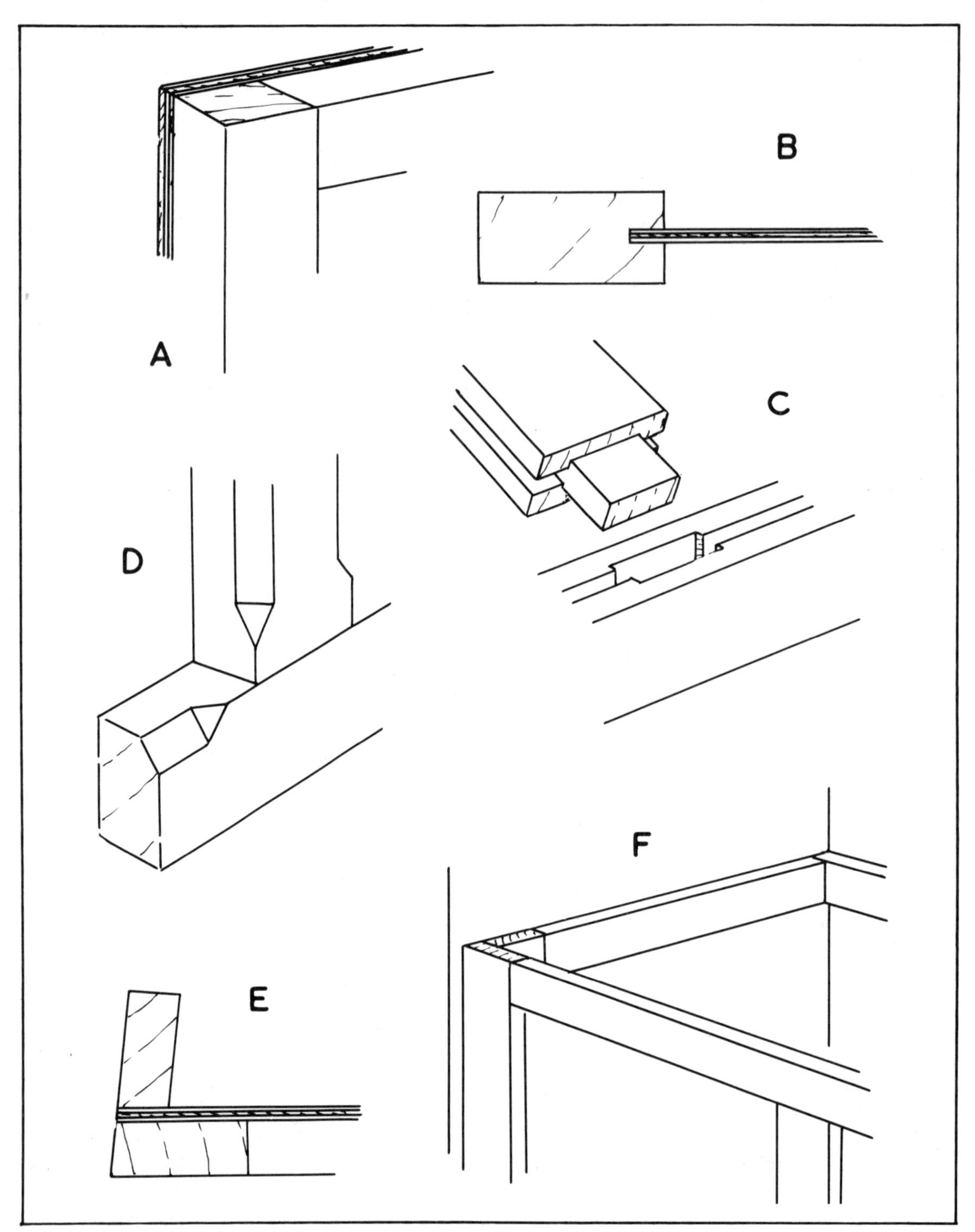

Fig. 9-25. Framing details of a window recess seat.

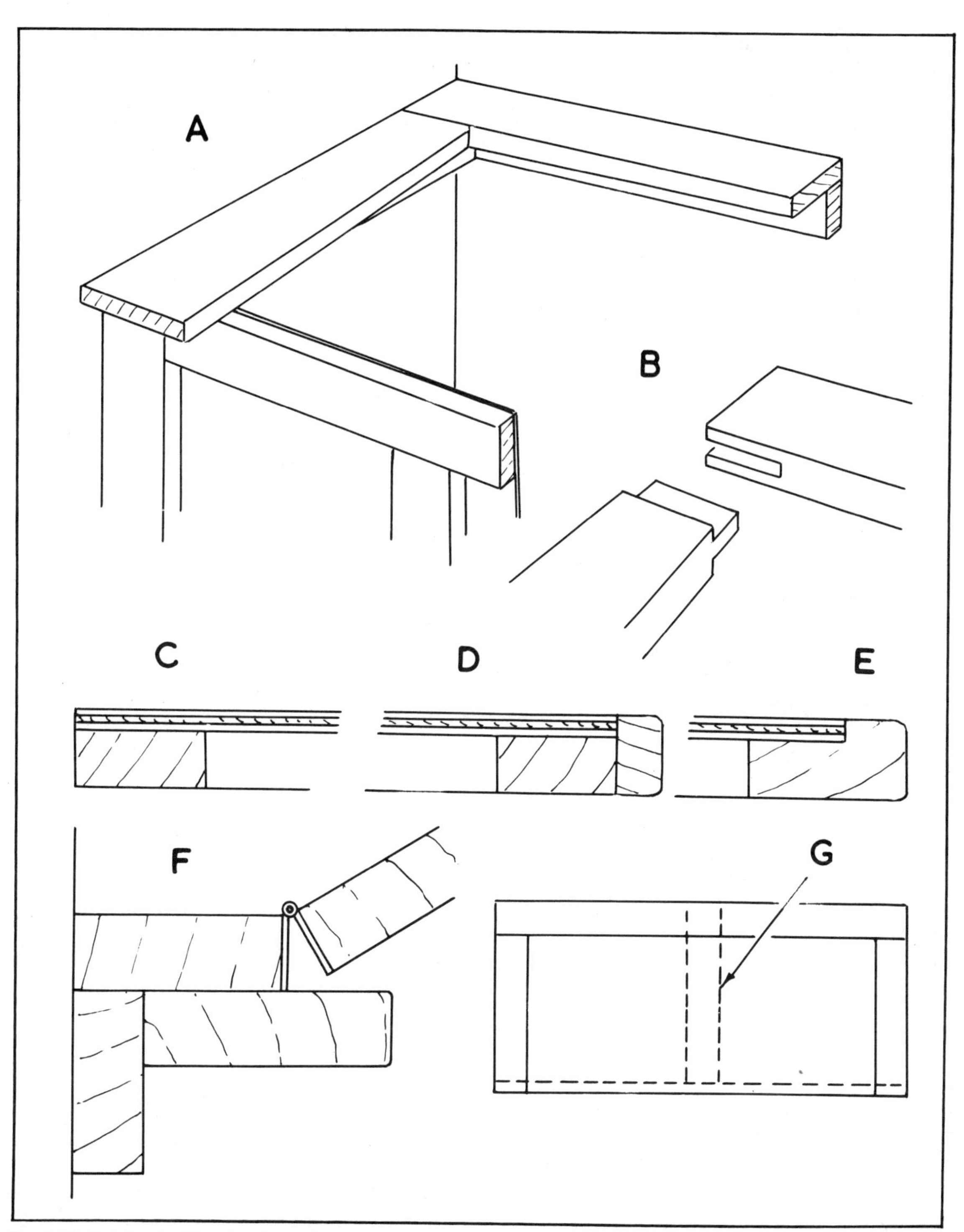

Fig. 9-26. Details of a lifting top for a window recess seat.

More than two hinges will probably be needed to make a strong joint. Put a hinge near each end and others at not more than 18-inch intervals. The hinges may take the load, but for long-term use it is worthwhile putting a supporting strip under the joint (Fig. 9-26F). If the seat is very long, there may be an intermediate support to brace the front and prevent the seat from sagging (Fig. 9-26G).

Chapter 10

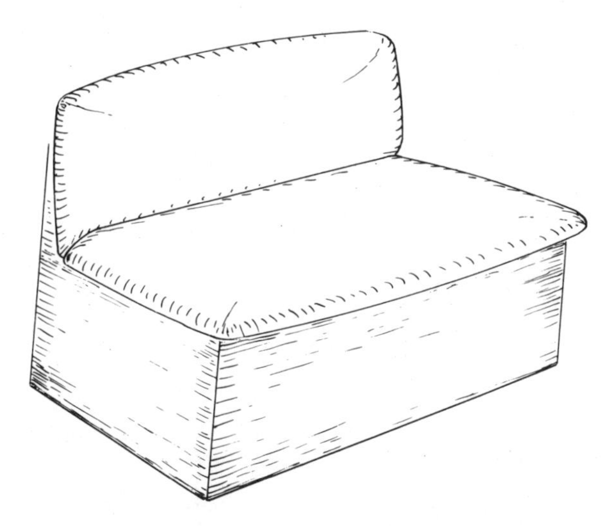

Living Room Furniture

THE ROOM THAT GETS MOST USE BY THE FAMILY needs chairs, tables, and storage space. If it is a large room, many of these things may be free-standing. Even if there is plenty of space, it may be better to attach some furniture to the walls so it does not get moved about or knocked over. If the room is not as big as you want, making built-in furniture will usually mean that the item is just as useful, but does not occupy as much floor space as a freestanding piece for the same purpose.

Many pieces of furniture described elsewhere in this book can also be used in a living room or family room. If the room is multi-purpose, you may want to equip one corner as an office or den and have dining facilities in part of the room. Folding tables can be used in many other places. Differences may be in the quality of finish. You usually want nicely finished hardwood in a family room, but in a den a similar thing can be made of softwood. It may be better painted for use outside.

Some furniture pieces have to be deeper back to front to insure stability when freestanding. Some examples described here are shallower as the wall provides rigidity. They are simpler and cheaper to build, while still being of sufficient size to adequately serve their purpose. If you want a table or other item to fold, it can be brought to a much thinner folded form when it is attached to a wall than if it has to be stable when not supported in this way.

GATELEG FLAP TABLE

A simple flap table with a bracket support depends entirely on the security of attachment to the wall. If the support can be arranged with a leg to the floor, much of the load on the wall fastenings will be reduced. This is preferable for a large table or one expected to carry heavy loads.

The example (Figs. 10-1 and 10-2) has a flap hinged to a part attached to the wall. The support is similar to one of the pair of gates provided for a freestanding gateleg table. See Table 10-1.

The tabletop can be made of several pieces of solid wood glued to make up the width. It can be plywood or particle board. To reduce the risk of solid wood warping, two battens may be screwed across underneath. Keep them outside the swing of

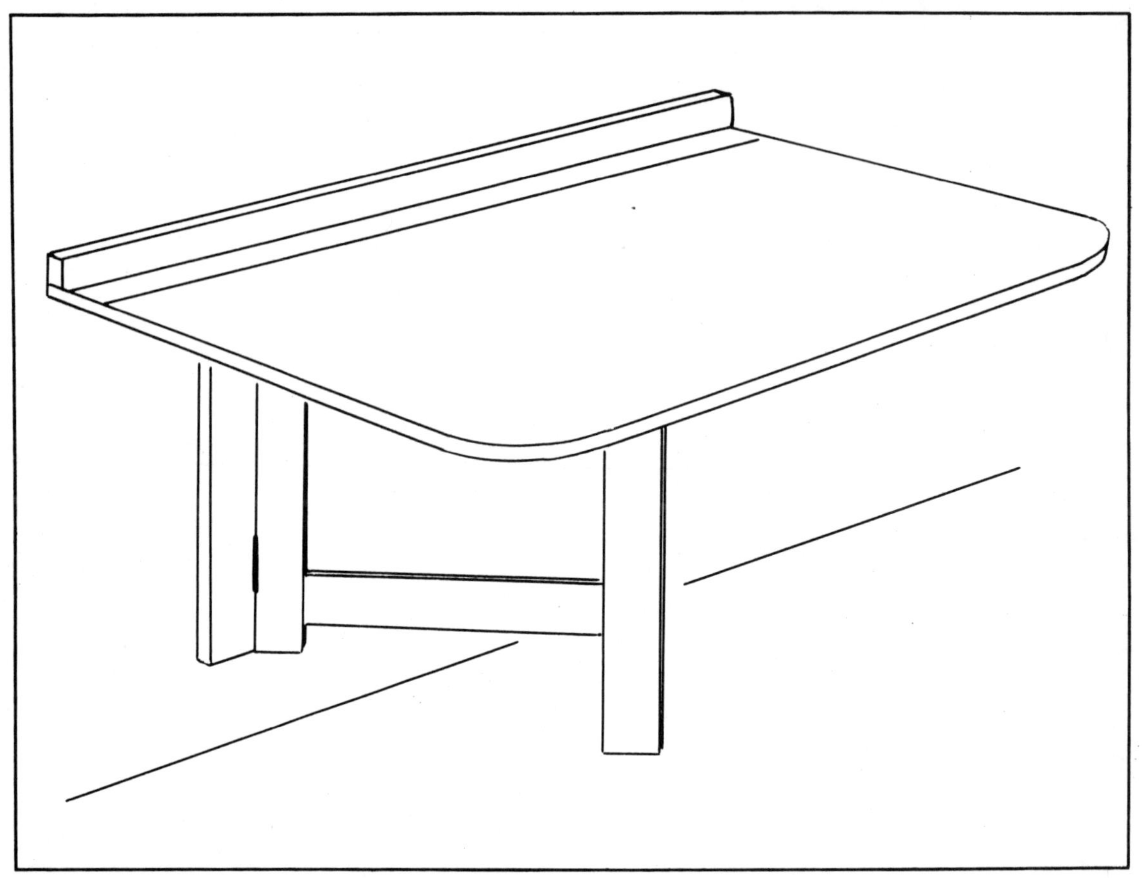

Fig. 10-1. A gateleg flap table that folds against the wall.

the leg. To allow for expansion and contraction of a solid wood top, put the screw in each batten through a round hole near the wall edge. Make the other holes into slots (Fig. 10-3A), increasing their lengths as they get further from the wall. Do not use glue on the battens.

The back is screwed upward into the strip that attaches to the wall. Join the flap to this with T hinges. Have one hinge near each end and space two hinges more evenly between them. The strip on which the gateleg pivots should be screwed to the wall, so the gateleg is central when folded. Keep it short enough not to show when the flap is lowered.

Make the leg high enough to keep the top level when it fits into a stop. The assembly then comes against the pivot piece (Fig. 10-3B) where two hinges hold it. The best joints are mortise and tenons (Fig. 10-33C), but it is simpler to halve the parts together (Fig. 10-3D). Use screws or dowels across halved joints.

The top can have square corners or be rounded. The flap may be a semicircle or half an octagon. Round or mold the exposed edges in any case.

Table 10-1. Materials List for Gateleg Flap Table.

Part	Size
1 top	25 × 43 × 1
2 top battens	3 × 22 × 1
1 back	2½ × 43 × 1
1 back suport	3 × 43 × 1
1 leg support	3 × 24 × 1
1 leg	3 × 30 × 1
1 leg pivot	3 × 24 × 1
2 leg rails	3 × 24 × 1

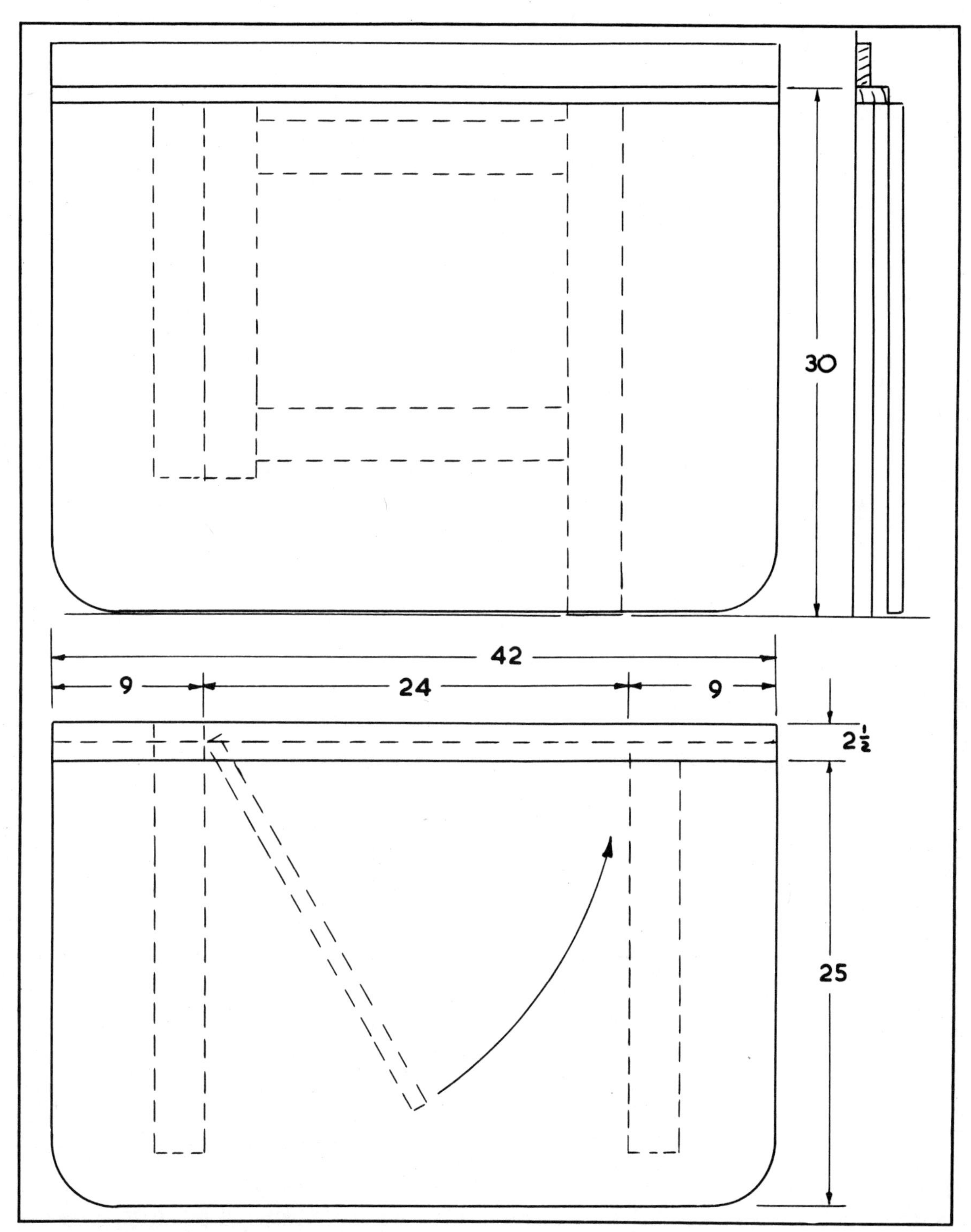

Fig. 10-2. Suggested sizes for a gateleg flap table.

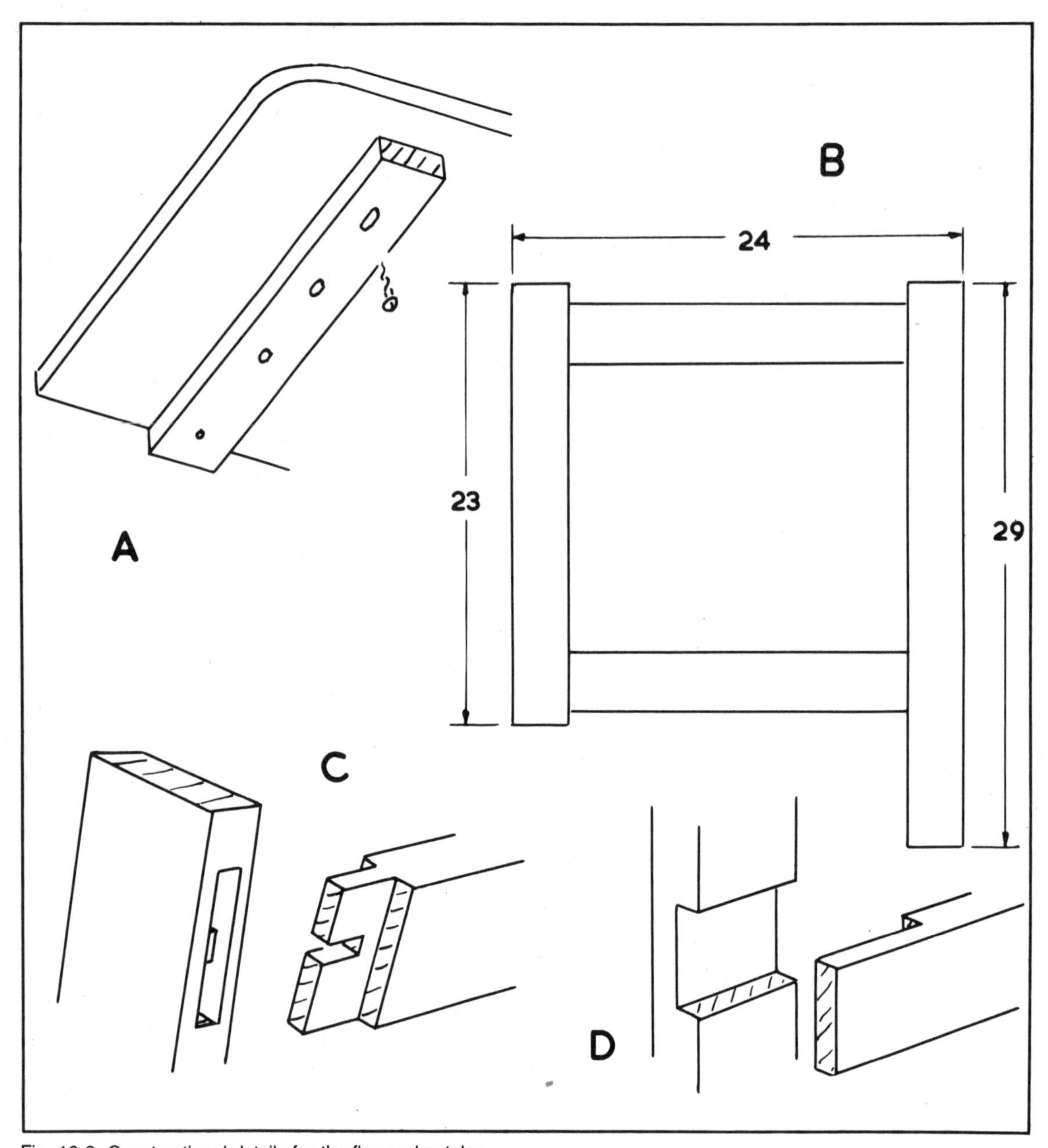

Fig. 10-3. Constructional details for the flap and gateleg.

RULE JOINT FLAP

A plain flap with hinges below pivots about the center of the hinge knuckle. When the flap is hanging, the square edges are exposed. There is a gap between them (Fig. 10-4A). This is satisfactory for many purposes, but for good quality cabinetry a special hinge is used to make a molded appearance when the flap is hanging.

An ordinary hinge will not move far in the direction opposite to closing. A backflap hinge is made to turn back an additional 90° (Fig. 10-4B). Its screw holes are countersunk on the opposite side to normal, so it can be mounted with the knuckles within the thickness of the wood. The edges of the wood are cut to curves having the knuckles as their center (Fig. 10-4C). Because of the similarity of the section to one form of folding rule, this is called a *rule joint.* To get the shapes to make the edge sections, set out an end view full-size.

The inner part can be started with a rabbet (Fig. 10-4D). Rounding may be done with a rabbet plane if a suitable curved plane or spindle is unavailable (Fig. 10-4E). The other part is best made with a spindle or curved plane, but there can be a series of rabbets (Fig. 10-4F) followed by sanding with abrasive paper on a shaped block.

A rule joint can be used with a flap that has square or other molded outer edges. It looks best if the edges are molded in a similar way to the rule joint (Fig. 10-4G).

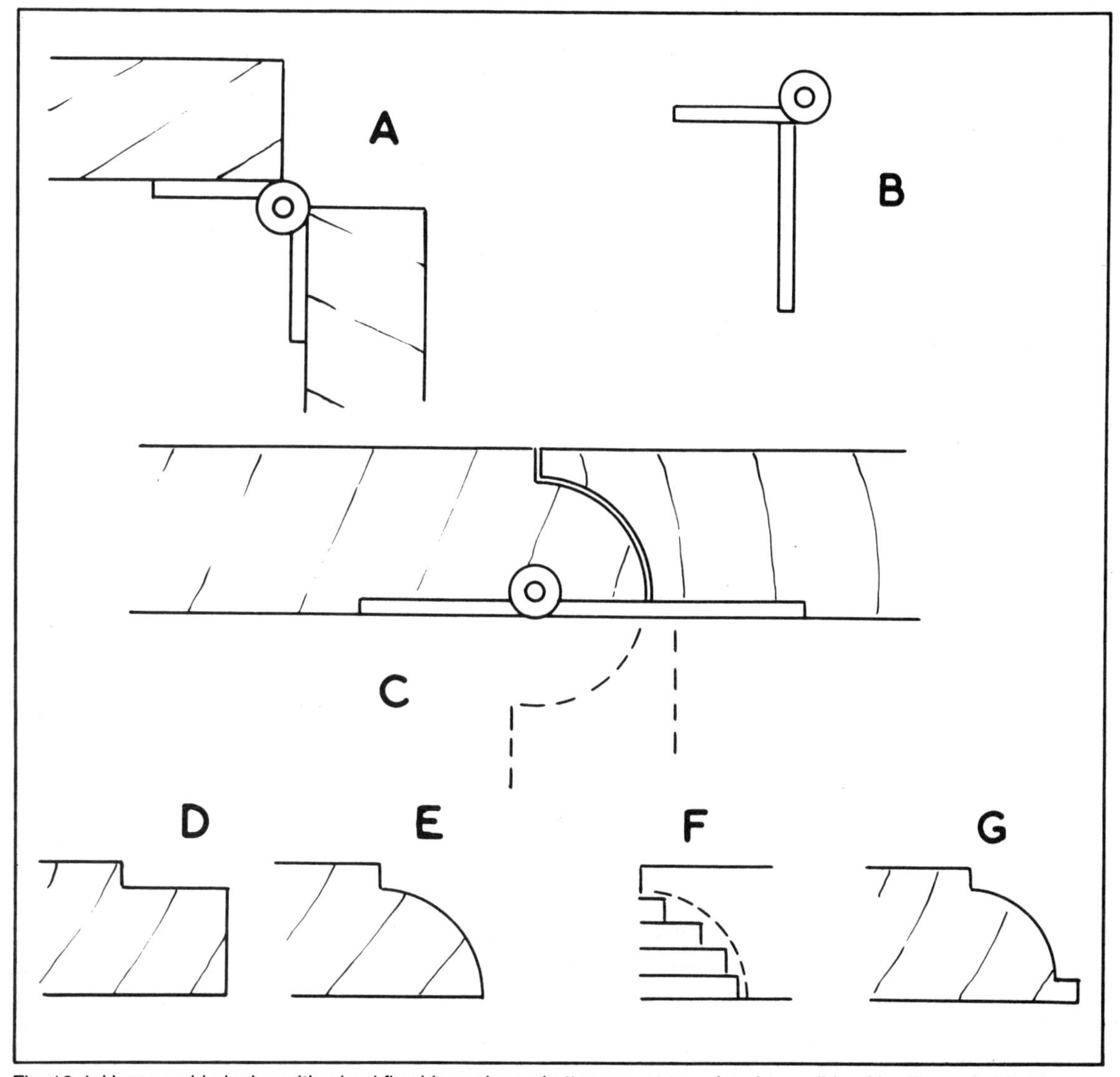

Fig. 10-4. How a molded edge with a backflap hinge gives a better appearance than is possible with a flap and plain hinge.

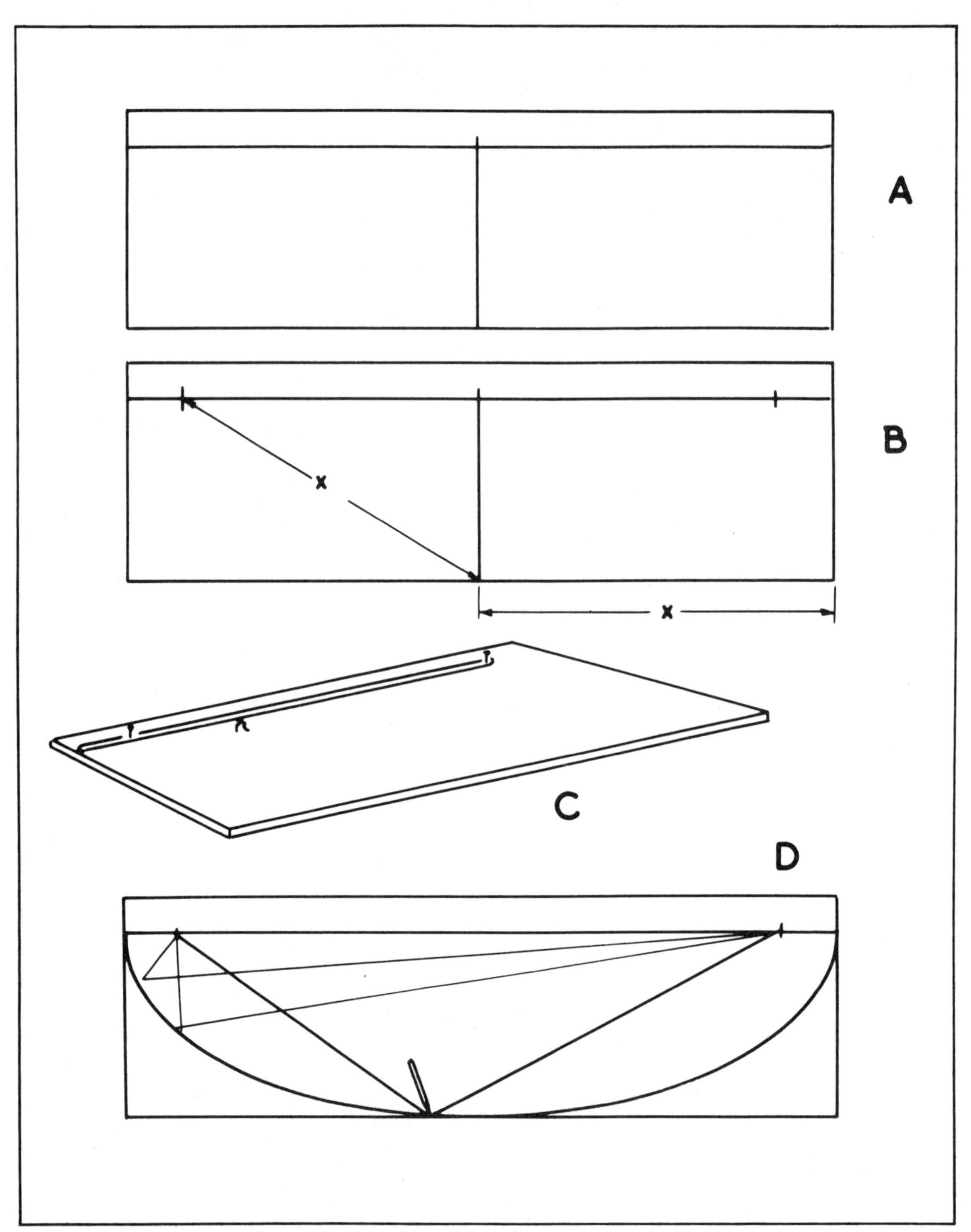

Fig. 10-5. A flap can be given a half-elliptical shape by drawing with the aid of string, nails, and pencil.

ELLIPTICAL FLAP

A drop flap or leaf can have any outline you wish. Square corners will give a maximum useful area, but the corners are liable to be knocked and can be a nuisance in a restricted space. Of the many possible outlines, a half-ellipse gives one of the more pleasing shapes. The problem is how to draw it.

Allow for the edge being straight for an inch or so in the vicinity of the joint. Lay out the shape with a base line parallel with the joint (Fig. 10-5A). Draw a center line the other way. Work on the undersurface. Measure half the base line and use this distance from the top of the center line to mark on the base line (Fig. 10-5B). These are the two foci about which the half-ellipse is drawn. Drive two thin nails lightly into each of these points. Make a loop of nonstretch string around the nails and to one end (Fig. 10-5C). Put the point of a pencil in the loop and move it around, keeping a tension on the string (Fig. 10-5D). If the first trial does not give quite the shape you want, move the nails in or out and adjust the size of the string loop.

LIFT-OFF TABLE

A drop-flap table is limited in its projection from the wall by its height. If it pivots at 30 inches from the floor, it has to hang there and can only project as much as will clear the floor—30 inches or less. If you want to use a longer table, you must be able to remove it from the wall and store it leaning against the wall or elsewhere.

Table 10-2. Materials List for Lift-Off Table.

1 top	24	×	50	×	¾ plywood
2 stiffeners	1	×	48	×	1
1 stiffener	1	×	20	×	1
1 leg	3	×	30	×	1
1 leg top	3	×	20	×	1
1 wall fitment	3	×	24	×	¼ plywood
1 wall fitment	1	×	24	×	1
1 wall fitment	¾	×	24	×	⅝
1 wall fitment	1	×	24	×	⅜
1 table end	½	×	24	×	½
1 leg gusset	9	×	9	×	¼ plywood

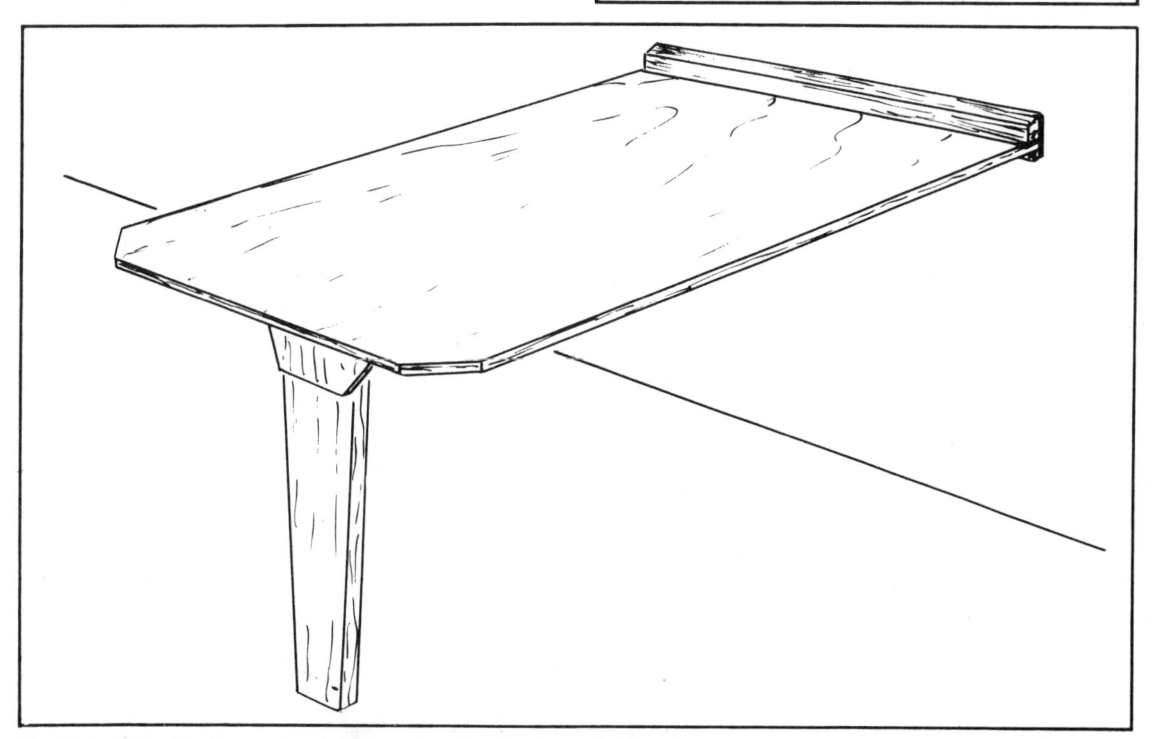

Fig. 10-6. A lift-off table can be made to extend further than a folding flap top.

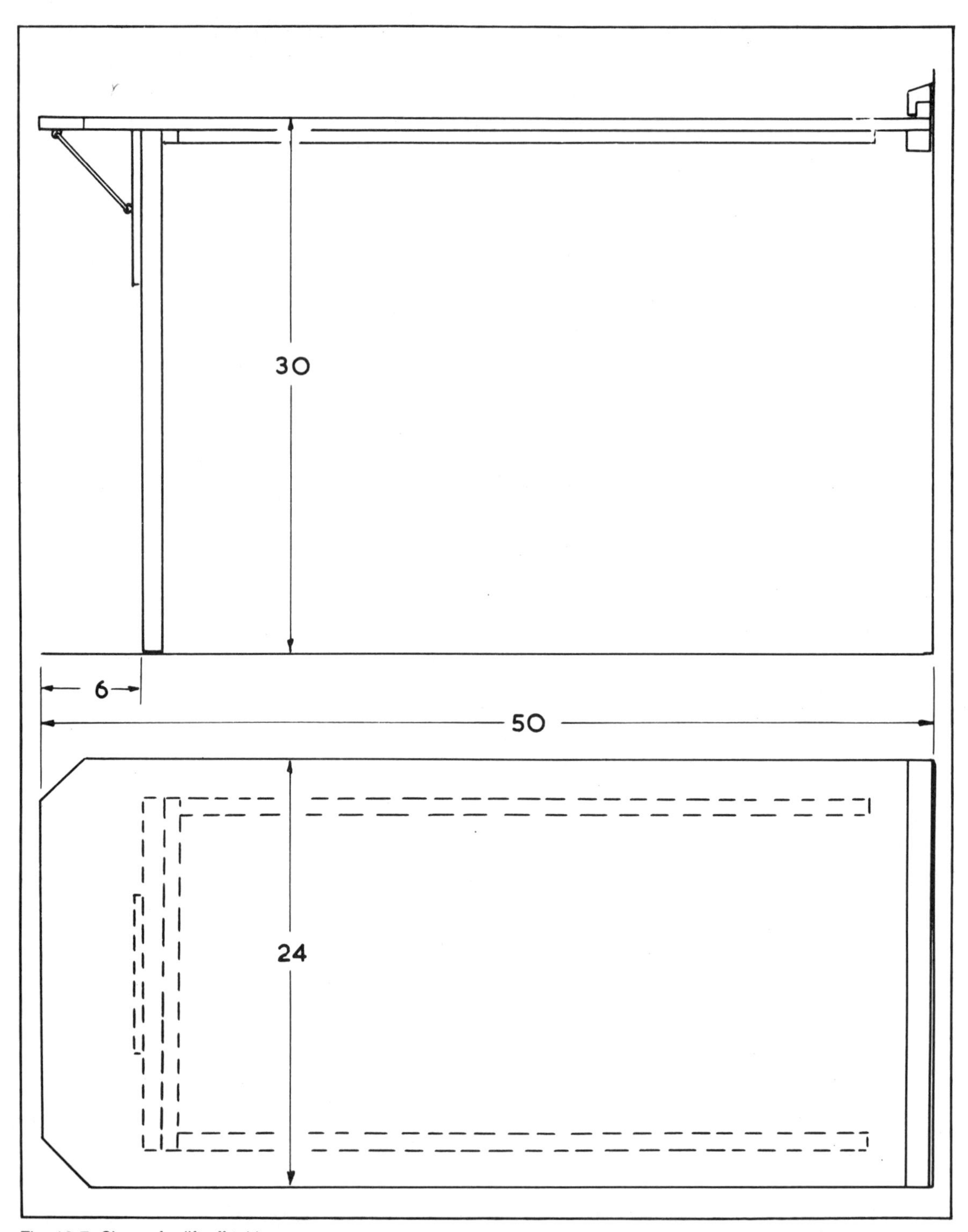

Fig. 10-7. Sizes of a lift-off table.

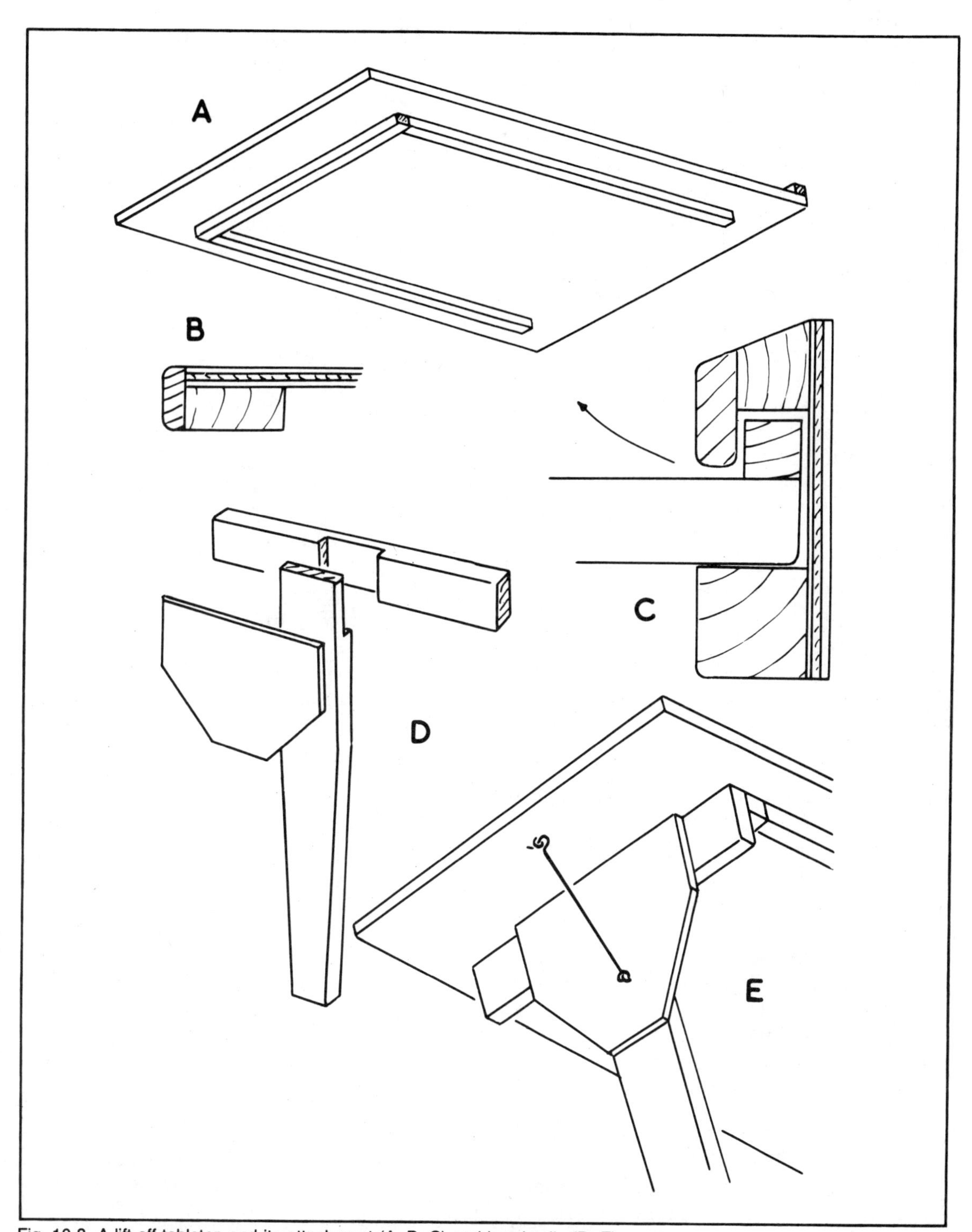

Fig. 10-8. A lift-off tabletop and its attachment (A, B, C) and leg details (D, E).

The suggested table (Fig. 10-6) has a single leg, but a larger table can have a frame with two legs hinged in a similar way. The sizes shown (Fig. 10-7 and Table 10-2) give suitable proportions, but overall sizes can be varied widely to suit your needs.

The simplest tabletop is a piece of ¾-inch or thicker plywood or particle board, with no framing. If some stiffening is needed, strips can be cut short at the ends (Fig. 10-8A). Thinner plywood may be framed fully and edged (Fig. 10-8B). You can use a Formica laminated plastic top with wood or plastic edging. Whatever top is used, consider the method of hooking to the wall and the need for the leg to fold. Make the top first, so the other parts can be fitted to it.

There is a built-up fitment at the wall, which is securely attached and the same length as the width of the table. It is made on a thin plywood back, which can have screws hidden in the gap. The lower piece takes the load on the table. The upper part keeps it in place. Round the lip so the table can be swung upward to release it. The table and its crosspiece do not have to make a tight fit. Experiment with the fit before locating the top part of the fitment. Rounding the table end will make it easier to tilt it up and out (Fig. 10-8C).

The leg and its crossbar can be joined with a mortise and tenon joint, but there should be a plywood gusset over the joint for extra strength. A T-halving joint is simpler to make (Fig. 10-8D). Arrange the hinges so when the leg is upright, the top and the load are not taken by the hinge knuckles. The easiest way to secure the leg upright is to use a hook and eye (Fig. 10-8E).

Instead of the hook and eye, you can use a folding strut on the inner side of the leg. Suitable metal struts can be bought to go inside or on the edge of the leg. Instead of the wooden wall support, you can get metal fittings that link in a similar way from suppliers of equipment for motor homes. They do not project as much when the table is removed.

CORNER TV STAND

A portable TV is best supported at about eye level. A convenient place for it is the corner of a room where it can be kept out of the way. Its shelf can be arranged at a height that will not interfere with chairs or other furniture that may be pushed into the corner.

There can be just a simple shelf. The suggested stand (Fig. 10-9) is a double shelf that provides storage space for magazines or other things. You need not have projecting brackets underneath.

The suggested material is veneered particle board, which can have exposed edges covered with self-adhesive veneer or molded plasticstrips. Solid wood can be used, but several pieces will have to be glued to make up the width. Arrange the grain to be diagonal across the corner. If plywood is used, the edges will have to be lipped with solid wood.

The sizes suggested should suit most small portable TVs. See Table 10-3. If you want to use a particular set, draw a plan view of it with a center line through it. From that line, draw other lines at 45° to represent the walls and add the front lines (Fig. 10-10A). This shape allows for the set being viewed at about 45°, but it does not have to be that way. In a long room you may prefer to use a shelf longer one way (Fig. 10-10B). Draw your plan view of the set at the angle you want it and fit a suitable shelf shape around it. The projection of the sides from the wall should be 6 inches or less.

Check the angle of the room's corner. If it is not square, make the top and bottom to suit and check that they match each other.

The two back pieces come between the top and bottom and inside the ends. You can screw downward through the top, using counterbored holes and plastic plugs in veneered particle board (Fig. 10-11A) or wood plugs in wood or plywood. If you will prefer not to have the fasteners showing on top, use a strip of wood for screws both ways (Fig. 10-11B). Join the backs to the top first. Add the ends in the same way, with strips inside (Fig. 10-11C). Drill for the screws that will go through the backs into the

Table 10-3. Materials List for Corner TV Stand.

2 panels	22 × 36 × ¾
2 backs	6 × 24 × ¾
2 ends	6 × 7 × ¾

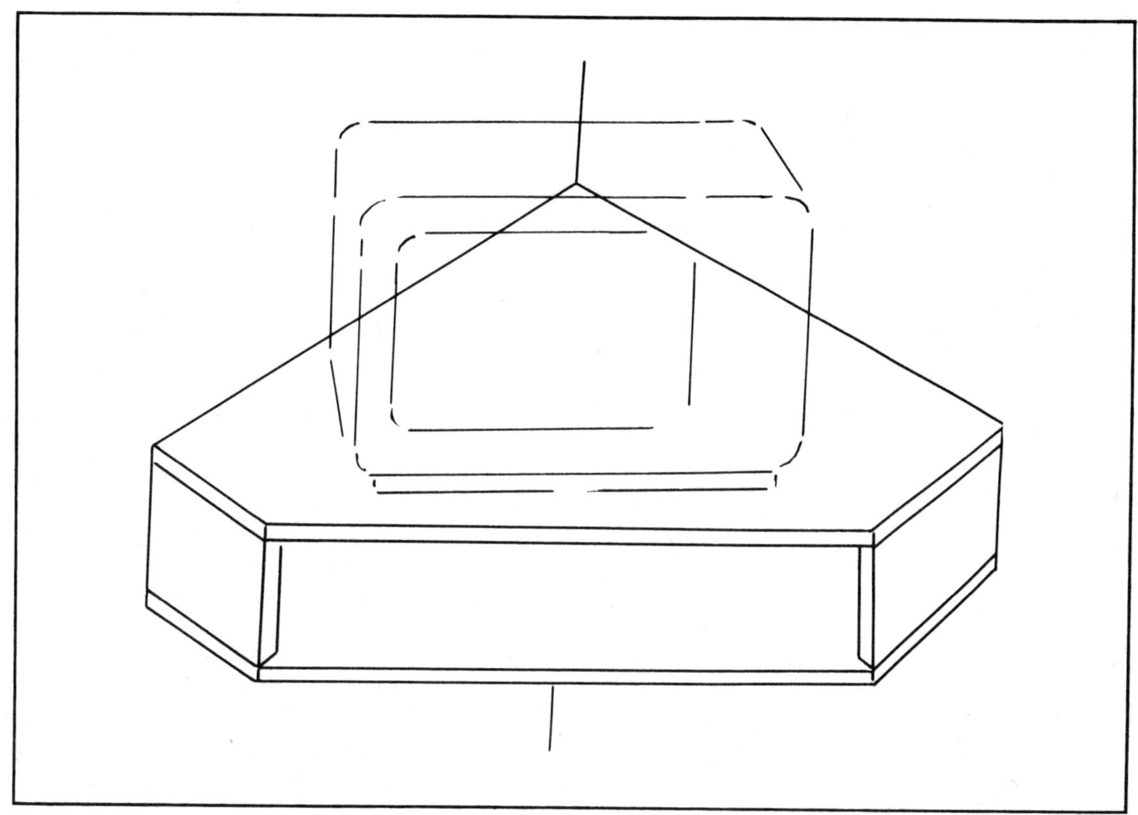

Fig. 10-9. A corner TV table.

walls fairly high (Fig. 10-11D), where they can best take the load. Add the bottom by screwing upward (Fig. 10-11E). As the low surface will be below normal eye level, screwheads there will not matter.

The ends are shown level with the edges of the other parts. They can be set back a short distance if the top and bottom edges are covered by moldings. If you think there is a risk of the TV being knocked off the shelf, a lip can be arranged around the edge with a square strip on top, either across the diagonal edge only or all around.

DUAL SEAT/CHEST

A seat attached to the wall can be located where people may want to rest, but you do not want them to move furniture. Such a seat may also be useful in a dining alcove, with the table in front of it and loose chairs at the other side. If the seat can also be opened and its base used as a chest, it is doubly useful.

This seat/chest (Fig. 10-12) is wide enough for two people and has an upholstered seat and back, with the seat part lifting away to give access to the interior. See Table 10-4. The back may not move, or it can be hinged at the top, so it will swing up and allow you to put tall flat things behind it. The woodwork can be left exposed and finished to match

Table 10-4. Materials List for Dual Seat/Chest.

2 ends	22	×	30	×	½ plywood
1 front	15	×	36	×	½ plywood
1 seat	19	×	37	×	½ plywood
1 back	16	×	37	×	½ plywood
8 frame strips	2	×	22	×	1
2 frame strips	2	×	28	×	1
7 frame strips	2	×	36	×	1
2 seat strips	2	×	32	×	1

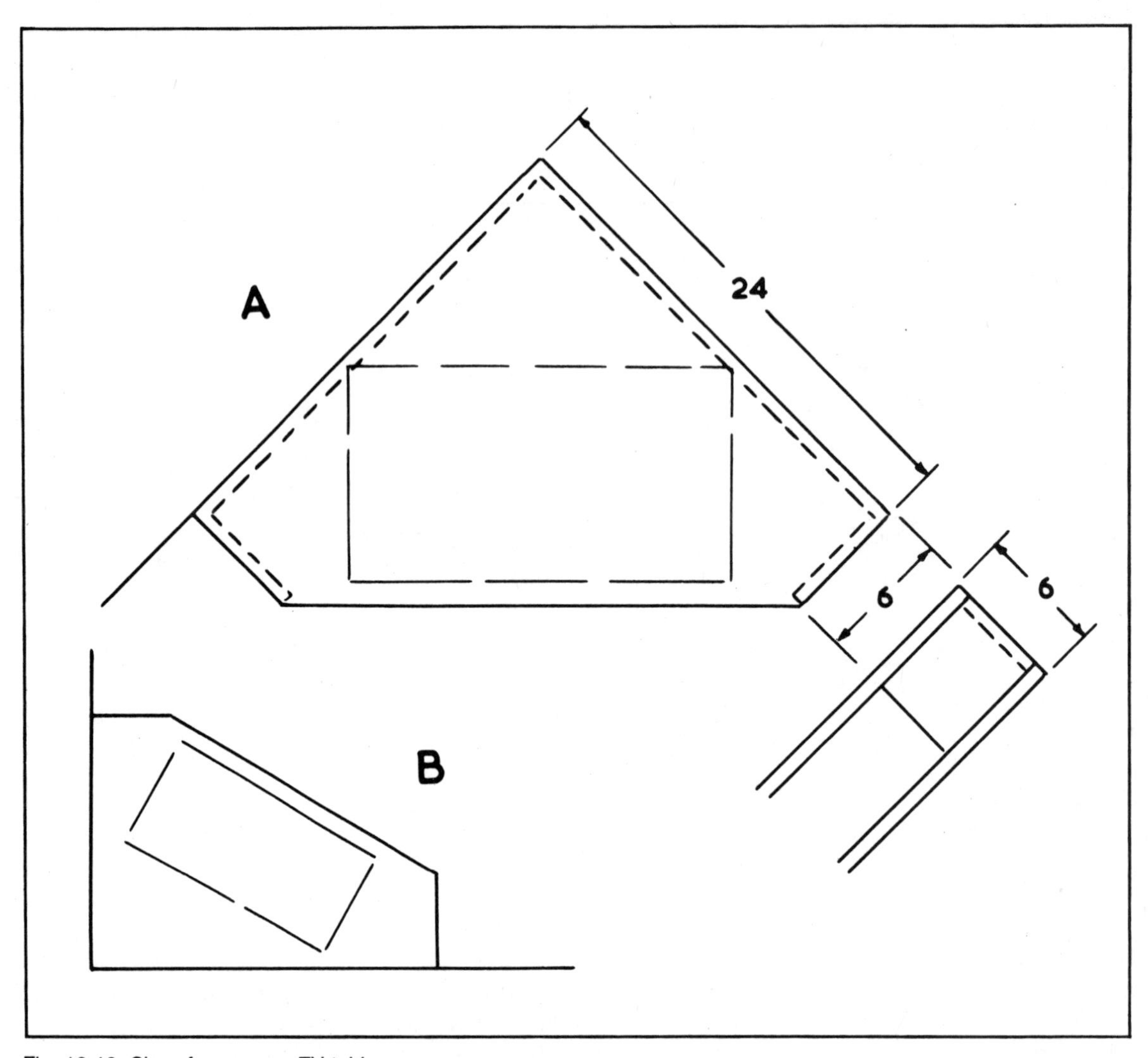

Fig. 10-10. Sizes for a corner TV table.

other furniture, but it will look well covered with cloth. The cloth can be the same as that on the cushions or a plain darker color that will show off the upholstered parts.

The suggested construction is of ½-inch plywood and 1-inch-by-2-inch strips throughout. Wall and floor form the back and bottom (Fig. 10-13). The assembly may be glued and nailed without any special joints between the framing parts.

The important parts are the ends (Fig. 10-14A). Make a matching pair. It is unlikely that the wall and floor will be out of square, but check the ends in position. Frame the ends (Fig. 10-14B) and leave gaps for the lengthwise parts. The parts are edgewise to the plywood, except the strip below the seat.

Put in the lengthwise strips and nail on the front plywood. To stiffen the strip that will support the rear of the seat, put another strip on edge beneath it (Fig. 10-14C). Nail its ends through or notch it into the end crossbar.

Make the plywood back the full height of the framing. Drill some holes in it for air to move in and

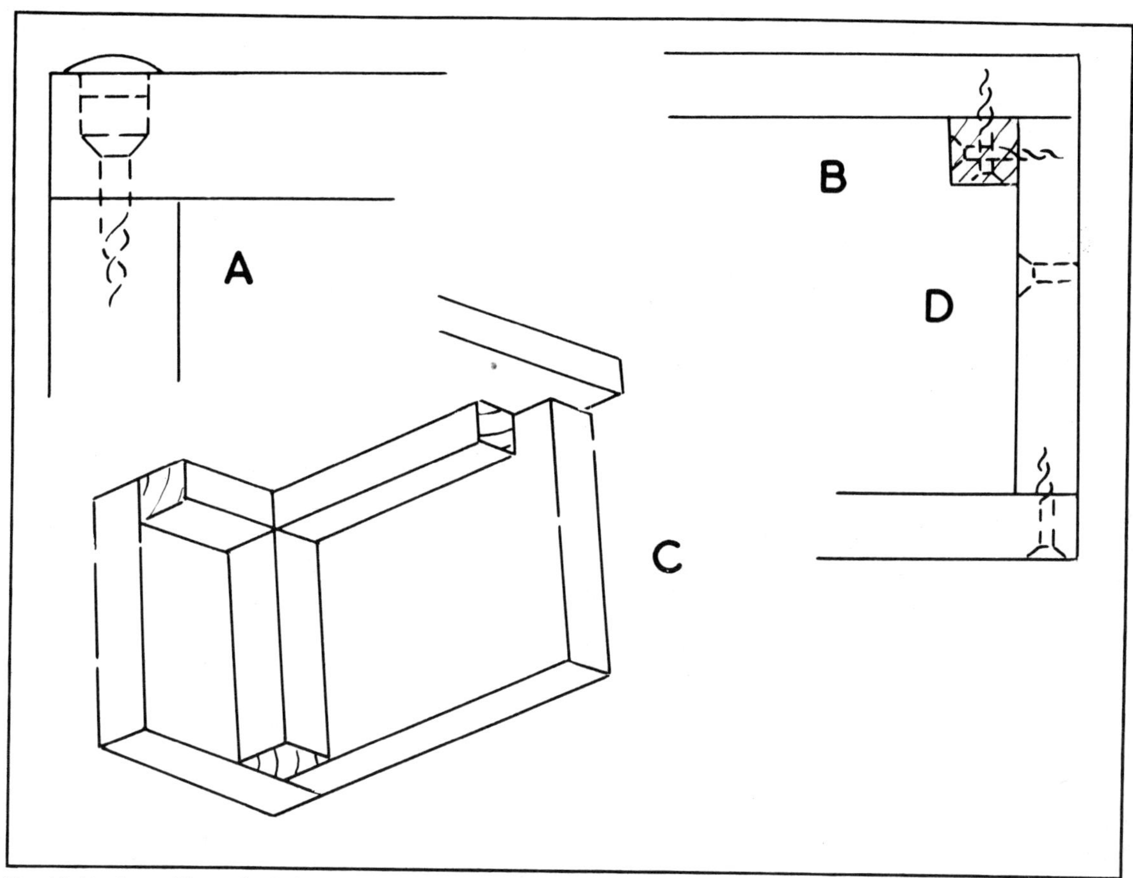

Fig. 10-11. Assembly methods for the corner TV table.

Fig. 10-12. An upholstered dual seat/chest.

out of the stuffing. Fit hinges to the top edge (Fig. 10-14D), but do not screw the hinges to the framing until after the wood is upholstered.

Make the plywood seat so it overhangs at the front. Drill a few holes in it and put strips under it (Fig. 10-14E). It should fit loosely in front of the back plywood.

Stretch cloth over the plywood and tack or staple it in place. It can go over the edges to tack inside (Fig. 10-15A). Turn the cloth under around the bottom and cover it with plywood (Fig. 10-15B), which will protect it from shoes.

The seat and back are upholstered as described in Chapter 5. Use 2-inch thick foam and bevel it underneath to produce rounded edges. Cut away a little more where the two cushions meet so they fit against each other. The covering material is pulled over and tacked underneath (Fig. 10-15C). Cover the tacked parts with gimp, webbing, or strips of covering material folded under to act as padding over the case edges and give a neater appearance when the parts are raised (Fig. 10-15D).

GLASS-FRONTED CABINET

This is a straightforward block of shelves with a glass door. See Table 10-5. The shaped top lends a Colonial quality to the cabinet, but that part can be omitted. The top and bottom overlap the door (Figs. 10-16 and 10-17). Arrange the door to hinge at the side most convenient for access or the side least likely to obstruct available light.

Rabbet the four main parts to take the plywood back. The best joints for the sides into the top and bottom are stopped dovetails (Fig. 10-18A). It is simpler to notch the wide pieces for the sides (Fig. 10-18B) and attach them with screws or dowels. In both cases use the rabbet depth as the limit and carry the rabbet in the sides through, so there is no visible gap outside.

The shelves fit into stopped dadoes. As they are narrower than the sides, there is no need to notch them (Fig. 10-18C).

If the ornamental top is to be used, make a template of half of it (Fig. 10-18D). Turn this over on the center line of the wood to get a symmetrical shape. The turned finial at the center may be bought, but a shape is suggested for turning on your own lathe (Fig. 10-18E). There can be some carving on the front of the top piece.

The four parts of the door frame are shown the same width, but making the bottom slightly deeper may improve appearance. Cut the rabbets so that the glass can be held with square fillets (Fig. 10-

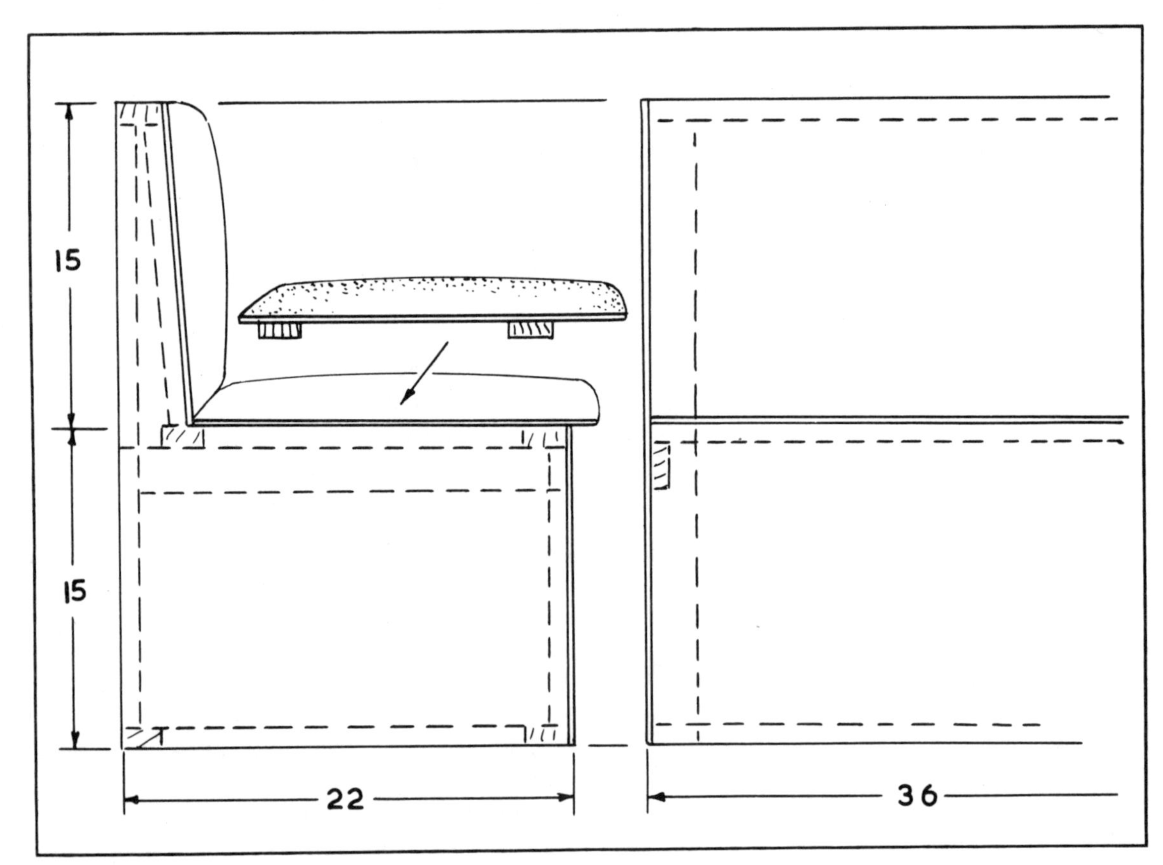

Fig. 10-13. Sizes of a dual seat/chest.

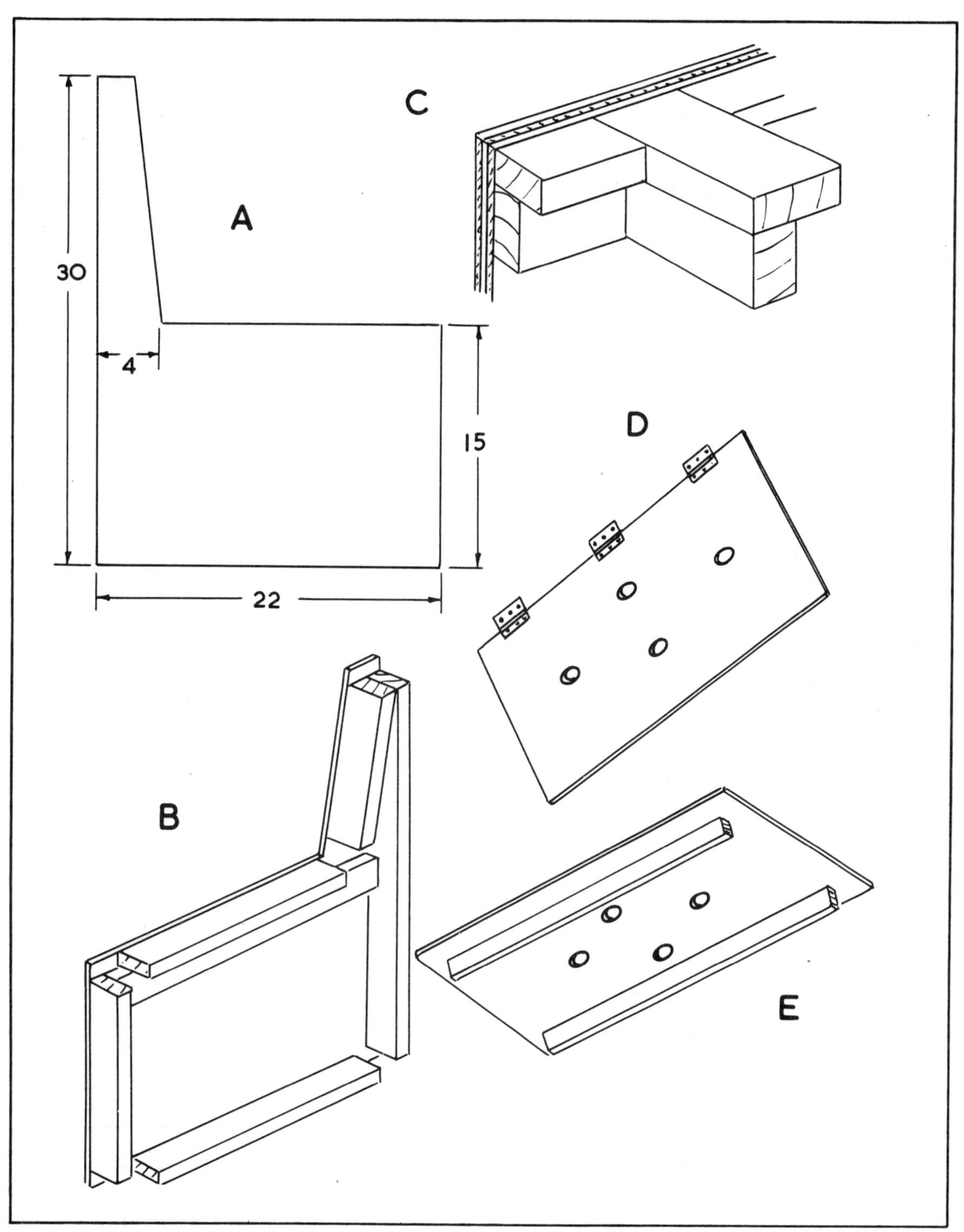

Fig. 10-14. Ends, seat, and back for the chest.

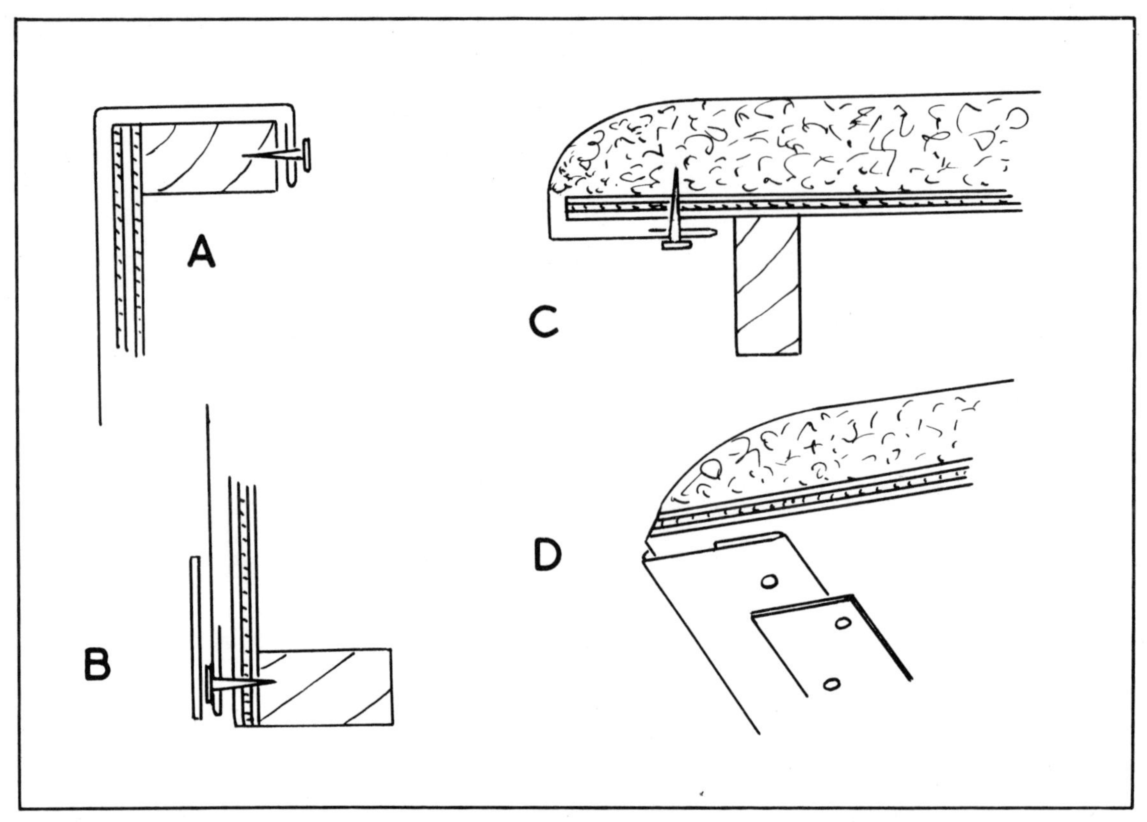

Fig. 10-15. How to cover the chest with cloth (A, B) and the seat and back with padding (C, D).

19A). Tenon the corners (Fig. 10-19B). Do not make the tenons too narrow and take them as deep as you reasonably can into the sides. The door must hold its shape.

There are two ways of hinging the door. Plain hinges can be let partly into the sides and partly into the door frame (Fig. 10-19C). The overhang of top and bottom can be used to enclose pivots. Drill through the overhangs into the door, so the hole goes into the door at half the thickness at the center of a curve planed on the outside edge (Fig. 10-19D). You can drive a screw top and bottom or use thin dowels. In either case, put a washer between the door and the bottom to provide clearance (Fig. 10-19E). The door edge must be rounded, at least on the inner edge, so it clears the cabinet side when it swings open.

Table 10-5. Materials List for Glass-Fronted Cabinet.

2 sides	6	×	30	×	5/8	
2 ends	7	×	25	×	5/8	
2 shelves	5½	×	24	×	5/8	
1 back	24	×	30	×	¼	plywood
1 top	3	×	25	×	¾	
2 door sides	1½	×	30	×	¾	
2 door ends	1½	×	25	×	¾	
2 fillets	3/8	×	30	×	3/8	
2 fillets	3/8	×	25	×	3/8	

You can have a catch and knob at the other side. If a projecting knob or handle is a nuisance, a simple hook can be on the side (Fig. 10-19F).

If the cabinet is to be used to display plates behind other things, a groove near the back of each shelf (Fig. 10-19G) will prevent slipping. Another way of getting a similar result is to put narrow strips across the shelves (Fig. 10-19H).

Fit the glass after finishing the woodwork. Use

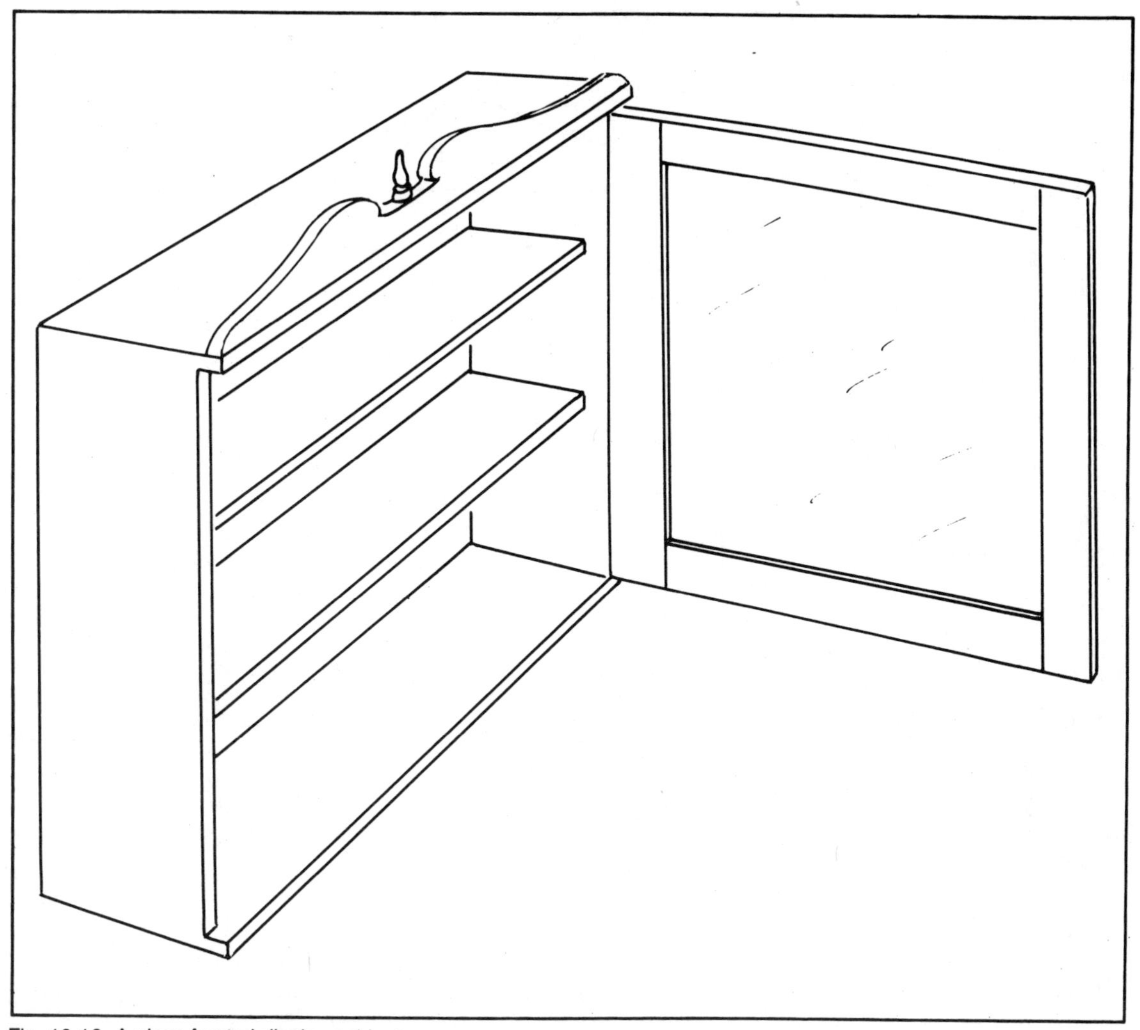

Fig. 10-16. A glass-fronted display cabinet.

fine nails to hold the fillets. Do not glue them, then they can be removed if you ever need to replace the glass.

SERVER OR SIDEBOARD

A side table is nice in a dining room when a meal is being served, but in a small room there may not be enough space for a freestanding table or server. This piece of furniture does not project far from the wall (Figs. 10-20 and 10-21). The server can be attached to the wall to prevent it from tilting forward. Its working top is at table height. There are drawers for silverware and other small items, together with useful storage space behind doors below. The shelves above will hold plates and other items briefly while a meal is served, but they are also useful at other times for displaying cups, plates, and souvenirs. The back of this part is shown as plywood, the same as the carcass below it, but you can use a mirror behind the shelves. See Table 10-6.

Construction can be arranged in stages. First is the main carcass, then its doors and drawers, followed by its plinth. The shelves and their ends

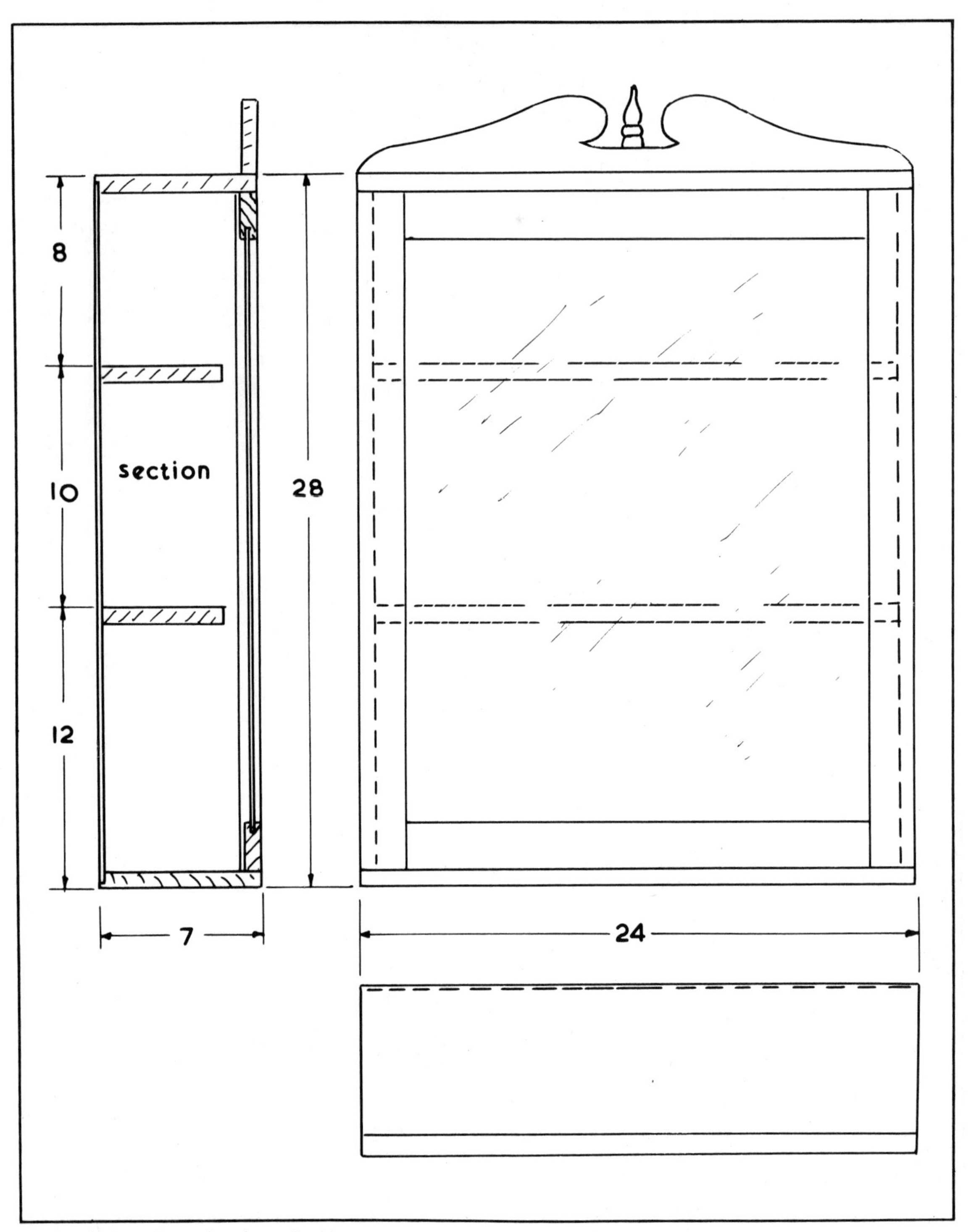

Fig. 10-17. Sizes for a glass-fronted cabinet.

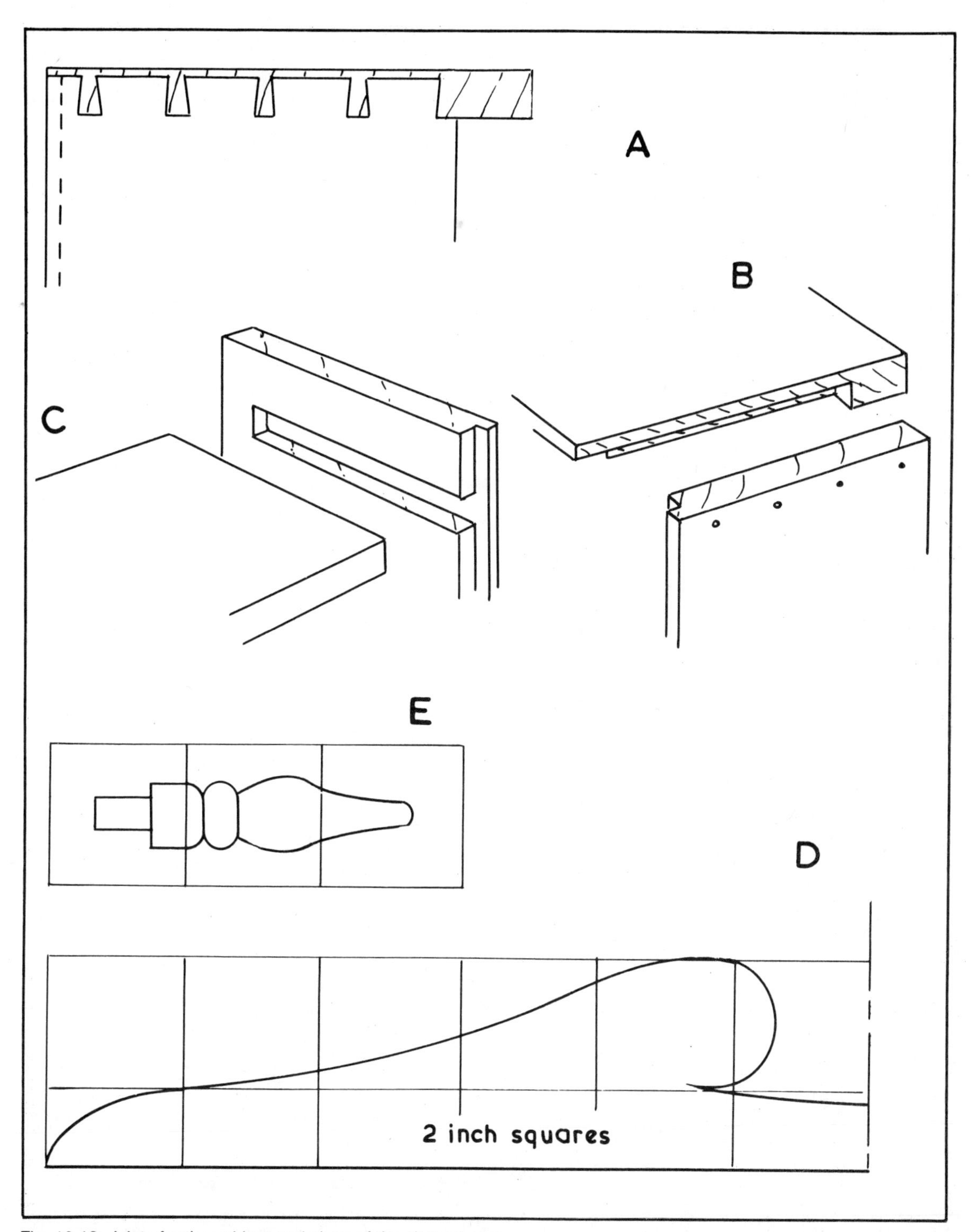

Fig. 10-18. Joints for the cabinet and sizes of the shaped parts.

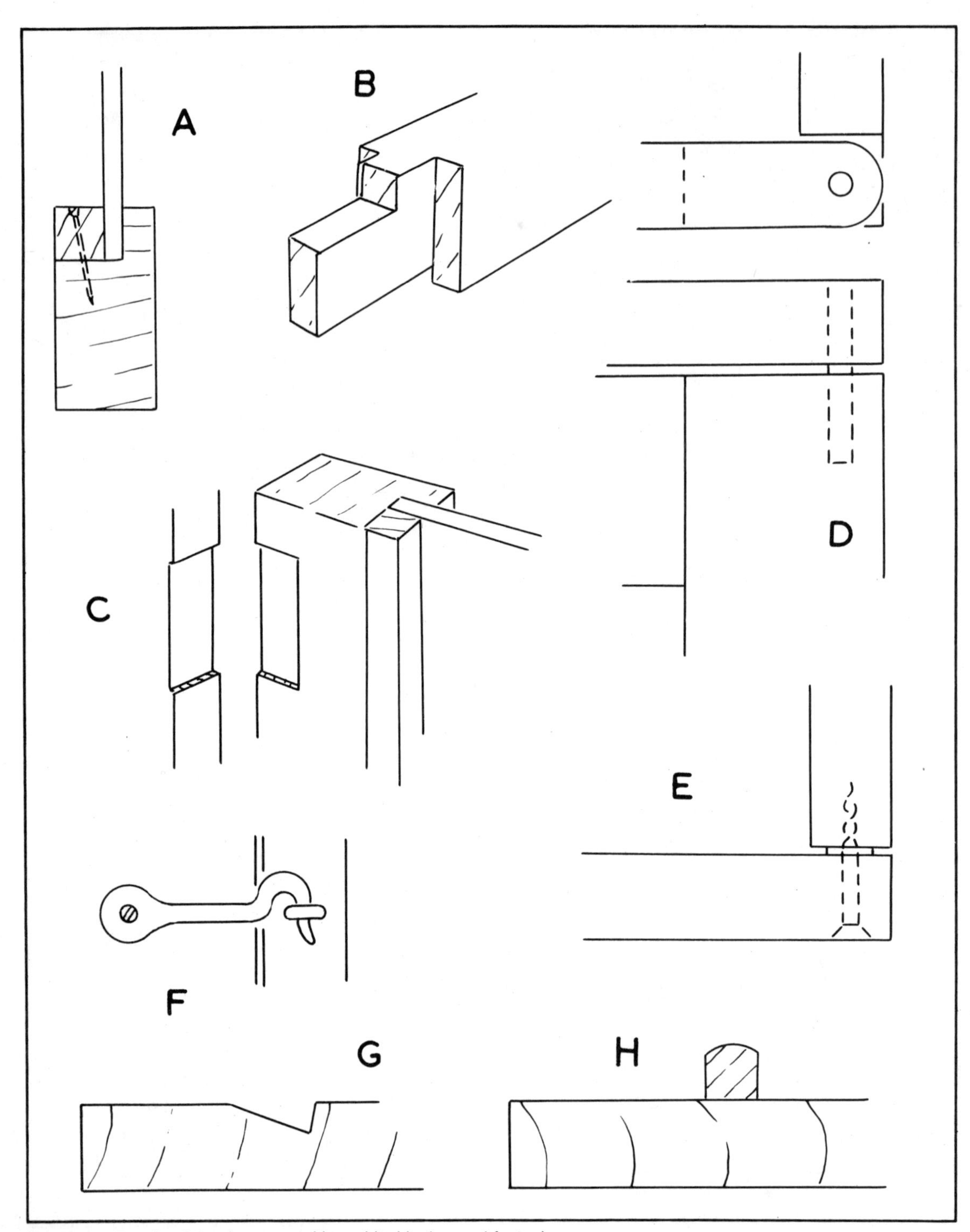

Fig. 10-19. Details of the door assembly and its hinging and fastening.

Fig. 10-20. A server or sideboard.

are made up as a unit, then attached to the carcass top.

Solid wood can be used, but for some of the wide parts it may be more convenient to use veneered particle board. If that is used for the shelf ends and the back over the top shelf, their edges may be better kept straight.

Make the pair of carcass ends (Fig. 10-22A), with the rear edges rabbeted for the back. The bottom can be dovetailed to the ends, but it is simpler to use dowels. Dovetails will not suit particle board in any case. Cut back the front edge of the bottom by the thickness of the doors. The two

Table 10-6. Materials List for Server.

2 ends	12	×	27	×	3/4
1 top	13	×	39	×	3/4
1 bottom	12	×	37	×	3/4
2 drawer rails	3	×	37	×	3/4
2 drawer dividers	6	×	12	×	3/4
2 drawer dividers	3	×	12	×	3/4
1 drawer front	6	×	16	×	3/4
2 drawer fronts	6	×	11	×	3/4
6 drawer sides	6	×	12	×	5/8
2 drawer backs	6	×	10	×	5/8
1 drawer back	6	×	15	×	5/8
1 drawer bottom	12	×	14	×	1/4 plywood
2 drawer bottoms	10	×	12	×	1/4 plywood
1 back	27	×	36	×	1/4 plywood
1 plinth	3	×	36	×	3/4
2 plinths	3	×	12	×	3/4
4 door frames	3	×	27	×	1
4 door frames	3	×	18	×	1
2 door panels	14	×	23	×	1/4 plywood
1 door post	3	×	27	×	1
1 divider	10	×	27	×	1/4 plywood
2 shelf ends	5	×	18	×	3/4
1 top shelf	6	×	39	×	3/4
1 lower shelf	4	×	39	×	3/4
1 back	4	×	39	×	3/4
1 back	18	×	36	×	1/4 plywood

drawer rails also go across, but there is nothing across under the top. Make the long drawer rails with the two short ones joined to them (Fig. 10-22B), either with dowels or stub tenons (Fig. 10-22C).

Make pieces to go between the drawers (Fig. 10-22D) and a door post between the long shelf rail and the bottom (Fig. 10-22E). Both are set back from the front, so drawers and door will finish flush. The door post may be grooved for the plywood divider, or it can be nailed to one side of it.

Assemble the bottom and drawer rails to the ends and the door post between them. The back plywood may be lightly nailed in to keep the assembly square, but you will probably want to remove it while adjusting the fit of the drawers. The back does not have to go behind the plinth. It can be cut level with the bottom, but allow for it going half over the edge of the top. The plywood behind the shelves can come down to meet it (Fig. 10-22F).

Make the plywood divider, which is attached to the door post and held at top and bottom between

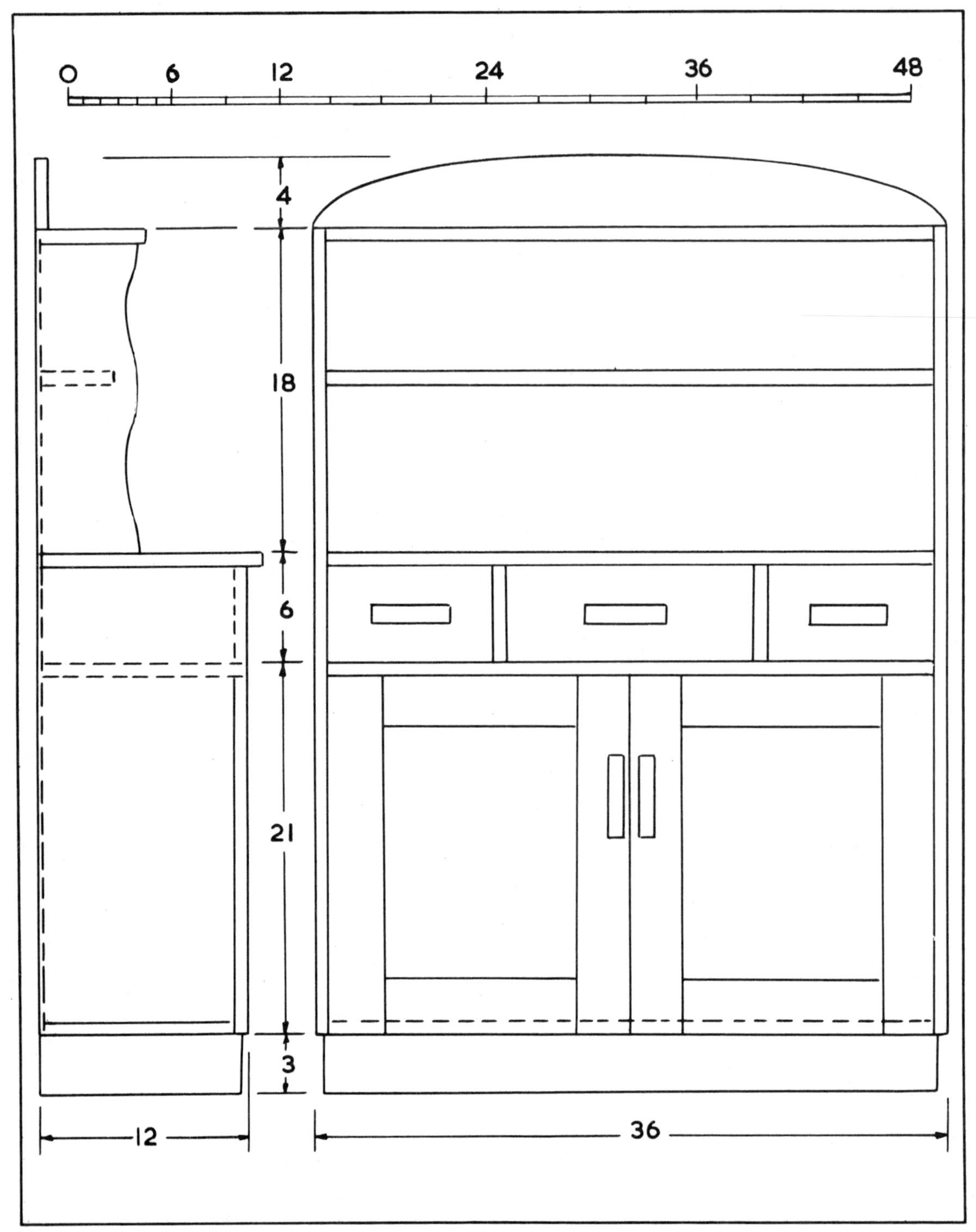

Fig. 10-21. Main dimensions of a server.

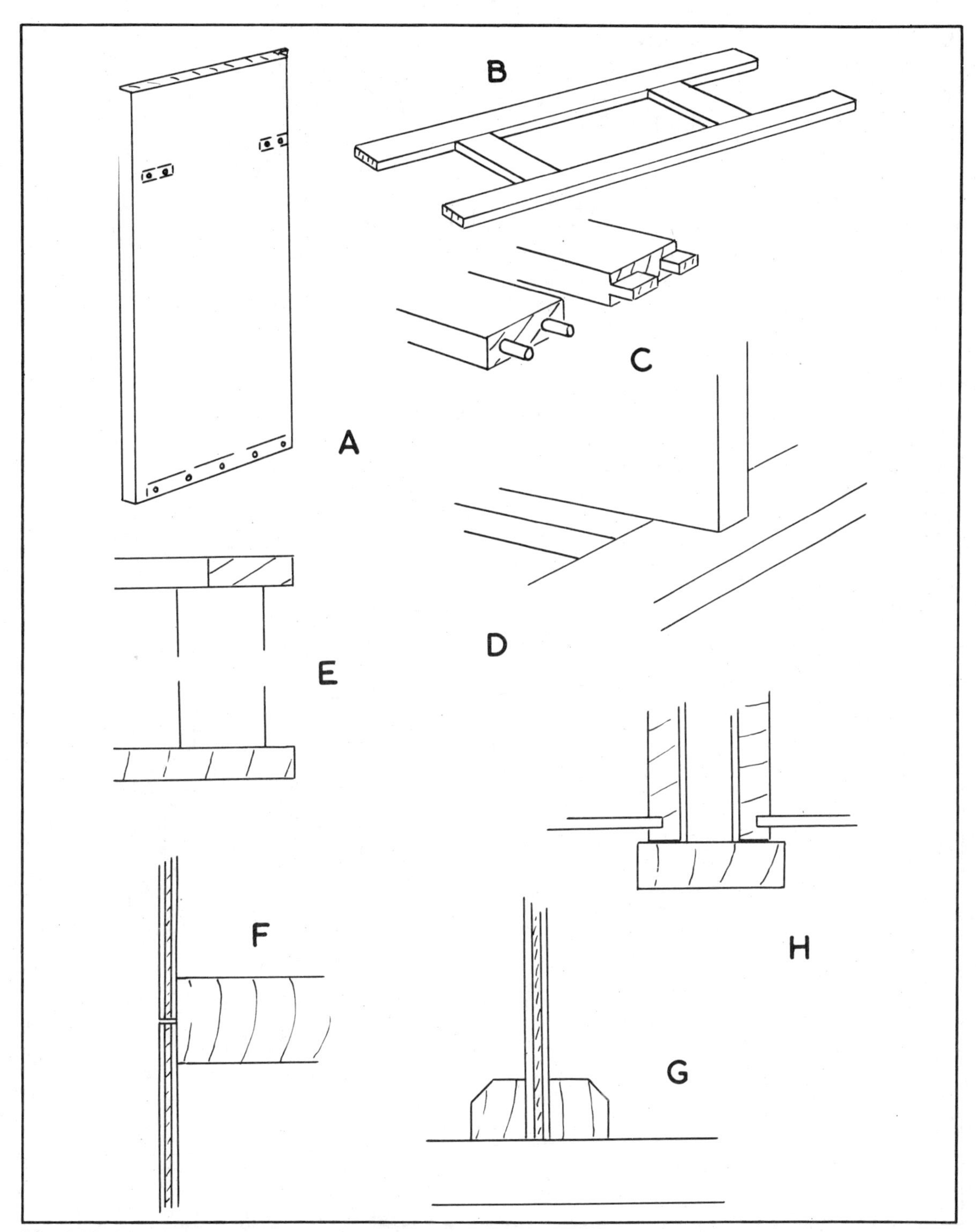

Fig. 10-22. Joints for the carcass, drawer slides, and divisions of the server.

strips (Fig. 10-22G). The pieces between the drawers may be held to the centers of the short drawer rails by screws from below. The rails projecting on each side then act as drawer runners (Fig. 10-22H). Get these square to the front rail for easy drawer movement.

Make the top to overhang at ends and front. Mold or round the edges. Use dowels between the ends and the drawer dividers and the top.

The drawer fronts fit inside the top and drawer rail. The outside drawers also come inside the ends, but where the drawers meet the fronts overlap the drawer dividers, with a little clearance between them (Fig. 10-23A). The drawer sides can go into the fronts at these overlaps with dadoes, preferably with dovetail sections (Fig. 10-23B), or they can be doweled. The outer corners of the two outer drawers can have any of the typical drawer front joints. Make the other parts of the drawers in the usual way, with the plywood bottoms grooved in. Make the drawers so their fronts stop them before their backs hit the plywood at the back of the carcass.

Each door can be made from a piece of veneered particle board. A door will keep its shape and look better, though, if it is framed and paneled. The doors fit within the carcass ends and the drawer rail, but they overhang the bottom and where they meet on the door post.

Groove the frame parts for the plywood panels. The corners can be doweled, but the traditional joint has tenons on the horizontal parts (Fig. 10-23C). Two 3-inch hinges on each door should be sufficient. Put spring or magnetic catches between the doors and the door post. Put matching handles on the drawers and doors, keeping them above center in both cases.

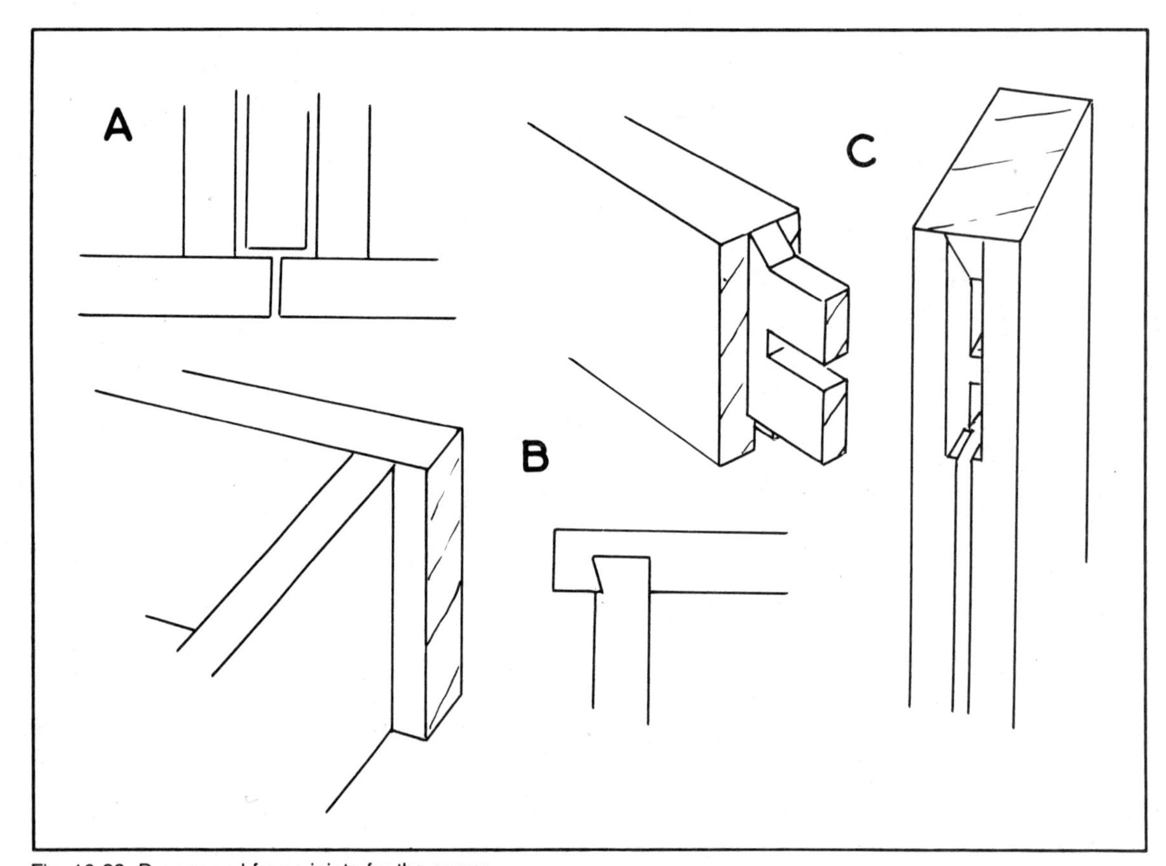

Fig. 10-23. Drawer and frame joints for the server.

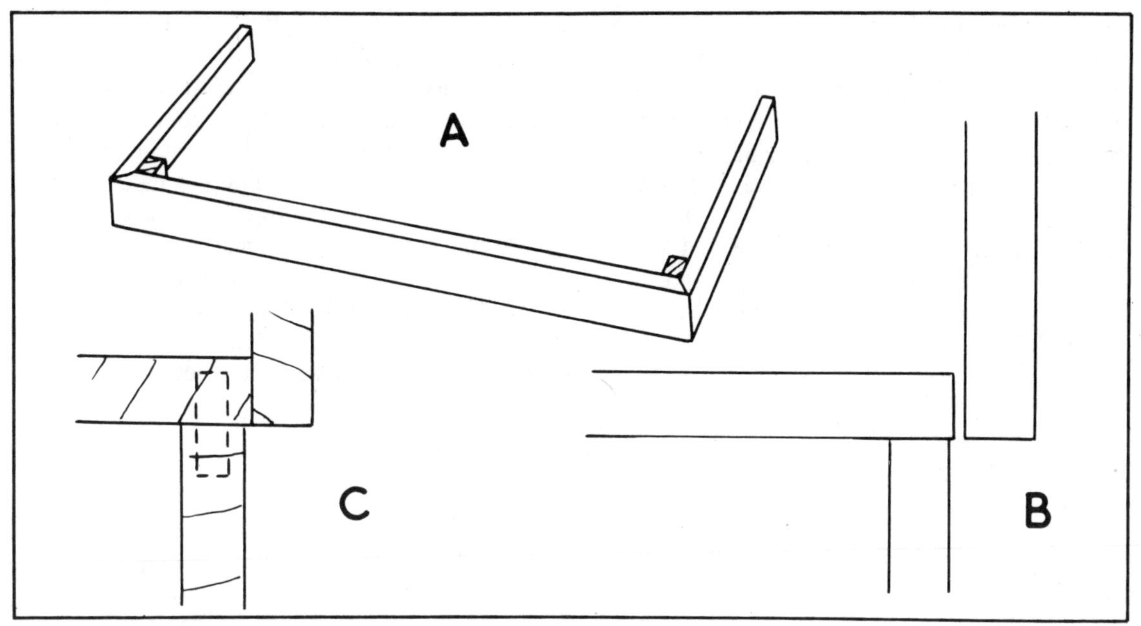

Fig. 10-24. Plinth details for the server.

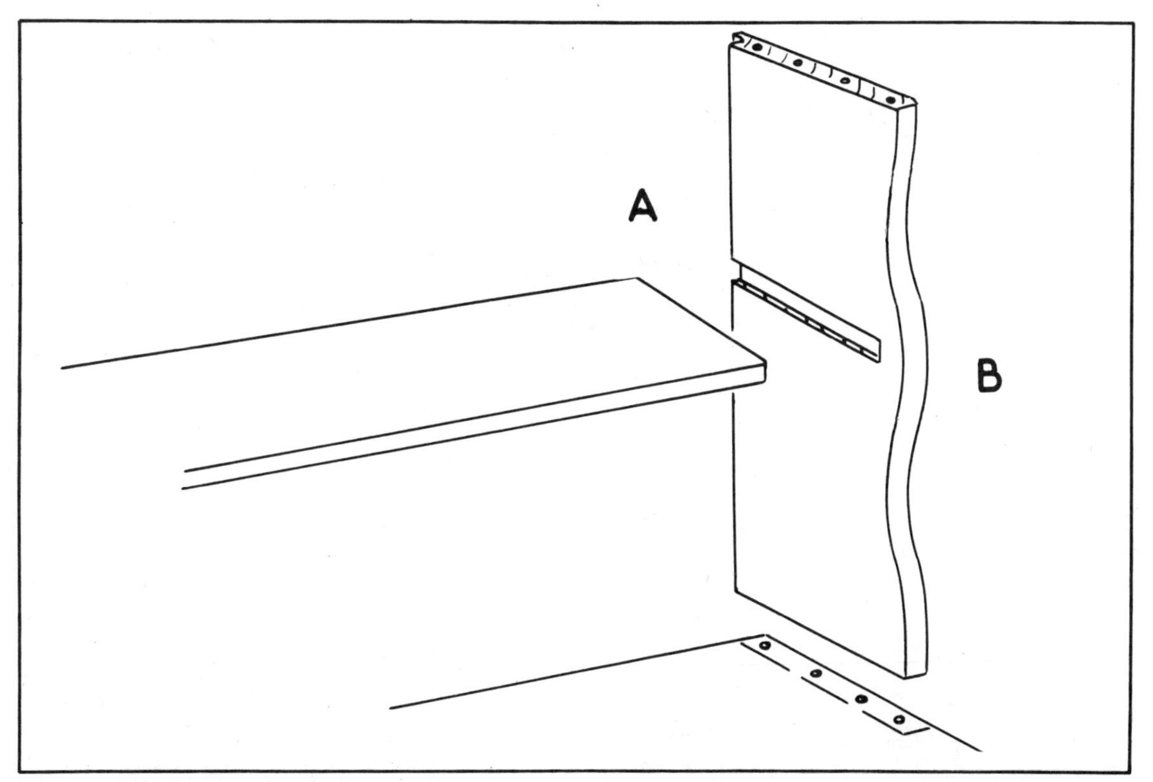

Fig. 10-25. The server shelf and end assembly.

The plinth is made with the corners mitered and strengthened with blocks (Fig. 10-24A). Set back the plinth by slightly more than the thickness of the doors at the front and the same distance in at the ends (Fig. 10-24B). Fit it by screwing down through the bottom. If you do not want screwheads showing inside, either screw upward with pocket screws from inside or use dowels (Fig. 10-24C).

The top shelf should be the same length as the carcass top. Its ends and front should be finished to match. The shelf ends have to be spaced so they come directly over the carcass ends, with dowels into the carcass top and the top shelf. The other shelf can be doweled, but it is better taken into a stopped dado groove (Fig. 10-25A). The front edge curves may be drawn freehand (Fig. 10-25B). They are prominent in the finished server, so make sure they match and are cleaned off completely.

The back above the top shelf is not essential, but it improves appearance and prevents items on the shelf from marking the wall. Use dowels between the back and shelf. Assemble the shelf parts together and to the carcass, then add the plywood back behind the shelves to complete construction.

Chapter 11

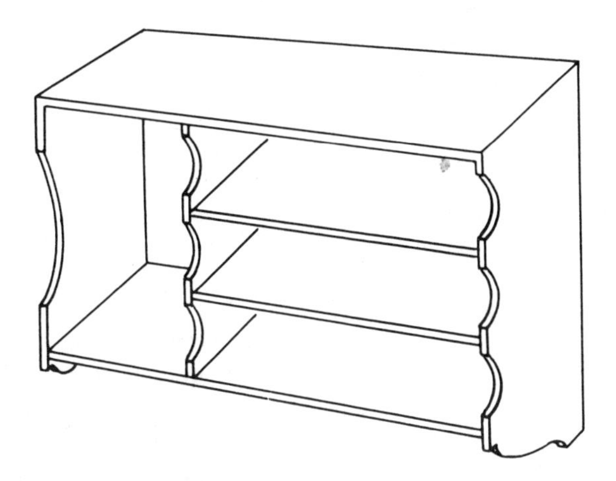

Kitchen Furniture

Many kitchen activities require work surfaces that can not move, both for safety and convenience. Items such as cookers and dishwashers have to be attached firmly in one place because of plumbing and connections for gas or electricity. Furniture that is to adjoin any of these immovable items is usually better built in to line up in size and levels with them than made as pieces of furniture that can be moved about.

Laundry furniture is not given separate space in this book. Many things made for the kitchen can also be used alongside washing machines and dryers where their rigidity is an advantage. Some items may also have uses in other rooms in the house, particularly in a dining nook or elsewhere that facilities are provided for preparing or serving food.

In planning an extensive program of built-in furniture in a kitchen, settle on those things that have to be bought and will then be fixtures. Your plans should include a cooker and other items that you plan to keep for some time.

Many of these things are standardized. If a change will mean altering something you have made, that will be a nuisance. It is always difficult to make a modification that appears as good as the furniture before modification.

If you are able to start planning a kitchen layout from scratch, draw a plan of the kitchen to scale. Cut out pieces of paper of the known sizes of what you hope to include, so you can move them around and get the best positions and sizes of the things you intend to make. It may help to have similarly scaled drawings of walls where you intend to build in and test the sizes of what goes there to see if your scheme is feasible. An advantage of doing your own building in is that you make most use of the available height. You may be able to work around a cooker or other item to get more storage or working space.

Manufacturers have settled mostly on standard heights, so you can get working surfaces level between bought things. If you want to build into a partly equipped kitchen, measure around and try to make the most use of gaps—both horizontally and vertically. Planning time is important; it is disconcerting to start making something and then have to alter it. Check with the lady of the house or whoever has to use the kitchen. Building in makes the most economical use of space, but be careful to leave room to move around. Think of related actions. Try to avoid the need to go from one side to the other for a particular food preparation process. You may be able to arrange for a mixer to be kept where it is most frequently used, even if storage for it seems easier to arrange elsewhere.

Many commercially-produced kitchen furniture units are intended to be built in. Examination of these units or of the manufacturers' catalogs may give you ideas, even if you do not intend to use the particular products. We can all learn from other people's experience, and the professionals have had plenty of experience.

Not all kitchen built-in furniture has to be large, extensive, or complicated. Many small items can be made to ease the work of a cook or housewife, and some examples are described first.

STORAGE IN WALL

A hollow wall may have one side cut through so shelves can be put in the thickness of the wall. If a glass-paneled door is fitted over the shelves, the effect is rather like a picture hung on the wall. Items such as spice jars are displayed behind the glass (Fig. 11-1).

You should not cut into an exterior wall containing insulation. There are inside walls where cutting away will not affect comfort or the structure.

You can usually identify stud positions on the surface. If you are uncertain, tap the wall. The hollow note produced will tell you when you are between studs. Make a hole, open it out to the studs, and square across for top and bottom.

The top and bottom cut edges of paneling may be rather loose and springy. That does not matter at this stage, but make sure the edges are trimmed straight.

Whether you make a back to the shelves or not depends on the appearance of the panel's rear at the far side. There is not much depth of shelving, so try to avoid reducing it with a back. You may paint the panel or cover it with cloth. Otherwise, you can use hardboard behind the shelves.

Make top and bottom pieces ½-inch thick to fit tightly between the studs, with thicker strips to support the surface panel (Fig. 11-2A). Fit these in place and cut side strips to go between them (Fig. 11-2B). The shelves may be notched into them (Fig. 11-2C), but then the shelves have to be put in at the same time as the sides. If you want to be able to lift the shelves out, they can rest on small cleats (Fig. 11-2D).

Make the door so its inner edges hide the edges of the framing in the wall. The outer edges should be far enough out to give a frame width proportional to the overall size. Top and bottom are shown curved (Fig. 11-1), but they can be straight. The glass is held in with fillets (Fig. 11-3A) and fine nails. Do not use glue under the fillets. They should be easy to remove if you ever have to replace the glass.

The sides go to the full height, then the top and bottom are tenoned into them. Shoulder the tenons over the rabbet (Fig. 11-3B). You can shoulder the ends without tenons and use dowels (Fig. 11-3C). Mark and cut the joints before shaping the top and bottom, but allow for the amount you will be cutting down. Round the exposed outer and inner edges after assembly.

If you are using ordinary hinges, let them into the door surface only (Fig. 11-3D). There can be a spring or magnetic catch at the other side to hold the door closed. If you do not want to use a knob or handle projecting from the surface, make a hollow under the edge (Fig. 11-3E) to get your fingers behind to pull.

DOMESTIC TOOL RACK

The many tools and implements used to keep a home clean range from simple hand brushes to an assortment of vacuum cleaner attachments. Most of them are better hung from a wall than thrown together in a corner. They will take up less room, be more accessible, and are less likely to get damaged.

The arrangement of the rack depends on the available wall space and what tools have to be accommodated. There is no need for complication. If a nail is the only thing needed from which to hang something, that may be satisfactory, but no

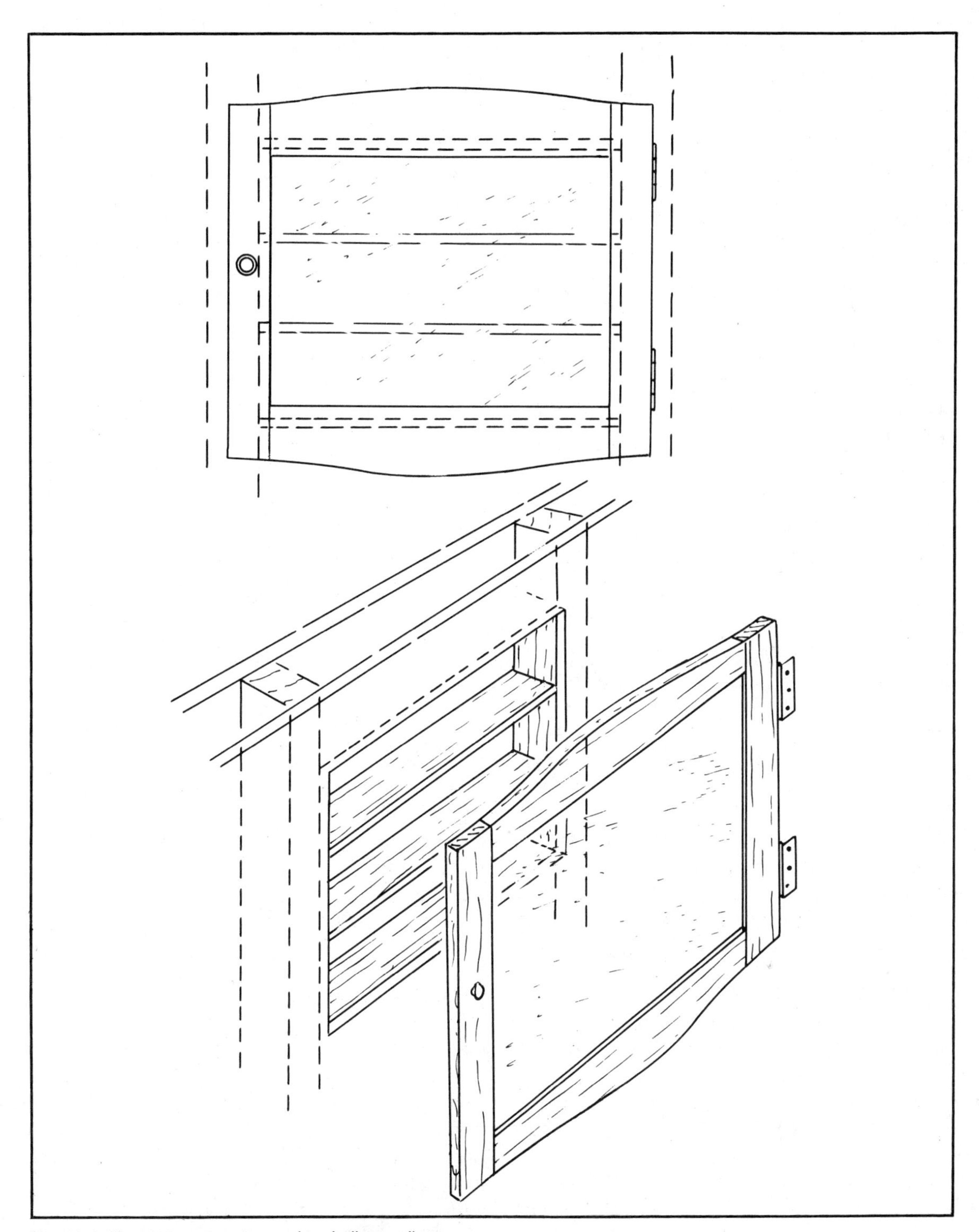

Fig. 11-1. How to arrange storage in a hollow wall.

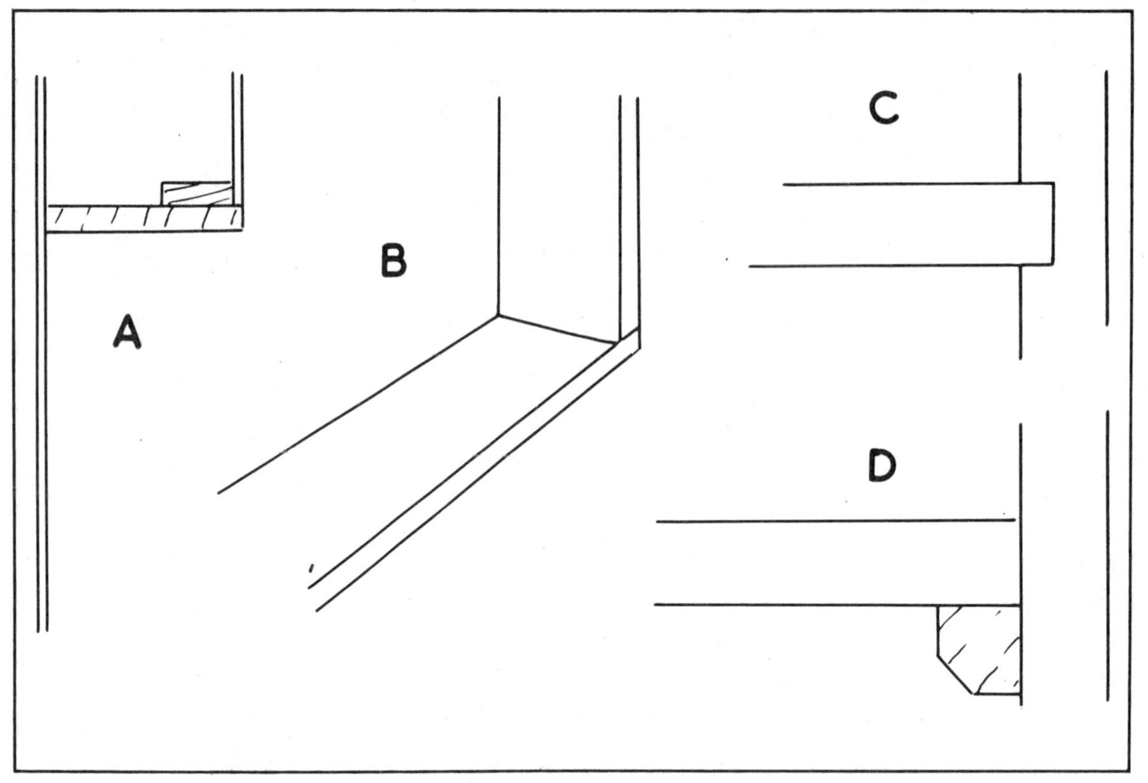

Fig. 11-2. The parts to be built into a hollow wall.

craftsman will be happy about it. A better arrangement is a screw hook. A cup hook (Fig. 11-4A) is particularly suitable.

If something thicker than a nail or metal hook is required, you can use a piece of dowel rod. Slope it upward slightly (Fig. 11-4B). If there will be several pegs in a row, make sure you drill for them at the same angle for a uniform appearance. It may be sufficient to glue a dowel in a hole, but you can make the joint stronger by making a saw cut in the dowel. Fit it with that across the grain of the back, so a wedge can be driven to tighten it (Fig. 11-4C). The back can be planed level after the glue has set.

Shaker pegs can be bought, or you can turn your own on a small lathe (Fig. 11-4D). You can originate your own design. The important need is a large knob to prevent things from falling off.

A pair of dowels or pegs can support a broom or anything else with a large end upward. Arrange them only far enough apart for the handle to slip between. Neat alternatives can be shaped from flat wood, with the ends as tenons into the back (Fig. 11-4E). Length must be enough to keep the head of the tool away from the wall (Fig. 11-4F). These or any other pegs can be used for coiled rope or electric wires. Space them to suit the usual size of coil and angle them outward (Fig. 11-4G).

Some small items may fit through holes in a shelf. If there is nothing in the tool to prevent it from falling through, there can be a second shelf with a hole drilled only partly through (Fig. 11-4H).

Not all tools can be dropped through a hole, particularly if they are long. In that case the hole can be cut into to make a slot. There are several ways to keep tools from falling forward. A turn button can be used (Fig. 11-4J). Making a groove along the top of the shelf will reduce the possibility of most things coming out (Fig. 11-4K). A similar effect is obtained with a strip at the front (Fig. 11-4L).

An ingenious way of hanging any long-handled

tool with its large end downward uses gravity to secure it (Fig. 11-4M). For a broom handle 1⅛-inch diameter, the pivot piece may be 1 inch thick with a 1½-inch diameter hole. The size of the lug into the slotted back is not critical, but the parts should be linked loosely with a nail. The handle is pushed upward through the hole and released. Its weight will pull the holed part down so it is gripped.

PAN LID RACK

If pan lids are arranged vertically in this rack (Fig. 11-5A), they form a decorative feature on the kitchen wall. There can be any number of lids, providing there is wall space to take them.

Exact sizes will have to suit the particular lids to be stored, but for usual sizes the back can be 5-inch-by-½-inch section. The fronts are ¼-inch plywood. The spacers will have to be made to suit the lids, with the smallest at the top.

The suggested design is shown with the lids overlapping slightly. For greater compactness you can tilt the lids forward more, so each lid comes almost as high as the handle of the lid above.

Start with some excess length in the back-

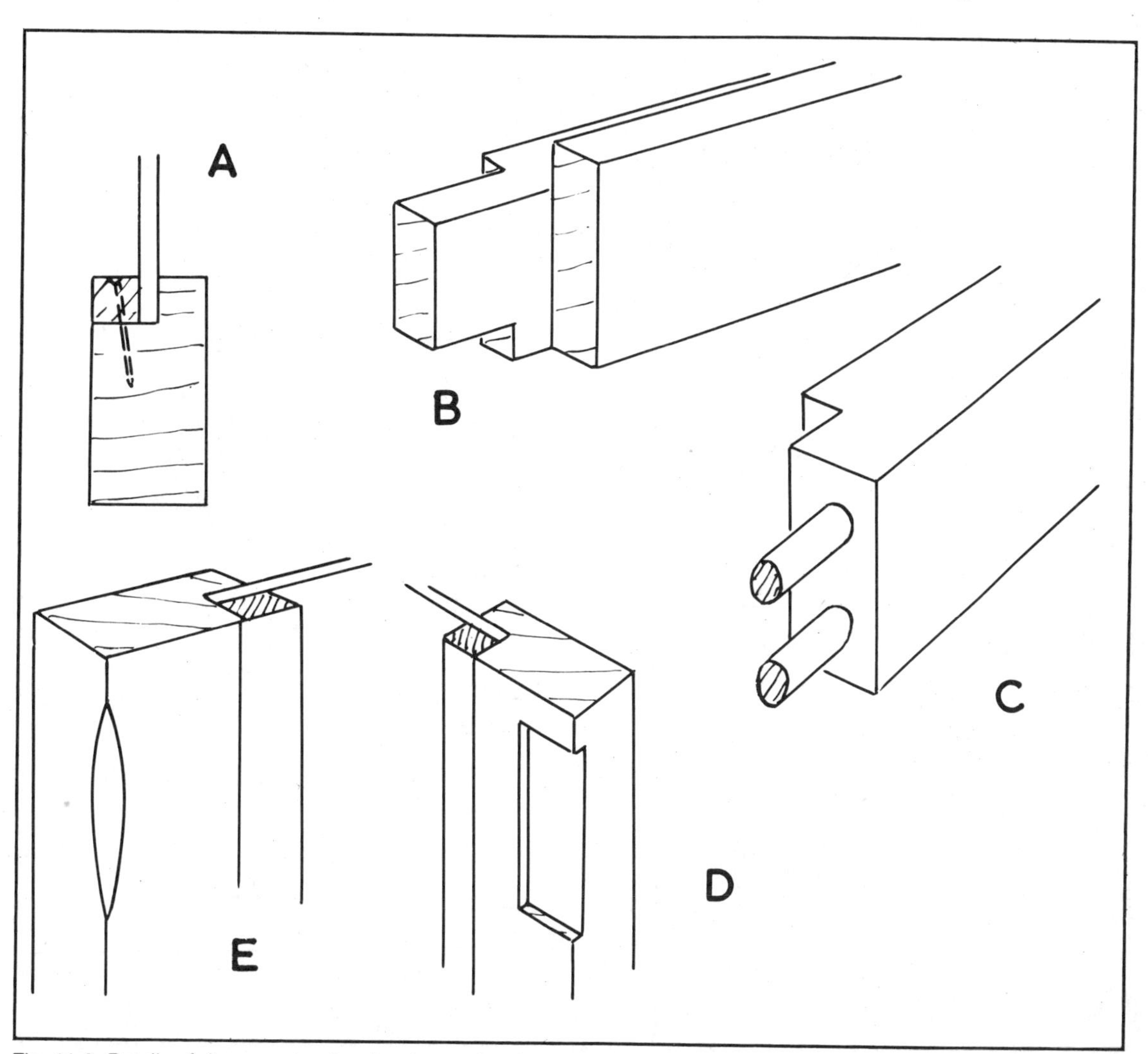

Fig. 11-3. Details of door construction for storage in a hollow wall.

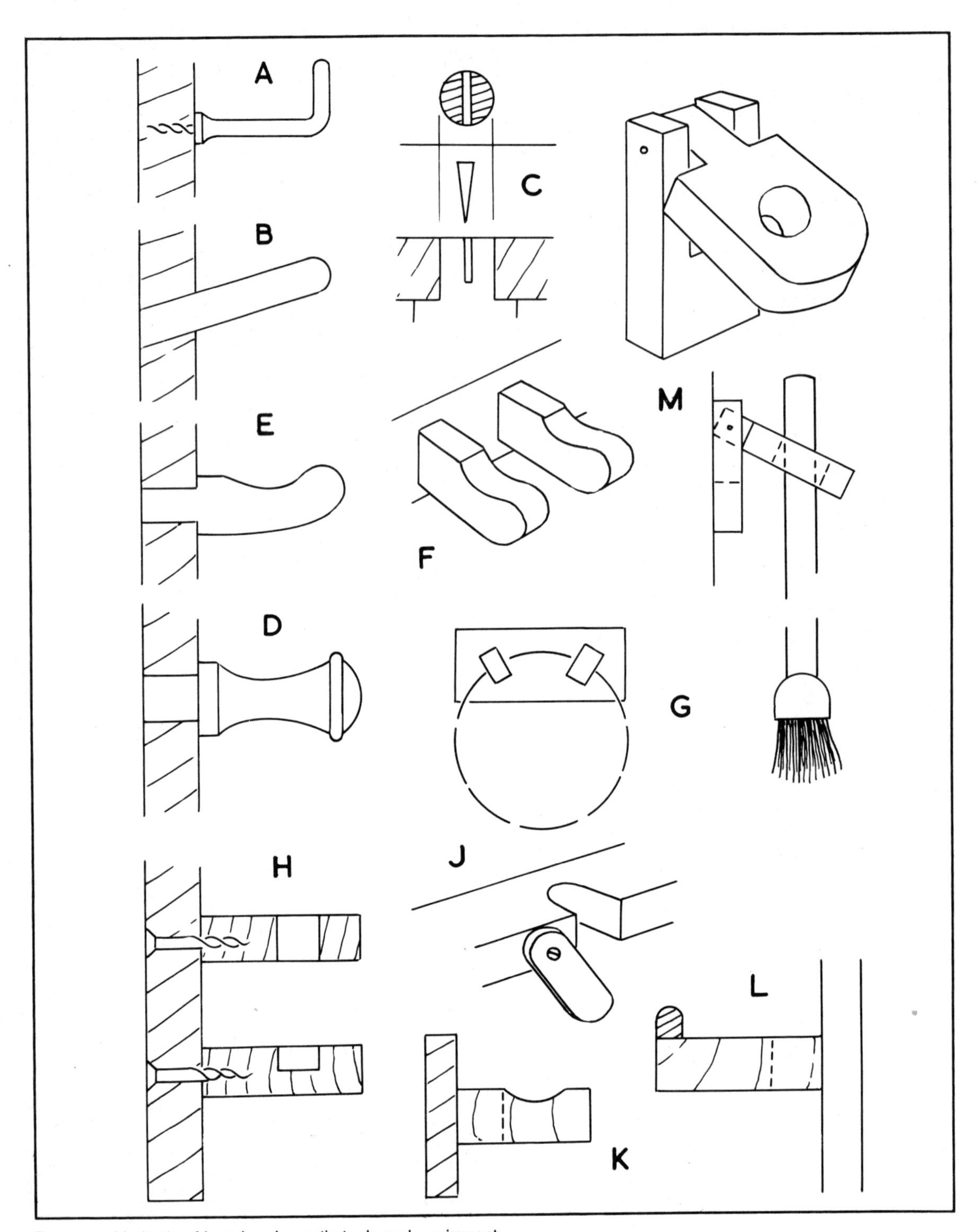

Fig. 11-4. Methods of hanging domestic tools and equipment.

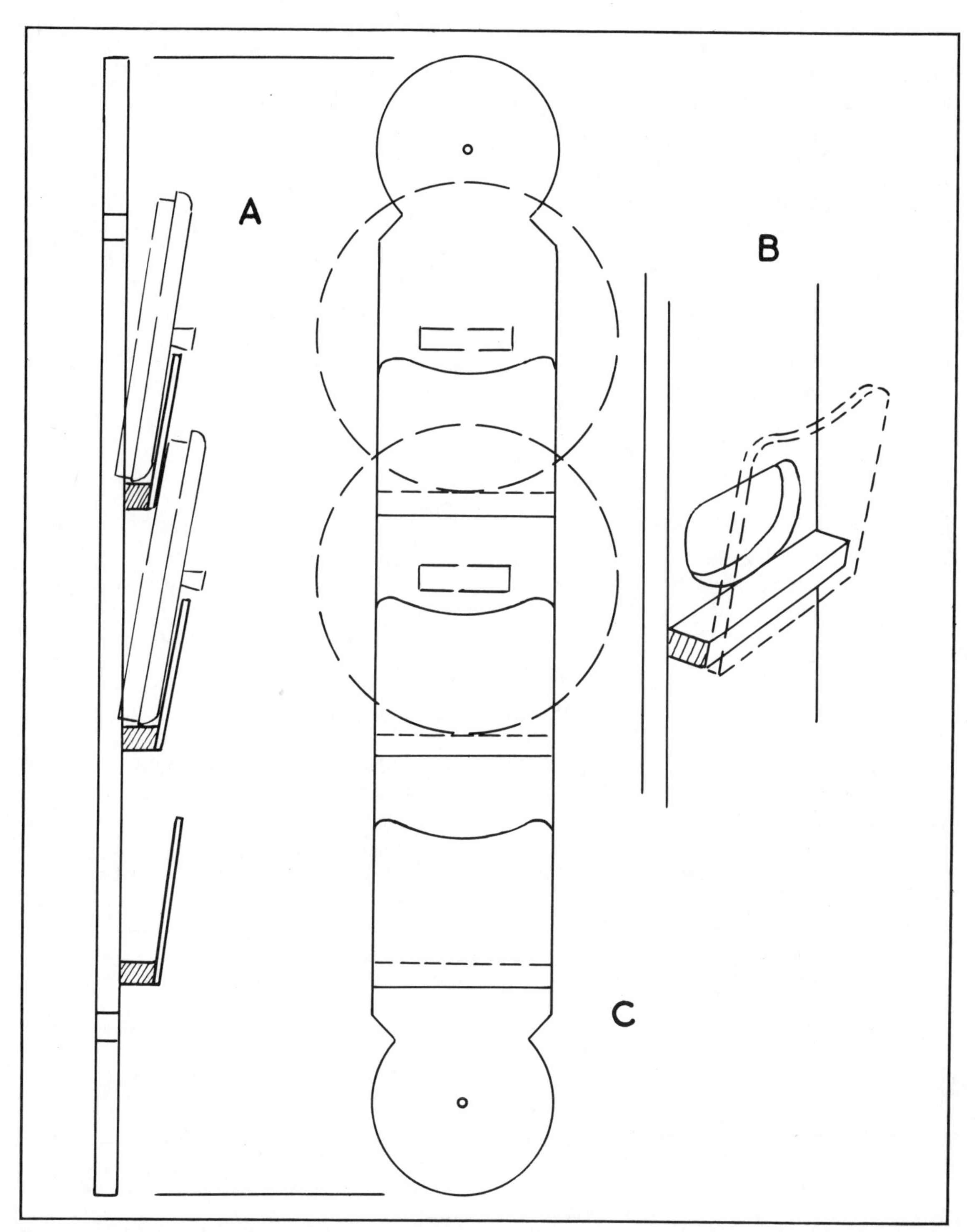

Fig. 11-5. A wall-mounted pan lid rack.

board, then make up a bracket that you expect will suit the top lid. Cut away the backboard so part of the lid will go through it (Fig. 11-5B). Try the lid and bracket against the hole. Perhaps you can reduce the thickness of the spacer, so the lid fits close enough in the hole to not roll.

Do the same with the next lid, arranging it so it overlaps the first bracket. The height it can come depends on the angle that it slopes forward. When that lid is fitted, move on to the third one and any others.

Shape the ends of the backboard in whatever style you like, but the rounded design shown (Fig. 11-5C) follows through the round shape of the lids. Screws can go through the centers of the circles.

You can put one or two hooks on the bottom bracket for hanging ladles and other equipment.

FOLDING TOWEL RAILS

A pack of rails for drying towels and other clothes is useful, particularly if it folds flat. The suggested design (Fig. 11-6A) has four or five rails on one pivot, so they can be folded flat against the wall or be fanned out. See Table 11-1.

The four rails settle the size of the bracket, so make them first (Fig. 11-6B). The holes are to suit the pivot, which can be 3/16-inch rod or bolt. Curve the end with the hole position as the center for the compass, so it will clear inside the bracket. Leave each rod square for about 2 inches. Round the rods first by planing them octagonal, then by taking off the angles and doing final sanding. Round the extreme ends well.

An interesting variation is a composite construction. The inner ends should be a close-grained hardwood for strength. The rest of each piece can be a light softwood. If you join a dark hardwood to a pale softwood, the contrasting colors give an individual appearance to your rails. Use a plain scarf joint (Fig. 11-6C). A simple way to cut this is to clamp a pair together (Fig. 11-6D) and saw and plane them together, so both angles will be the same.

Put the four rails together and measure their combined thickness for the distance between the projections on the bracket. You can screw the projections from behind or they can be doweled, but the strongest joints are mortise and tenon (Fig. 11-6E). Shape the top and bottom of the back in any way you wish, but allow for the screws to the wall. Round the extending front ends and drill the two pieces together. The pivot must be upright.

The pivot can be a long bolt. This allows you to adjust the friction on the rails. If you have marked out correctly, though, there should be no trouble. If you use a plain rod, make it brass or aluminum so you will not be troubled with corrosion. Make a trial assembly, then drive the rod out with a punch, so you can varnish, or otherwise finish, the wood before final assembly.

KITCHEN LAYOUT

If you are equipping a new kitchen or extensively reorganizing an existing one, start with a plan showing the sizes and positions of things that have set positions. Arrange other things around them to make the best use of space. You need as much working space as possible at table or counter level. Plenty of storage space can go on the walls, either high enough to allow for bending over the working surfaces or kept shallow and far enough back to rest on them without impeding work.

Decide on the style of work tops so they match. Other prominent things are doors and drawers, both of which contribute to the overall appearance of the kitchen. With work tops and these frontages giving a pleasing appearance, the rest is largely straightforward constructional work that is mostly hidden.

Modern work tops are usually Formica or similar laminated plastic, and that material needs a stable backing. Solid wood tends to expand and contract. Make tops of particle board, stout plywood, or other manufactured board thick enough to withstand hammering or chopping. Constructional framing underneath will also provide stiffening. If there are large unsupported areas, include some framing under the top.

The front edge is prominent and gets the roughest treatment. You can edge the top with more Formica laminated plastic (Fig. 11-7A). Thickening the backing gives a more solid appearance (Fig.

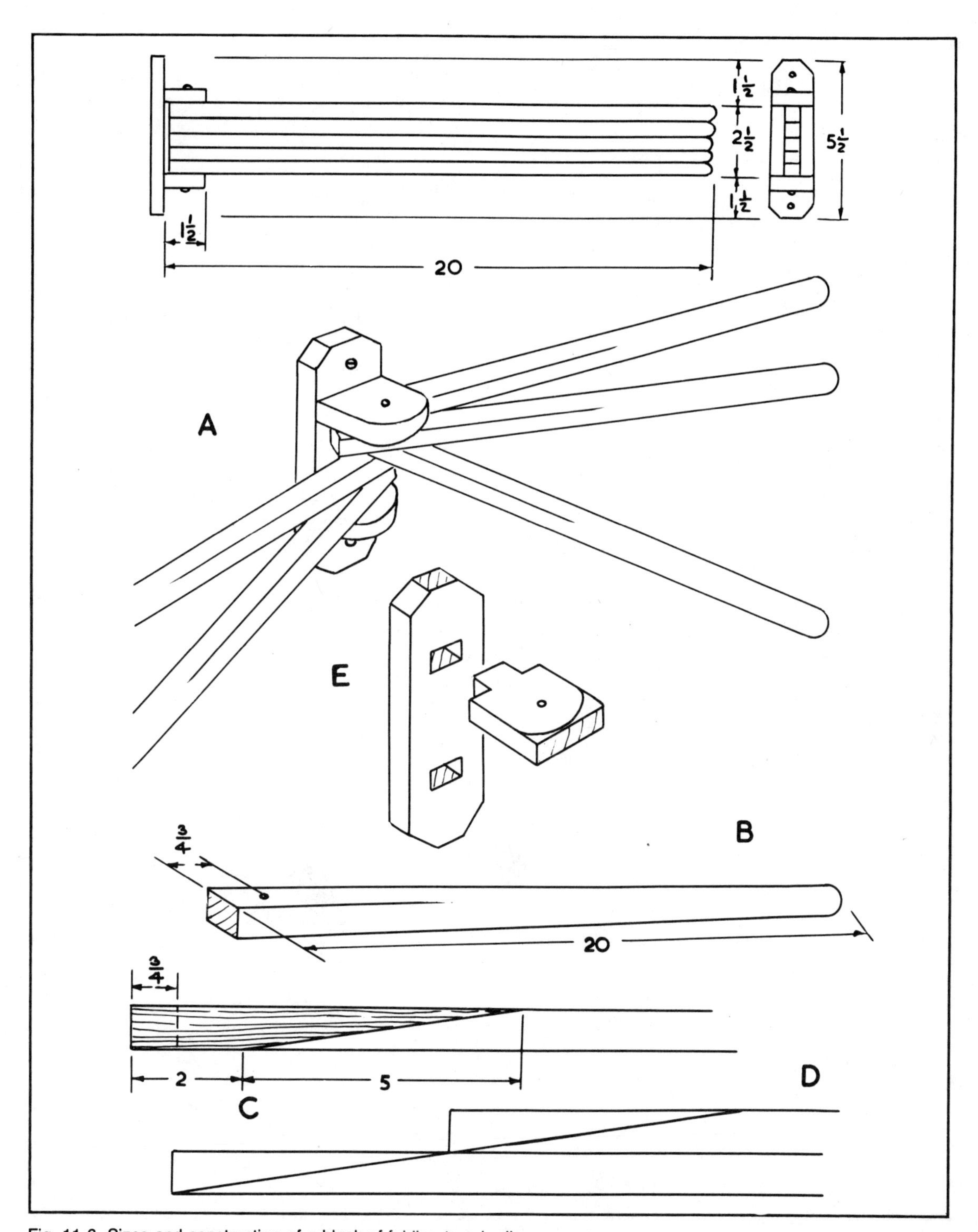

Fig. 11-6. Sizes and construction of a block of folding towel rails.

Table 11-1. Materials List for Folding Towel Rails.

4 rails	5/8	×	20	×	5/8
bracket from	1½	×	12	×	½

11-7B). A varnished hardwood edge is attractive (Fig. 11-7C), but occasionally it will require revarnishing. Otherwise, the bare wood will absorb dirt and moisture and become discolored. Aluminum and plastic edge moldings are available. One type has a narrow lip over the surface. It is attached with nails that are then covered by a plastic insert (Fig. 11-7D). This protects the surface material, but the lip makes wiping the top slightly more difficult.

DOORS AND DRAWERS

Doors can be made in many ways. Plastic-coated particle board has a rather clinical appearance. You can use modern synthetic finishes to seal wood with what amounts to a clear plastic coating. As long as the covering remains intact, there is no fear of the porous wood absorbing anything.

Doors and drawer fronts are usually made to overlap their frames (Fig. 11-8A). Putting them within the frames calls for more careful fitting (Fig. 11-8B). Hidden hinges allow doors to swing clear. You can use plain butt hinges of preferably brass or other metal that resists rust.

Plain doors and drawer fronts made of plastic-coated particle board can be improved with half-round molding (Fig. 11-8C), preferably wood varnished before attaching. Handles in contrasting colors can also be regarded as decorations (Fig. 11-8D).

You can frame plywood in the usual way (Fig. 11-8E) and put false fronts on drawers made up in a similar fashion (Fig. 11-8F). If you are able to mold around the panels, a better appearance results (Fig. 11-8G). Small prepared moldings can be put in squared frames to get the same effect. You get a luxurious appearance if you are able to mold the panels (Fig. 11-8H). A panel ideally is solid wood with its edges reduced. You can get a comparable effect by putting wood on the surface of a plywood panel, preferably with its edge molded or a molding added (Fig. 11-8J).

In most kitchens you will have to make many matching doors and drawer fronts, so choose designs that will not be too laborious. One complicated design may be acceptable for a particular door, but you may not want to spend a long time making a lot more in the same way.

Flush plywood doors can have the plywood in rabbeted frames (Fig. 11-8K) and will look good with nicely veneered plywood. It helps in ensuring a door's rigidity to have another piece of plywood inside (Fig. 11-8L). There is the practical problem

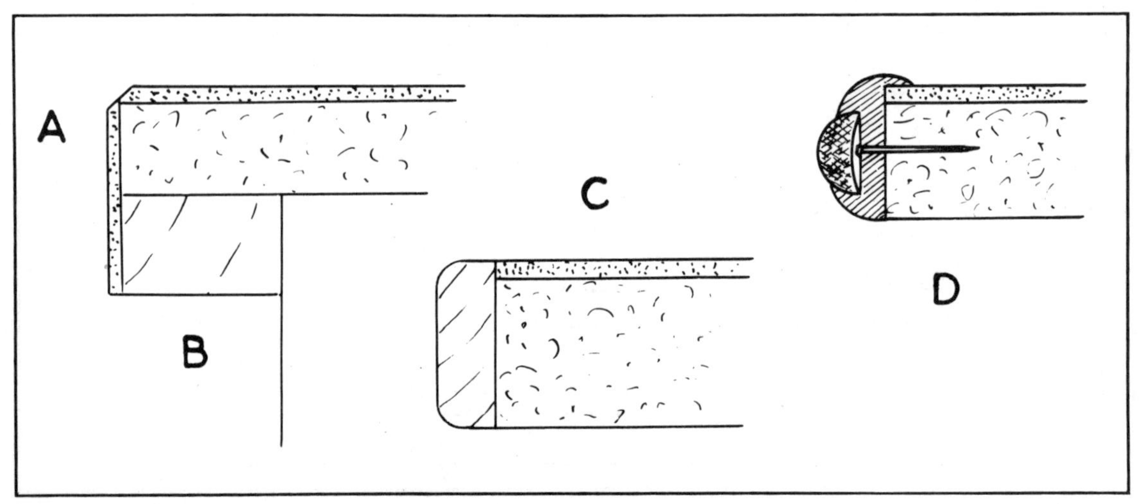

Fig. 11-7. A laminated plastic top may be edged with the same material, wood, or a special molding.

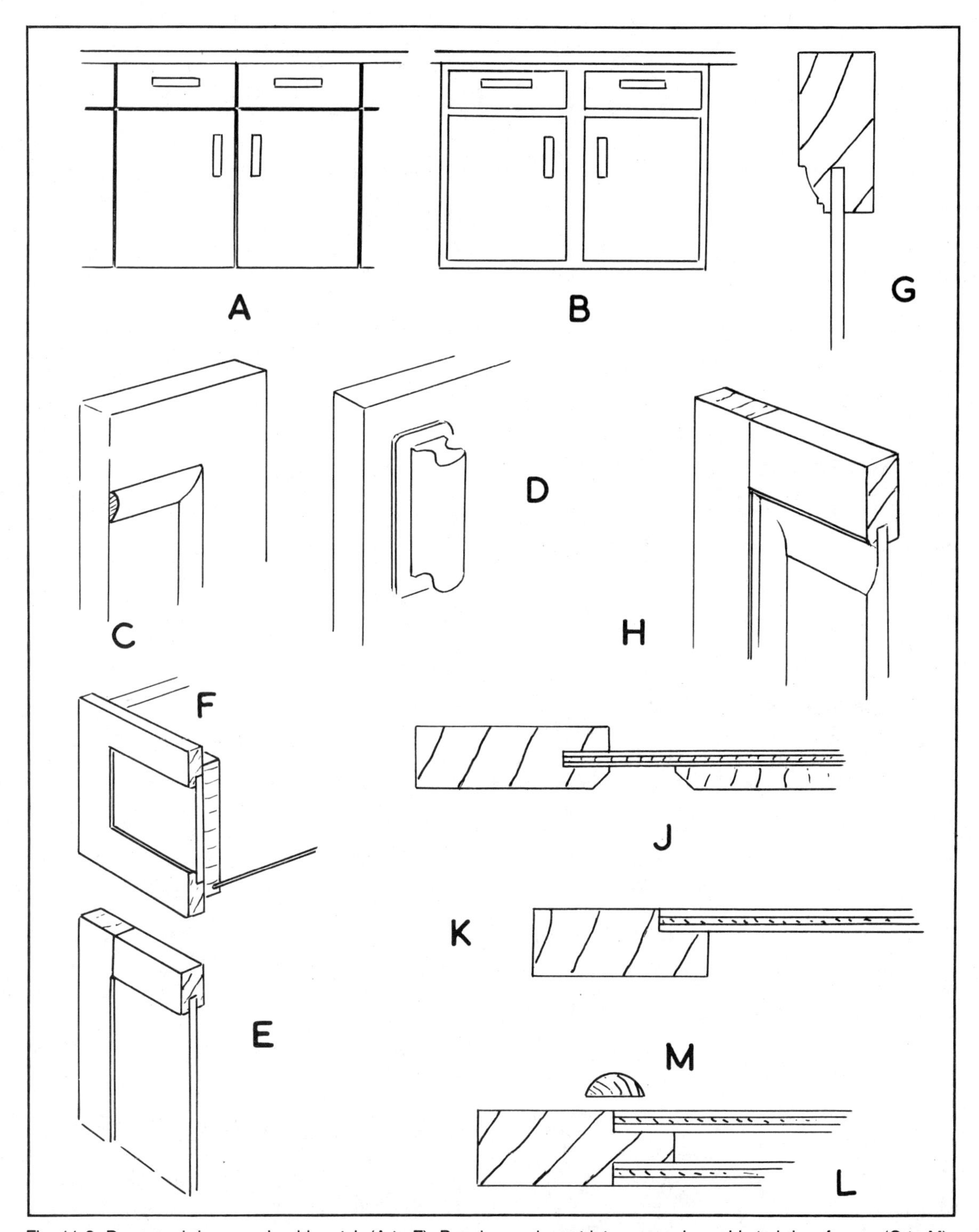

Fig. 11-8. Doors and drawers should match (A to F). Panels may be set into grooved or rabbeted door frames (G to M).

of getting the plywood to fit well in the rabbets, but you can disguise the joint with half-round molding (Fig. 11-8M). Doors made up of plywood panels each side of solid wood strips may have uses for larger parts, but they tend to be thicker than necessary for doors under work tops.

You can allow for a plinth about 4 inches high, but with doors mounted on the surface the framing itself may be set back enough to act as a plinth (Fig. 11-9A). If you want more toe room, the base can be set back (Fig. 11-9B).

CABINETS

It is best to treat all units along one wall as a single structure. This gives you an advantage over the suppliers of mass-produced kitchen furniture, who may have to put joints between prefabricated units where they are not really needed. It helps to adopt standard sections. For upright posts and other parts, 2-inch-by-2-inch provides strength and enough wood for cutting joints. Most other framing can be 1-inch-by-2-inch section. You can make many things on the bench, but much of the assembly is best done in position. Watch the levels as you fit parts. Get a front horizontal member true, then check the supports that go against the wall with a level on a strip of wood (Fig. 11-9C). Halving joints are suitable for much of the construction (Fig. 11-9D). They are easy to cut and have the advantage over dowels of positively locating parts in relation to each other.

At the bottom you will have to allow for a piece of plywood at the plinth level. Never leave a plywood edge exposed. Make sure it is covered with solid wood bedded in glue (Fig. 11-9E). If plumbing or electrical wiring goes under the unit, leave the bottom loose so it can be lifted out for access.

It is unusual to close the gap between the drawers and the space below, but you can include plywood there. Drawers have to be provided with runners and kickers unless you use metal guides. Put rails back to front at drawer level, preferably wide enough to act as runners (Fig. 11-9F), although you can put strips on narrower rails. Add a strip above as a guide (Fig. 11-9G). A narrow rail located higher can have a bearer on it and make its own guide (Fig. 11-9H). Above the drawer, arrange another rail wide enough to form a kicker (Fig. 11-9J). Get parts square to each other, or you will have difficulty in making a drawer run smoothly.

You can arrange a block of drawers for the full depth instead of a cupboard, but an alternative is to make a stack of trays that come behind a door. You may use plastic or wire mesh trays and build the other parts to suit. Light wood trays that can be taken out will hold cutlery and the many small items used in a kitchen. Arrange plywood sides and put runners on them (Fig. 11-10A). Trays have their fronts cut down for gripping (Fig. 11-10B), so they can be made almost out to the door. Put stops on the runners if the trays do not go back the full width of the compartment.

If you continue the assembly under a sink, the long top member provides strength and continuity. There will still be space lower down for doors, but the depth of the sink prevents continuation of a line of drawers. You can fit a dummy drawer front as a matching panel for a better appearance (Fig. 11-10C). Consider the depth you will have to allow for this when settling the height of the drawer rail for the units further along.

CORNERS

If the working surface is to be continued or around a corner, there is a problem of how to deal with the space below so it is accessible. Whatever you do with a closed corner, it will be difficult to get at things stored there. Usually it is best to stop drawers (Fig. 11-11A) and leave the space at drawer height in the corner to allow for tall things to extend there. You can make a drawer with a curved back to swing there (Fig. 11-11B), but its usefulness is doubtful. If the doors below swing away from the corner, you will have allowed maximum access (Fig. 11-11C).

Another treatment is to arrange for a diagonal piece across the corner (Fig. 11-11D). You can then allow for a narrow drawer and a door below it. If the diagonal part will be wide enough to be useful, it comes out into the room and may be inadvisable if floor space is already small.

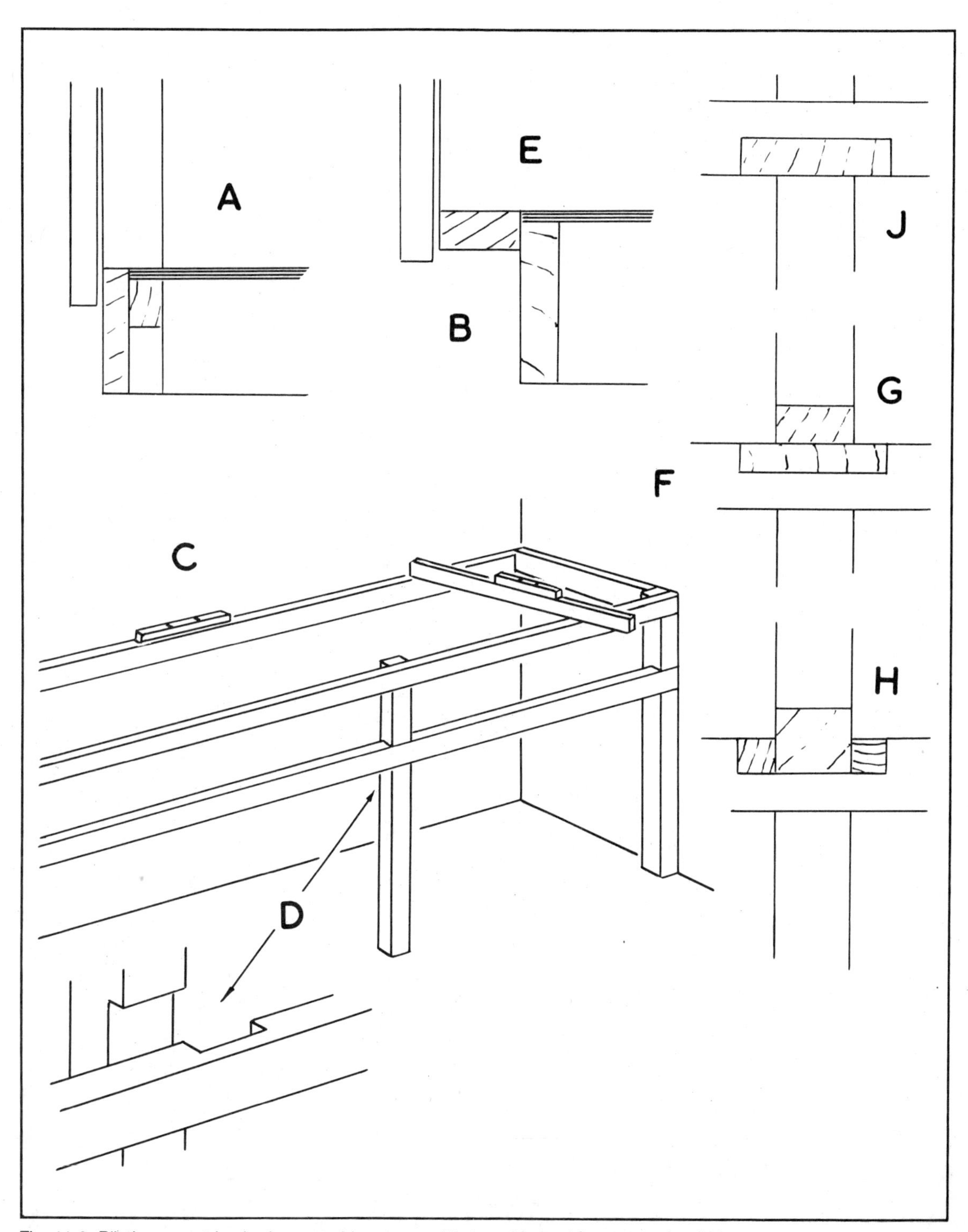

Fig. 11-9. Plinths are set back, drawer guides are provided, and halved frames are leveled.

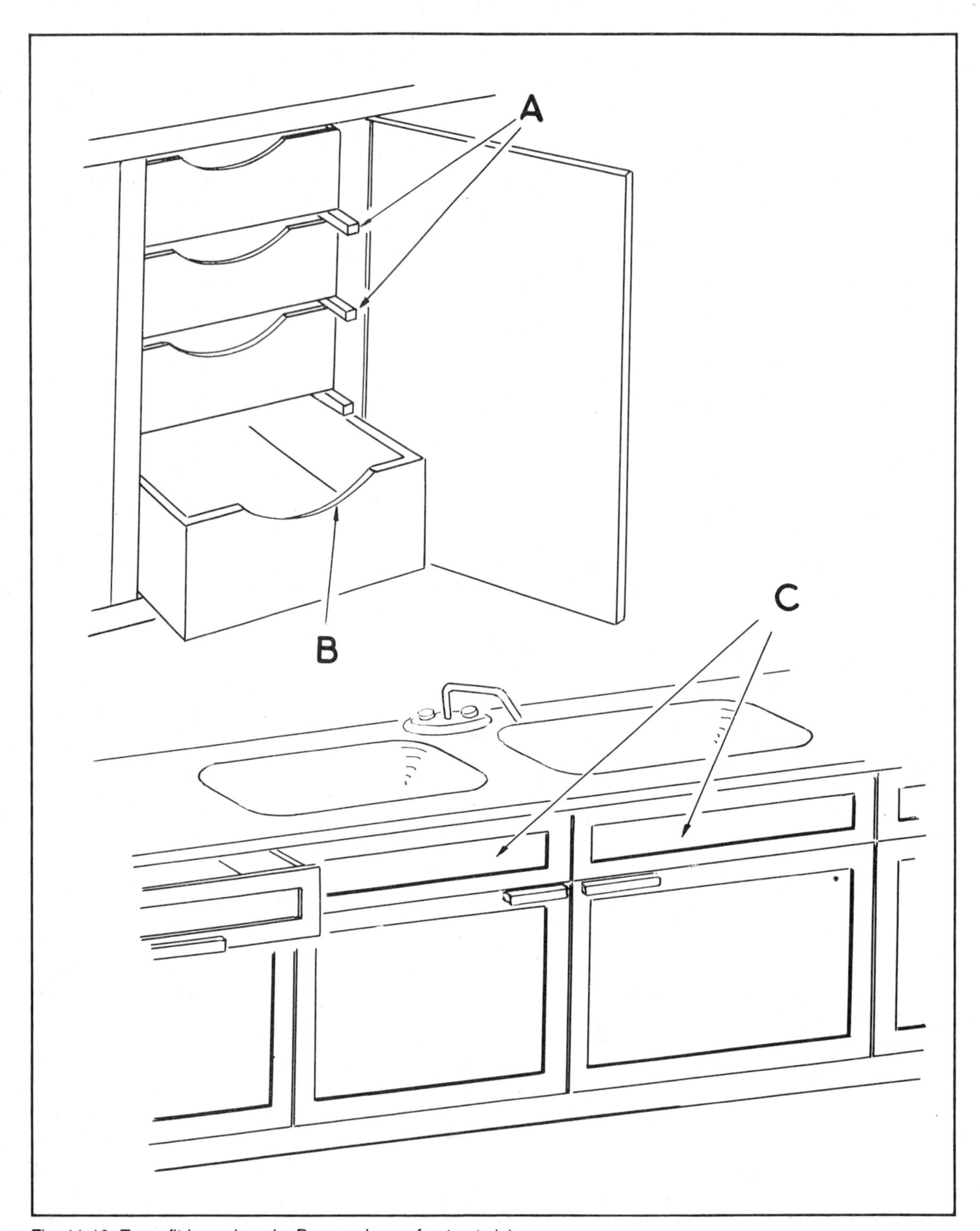

Fig. 11-10. Trays fit in cupboards. Dummy drawer fronts at sink.

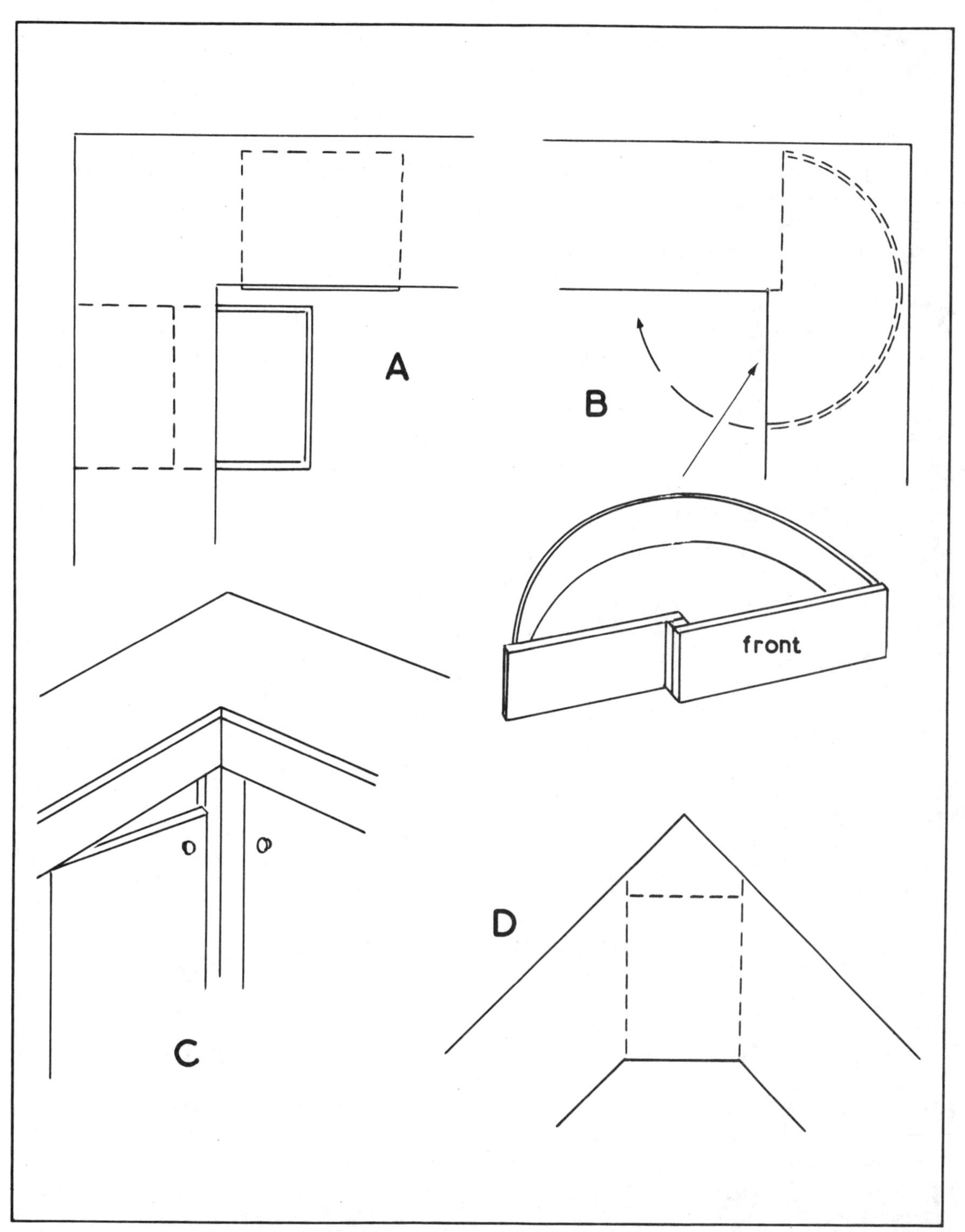

Fig. 11-11. At a corner drawers and doors must be arranged to clear each other. A curved drawer may swing.

While not using every bit of corner space, you can make curved trays that will use a large part of the volume and become easily accessible when opened. One idea is a door hinged in the corner so it can swing to the other side through 90° (Fig. 11-12A). Semicircular trays are attached to this at two levels. When the door is opened, half of the trays comes out, and the other half should be easy to reach. Use stout plywood for the trays and edge them with thin plywood sprung round. Struts between the trays provide rigidity (Fig. 11-12B). Quarter-round trays can be fitted in a similar way to other doors. They are convenient for getting at things, but they do not provide as much storage space as a plain cupboard. If maximum storage is needed, restrict their use to places where convenience outweighs capacity.

SPECIAL EQUIPMENT

In planning the layout there often is a narrow part left when space for drawers and doors of a useful width has been allowed. A narrow drawer is no problem, but a narrow space behind a door may go too far back to be reached for general storage. One use is space for serving trays, chopping boards, and oven trays. A solid or framed division will prevent the contents from falling over (Fig. 11-12C).

Another use is for a trash container. Although the front may look like a door, the whole thing slides out like a drawer (Fig. 11-12D). The bottom slides on guides. Strips near the top may also support the trash bag. They are joined across at the back and run between more guides (Fig. 11-12E). This provides space for a large container and should be located near the sink and the most used part of the work top. A smaller pedal bin or similar container can be attached inside an ordinary door.

Many storage devices may be included in your kitchen units, but check what is available and what you want to use before starting construction. Some supports swing out and up after you have opened a door, and others will slide out as you move the door. There may be storage jars and other containers for which you can make compartments in drawers or on the backs of doors.

The backs of doors will take many things and keep them within reach. A rack of small shelves (Fig. 11-13A) will hold many items. Leave gaps below the rails so the shelves can be wiped clean (Fig. 11-13B). Wider things like chopping boards may drop into slots (Fig. 11-13C). Some things will fit into holes (Fig. 11-13D). Think about what has to be stowed, then make a combined fitting inside the door. Because you can add these racks after the kitchen has been put into use, you may want to delay making them until you know the most suitable arrangements.

Will a work or serving trolley be useful? You can make what looks like a cupboard front, but the whole thing pulls out on casters and can be taken where you wish. You can get at all sides when the trolley is out, so you can arrange storage and drawers in any direction to suit your needs. The casters are inside a frame like a plinth (Fig. 11-14). The parts can be faced particle board held together with dowels. The top flap slides in either direction and can be faced with asbestos or other head-resistant material to take hot pans. The drawers may also go either way, or you can arrange one each way. Heavier things stored below will aid stability.

Items like a refrigerator and an eye level cooker will go higher than the work top. Alongside you may put a tall storage space, possibly with a bank of shelves for storing groceries and other things that do not require refrigeration. You can also use the height to accommodate brooms and other long-handled things. These tall compartments may link with any higher wall storage that you are providing, and they should be built in with that.

HIGHER STORAGE

Storage on the walls above the working surfaces has the advantage of putting things at the most convenient height near eye level. Larger things and those less frequently needed may go in the drawers, but what is right in front of you gets most attention. This also applies to appearance as well as convenience. The ordinary observer does not look up or down very much, but his attention is directed mostly to what he can see ahead. The focus of your layout should be on the parts between about 4 feet

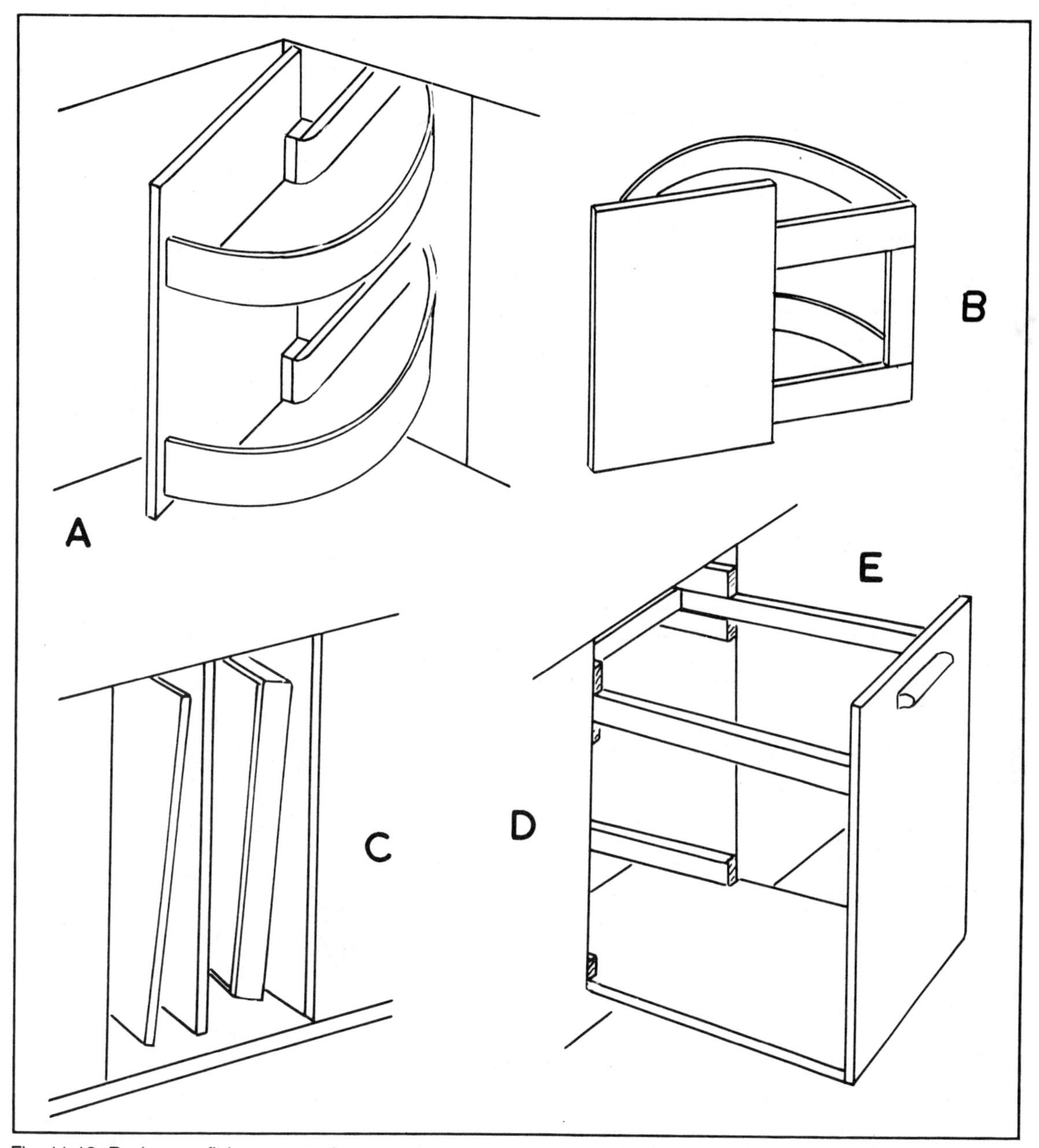

Fig. 11-12. Racks may fit in a corner door or a narrow space. A compartment may be arranged to slide.

and 7 feet from the floor (Fig. 11-15).

Some storage can come down to the work top. Anything with much projection from the wall should have its bottom high enough for you to see right to the back of the work surface and bend to do things on it without hitting your head (Fig. 11-16).

Basic wall units will usually be blocks of shelves with doors and plywood backs. Veneered or plastic-coated particle board may be used. White interiors look hygienic and are easy to clean. Most

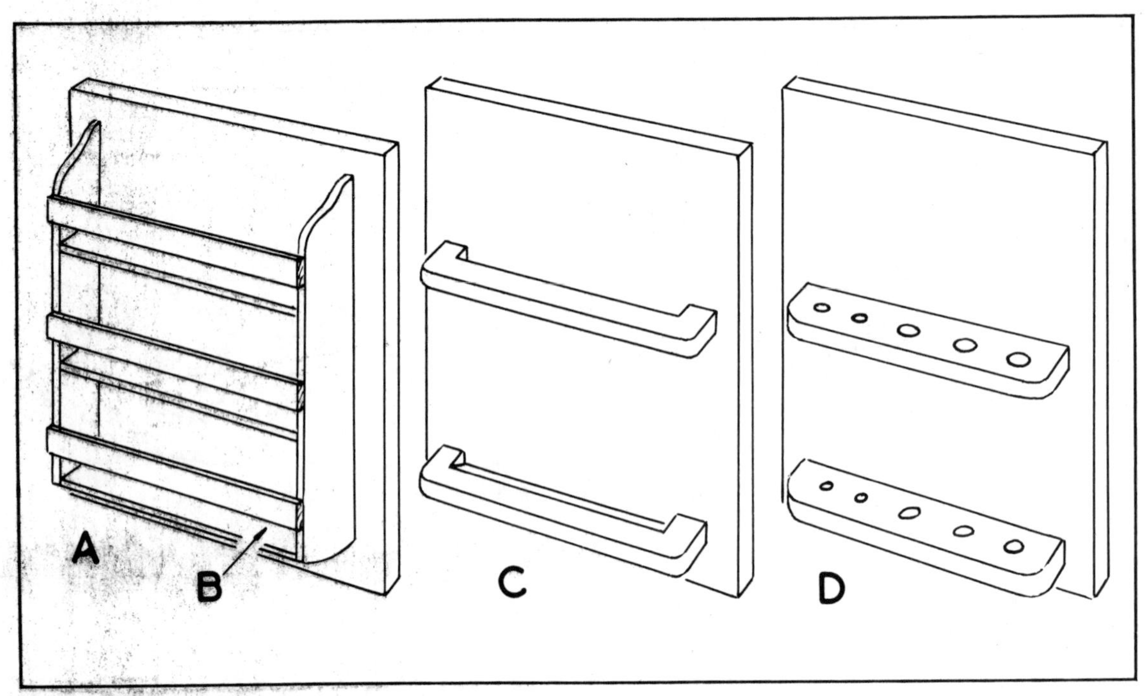

Fig. 11-13. Racks provide storage inside doors.

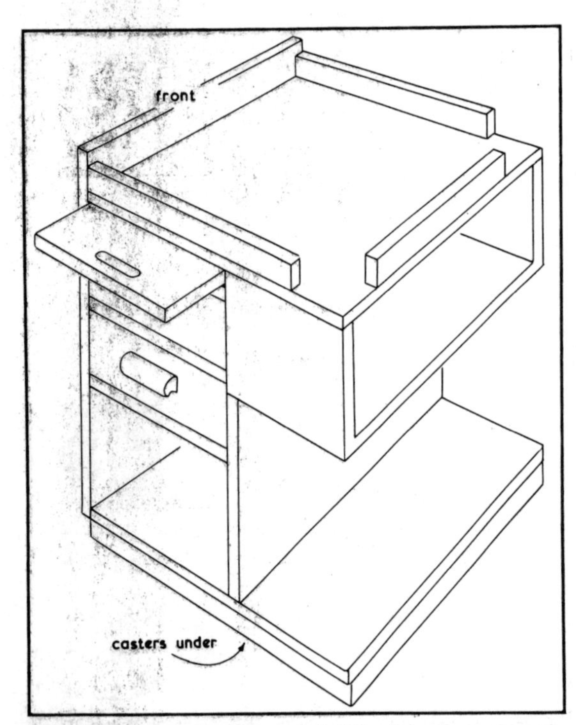

Fig. 11-14. A trolley can be made to fit in place of a cupboard.

items can be stored in a 6-inch width, but you may go to 9 inches if that will not project too much. It may be possible to step the widths along a wall, with a narrow section between wider ones, or the other way around.

For a long run, carry the top and bottom right through, with the ends doweled or dovetailed (Fig. 11-17A). Intermediate uprights can be doweled in place (Fig. 11-17B). The width of compartments depends on the intended doors. The arrangement looks best if the doors are not wider than they are high. It will be best if doors do not swing out further than the width of the work top. You must make a single-door compartment fairly narrow (Fig. 11-17C). It is better to use a pair of doors for most compartments (Fig. 11-17D). In some places you may make the door to swing up (Fig. 11-17E), preferably with a friction strut that holds it at any degree of opening. Vertically-hinged doors are preferable for most situations.

The shelves may be arranged as you wish. It is better to have them at different heights each side of an upright for easy construction (Fig. 11-17F). You may use dowels with particle board. For shelves at the same level, dowels can go right through (Fig. 11-17G). You may use dowels with solid wood, but dado joints are alternatives. If you are uncertain of the best shelf spacing or you want to alter positions later, shelves can be loose and supported on pegs in the same way as suggested for some bookcases (Fig. 11-17H). Shelves can come out to the full width or be set back slightly, particularly if you want to put anything on the inside of a door. It may

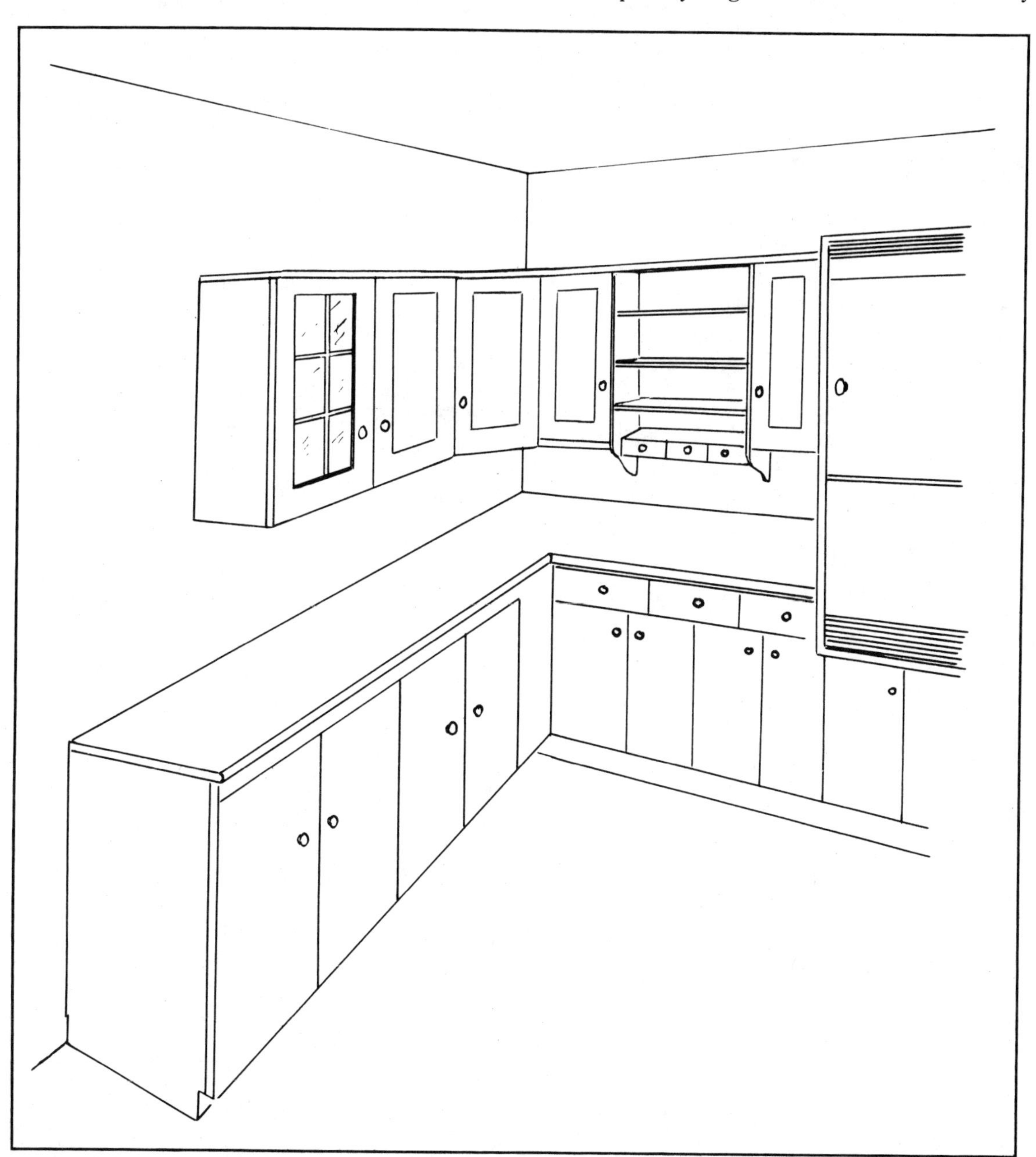

Fig. 11-15. Upper and lower parts must match and use space economically.

Fig. 11-16. The corner space near a cooker has been fully used with closed storage and a rack for cookbooks.

be useful in some places to provide a rim in front of shelves (Fig. 11-17J).

Doors can be similar to those below, although they do not have to be exact matches. You may prefer a different scheme at that level. With a gap between the two lines of doors, you can provide a different appearance by using related but different doors. Put handles where they can be reached. The balanced pull on any door has the handle at the middle, but you will want the handles lower than that for a comfortable reach.

Too long an expanse of identical doors looks monotonous. You can break the pattern with a glass door (Fig. 11-18A) and use the shelves behind to display special dishes rather than a collection of canned goods. Fit the glass in rabbets with fillets (Fig. 11-18B). Although plain glass may look satisfactory in a small door, it is better broken into panels for a larger one. You can do this with narrow strips of wood (Fig. 11-18C), but leaded glass is particularly appropriate. It need not be fitted in the traditional way. Lead strips and adhesives are available for putting on the surface. Appearance is improved if you arrange divisions on the glass in line with shelves inside (Fig. 11-18D).

SHELVES

Compartments with doors can be separated by open shelves. These may be the same as inside the compartments. If you have made the closed compartments with plastic-surfaced particle board, solid wood open shelving makes a good contrast, particularly if other exposed woodwork is the same. Any kitchen woodwork should be given several

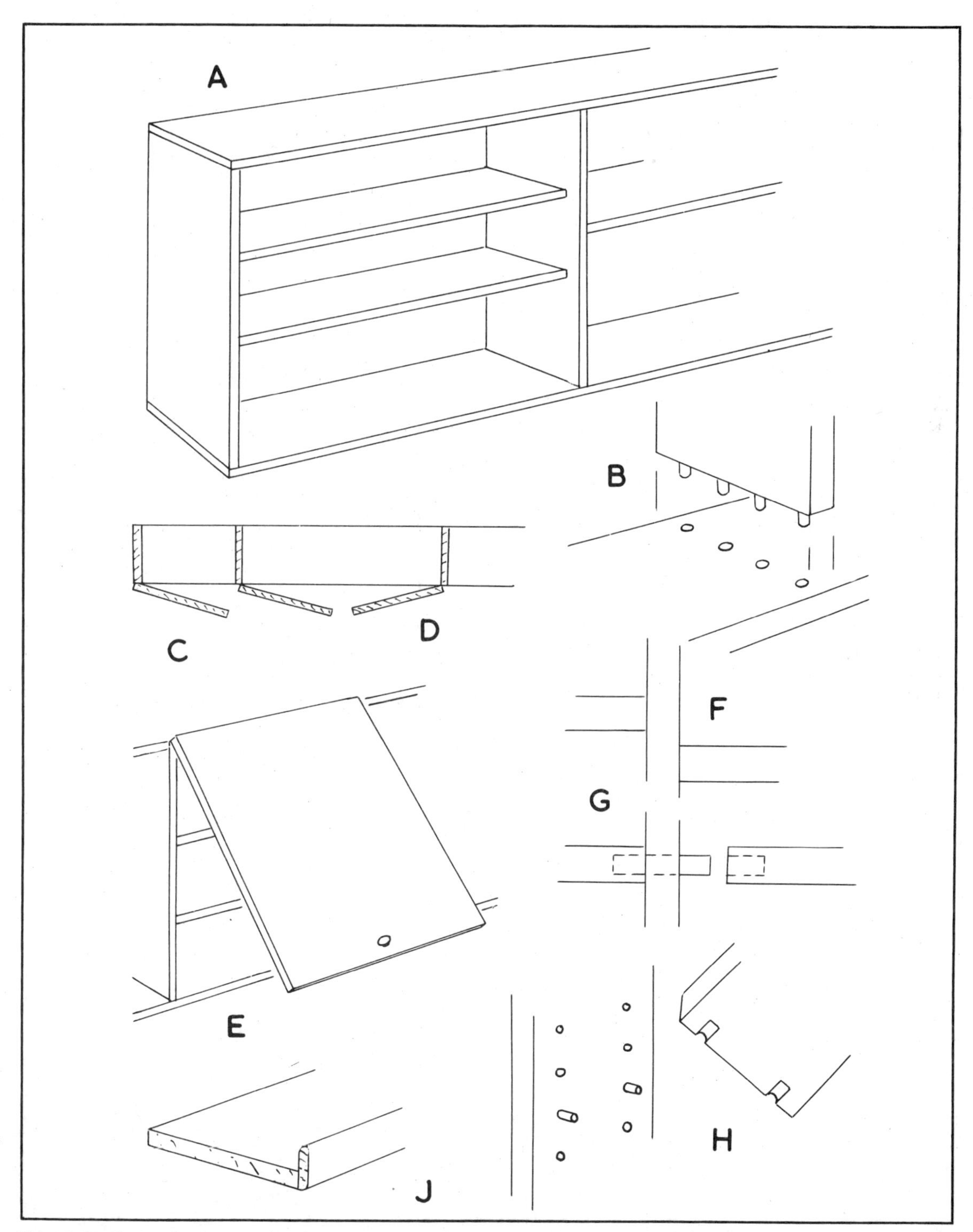

Fig. 11-17. Shelves in upper compartments may be fixed or adjustable.

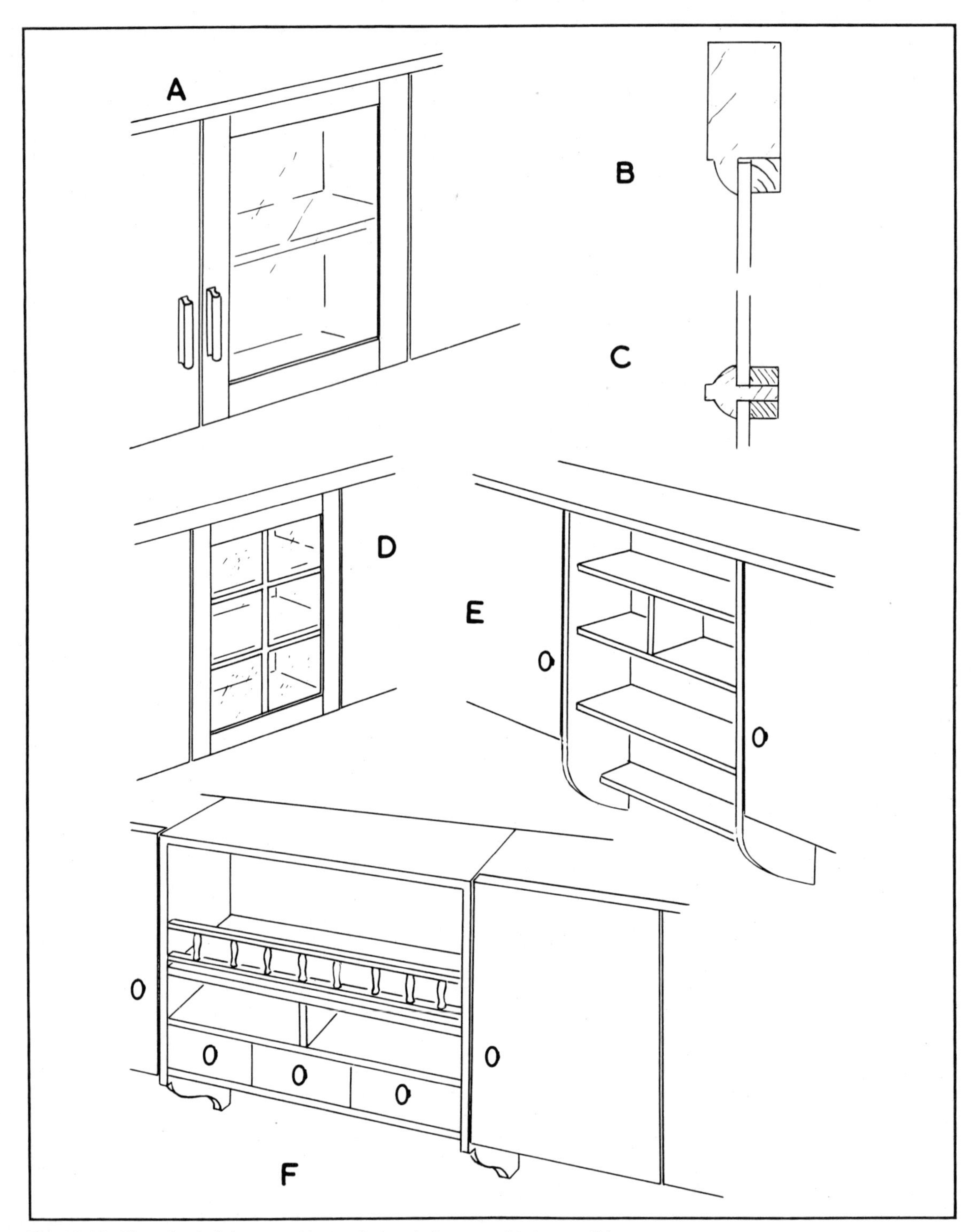

Fig. 11-18. Glass-fronted doors and open shelves between solid doors will improve appearance.

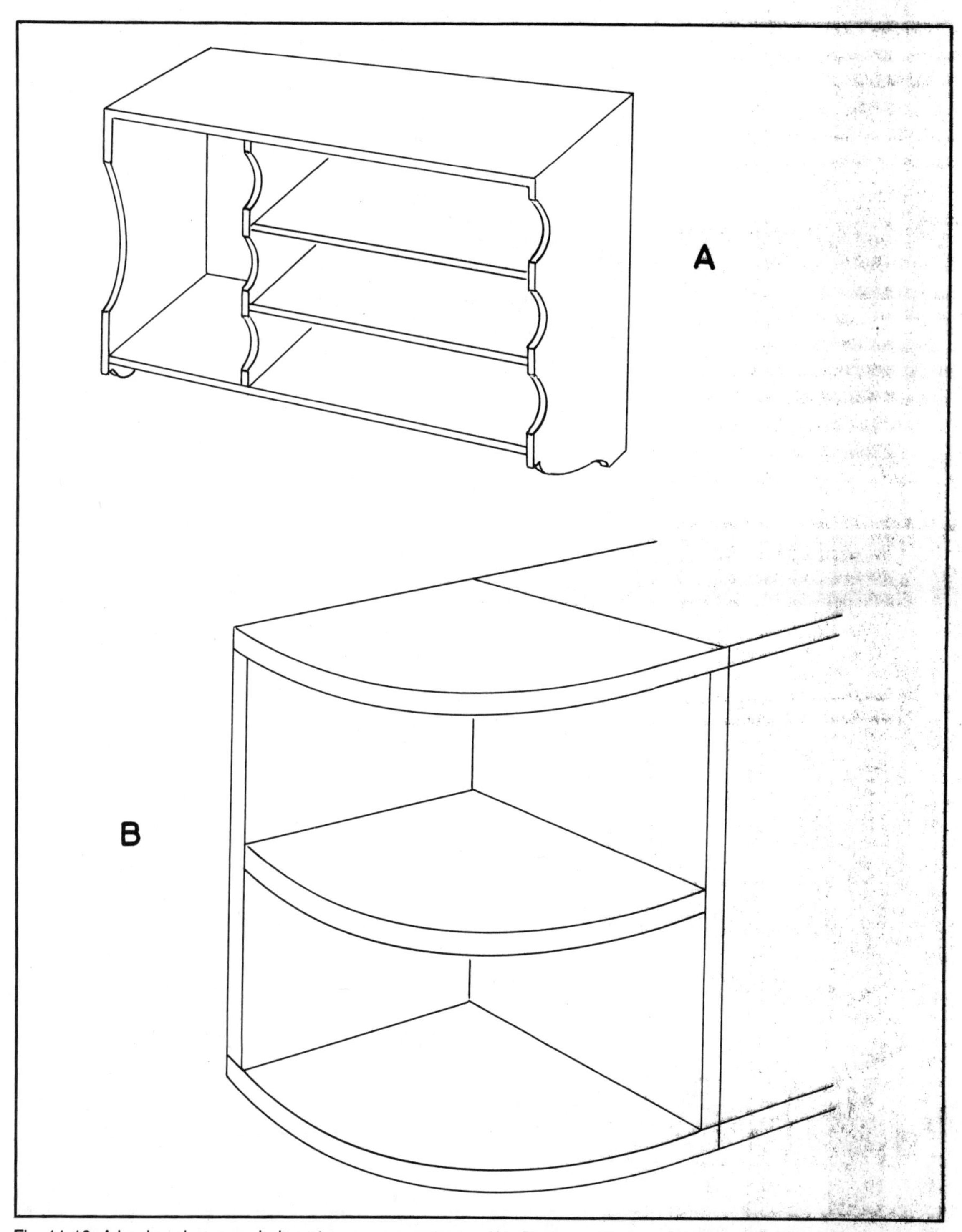

Fig. 11-19. A book rack may go below storage compartments (A). Shelves with curved edges will finish a line of racks (B).

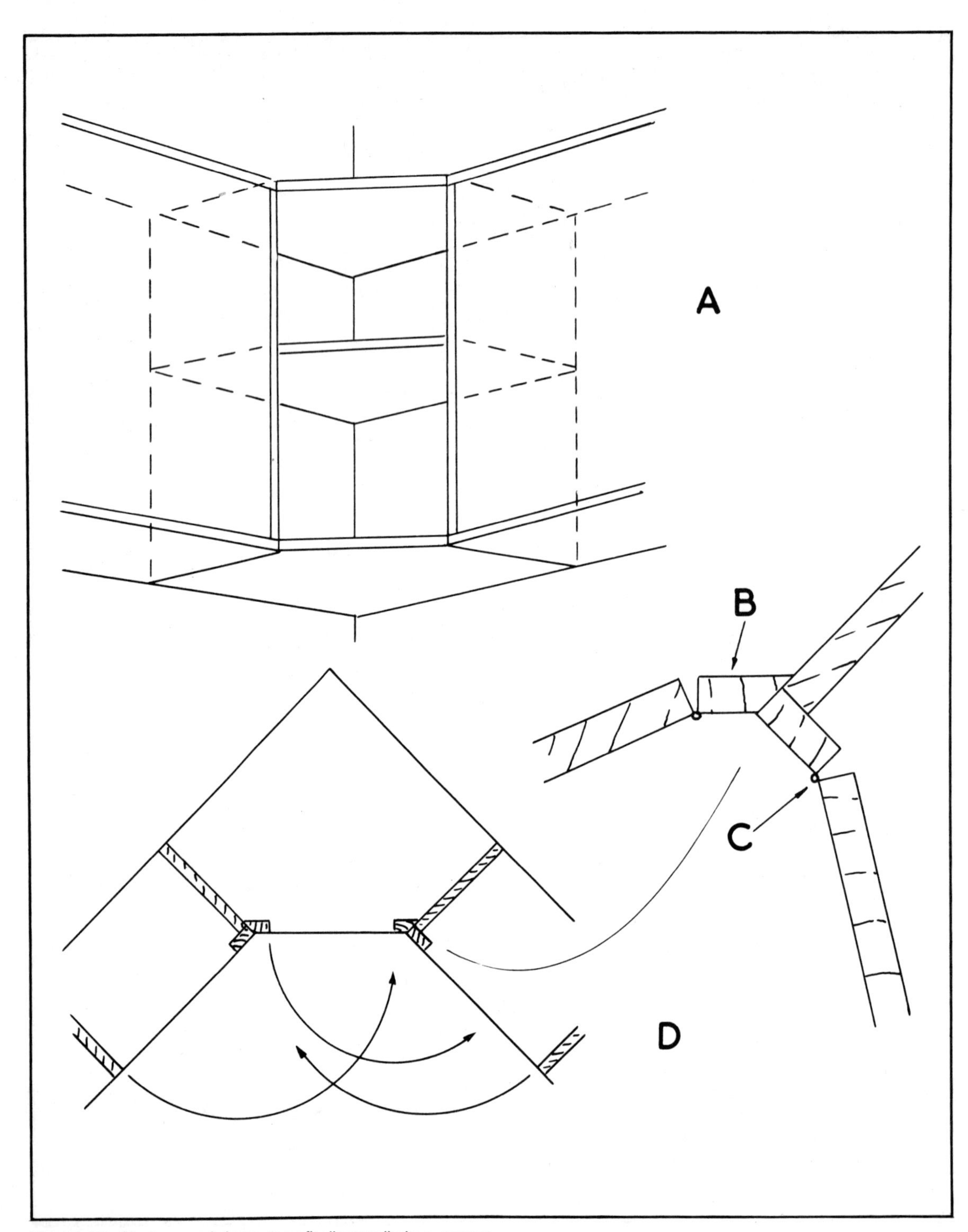

Fig. 11-20. Shelves and doors may fit diagonally in a corner.

coats of a good waterproof varnish.

Make up an open unit with its own sides to go against the sides of closed compartments. A simple unit (Fig. 11-18E) may extend below the line of doors. You can make a more decorative unit with the sides shaped as they go below and rails supported with little turned spindles (Fig. 11-18F) in front of shelves. You can include drawers, but they will not be very large. They should not be too wide if they are to slide easily.

Somewhere you should include a rack for cookbooks. They may be most accessible in a wooden rack below a closed compartment (Fig. 11-19A). Measure the books. Some cookbooks tend to be large. You may have to allow for them being put flat instead of on edge. The same rack can carry more personal things such as a diary, pens, notebook, and leaflets or brochures.

The end of a block of closed units may finish squarely. You can make a corner unit to go there, preferably with a wood finish to match open shelving further along (Fig. 11-19B). Dowel the parts together. Veneer around the curved edges of the shelves. You can spring thin plywood around to make lips. This unit is probably best used for plants or flowers.

HIGH CORNERS

If you look diagonally into a corner, the work top is wider. There is more head clearance as you lean

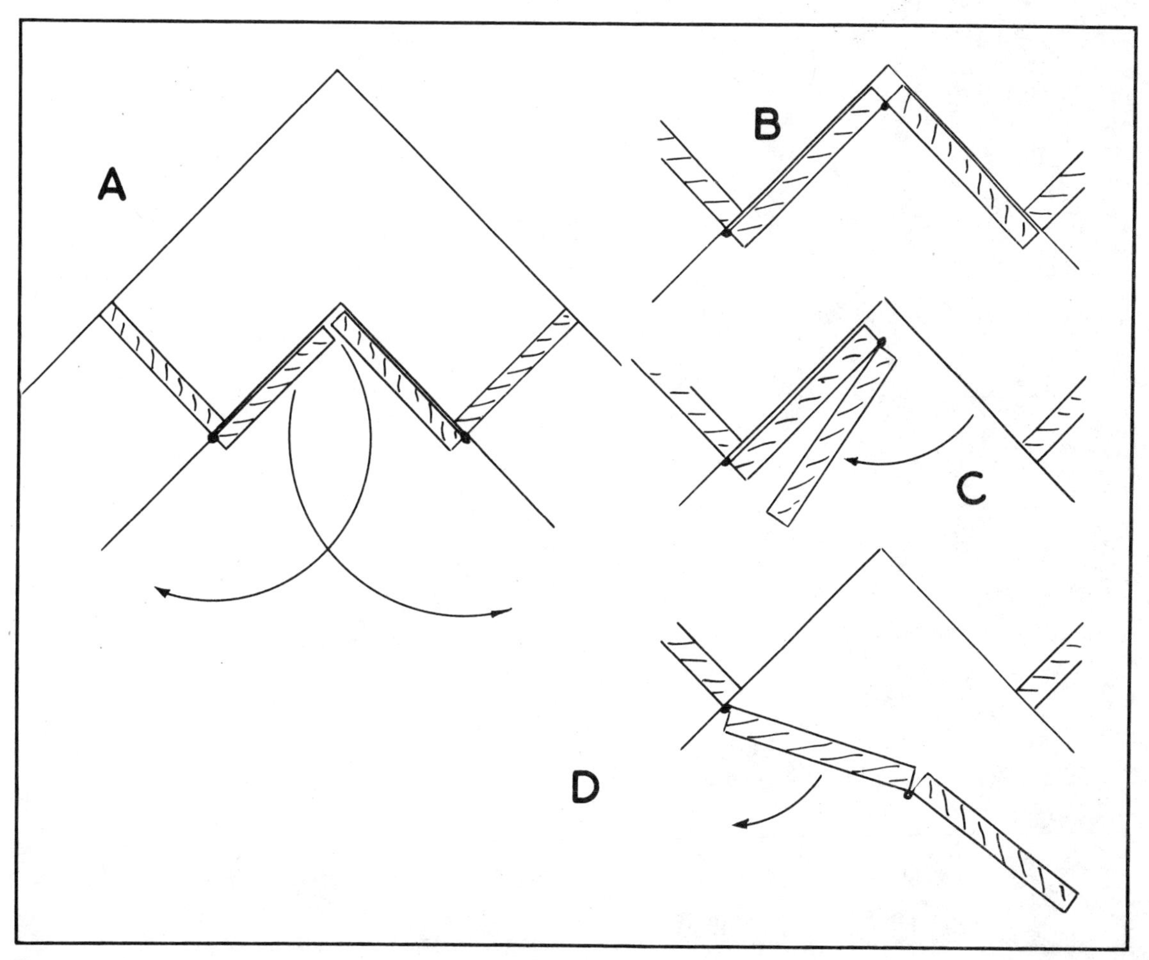

Fig. 11-21. Doors may be hinged to swing clear in a corner.

Fig. 11-22. This door to a corner compartment is in two parts hinged together.

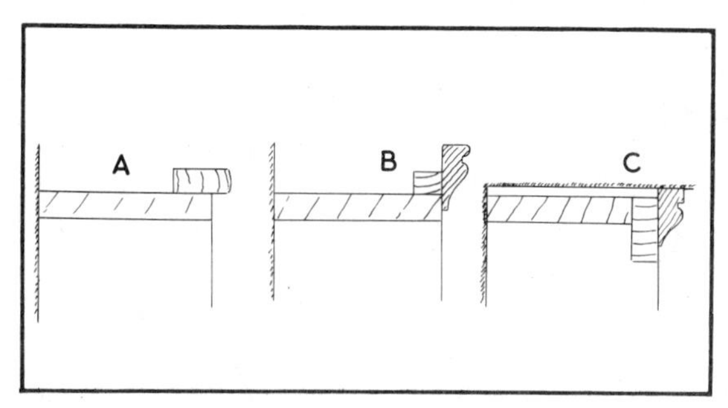

Fig. 11-23. The top of a cabinet is improved with an edging, which may close the gap at the ceiling.

over, so you can bring a corner unit further forward without obstruction. You can make the best use of a corner with a diagonal frontage. You can make open shelves between the units along the walls (Fig. 11-20A). Things that will not go conveniently into other shelf spaces can be stored there. The shelves can be spaced to take bottles, tall cans, or a food mixer that will not go anywhere else.

If you want to close the corner, there are a few considerations. That door and any adjoining ones must be able to swing without touching each other. Allow for clearance for the thickness of handles. Instead of a door going to the edge, it will be better to have a narrow width against it (Fig. 11-20B). Adjoining doors are best hinged at the corner edges (Fig. 11-20C). A narrow strip each side of the diagonal door will allow all doors to be opened, but not at the same time (Fig. 11-20D).

Another way to deal with a corner is to keep the shelving square and fit doors. Two ordinary doors can meet in the corner, but one will have to overlap the other when closed (Fig. 11-21A). They have to be opened and closed in sequence. Another interesting way of fitting doors is to join them with a piano hinge at the corner, so only one is hinged to the unit (Fig. 11-21B) and the other has the catch. The door folds back on itself in the first opening (Fig. 11-21C), then is straightened as it is pulled further (Fig. 11-21D). See Fig. 11-22.

The upper part of the wall toward the ceiling is too high to be reached comfortably while standing on the floor. If maximum storage space is important, you can put units there, possibly in the way high storage has been described. Otherwise, it is usually better to stop the units between 18 inches and 24 inches from the ceiling. This leaves open space on which you can put things that are not often required.

The tops of the units may just finish as they are, or you may add a top to give a cleaner line. This can be just an edge with an overhang (Fig. 11-23A), or you may use a length of molding held up with a strip behind (Fig. 11-23B). In both ways the edgings also act as retainers to prevent things put on top from falling off. If units are taken to near ceiling height, similar moldings will fill the gap (Fig. 11-23C). It is easier to make the units without actually touching the ceiling, then cover the gap to allow for slight level variations.

Chapter 12

Bedroom and Bathroom Furniture

MOST BEDROOMS DO NOT HAVE MUCH SPACE for moving things about. A main bedroom may be fairly large, but others may be very small to get as many rooms as possible into the house or allow for other daytime rooms being larger. There is often a need for built-in furniture that will take up little floor space and be rigidly held, despite projecting no more than necessary from a wall.

Nothing much can be done about the size of the bed, but it is possible to plan a room so other furniture is adequate, yet uses very little space. You thus get furniture for all your needs. There is more of a sense of spaciousness, despite the limits of room size, due to more open floor area. If a room is being furnished for the first time, draw a scale plan of it, with windows and doors marked, so you can move around other pieces of paper representing the bed and furniture you hope to build in. Get the best locations and modify sizes before you start making anything. Don't put something where it may shade something else from window light or limit the opening of a door.

Some items can be made to fold or otherwise reduce in size when not being used. If the folded furniture goes closer against a wall, there is more available floor space. A very small room can be provided with a dresser or other piece of furniture where a freestanding or full-size built-in one could not be accommodated. You can combine items so one piece of furniture takes the place of two or more, but occupies much less space, and is just as serviceable. You also can arrange a combined assembly to occupy a whole wall and give a better appearance than separate pieces of furniture. A combined assembly will usually be more functional.

A bathroom may be even smaller than a bedroom. Making bathroom furniture to be built-in and possibly folding may be the only alternative. If the bathroom also has to be used for drying clothing or another secondary purpose, the additional equipment needed has to be as compact as possible, particularly when it is not being used. Some ideas given in this chapter, may have to be adapted to suit the existing size and layout of a bathroom.

FOLD-FLAT DRESSER

Wall mirrors are always useful. While you are using one, you often need a shelf for brush and comb or cosmetics. A projecting shelf is a nuisance at other times, particularly in a confined space. This mirror has a shelf of useful size that will fold down when not being used, so the total projection from the wall is no more than 1½ inches (Fig. 12-1). Suggested sizes (Fig. 12-2 and Table 12-1) will make a small dresser, but they can be modified. Note that the shelf hangs to the same level as the sides and hides the brackets that fold back between the sides. If sizes are altered, allow enough space between the sides for the brackets to fold without touching and enough depth in the bottom part of the lowered shelf to hang at the same depth as the sides.

Prepare the four parts that will frame the mirror by cutting rabbets deep enough to take the glass and strips behind (Fig. 12-3A). Cut back the sides to the bottoms of the rabbets below where the crosspiece will come (Fig. 12-3B). You can draw the shaping of the top, but delay cutting it until you have prepared the joints.

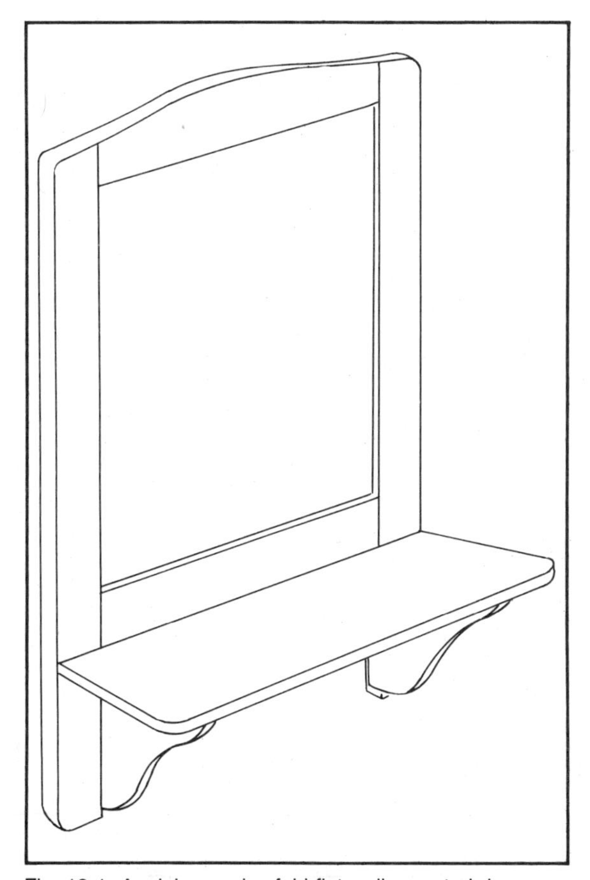

Fig. 12-1. A minimum-size fold-flat wall-mounted dresser.

It may be simplest to dowel the joints. The fronts of the crosspieces must be cut back to fit over the sides and the dowel holes drilled inside (Fig. 12-3C). You can use tenons, again with the fronts shouldered (Fig. 12-3D). Keep the dowels or tenons at the tops low enough to allow for shaping the edges.

Assemble these four parts. Take care that the sides are parallel and the frame is square. Cut the shelf to match the width of the frame. It will be hinged in front of the crosspiece and will hang to the bottom of the sides (Fig. 12-4A), with its corners and those of the sides rounded to match.

The hinges are let into the edge of the shelf so its lower surface is level with the bottom edge of the crosspiece when it is raised (Fig. 12-4B). Most plywood does not provide a very good grip for screws driven into its edge. To make the hinge screws hold better, put dowels of ¼-inch diameter through the plywood. They need not reach the top surface (Fig. 12-4C).

Draw the shape of a bracket (Fig. 12-4D), then use it as a pattern for the other. Notice that the top edges are cut down, so as not to rub under the shelf and ensure that the extreme ends provide support.

Use hinges at the edges of the brackets with screws into dowels in a similar way to the shelf. As the bracket edges will not show, the dowels may go right through. Set the brackets back slightly into the thickness of the frames, so the hinge knuckles will not interfere with the hanging shelf (Fig. 12-4E).

Make a trial assembly to see that the folding parts open and close correctly, then unscrew the hinges so the wood can be finished. Paint or stain black inside the rabbets to reduce edge reflections. When securing the glass, lay cardboard over it where a hammer will be used. Drive the brads partly through the strips before putting them in position (Fig. 12-4F). Cloth strips under the wood strips will cushion the glass.

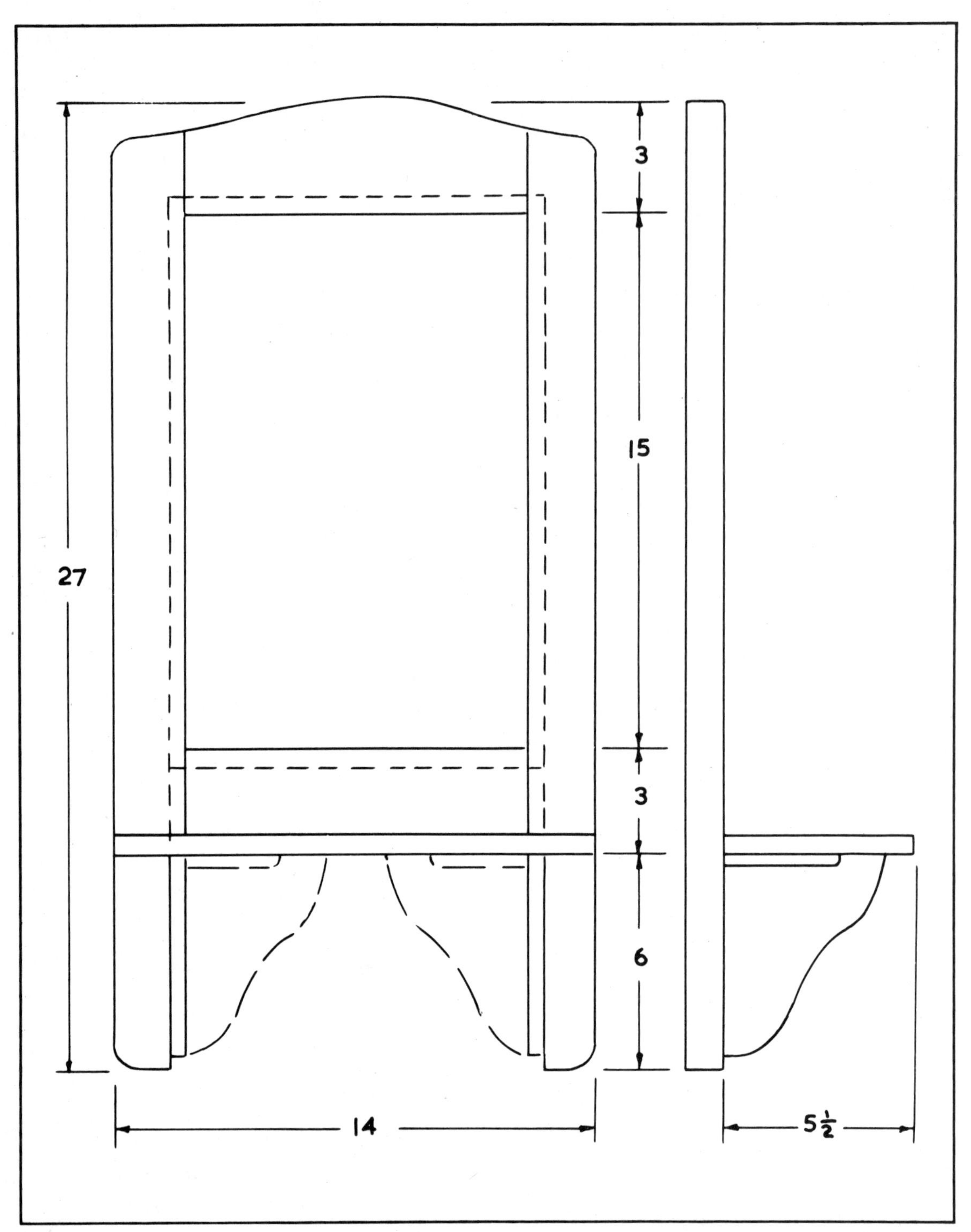

Fig. 12-2. Sizes for a fold-flat dresser.

Table 12-1. Materials List for Fold-Flat Dresser.

2 sides	2	×	27	×	1	
2 cross members	3	×	12	×	1	
1 shelf	6	×	14	×	½ plywood	
2 brackets	5	×	6	×	½ plywood	
2 mirror strips	⅜	×	16	×	⅜	
2 mirror strips	⅜	×	12	×	⅜	

WALL DRESSER

This dresser can be used in a small bedroom or where there is limited space beside a bed. The mirror is shown separately, as it is easier to construct that way. It can be brought against the shelf without the narrow back between. By having the mirror separate, you can locate it at a height to suit the user.

The design is shown with curved edge decoration (Figs. 12-5 and 12-6). These parts can be made straight or with simple bevels, if that will suit your equipment better or be a better match for other furniture.

Make the main shelf and the back first. There is no need to do the edge shaping until after the joints have been prepared (Fig. 12-7A). The shelves are screwed through the back, but most other joints can be made with ¼-inch dowels at about 1-inch spacing (Fig. 12-7B).

Mark the top shelf from the other to get spacing exact. Mark the large end to size without cutting the curves (Fig. 12-7C). Mark the other end from it. Draw the curve for the underside of an end (Fig. 12-7D) on a piece of cardboard or hardboard. Cut this out for use as a template. You will have to modify it freehand at some other places to suit different sizes, but using the template will ensure a uniformity of design. When the dowel holes have

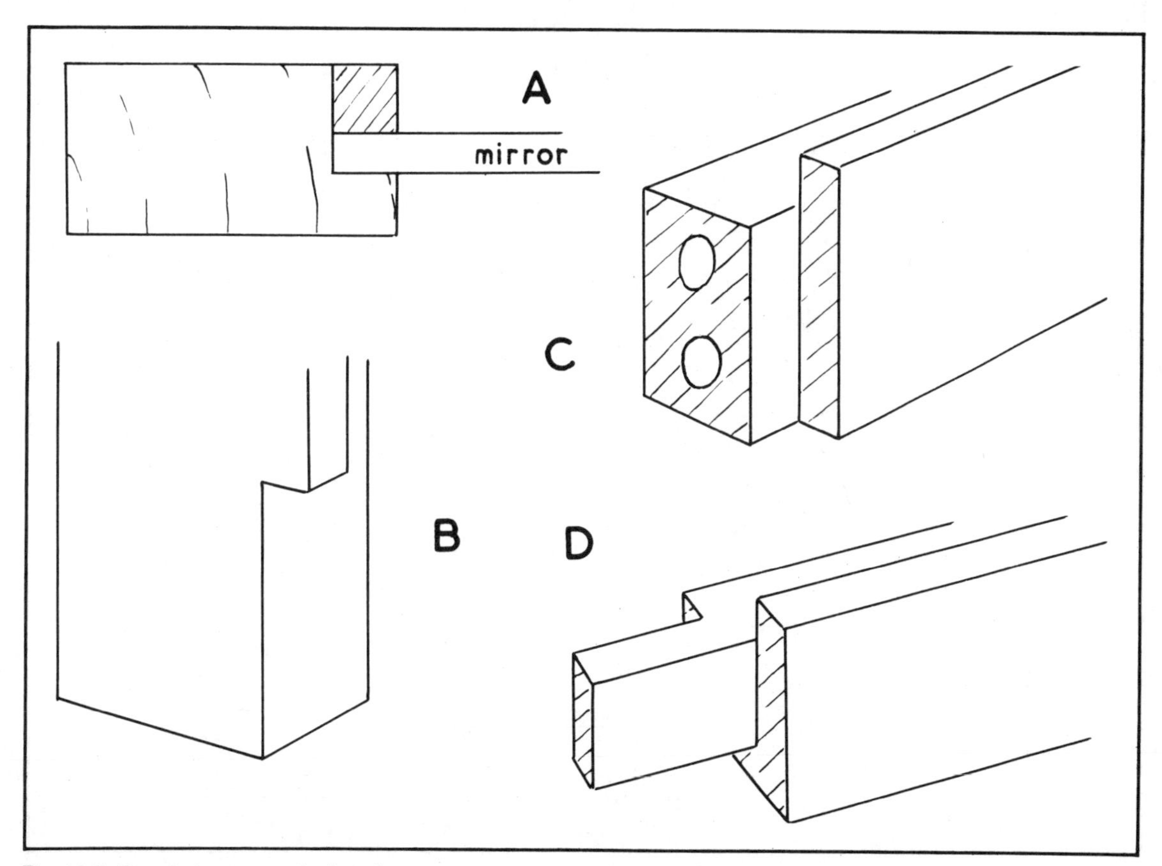

Fig. 12-3. Doweled or tenoned mirror frame.

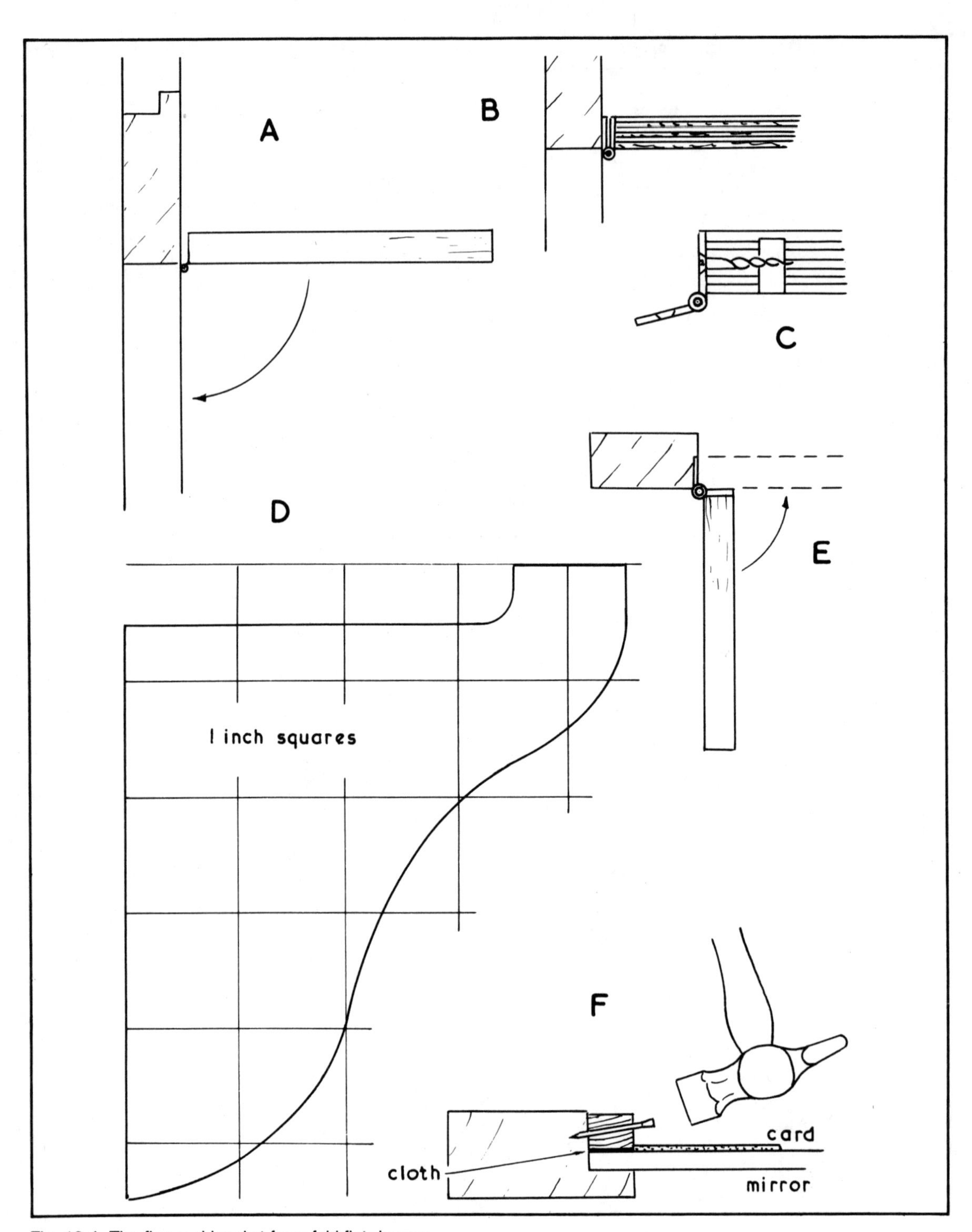

Fig. 12-4. The flap and bracket for a fold-flat dresser.

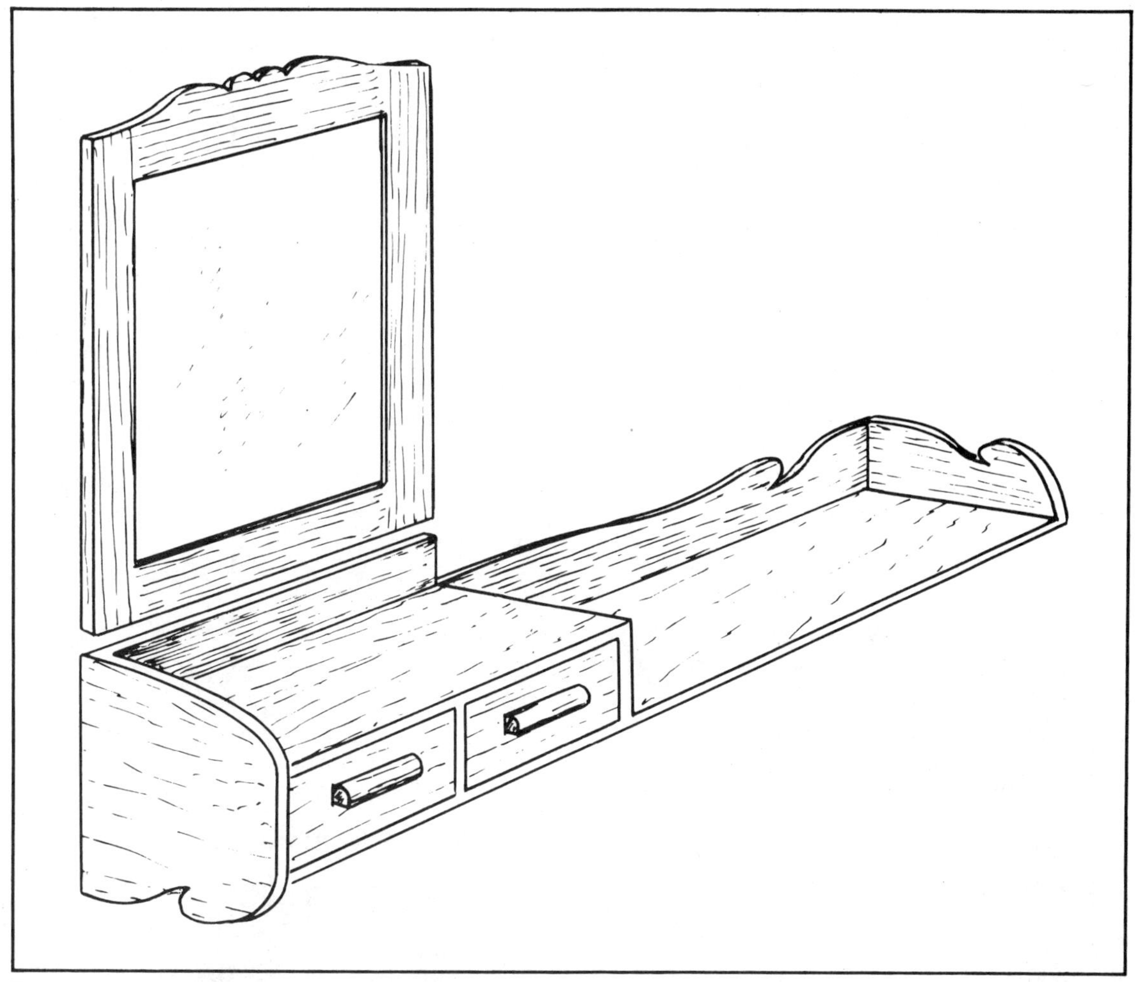

Fig. 12-5. A wall dresser with mirror, drawers, and table.

been drilled, cut the shaped edges and clean them with files and sandpaper.

Make the drawer divider with the grain vertical, so all the assembled parts will have their grain the same way. There should be no risk of cracks due to uneven shrinkage. Assemble the dividers to the shelves, then the shelves to the back, before adding the ends. Make and fit the narrow back above the drawers if the mirror is not to come down to the shelf. If you marked out carefully, the assembly should finish squarely. Check squareness before the glue has set.

Finish the drawers level with the shelf fronts. They can have false fronts, but that will increase the total projection from the wall, which may be important in a confined space. For the least projection, allow for handles that let into the thickness of the fronts.

It is best to dovetail the sides for flush fronts (Fig. 12-7E), although they can be notched and screwed (Fig. 12-7F). Slide the plywood bottoms into grooves and put the backs above the bottom in the usual way. Allow for planing off projecting ends of the sides, so the fronts finish flush when the sides hit the back.

The mirror frame parts have to be rabbeted, but the size to work has to be found by putting together everything that will go in the rabbet. Put

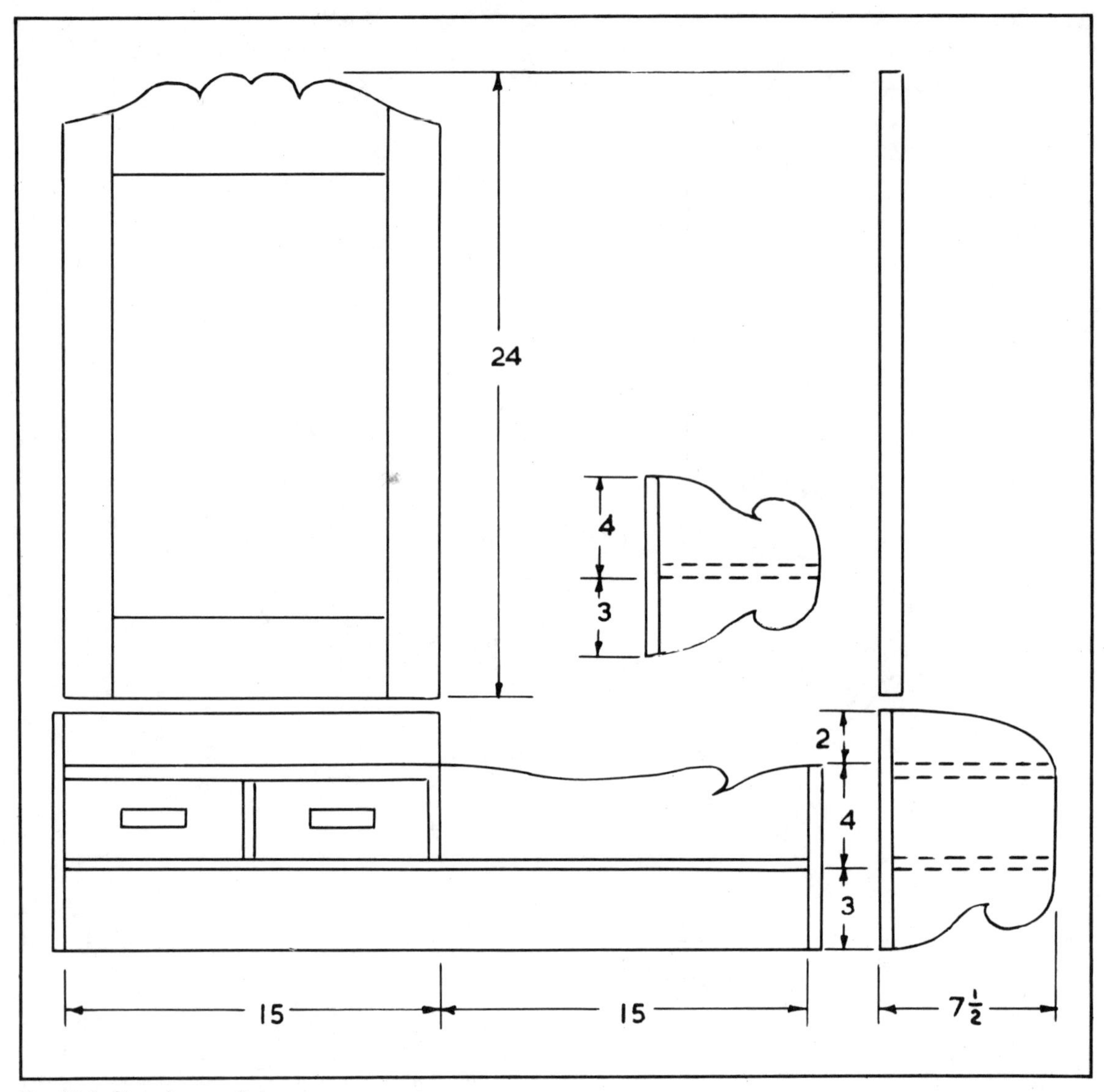

Fig. 12-6. Sizes for a wall dresser.

paper or cardboard between the mirror and the plywood, which will be held in place with small nails (Fig. 12-8A).

The two sides go the full height, and the top and bottom are tenoned to them. The joints are similar, but the top has shallower joints because of its shaping. Arrange one side of each tenon inside the rabbet, then step the shoulders (Fig. 12-8B). Mark the top shaping so you know what space to allow for the joints, but cut the joints before cutting the curves (Fig. 12-8C). Do not make the frame too close a fit on the mirror's edges. If you can find a stock mirror size, the size of rabbets or the whole design may be altered to avoid having a mirror specially cut.

Paint or stain the insides of the rabbets black, so the wood grain is not reflected in the glass. Drive the nails closely and carefully, so the mirror is held

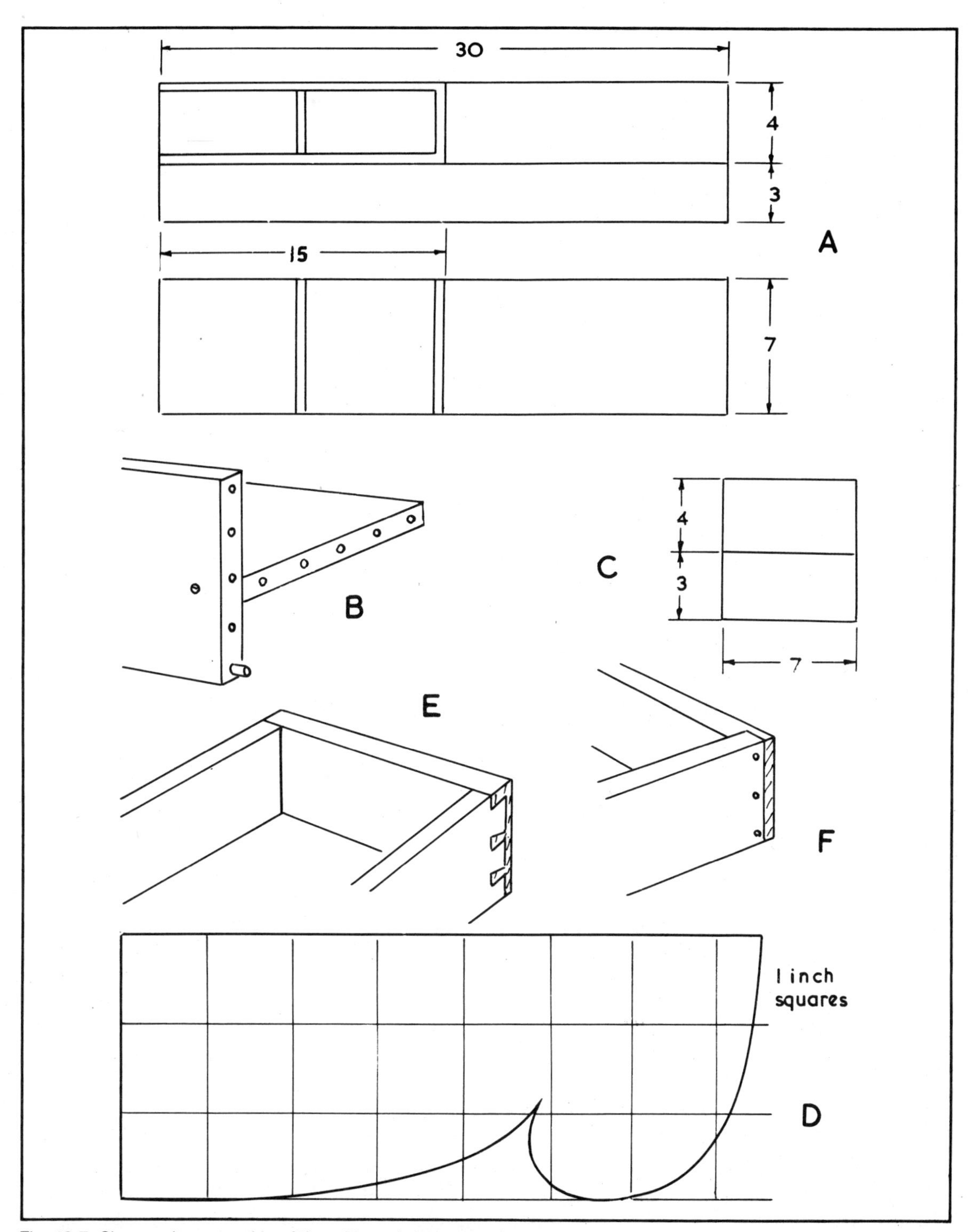

Fig. 12-7. Sizes and construction of the table and drawer section.

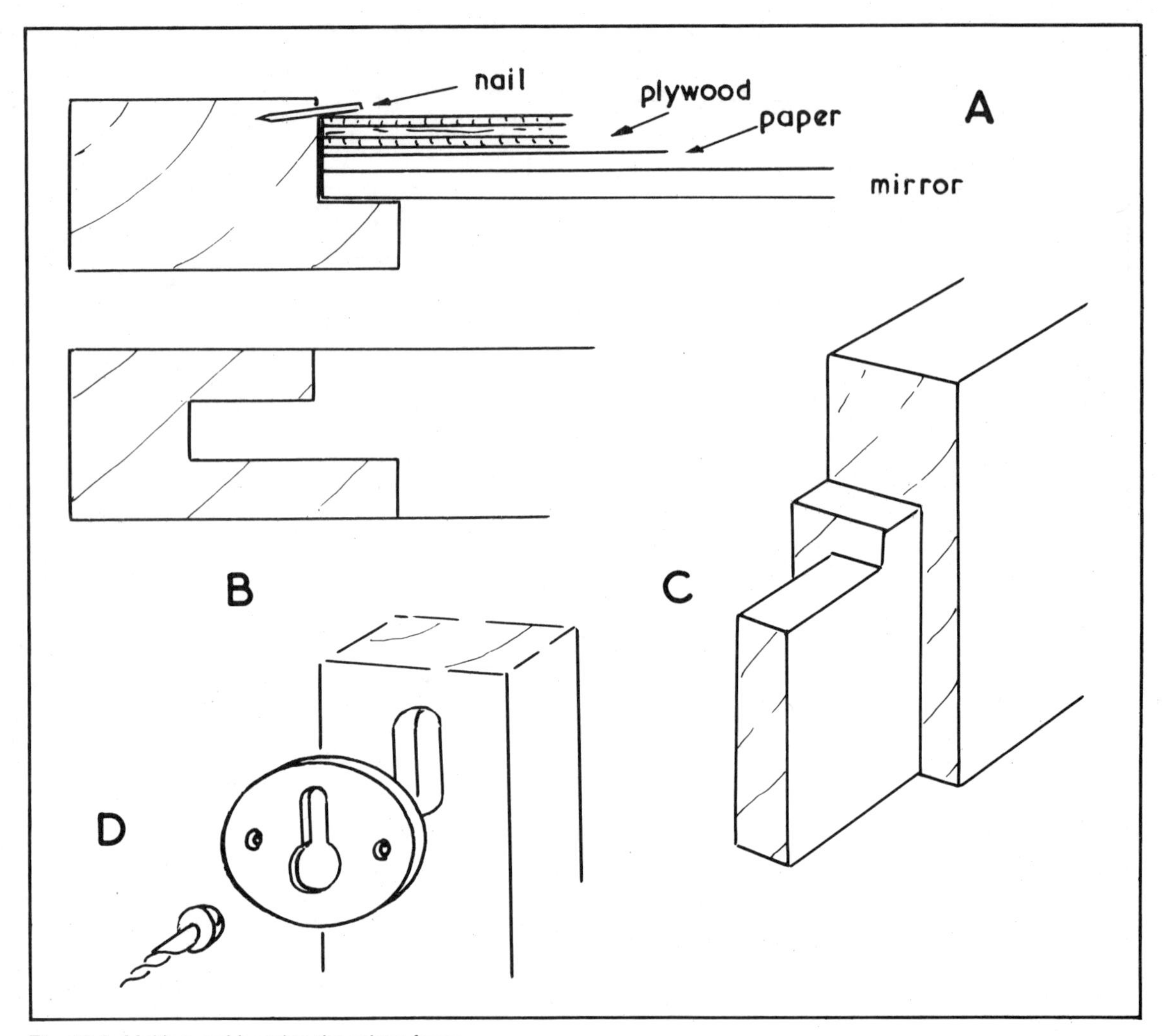

Fig. 12-8. Making and hanging the mirror frame.

tightly against the front of the rabbet. Masking or other tape can be put over the gap at the back to keep out dampness and dust.

The lower part of the dresser can be screwed to the wall, with the screws arranged inconspicuously. It is not so easy to hide screws through the mirror frame. There can be a screw on each side above the center, with a decorative plug over its head. For concealed screws, make thin metal plates with keyhole slots to fit over the screws and cut slots to clear the screwheads in the wood (Fig. 12-8D). The mirror will hang safely, but it can always be lifted off.

UNIT DRESSER

This piece of furniture is based on a drawer unit, which may be repeated, and supporting legs. The leg assemblies attach to the wall, but the drawer units may be lifted off, which may be convenient for cleaning or access. A wall-mounted mirror may be with the dresser, but it is not an integral part of the dresser.

One unit is used in its simplest form (Fig. 12-9A). A second unit may rest on it, with more legs (Fig. 12-9B). If the assembly can come in a corner, one unit can rest on a batten screwed to the wall (Fig. 12-9C). Three units make a very spacious dresser (Fig. 12-9D) if the wall is long enough.

The tops and ends of the units can be solid wood, possibly with pieces glued together to make up the width. The ends should be arranged with their grain vertical. Plywood can be used, but its edges must be lipped with solid wood strips where they are exposed. Veneered particle board may be used for these parts. The drawer fronts and other visible wood should match. The legs and their framing may also match, but a pleasing effect can be obtained by having them a different color—usually darker.

Instructions are given for a two-unit assembly (Fig. 12-10), as that includes all the parts found in the other assemblies. See Table 12-2. Cut and square the tops and ends for each unit. Drill for dowels from the ends into the top and mark where the other parts will come (Fig. 12-11A). The back rail acts as a drawer stop. The top should be stiff enough, but allow for another rail under its rear edge if you think it needs support.

Make the lengthwise rails and drill them for two dowels each into the ends. Screw the drawer runners to the ends, but make sure their top surfaces are level with the front rail (Fig. 12-11B). Assemble each unit. Check squareness and be careful that the front of the drawer opening is not narrower than the back.

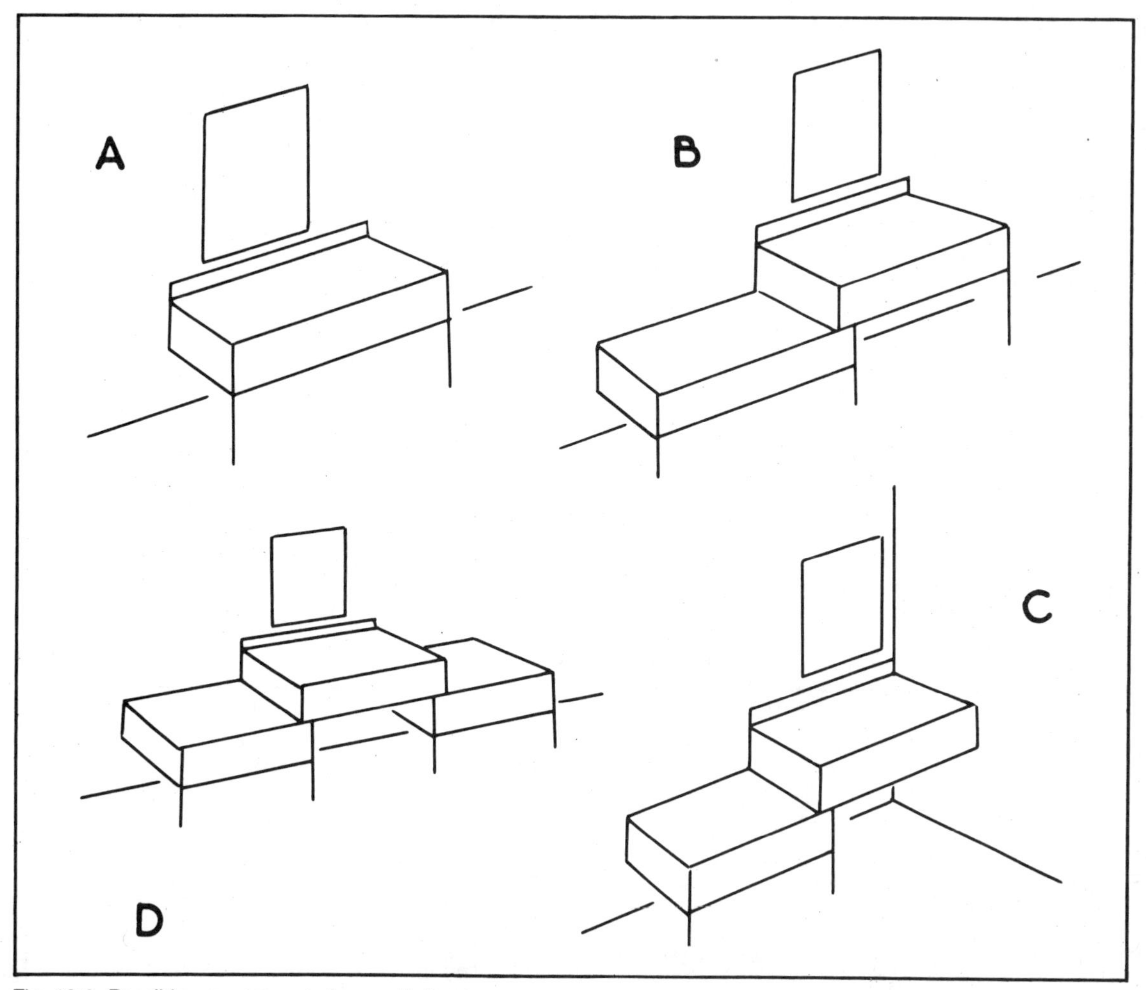

Fig. 12-9. Possible arrangements for a unit dresser.

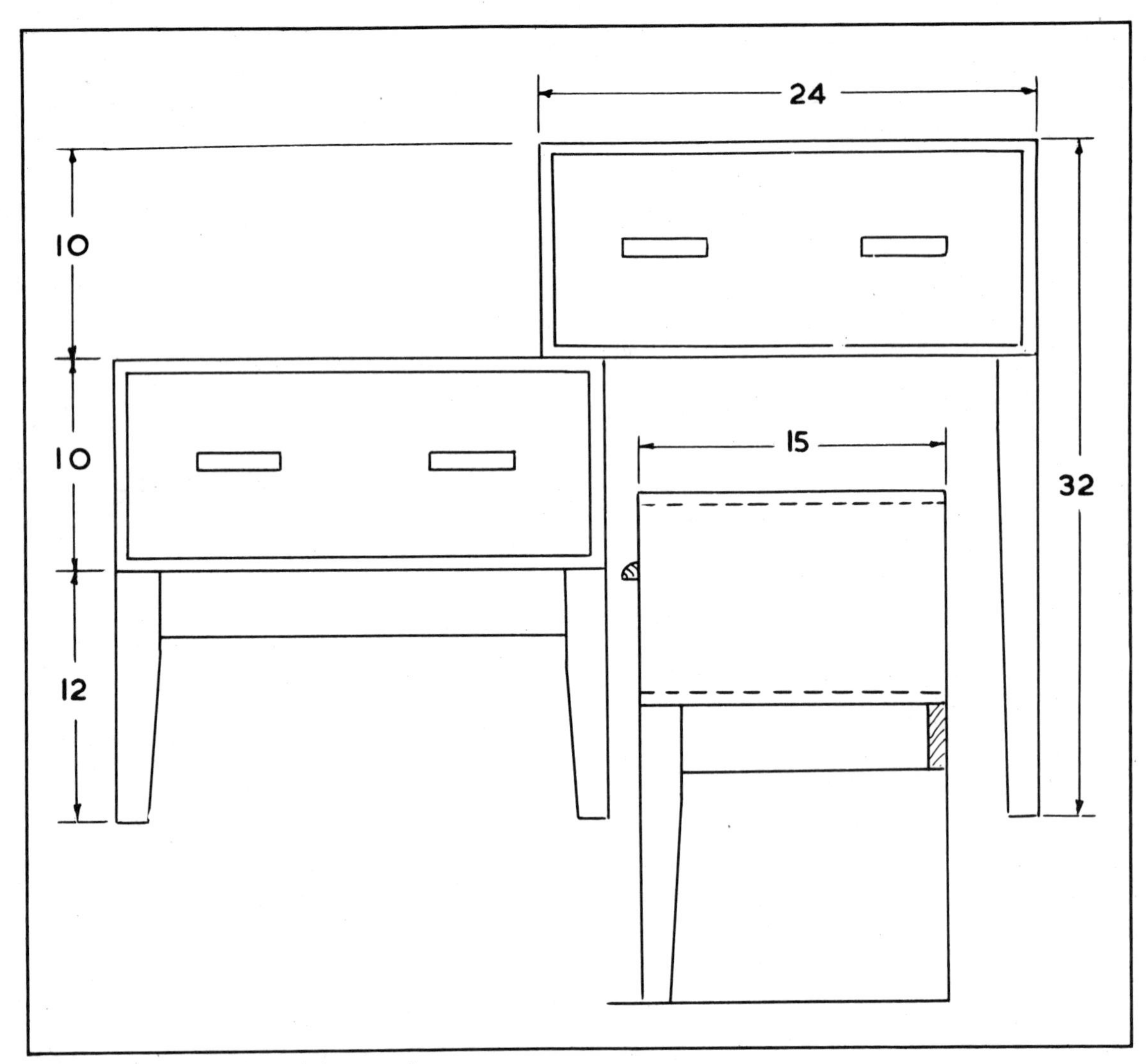

Fig. 12-10. Suggested sizes of dresser units.

Table 12-2. Materials List for Unit Dresser.

Each unit						
1 top	15	×	25	×	7/8	
2 ends	15	×	10	×	7/8	
1 front	1 7/8	×	25	×	7/8	
1 back	1 7/8	×	25	×	7/8	
2 runners	7/8	×	15	×	7/8	
1 drawer front	9	×	24	×	3/4	
1 false drawer front	9 1/2	×	24	×	5/8	
1 drawer back	8	×	24	×	5/8	
2 drawer sides	8 1/4	×	15	×	5/8	
1 drawer bottom	15	×	24	×	1/4	plywood
1 rear top strip	2 7/8	×	25	×	7/8	

Each low support					
2 legs	1 7/8	×	13	×	1 7/8
2 rails	2 7/8	×	24	×	7/8
2 rails	2 7/8	×	15	×	7/8
2 locating strips	1 3/8	×	15	×	7/8
2 locating strips	3/4	×	15	×	3/4
High support					
1 leg	1 7/8	×	23	×	1 7/8
1 rail	2 7/8	×	15	×	7/8
1 locating strip	1 3/8	×	15	×	7/8
1 locating strip	3/4	×	15	×	3/4
1 rear rail	2 7/8	×	24	×	7/8

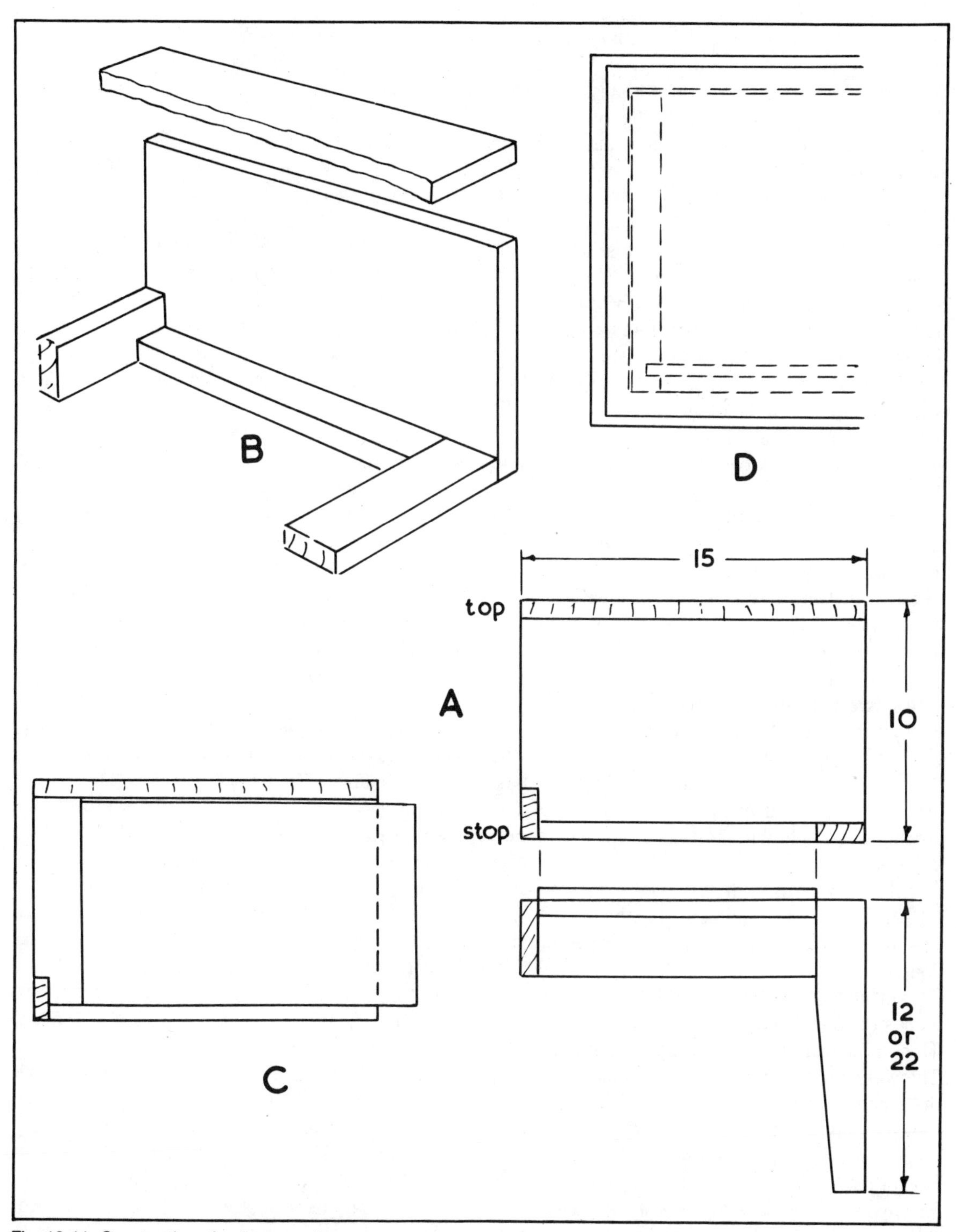

Fig. 12-11. Construction of a drawer unit.

Make the drawer sides to length and width to slide easily in their positions (Fig. 12-11C). Plow grooves in them to take the bottom plywood.

Make the front to match the opening and groove it for the plywood. Cut dovetails or other joints between the front and sides (see Chapter 4). Make the drawer back to come above the plywood. Assemble the front to the sides and slide in the bottom. Try this in the carcass and test its width at the rear. When this is satisfactory, add the drawer back. As the back and bottom of the carcass are open, you can see how the drawer slides and do any planing necessary if it has to be eased.

That construction assumes the drawer sides will slide directly on the runners. If you prefer to fit metal runners at the sides, allow ½ inch or other suitable clearance between the drawer sides and the carcass ends.

With the drawer fitted satisfactorily, make its false front to match the carcass shape—about ¼ inch in all around (Fig. 12-11D). Mold its edges and join it with glue and screws from inside the drawer. If the handles bolt through, they will also help keep the parts together.

The low support (Fig. 12-12A), or a high one for a single unit with longer legs, is made like a table without rear legs. The legs are shown straight outside and tapered inside (Fig. 12-12B). Keep the tops parallel to below the joints, which are best made as mortise and tenons (Fig. 12-12C). The rails are shown straight, but they can be shaped on their undersides.

At the wall the side rails join a rear rail (Fig. 12-12D), which will be screwed to the wall. As you assemble, check sizes against those of the unit that goes on top.

Fit locating strips inside the short rails, with pieces to come inside the unit ends (Fig. 12-12E). This can be done accurately with the parts inverted. The weight of a unit will keep it in place, but make the locating strips a reasonably tight fit.

To support the high unit, make a matching longer leg, with a side and rear rail (Fig. 12-12F). Do not make a front rail, as that will limit leg room for anyone sitting. The top unit should overlap the other by about 3 inches. When you make the final assembly, put one screw through the upper front rail into the top of the lower unit.

The assembly can be used as it is, but it will be better with a strip along the back of one or both units (Fig. 12-12G) and held with a few screws from below. If the unit goes in the corner of a room, put a strip along the other wall, too.

CLOTHES CLOSET/DRESSER

Many built-in furniture items are made completely with backs and sides before being installed in position. This is advisable if the furniture has to be moved to another position at some future time, or if the conditions of the walls and ceiling make them unsuitable for being exposed inside the furniture. If the walls are in good condition and their appearance is satisfactory, there is no need to fit plywood or other panels against them. It may even be attractive to have the wall the same inside as outside the furniture. Alternatively, wallpaper or similar covering can be used inside the furniture.

This combined clothes closet and dresser design makes full use of the walls, ceiling, and floor (Fig. 12-13). Except for necessary framing, there are no parts used where the house can provide a surface.

To make this piece of furniture, you have to do much of the construction in position. You can prefabricate some parts on your bench, but much of the basic assembly work is done in place, proceeding one piece of wood at a time.

Sizes will have to be related to the corner of the room and the space available. You may be able to extend some way along a wall, or you may have to reduce sizes if there is little space beside a bed or other furniture. To make the best use of the closet, clothing should hang square to the wall. If you cannot allow enough distance back to front, hangers may still be used diagonally, but you will not get in as much. When planning the sizes, make sure that doors and drawers can open fully. Some suggested sizes are given (Fig. 12-14) as a guide to detail work, but check your own situation.

Check that walls are plumb and all surfaces are flat and square to each other. Slight errors will not matter, but it is better to square the furniture than

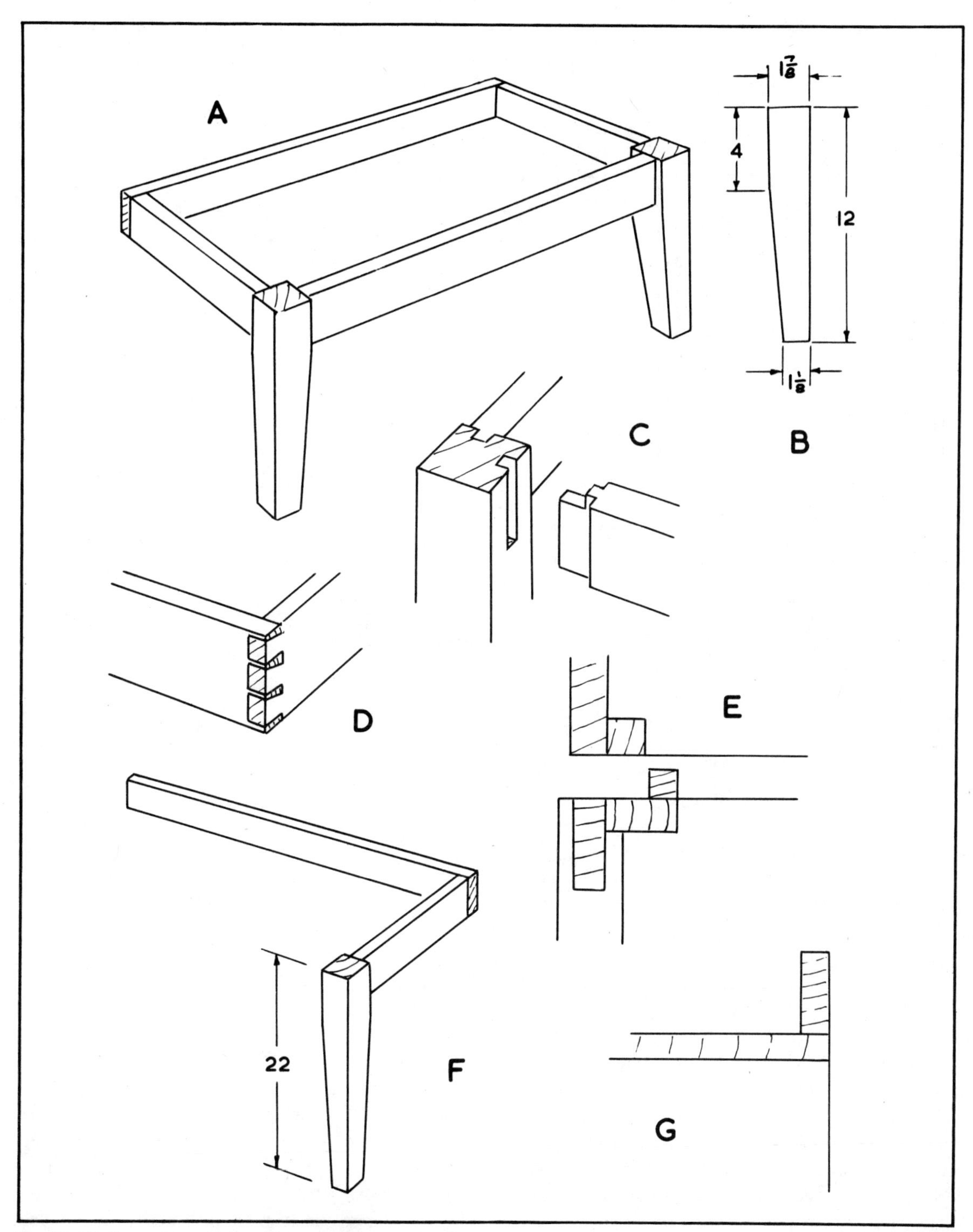

Fig. 12-12. Supports and joints between units of a dresser.

Fig. 12-13. A corner clothes closet/dresser.

to let it follow very inaccurate outlines. Pencil guidelines on all the surfaces that will be affected. While doing this, check that the exposed corner of the clothes closet will be upright by using a weighted string (plumb line) from the corner marked on the ceiling to that on the floor. Any error on this prominent edge will be very obvious to even a casual viewer.

Closet

The key to most sizes is in the front assembly of the clothes closet, so make that first (Fig. 12-15). The front parts are 1-inch-by-2-inch section. Parts can be joined with two ½-inch dowels in each position (Fig. 12-15A), or you can use stub tenons (Fig. 12-15B). Once the front is attached to the house surfaces, there will not be much strain on individual joints. Be careful how you handle the assembly before it is put in position. You may make the front the full height so it fits tight against the ceiling. It may be easier to allow a small clearance, particularly if there is any unevenness in the ceiling (Fig. 12-15C). Cover the gap with a quarter-round molding.

Where the frame meets floor, wall, and ceiling, there are strips inside attached to the frame and with screws into the adjoining surfaces (Fig. 12-

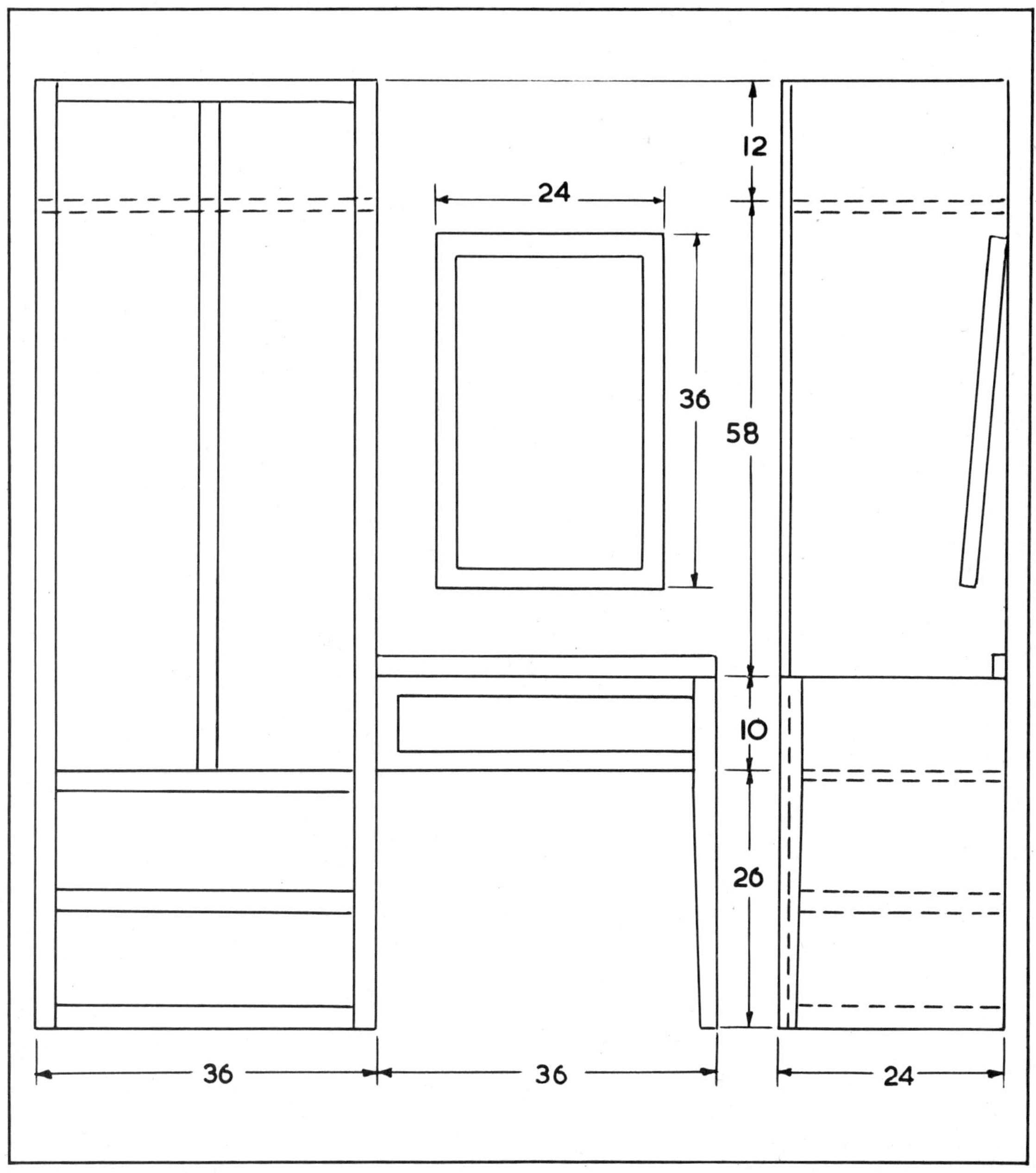

Fig. 12-14. Sizes for a clothes closet/dresser.

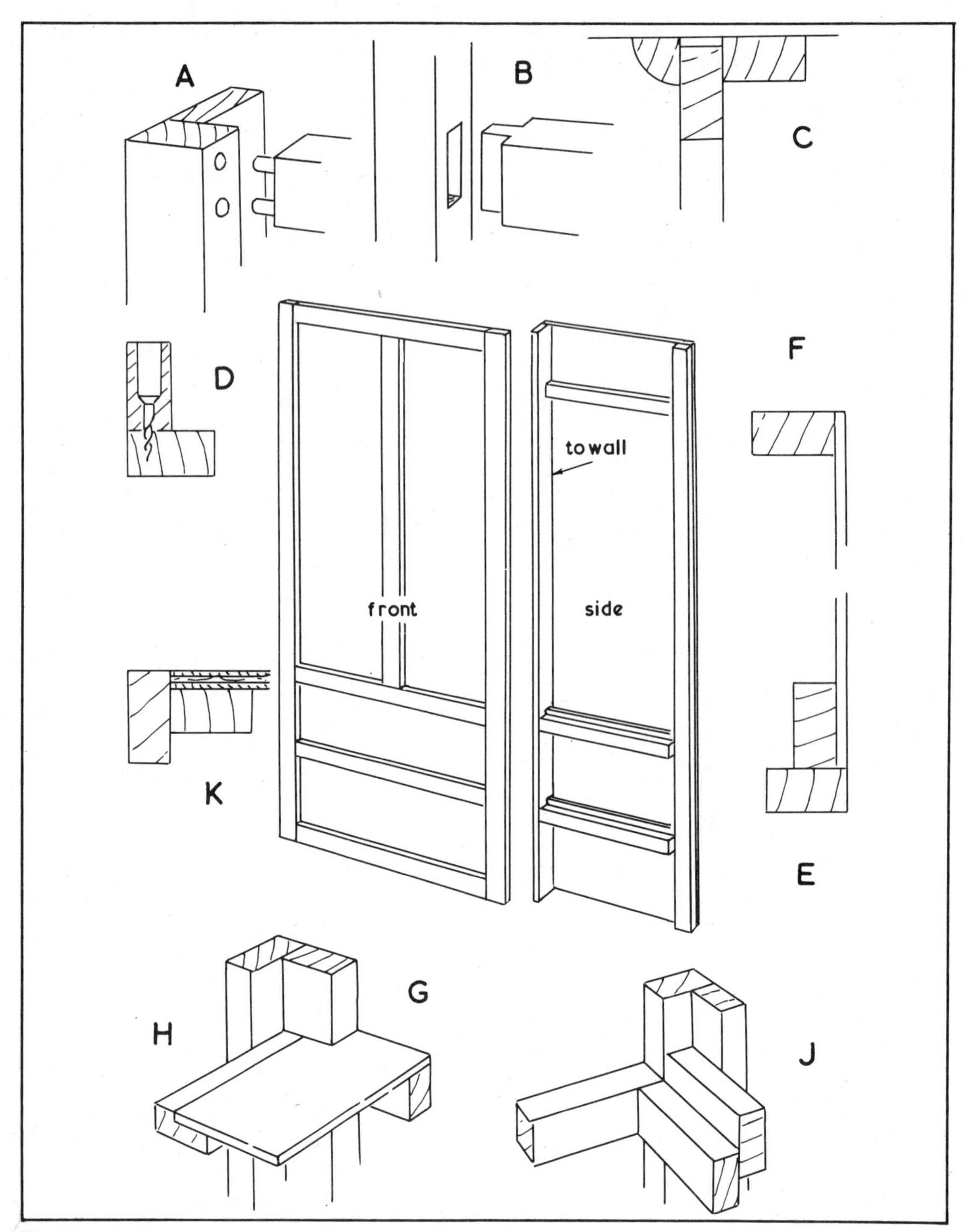

Fig. 12-15. Details of clothes closet parts.

15D). Screwheads on the front surface will look ugly even if they are counterbored and plugged, so it is better to screw from inside. Choose screws that can be counterbored enough to give a good grip without the points reaching the front surface. Have a stop on the bit or the drill press to get all the counterbores the same. Use glue and screws in all joints.

The closet side is a piece of plywood, with a surface to match the other wood in the closet or that used to line the room. Get its front edge absolutely straight, then back it with a strip screwed into the front framing (Fig. 12-15E). Have another piece at the rear for screwing to the wall (Fig. 12-15F). Arrange a similar piece across the top for screwing to the ceiling and another at the bottom for screwing to the floor.

The shelf rests on a bearer inside the plywood side and another in a matching position on the opposite wall (Fig. 12-15G). When you make the shelf from plywood, it will look better if you can cover the front edge with a rabbeted strip (Fig. 12-15H). The plywood should then be stiff enough without extra support. If you think more strength is needed, put a strip across the back and screw it to the wall.

Use two pieces in each side where the bottoms of the two drawers will come. One piece is raised to act as a guide to prevent its drawer moving sideways, and the other piece inside it serves as a runner (Fig. 12-15J). Make sure the inner surface of the guide and the upper surface of the runner match the adjoining parts of the front frame in each position.

The bottom of the closet is a piece of plywood resting on bearers each side and on a strip inside the front framing. You can prepare these parts as you build up the closet in position. Leave final fitting until after you have made and fitted the drawers, so you are better able to see their movement and make adjustments.

The clothes rail can be a piece of ¾-inch or 1-inch dowel rod, but a ¾-inch metal tube is less likely to sag. The ends of the rail can go into holes in the shelf bearers during assembly. If you want to add the rail after assembling the other parts, one end may go in a separate block (Fig. 12-16A). If you want to give the rail extra support, make another block to join it to the shelf (Fig. 12-16B).

The doors may be made in several ways, but they should match the fronts of the drawers. You can frame them with plywood panels let into plowed grooves. They can be made with thin plywood panels each side of thin solid wood framing to present a smooth appearance on both sides. In both cases the doors will have to be fitted inside the front framing.

The doors suggested overlap the framing. There does not have to be such a precise fit, and construction is simplified. A door has an inner ½-inch plywood part that fits easily into its opening. Make a solid wood frame around another piece of plywood outside. It should overhang about ⅜ inch on all edges (Fig. 12-17A). Assemble with glue and fine nails driven from inside and miter the corners of the frame (Fig. 12-17B). Make sure the plywood pieces are pulled close near their centers and

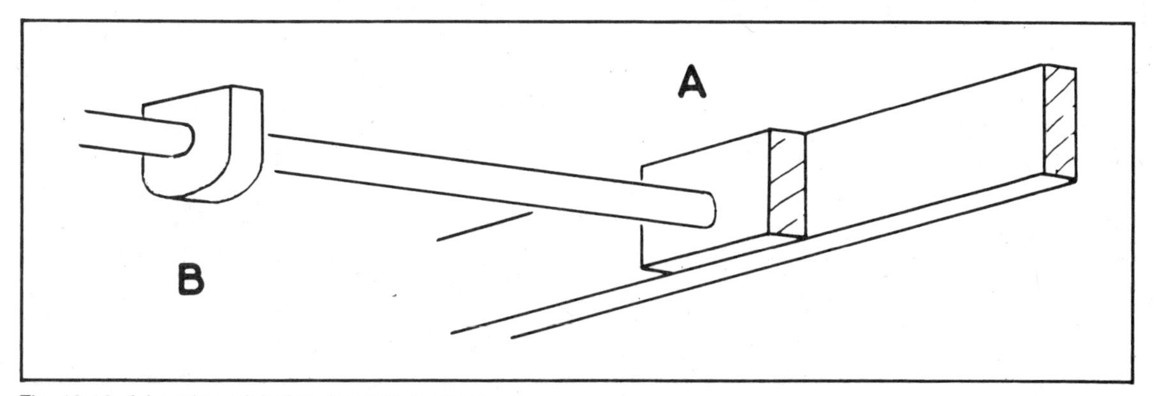

Fig. 12-16. A hanging rail inside the clothes closet.

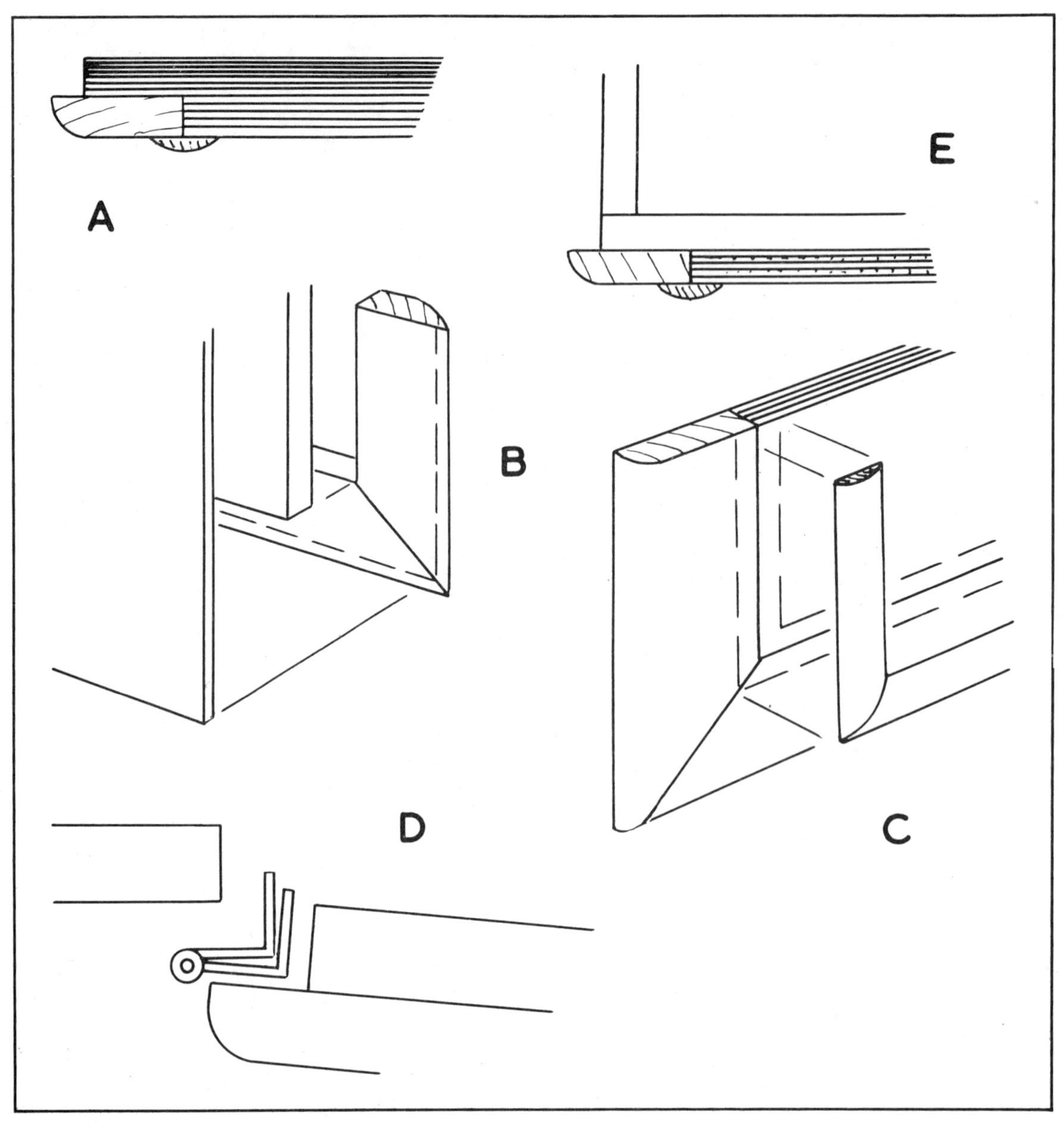

Fig. 12-17. Door details for the clothes closet.

around their edges. The outer plywood will look best if it has a veneer to match other parts of the closet.

The door framing is shown with a simple rounded edge, but the edge can be molded if you have suitable tools. When you have these parts joined and the glue has set, check the doors in place. See that their edges are parallel with adjoining parts, even if that means planing a little off. When you are satisfied, cover the front joints with half-round molding (Fig. 12-17C) and make sure it is parallel with the door edges, even if it may not be exactly central over its joint. The hinges come outside (Fig. 12-17D). You can get a type to fit on the surface with a decorative outline exposed or a plainer type that is hidden behind the door. If you choose the exposed type, it should be part of a matching set with door and drawer handles. If you prefer to make wooden handles, there should be hidden hinges.

The two drawers can be made in any of the usual ways, with the sides sliding on the runners and extending almost to the wall at the back. To match the doors, make the inner fronts to come level with the front closet frame. Add similar false fronts (Fig. 12-17E) with the same amount of overlap. Check the action of the bottom drawer first by looking into it from where the closet bottom will be. When that is satisfactory, do the same with the upper drawer. In both cases the false fronts should close tightly to the closet fronts without the backs of the drawers touching the wall. Fit the closet bottom.

Use knobs or pulls on the drawers to match those on the doors above them. This completes the clothes closet. It can be used without the dresser, or that can be added later.

Dresser

You can regard the dresser as a table with a drawer, but only one leg is required. The back is supported by a wall, and one end is attached to the clothes closet. Sizes can be altered to suit situations, but the dresser and closet should blend together for a better appearance. Sizes are shown with the rail below the drawer following across the line at the bottom of the closet. The drawer should be finished in a way that matches the other two drawers. The dresser top is shown coming flush with its supports at the edges, but it can overhang. The top may be veneered plywood with solid wood edging, or you can use particle board bought already veneered to match the other wood.

Mark out the leg (Fig. 12-18A). Its outer corner should remain straight, but taper toward it on the inner surfaces from 1 inch below the joint positions.

Frame the front in a similar manner to the clothes closet (Fig. 12-18B). Where the frame comes against the closet side, put a rail across, with another to act as a kicker for the drawer (Fig. 12-18C). Make two rails at the bottom to act as guide and runner (Fig. 12-18D). Between the top and bottom rails, put a short piece behind the upright part of the front frame. These parts can be screwed through the plywood side of the closet.

At the leg side there have to be similar parts to guide the drawer, but you have to close the side. This can be done with a piece of plywood, then the other parts are set back behind it (Fig. 12-18E). Dowel or tenon their ends into the leg and at the back join them to rails attached to the wall. Have a top rail going across the wall to support the dresser top.

Make the top a close fit against the wall and the side of the dresser, then get the front and open side true. Veneer the edges or lip plywood to give an attractive edge.

Before fitting the top, make the drawer in the same way as the drawers under the closet. Check the action while viewing from above. See that all three drawers match. Get the handles similarly located just above their centers. Fit the top by screwing from below. Make sure the visible edges are pulled tight. Make a narrow rail to go across the the back, so things used on the top do not knock or mark the wall (Fig. 12-18F).

MIRROR

The mirror can be any size to suit the available space. It may be convenient to buy one of a stock size. The suggested size is 24 inches by 36 inches. Glass is a heavy material, and you must support it strongly. If you have a mirror with polished or beveled edges, it can be mounted on a piece of ½-inch plywood, with clips around the edge (Fig. 12-19A). Either put a strip across the lower edge (Fig. 12-19B) or use extra clips there to prevent slipping.

You can frame the mirror using rabbeted strip. Fit the mirror with pieces to hold it close. Cover the back with plywood (Fig. 12-19C), which will strengthen the frame and keep out dust.

It may be possible to hinge the top of the mirror directly to the wall, or it may be better to put a batten across and hinge the mirror to that. The

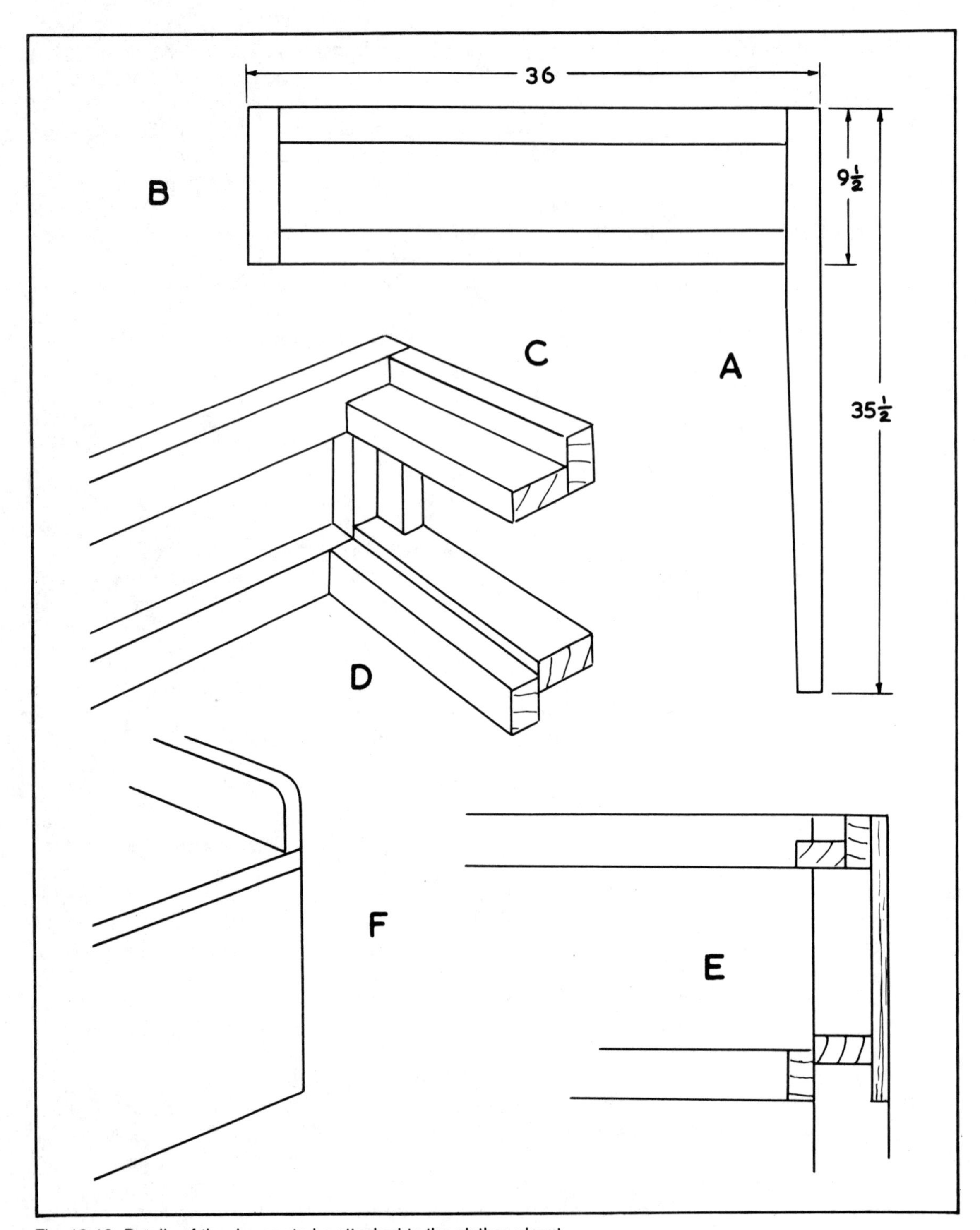

Fig. 12-18. Details of the dresser to be attached to the clothes closet.

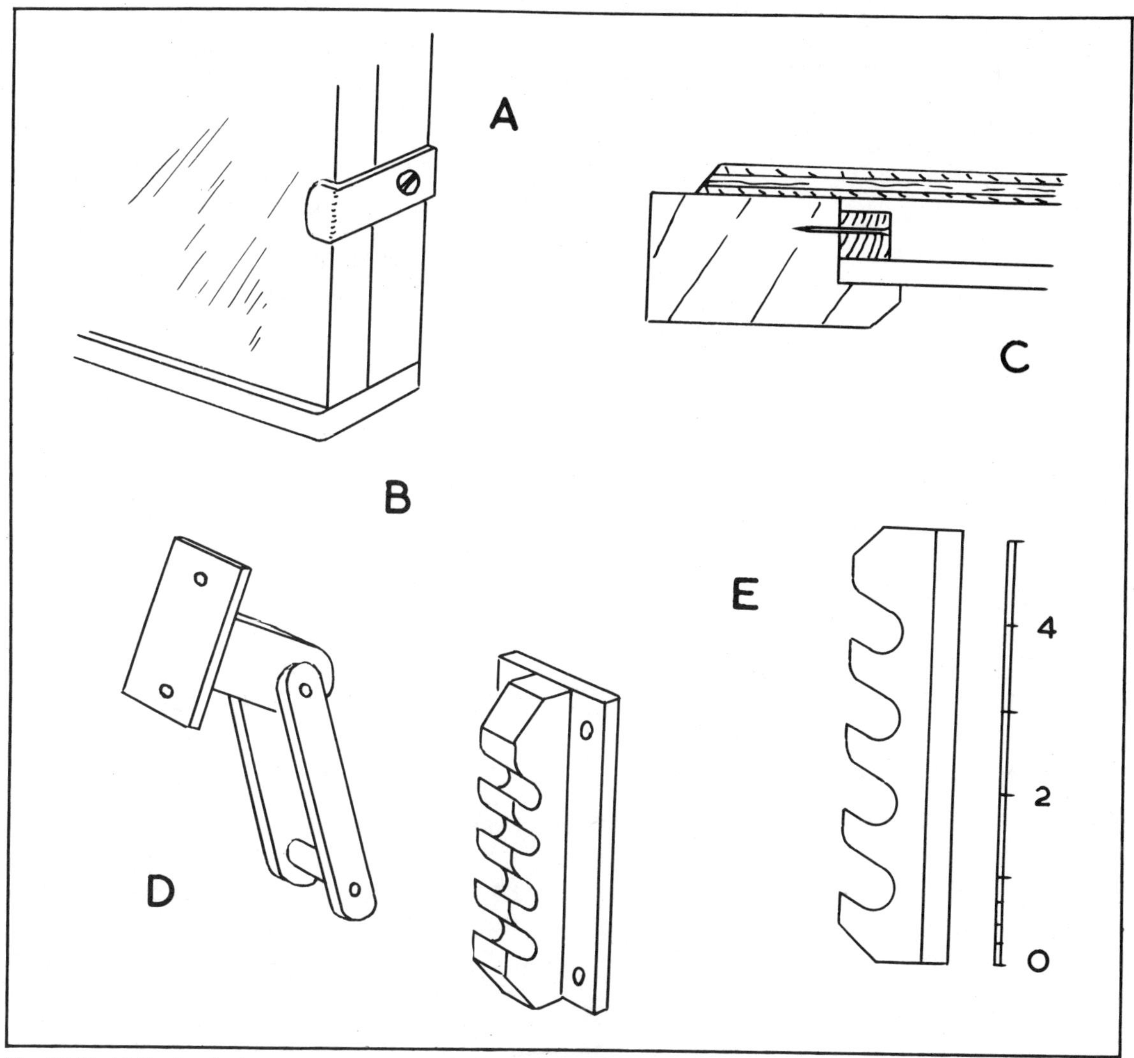

Fig. 12-19. Methods of mirror construction and its tilt adjustment.

best pivot is a piece of piano hinge going right across, but otherwise you can use two 3-inch or 4-inch hinges.

If you have a very deep mirror, it may be satisfactory fitted flat against the wall. It is convenient for most users to be able to adjust the amount of tilt according to whether they are standing or sitting. Metal struts are available with an adjustment or a friction joint to hold the mirror angle where required, but a wood strut is better (Fig. 12-19D). Suitable sizes are given (Fig. 12-19E), but you may wish to hang the mirror and experiment with angles before settling on strut sizes and position.

RECESS HANGING CLOTHES CLOSET

If there is a recess in a bedroom that gives three enclosed sides (Fig. 12-20A), it can be made into a place to hang clothing, even if the depth of the alcove is not as great as the width of hangers. They can be arranged diagonally (Fig. 12-20B), although the nearer they are to square to the back wall, the

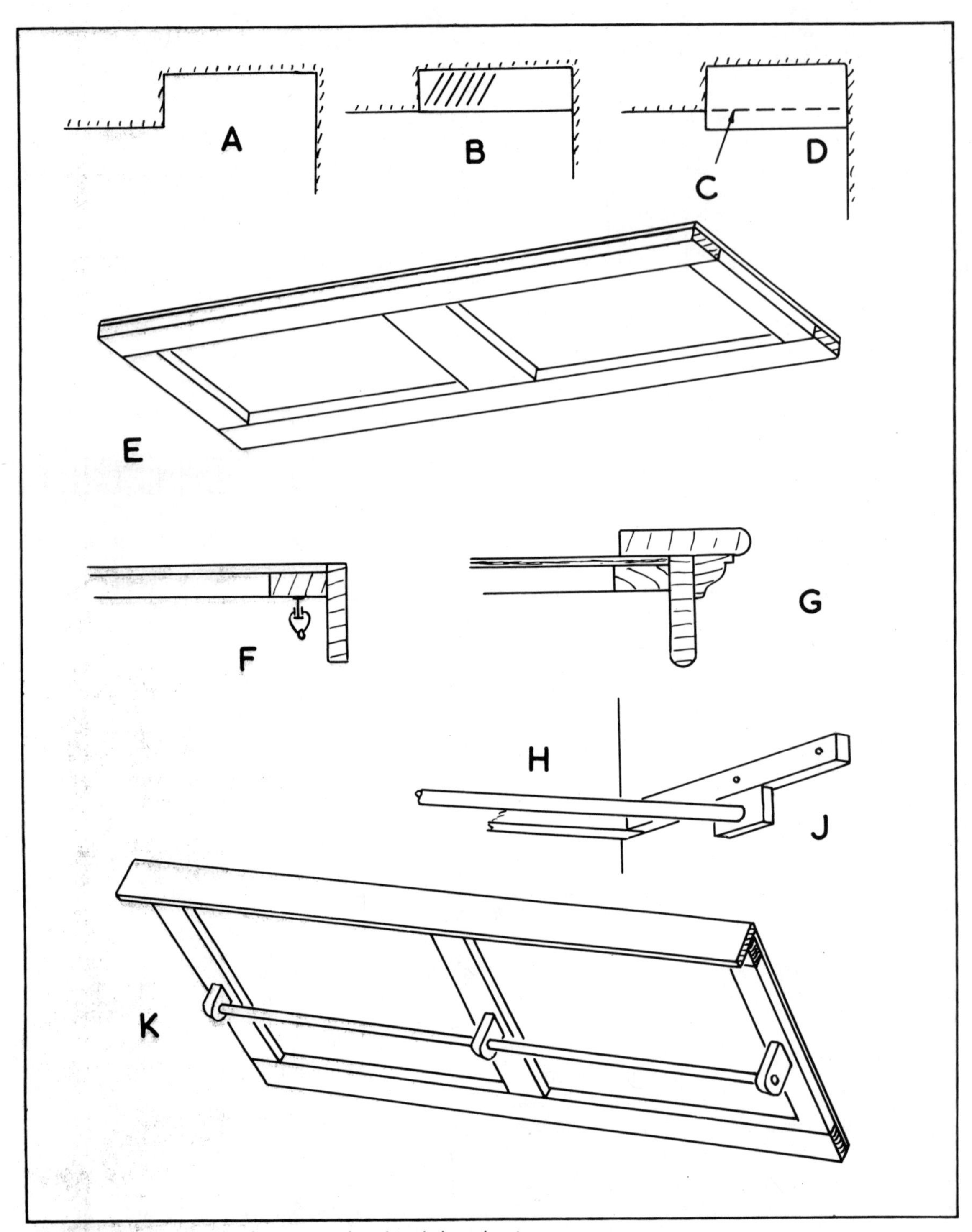

Fig. 12-20. Details of the top for a recess hanging clothes closet.

more you can get into a particular length.

The arrangement of the top of the closet depends on the existing wall. If there is a picture rail, the top may rest on it. Some picture rails are not very securely attached, and you may have to add more fasteners. If the wall is plain, it will usually be best to have the top about 6 feet from the floor. There will be space below hanging clothing for shoes and other smaller things. The space on top of the closet can be left open for general storage, or there can be doors for a neater appearance.

The simplest top comes completely within the alcove (Fig. 12-20C). If the recess space is too narrow, you can make it wider (Fig. 12-20D), although coming out too far will create a support problem. The hanging drape will have to travel around the corner.

The top can be solid wood, but it does not have to take much load. You can use thin plywood or hardboard on framing. If the top will be more than 36 inches long, put a piece across the center to take an intermediate support (Fig. 12-20E). At the front put a strip deep enough to hide the top of the drape suspended from a track (Fig. 12-20F). Another piece may be on top, with molding below to stiffen the front and give a more substantial appearance (Fig. 12-20G).

If the wall is plain, arrange supports for the top at the ends and back (Fig. 12-20H). Be careful that the opposite ends are both level, and therefore parallel with each other, so you do not put a twist in the top when it is screwed to them.

The rail from which the clothes hang can be dowel rod of ¾-inch or 1-inch diameter, although a piece of metal tube will be stiffer. If the top is to be permanently in position, the rod end supports can be wood blocks on the wall (Fig. 12-20J). If the top is resting on a picture rail or you want to remove it, the end supports can project down from the top framing (Fig. 12-20K). If there is to be an intermediate support, make that in the same way. Thread the rod through the supports before putting them in position, or you may not get it in.

Fit the track under the front framing as close as it can reasonably be put to the vertical front strip.

If you want to put doors above, make framing against the walls and ceiling (Fig. 12-21A). The framing can be facing pieces on other strips screwed in place (Fig. 12-21B). Check that the opening you leave has square corners. If there is any unevenness of wall or ceiling, adjust the edge of the wood. The doors are better with square corners than shapes parallel to inaccurate walls. If it is difficult to get a good fit, your wood can be allowed to make the opening square. Any gap may be hidden by quarter-round molding (Fig. 12-21C).

Doors that are wide in relation to their height do not hang well with hinges at the sides. You may have to divide a long space (Fig. 12-21D) with uprights.

If you don't want divisions, the single door can be hinged at the top (Fig. 12-21E). This gives very good access, but it is high and cannot be lifted fully while standing on the floor. That may not matter for occasional use, and you can arrange for the door to clip up to the ceiling with a turn button (Fig. 12-21F).

Doors can be single pieces of thick plywood or two pieces of thin plywood with solid framing between (Fig. 12-21G). You can make the door in the traditional way with plywood panels grooved into solid framing (Fig. 12-21H).

If you want to store shoes below the hanging clothing, make a simple rack to keep them tidy. The rack can be freestanding or attached to the wall or floor. Two dowel rods are held by wood brackets to the wall (Fig. 12-22A) or floor (Fig. 12-22B). You can use ½-inch dowel rods and place brackets at about 18-inch intervals. Check rod spacings in relation to the shoes and modify accordingly. High-heeled shoes may need a different spacing from heavy boots. If there is much depth available, you can make a shoe rack in two tiers. If you arrange shoes with toes facing forward, you are able to see them better, but for two rows of shoes you can make a more compact rack with the toes toward the back.

A different shoe rack has a row of dowel rods inclined and projecting from a board (Fig. 12-22C). Fit it high enough for the shoes to clear the floor. If space is restricted, this rack allows you to hang shoes partly behind clothing.

On the end walls you can arrange racks that do

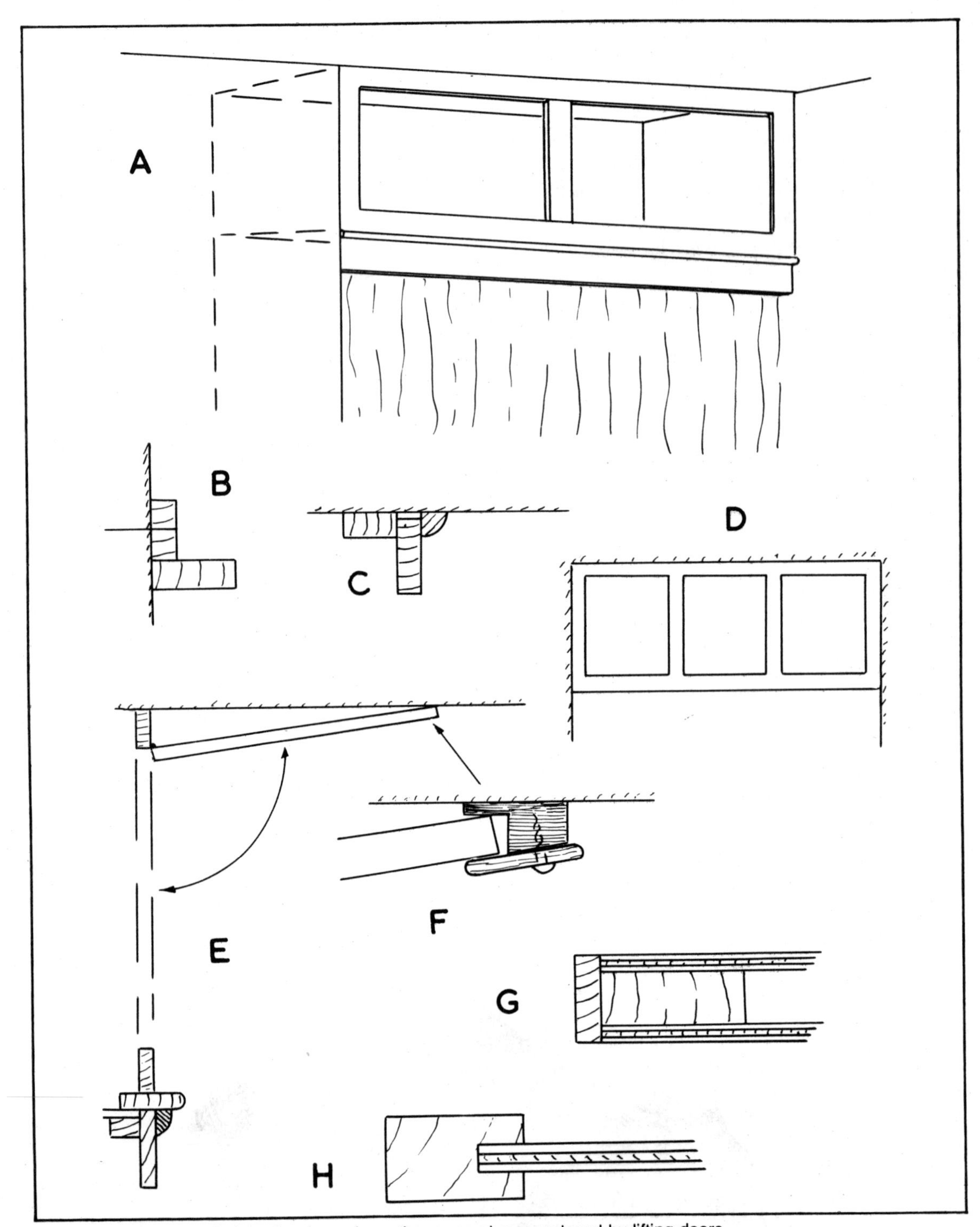

Fig. 12-21. A hanging clothes closet may have the space above enclosed by lifting doors.

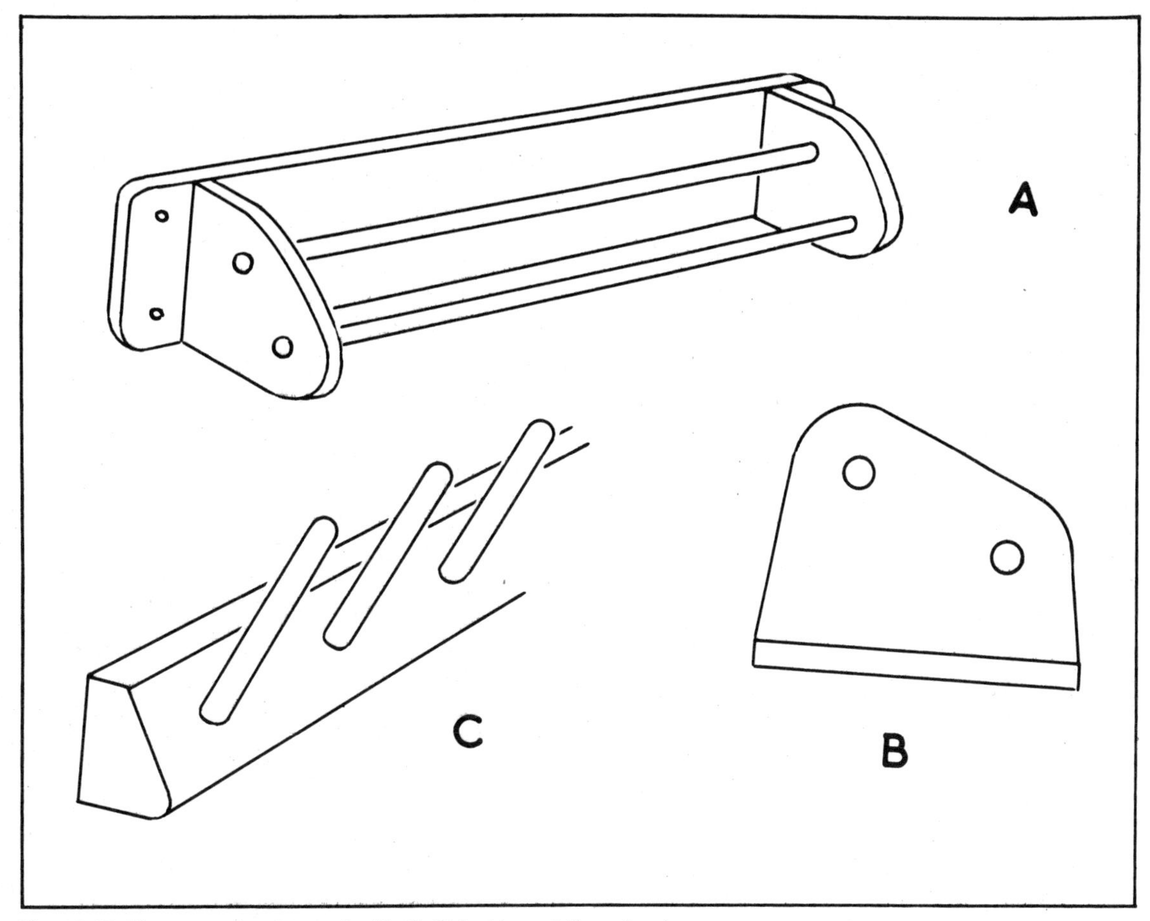

Fig. 12-22. There may be shoe racks (A, B, C) inside a clothes closet.

not project far enough to obstruct hanging clothes. A simple rail quite close to the wall will take ties or socks (Fig. 12-23A). A shelf with a rail in front can hold jewelry and other small items. A gap in the rail makes it easy to remove things like pins (Fig. 12-23B). Several rails and shelves can be individually mounted on a wall, or they can be on one piece of plywood.

CORNER HANGING CLOTHES CLOSET

When space is restricted in a bedroom, yet storage has to be provided for hanging clothing, you may have to arrange it in a corner. There are limitations as to what can be hung in this way. If there is no alternative, you can provide some hanging space in an area that may not otherwise be used.

The simplest arrangement is a triangular top with a drape across (Fig. 12-24A), but you can increase the useful area by squaring the corners (Fig. 12-24B). Under this top you can arrange hooks along each wall, but clothing on hangers will go on a rail projecting from the corner (Fig. 12-24C). As the available width gets less toward the corner, the useful accommodation depends on how big you make the top. If it extends 24 inches along each wall, you can use a few hangers, but you can use many more hangers if you make it 36 inches.

Another variation that may better suit the use of the room and get more hangers in is to make the wall sides of the triangle uneven. The hangers can be slightly askew (Fig. 12-24D).

The general arrangement of the top is very

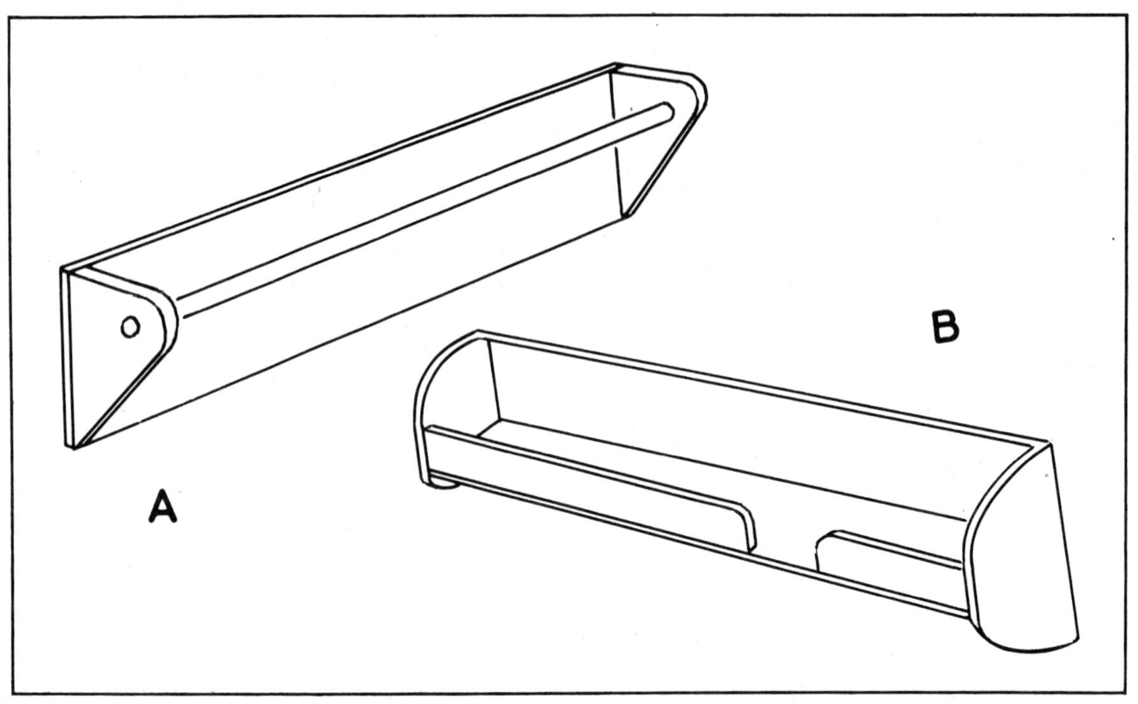

Fig. 12-23. Ties or socks can hang on a rail (A). Small things go on a shelf (B).

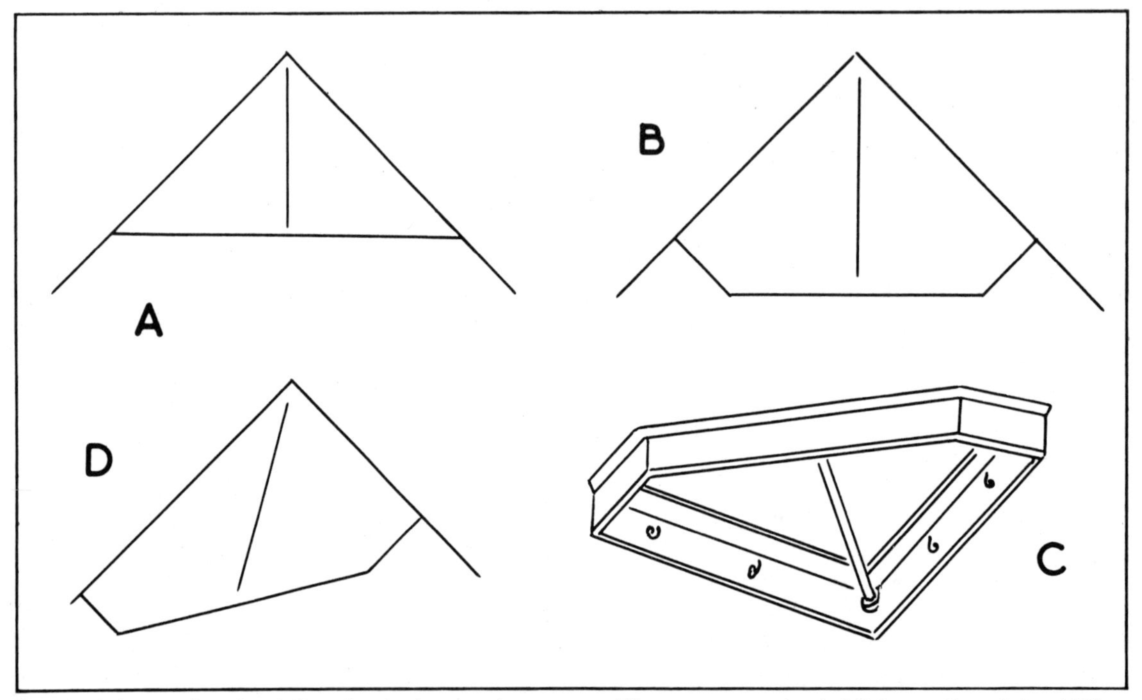

Fig. 12-24. A corner hanging clothes closet gets more storage space if its corners are extended. It does not have to be at 45°.

similar to the recess hanging clothes closet. Frame under plywood or hardboard and build up the front section (Fig. 12-25A). Miter the front piece if you use squared corners. The supporting pieces screwed to the wall should be deep enough to take hooks. If they are the same depth as the front, you can make a strong joint between them (Fig. 12-25B).

Allow space for the drape and its track across the front, then hang a post to take the end of a rail. It can be tenoned (Fig. 12-25C). Although full width clothes hangers cannot go close to the corner, the rail may go as far as possible so other narrower things may be hung from it. The post may go into the edge framing, or you may have to put a piece across the corner to take it (Fig. 12-25D). If you have made the shape longer on one wall than the other, bring the rail to the center of the front.

You can enclose the space above with doors as described for the recess hanging clothes closet, but the amount of storage space available is not great. You can also fit some of the racks and shelves described for that closet. If clothes are to be hung from hooks, there may be interference between them.

BEDSIDE RACK

This rack takes the place of a bedside table. It is supported on the wall. There are no legs or other projections to the floor (Figs. 12-26 and 12-27). It can be at one side of a bed or arranged between two beds. A pair can be arranged at opposite sides of a bed. Instead of the individual backboard, the bed headboard can be extended to accommodate the rack.

Construction can be in solid wood or veneered

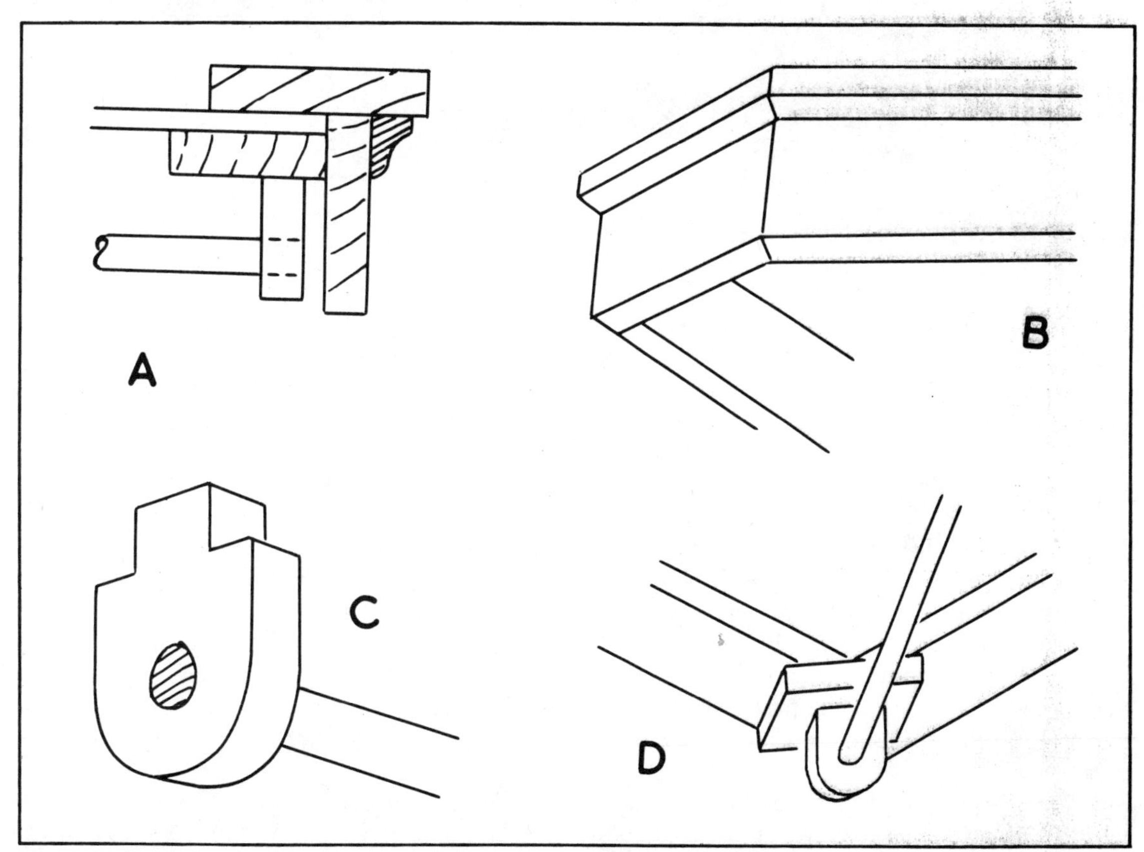

Fig. 12-25. How the corner hanging clothes closet is made and the central rail fitted.

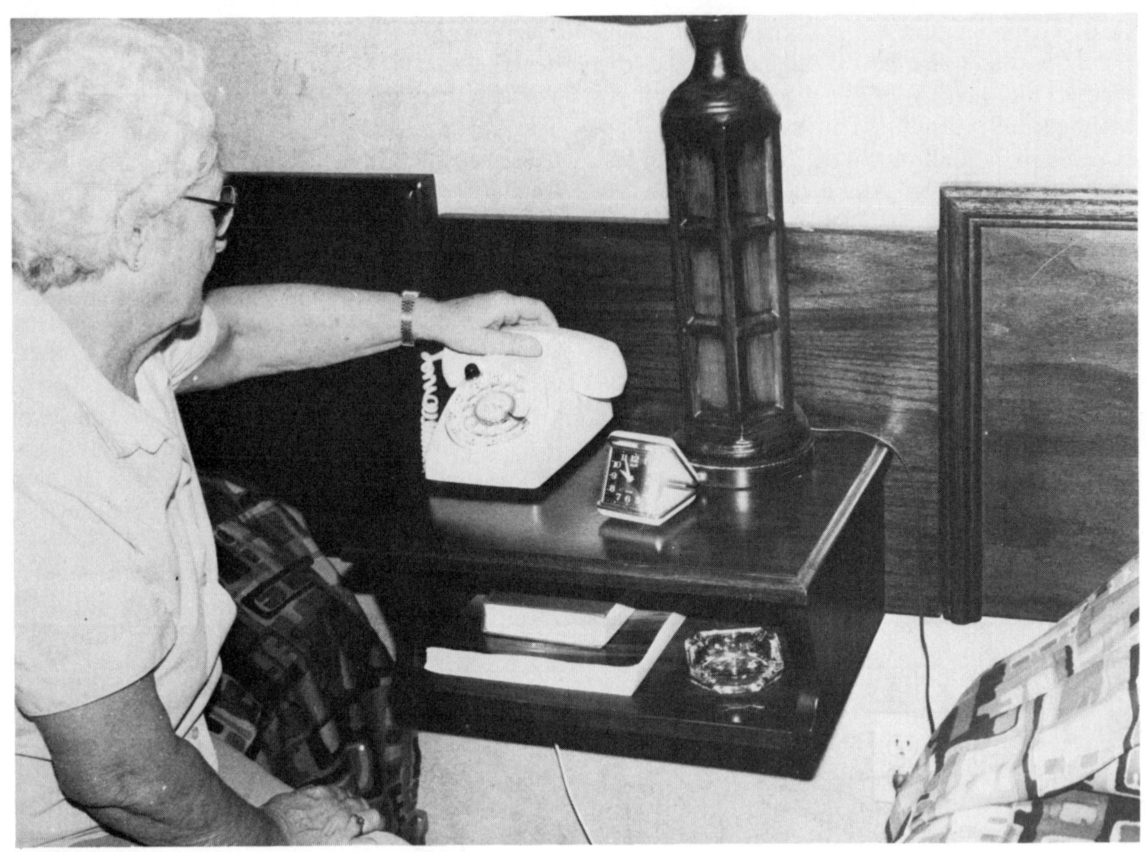

Fig. 12-26. A rack with a shelf below can form a table beside or between beds.

particle board. Although other joints can be used, it is simplest to use dowels throughout, whatever the chosen material. The sizes given are suggestions and will have to be adapted to suit circumstances. See Table 12-3. If solid wood is used, it will be strongest to have the sides with the grain vertical.

Start with the sides (Fig. 12-28A). Make sure the top and rear edge are square with each other. The lower edge can be level with the shelf or given a slight slope. Shape the front edge and allow for the top projecting further from the wall than the shelf. If you are using solid wood, round the section of the shaped part. If you are using particle board, cut squarely across the shaping, so you can veneer the edge.

Make the shelf to fit between the sides (Fig. 12-28B). Round the front edge if you are using solid wood. Mark and drill for dowels (Fig. 12-28C).

Allow for the top overlapping the sides. The exposed edges may be left square, or they can be rounded (Fig. 12-28D). If you have the facilities for doing so, you can mold the edges (Fig. 12-28E). Drill for dowels (Fig. 12-28F) in a similar way to the shelf, but with the dowels upward into the top.

Assemble these parts and take care to get the corners square. If necessary, level the rear edges so they will go flat against the back.

The method for making the back depends on what comes against it. It can be cut squarely to fit between two bedheads. Otherwise, it may look better to shape its top edge (Fig. 12-28G), which can also be molded to match any molding on the rack top.

Put the assembled part on the back and mark its outline inside and out. With this as a guide, mark and drill for dowels, which can go right through as

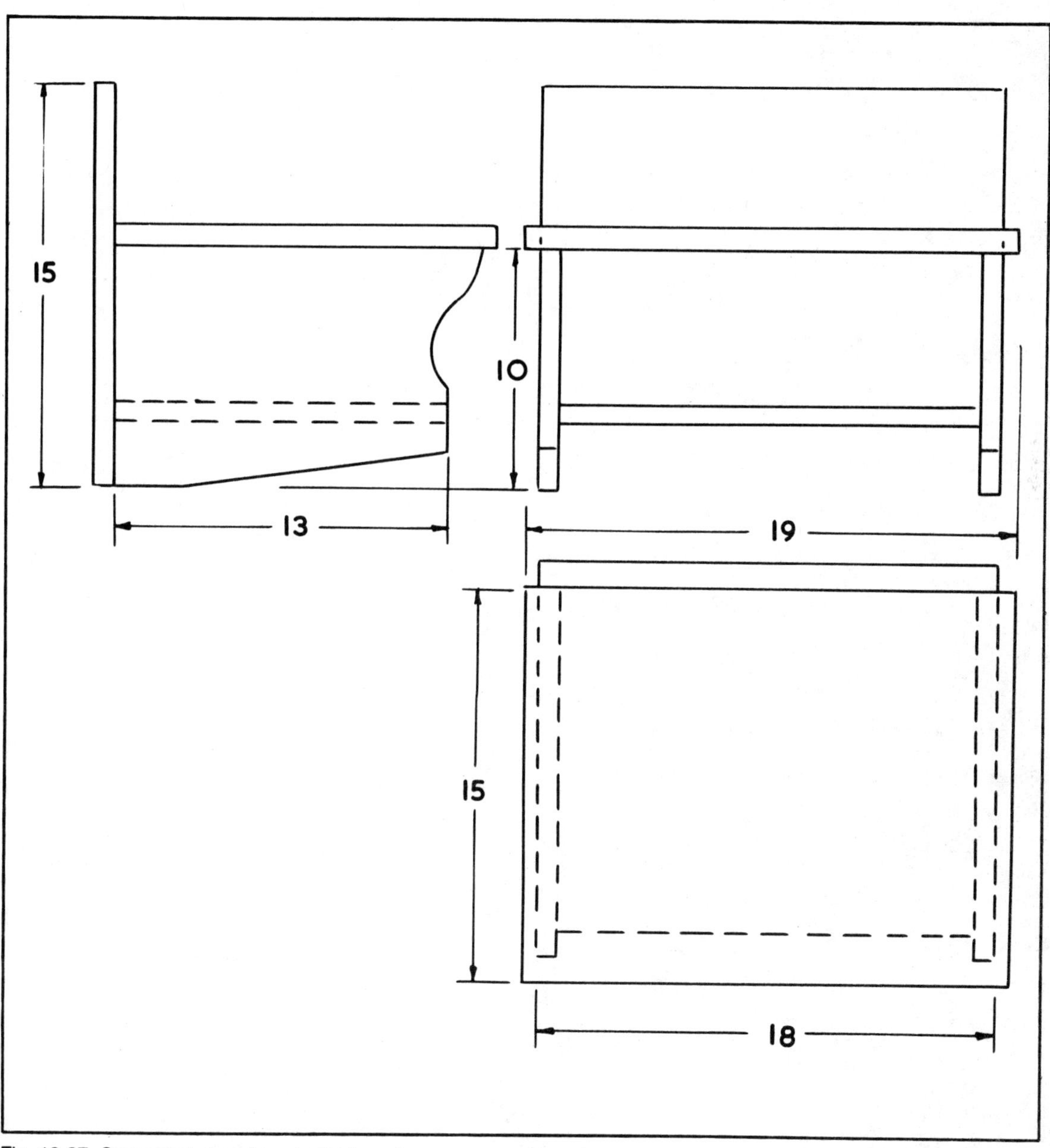

Fig. 12-27. Suggested sizes for a bedside rack.

Table 12-3. Materials List for Bedside Rack.

1 top	15 × 20 × ¾ or ⅞
2 sides	14 × 11 × ¾
1 shelf	13 × 17 × ¾
1 back	12 × 19 × ¾

their ends will not show. Using the penciled lines as a guide, drill through into the front assembly at two positions on opposite sides. Apply glue to the meeting surfaces and start assembly with dowels in the first two holes. These will keep the parts correctly related, and you can drill and drive the other

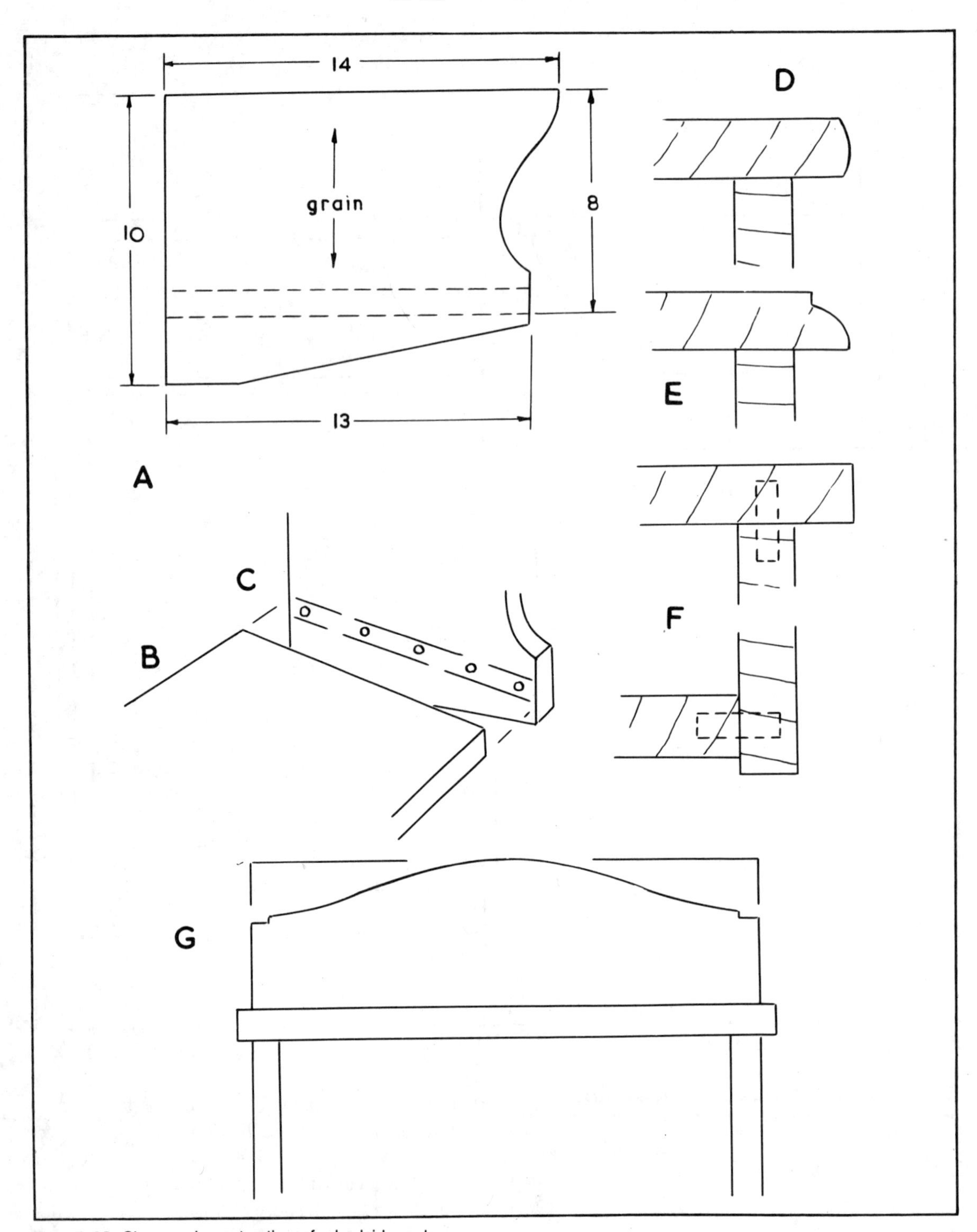

Fig. 12-28. Sizes and construction of a bedside rack.

dowels. If you prefer, the back can be screwed to the other assembled parts.

BEDHEAD WITH CABINETS

A bed is often provided with a headboard, then side tables or cabinets are separate, so they tend to be moved around and may be unstable. This unit (Fig. 12-29) has its cabinets built in, and the bed goes between them. Two possible cabinet designs are shown. The one with the edge extended upward is particularly suitable in the corner of a room. Sizes are given (Fig. 12-30 and Table 12-4) to suit a 48-inch-wide bed, but the width can be adjusted to suit any bed.

The headboard is framed plywood, but the framing must be arranged so some parts of it provide stiffness where the cabinets are attached. Use veneered plywood, which can be backed with softwood framing and edged with matching hardwood (Fig. 12-31A). The bottom need not be edged. Assemble with glue and sink any pins used, so they can be covered with matching stopping.

You can use plywood, particle board, or solid wood with its grain across for a plain drop-front cabinet. Corner joints can be made with fillets inside the top and under the bottom (Fig. 12-31B). At the back include more fillets for attaching to the headboard. The greatest load comes at the top, so have a wider piece there (Fig. 12-31C). Bolt through at the top for greatest strength.

The fall front may be a piece hinged at the bottom and fitted between the sides (Fig. 12-31D). Use a spring or magnetic catch at the top and put a knob on the door near the bedside. Fit a folding strut

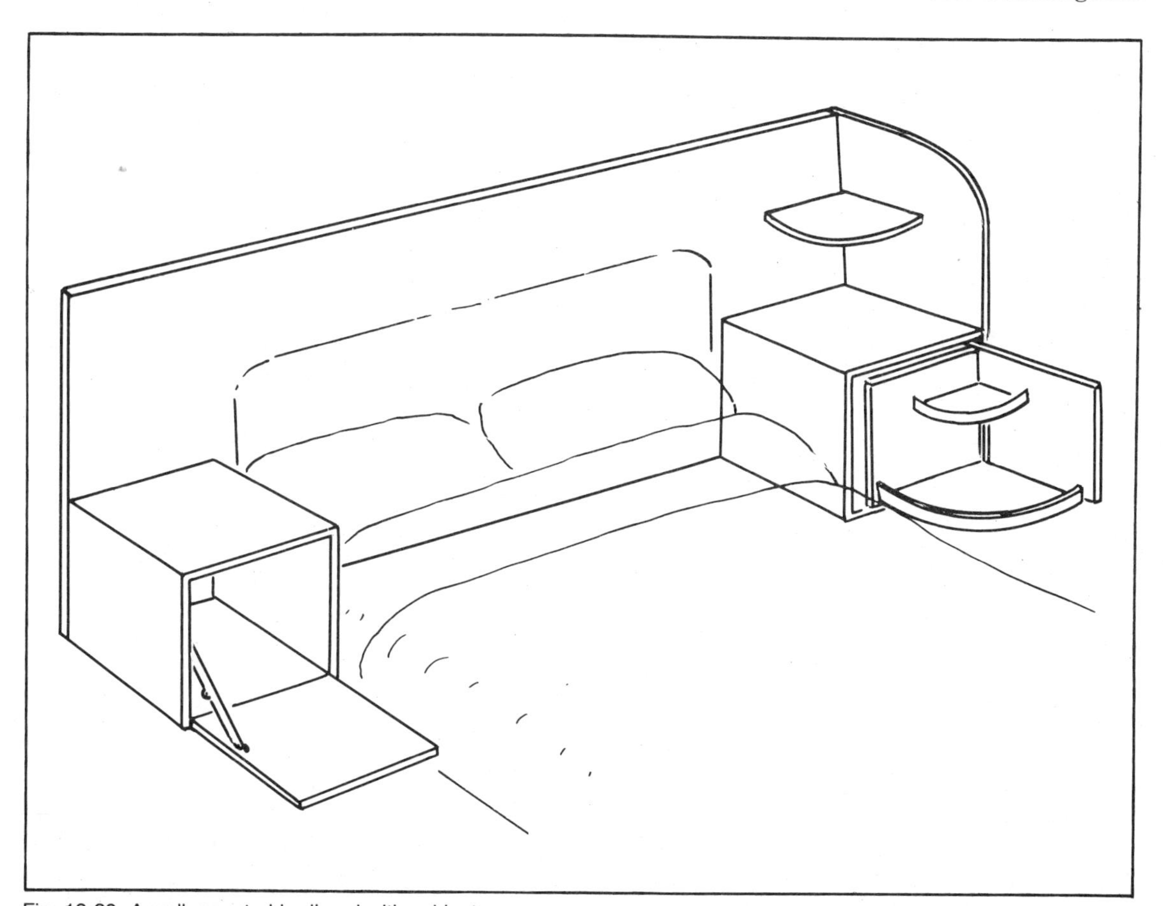

Fig. 12-29. A wall-mounted bedhead with cabinets.

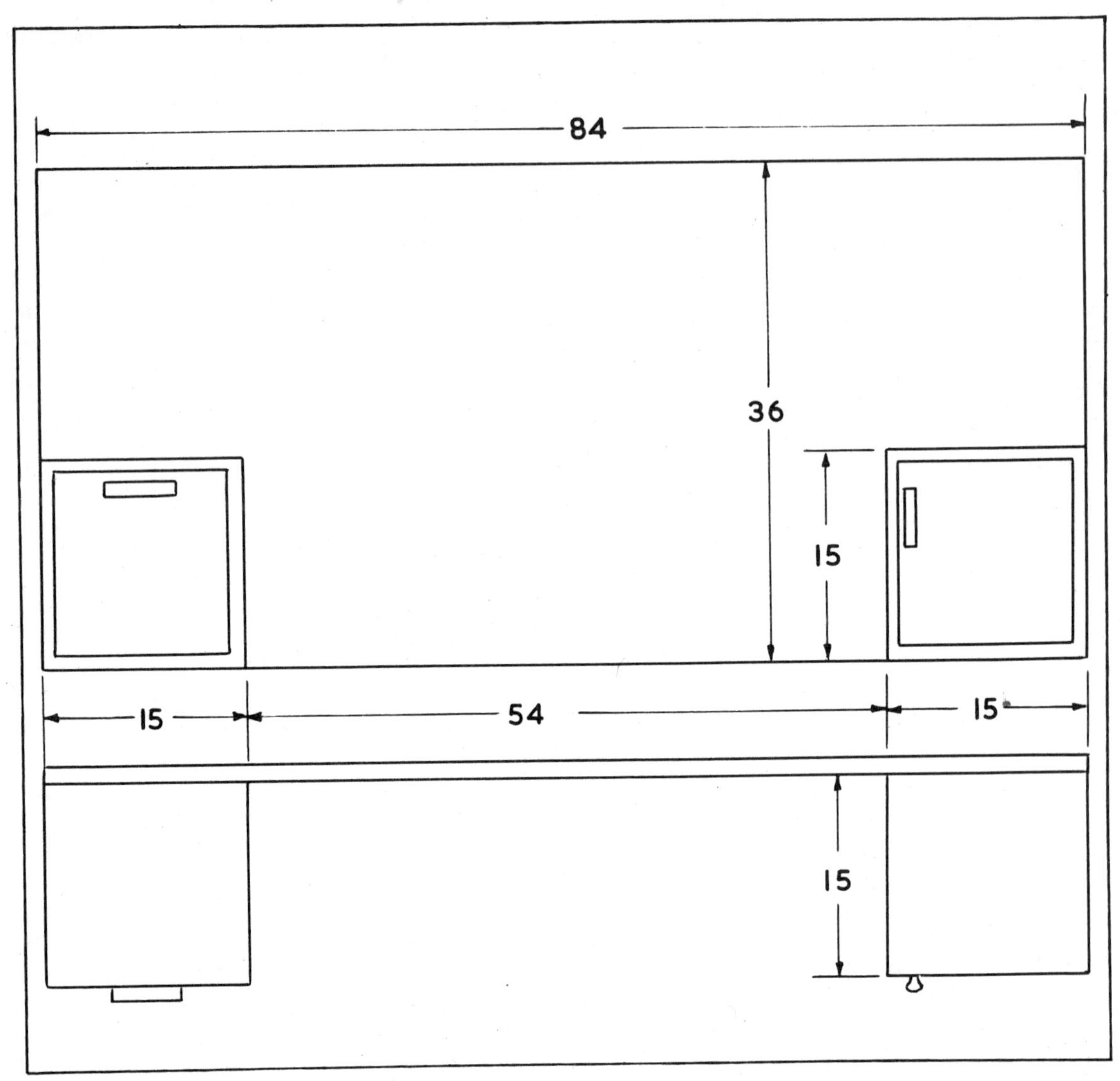

Fig. 12-30. Sizes for a bedhead with cabinets.

Table 12-4. Materials List for Bedhead with Cabinets.

1 back	36 × 84 × ¼ plywood
3 back frames	2 × 84 × 1
4 back frames	2 × 36 × 1
2 back frames	2 × 20 × 1
4 cabinet sides	15 × 18 × ¾
4 cabinet sides	15 × 15 × ¾
2 cabinet doors	15 × 18 × ¾
12 fillets	¾ × 18 × ¾
2 fillets	2 × 15 × ¾

of the type intended for a desk flap to hold the door level when it is open. Alternatively, use a piece of thin chain between screw eyes.

If the outside of a cabinet can project up the side of the headboard, it provides valuable strength (Fig. 12-32A). It can take the place of the edging on that side of the headboard (Fig. 12-32B). The other parts have to be joined to the headboard in the same way as the first cabinet. There can be a fall front or a door hinged at the side.

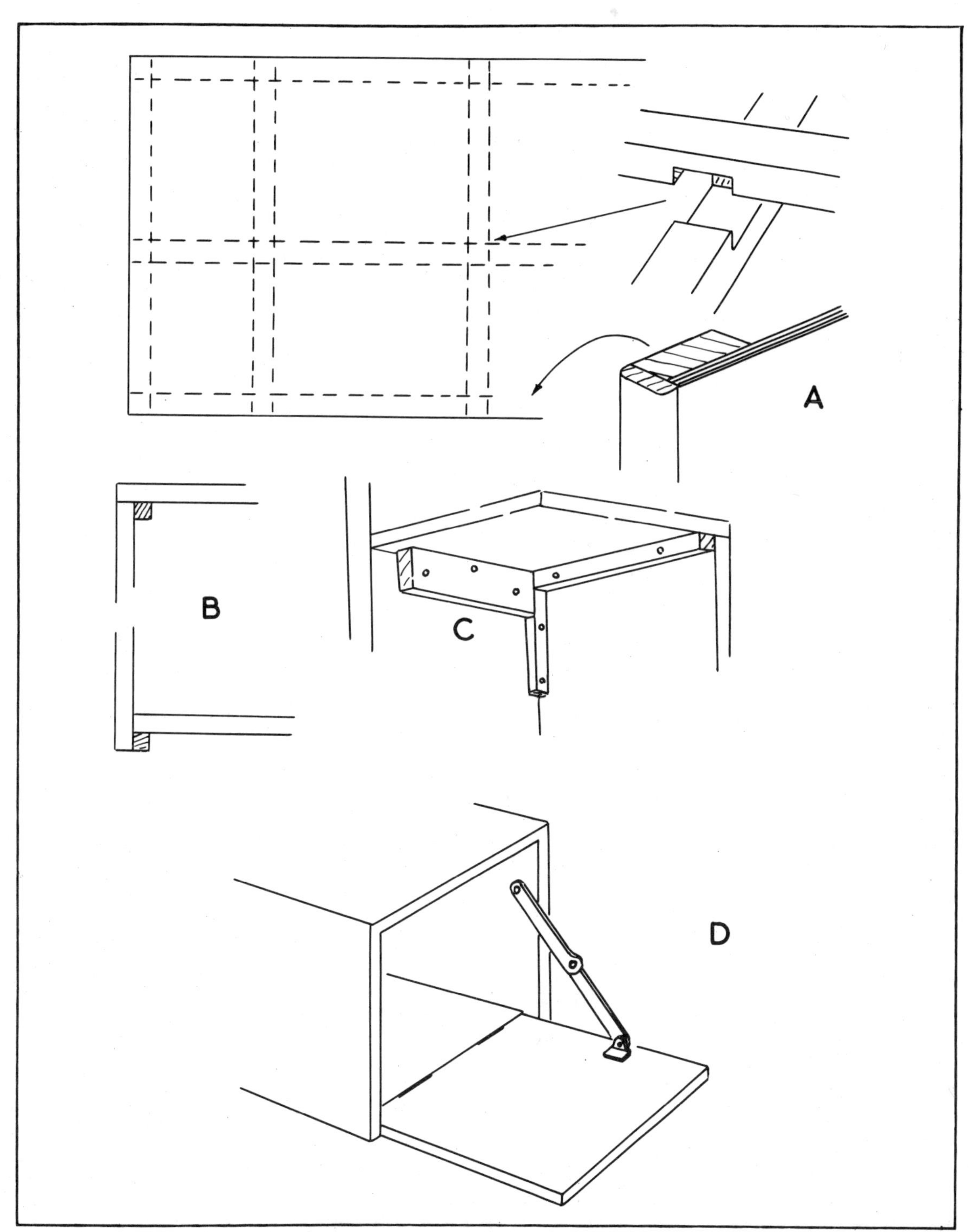

Fig. 12-31. The built-up back (A) and cabinet details (B, C, D).

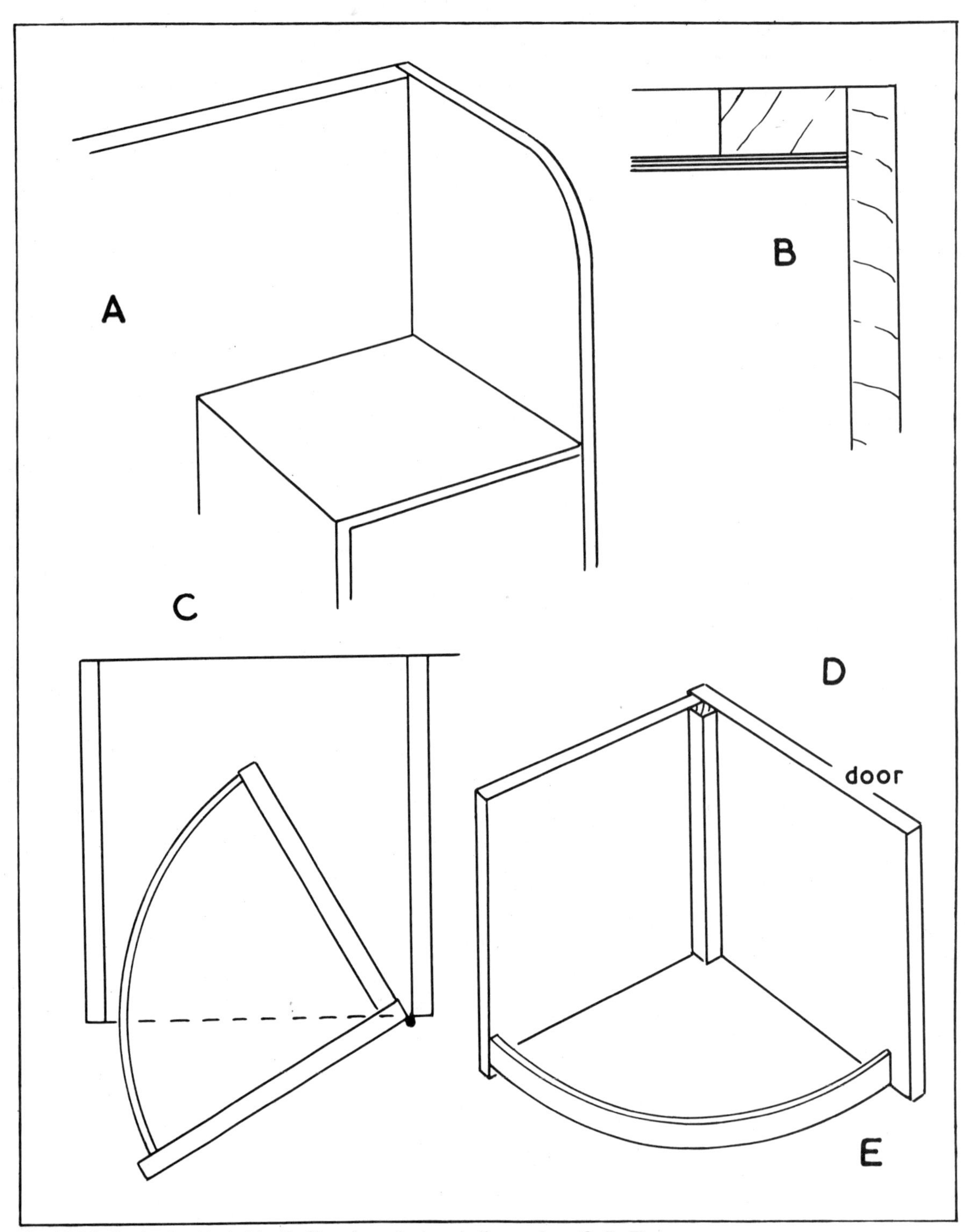

Fig. 12-32. A raised cabinet side (A, B) and a swinging shelf on a door (C, D, E).

If a door is hinged at the side, it can be fitted with curved trays. The trays bring their contents out as the door is opened, but the capacity of the cupboard is not much more than half that of a plain cupboard.

To get the maximum size of curved shelf, draw a plan view of the cupboard full-size, with the door closed. Use a compass with its point at the center of the hinge knuckles and draw a curve that will clear the side of the case (Fig. 12-32C). That will be the outside of a tray. Put a piece square to the door near the cabinet side when the door is closed. Use a fillet inside if you do not want screwheads to show on the front (Fig. 12-32D).

Make a quarter-circle shelf attached to that and the door, with a lip around it (Fig. 12-32E). The lip can be thin plywood, cut so the grain of the outside plies is the short way, for easy bending. You can also use semiflexible plastic strips.

If you fit a second curved shelf, make it smaller. Otherwise, it is made and fitted in the same way. To prevent the door and curved shelves from opening too far, put a small block of wood under the top so the piece behind the shelf hits it when the door is open far enough.

If the cabinet side projects upward, you can put a shelf similar to that inside the cabinet further up the side. The shelf should not interfere with a reading lamp.

DRIP-DRY AIRER

Some clothes cannot be dried by machine, and the obvious place to dry them indoors is in the bathroom. This rack (Fig. 12-33) hangs vertically

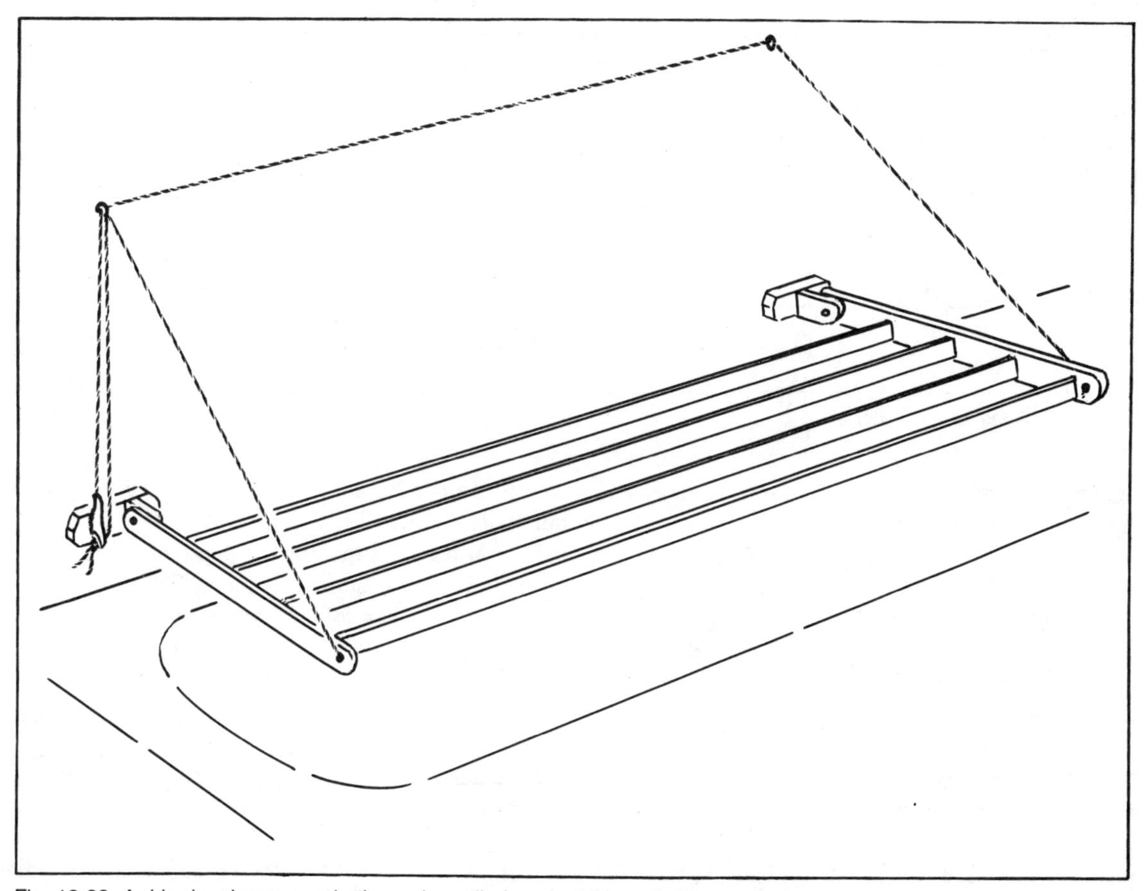

Fig. 12-33. A drip-dry airer over a bath can be pulled against the wall when not being used.

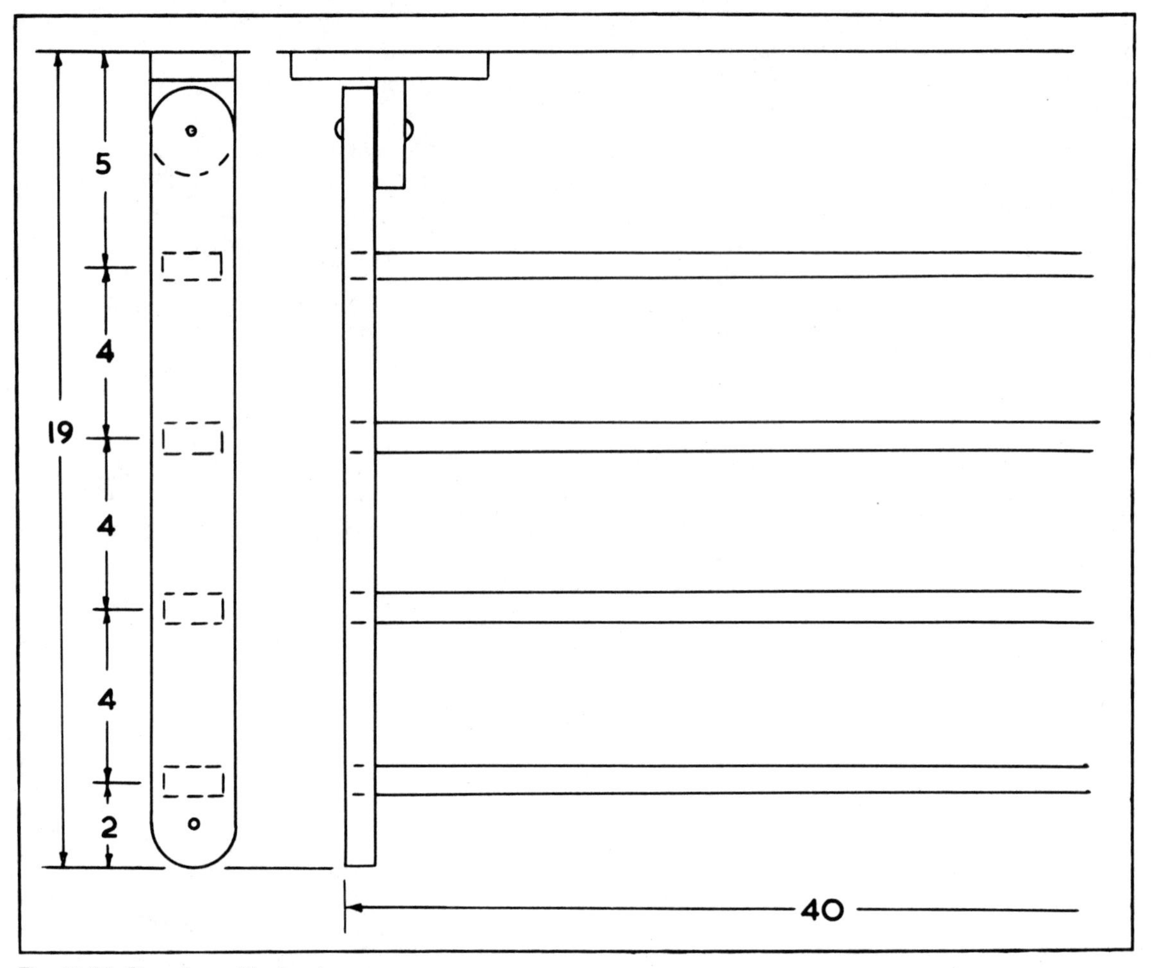

Fig. 12-34. Sizes for a drip-dry airer.

against the wall when not being used, but it can be lifted to horizontal with cords. Its four rails will allow wet clothing to drip into the bath. There are other applications, too. It can be used outside for clothes drying or airing. A smaller version may be used in the kitchen for smaller clothes. A draftsman can drape large drawings over the rails to avoid folding and creases.

Table 12-5. Materials List for Drip-Dry Airer.

2 ends	2	×	20	×	3/4
4 rails	1½	×	42	×	5/8
Brackets from	2	×	18	×	3/4

Sizes can be adapted to suit available space, but those shown (Fig. 12-34 and Table 12-5) will suit most baths. Allow for the depth of the vertical airer and for the adjusting cords. There are two ways the airer can fold. It may be high enough to clear the bath when down, with space above for the cord at about 45° when the rack is in use (Fig. 12-35A). You can arrange the airer lower so it folds upward, but the cord points on the wall must be a few inches above the vertical airer (Fig. 12-35B). The first way is more acceptable if there is enough space.

The best wood is close-grained hardwood, preferably light in color. It can be used without any

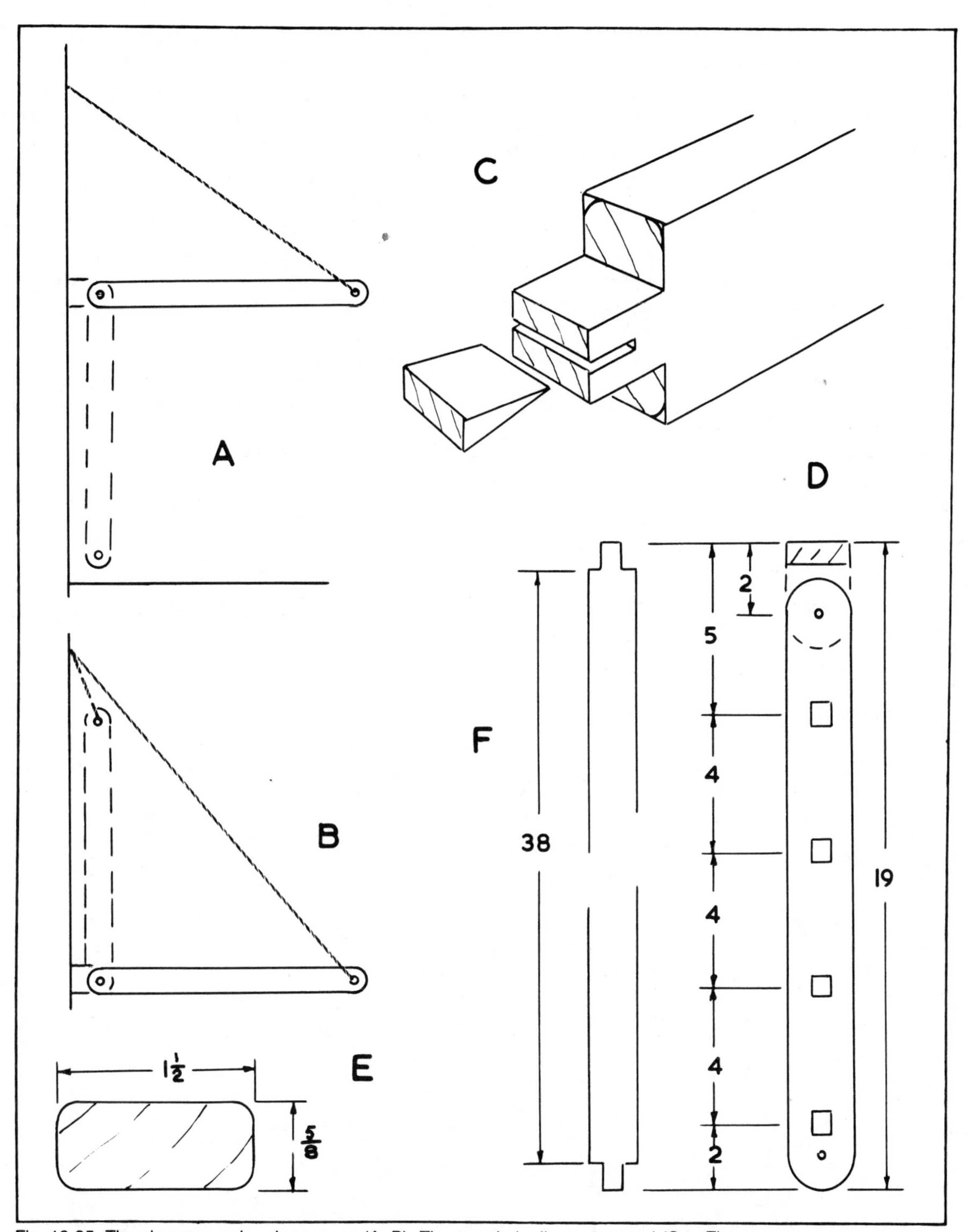

Fig. 12-35. The airer may swing down or up (A, B). The rounded rails are tenoned (C to E).

surface finish. Otherwise, you can apply paint or a clear waterproof varnish or lacquer.

The rails should be tenoned into the ends and tenons locked with wedges and waterproof glue (Fig. 12-35C). The assembly will hold its shape better with these joints than if the joints are screwed or doweled.

Mark out the ends (Fig. 12-35D). The hole at the outer end should suit the cord chosen. The load is not great, and a soft flexible synthetic cord of ⅛-inch or 3/16-inch diameter will do. The inner end should suit pivot bolts, which can be ¼-inch diameter and preferably of a metal that will not corrode.

The rails have their angles rounded (Fig. 12-35E). Mark them together to get the distances between shoulders the same (Fig. 12-35F). Allow a little excess length on the tenons for planing level after assembly.

The brackets (Fig. 12-36A) should also be tenoned. Allow for screwing to the wall. Make one bracket a little longer to take the cleat to which the cords will be attached. The cleat can be a metal or plastic one, but you can make a suitable wooden one (Fig. 12-36B).

The operating cords go from the airer ends up to points on the wall, then the further one is brought along so they go down to the cleat together (Fig. 12-36C). Small pulleys can be attached to the wall, but the simplest arrangement uses two screw eyes (Fig. 12-36D). You can put a knot in the pair of cords

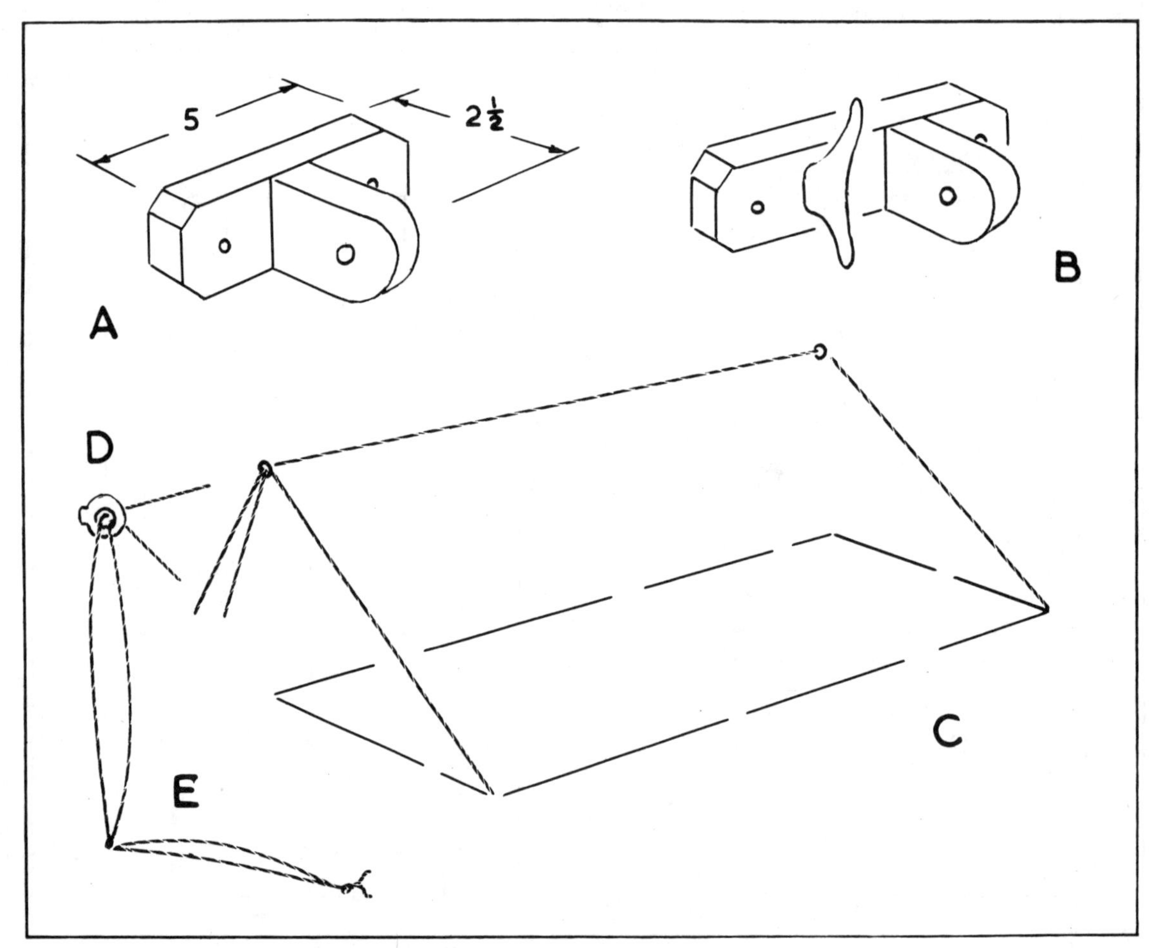

Fig. 12-36. Pivot and cord arrangements for the drip-dry airer.

Fig. 12-37. A cupboard below a shelf gives good combined storage space.

to hook under the cleat at the raised position (Fig. 12-36E), then the cord tails are wound around the cleat when the airer is lowered. Seal the ends of the cords with a flame so the fibers will not fray.

SHELF WITH CABINET

A shelf needs support at intervals and at the ends. If you can include a closet or cabinet within the length, that can take the place of at least one bracket and offer storage space, too. One use is in a bathroom. A shelf can be arranged fairly high, and a cabinet with a mirrored door may be put underneath and used to store toilet articles (Fig. 12-37).

Sizes will depend on the available space. A shelf width between 5 inches and 7 inches is suitable. One end may go into a corner and be supported on a cleat (Fig. 12-38A). A free end can rest on a metal shelf bracket, or you can shape a wood end (Fig. 12-38B), with the shelf in a dado joint and blocks for screws against the wall. Put a back along the shelf for screws, either on top (Fig. 12-38C) or behind it (Fig. 12-38D).

Make the cabinet as a unit to be screwed upward into the shelf and to the wall. Rabbet a plywood back (Fig. 12-38E). Use a waterproof grade if the cabinet will be in a damp atmosphere. The top and bottom should extend over the door (Fig. 12-38F). Use ½-inch or ⅝-inch wood for a small assembly. The best joints are dovetails (Fig. 12-38G), but you can nail rabbets (Fig. 12-38H) or merely screw the corners (Fig. 12-38J).

The door can be a piece of plywood ½ inch or thicker with the mirror held to it with metal clips (Fig. 12-38K). The alternative is to make a framed door with the mirror set in rabbets, in a similar way to a picture, but with plywood behind the mirror. A glazier will cut a mirror for you, but it may be cheaper to use a stock size and design the cabinet to suit it.

The door can be hinged in the usual way at one side, with a spring or magnetic catch at the other side. Another way is to put screws through the top and bottom into the door. Include a washer at the bottom to give clearance to the door (Fig. 12-38L). Round the inner corner of the door, so it clears the side as it opens (Fig. 12-38M).

There may be a knob or handle at the opening side. If the mirror is full-size, a hole has to be drilled through the glass. A hollow for fingers behind the edge is simpler for any type of door (Fig. 12-38N).

Whether you put shelves inside depends on the intended contents. There can be one or two glass shelves for small toilet articles. They should have their edges rounded and drop into notched cleats on the sides (Fig. 12-38P). Wood shelves can be fitted in the same way, or they can be included in dadoes

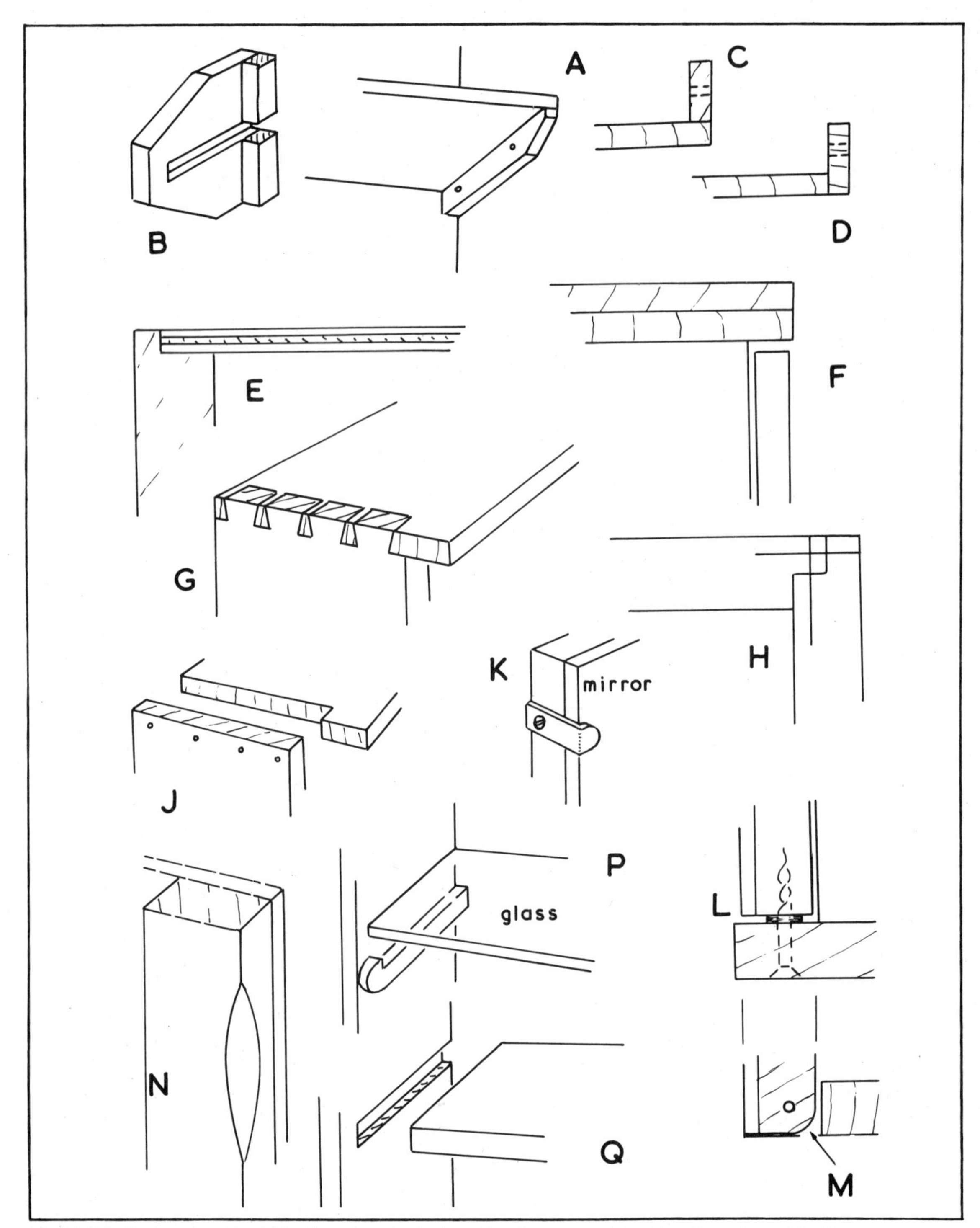

Fig. 12-38. Shelf construction (A to D) and methods of making the cupboard and its mirror door (E to Q).

during construction (Fig. 12-38Q).

A gloss paint is usually the best finish if the woodwork is going into a bathroom. A good finish is easiest to obtain before fitting the glass and screwing to the wall.

BATHROOM TOWEL RACK

In a small bathroom you may want to use all available space. One wall area often left vacant is above the toilet cistern. Shelves can be attached to the wall, but this rack (Fig. 12-39) will provide storage for folded towels and similar things in a way that allows you to move the whole rack. If you move to another home, you can take it with you. Alternatively, the rack can be screwed to the wall, floor, and ceiling. The rack fits over the cistern with the two sides braced between floor and ceiling. You can make the shelf positions variable if you wish.

Sizes will have to be arranged to suit the actual situation, but some typical sizes are shown (Fig. 12-40A and Table 12-6) as a guide to proportions. The following instructions are mainly related to a rack that braces itself between floor and ceiling and has shelves that can be removed.

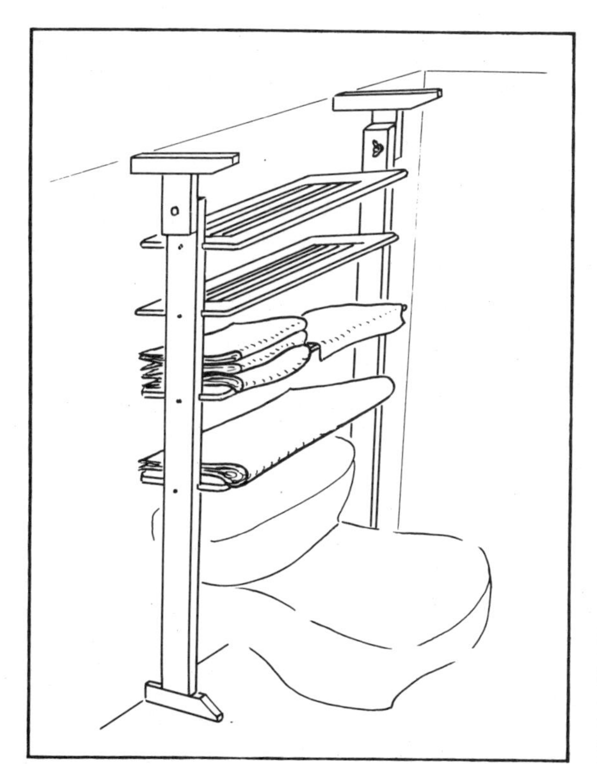

Fig. 12-39. A bathroom towel rack may fit above the toilet seat.

Start with the shelves, which are all the same. There are four in the example. The best shelves have all the parts at the same level (Fig. 12-41A). Note that the sides overlap the ends, but the inner parts are between the ends. All the joints can be doweled (Fig. 12-41B) or tenoned (Fig. 12-41C).

For simpler construction, the four long parts can merely overlap the ends and be joined to them with nails or screws (Fig. 12-41D). Keep the ends of the inner parts far enough back to allow the joints to fit.

The upright sides will have shallow dado slots for the shelves to fit in. The ends of the shelves are notched, so their visible edges will be at about half the thickness of the uprights (Fig. 12-41E).

The uprights each have a sliding top section, which can be locked when tight (Fig. 12-42A), so the rack can be tightened between floor and ceiling. Suitable sizes are suggested (Fig. 12-40B). There does not have to be much movement. If you measure the overall size from floor to ceiling and make the assembled sides so you can shorten about ½ inch for positioning, then allow ½ inch the other way for tightening, that will be enough.

Cut the slot and guide piece to allow easy movement, but not so slack that the assembly can wobble (Fig. 12-42B). A ⅜-inch coach bolt should be suitable for locking each joint. You may put a metal washer under each butterfly nut, but a plywood disk (Fig. 12-42C) will provide friction and prevent slipping.

The bearers, which act like feet against floor and ceiling, also act as spacers to hold the rack parallel to the wall. Make them square to the wall,

Table 12-6. Materials List for Bathroom Towel Rack.

2 sides	3	×	93	×	1
4 bearers	2	×	13	×	1
2 upper sides	3	×	10	×	1
8 shelf sides	2	×	25	×	1
8 shelf parts	2	×	23	×	1
8 shelf ends	2	×	12	×	1

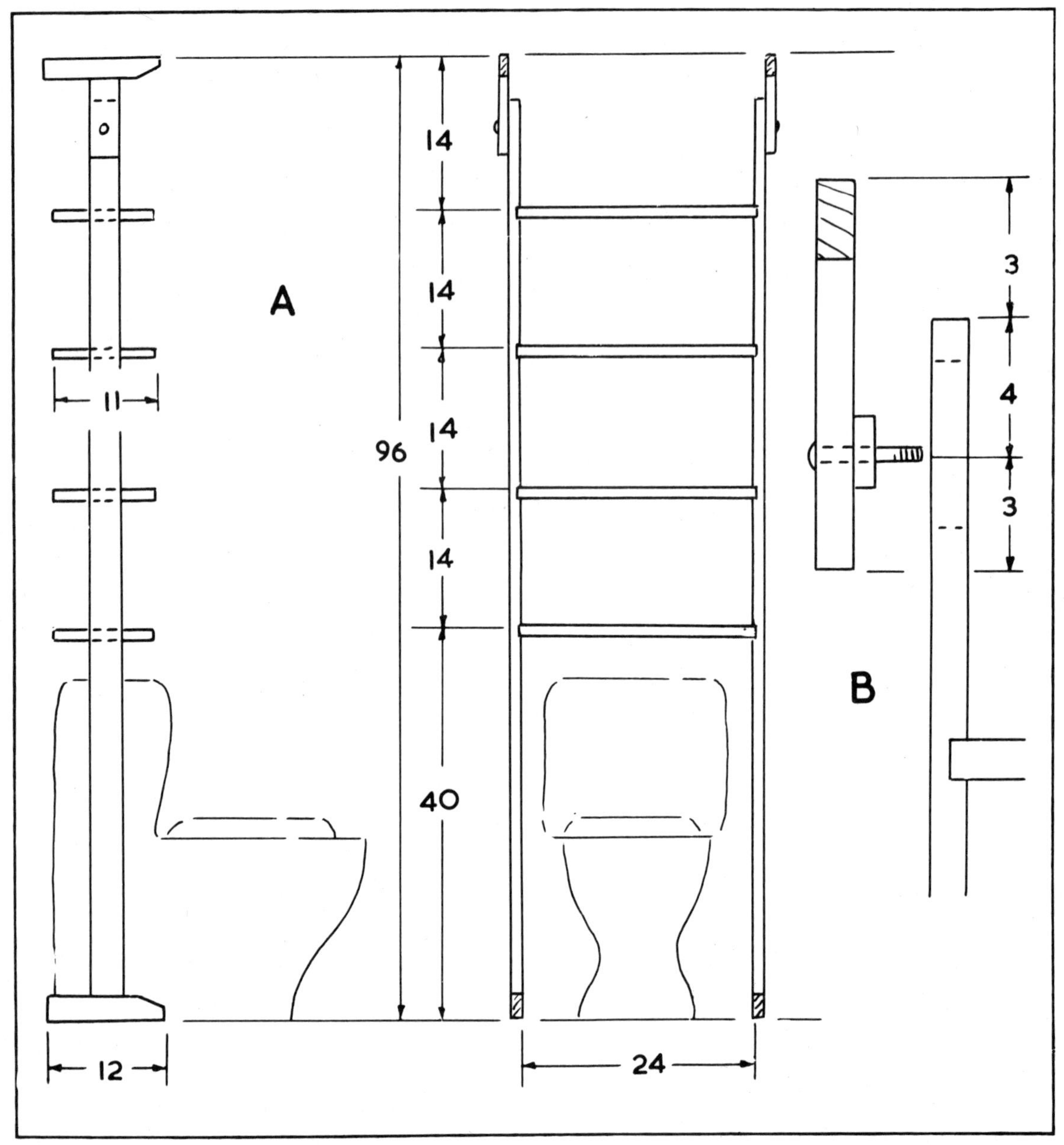

Fig. 12-40. Suggested sizes for a bathroom towel rack.

but taper the outer ends (Fig. 12-42D). If there is a baseboard at the floor, shorten the bearers there to keep the sides parallel to the wall. Either tenon (Fig. 12-42E) or dowel the uprights to the bearers. To give the bearers a better grip, glue cloth or rubber to their edges (Fig. 12-42F).

Shelf positions are suggested, but measure the height of the cistern and check how it has to be opened for maintenance. Allow enough clearance under the bottom shelf so the rack does not have to be moved to open the cistern.

You can allow other positions on the sides so

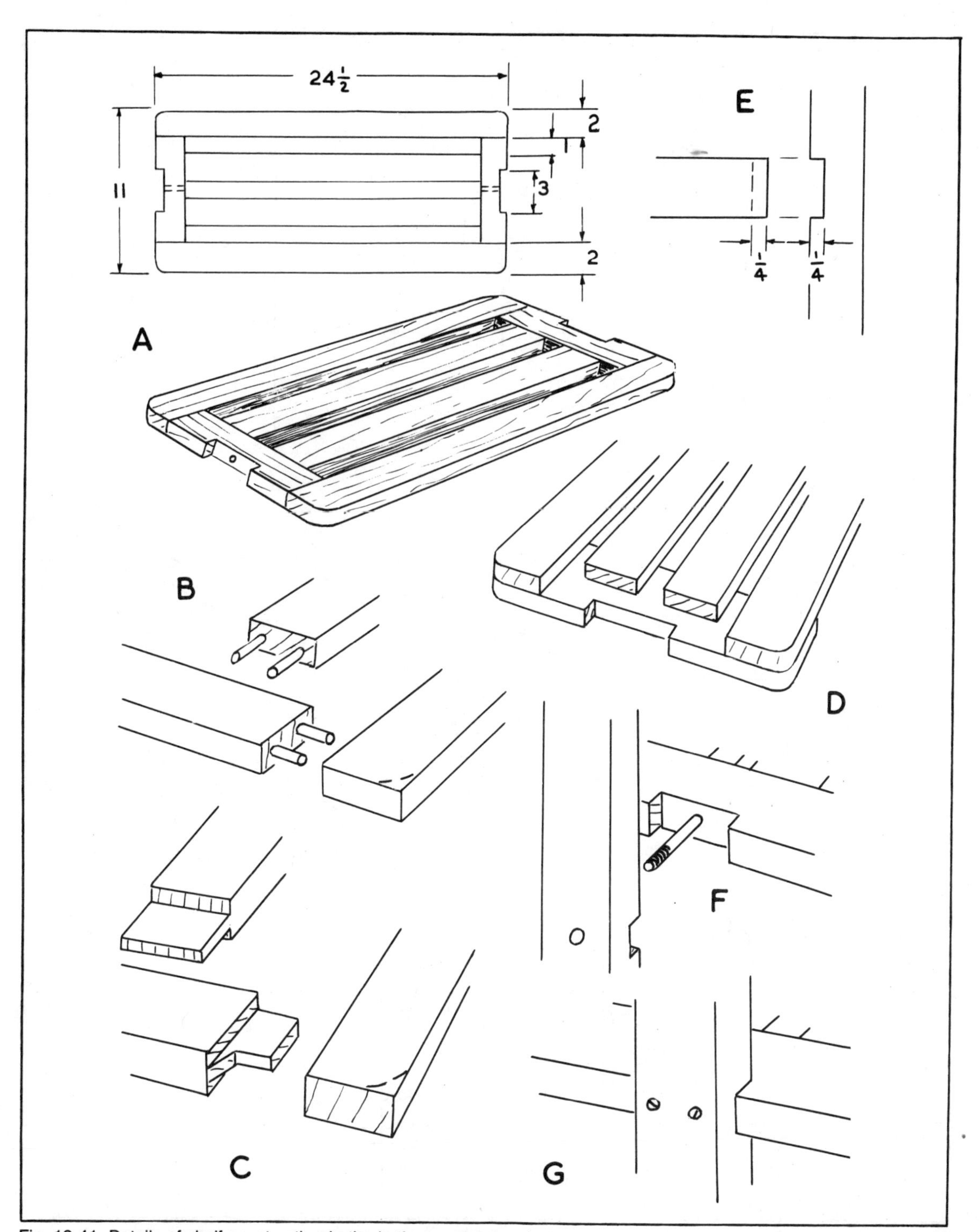

Fig. 12-41. Details of shelf construction in the bathroom towel rack.

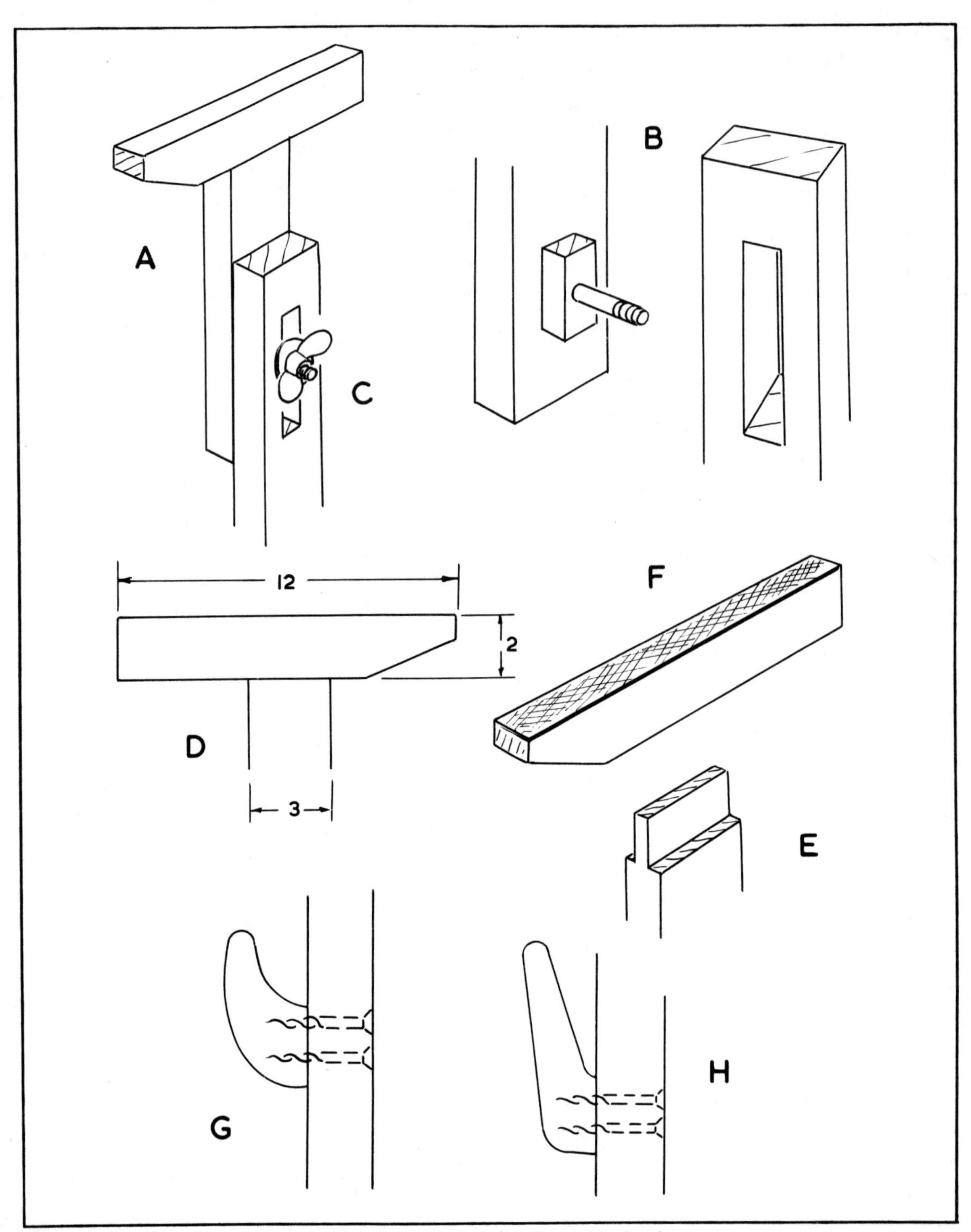

Fig. 12-42. Details of the uprights and their adjustments in the bathroom towel rack.

there are more shelf locations available. Much depends on the uses of the rack and possible changes. If the rack is being made so it can be taken apart, use 5/16-inch or 3/8-inch coach bolts (Fig. 12-41F) with washers and butterfly nuts.

If the rack is to be more permanent, use two screws or dowels at each joint (Fig. 12-41G). Screws should be of a noncorrodible metal, or sink them below the surface so they are protected from attack by moisture with stopping or plugs. Paint over steel screwheads will not delay rust very long.

When you position the rack, check squareness. The light structure is easily pushed out of shape before it is braced in position. Measure diagonals or check that the uprights are parallel to a sidewall.

Things like coat hooks or towel holders can be attached to the outsides of one or both uprights. Bolts from shelves may also hold racks or hangers. You can make wooden hooks (Fig. 12-42G) or use metal coat hooks. A hook with an acute V inside (Fig. 12-42H) will grip a towel or other cloth pressed into it, yet it can be lifted out.

Chapter 13

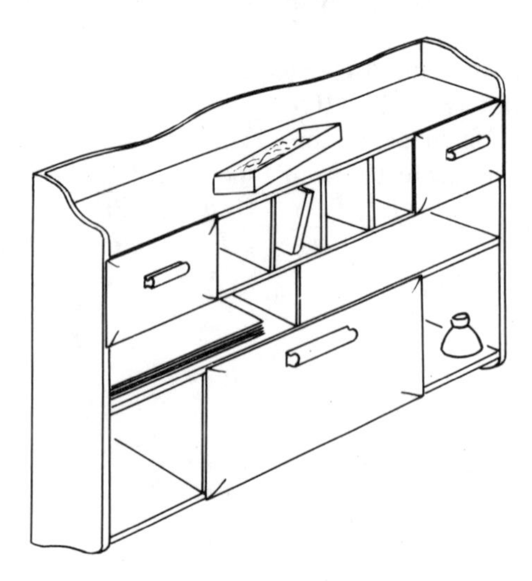

Personal Furniture

MOST OF US HAVE PLACES WE CALL OUR OWN where we tend to settle when there is no need to go to another part of the house. The place may be a den, a study, a playroom, or just a corner of a large room used mainly for other things. We need a place to deal with paperwork and finance, even if it is just a corner that is not big enough to qualify as an office.

Furniture for any of these places has to help us in our relaxation or work. Its appearance is secondary but important. Any furniture is best appreciated if it is both functional and attractive. It has to be designed to fit available space and arranged to serve its purpose as well as possible. Usually it has to be compact, so it provides all your needs in a minimum space. If you can spread yourself, though, that is fine.

Building in lets you get the most out of space and possibly arrange furniture with a depth that will be unsteady in freestanding furniture. The built-in furniture should project far enough from the wall to serve its purpose adequately. This leaves more free floor area and gives a rigid piece of furniture on which to work or play.

A table or desk can be suitable in a living room or bedroom. A bar may make a working or serving surface in a kitchen, just as well as it does in a playroom or den. Similarly, furniture pieces described elsewhere in this book may also have uses in your personal room, but those that follow are particularly suited.

TYPING TABLE

If a typewriter is to be used on a desk, it tends to take up so much space that there is little room for other things. It is better if the typewriter can be supported to one side, then you can turn to type without disturbing the papers on the main surface. This desk (Fig. 13-1) can go in the corner of the room and occupy a space 24 inches by 48 inches, but that can be extended along the other wall when required to take a typewriter. The extension slides into the width of the main desk when not needed. You will have to decide which way you prefer to turn

Fig. 13-1. A typing table with a stowable sliding flap.

to use the typewriter. As shown (Fig. 13-2), you will be looking to your left when you refer to papers. The extension size shown should have plenty of space for a portable typewriter, but measure your own machine before deciding on a size. The typing table is a little lower than the main table, which is an advantage. See Table 13-1.

Make the main top first. It can be a piece of plywood, with solid wood at the edge, or entirely solid wood, made from strips glued together. Shape it to fit the corner of the room. Make the back and end strips. These strips hold the desk to the wall, so glue and screw them securely (Fig. 13-3A).

A rail goes under the end and is joined into the leg. A front rail goes into the leg the other way, but the sizes depend on parts of the extension. The extension top has its leg attached to a rail (Fig. 13-3B). The leg and rail must come under the main top when folded (Fig. 13-3C), so the long front rail must be set back far enough to allow for that. This decides where the leg comes. Either tenon or dowel the rails into the top of the leg, which may be tapered or turned.

Cut away the front rail so as to easily pass the

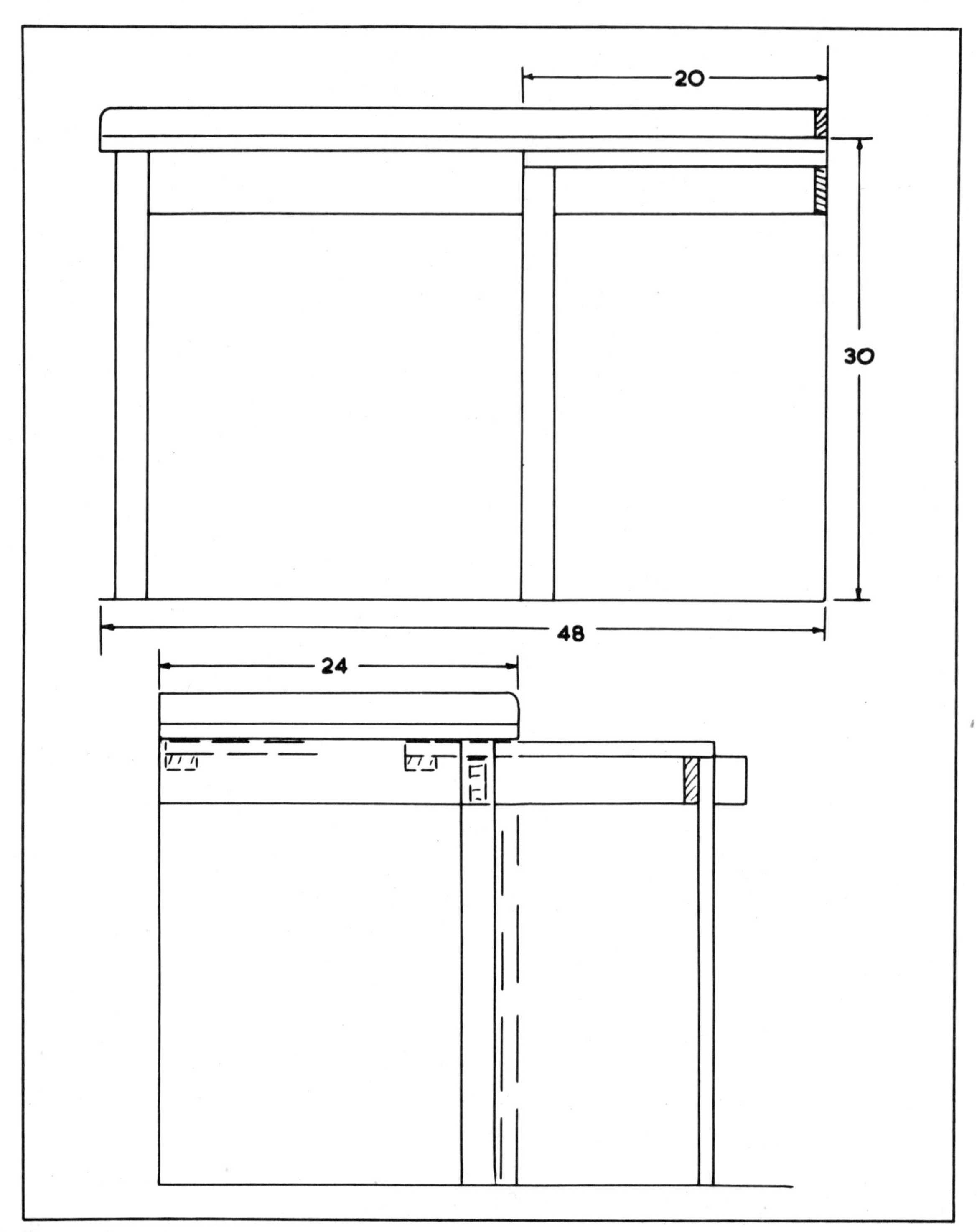

Fig. 13-2. Sizes of the typing table.

Table 13-1. Materials List for Typing Table.

Part	Size
1 top	24 × 48 × ¾
1 typing top	20 × 24 × ¾
1 leg	2 × 30 × 2
1 back	2 × 48 × ¾
1 end	2 × 25 × ¾
1 end rail	4 × 24 × ¾
1 front rail	4 × 48 × ¾
1 slide rail	3¼ × 48 × ¾
1 table slide	3 × 24 × ⅞
1 table slide	4 × 24 × ¾
1 extension leg	2 × 30 × 1
1 extension rail	3 × 22 × 1
1 extension stop	2 × 20 × 1

extension top. There will be a slide rail against the wall, extending as far as the extending top is to go (Fig. 13-3D). Arrange a guide (Fig. 13-3E) under the main top at the other side on which the extension slides.

Attach the extension leg and rail securely to the extension top. Because of the need to keep this joint narrow, tight gluing and screwing are necessary for rigidity.

Have the main leg and its rails attach to the top. Blocks or strips inside and screwed both ways (Fig. 13-3F) make strong joints. Bring the table into position and get the top level both ways before screwing to the wall. Arrange the slide rail along the second wall at a height that will give the extension top easy clearance under the main top. Test the action of the extension. Keep the extension leg slightly short, so it does not drag on the floor when pulled out. If the extension movement is satisfactory, screw on the guide that holds the edge of the extension top under the main top. Put a stop piece across the underside of the extension top to prevent it from pulling right out (Fig. 13-3G).

CORNER DESK

A desk attached to a wall takes up less space in a room than a freestanding desk. It needs less wood as the wall takes the place of at least two legs. It is more rigid and cannot be pushed around. A lamp mounted on the wall does not use up valuable desk space. It can shine the light just where you want if it is on a flexible or hinged arm. The desk shown (Figs. 13-4 and 13-5) is intended to fit into a corner, but it can be adapted to suit a flat wall by adding another leg. See Table 13-2.

Make the top first as that controls certain other sizes. The top can be solid wood, but it is shown as framed plywood with leathercloth glued on the panel (Fig. 13-6A). Rabbets have to be cut deep enough to allow the leathercloth to finish level with the frame (Fig. 13-6B). With the plywood to hold the mitered corners, it may be sufficient to merely glue them. Dowels can be put through diagonally for extra strength (Fig. 13-6C). Assemble the top on a flat surface and sight across to see that it is not twisted.

Taper the inner surfaces of the front leg (Fig. 13-7A), but the wall leg remains square (Fig. 13-7B). Put rails between them so the top will overhang about 1 inch at the front. Tenon the rails and allow for similar joints into the tops of the legs the other way. Dowel the rails to the legs if you wish, but tenons are stronger. The back rail goes the full length under the top and will be screwed to the wall. The front rail is similar, but it will be doweled to the drawer block side.

The drawer block sides are shown as solid wood with the grain upward (Fig. 13-8A). They can be thick plywood with solid wood on the front edge, or there can be thin plywood framed round with the smooth surface inward (Fig. 13-8B).

Mark out the sides and allow for notching around the back rail (Fig. 13-8C). The rails are 1 inch square. Attach those that act as runners and kickers to the sides (Fig. 13-8D). Arrange the front rails between them and the top and bottom rails across the back, so the assembly makes up as a unit (Fig. 13-8E). Leave it unattached to the top until after you have made the drawers. You will screw it to the top, the back rail, and the wall.

Make the drawers in the usual way, with dovetails or notched joints and the plywood bottoms slid into grooves (Fig. 13-8F). Fit the false fronts to overlap the front framing. Let their adjoining edges come close (Fig. 13-8G). Put handles just above the centers of the drawer fronts.

When you are satisfied that the drawers will slide properly, assemble the desk parts. The rails

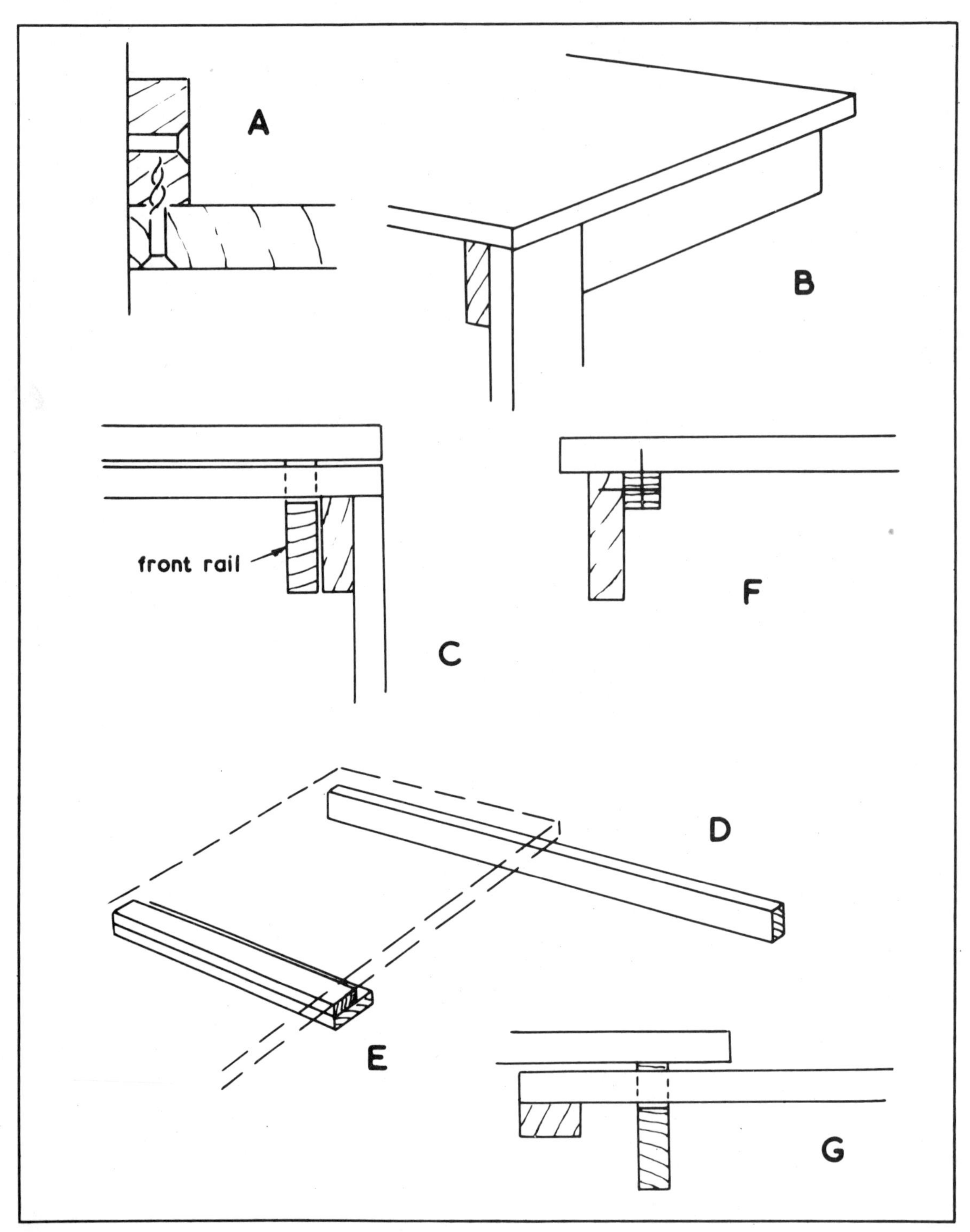

Fig. 13-3. Construction and the sliding arrangements of the typing table.

Fig. 13-4. A corner desk with drawers.

may be attached to the top from below with a few pocket screws (Fig. 13-8H). Check levels as you attach parts to the walls. If necessary, trim the edges of the top to make a close fit to the walls. Strips can be put against the walls to protect them, or the strips can be built up further to form racks for paper and pens.

BEHIND-DESK RACK

If a flattop desk or table is used against a wall, it can become so littered with papers and writing or drawing equipment that little space is left on which to work. A rack on the wall can take over storage and leave the working surface free for its intended purpose. There are many ways that this can be

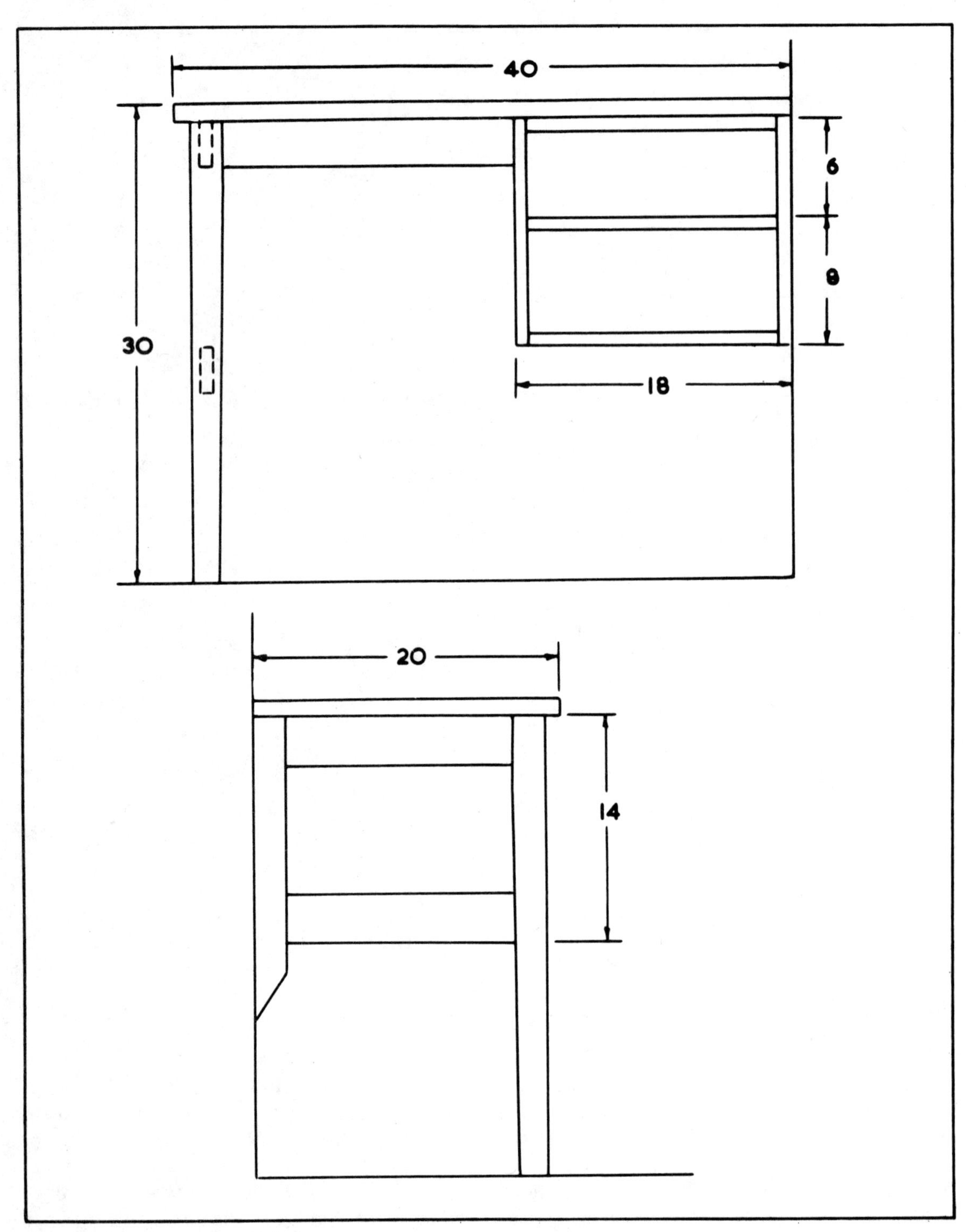

Fig. 13-5. Sizes for a corner desk.

Table 13-2. Materials List for Corner Desk.

2 top frames	3 × 41 × 1
2 top frames	3 × 21 × 1
1 top panel	17 × 37 × ½ plywood
1 leg	2 × 30 × 2
1 wall leg	2 × 18 × 2
2 end rails	3 × 18 × 1
1 front rail	3 × 22 × 1
1 back rail	3 × 40 × 1
2 drawer block sides	14 × 20 × ¾
5 front and back drawer rails	1 × 18 × 1
6 drawer rails	1 × 20 × 1
2 drawer sides	5 × 20 × ⅝
2 drawer sides	7 × 20 × ⅝
1 drawer back	5 × 17 × ⅝
1 drawer back	7 × 17 × ⅝
1 drawer front	5 × 17 × ⅝
1 drawer front	7 × 17 × ⅝
1 false drawer front	6 × 18 × ⅝
1 false drawer front	8 × 18 × ⅝
2 drawer bottoms	17 × 20 × ¼ plywood

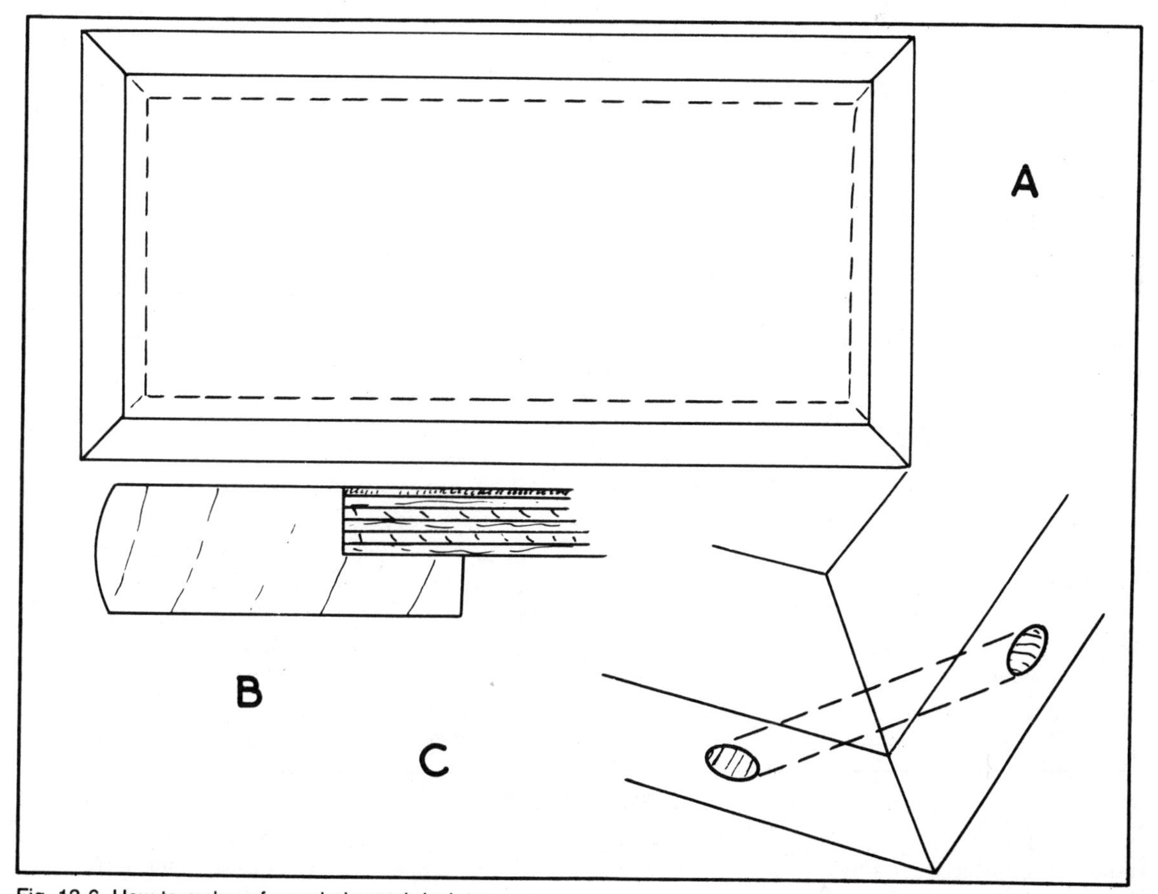

Fig. 13-6. How to make a framed plywood desk top.

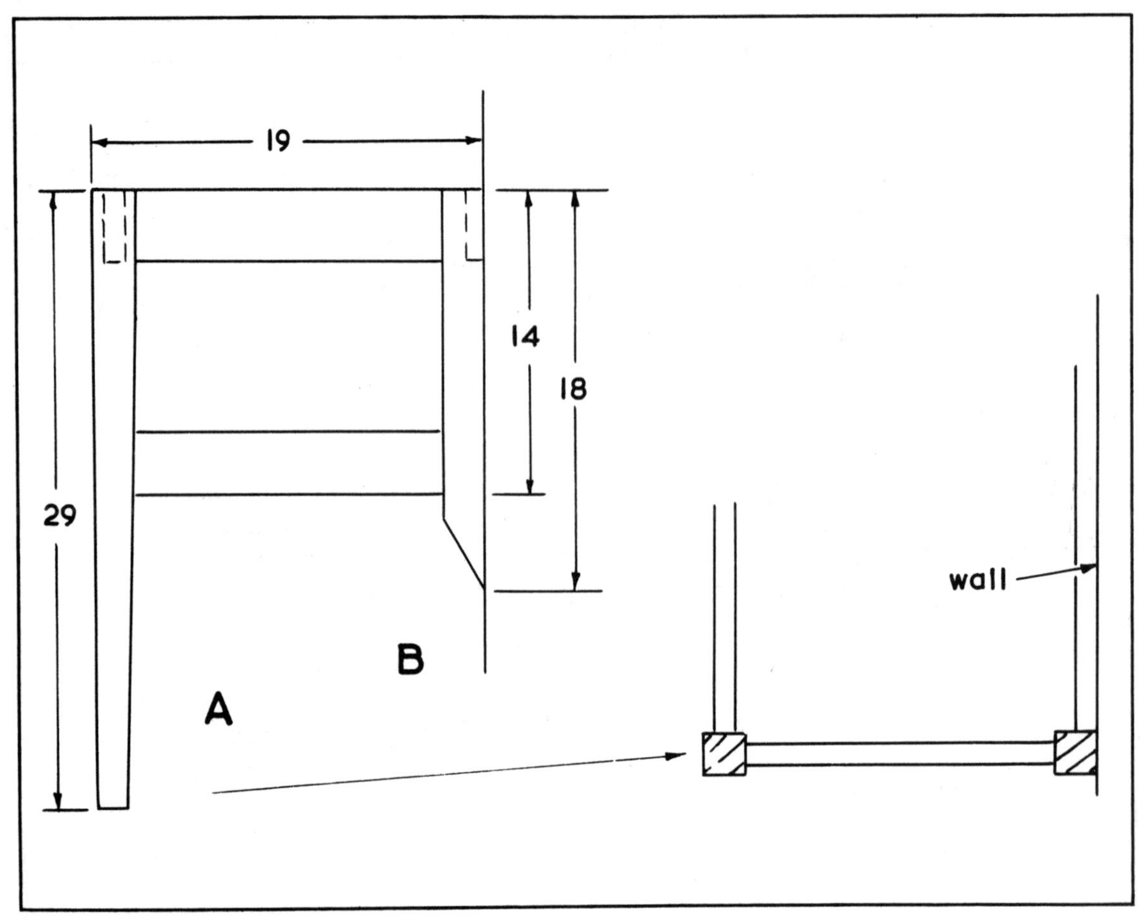

Fig. 13-7. The desk leg assembly.

arranged and spaces may be allowed for particular items. Don't get too detailed and specific, or you may find that the whole rack is a mass of carefully fitted compartments. If you change your stapler for a bigger one or decide to add a calculator, you may find there is nowhere to put it.

The rack shown (Fig. 13-9) has shelves for papers and envelopes, a rack for reference books, a drawer for small items, a shelf for pens and pencils, and a central broad area for the many other items you will find indispensable for your work at the desk. Sizes may have to be adjusted to suit your desk, but those shown (Fig. 13-10 and Table 13-3) will give plenty of useful space. The back can extend down to the desk top below the main shelf. That area may be used as a bulletin board, or you can put spring clips on it to hang rubber stamps or other items.

Plywood can be used for most parts. The edges will be exposed, so cut them carefully and finish them smooth. Ragged broken-out plywood will spoil the appearance of the rack. If ½-inch plywood is used, it is thick enough to take screws edgewise if suitable holes are drilled first.

Mark out the back with the positions of the other parts on it. Drill for the screws that will be driven through from the rear. Countersink them so there will be no metal projecting against the wall.

The key parts are the four shaped dividers. Draw one full-size (Fig. 13-11). Each shape is a quarter circle. The shelves for paper and envelopes are too thin to take screws. Although dado grooves

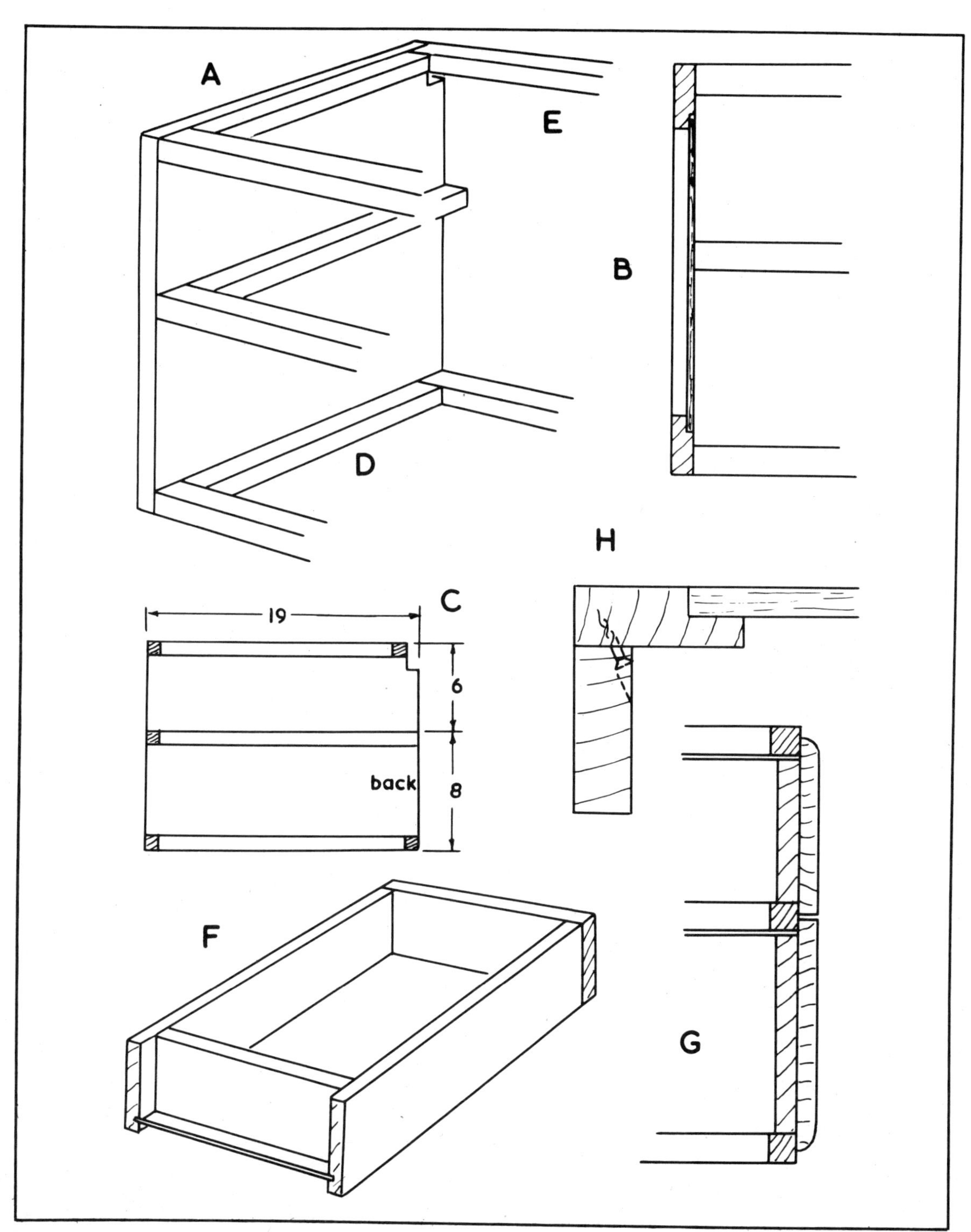

Fig. 13-8. Details of the block of drawers under the desk top.

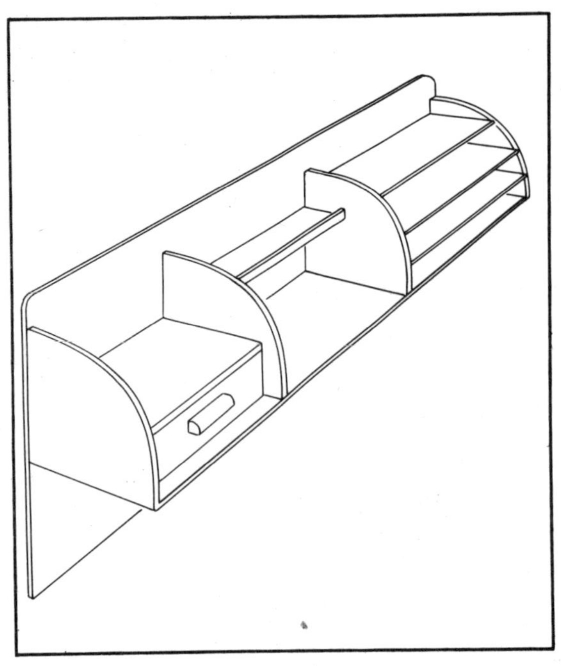

Fig. 13-9. A wall-mounted behind-desk rack.

may be cut for them, it is simpler to make V-shaped grooves (Fig. 13-12A). Round the front edges of the shelves.

At the other side the shelf above the drawer can fit into grooves. If it is carefully squared, its ends may be screwed directly through the dividers.

Assemble the bottom to the back. Put the end dividers in place and screw them. Put in the other two dividers with their shelves between them. Don't make the pen shelf until you can measure where it is to go. Make it with a front ledge (Fig. 13-12B) or a strip on top. A gap at the center aids cleaning and picking up pens (Fig. 13-12C). Be careful when assembling the drawer compartment that it is parallel, so the drawer will slide properly.

The drawer can be made in any of the usual ways, but a simpler construction is satisfactory. If you make it as a box, put strips under the sides as runners (Fig. 13-12D). Inside there can be thin plywood divisions fitted into V grooves, like the paper shelves (Fig. 13-12E). If you fit them without

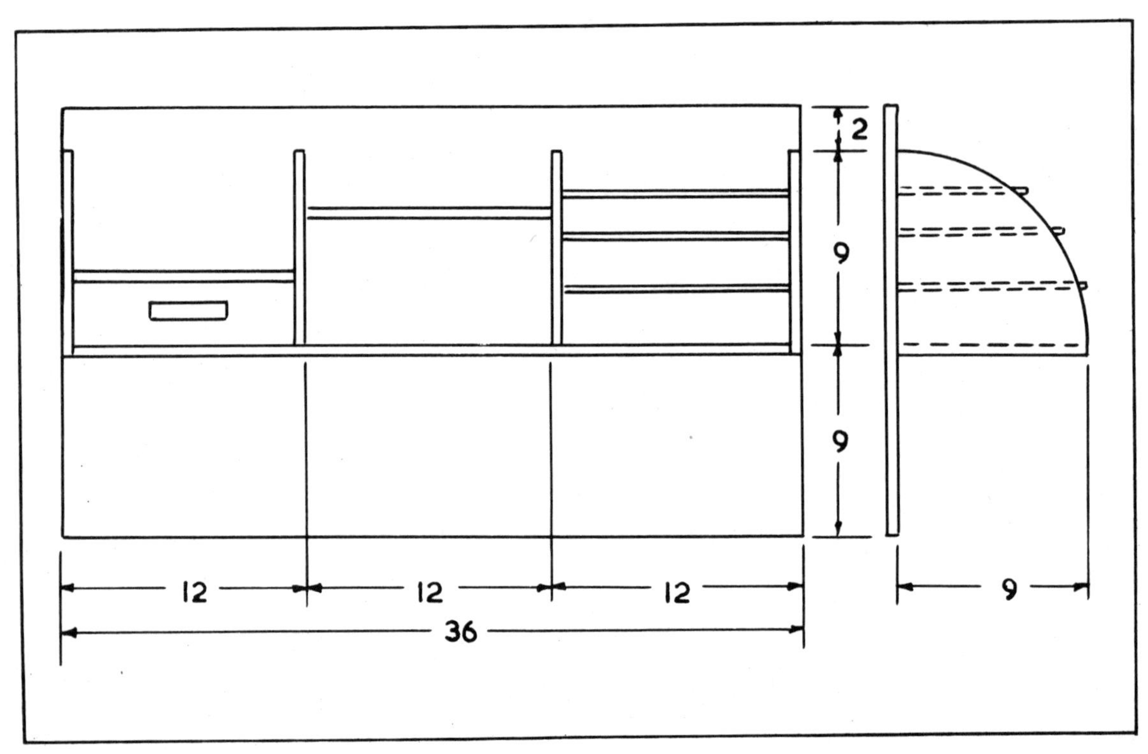

Fig. 13-10. Sizes for the behind-desk rack.

Table 13-3. Materials List for Behind-Desk Rack.

1 back	20	×	36	×	½ plywood
1 bottom	9	×	36	×	½ plywood
4 shapes	9	×	9	×	½ plywood
1 book base	9	×	12	×	½ plywood
1 paper shelf	8¾	×	12	×	¼ plywood
1 paper shelf	7½	×	12	×	¼ plywood
1 paper shelf	5½	×	12	×	¼ plywood
1 center shelf	4	×	12	×	½ plywood
2 drawer sides	3	×	8	×	½
1 drawer front	3	×	12	×	½
1 drawer back	3	×	12	×	½
1 drawer bottom	8	×	12	×	¼ plywood

glue, you can withdraw them easily if you want to rearrange the drawers' contents.

READING DESK

If you have a large dictionary or encyclopedia that you take down from a shelf for occasional reference, it may be heavy to hold. There may be nowhere to conveniently rest it. This is particularly so in some libraries. A wall-mounted desk that can be swung into position takes up little room and can be arranged for comfortable use when standing or sitting (Fig. 13-13).

The size can be made to suit particular books. If space is available, a large desk is more useful than a small one. The suggested sizes should hold most books (Fig. 13-14 and Table 13-4).

The desk looks best if made in solid wood finished to match nearby furniture. If possible, make the front from wood that has been cut radially from the log, so there is no risk of warping. The traditional way to secure the front is to put cleats across the ends with tongue and groove joints (Fig. 13-15A). A simpler way is to screw a batten underneath near each end (Fig. 13-15B), far enough out to be clear of the swinging bracket.

Make a full-size side view (Fig. 13-15C). The slope to allow depends on the height the desk is located in relation to the user. Put a book on a scrap piece of plywood in the position you want and try tilting it to get the most useful angle—30° is about right.

Make the front and attach a ledge to it (Fig. 13-15D). Round all the exposed edges and corners. Make the top two pieces and glue them together, with the one piece angled to match the front and take two hinges let into the edges (Fig. 13-15E). The lower part will have two or more screws into the wall.

Cut the bracket with its grain diagonal (Fig. 13-15F). The post comes slightly off-center so the bracket is about central when the front is held up. The post can be just screwed to the wall, but it is more accurately located with a mortise and tenon joint (Fig. 13-15G).

A long piece of piano hinge can be used between the bracket and post. If you use two ordinary hinges, arrange them near the top and bottom of the joint to resist any tendency of the bracket to twist on the post. The bracket will probably stay in its open position when turned, but you can put a small stop under the top if you find it necessary.

WALL TIDY

This arrangement of storage spaces can be useful on the wall over a desk for the many items of office equipment that accumulate (Figs. 13-16 and 13-17). It may be located near the telephone. The racks will take envelopes and postcards, jotting pads, and notebooks or address books. The drawers can hold small things like rubber bands and paper clips, while the drop-front compartment will hold larger

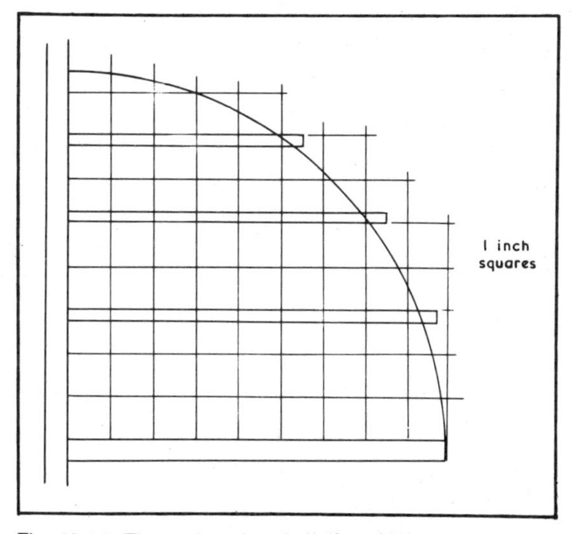

Fig. 13-11. The rack end and shelf positions.

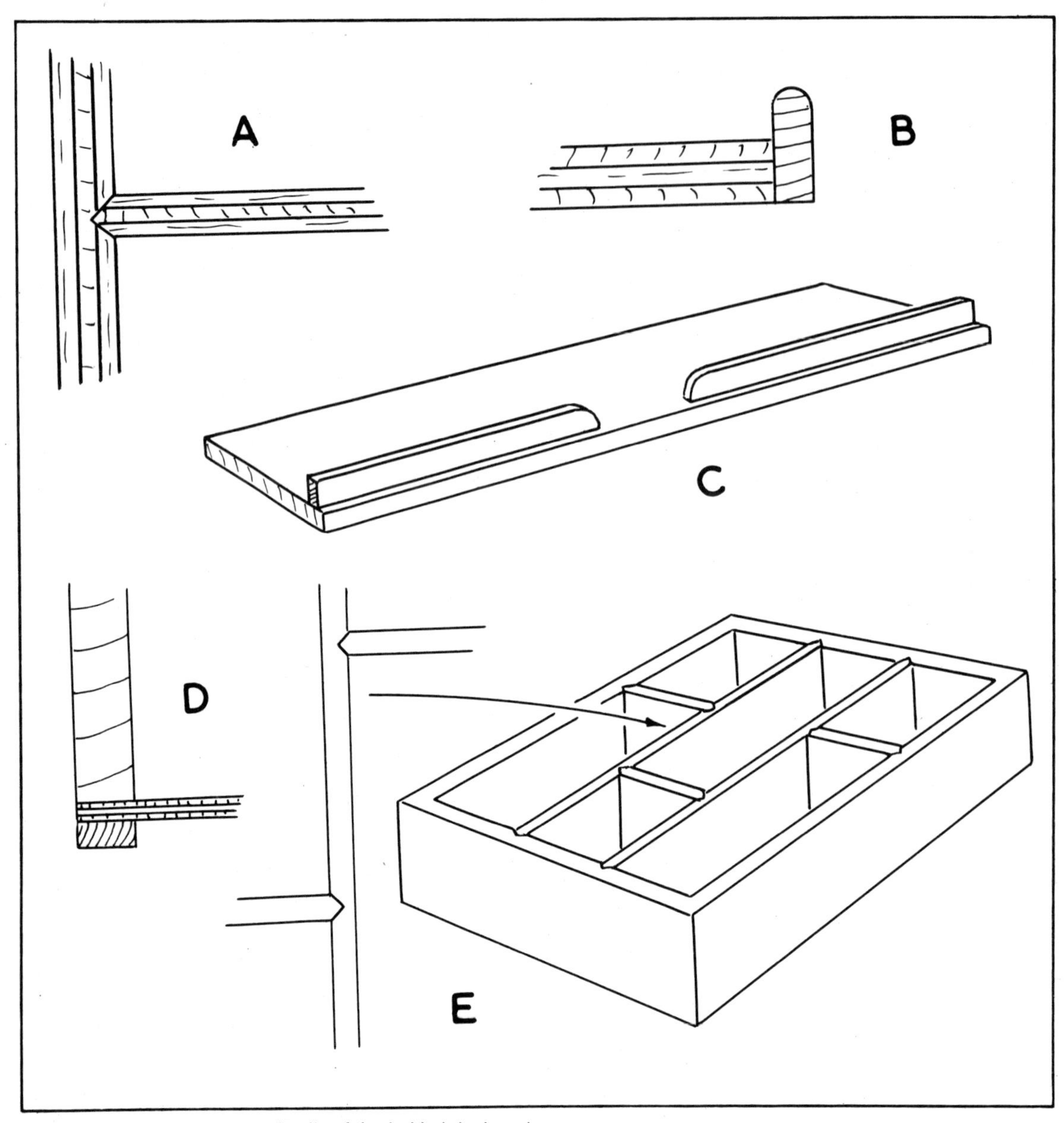

Fig. 13-12. Shelf and drawer details of the behind-desk rack.

items. The tidy can also be used above a craft bench for the many tools and small items that have to be stored.

The shaped ends and back give the tidy a Colonial appearance. Most parts are 4 inches wide and ½ inches thick and can be softwood, given a clear varnish or lacquer finish. If a hardwood will match existing furniture, that is equally suitable. See Table 13-5.

There are several ways of joining the parts. To follow through the simple Colonial theme, they can be nailed, with the heads set in and stopped (Fig. 13-18A). If you are careful with sizes and squareness, this can produce a satisfactory finish. The

Fig. 13-13. A reading desk that folds against the wall when out of use.

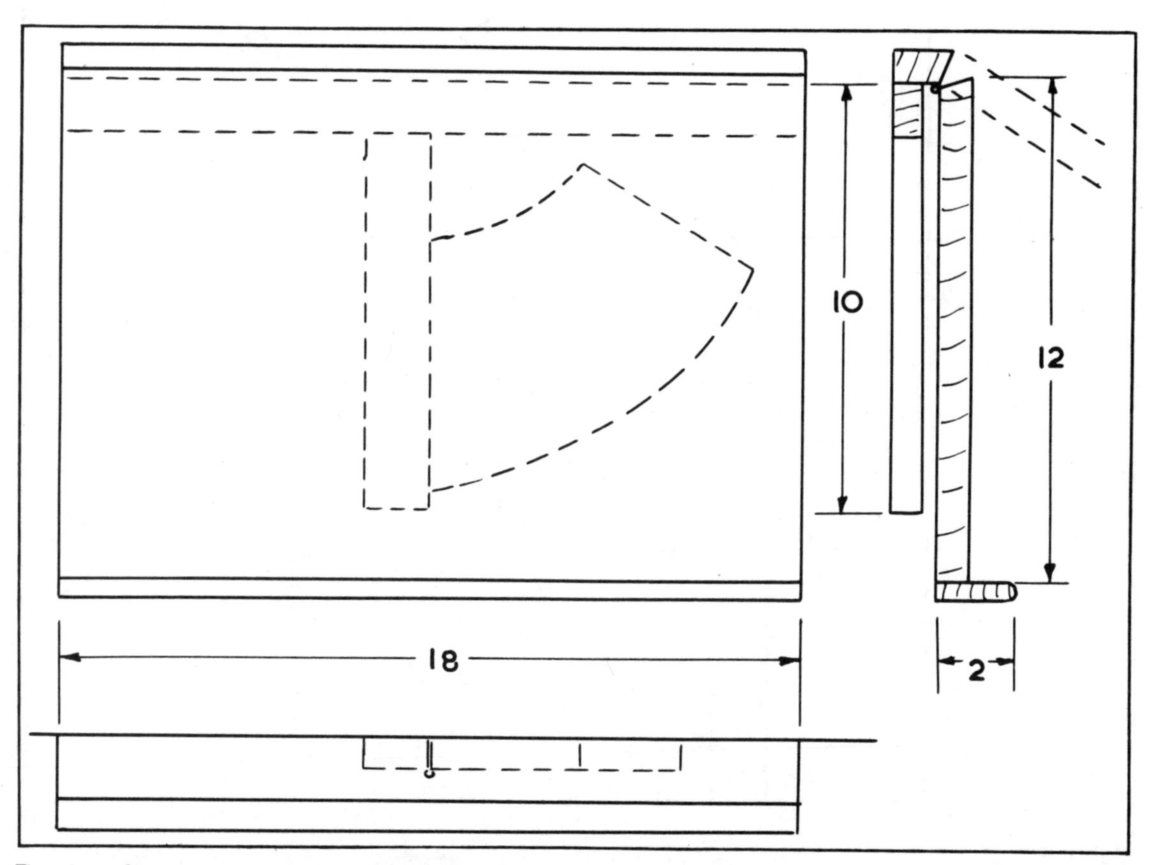

Fig. 13-14. Suggested sizes for the folding reading desk.

Table 13-4. Materials List for Reading Desk.

1 front	12	×	19	×	3/4
2 tops	1 1/2	×	19	×	3/4
1 ledge	2	×	19	×	1/2
1 post	1 1/2	×	10	×	3/4
1 bracket	27	×	38	×	3/4

wood is too thin for the use of dowels. It is better to use dado joints, which can go right through (Fig. 13-18B) or be stopped at the front (Fig. 13-18C). The joints are the same, so if you use a dado head, it will be at one setting. The back plywood or hardboard fits into rabbets in the sides (Fig. 13-18D).

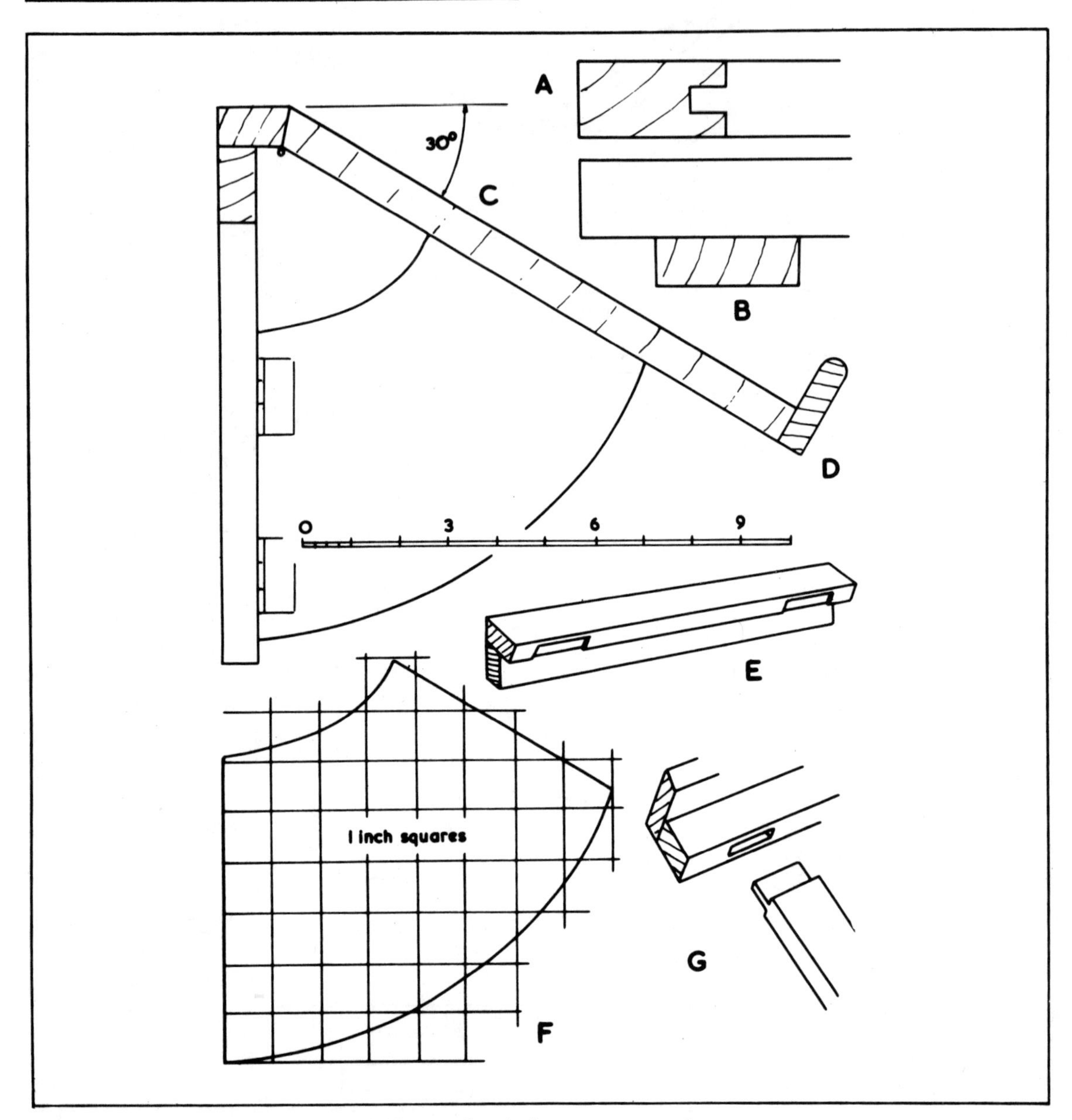

Fig. 13-15. The flap and bracket for the folding reading desk.

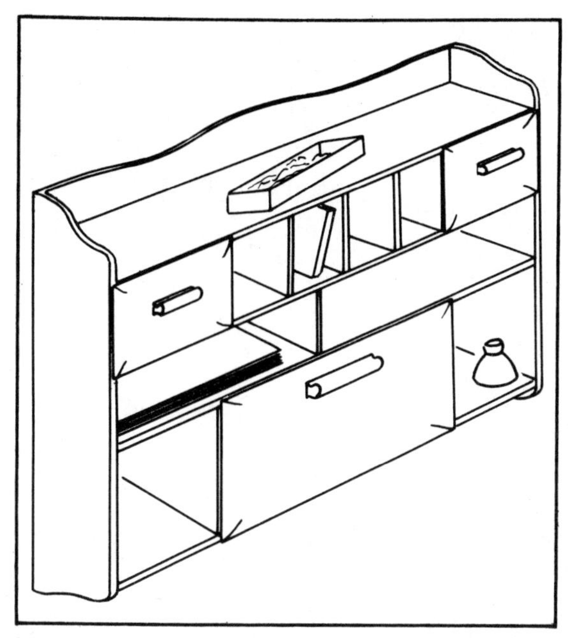

Fig. 13-16. A wall tidy with compartments for stowing many things.

Make the pair of sides first (Fig. 13-19A). Cut the joints before shaping the ends. Make the four shelves to identical lengths, but mark and cut the dadoes as required (Fig. 13-19B). Parts that should match must be exactly the same, as any lack of squareness will be very obvious. The sides can be used as guides to the lengths of dividers—the spaces plus depths of grooves.

Join the top two shelves with their five dividers and the bottom two shelves with their two

Table 13-5. Materials List for Wall Tidy.

2 sides	4¼	×	18	×	½	
4 shelves	4	×	22	×	½	
5 dividers	4	×	5	×	½	
1 divider	4	×	4	×	½	
2 dividers	4	×	7	×	½	
1 back	18	×	22	×	¼	plywood
1 door	7	×	14	×	½	
2 drawer fronts	5	×	6	×	½	
6 drawer parts	4	×	5	×	½	
2 drawer bottoms	4	×	5	×	¼	plywood

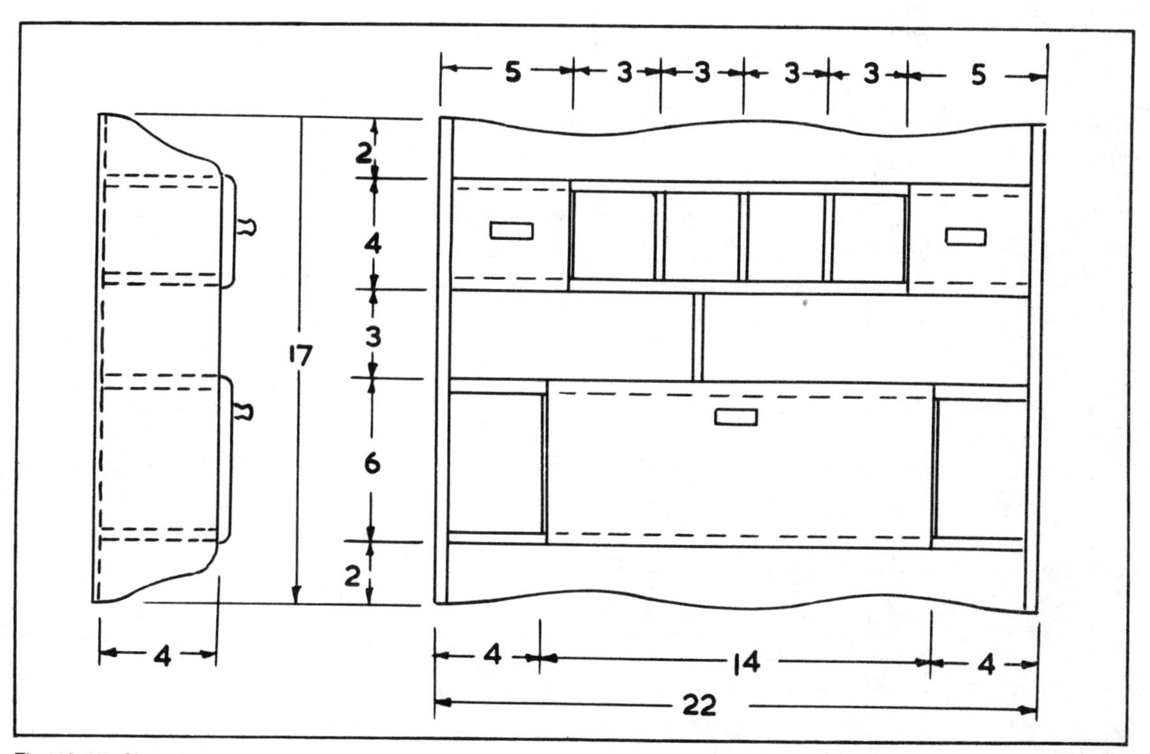

Fig. 13-17. Sizes for the wall tidy.

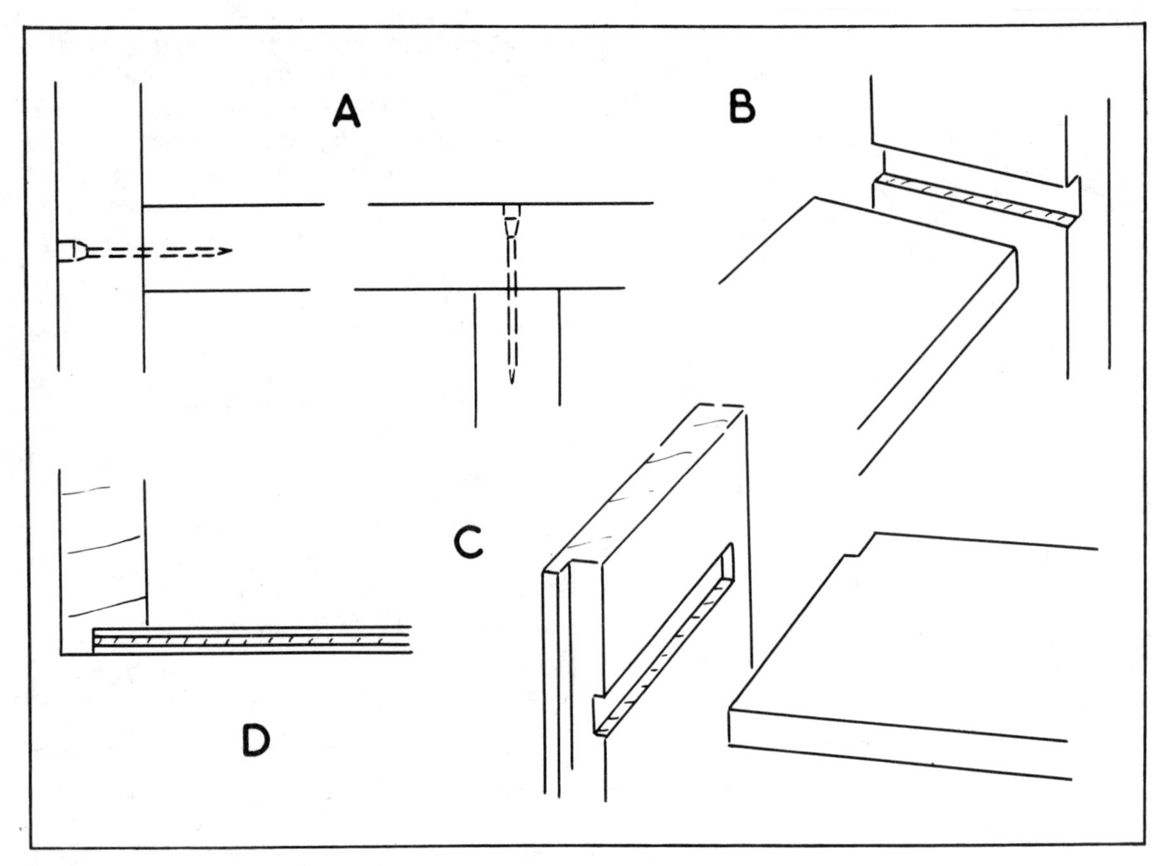

Fig. 13-18. Joints used in the wall tidy.

dividers. Pull the joints close with clamps. When the glue has set, put in the middle divider and clamp on the sides. While still in the clamps, you can cut and fit the plywood back, so all glue can be set before the clamps are released.

Make the door over the lower compartment so its bottom edge is level, but the other edges go halfway over the other parts (Fig. 13-20A). Let two 2-inch hinges into the shelf. The door may be allowed to drop vertically. If it will be more useful stopped horizontally when open, put a cord or light chain between screw eyes at one side (Fig. 13-20B). Use a magnetic or spring catch to keep the door closed.

The two drawers can be made in the usual way, with the bottom grooved in and dovetail joints, but in this small size a simpler construction may be acceptable. The sides and back are shown nailed; then the bottom is nailed on (Fig. 13-20C). The front is level at the bottom, but it goes halfway over the other parts, with the drawer sides into grooves (Fig. 13-20D).

Round the outer edges of the drawers and door. Put matching handles on these parts. They can be bought metal ones, or you can make a piece of wood to a suitable section (Fig. 13-20E), then cut off lengths that can be screwed from the back. If holes for screws to the wall are drilled through the plywood at the backs of the drawer compartments, they will be hidden in use.

SIMPLE BAR

This bar is suitable for a den or playroom, where it can be located with its end attached to one wall and far enough from a corner for someone to stand behind it to serve. It is at a height suitable for standing beside or sitting on a high stool. The front is enclosed, with a plinth set back to give foot room, while the top projects with a rounded end (Fig. 13-21). The top may be covered with Formica laminated plastic or other drink-resistant material. The plywood front can be any of the decorated plywoods, with a simulated board pattern.

At the sizes shown (Fig. 13-22) the bar is large enough to store drinks and has a large enough top to be useful. It does not occupy much floor space. See Table 13-6.

Set out an end view full-size (Fig. 13-23A) on the floor or on the plywood that will form an end. Choose plywood with a good face for the outer end, but the other end will be hidden and can be made of less attractive plywood. Mark out and cut the pair of ends, with the outlines of other parts penciled on.

Plane the sections of the strips that come

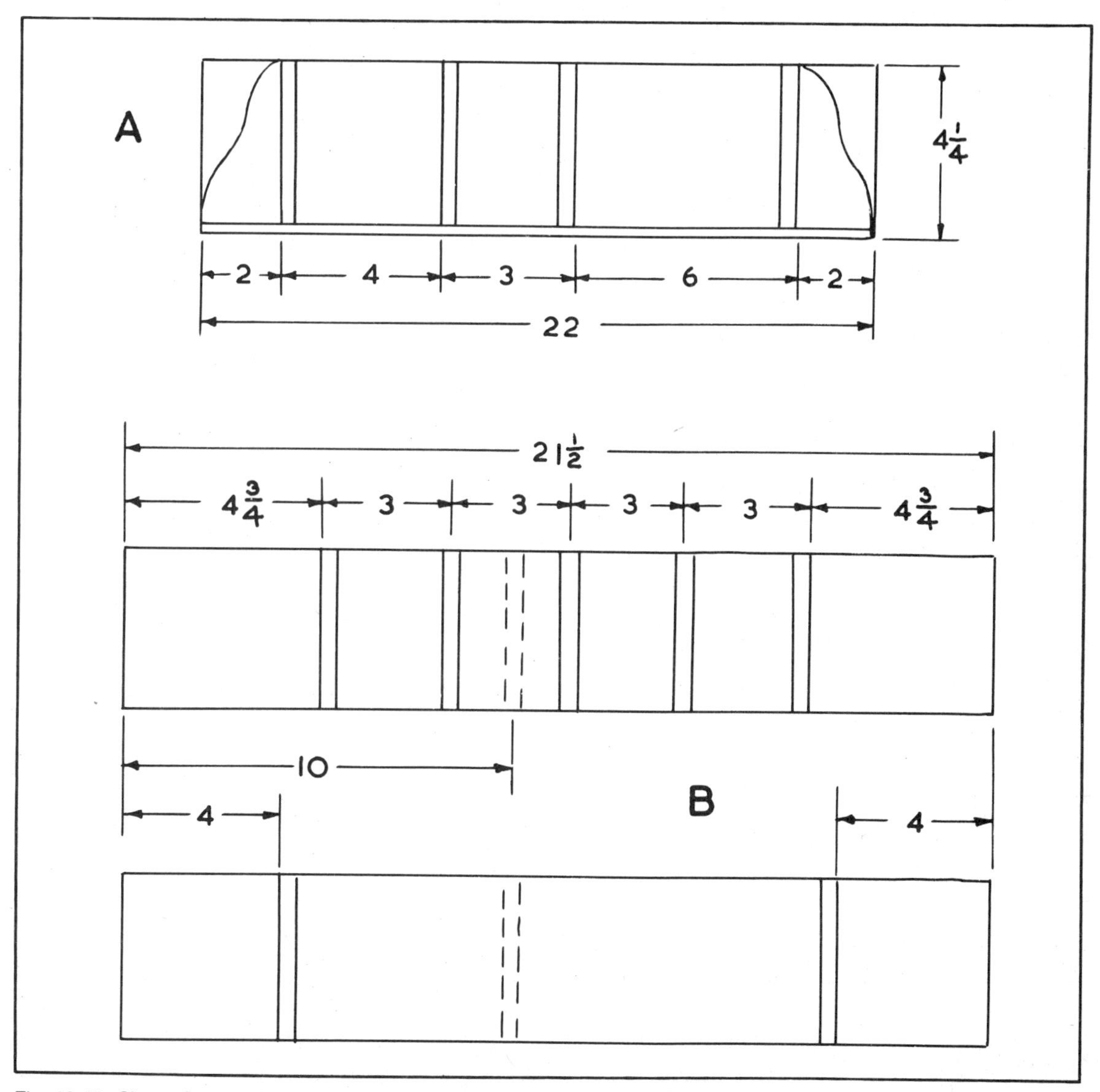

Fig. 13-19. Sizes of parts of the wall tidy.

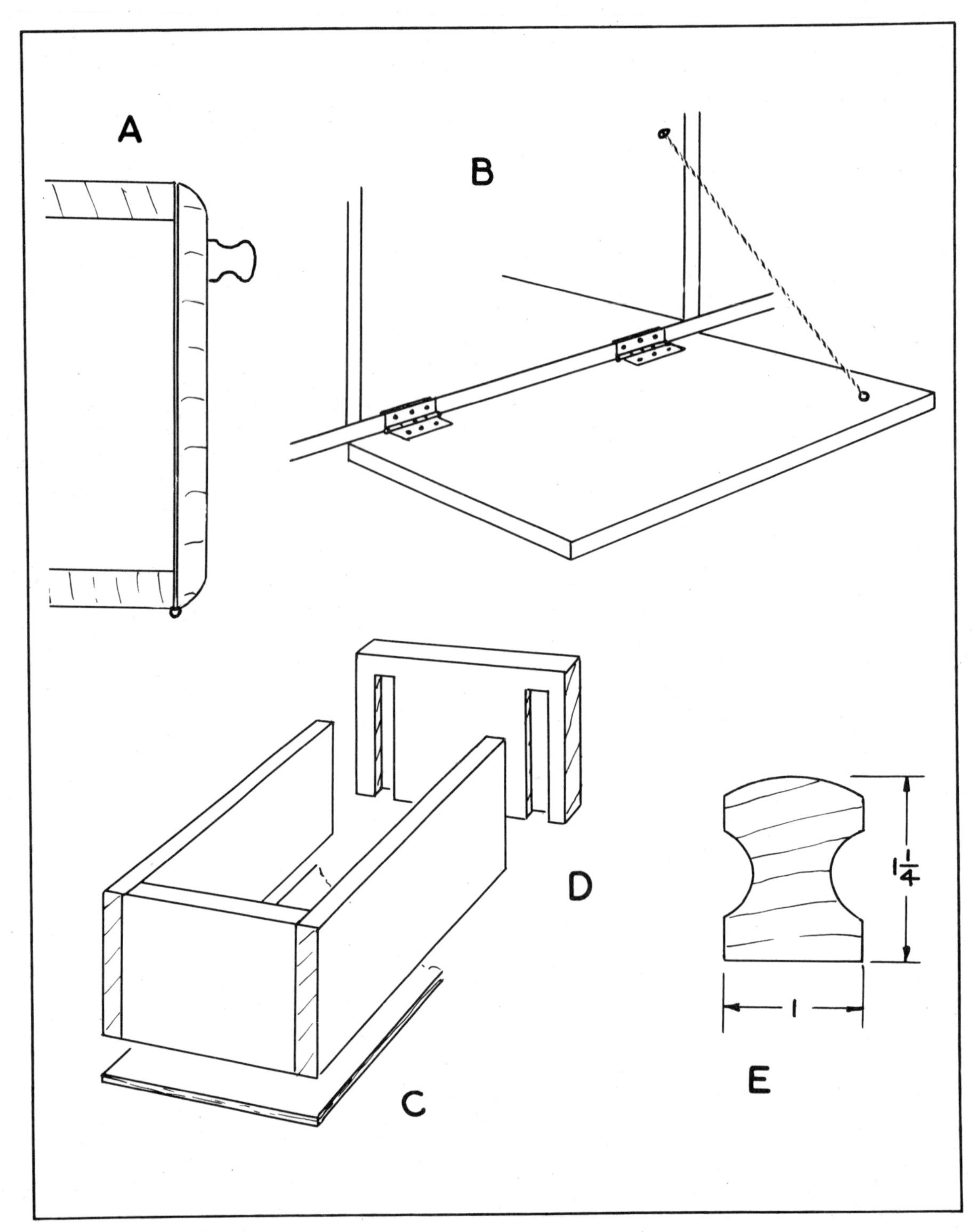

Fig. 13-20. Flap and drawer details for the wall tidy.

Fig. 13-21. A simple bar extending from the wall.

against the front to its angle. The other strips are square. Cut the bottom plywood and frame it on top (Fig. 13-23B). The 2-inch strip prevents things from falling out. Round its top edge. Use the bottom as a guide to the lengths of other parts, but get the widths of shelves from your drawing or a cut end. Frame the shelves on their undersides (Fig. 13-23C). You can use glue and nails for all these parts, and there is no need to cut joints between the meeting strips.

Prepare the strips that will come under the top (Fig. 13-23D). When you assemble, nail or screw the ends of the bottom and shelves to the ends. At the top, fasten the short pieces to the ends and screw the ends of the lengthwise parts to them. Make sure the assembly stands level without twist, then nail or screw the front panel to it. Nails into the shelves and around the edges should make a very rigid assembly.

The plinth can be of very simple construction. At the wall it is level, but elsewhere it is set in about ¾ inch. The long pieces can overlap the short ones at the wall (Fig. 13-23E), but at the other corners the plinth looks better mitered and strengthened with pieces inside (Fig. 13-23F). Attach it with screws down through the bottom.

The top can be glued strips of solid wood or thick plywood, but the most suitable material is particle board to which Formica laminated plastic can be glued. There will be no trouble with expansion and contraction. Curve the extending part of the top, which can be level with the open side of the bar and project at the other side. An aluminum or plastic edging makes a good finish to the top.

Screw upward through the 1-inch strips into the top (Fig. 13-23G). At the 2-inch deep strip drive screws diagonally upward from inside (Fig. 13-23H). Attach the end to the wall with screws. There can be protection for the wall with a narrow strip above the top, or you can put a higher panel there on which mugs or decorations can be hung.

COUNTER

This is a working surface projecting from a wall. It can be a hobby bench or a place to prepare food. It can divide a room, or it may be a place for two people to work from opposite sides. As shown (Fig. 13-24), there are two drawers that go right through and can be opened from either side. The lower part has doors on both sides. The drawers can be divided internally to suit your needs, and there can be shelves and other divisions below. Attachment to the wall should provide plenty of rigidity, but internal divisions will contribute to stiffness.

Construction can be in three parts, with the top assembly and its drawers made as a unit. The carcass is made and attached to it. This is finally

Table 13-6. Materials List for Simple Bar.

1 top	18	×	61	×	¾	
2 ends	17	×	40	×	½	plywood
1 shelf	18	×	51	×	½	plywood
1 shelf	17	×	51	×	½	plywood
1 bottom	16	×	51	×	½	plywood
8 end rails	1	×	18	×	1	
6 long rails	1	×	51	×	1	
2 long rails	2	×	51	×	1	
2 plinths	3	×	14	×	¾	
2 plinths	3	×	51	×	¾	
1 front	39	×	52	×	½	plywood

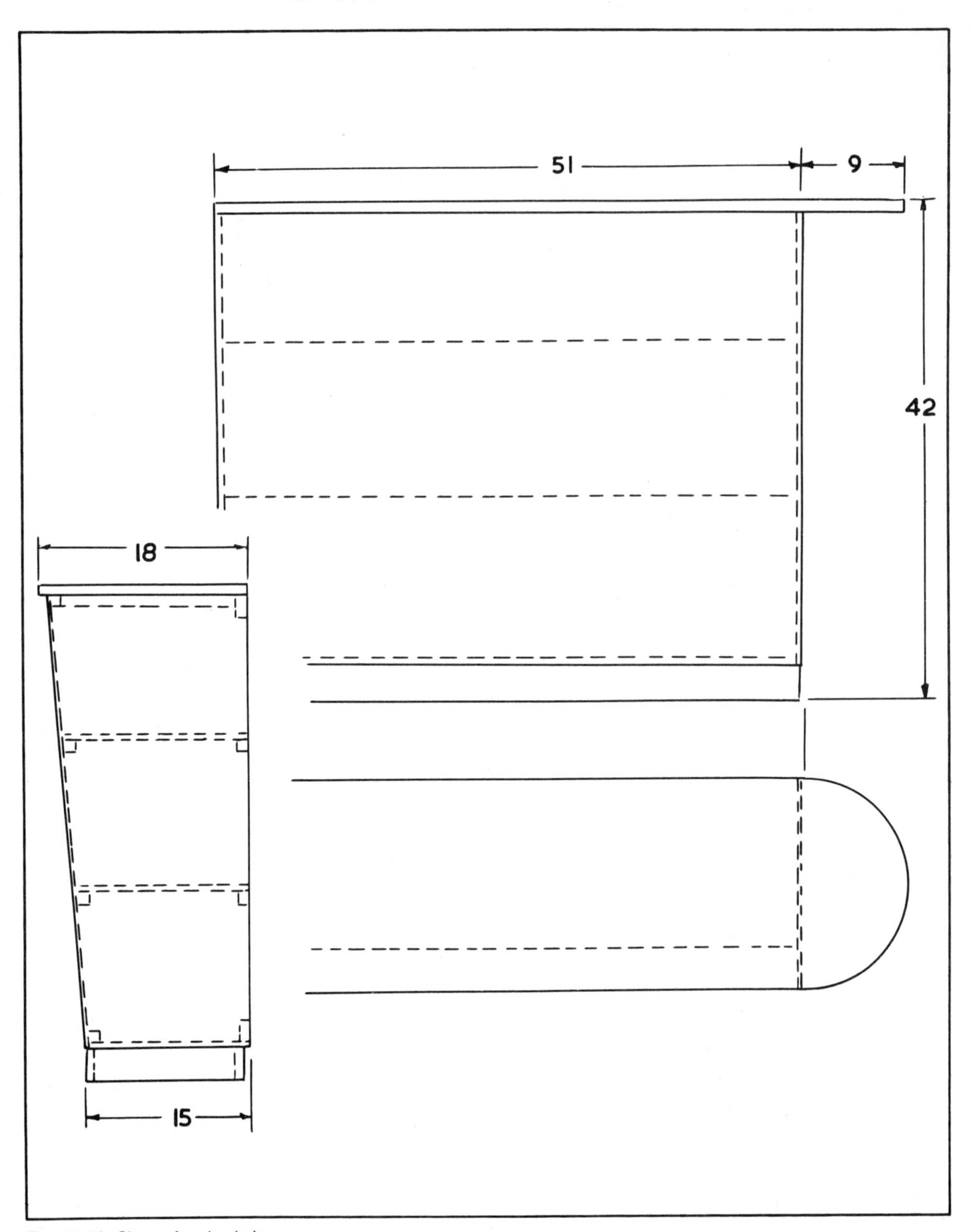

Fig. 13-22. Sizes of a simple bar.

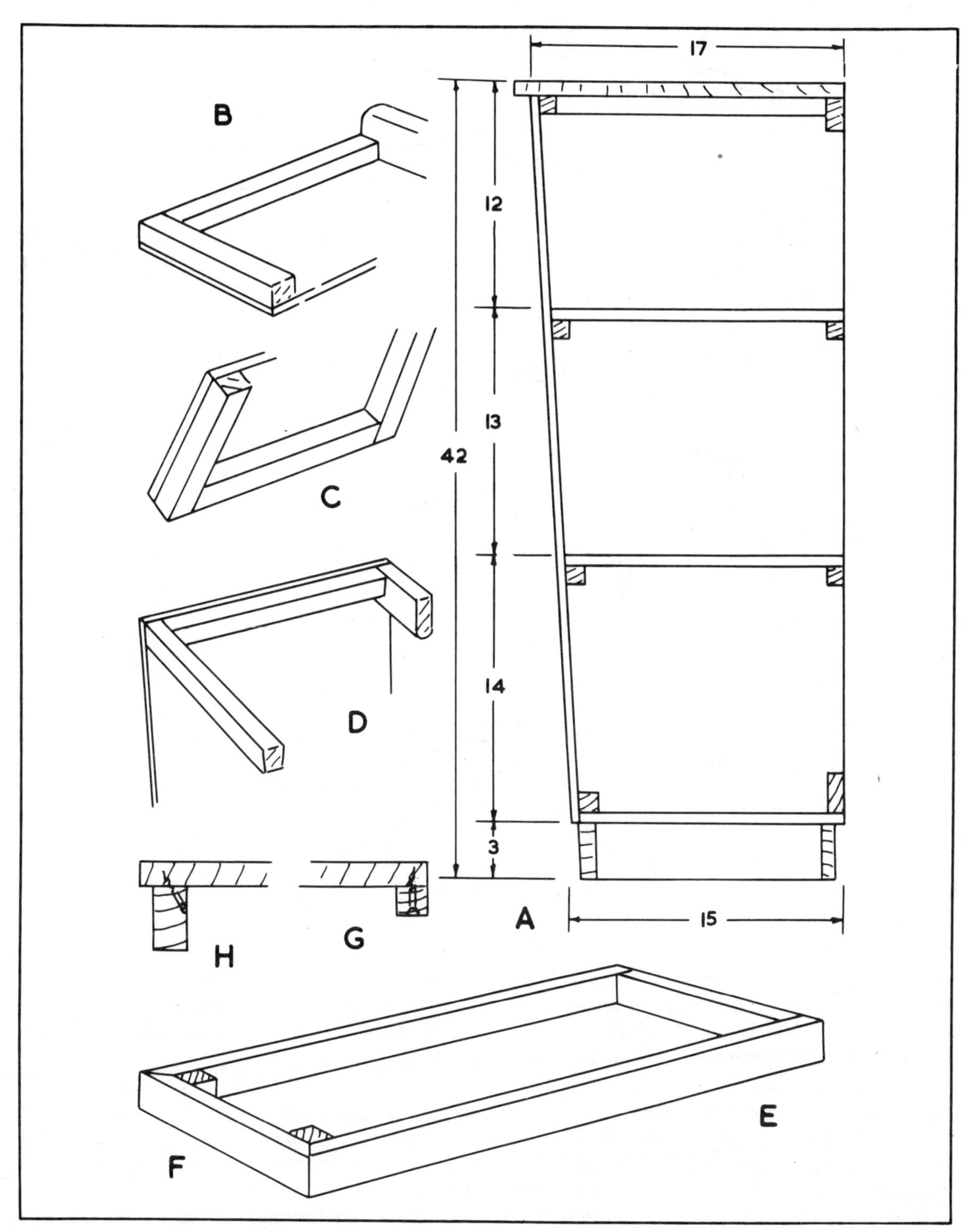

Fig. 13-23. The method of building up the bar.

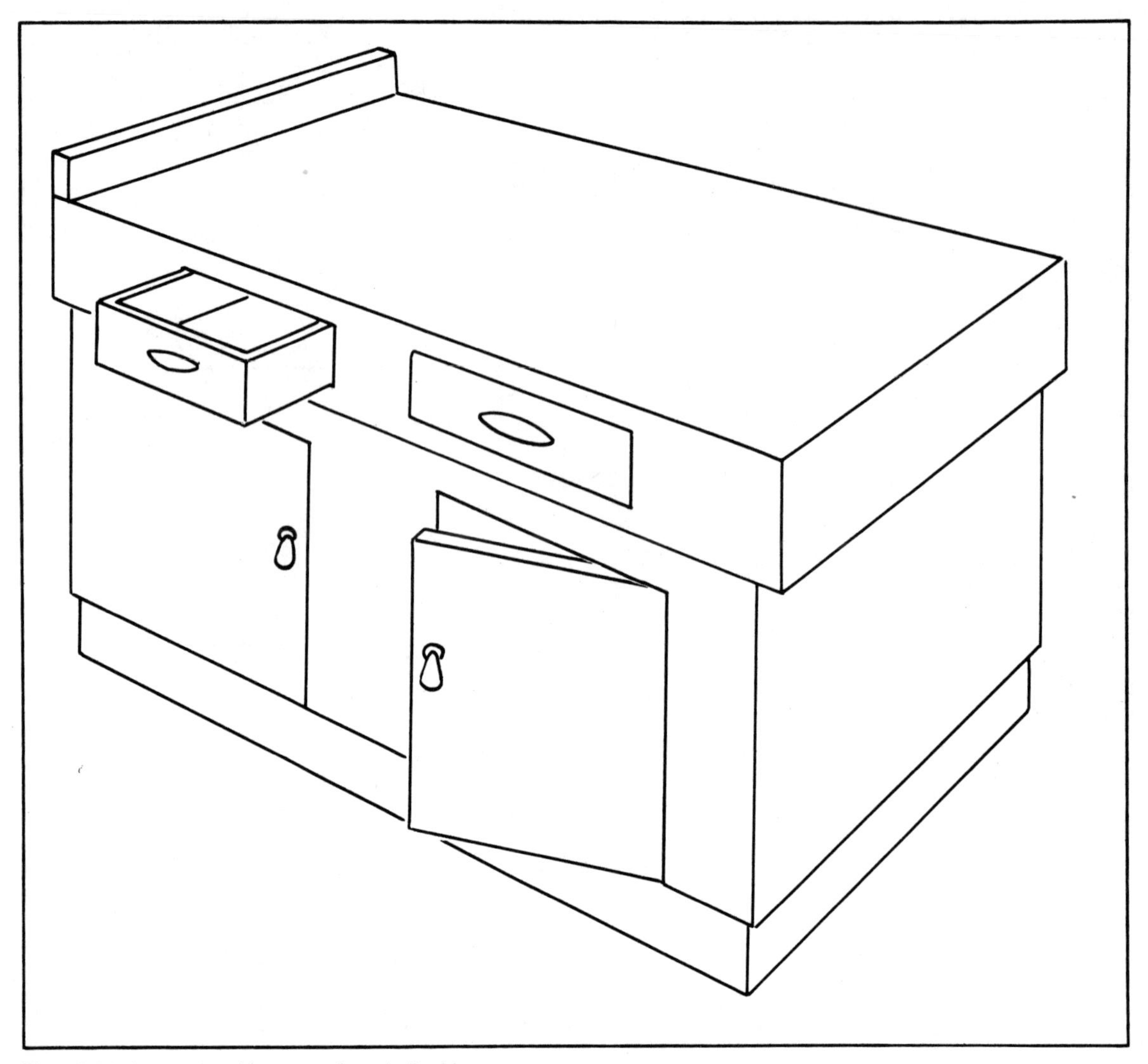

Fig. 13-24. A counter with access from both sides.

mounted on a plinth. One end is level against the wall, but each part overhangs the one below at the other end (Fig. 13-25 and Table 13-7).

If the counter is to be used for food, the top part may be covered with Formica laminated plastic over plywood or particle board with similar material around the sides. The lower part may then be made of solid wood and plywood finished with paint. If the top is to be used for hammering and cutting on while working at a hobby, it may be better made of thick plywood or strips of solid wood glued together. The lower part is intended to be framed and faced with plywood or hardboard.

Start by making the top section. The surface piece goes over a built-up box with places for the drawers (Fig. 13-26A). Lay out the sides (Fig. 13-26B). You can alter the drawer sizes. They need not both be the same, but keep the width of a front less than the distance across the top of the counter, or the drawer may not slide easily.

Cut out the openings for the drawers and see that the opposite sides match as a pair. At the ends you can have a simple lap or a miter, with a block inside (Fig. 13-26C) at the exposed end. Put flat strips inside at the bottom (Fig. 13-26D) for attaching to the carcass (Fig. 13-26E).

Make the drawer guides to fit between the sides and notch over the flat bottom pieces (Fig. 13-26F). Put runners and kickers to line up with the tops and bottoms of the openings. There can be blocks on the other sides for screwing to the sides.

Join all the parts of the top section and be careful of squareness, particularly through the drawer spaces. Otherwise, there will be difficulty in making the drawers a neat fit. Do not add the surface piece yet. It is better to leave the assembly

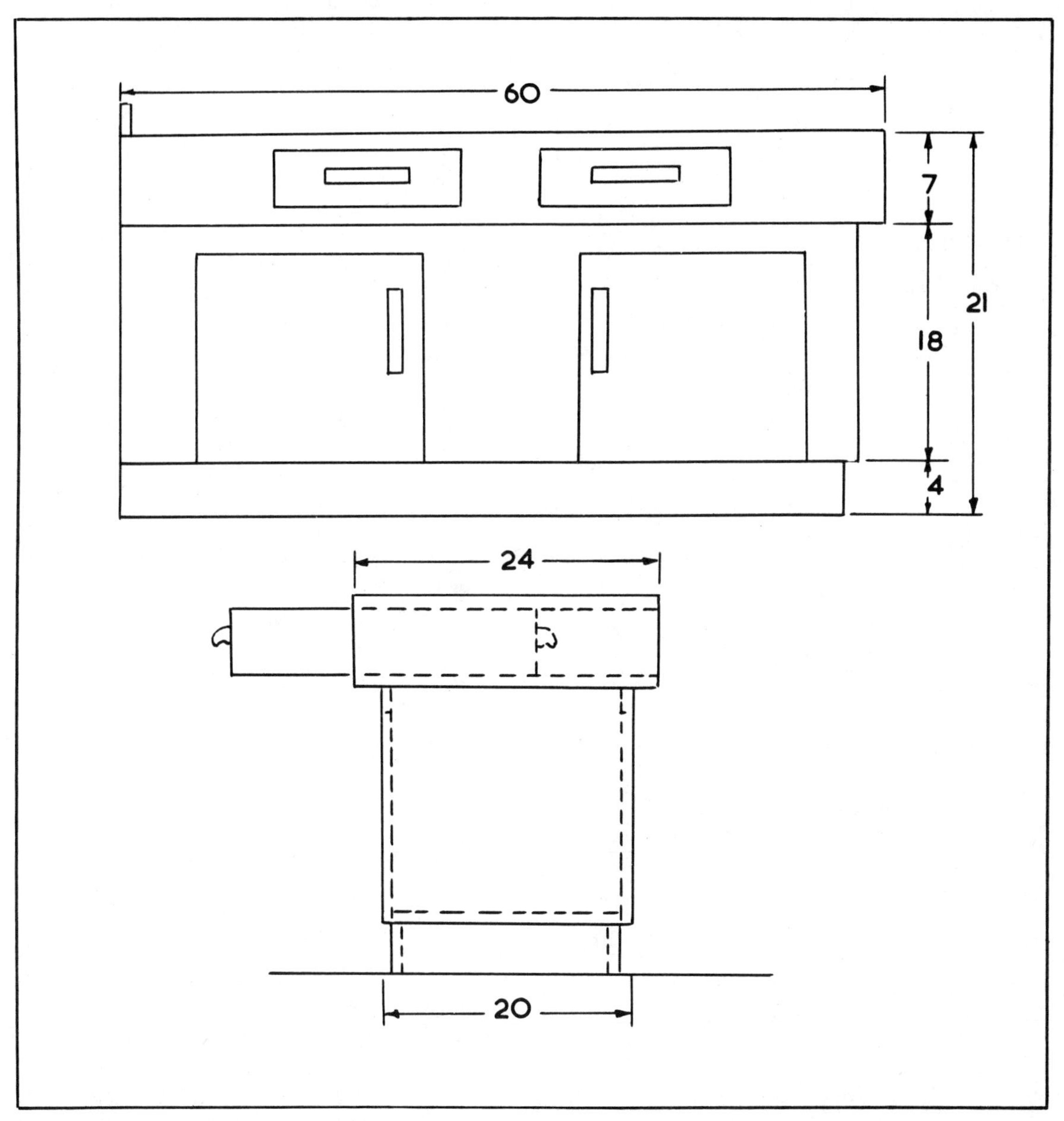

Fig. 13-25. Suggested sizes for a counter.

Table 13-7. Materials List for Counter.

Part	Size
Top section	
1 top	24 × 60 × ¾
2 sides	6¼ × 60 × ¾
2 ends	6¼ × 24 × ¾
2 bottoms	3 × 60 × ¾
2 bottoms	3 × 24 × ¾
4 drawer guides	6¼ × 24 × ¾
8 drawer guides	¾ × 24 × ¾
4 drawer fronts	4¾ × 15 × ¾
4 drawer sides	4¾ × 24 × ⅝
2 drawer bottoms	14 × 24 × ¼ plywood
1 wall end	3 × 24 × ¾
Carcass	
2 ends	18 × 20 × ½ plywood
4 end frames	2 × 20 × 1
4 end frames	2 × 18 × 1
1 bottom	20 × 58 × ½ plywood
2 bottom frames	2 × 58 × 1
2 bottom frames	2 × 20 × 1
2 top strips	2 × 58 × 1
4 door strips	2 × 19 × 1
2 side panels	18 × 58 × ⅛ or ¼ plywood or hardboard
8 door panels	18 × 18 × ⅛ or ¼ plywood or hardboard
16 door frames	1½ × 19 × ¾
Plinth	
2 sides	4 × 58 × ¾
2 ends	4 × 19 × ¾

open until after the drawers have been fitted.

As the drawers have to move both ways, they cannot be made in the usual way. You have to treat them as having two fronts. Prepare the parts with grooves for the bottom plywood. Make the fronts and the sides with notched or dovetailed joints (Fig. 13-26G). Try a dry assembly without a bottom. If necessary, plane off parts until a drawer slides easily and closes with both fronts level. Take the drawer apart and fit the bottom plywood as you glue the joints.

You must do something to hold a drawer closed, yet allow it to be pulled out either way. One or more spring ball catches in each front can be used (Fig. 13-26H). If the drawers are to move both ways, you cannot provide stops to prevent them from being pulled fully out, except at the middle, and that will only allow opening halfway.

The carcass ends can be made of plywood framed with solid wood inside (Fig. 13-27A). Notch for the lengthwise pieces that will come under the top.

The carcass bottom can be a single thick piece of plywood or thinner plywood framed in the same way as the ends. Keep the bottom narrow by the thickness the overlapping doors will be (Fig. 13-27B). The bottom can be screwed from below into the ends during assembly.

Make the top strips. A panel comes between the doors. The surfaces are faced with plywood or hardboard, so the panel has to be built with the facing supported by strips notched at the top and bottom (Fig. 13-27C).

There are several ways of making the doors. Pieces of ¾-inch plywood or particle board can be used without framing. Each door can be framed from solid wood with thin panels in grooves. Don't frame thinner plywood with solid wood on the inside only, as changes in the wood may cause warping. If thinner plywood or hardwood is used, it is better to have panels on both sides of the solid wood (Fig. 13-27D). The doors fit inside the counter sides at their tops and edges, but the lower edges overlap the carcass bottom. The top corners of the door framing should be mitered for neatness. As the bottom will not show, the sides can carry through. Hinge the doors in the usual way and fit handles and catches.

The plinth is a simple box shape (Fig. 13-28). Set it back under the sides and exposed end of the carcass, with the outer corners mitered and blocks inside in the same way as the corners of the top section (Fig. 13-26C). Screw down through the bottom into the plinth.

When the counter is attached to the wall, put a matching strip across, so that things used on the surface do not knock and damage the wall.

CORNER BAR

The usual design that comes to mind when a bar is mentioned is a form of counter where a person at one side serves drinks to people on the other side. Any storage or washing of glasses is done elsewhere. If the bar is to serve the needs of only two or three people, it may be better to put the bar against a wall, where storage can be on shelves

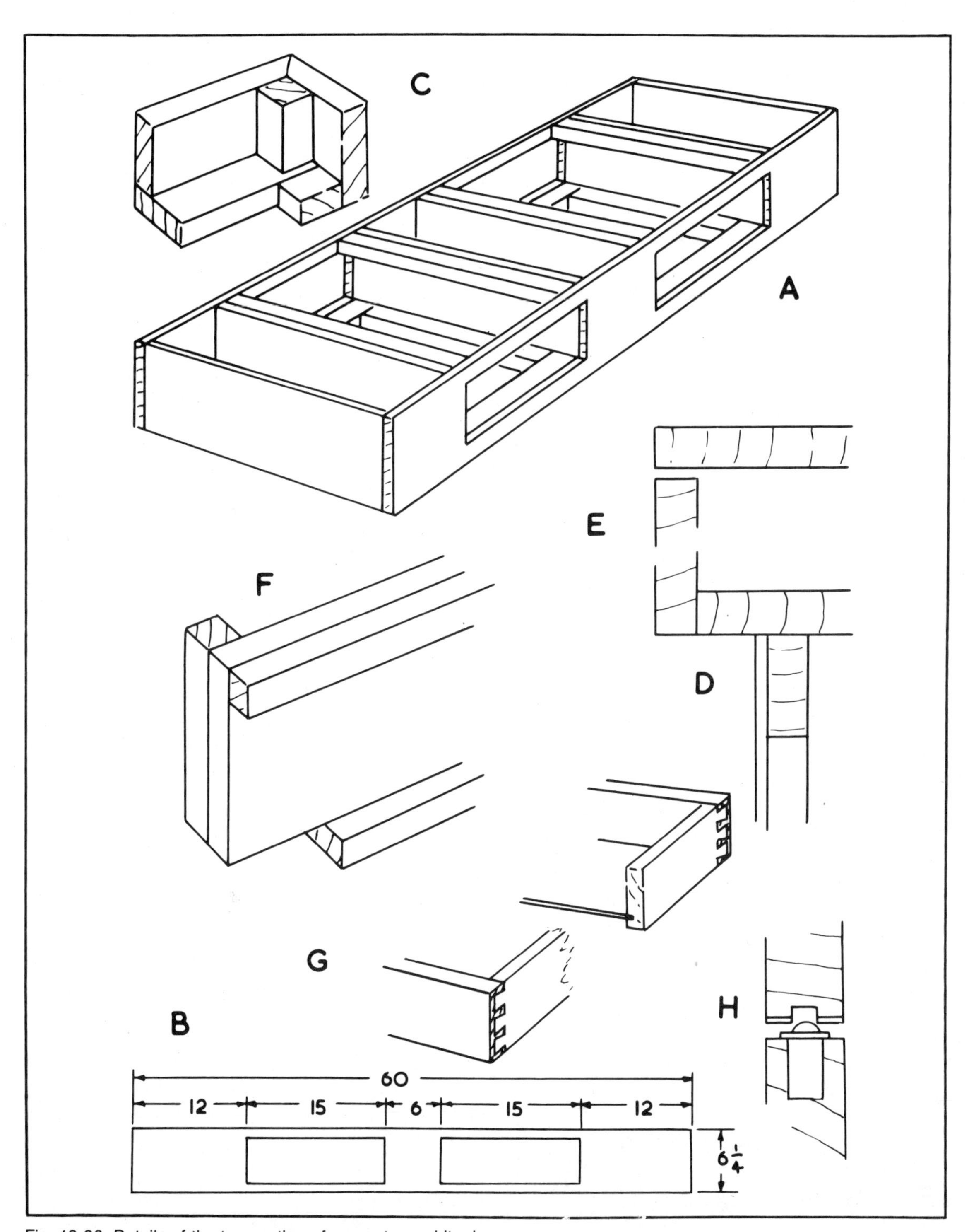

Fig. 13-26. Details of the top section of a counter and its drawers.

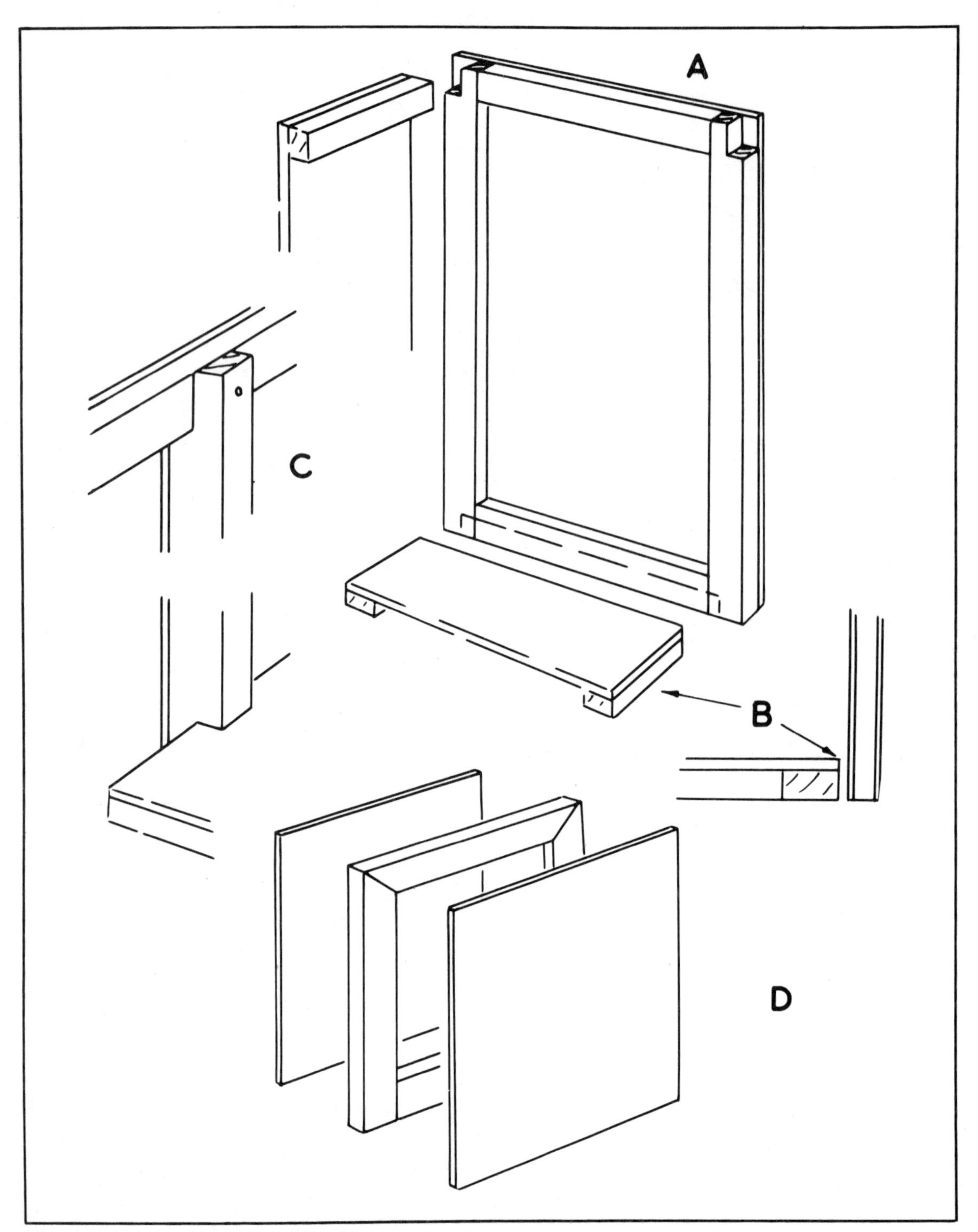

Fig. 13-27. Framing the bottom section of a counter and its doors.

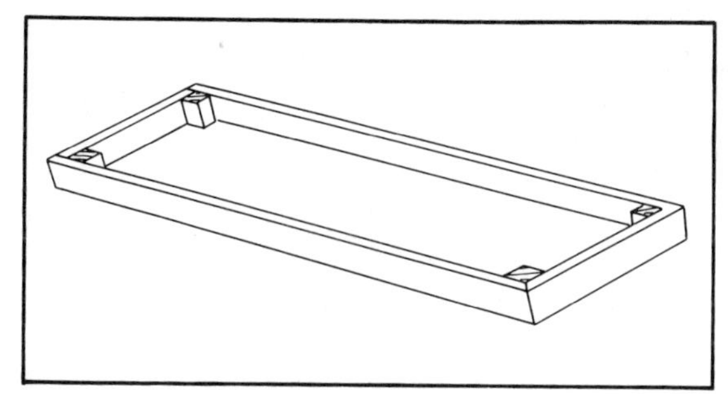

Fig. 13-28. The plinth to go under the bottom section of a counter.

above and in cupboards beneath. The bar described here (Fig. 13-29) is intended to be fairly self-contained. There is a sink with a faucet and space for a refrigerator in half of the cupboard. Glasses can go on shelves on the wall above the bar, then there is an extension to the side suitable for two persons to sit on high stools.

Some details will depend on the possibility of plumbing and electrical connections. The sink can be plastic or stainless steel and of the type intended for recreation vehicles. One or two faucets can also be of the recreation vehicle type. If you are unable to connect with home plumbing, it may still be possible to use portable containers and an electric or hand pump. You can stow plastic 5-gallon containers for fresh and waste water in the cupboard, with plastic pipes into them, from the sink and to a pump serving the faucet. The refrigerator can be any small type, such as intended for a recreation vehicle. If it does not have a built-in light, you can mount one inside the cupboard. Check your sink, refrigerator, and other equipment in relation to the

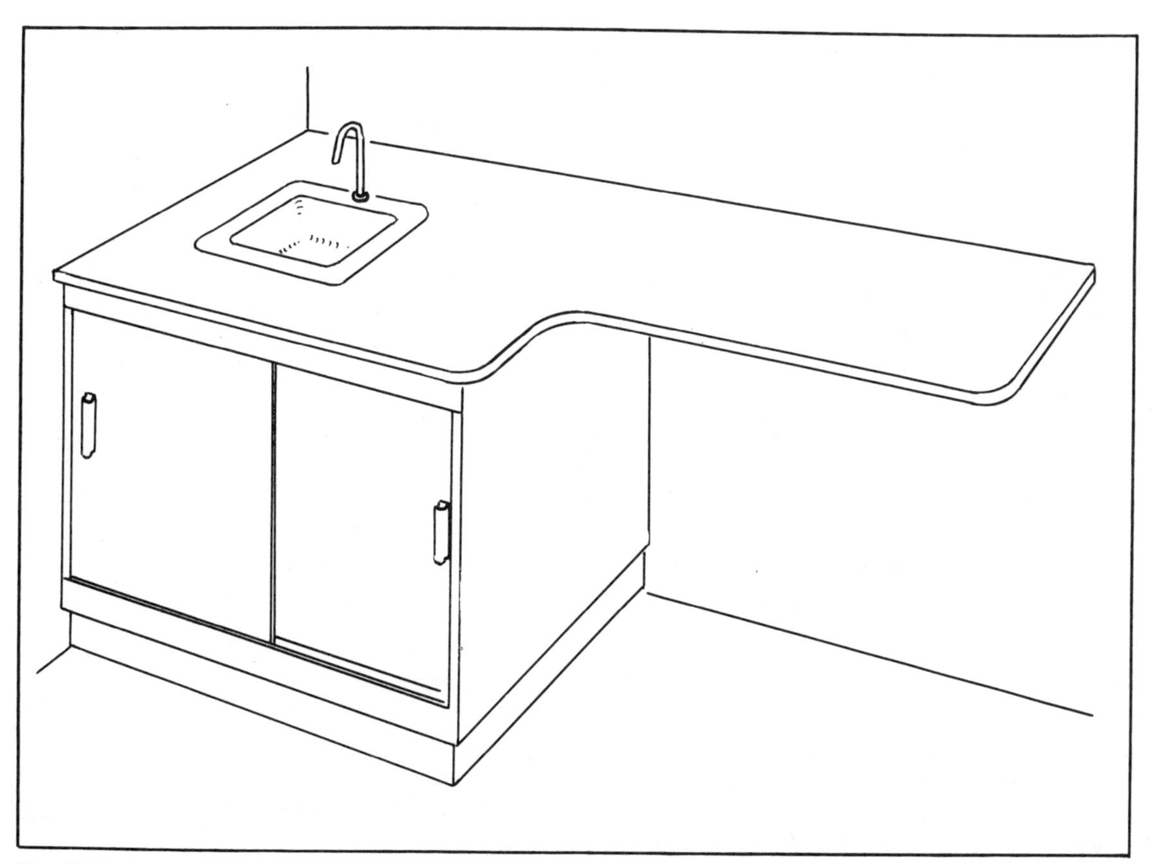

Fig. 13-29. A corner bar uses the walls and has built-in facilities.

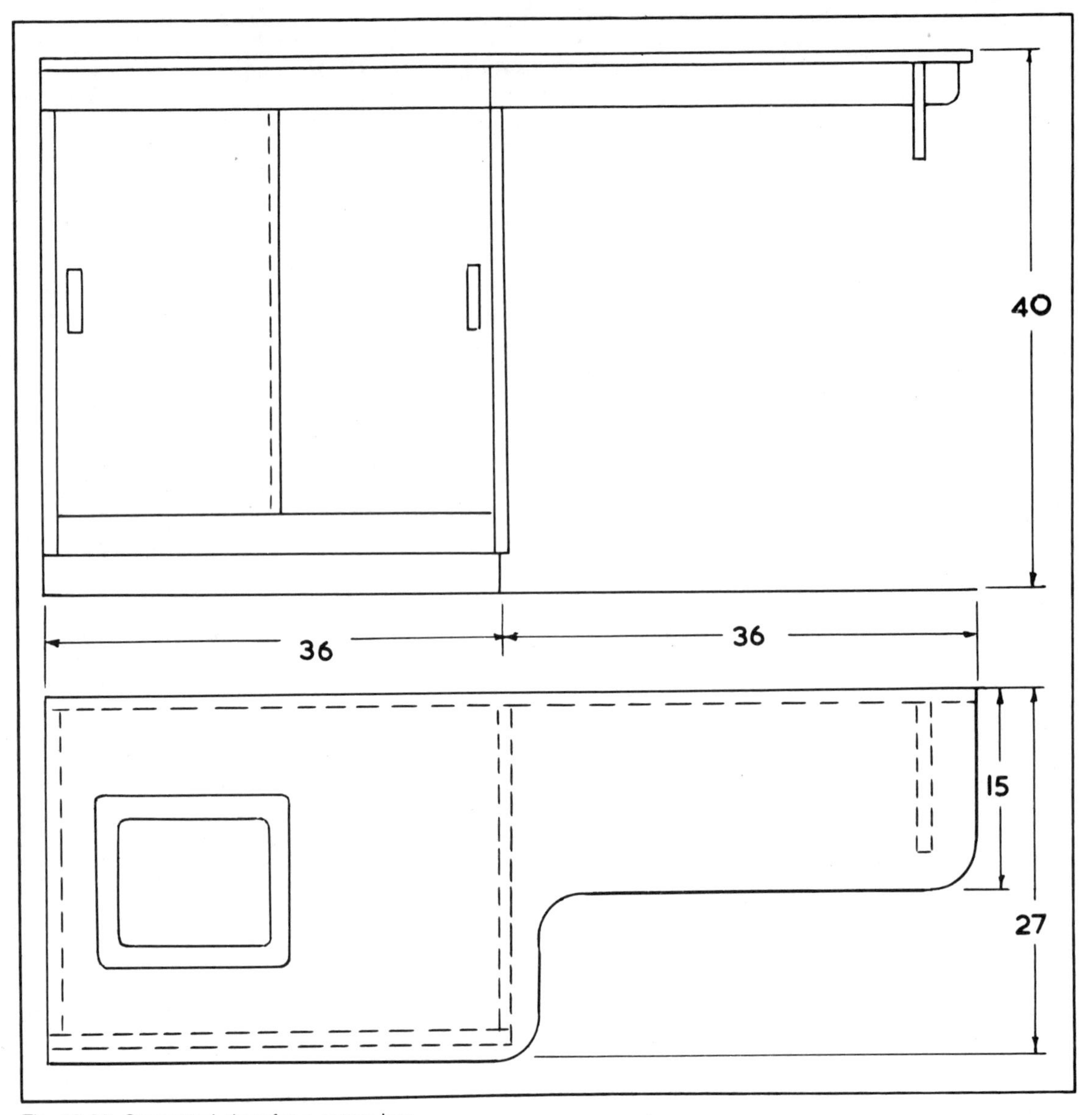

Fig. 13-30. Suggested sizes for a corner bar.

sizes you intend to make the woodwork (Fig. 13-30 and Table 13-8).

Make the bar top first, then make the other parts to match it. The working surface should be Formica laminated plastic or a similar material that will resist most liquids. Beneath it can come plywood or particle board, but the top looks best if it appears to be thick. You can increase the thickness around the edges with strips, then cover with plastic edging (Fig. 13-31A). At the back there should be an upright strip going the full length (Fig. 13-31B) and a supporting bracket toward the end of the extension (Fig. 13-31C).

The important part of the cupboard design is the arrangement of the sliding doors. These are pieces of ¼-inch or ⅜-inch plywood without fram-

Table 13-8. Materials List for Corner Bar.

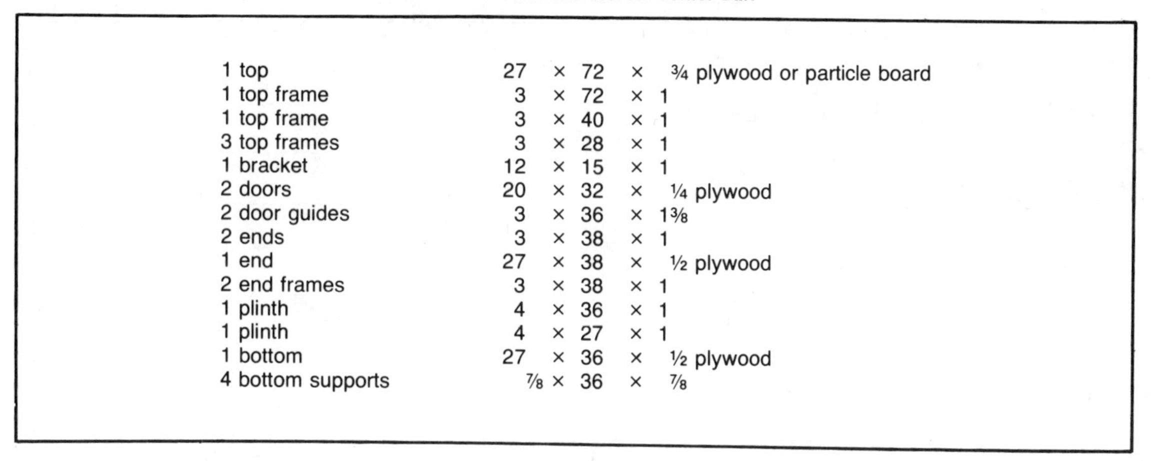

1 top	27	×	72	×	¾	plywood or particle board
1 top frame	3	×	72	×	1	
1 top frame	3	×	40	×	1	
3 top frames	3	×	28	×	1	
1 bracket	12	×	15	×	1	
2 doors	20	×	32	×	¼	plywood
2 door guides	3	×	36	×	1⅜	
2 ends	3	×	38	×	1	
1 end	27	×	38	×	½	plywood
2 end frames	3	×	38	×	1	
1 plinth	4	×	36	×	1	
1 plinth	4	×	27	×	1	
1 bottom	27	×	36	×	½	plywood
4 bottom supports	⅞	×	36	×	⅞	

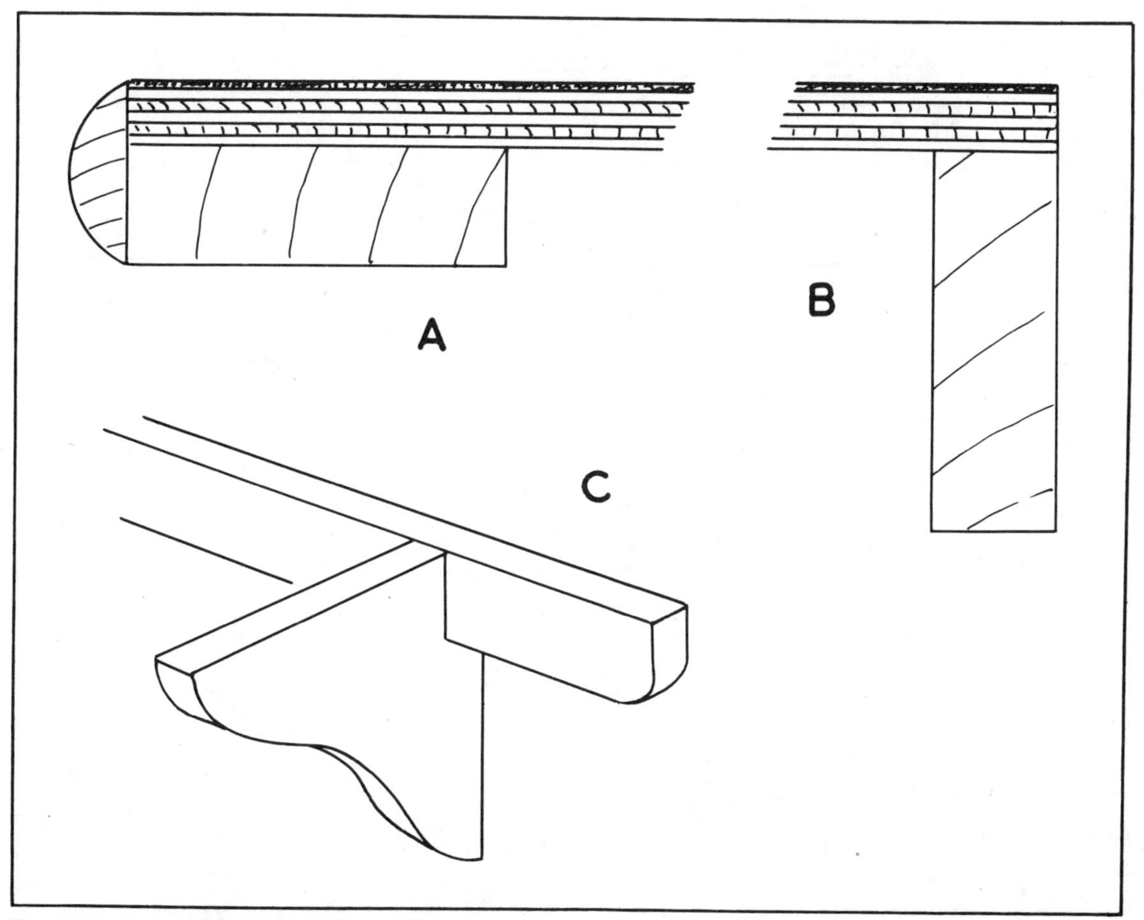

Fig. 13-31. Top and bracket details for a corner bar.

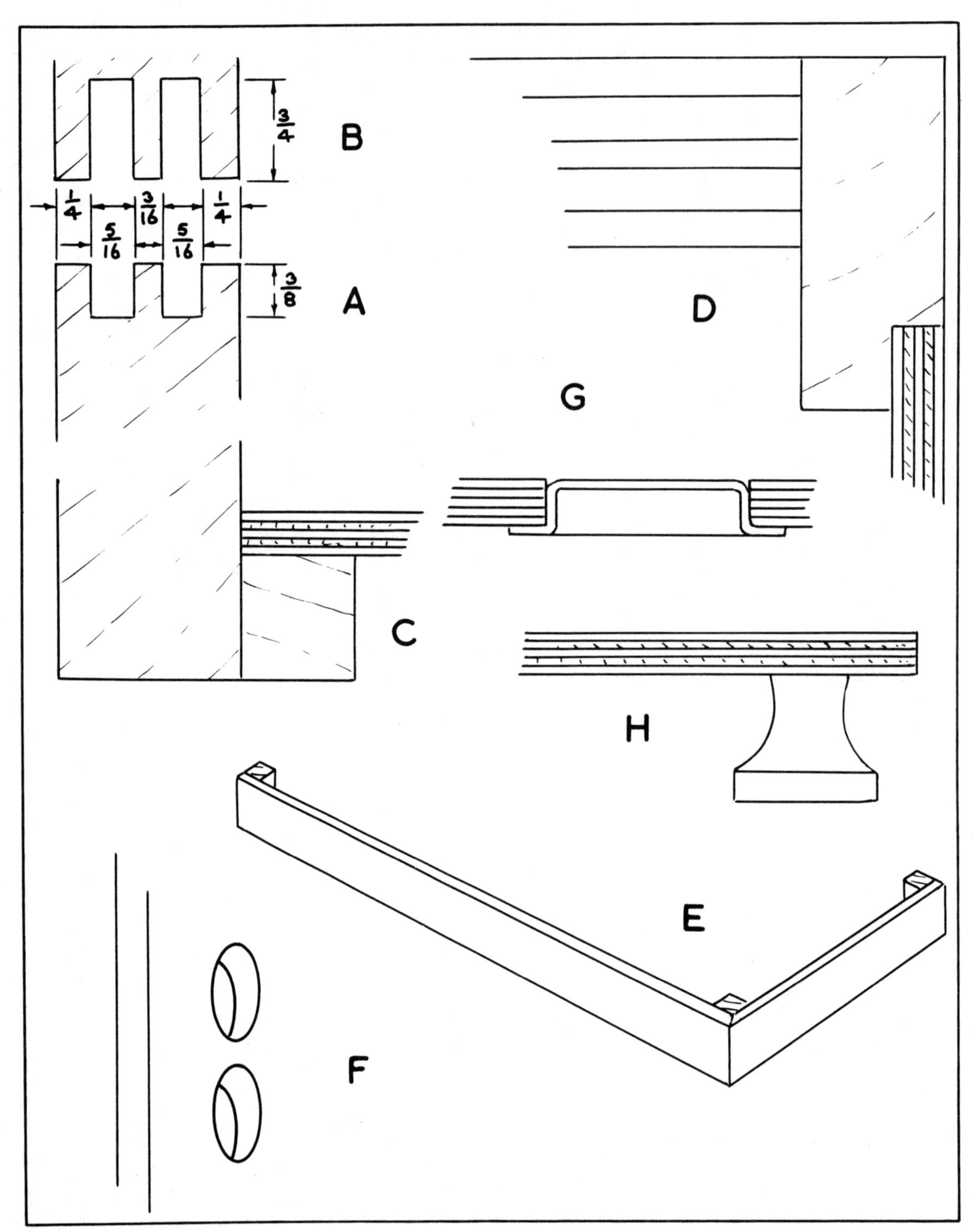

Fig. 13-32. Sliding door and plinth arrangements for a corner bar.

ing, running in grooves. In the bottom guide piece the grooves are plowed about ⅜ inch deep (Fig. 13-32A). In the top guide piece the grooves have a similar spacing, but they are twice as deep (Fig. 13-32B). This allows you to lift the doors clear of the bottom grooves for removal and easier access to the interior.

The door guides come against an upright attached to the wall. Dowel or tenon these joints. The cupboard bottom is a piece of ½-inch plywood on supporting strips at the front (Fig. 13-32C) and at the wall. Keep the strips at the front level with the lower edge for ease in fitting the plinth.

The other ends of the door guides join the cupboard end, which can be plywood with a rabbeted lip at the front (Fig. 13-32D) and strips inside to support the bottom and take screws to the wall. Notch the plywood around the strip under the back of the top. If plumbing and electrical work have to be done after the bar is installed, you may wish to leave the bottom loose, so it will be easier to make cuts in it for pipes and wires. Make all cuts necessary in the top for sink and faucets before building in the bar.

The cupboard has to be supported on a plinth set back ½ inch from the front and end. Attach it with blocks to the walls (Fig. 13-32E). There can be a few screws down through the bottom supports. When the whole assembly has been attached to the walls, there will be no movement of parts in relation to each other.

The doors may be drilled for finger holes (Fig. 13-32F), a plastic handle may be let in (Fig. 13-32G), or you can put handles or knobs near the outer edges (Fig. 13-32H).

Chapter 14

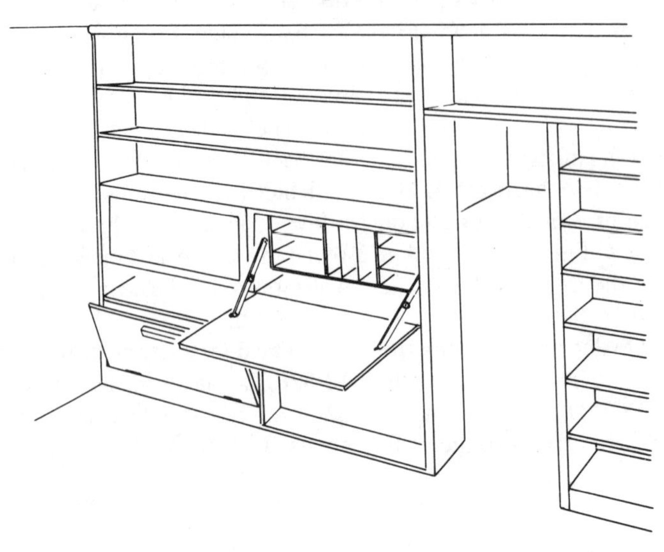

Room Dividers

IF PARTS OF A ROOM HAVE TWO DISTINCT PURposes, it will probably be worthwhile arranging some sort of a divider. If part of a family room also has to be used as an office or study, a divider can provide storage space at one or both sides, so books and files or other things needed on the office side do not spoil the appearance of the general living area on the other side. If part of a room is used for cooking and the other side for eating, a divider can double as a serving bar. The cooking equipment can be kept away from the dining area, which can be laid out neatly.

Even if both sides of the proposed divider are used for similar purposes, its many shelves can provide extra storage space for books, magazines, records, radio, and similar things. The divider does not have to project very far into the room, but it may be regarded as shelves arranged square to the wall instead of against it. You may also have shelves along a wall and arrange a block of projecting shelves square to them.

How opaque you make the divider depends on how separate the two areas will be. If you are really dividing one room into two rooms that will have different uses, you may make the divider almost solid with a door. In most cases it may be better if there are spaces that allow communication between occupants of the two areas. Another problem may be natural light. If there is a window only on one side of where you hope to put the divider, you will have to consider how the far side will get light. If you make a very open divider, there may be plenty of light still getting through. If you have closed racks or doors, you may shut off a lot of light. If the divider only projects a short way from the wall, it may not matter much if it is closed. If you are taking it across the room, decide about lighting before you start.

Another consideration is stability. Most built-in furniture has its longer dimension against the wall, so it is easily secured with only a few fasteners. A divider has only a narrow surface against a wall, but its base has a long narrow contact with the floor. Allow for screwing downward in a few key places. The higher part is more vulnerable. It is liable to get knocked in the same way as a house wall does. To be certain of withstanding these shocks, it is best taken up and secured to the ceiling. A divider that does not go that high needs a much stronger construction, particularly if it is narrow and of open design.

In planning a divider, consider altering some of the built-in furniture intended to be attached flat against a wall. Some of these things can be turned edgewise and modified so what was the back becomes presentable in one part of the room. If on one side you want to mount maps or other large pieces of paper, a large expanse of plywood may be what you want. Otherwise, allow the shelves to be open to both sides.

SIMPLE ROOM DIVIDER

A room divider does not have to divide one room into two completely. It may go only partly across the room so it is easy to pass by or through. It may be partly open, so it is possible to see through, or there can be access to things on shelves from both sides. Usually it is better to enclose the lower part up to about table height. This suggestion (Fig. 14-1) incorporates those requirements in an assembly that is of basic construction and can be adapted to other sizes. Construction can be with all standard width boards, or you can use prepared particle board already veneered with wood or plastic on surfaces and edges. Some joints in solid wood can be mortise and tenon or dado. It is better to use dowels for particle board and usually for solid wood.

Sizes are given for convenience in describing construction, but you must first measure the actual room and decide on the size and position of your divider. See Table 14-1. It helps to pencil or chalk on the wall, ceiling, and floor. Supporting a few boards temporarily in position will help you and others to visualize what the results will be and allow you to make modifications before going far with the actual assembly.

There is little difficulty in securing the divider to the wall and floor. It is not always easy to get a close fit against the ceiling, particularly as the ceiling may not be perfectly flat or exactly parallel with the floor. You can make the top piece a little low, then put packings at intervals between it and the ceiling. This is hidden by strips outside (Fig. 14-2A). The strips can be taken around the end with mitered corners. They can just be flat pieces or lengths of molding (Figs. 14-2B and 14-2C). Laying out the divider with some clearance at the top allows you to preassemble it and bring it into position without the risk of a closely fitting top scratching or marking the ceiling as it is moved into place.

Table 14-1. Materials List for Simple Room Divider.

3 shelves	9	×	84	×	¾
1 shelf	9	×	75	×	¾
2 shelves	9	×	66	×	¾
3 uprights	9	×	13	×	¾
2 uprights	9	×	15	×	¾
3 uprights	9	×	18	×	¾
2 uprights	9	×	20	×	¾
2 top strips	2	×	85	×	¾
1 top strip	2	×	11	×	¾
2 plinths	4	×	85	×	¾
1 plinth	4	×	11	×	¾
5 partitions	7½	×	26	×	¾
2 panels	6	×	26	×	¾
4 panels	18	×	26	×	¾
4 doors	18	×	26	×	¾
4 shelves	7½	×	18	×	¾

Mark the positions of shelves on the backboard (Fig. 14-1) and use this as a guide to sizes of the other upright parts. Prepare all the doweled joints (Fig. 14-2D). At the bottom you can make the plinth to match the strips at the ceiling (Fig. 14-2E).

The lower part is open at the exposed end, then it is divided with doors alternating on opposite sides. If veneered particle board is being used, the doors can be broad pieces of the same material. Otherwise, the doors can be made in any of the ways described for other projects. Inside you can make shelves that are wide enough to act as doorstops—the same as the vertical partitions.

OPEN DIVIDER

If the divider will not hide one part of the room from the other, it can be made with an open framework. This allows light through and is particularly appropriate if you want to put climbing plants on the divider. The size depends on the room and your needs, but to have an effective appearance it should not extend more than about half the width of the room.

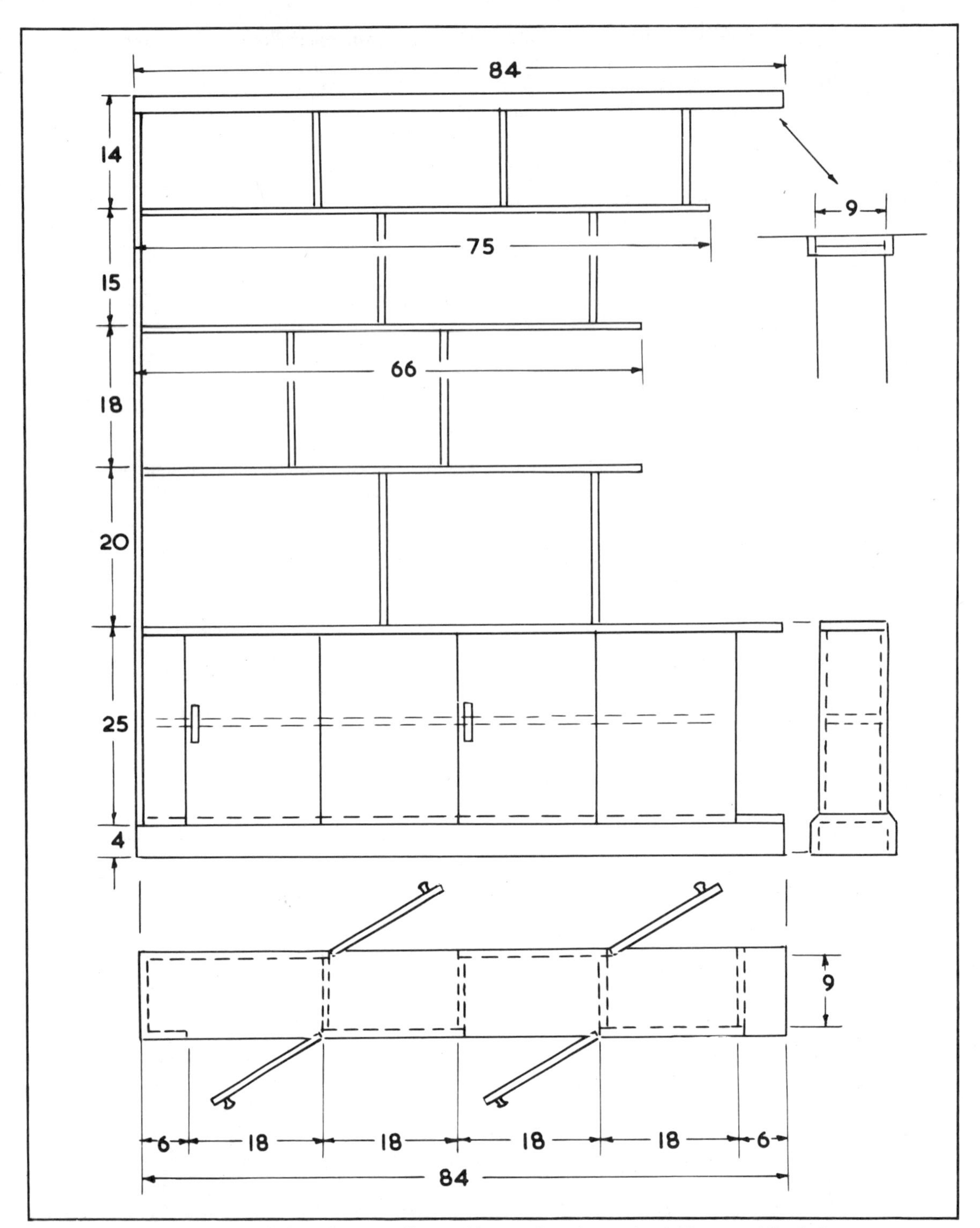

Fig. 14-1. This room divider goes from floor to ceiling and has cupboards opening both ways at the bottom.

This divider (Fig. 14-3) has one shelf at working height to serve as a table, bar, or counter. There is a cupboard below that provides stiffness and storage space. Instead of a plinth there are legs, leaving a space underneath deep enough to permit a brush, vacuum cleaner, or even your cat. The higher shelves have rails that prevent books or other things from being pushed right through. Suggested sizes are given (Fig. 14-4 and Table 14-2), but you will have to check the intended position for actual measurements.

The shelves and the back can be solid wood or veneered particle board, but the other parts should be strong hardwood. The uprights and the shelves can be in contrasting colors. The long parts must be flat and straight. If solid wood is used for the shelves, you may have to put strips across as cleats between the uprights to prevent warping.

Make the back to extend from floor to ceiling. On it mark the positions of the other parts and use it as a guide when marking out the upright strips. The shelves can be set into dado slots in the back, but it is probably simpler to use dowels (Fig. 14-5A), particularly if you are using particle board.

Mark the uprights from the back. Take care to get the shelf spacing exactly the same on all of them. Any variation will be very obvious in the finished divider. Mark out all the shelves together to get the upright spacings the same. Where the uprights and shelves cross, cut half thickness out of each of them (Fig. 14-5B). When you make the final assembly, close fitting joints should be strong enough with glue only. You can use a screw in each place, with its head counterbored and covered with a plastic plug.

Table 14-2. Materials List for Open Divider.

1 back	12	× 96	×	¾	
2 uprights	2	× 96	×	1	
2 uprights	2	× 56	×	1	
3 rails	2	× 24	×	1	
3 shelves	12	× 37	×	¾	
3 shelves	12	× 73	×	¾	
1 shelf	12	× 48	×	¾	
1 side	24	× 24	×	¾	
1 front	6	× 24	×	¾	
1 door	18	× 24	×	¾	
1 divider	12	× 24	×	¾	
1 inner shelf	12	× 24	×	¾	

The ends of the shelves are shown rounded. This is easy with solid wood, but taking veneer around curved particle board may not be satisfactory. The corners may have to be left square or given a 45° bevel.

There is a strip between the uprights to make the end of the cupboard (Fig. 14-5C). It can be glued and doweled in. At one side there is a solid piece to make a back to the cupboard. This can be solid wood or particle board, or you can frame around a thin piece of plywood. Glue the panel with a few dowels between the surrounding parts to ensure a strong construction.

The piece that comes beside the door is doweled to the shelves and back, and the door is hinged to it. If necessary, stiffen the edge with a piece inside (Fig. 14-5D). A single piece of particle board will make the door, or you can make a framed and paneled door if that will match other furniture in the room. At the side where the door closes, you can put a stop at top and bottom (Fig. 14-5E) or arrange one near the middle of the upright, if that better suits the type of catch you use. Arrange the handle fairly high on the door so you do not have to bend to use it. A shelf can be put inside, resting on battens (Fig. 14-5F), if that suits your storage needs.

On a hard floor the feet formed by the extended uprights can rest directly without trouble. If there is a carpet or other soft surface, it will be better to spread the load, either by putting other pieces inside the feet to increase area or by linking opposite feet with strips across.

DIVIDER WITH DOORWAY

If a room is to be divided into two, there can be a partition erected using studding and any of the surfacing boards used on inside walls. The effect will be to give each room a wall similar in appearance to the other walls. This is an opportunity to provide built-in furniture in both rooms by making a closed divider with shelves, racks, or whatever is required on opposite sides. If a plain wall is needed in one room, that can be made, but the other side may be

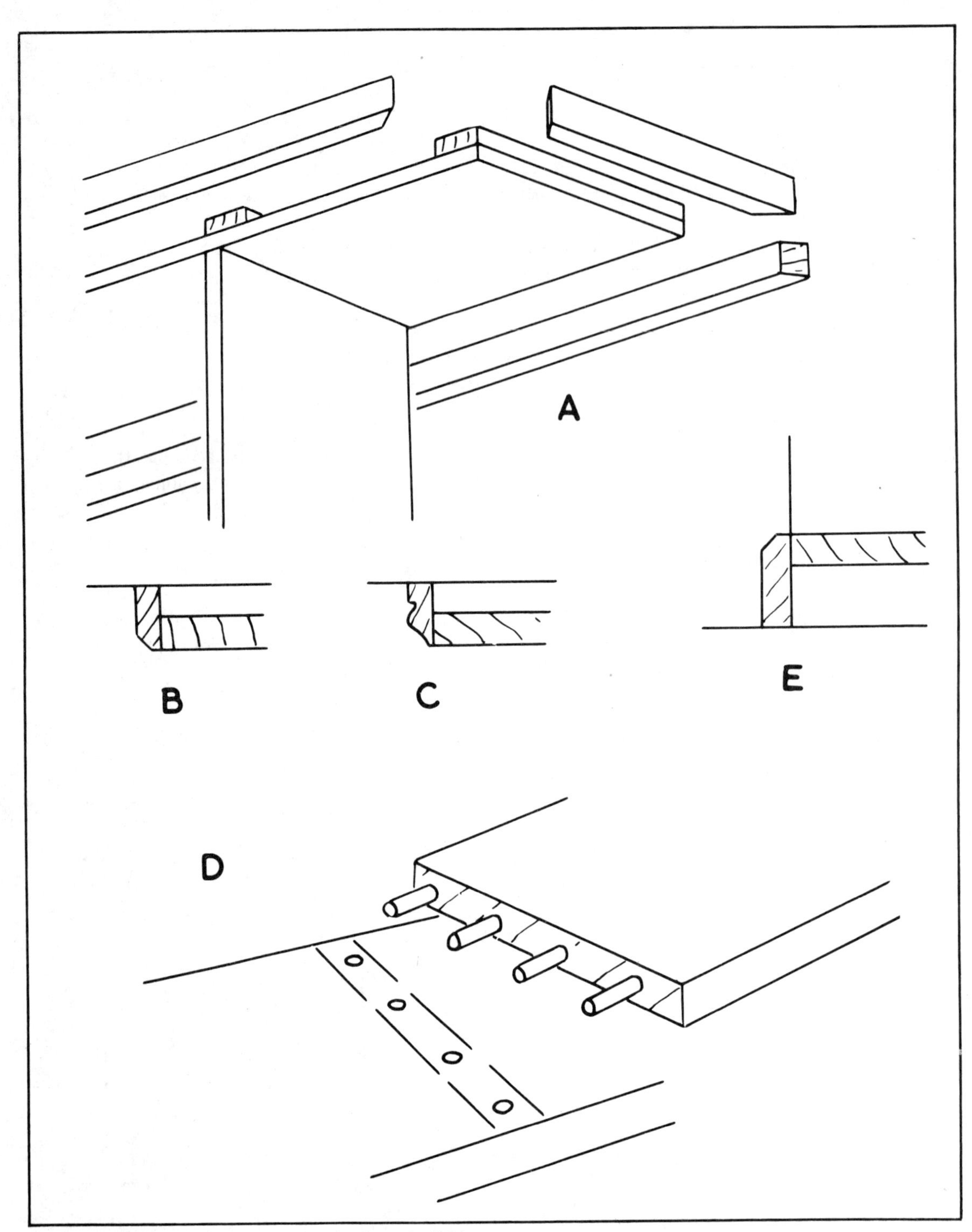

Fig. 14-2. Constructional details of the simple room divider.

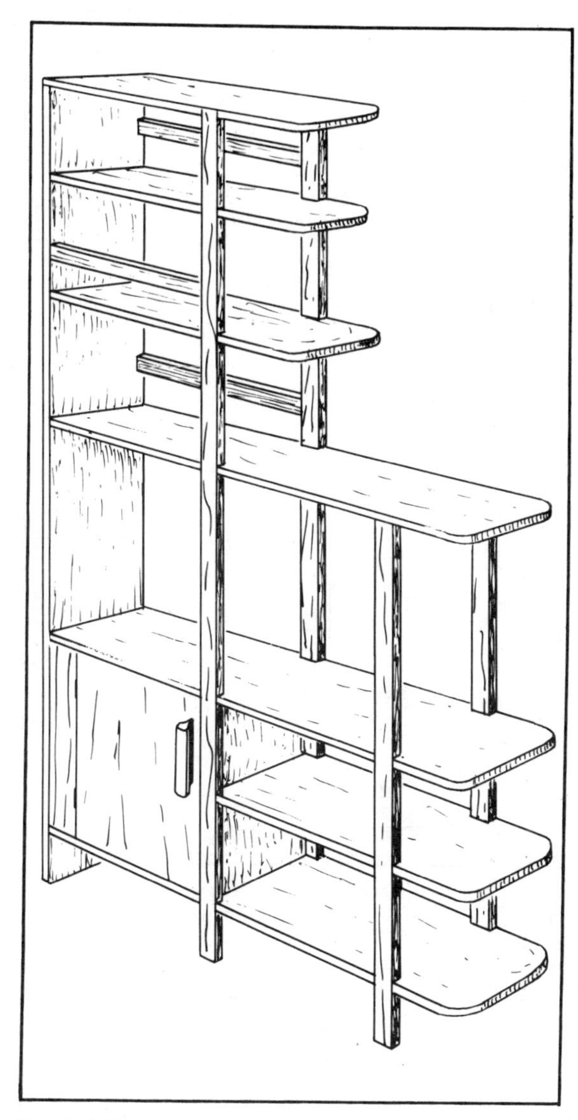

Fig. 14-3. This room divider is mainly open for light to pass through.

equipped in any way you wish. A doorway can be provided, either close to one existing wall of anywhere that is convenient in the divider. It may be left open. You can swing a normal interior door in it or provide a curtain, possibly of the hanging bead type.

The thickness of the divider will reduce the floor space in each room, but against that you are providing furniture that may otherwise have been freestanding and take up more space. It is possible to arrange shelves and other things both ways in quite a thin divider, providing when you want a wide shelf one way, the other side has just a flat surface. If you want to arrange shelves on opposite sides of the same position, the divider has to be wider. If the total width is 12 inches, you can put many books on shelves that come back-to-back.

The suggested design (Fig. 14-6) has a writing flap and storage for papers and magazines, as well as plenty of books on one side. The other side can have a similar flap arrangement, but behind it may be a cocktail cabinet. Shelves can be used to display souvenirs, trophies, and more books. Most arrangements can be back-to-back, but the writing compartment and the cocktail cabinet are better carried through to give ample storage space inside. That will mean staggering their positions, as they need to be about the same level. Their opposite sides may serve as bulletin boards or positions for pictures.

The final sizes will have to be made to suit the room, but the drawing (Fig. 14-7) shows a suggested layout. The divider can completely obscure one room from the other, but it can be made with gaps for ornaments or plants to be visible from both sides. There may be just a small access flap or door, so the person working on the writing flap can be passed a drink from the cocktail cabinet.

The two uprights at the walls go the full depth. In the example it is assumed that they are 12 inches wide and ¾ inch thick. Mark them out with the positions of the shelves. If the doorway will take a standard door, it must be made to suit. Otherwise, a height of 78 inches and a width of 30 inches should be satisfactory. It helps in planning the divider and for strength if one door post goes to the ceiling, particularly if a door is to be hinged on it. Make this 1 inch or more thick. A shelf goes from it to one wall upright, and the other door post is under that. All these joints can be doweled.

Other shelves are at the other side of the doorway, but they need not all be at the same level on the divider. It helps in laying out the parts to have the shelves that make the tops and bottom of the writing cabinet and the cocktail cabinet in single

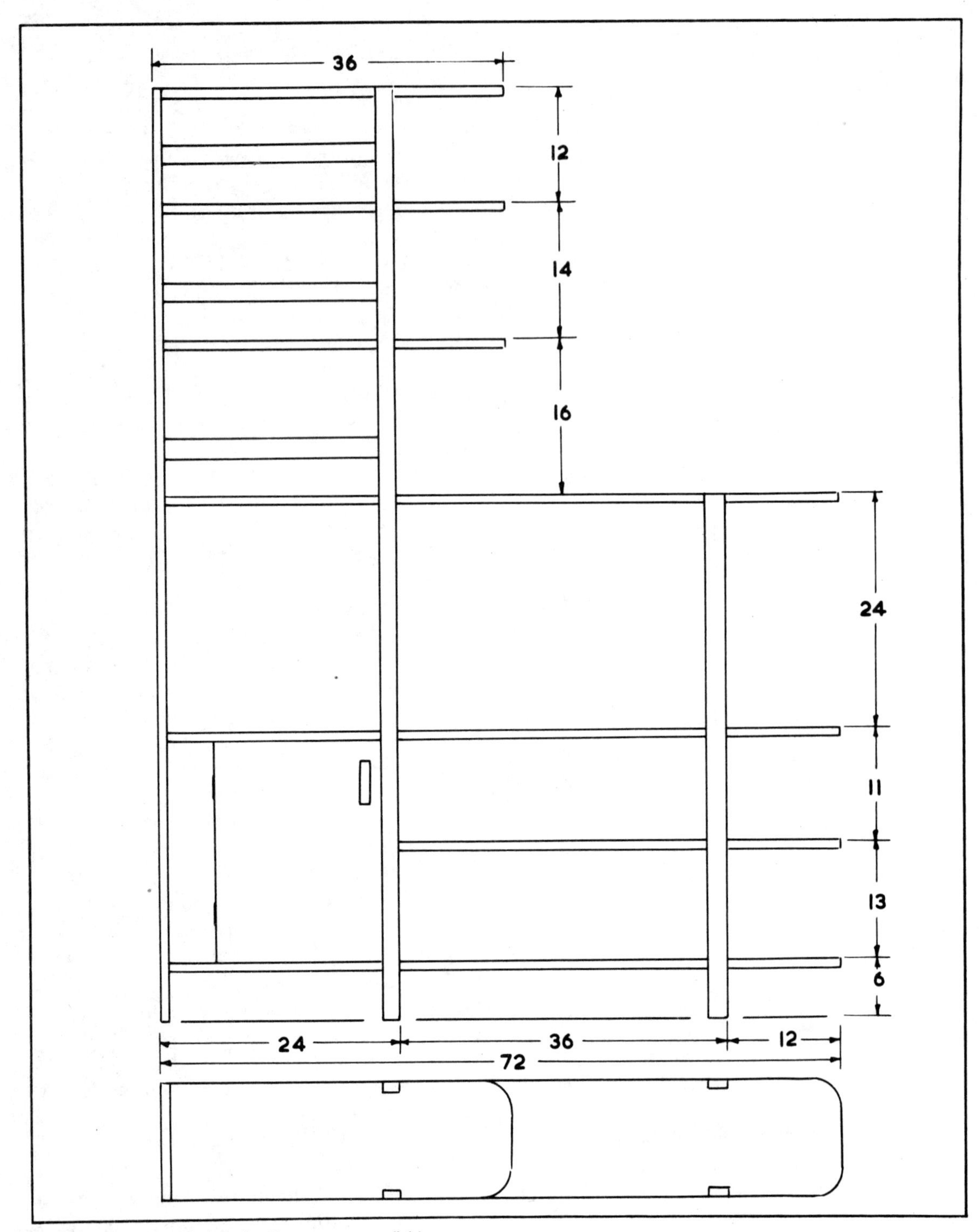

Fig. 14-4. Suggested sizes for the open room divider.

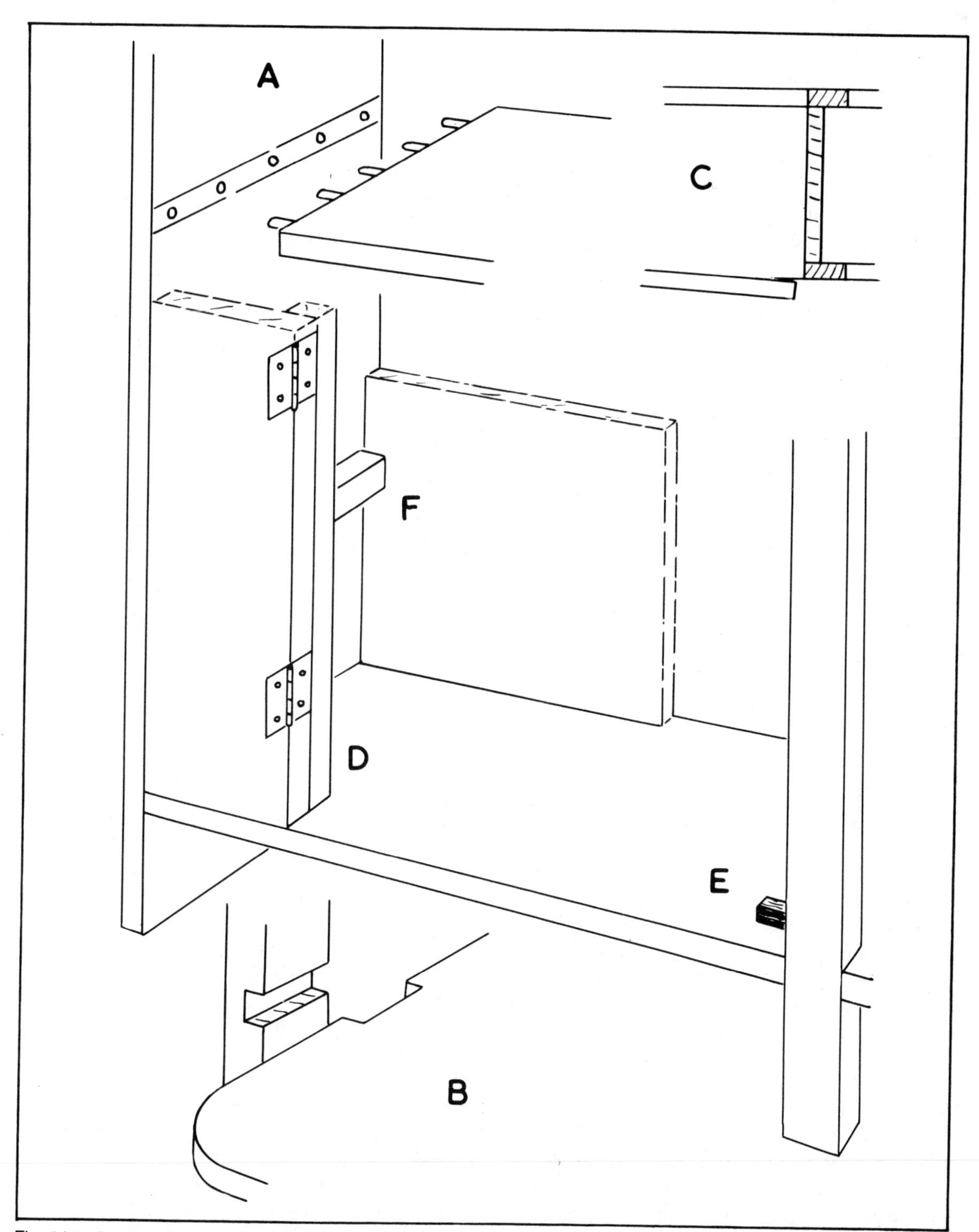

Fig. 14-5. Cupboard and shelf construction for the open room divider.

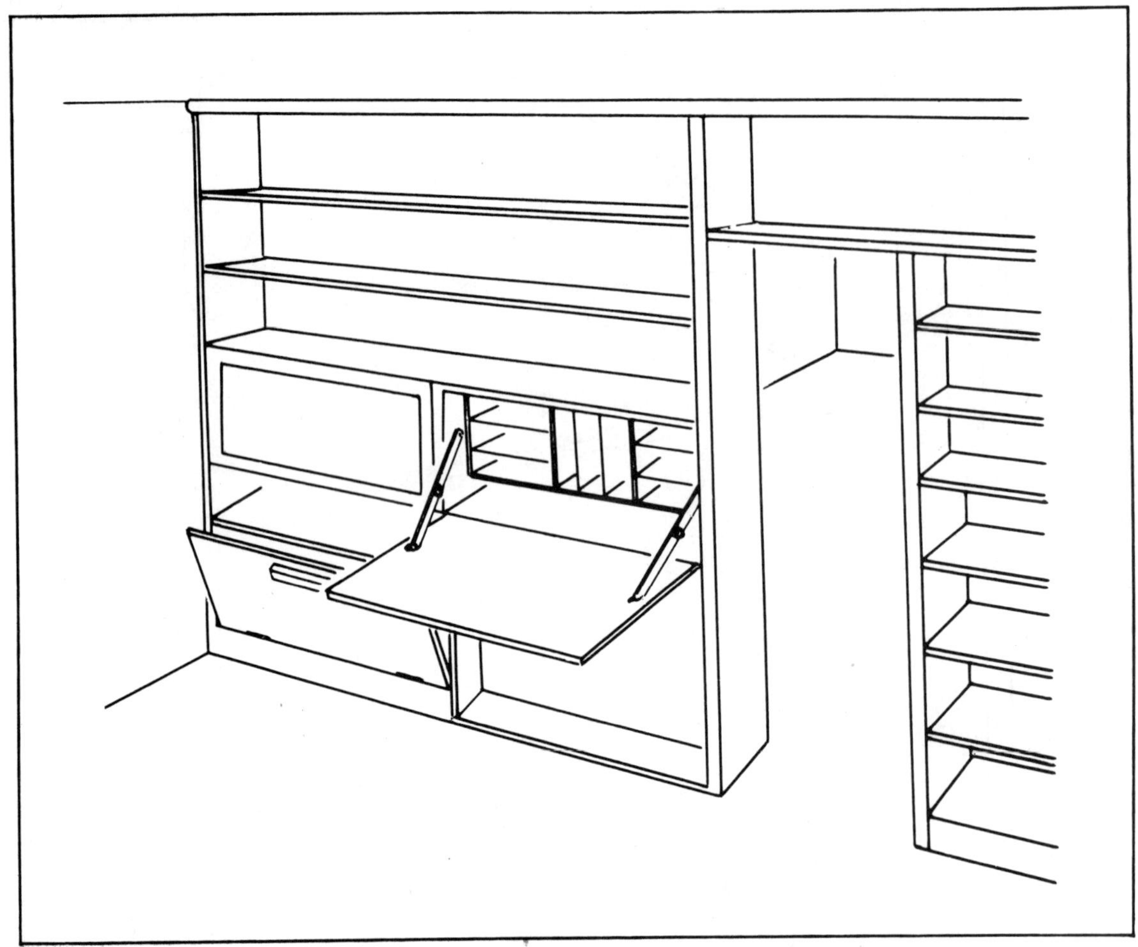

Fig. 14-6. A divider across a room may have a doorway and fitted arrangements that are different on opposite sides.

widths right through. If the book shelves above these cabinets are to be the same both sides and of equal width, put a piece of plywood centrally in the space above the cabinet shelf, with small fillets to hold it (Fig. 14-8A). One shelf can be screwed through the plywood (Fig. 14-8B), but the other will need a fillet and fine screws if it is at the same level (Fig. 14-8C).

Behind the cabinets or anywhere else that the division is to come off-center, you can move the plywood to suit. If you want to put it near the edge, it is better to frame around plywood (Fig. 14-8D).

The compartment for papers has a flap front. Make a bottom a few inches from the floor with a short length of plinth. Arrange the flap to be hinged along the bottom, so it will swing out and be restrained by a cord or chain (Fig. 14-8E). Put a long handle outside and one or two positive catches to keep the flap against its shelf. Magnetic or spring catches will not hold against a compressed pad of paper.

The two opening compartments have flaps hinged at the bottom. A long piano hinge will be ideal, but you may have to use two butt hinges. There can be a restraining cord to keep a flap level when it is down, but folding metal struts are better. Inside there can be sections to hold paper and your writing things. In the cocktail part you can make racks for glasses and bottles.

The top of this divider may be more easily

made if you keep the top board a short distance below the ceiling. You can fill the gap with molding carried across each side (Fig. 14-8F).

DRAFT SCREEN

At one time houses were much more drafty than most homes today. A draft screen was often placed near a door to deflect the stream of air when the door was opened. Similar screens were made to divide eating areas to provide some privacy. Such a screen can have uses today in a home to provide a dining nook in a corner of a room or to allow a group playing cards to be protected from others playing more active games. Such a divider need not extend very far or be very high, but it is usual to give it a fairly substantial construction.

The suggested design (Fig. 14-9) is intended to be made of an attractive hardwood, although it can be made of softwood and painted. See Table 14-3. It may be made with wood of square sections with minimal rounding, but as shown it is assumed that some molding facilities are available to work beads and hollows. The upper panel is plywood and needs grooves (suggested ½ inch), but the lower panel is made up of matched boards. The boards may be bought already prepared, or the edges can be worked with suitable spindle cutters (Fig. 14-10A). These fit into wider grooves (suggested ¾ inch). If these cannot be made with one cutter, they can usually be made with two or more passes.

There is a post attached to the wall. Another is shown going from floor to ceiling. It may be cut off just above the screen and a turned finial mounted on top, but that is weaker. The outer corner can be put under considerable strain if given an inadvertent sideways knock. A post to the ceiling is advisable.

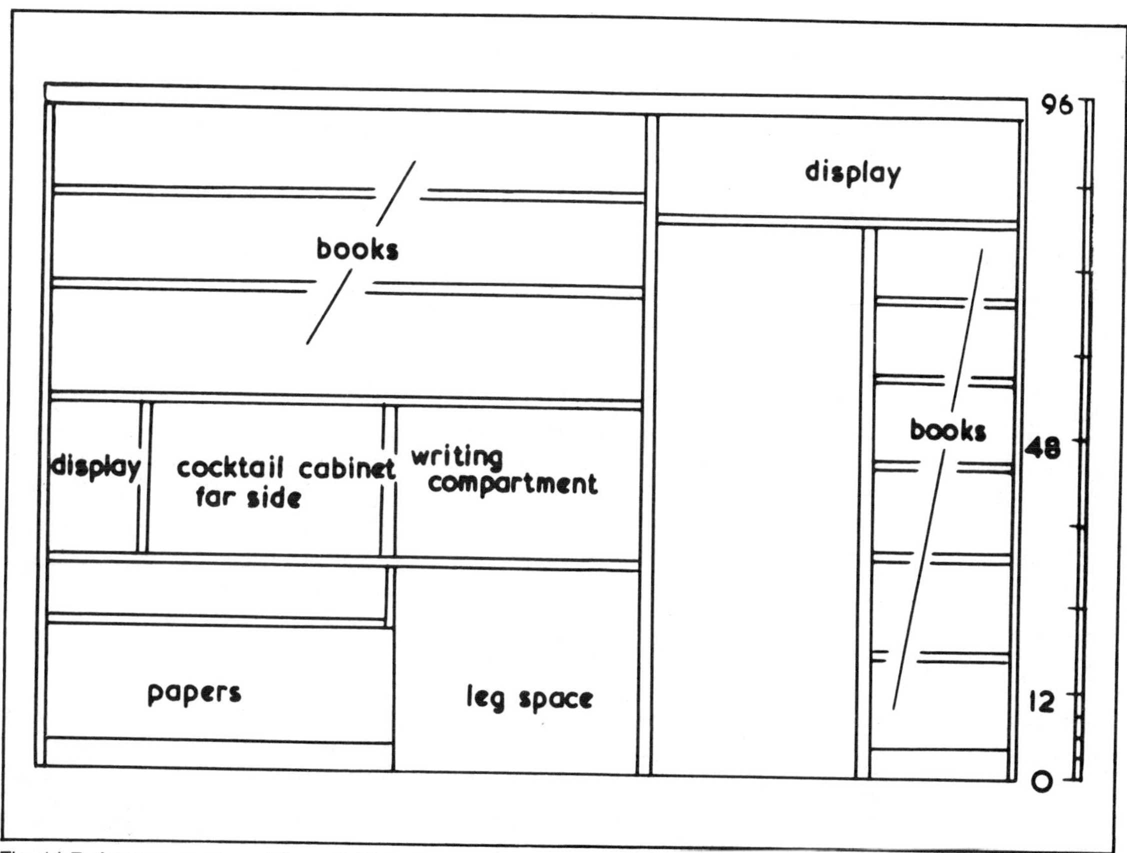

Fig. 14-7. A suggested layout for a divider with a doorway.

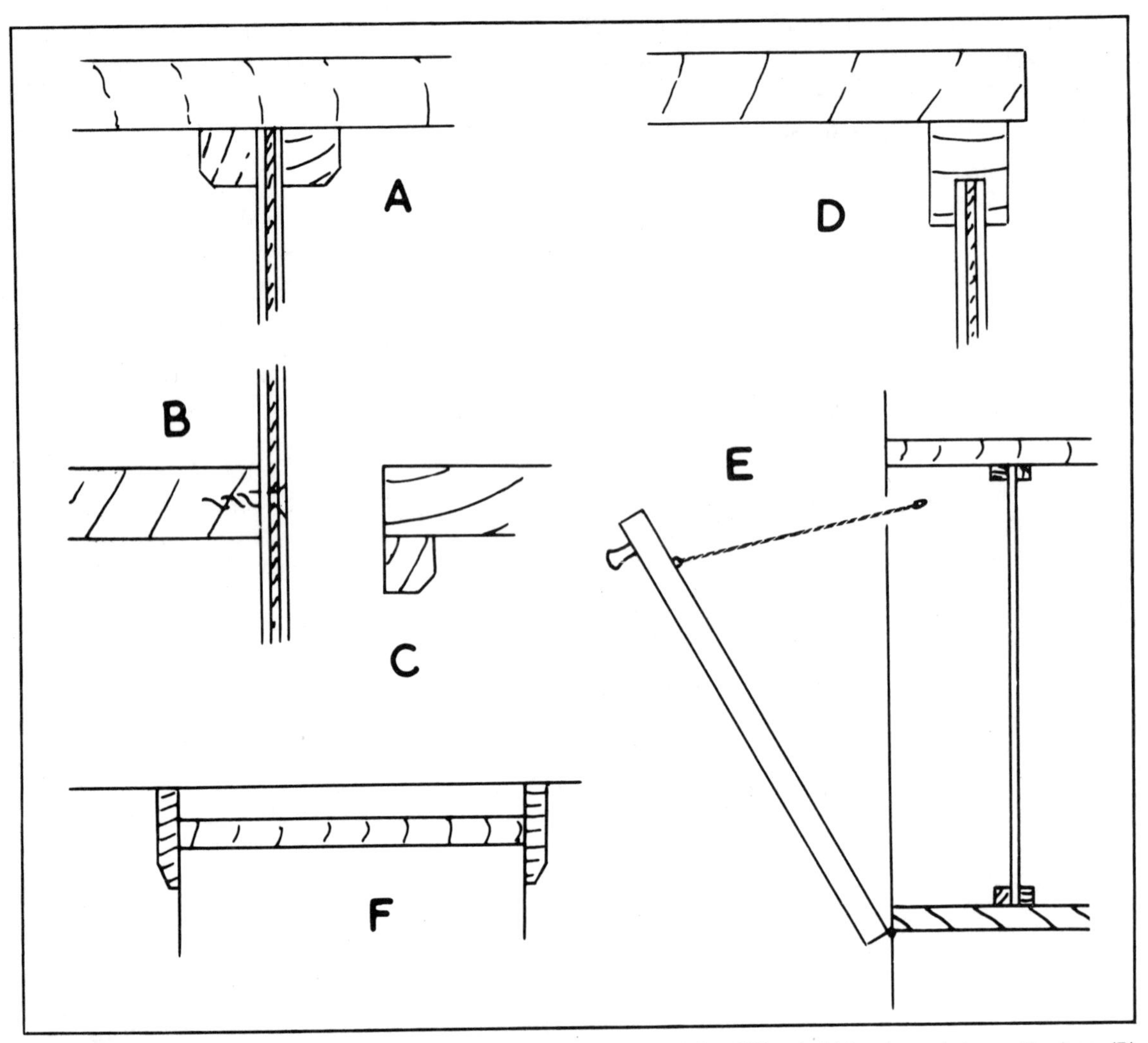

Fig. 14-8. Divisions and flap arrangements in the divider with a doorway. (A) Small fillets hold the piece of plywood in place. (B) One shelf can be screwed through the plywood. (C) The other shelf will need a fillet and fine screws if it is at the same level. (D) You may want to frame around plywood. (E) The flap is restrained by a cord or chain. (F) Molding can be carried across each side.

The upper part carries seven identical turned spindles. If you have a lathe, they can be made with ¾-inch dowels on the ends (Fig. 14-10B). Otherwise, it may be possible to buy spindles of about the size shown, then adapt the design to suit them. You should know what turned parts you will be using before laying out the other parts. An alternative to turned spindles is square posts, either set parallel to the divider or turned diagonally to give a diamond effect.

Table 14-3. Materials List for Draft Screen.

4 rails	3	×	72	×	3
1 post	3	×	76	×	3
1 post	3	×	96	×	3
11 matched boards	6	×	36	×	¾
1 panel	22	×	68	×	½ plywood
7 spindles	3	×	12	×	3
4 moldings	⅞	×	68	×	⅞ quarter round
4 moldings	⅞	×	22	×	⅞ quarter round

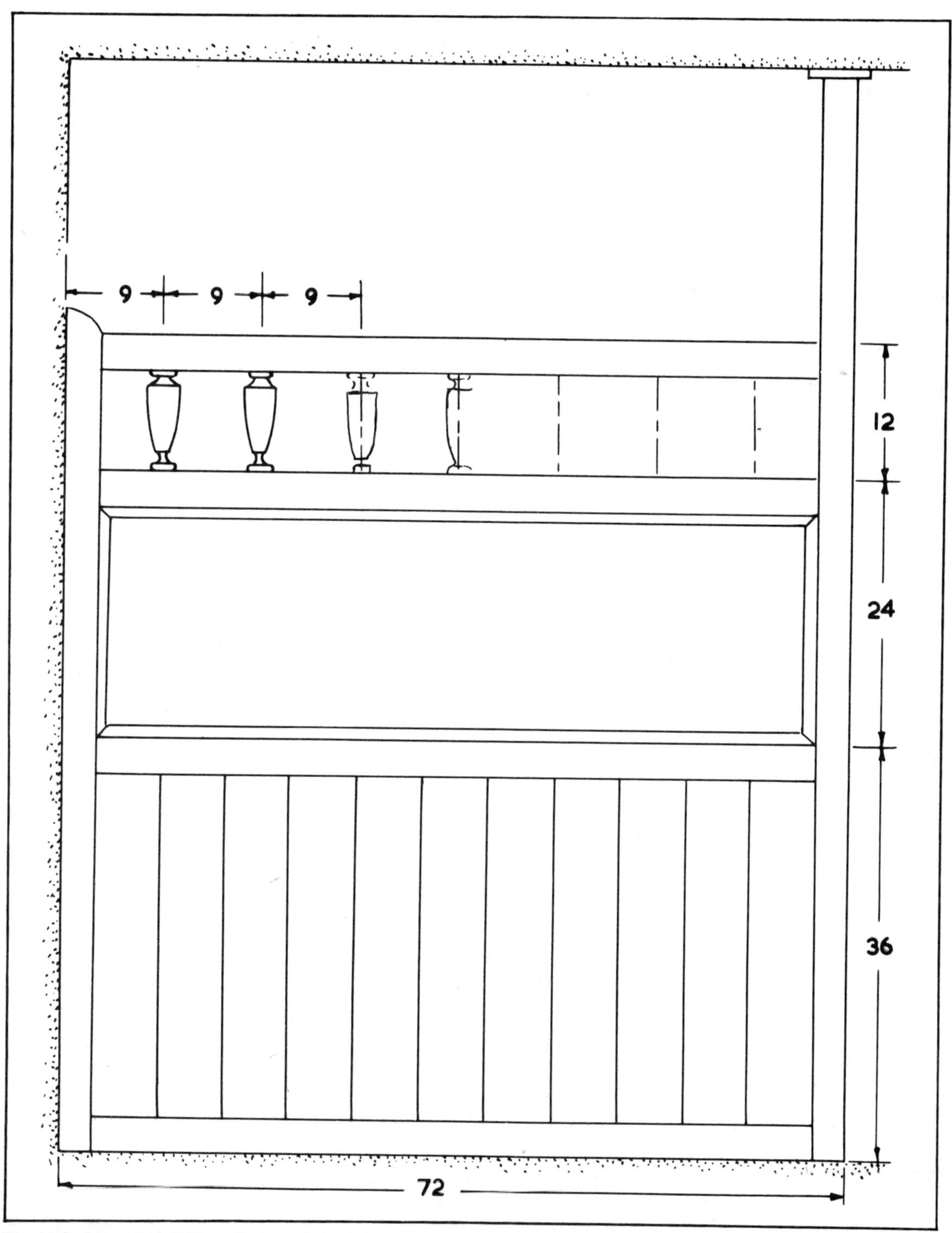

Fig. 14-9. A paneled divider with turned decoration and a post to the ceiling.

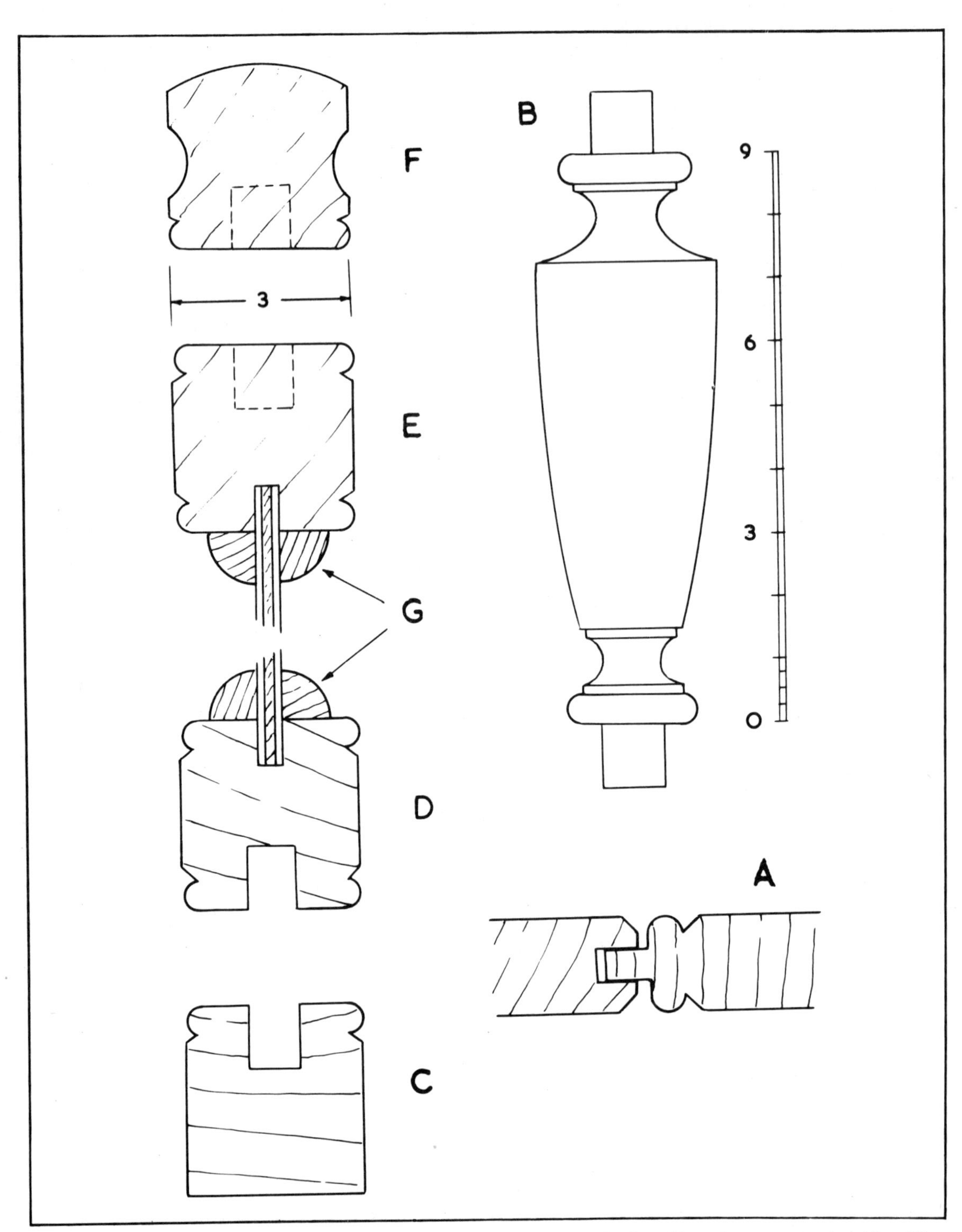

Fig. 14-10. The matched boarding (A), turned details (B), sections of the rails (C to F), and quarter-round molding (G).

Assemble all the wood first and plane it true before working it to the various sections. At the floor the rail is given beads on the upper edges and a full-length groove to suit the matched boards (Fig. 14-10C). The rail at the top of the matched boards (Fig. 14-10D) has a similar groove on its lower side and one to suit the ½-inch plywood on its top side. All corners have beads worked on the outer edges. The rail at the top of the plywood has a similar groove, but the top is drilled for the turned spindles (Fig. 14-10E) and matching beads.

The top rail (Fig. 14-10F) looks best with the top rounded and hollows worked along the sides, then beads at the lower edges. Mark out matching holes for the spindles on this and the next rail together to get the spacing exact.

The front rail to the ceiling can have a pair of beads the full length on the outer corners similar to the bottom rail (Fig. 14-10C), but without the groove. The back rail against the wall is made square without any beads or grooves. Mark the joint positions on the two uprights together. Traditionally, the joints were mortise and tenon, but it will be satisfactory to use dowels.

If you have to reduce the width the tongued and groove boards make up, take a similar amount off each outer board to keep the pattern of joints between boards symmetrical. As you assemble the screen, do not glue the tongues and grooves. Put varnish or other finish in the grooves as you push in the tongues.

Assemble the screen with the plywood and tongued and grooved boards in their slots. Check squareness or the fit of the screen in position if the wall or floor is out of true. Put quarter-round molding all around the plywood panel (Fig. 14-10G) and down the sides of the lower panel. Where the long post touches the ceiling, you can put a frame of about ¾-inch mitered square strips around it. Drive screws upward through them. For attachments to the wall and floor, counterbore long screws and cover the heads with wood plugs.

Chapter 15

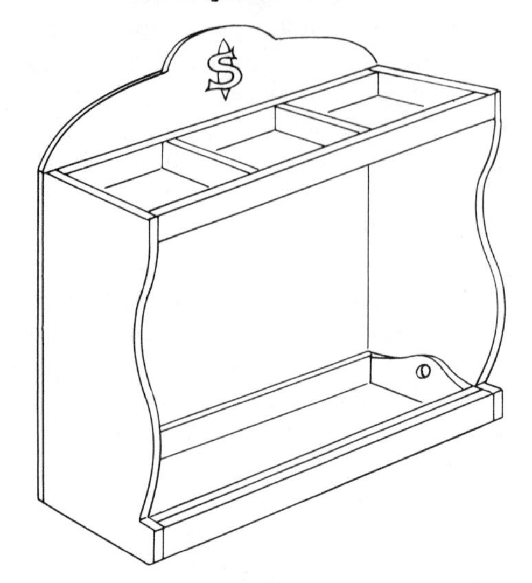

Hall Furniture

The area inside the front or other outside door often forms a hall or vestibule that is kept as small as reasonably possible so as not to take space that is considered more valuable in adjoining rooms. There is little space for freestanding furniture. It is helpful to provide racks, mirrors, and storage on the wall, either resting on the floor or kept high on the wall so as not to use up floor space.

You can take care of outdoor clothing so it does not have to be taken further into the house. Obviously, hall furniture should not interfere with free passage. It should not get in the way of the outside door, nor any inside one. It is usually possible to place useful pieces of furniture so they serve their purpose without becoming obstructive.

Some suggested items may have uses elsewhere. You can arrange for visitors to hang clothing or leave wet boots and umbrellas on the patio or under a shelter adjoining a deck. Public meeting rooms may benefit from coat hooks and other items.

COAT RACK

This rack combines plenty of hanging space for clothing with a mirror and a small shelf (Fig. 15-1). The suggested mirror is about 11 inches by 13 inches, but you should obtain a mirror before settling on other sizes. It is easier to alter wood than glass (Fig. 15-2 and Table 15-1).

The mirror has to be let into rabbets that do not extend the full length of a piece of wood. The usual method of cutting through-rabbets cannot be used. If a spindle or a router is available, a rabbet can be cut of the length needed, but with rounded ends (Fig. 15-3A). The corners can be squared with a chisel (Fig. 15-3B). Otherwise, the whole rabbet will have to be cut by hand. Allow for glass and retaining fillets (Fig. 15-3C).

Prepare the top and the uprights, including their rounded ends. You can use dowels between these parts (Fig. 15-3D) or tenons (Fig. 15-3E). The bottom may be joined in either of these ways. Match the rabbets so the mirror can be fitted in from the

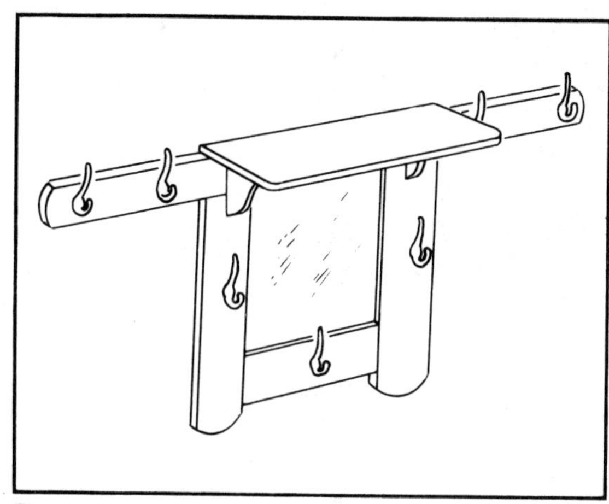

Fig. 15-1. A hanging coat rack with a mirror and shelf.

back. Mark out and cut the joints before completing the rabbets, so you are able to mark their limits accurately.

Assemble these four main parts. Mark where the shelf will come on the top. Go all around the front edges with bevels, rounds, or molding (Fig. 15-3F). If you have a suitable router molding cutter, you can make an attractive design that meets with miters in the corners. Otherwise, simple bevels or rounds are effective.

As the shelf comes above eye level and screwheads will not show, it can be screwed downward into the top (Fig. 15-4A). Shape its edges to match the other woodwork. Draw the bracket shapes (Fig. 15-4B) and treat the exposed edges in a

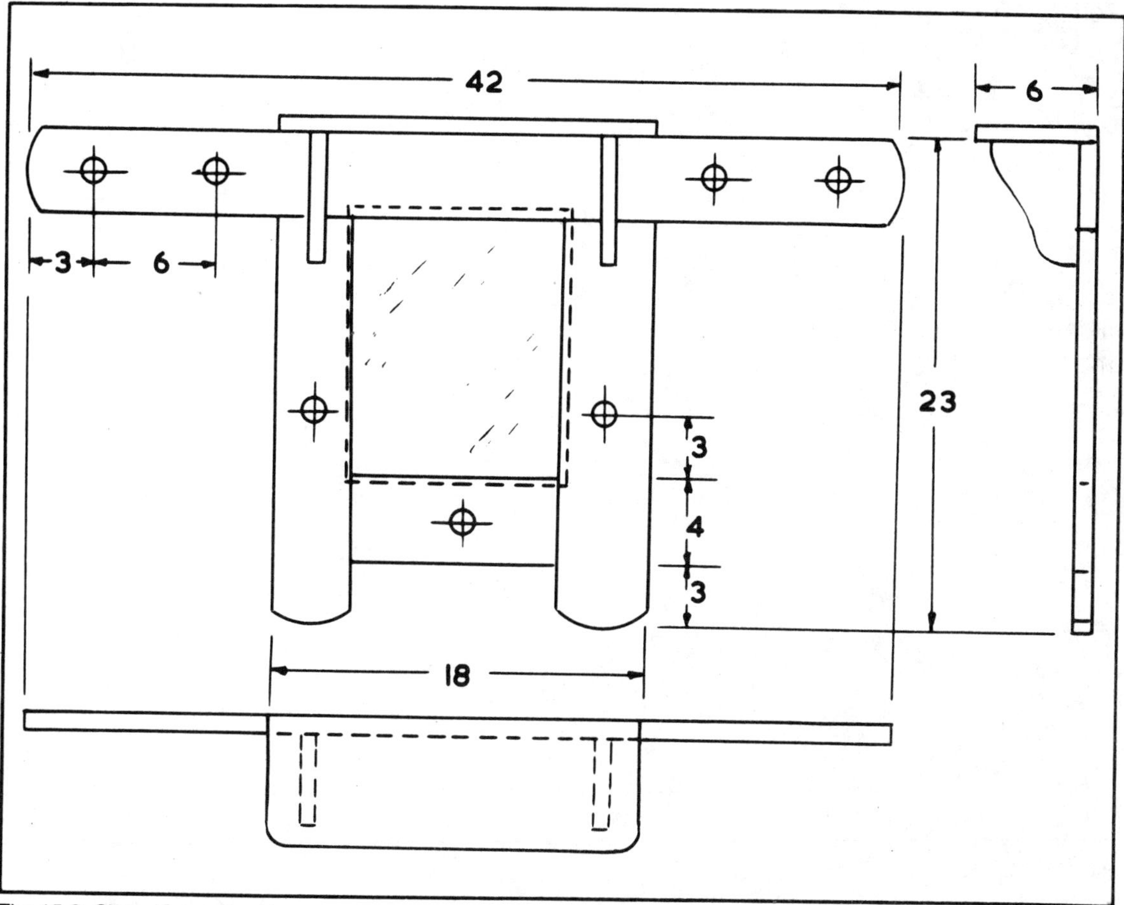

Fig. 15-2. Sizes of a coat rack.

Table 15-1. Materials List for Coat Rack.

1 top	4	×	42	×	7/8
2 uprights	4	×	22	×	7/8
1 bottom	4	×	17	×	7/8
1 shelf	6	×	19	×	5/8
2 brackets	4	×	7	×	5/8

similar way to the other parts. Get both brackets exactly alike and remove all signs of sawing or other tool work. Attach the brackets centrally over the uprights with screws through (Fig. 15-4C).

Make sure the mirror will fit, but apply finish to the wood before finally securing it. To avoid damage to the mirror, put cloth or thick paper under

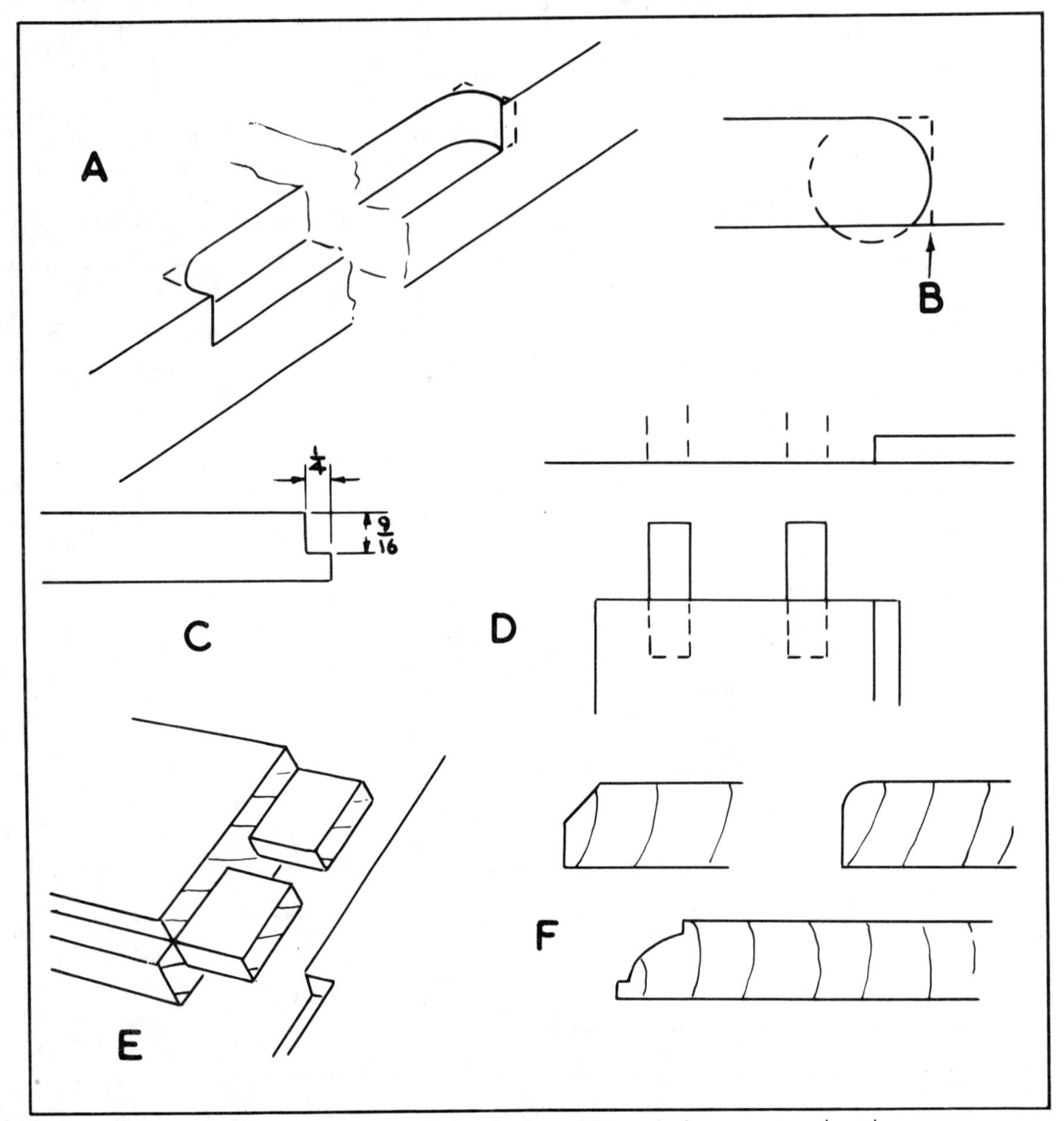

Fig. 15-3. Preparation of the coat rack parts with dowel or tenon joints and edges square or shaped.

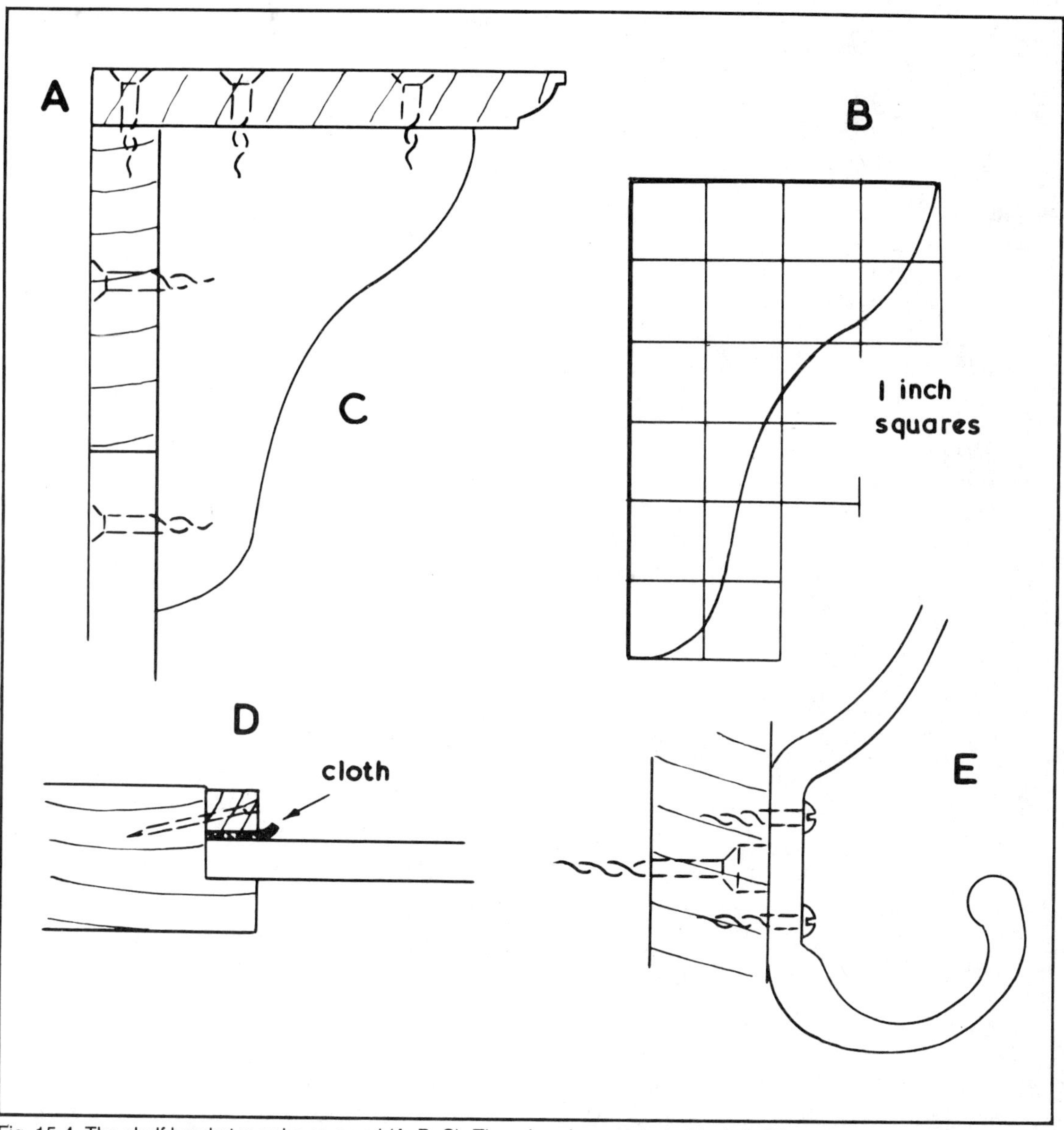

Fig. 15-4. The shelf bracket may be screwed (A, B, C). The mirror is protected with cloth (D), and screws to the wall may be hidden behind hooks (E).

the fillets and nail carefully (Fig. 15-4D) with widely spaced thin brads.

The coat hooks can be turned pegs, but the usual double metal types are better. You can hang the rack so the screws do not show by putting them under hooks. Screws under the outer and bottom hooks should be enough. There will probably be enough spread of screw holes on the hook to allow you to counterbore the wall screw (Fig. 15-4E).

HALVED COAT RACK

A series of pegs can be arranged in many ways on a wall, so items of clothing can be hung from them without projecting far enough to obstruct space in a

Table 15-2. Materials List for Halved Coat Rack.

2 pieces	2 × 25 × 1
4 pieces	2 × 16 × 1
7 pegs	6 × 1¼ × 1¼

narrow passage or other restricted area. Something better looking than a plain row of hooks can be made by halving strips together. The basic idea can be adapted to many arrangements (Fig. 15-5 and Table 15-2). If the crossings are allowed to project below, pegs are brought within reach of children.

The method of construction is the same, and the example has only two squares (Figs. 15-6A and 15-6B). Other patterns extend the arms as needed.

The strips are all the same section, with half-lap joints at the crossings (Fig. 15-6C). The sizes of squares give an average spacing, but for bulky clothing they can be enlarged. The extending arms can be left square, but bevels improve appearance (Fig. 15-6D).

The pegs can be plain pieces of dowel rod glued into holes that will tilt them up about 15° (Fig. 15-6E). Shaker pegs (Fig. 15-6F) can go into holes drilled squarely. These are a standard design used by Shakers for hanging furniture and many other things. They can be bought ready-made, or you can turn them on a simple lathe (Fig. 15-6G). Assemble the framework before drilling centrally through each crossing.

In the basic rack the spaces are open and the wall shows through. It is possible to fill them. Plywood panels can be let in. The plywood can be covered with fabric. A mirror may be in the middle square or three. You can include a picture or photograph in a square, with or without glass over it.

For any of these arrangements, cut rabbets in the framing just far enough into the corner joints to let in the panel (Fig. 15-6H). For a mirror or glass over a picture, allow enough thickness for a piece of plywood or hardboard behind.

TELEPHONE SHELF

A support for a telephone should also provide a place to store directories, notebooks, and lists of numbers. There should also be space to open a directory and write notes. This double shelf (Fig. 15-7), bracketed to the wall, will serve all those purposes. The sizes (Fig. 15-8 and Table 15-3) should be ample to suit most instruments and directories. You should measure yours before starting work, though, particularly if the shelf must be as small as possible.

The shelf can be made of solid wood. The grain of the dividers should be upright. Veneered particle board is also suitable, but the fronts of the dividers and the slope of the bracket have to be straight for easy veneering. Plywood will need its exposed edges covered with veneer or solid strip. Both of these materials can have plastic strip put around them.

Set out the back first (Fig. 15-9A), with the positions of other parts on it. Round the corners and drill for screws into the shelves and the dividers. Make the two shelves and round their outer corners (Fig. 15-9B).

The spacers (Fig. 15-9C) are all the same. Besides the front shaping, round the wood there in section. The inner spacer should be located far enough from one end to take directories and leave the other space for pads and notebooks.

Make the bracket to notch around the back (Fig. 15-9D), where it will be screwed. Screw it centrally under the bottom shelf.

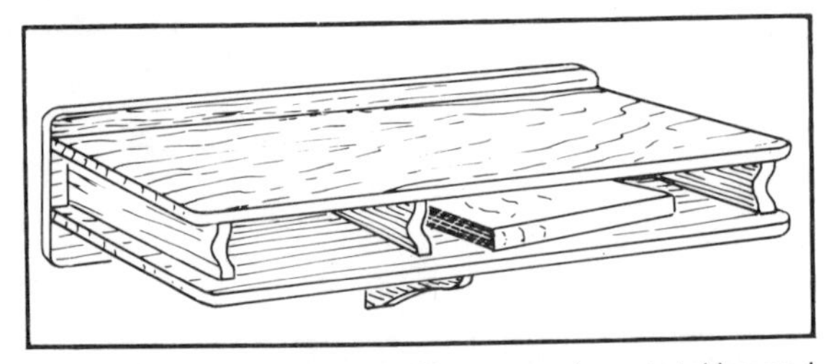

Fig. 15-7. This telephone shelf has space for note taking and storage for directories and other papers and books.

Table 15-3. Materials List for Telephone Shelf.

2 shelves	10 × 25 × ⅝
1 back	7 × 25 × ⅝
3 dividers	9 × 4 × ⅝
1 bracket	5 × 10 × ⅝

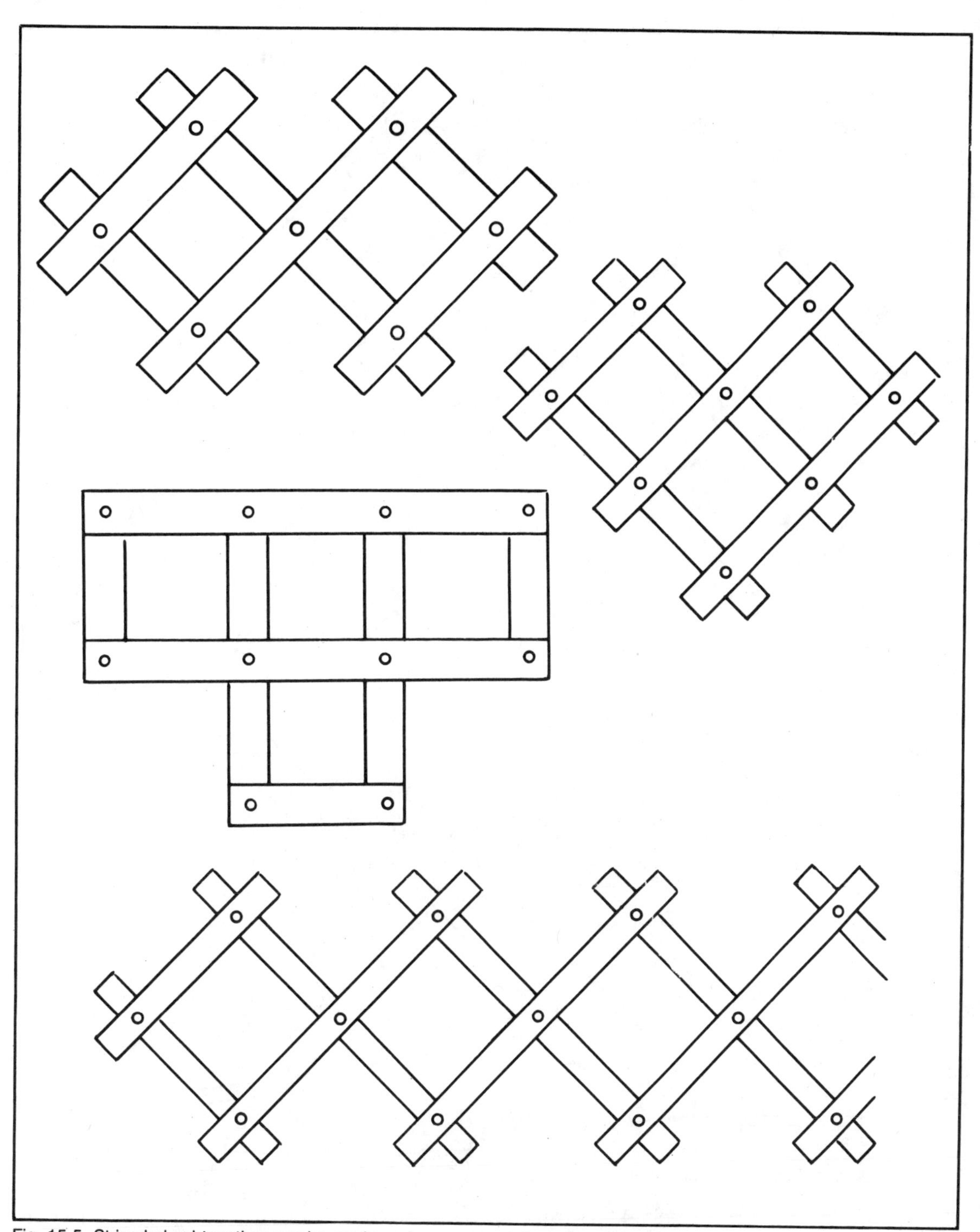

Fig. 15-5. Strips halved together can be made up in many ways to make coat racks.

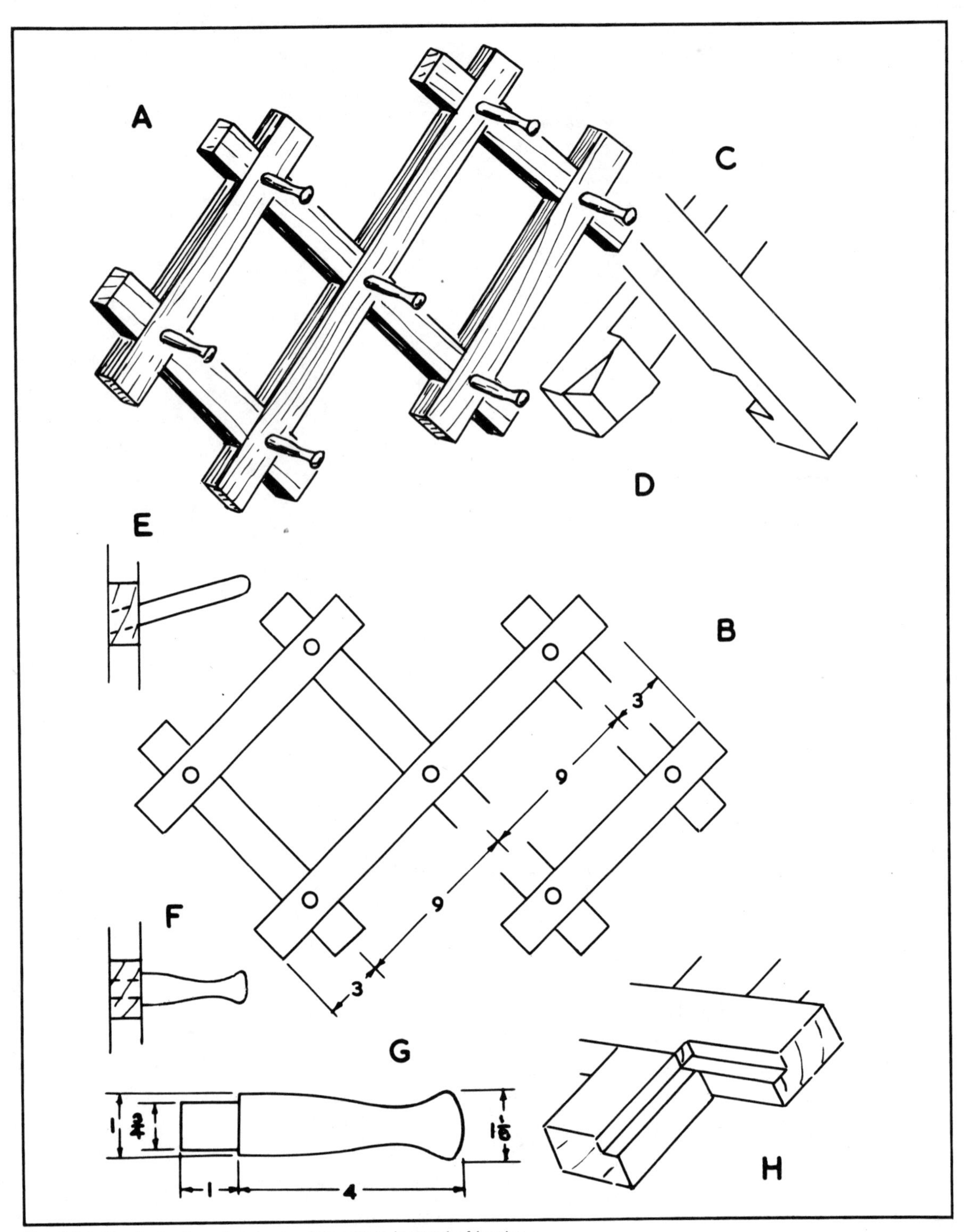

Fig. 15-6. The halved coat rack may have pegs instead of hooks.

Join the spacers to the shelves with dowels. The lower shelf surface is hidden, and you can drive screws upward there (Fig. 15-9E).

Screw the back to the other parts. Make sure the bracket continues straight down in line with the back, so it will bear against the wall. Screws to the wall can go through the back between the shelves and below the bottom shelf.

HALL LOCKER

This design (Fig. 15-10) is primarily intended for a piece of furniture to be located inside the main house door. Gloves, hats, and other outdoor clothing can be stored in the top compartment. The tilting bin below will house all kinds of footwear. A similar locker may have uses elsewhere. It can hold toys in a child's room or foodstuffs in a kitchen. With a stouter top it can be used in a workshop as a bench or the base for a machine. The description here assumes that it will be a hall locker.

The locker may be screwed through its back into the wall. If there is a baseboard to the wall, you can cut that back so the locker fits flat against the wall. If you do not want to disturb the baseboard, the locker should be cut to fit over it or a packing used behind it.

Most parts should be made of solid wood, but ½-inch plywood can be used for the shelf, the bottom, both doors, and bin parts. See Table 15-4. Check sizes in relation to the position the locker will occupy. Will it interfere with door movements? Are passersby liable to knock against it? One of the

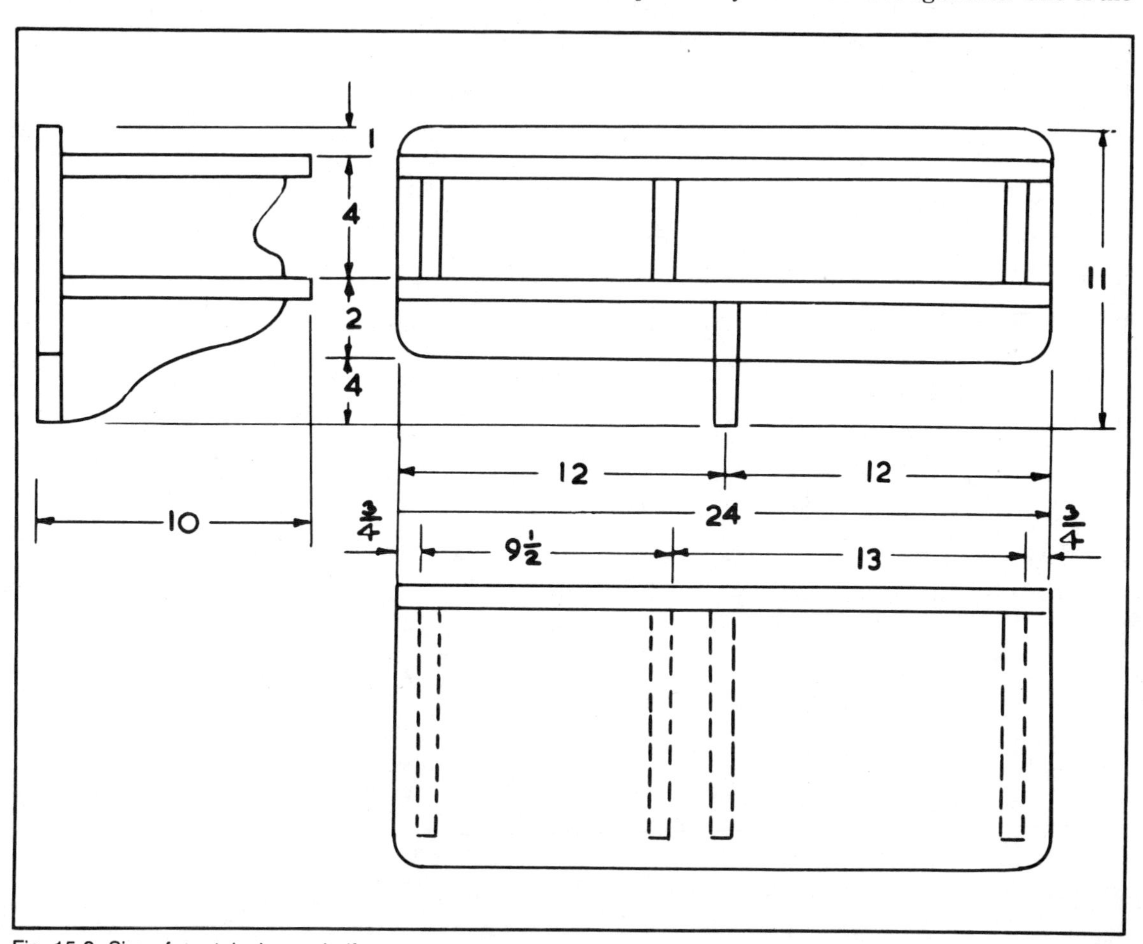

Fig. 15-8. Sizes for a telephone shelf.

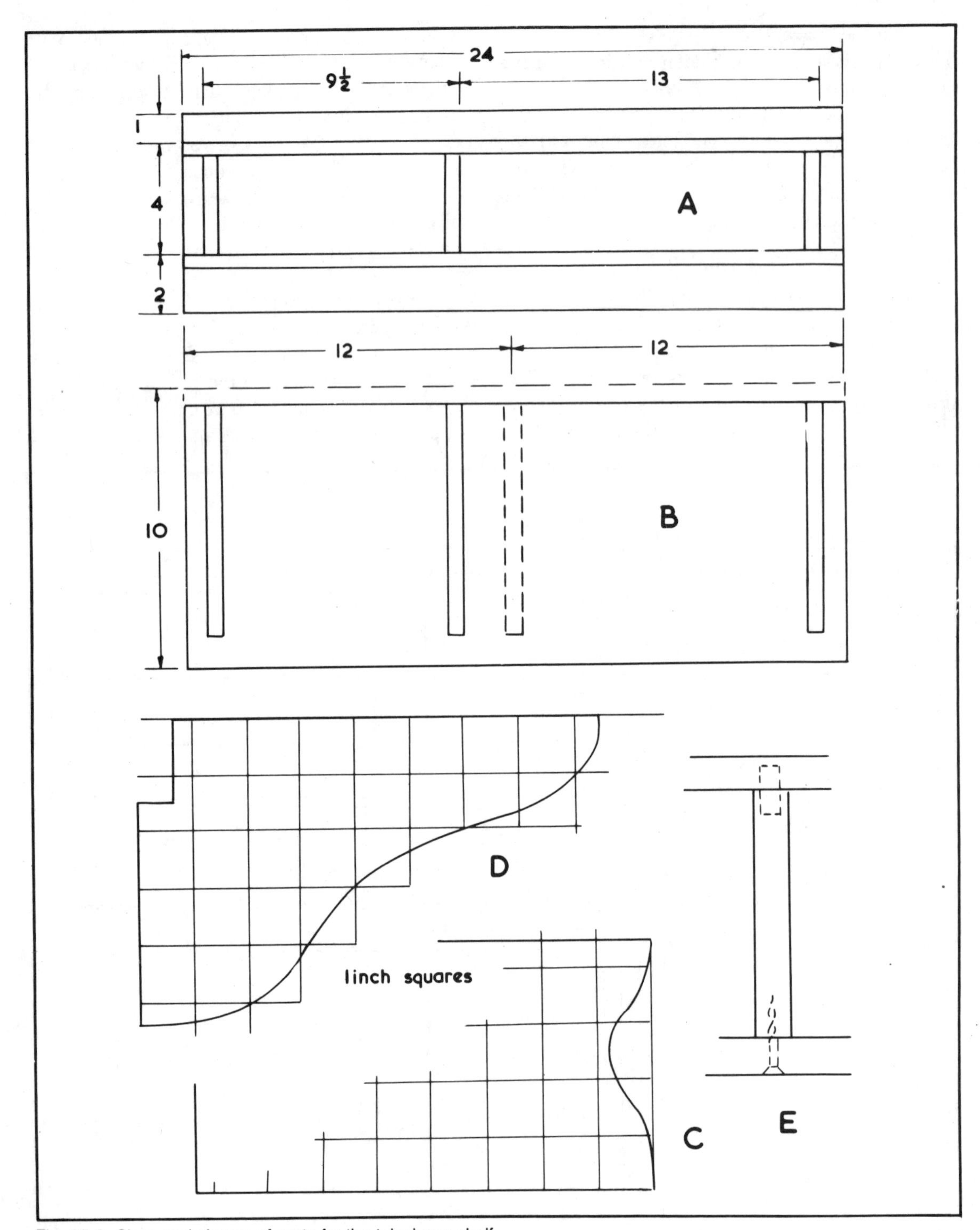

Fig. 15-9. Sizes and shapes of parts for the telephone shelf.

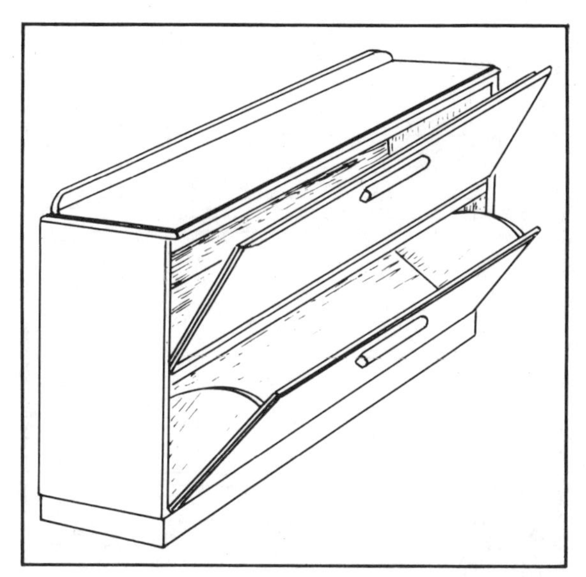

Fig. 15-10. A hall locker with a fall-front locker and a tilting bin below.

attractions of making your own furniture is that you can make it to exactly fit your needs and not have to compromise with a standard item. Consider the locker in relation to other things. There can be a mirror above it. An umbrella stand may go alongside it or be attached to it.

The end view (Fig. 15-11A) includes the controlling dimensions for the other parts. Draw it full-size. Allow for the actual sections of lengthwise parts, either on a spare piece of plywood or hardboard or on the wood that will make one end. If you do not draw everything, at least outline the details of the tilting bin (Fig. 15-11B). That pivots on the center of the hinge knuckle (Fig. 15-12A). When you draw the curve of the bin end, the compass point goes on the knuckle (Fig. 15-12B).

Make the pair of ends and allow for the rails, shelf, and bottom to be doweled (Fig. 15-12C). Rabbet the rear edges for the plywood back. The shelf goes behind its front rail. That joint can be glued and doweled, but it will be stronger rabbeted (Fig. 15-12D). If you are using solid wood throughout, you can economize at the bottom by using a frame of 2-inch strips instead of the solid piece. The bottom does not show, but wood around the edges is needed for attaching the plinth.

Table 15-4. Materials List for Hall Locker.

Part						
2 ends	15	×	33	×	3/4	
1 top	16	×	43	×	3/4	
1 shelf	15	×	43	×	3/4	
1 bottom	15	×	43	×	3/4	
3 rails	2	×	43	×	3/4	
1 front	12	×	42	×	3/4	
1 false front	12 1/2	×	42	×	3/4	
1 front	16	×	42	×	3/4	
1 false front	16 1/2	×	42	×	3/4	
2 bin ends	15	×	16	×	1/2	
1 bin back	7	×	42	×	1/2	
1 bin bottom	15	×	42	×	1/2	
1 locker back	32	×	42	×	1/4	plywood
1 plinth	4	×	42	×	3/4	
2 plinths	4	×	15	×	3/4	
2 handles	1 1/4	×	8	×	1 1/4	
1 back ledge	3	×	42	×	3/4	

Assemble the lengthwise parts to the ends and add the back. The back should hold the carcass square, but stand the assembly on a flat surface and check diagonals on the front before the glue sets.

Make the top door to fit easily into its opening. Allow for hinges let into the lower edge; three or four 2-inch or 3-inch hinges will be needed. You can fit the hinges and make a trial assembly before adding the false front, which overlaps at ends and top (Fig. 15-12E). The edges of the false fronts and top can be left square, rounded, or molded. A simple molding is shown (Fig. 15-12F), but other sections are equally suitable, depending on available cutters.

The door for the bottom compartment is made up in a similar way, and its front appearance should match the top door. The bin end shape should be obtained from your full-size drawing. At the front the load is best taken with dowels or screws into the ends of the door (Fig. 15-12G). Screw or dowel into the other parts and drive screws through the door and the bin back into the bin bottom (Fig. 15-12H). Round the top edges of the bin ends and back. Screw the hinges to the bin door first, then have the door tilted fully out so you can get at the screws into the bottom. It may be simpler to wait until you have fitted the plinth before doing this work.

The bin can swing out as far as possible when in use, but you should limit the drop of the top door to horizontal. Do so either with a folding strut sold

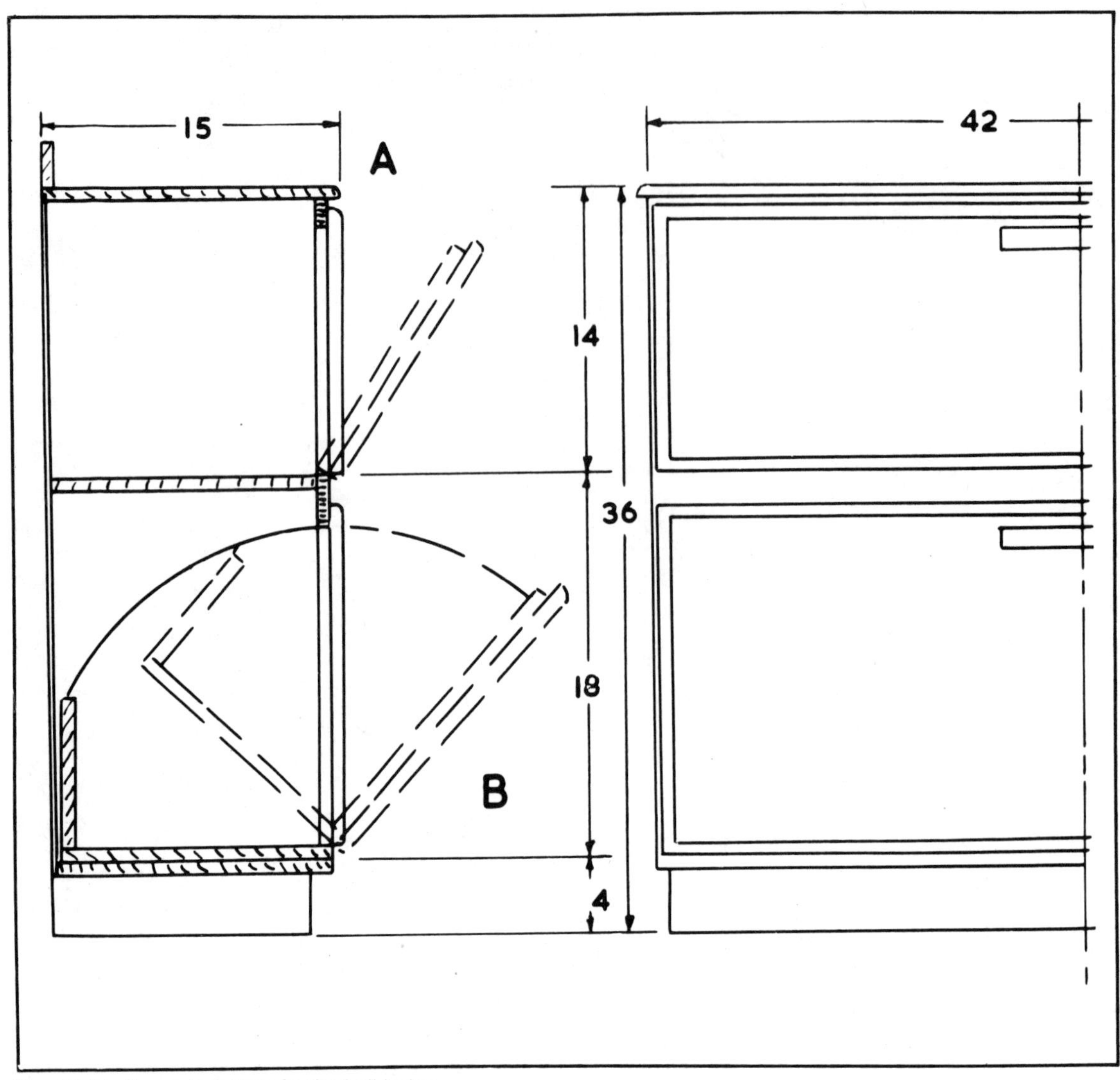

Fig. 15-11. Suggested sizes for the hall locker.

for this purpose or a cord between two screw eyes at one or both ends (Fig. 15-12J).

The plinth has a front and two ends (Fig. 15-13A) mitered at the corners with a block (Fig. 15-13B). There is no need for a back piece. Screw downward through the carcass bottom (Fig. 15-13C) or use pocket screws upward (Fig. 15-13D).

The top is the most prominent part of the locker, so choose an attractive piece of wood for it. If you have to glue pieces to make up the width, try to get the grain matching. Veneered plywood or particle board can be used, with molding added around the edges. Allow for an overlap and screws from below through the rails and through strips across the ends (Fig. 15-13D). You can counterbore through the rails (Fig. 15-13E) or use pocket screws (Fig. 15-13F). You can put a back ledge on to protect the wall.

The handles should be fairly long and near the tops of the doors, so you can reach any part of a

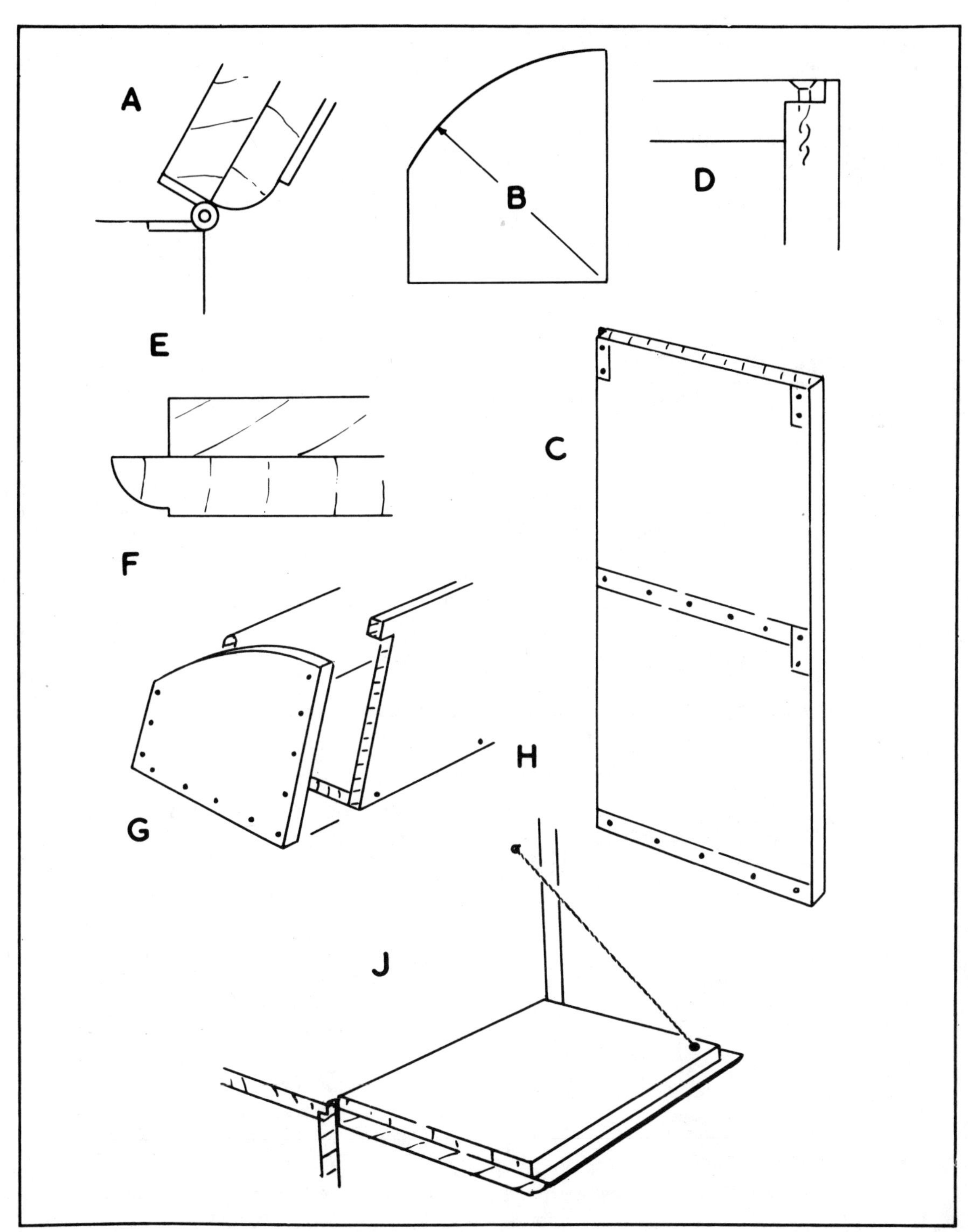

Fig. 15-12. Locker bin and door arrangements.

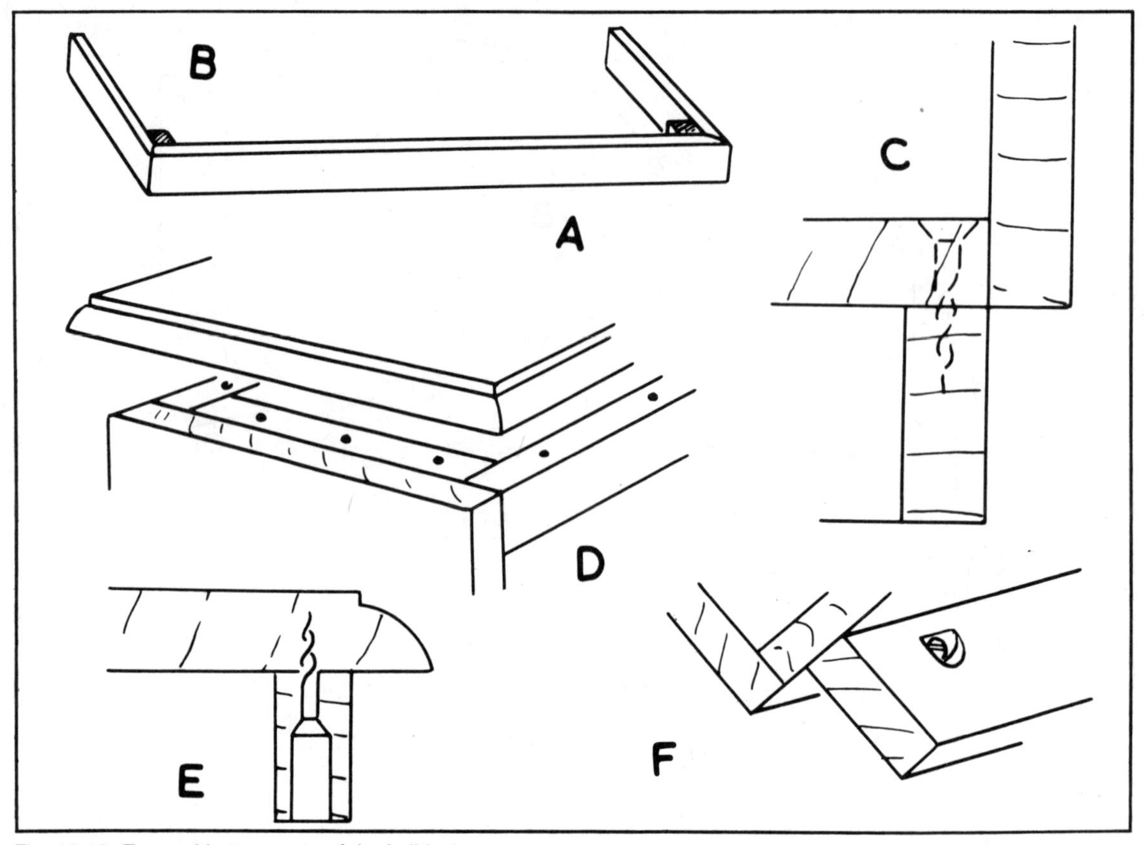

Fig. 15-13. Top and bottom parts of the hall locker.

Fig. 15-14. An umbrella stand with a lift-out tray.

handle to pull it. You can use bought metal or plastic handles, but blocks of wood hollowed on the underside may be made and screwed from inside the door.

UMBRELLA STAND

This stand is for umbrellas, walking canes, and other long narrow things such as fishing poles and some games equipment. It is intended to rest on the floor and be attached to the wall (Fig. 15-14). At the bottom is a lift-out tray, so drained water or dirt can be removed. The sizes (Fig. 15-15 and Table 15-5) show three roomy compartments, but the width can be made more or less. There are curves in some parts, but straight lines can be used for simplicity or to match other furniture.

Mark the pair of ends with rabbets for the plywood. The curve (Fig. 15-16A) is not critical, and you can draw a pleasing shape freehand. Allow

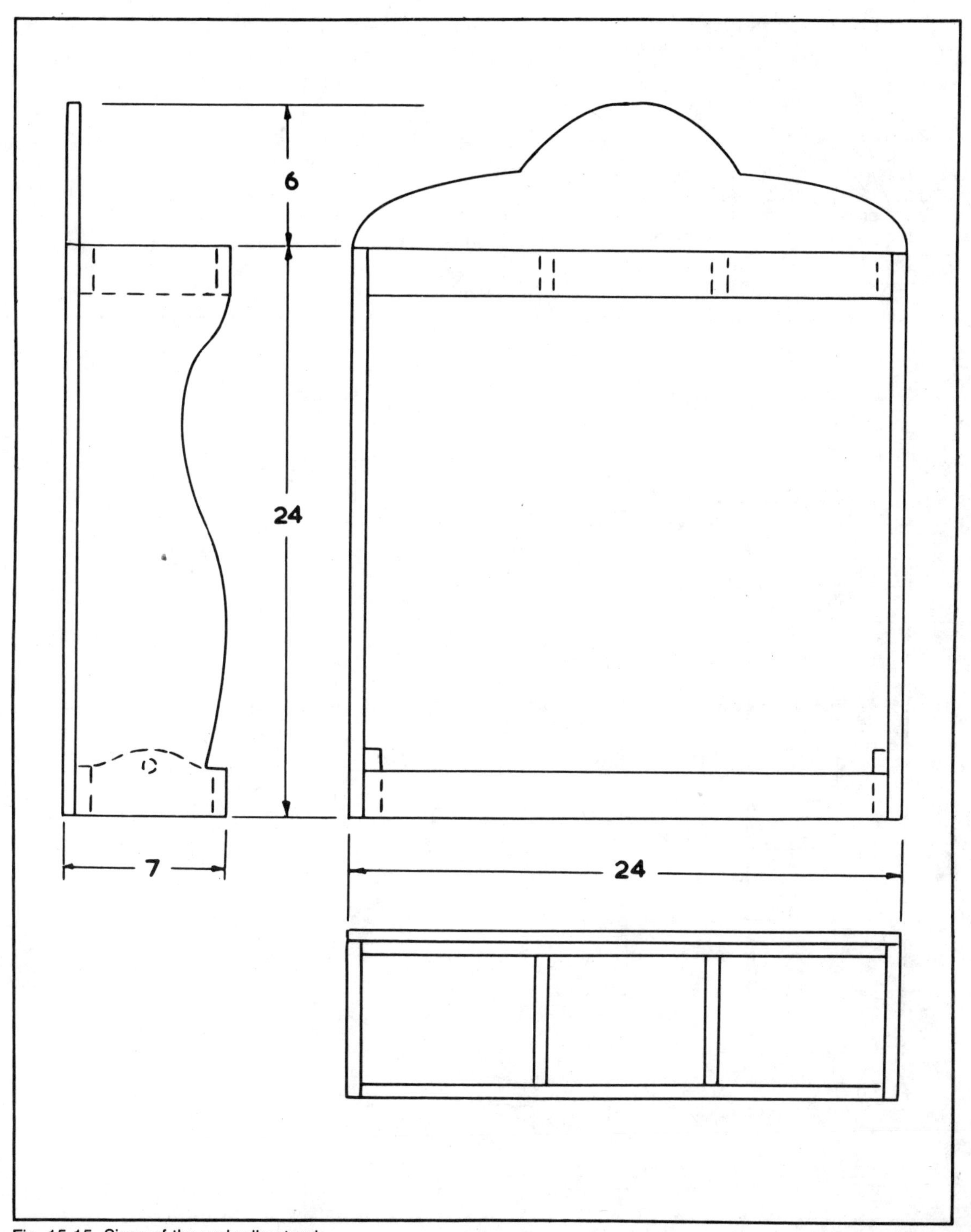

Fig. 15-15. Sizes of the umbrella stand.

Table 15-5. Materials List for Umbrella Stand.

1 back	24	×	30	×	½ plywood
2 ends	7	×	25	×	⅝
4 rails	2	×	25	×	⅝
2 dividers	2	×	8	×	⅝
2 tray sides	2	×	24	×	⅝
2 tray ends	3	×	6	×	⅝
1 tray bottom	6	×	24	×	¼ plywood

for doweling the rails to the ends and the dividers to the rails (Fig. 15-16B), although you can use stopped tenons if you prefer (Fig. 15-16C).

All parts can be joined without the back, but make sure the assembly is square in all directions.

The back is shown with its top edge shaped. Make a template of half the outline and turn it over to get the shape symmetrical (Fig. 15-16D). You can do some decorative piercing such as initials, a badge, or a leaf (Fig. 15-16E), with the outline cut in

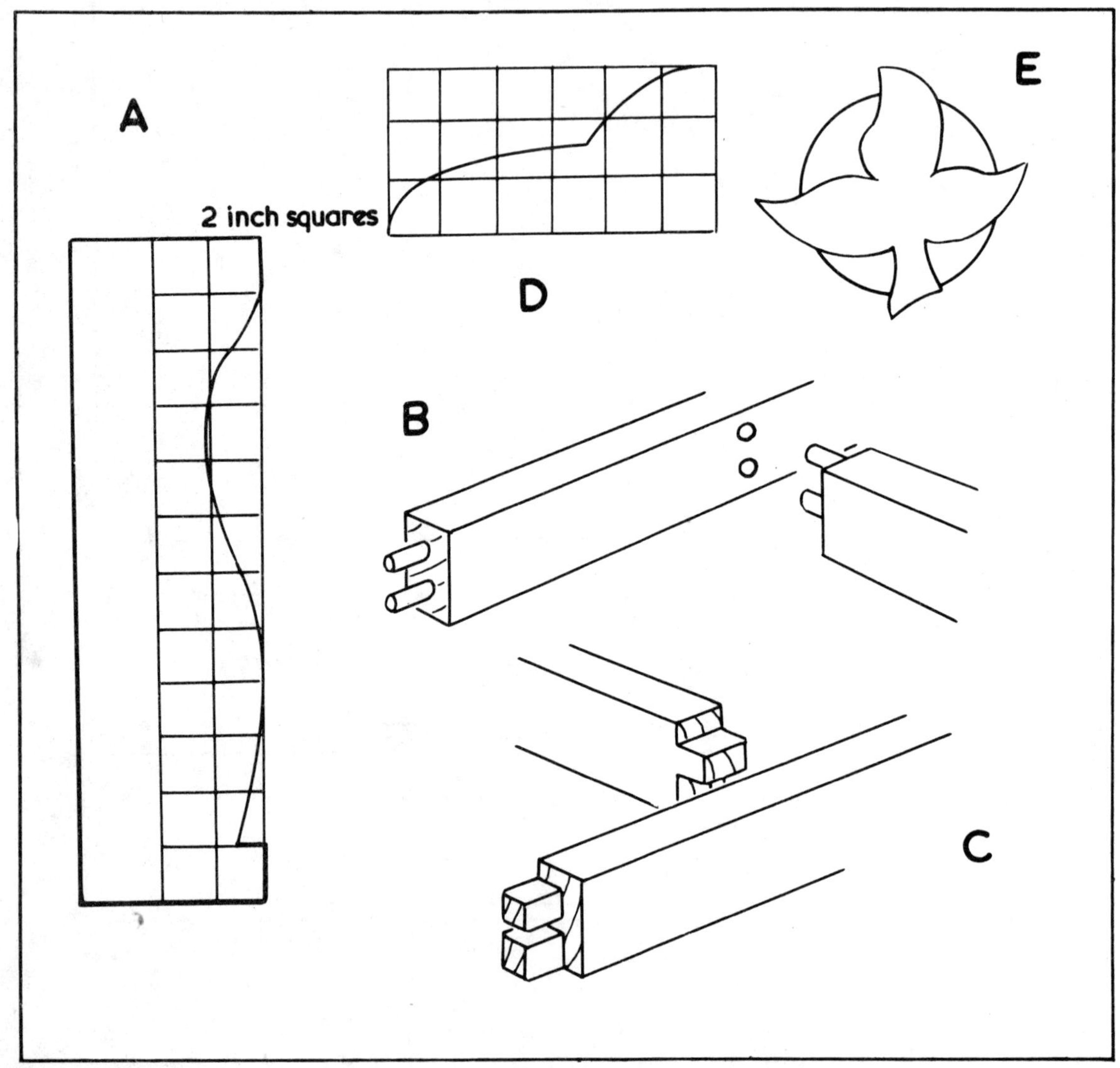

Fig. 15-16. Shaped and decorated parts and constructional methods.

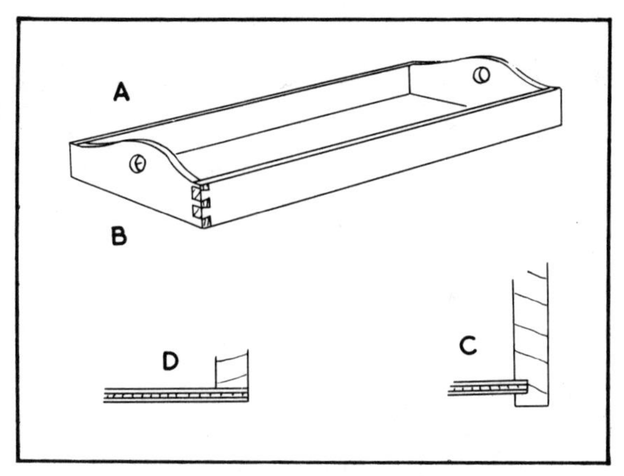

Fig. 15-17. The tray at the bottom of the umbrella stand.

with a chisel where it overlaps the cutout. Be careful that the plywood veneers do not break out. Round the exposed front edges.

The tray that goes in the bottom is a simple box, but it should be watertight. Use a waterproof glue in all the joints and preferably use marine grade plywood for the bottom. Coat the tray with boat varnish or something that resists water well.

The box ends are raised with holes for lifting out (Fig. 15-17A). Corners can be nailed, screwed, or dovetailed (Fig. 15-17B). The bottom can be let into a groove (Fig. 15-17C) or glued and screwed (Fig. 15-17D). Make the tray an easy fit in the base so it can be removed.

Chapter 16

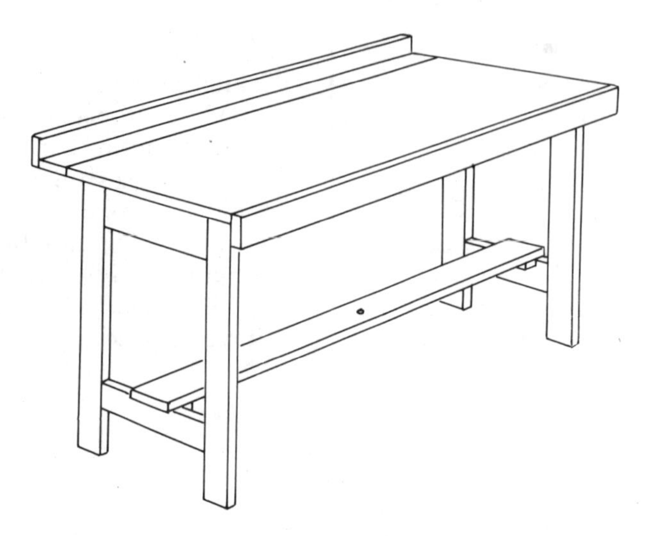

Workshop Built-Ins

YOUR WORKSHOP IS PROBABLY IN AS GREAT A need of built-in items as anywhere in the home. There is usually only limited space in which to work. The more things that can be put onto the walls, the more space there will be in which to work.

Racks with a specific place for each tool will help you work quickly and more efficiently. You also need to protect your cutting tools. Chisels and planes need sharpening frequently. If they are left around among other things on the bench, they are liable to get blunted and need even more frequent sharpening. If they have racks conveniently located near the bench and you return them there between use, their vital cutting edges will be kept in the best condition for as long as possible.

Squares and rules need to be protected from damage if they are to remain accurate. Another problem is the storage of tools that are important but less frequently used, as well as spare blades or other parts that you sometimes need to change. If they have their own storage places, you can find them without delay.

Every shop will have its own layout. Available wall space in relation to benches and windows has to be considered. If it is a new place, you may want to delay fitting racks and other built-in items until you have experimented with positions of benches and power tools. Allow for additional items that you hope to get later, particularly larger power tools such as a lathe or combination woodworker. Racks and other wall items are best made as units, so they can be taken down and repositioned with minimum trouble. Only attach shelves and racks individually to the wall to make up a group if you are certain you will not want to move them.

Some craftsmen make their own racks and shop furniture quite crudely. The racks may be functional, but a visitor to your shop may assess your skill as only being at the standard he sees there. A nicely finished and correctly constructed item on the wall inspires you to do better work on the furniture you are making on the bench. Sometimes a roughly made rack may be made, because the tools have to be stored and you are short of time. Take care that it does not then become the permanent rack. Find time later to produce a craftsman-like job.

OPEN TOOL RACKS

Important tools and those that have to be protected are best kept behind doors or in drawers, but other tools are more usefully kept open and within reach. Some racks can be similar to those described for use in a locker, but some special arrangements can be used.

The tools to be kept within reach often are not always the same, so you shouldn't make a rack system on the wall above the bench, with carefully fitted racks that each only take one tool. You should make racks that will keep tools off the bench and are of basic and general form.

One general rack is a fairly broad shelf, probably as long as the bench, with holes of various sizes and a strip held off to make a slot (Fig. 16-1A). The width of the shelf is useful for putting larger tools on temporarily. If many tools are put through a slot without restraint, they will fall over, so there should be stops at least at 6-inch intervals. They can be pieces of wood (Fig. 16-1B). You will use up less valuable space by drilling through pieces of dowel rod (Fig. 16-1C). For a metalworking rack, the bar at the front can be a strip of aluminum or mild steel, but that may blunt woodworking tools.

Several tools can be hung. Usually something better than a nail is needed. If its size does not matter, a piece of dowel rod, arranged to slope, can be used (Fig. 16-1D). If you want to hang a tool with a smaller hole, cut off the head of a long nail and file it round, or use a piece of steel or brass rod (Fig. 16-1E). The giant screw hooks obtainable at hardware stores will support many tools.

Some things are better on a bar. Many C-clamps can hang on a bar held out by spacers (Fig. 16-1F). You can bend a strip of metal, such as ⅛-inch-by-¾-inch section, to make a rack (Fig. 16-1G).

Magnetic tool racks are available. Each consists of two exposed iron strips, which are the opposite poles of a magnet (Fig. 16-1H). A magnet will only grip iron or steel, but any steel tool put across the strips will be held. Some surprisingly heavy steel tools can be held this way. Some of the magnetism will be transferred to the steel tool, though. That may not matter. In some instances it can be an advantage, as when a screwdriver attracts and holds a steel screw. At other times a tool may attract something when you do not want it to.

Perforated hardboard can be made into racks. The ⅛-inch hardboard is perforated cleanly at regular intervals. Hardboard may not be as strong as wood, but it will stand up to considerable use. Many fittings are available to hang different things from perforated hardboard. They are particularly suitable for the lighter tools needed for leatherwork, macrame, basketry, and canvas work. Many woodworking and metalworking tools can hang from hardboard.

The fittings are mostly made from stout wire, with a double bend to go through a hole (Fig. 16-2A). Some may go through more than one hole for additional strength or rigidity.

The perforated hardboard has to be held off the wall a short distance (½ inch is plenty). There can be spacers under screws (Fig. 16-2B) or strips put under the edges (Fig. 16-2C). The edges of hardboard wear first, so a rack will keep a good appearance longer if it is framed (Fig. 16-2D). If the board is very big, have attachments to the wall in the body of the board as well as around the edges to prevent buckling.

TOOL LOCKER

Many tools require protection if they are to be kept in best condition. Files must not be allowed to rub against each other, or they will soon be blunted. Some small tools should have specific storage places, or you may not be able to find them when needed.

The tool kit of an enthusiastic craftsman often changes, with tools being replaced and new ones added. It is very difficult to make a tool box or locker for everything and be certain there will not have to be alterations. Most craftsmen have certain basic tools, and it should be possible to devise a layout of a storage arrangement for them that will not need altering at least for some time. Other tools that you are uncertain about may be given tempor-

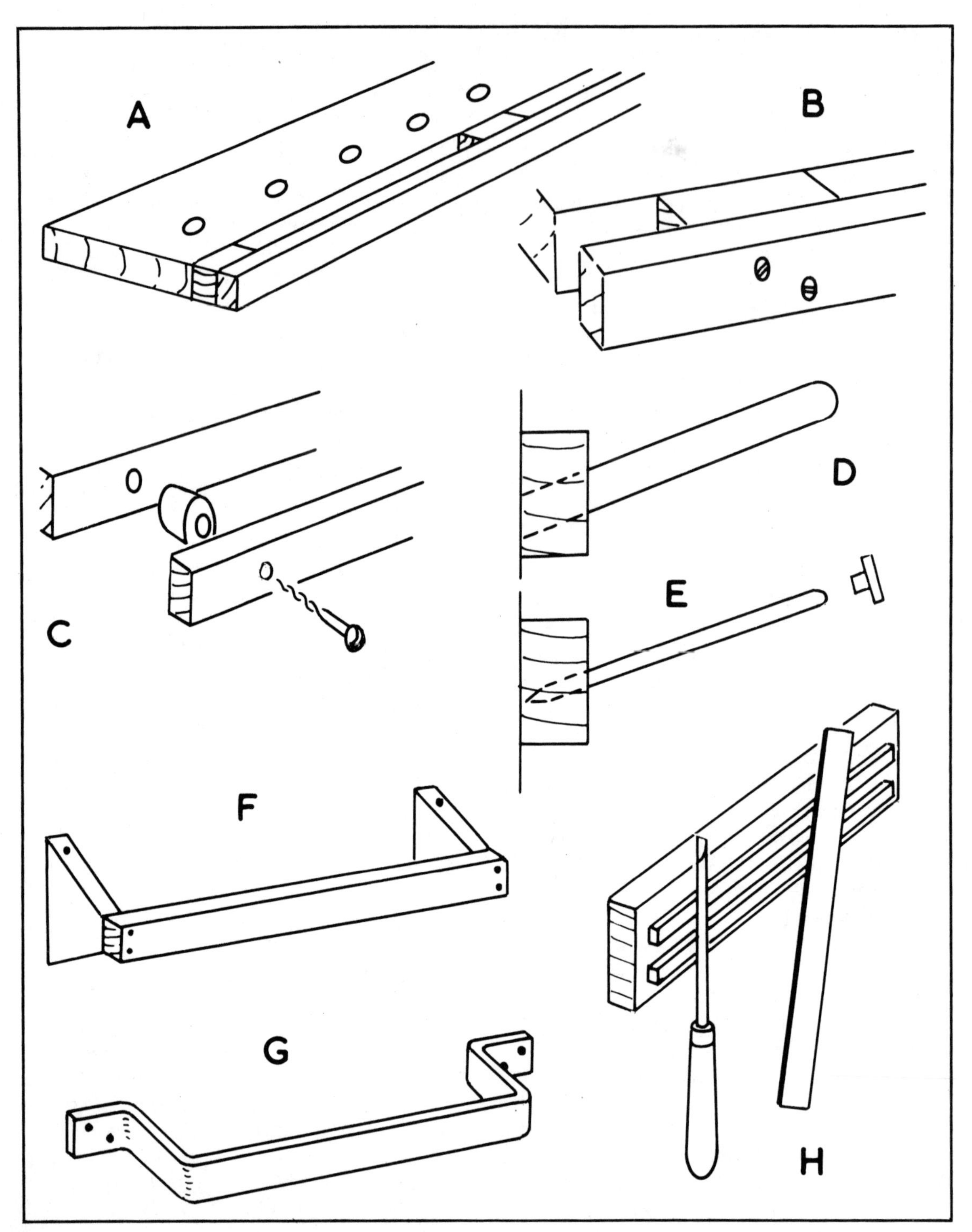

Fig. 16-1. Suggested arrangements of open tool racks with holes, hooks, slots, and bars to support tools.

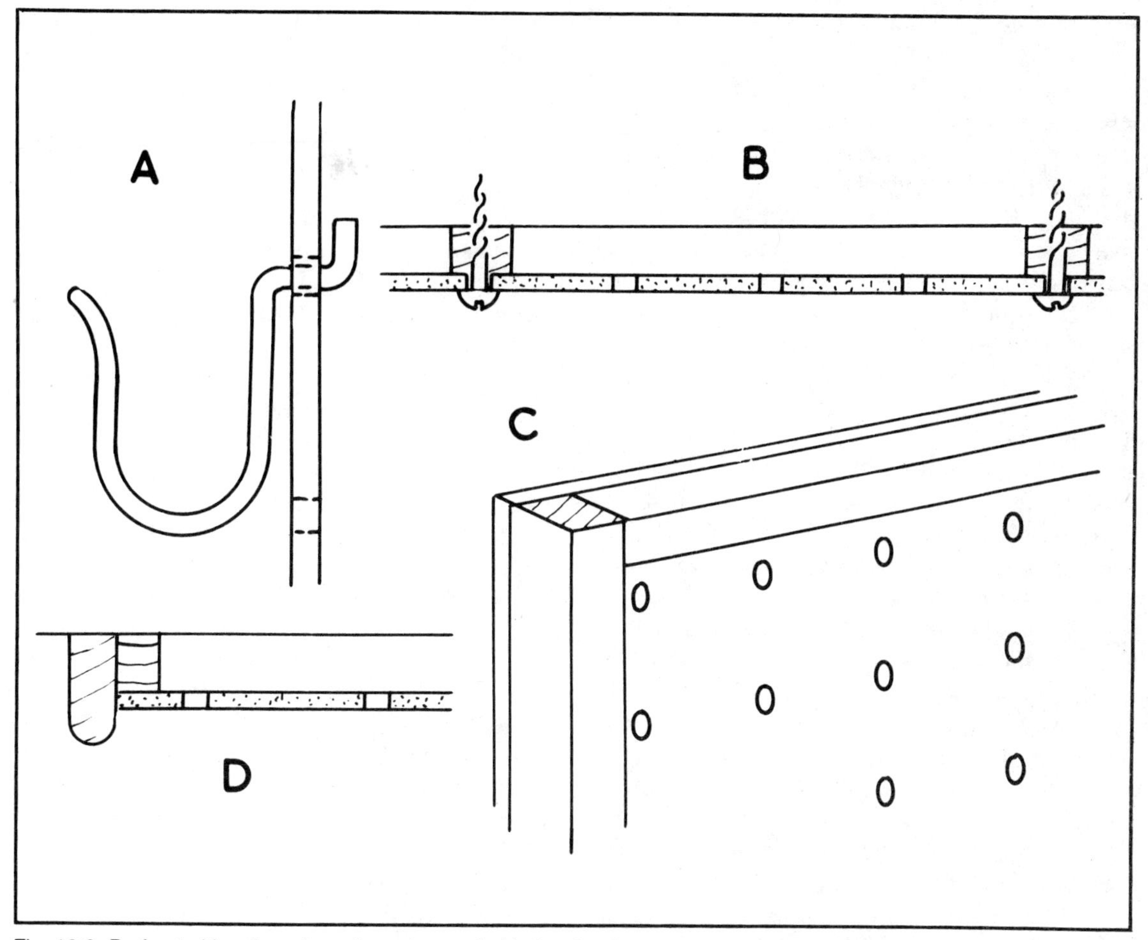

Fig. 16-2. Perforated hardboard can have frames behind so hooks may go through the holes.

ary accommodation in boxes or racks that can be changed. If you have enough space, you can arrange a wall locker for the basic tools and another with less permanent racks for other tools. Usually the amount of wall space available is not much, so rarely used tools will have to go under the bench or elsewhere. Some tools used frequently can go in open racks on the wall in front of the bench. If your shop is only used occasionally or the tools have to be protected from children, it is better to be able to close them behind doors. The tools must be visible and readily available when you are engaged on a project. Sliding doors always hide part of the contents. Let the doors swing to the sides if there is space. An advantage of this arrangement is that you can put some tools on racks inside the doors. If there is insufficient space for doors to swing, it is better for the doors to lift out than to slide.

The size of a locker or cabinet depends on the available wall space. Consider your reach when standing at the bench or in front of the locker. The tools needed frequently should be easy to reach. If the locker is taken to the ceiling, you may put some tools up high, but you may have to stand on something to reach them.

If you make any sort of tool rack, the tool and the rack will take up more space than the tool alone. This may seem very obvious, but it is too easy to make many ingenious and bulky racks, then find you cannot get as many tools into a space as you expected. Keep racks small and try to store tools so they fit closely.

Start by assembling all the tools you want to store, then try various layouts to see if they will go in the available space. Some things will go on the sides of the locker and others go on the insides of the doors. Sometimes you can arrange for a row of tools going through holes in a thick shelf. Others can be attached by clips to the front of the shelf.

The stored tools should be accessible. You should be able to reach out and remove a tool from its rack with a single action. In a few cases you may have to move a knob or other retainer, but there should never be anything that requires releasing a nut or screw. Avoid complications. If a tool can hang on a nail, that is fine, although a screw hook may be better. For something like a steel rule with a hole in the end, cut the head off a nail and drive it so it slopes upward.

Spring steel clips can be used for many tools with round handles. Some are supplied coated with plastic, so they will not scratch wood handles. The types with a double curve (Fig. 16-3A) have a greater movement as you press a tool in than those with single curves (Fig. 16-3B), so they are more tolerant of size variations. Use roundhead screws as large as will go through the holes in the springs. The holes are rather small.

Many round tools in handles such as spikes, awls, and many screwdrivers can be stored in racks with holes. Have the rack about 1 inch thick. With thinner wood, some loosely fitting tools may tilt. Countersink the holes for ease of tool entry. If you countersink underneath, that will reduce the risk of a tool's end breaking out the grain (Fig. 16-3C). A single shelf is all that is needed with most of these tools if the handle will prevent the tool from dropping through. For other tools, particularly if you want to protect the point, there may be a second shelf with a hole partly through (Fig. 16-3D). The handle sizes determine the spacing of holes. You can get more in a given length by making a zigzag arrangement of holes (Fig. 16-3E).

You can make racks for tools of other cross sections in a similar way. Chisels can have a row of slots (Fig. 16-3F). You can get more in by cutting the slots across (Fig. 16-3G) or at an angle (Fig. 16-3H). As with the other tools, handle sizes control spacing.

You may not always want to have the same chisels available for use. In that case a rack that is not tied to specific sizes is better. This can be made with a piece wide enough to give handles clearance at the back, then a strip is held off by spacers at intervals (Fig. 16-3J). If you want to protect the chisel edge yet keep them visible, a piece of Plexiglas or other rigid transparent plastic can hang in front of any rack (Fig. 16-3K). Files can be dealt with in any of the ways suggested for chisels.

A square can go into the ends of a slotted shelf (Fig. 16-4A), which can have clips or other storage on its front. A smaller square, such as a combination one, may be inserted into a slot at the front of a shelf.

Hammers and mallets are better put into a rack from the front. You can drive pieces of dowel rods into holes, so they slope upward slightly (Fig. 16-4B). You can make a shelf with its near edge beveled to give it a slope, then drill to clear the tool handle and cut into the hole to make a slot (Fig. 16-4C). An upward slope to this sort of rack is important. Shop vibrations may be enough to make a tool fall out of a level rack.

Pliers and pincers may have their handles over a rod (Fig. 16-4D), although a flat strip on edge is better (Fig. 16-4E). One pair of pliers can hook over a shaped block (Fig. 16-4F).

The wedge system in many planes allows you to hang them with a bar across the compartment (Fig. 16-5A). Make sure there is room to lift a long plane clear of the bar. You can put several planes together without spacers between them. Small or special planes can go on divided shelves or into compartments. If there are several blades for a plane, arrange racks or slots for them near their plane. It is a nuisance if things needed together are kept in different places.

Saws need protection for their teeth. If a saw goes into a cabinet near one end with its teeth to the back, that will be sufficient protection (Fig. 16-5B). If a saw can go inside a paneled door, the teeth may go toward the frame (Fig. 16-5C). To keep the saw

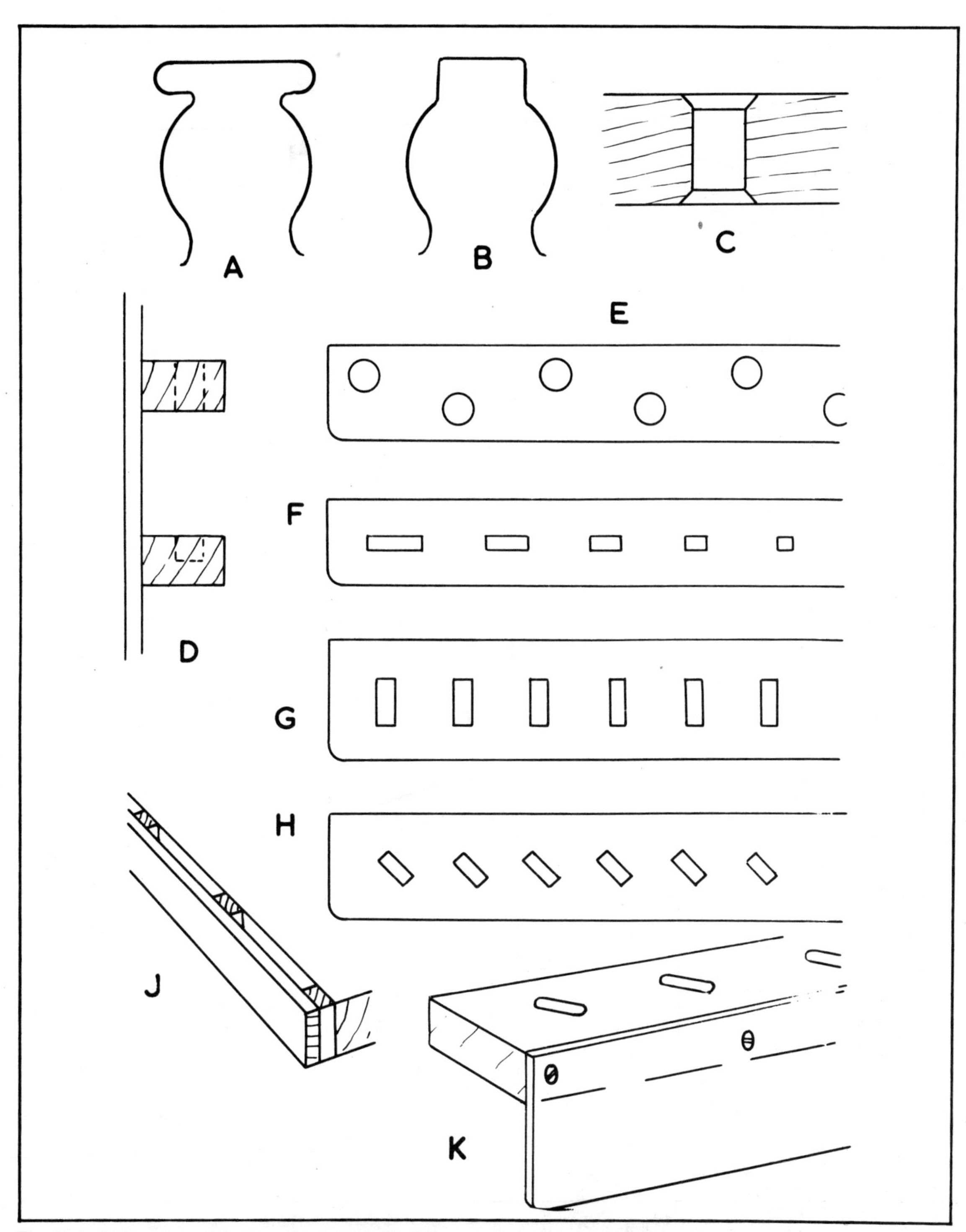

Fig. 16-3. Spring clips will hold some tools (A, B). Others go through holes and slots (C to K).

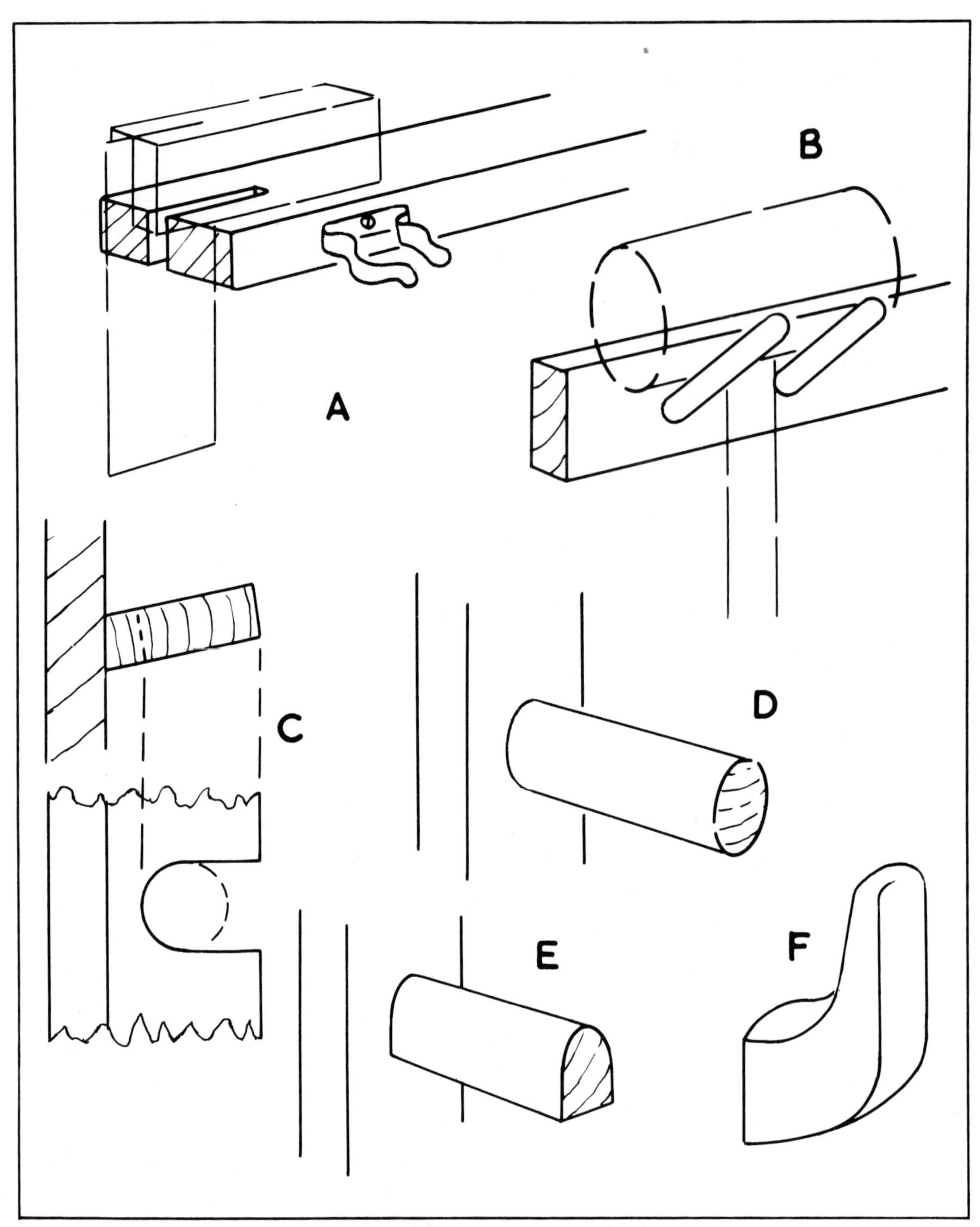

Fig. 16-4. Tools may go into slots (A). Tilting (B, C) prevents tools from falling forward. There can be rounded rails and hooks (D, E, F).

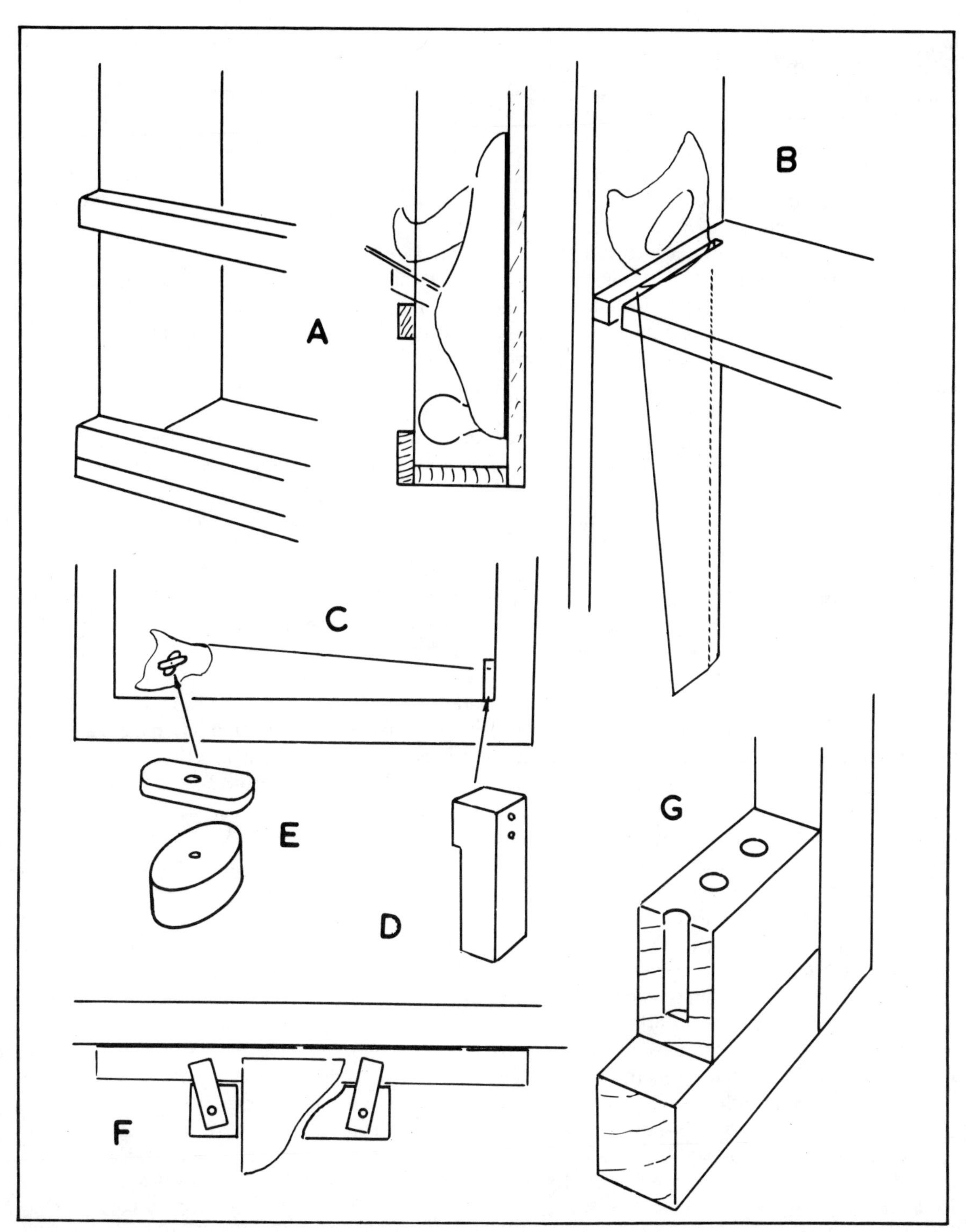

Fig. 16-5. Racks built into cabinets and doors are needed for some tools.

in place, there can be a notched block at one end (Fig. 16-5D) and a block and turn button through the handle (Fig. 16-5E). Hacksaws and backsaws can be treated in a similar way.

Some other flat tools can go inside doors, but in most cases you can have shaped blocks and turn buttons to keep the tools in place (Fig. 16-5F). Exceptions are punches and brace bits that can go into deep holes in a strip of wood (Fig. 16-5G).

No matter how carefully you scheme racks, there will be some tools left over. Include drawers or deep trays to take assorted small things that do not have racks. At the other extreme are some large tools that will take up too much space in a locker. Things like wrecking bars and long clamps may hang on the outsides of the locker. Arrange storage elsewhere for portable electric tools with their coiled cables.

When you plan the layout of racks inside the locker, some vertical divisions are needed to support the ends of racks that do not go right across (Fig. 16-6A). If possible, arrange racks of similar length above each other, so the vertical pieces can go through several levels. You may be able to use the upright pieces to carry their own racks (Fig. 16-6B).

Have the back of the locker thick enough to take screws from the front. When you make the first assembly, racks can be screwed from behind before the locker is attached to the wall.

Make the locker of wood at least ¾ inch thick, unless it is very small. Rabbet the rear edges for the back. Arrange for top and bottom to overhang the doors (Fig. 16-6C). Dovetails at the corners (Fig. 16-6D) may be nice. The depth that you make the locker back to front depends on available space and your tools. A plane dropping into a rack with its sole to the back may need 6 inches depth. A large handsaw with teeth to the rear may need as much. If you want to keep the locker shallower, these tools will have to be arranged another way.

How the doors are made depends on size. They can be pieces of thick plywood, or they may be framed with plywood in grooves (Fig. 16-6E). Racks in the doors will be screwed from outside. Plywood can be framed, using rabbets to bring most of the thickness inside (Fig. 16-6F), to give better space for inside racks and fittings. A pair of doors does not have to be the same size. If tool storage will be better on one wider door, or there is more room to one side of the cabinet than the other, the doors can be different widths. A single wide door with tools on it will put considerable load on its hinges and may develop a sag. Plus, more space will be needed at the side of its cabinet.

If there is no room for doors to swing and they have to be made to lift out, a simple arrangement uses two pieces of plywood (or one for a small cabinet). Arrange a strip across the bottom of the cabinet with a groove for the plywood (Fig. 16-7A) or groove the bottom of the cabinet. Have another piece at the top with a groove twice as deep (Fig. 16-7B). Make the doors deep enough to only go halfway into the top groove (Fig. 16-7C), then you can lift a door high enough to bring it clear of the bottom groove.

If you fit drawers, the best place for them is at the bottom (Fig. 16-8A). Put a strip over them as a false base to the rest of the locker. Make sure the end drawers will clear the doors. Do not make the drawers too wide, or they may not slide easily. A drawer should not be wider than twice its depth from front to back and preferably much narrower than that, but you must consider the lengths of tools to be put in them (Fig. 16-8B).

WHETSTONE CASE

Tools must be sharp to do quality work. A good craftsman spends more time sharpening planes, chisels, and other edge tools. A less expert worker will begrudge time spent sharpening and press on with blunt tools to do less satisfactory work. Usually there are two whetstones or oilstones in use: a fine one for the frequent touching up of an edge and a coarser one for use when more has to be taken off, as when the edge has struck a nail.

The stones should be kept clean if they are to sharpen properly. If they are kept loose on the bench, their oily surfaces collect dirt. Even if they have boxes, the lids may not always be replaced. This case can be attached to a wall so its flap can be lowered to about bench level, when the two stones

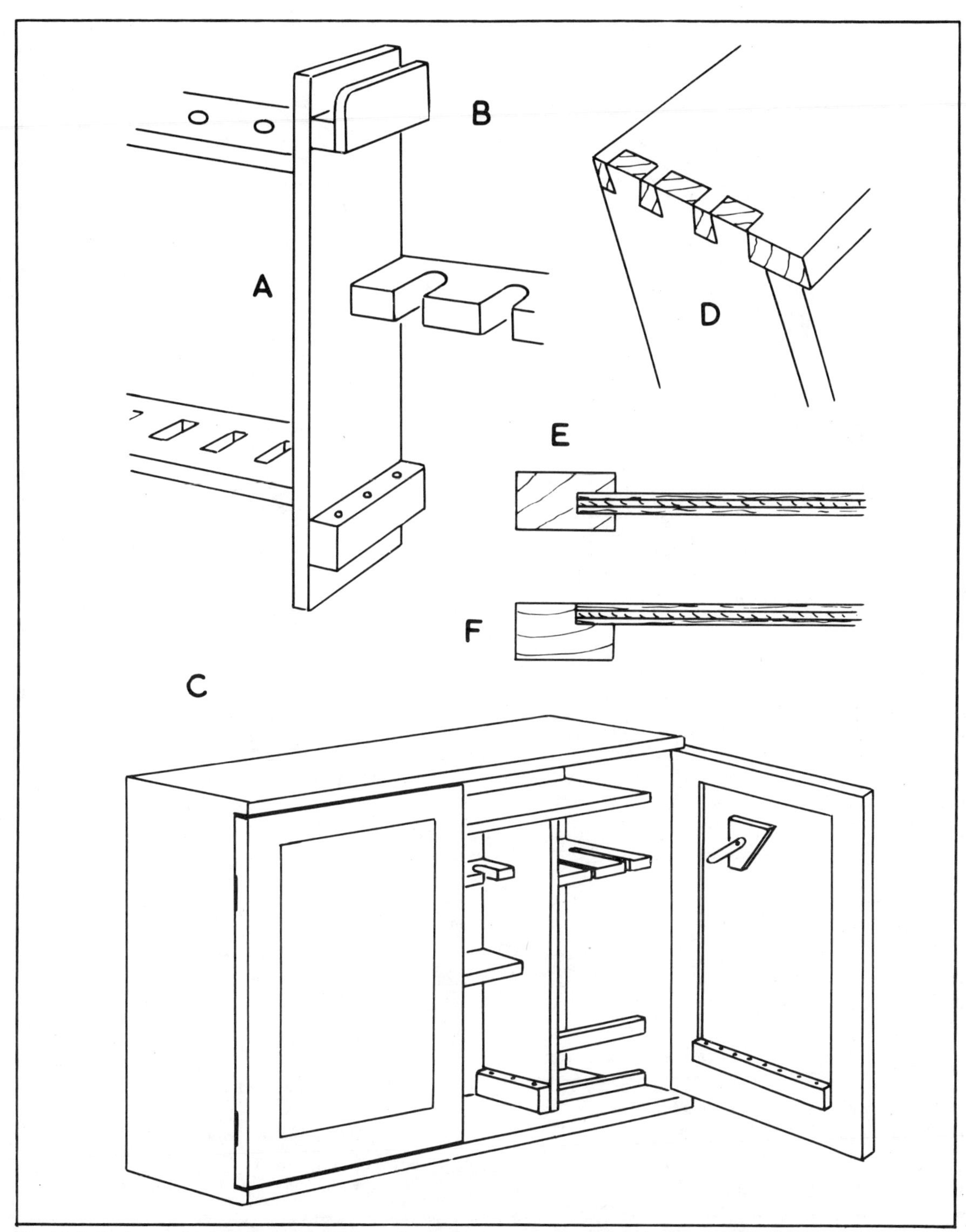

Fig. 16-6. Racks can be built into each other to give maximum storage capacity in the minimum space.

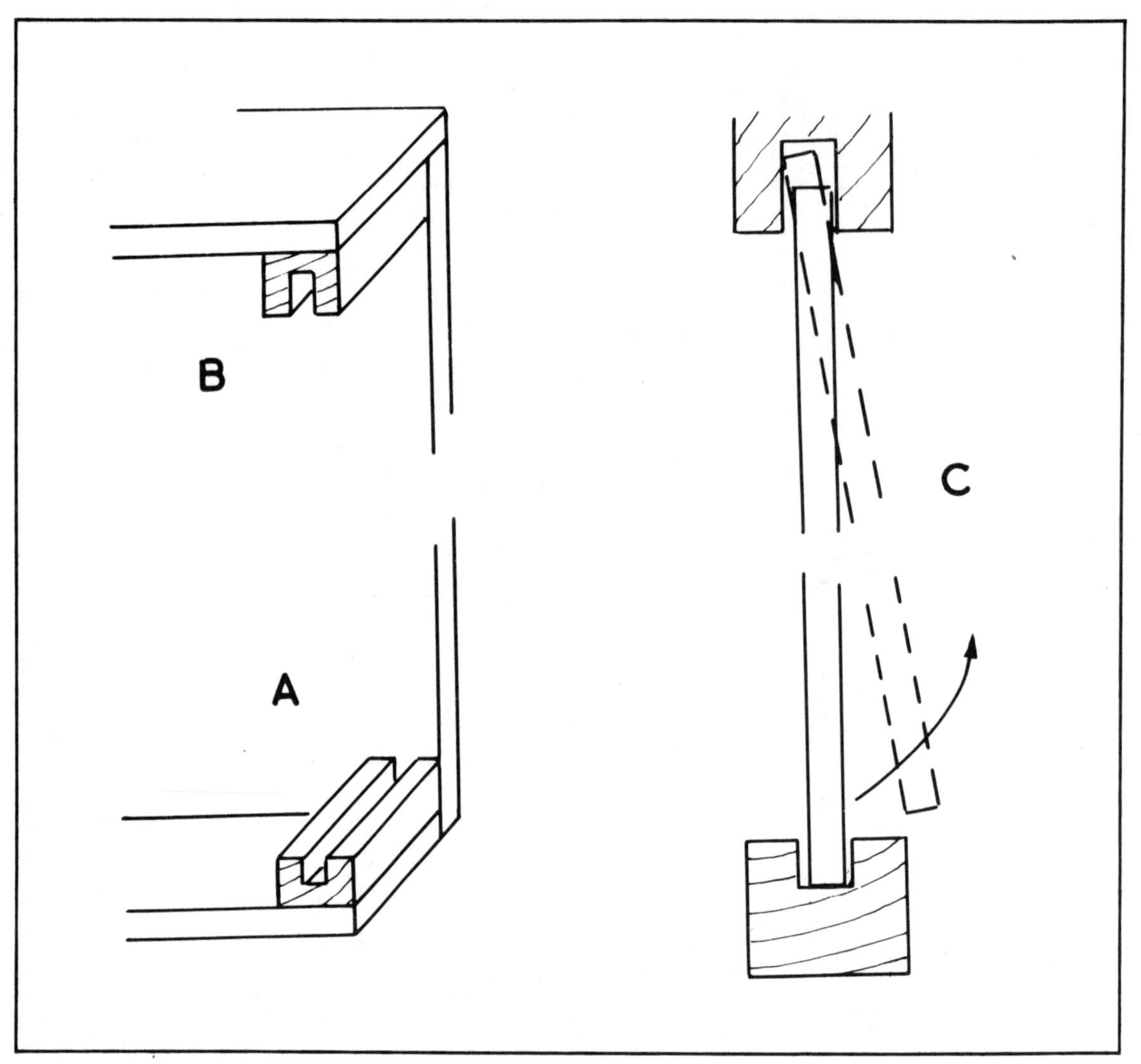

Fig. 16-7. A sliding door can lift out if the upper groove is deep enough.

will be at a convenient height for sharpening most tools. When not required, the flap tilts so the stones are inside the case and protected from dirt and damage. There is space inside the cabinet for a can of oil, slipstones for gouges and carving tools, and a cloth for wiping stones and tools. The stones are held by wedges. A stone has to be stood on edge for sharpening some tools. Removing a wedge will release the stone, which can then be secured by the wedge in the new position.

The most popular whetstones for sharpening general woodworking tools are about 8 inches long, 2 inches wide, and 1 inch thick. This case (Fig. 16-9) can hold two stones of this size. The parts are drawn to suit (Fig. 16-10), but obviously they can be modified to suit other sizes. See Table 16-1. If your craft requires unusual tools with handles at the side, you may prefer to have the stones further apart. Nearly all the parts may be made from ½-inch plywood.

Lay out the flap first (Fig. 16-10A). At the inner ends of the stones the parts go into recessed pieces (Fig. 16-10B). At the outer ends they are held by the

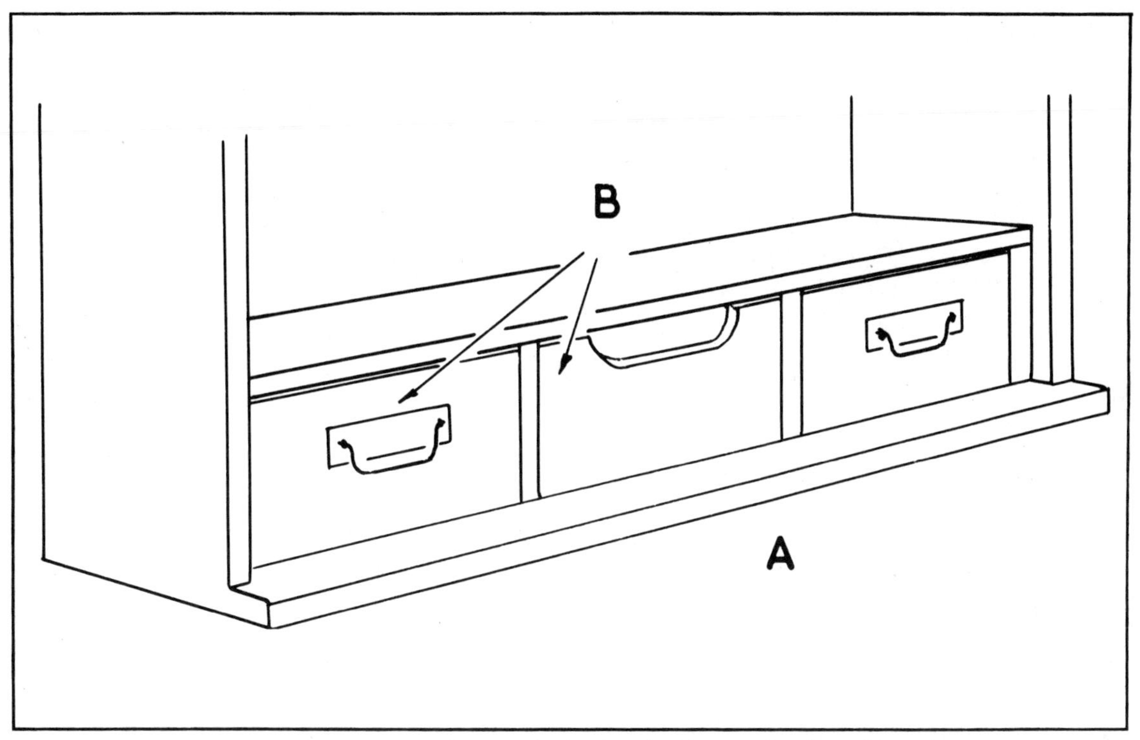

Fig. 16-8. Drawers in a tool cabinet should not have projecting handles that may interfere with closing the doors.

Fig. 16-9. This wall-mounted case holds two whetstones ready for use.

folding wedge principle, except that one of the wedges at each place is part of the stop (Fig. 16-10C). Join the parts together and check the fit of the stones. Behind the inner stop, put the 1-inch square pivot bar across. This will take the downward pressure when tools are being sharpened. Secure it with screws and glue. You can leave the rear end of the flap too long at this stage and trim it to length during assembly.

Set out a side (Fig. 16-10D). Mark the position of the pivot hole and use the flap you have made to check the position of the inner shelf, which acts as a lower stop, and the angle of the front, which should be parallel with the raised flap. That also gives you the position and section of the top stop. Cut the two sides to shape and make the back to fit between them.

To support the lowered flap in use, put two pieces of ¼-inch iron or brass round rod as pivots (Fig. 6-11A). Drill for them, but drive them from outside after assembly. It may be sufficient to attach

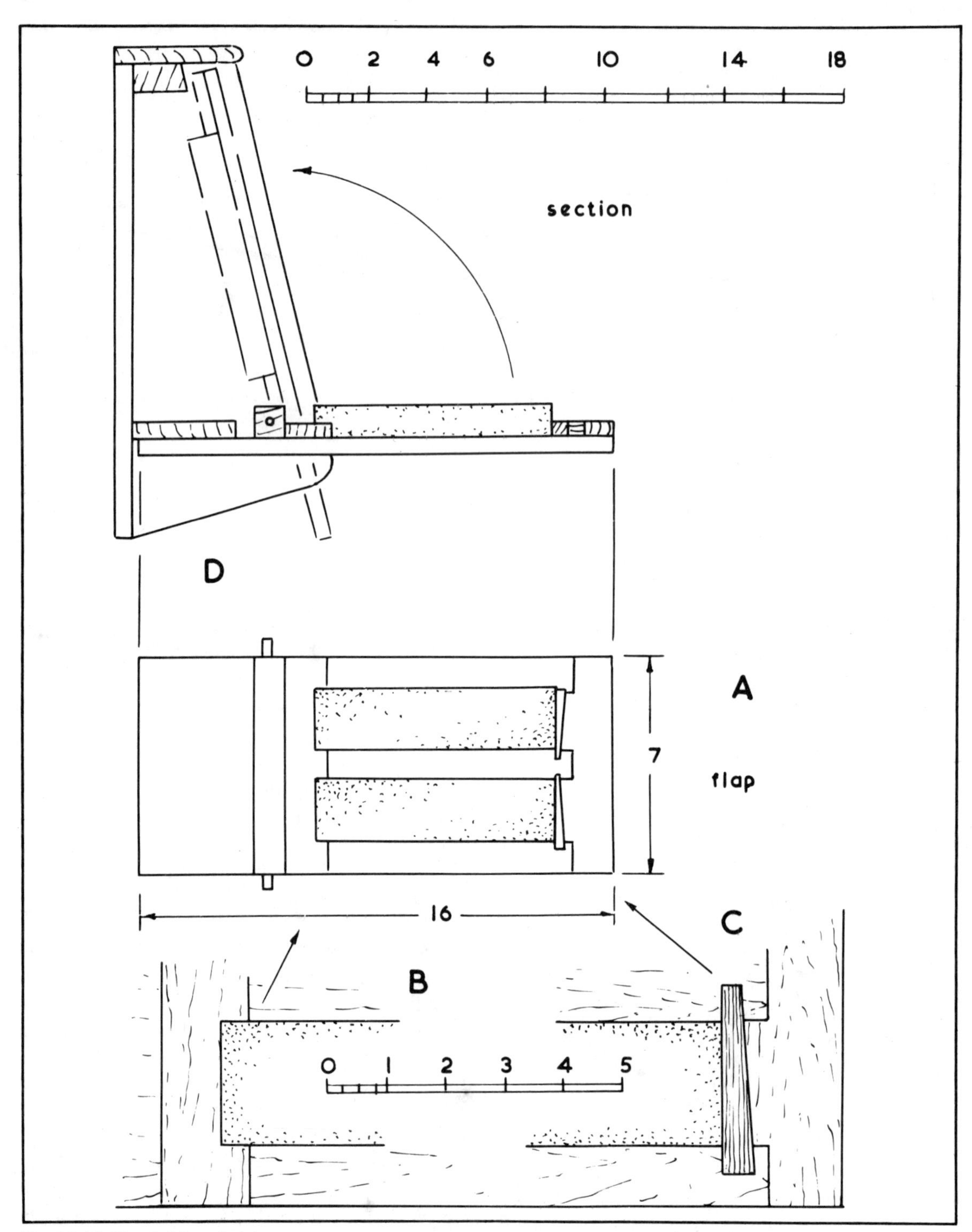

Fig. 16-10. Sizes of the whetstone case.

Table 16-1. Materials List for Whetstone Case.

1 flap	7 × 17 × ½
1 back	8 × 17 × ½
2 sides	8 × 17 × ½
1 top	4 × 9 × ½
1 shelf	3½ × 9 × ½
1 front stone piece	1¼ × 7 × ½
1 back stone piece	1¼ × 7 × ½
1 top stop	2 × 7 × 1
2 wedges	½ × 3 × ½
1 pivot bar	1 × 7 × 1

the shelf to the sides with screws only, but it will be better able to take the thrust of the flap if you make shallow dadoes to supplement the screws (Fig. 16-11B).

When you assemble, check the action of the flap with the pivot rods only partially inserted. You may have to take a few shavings off the sides of the flap to give it an easy action. When you are satisfied that the case works properly, apply several coats of varnish or other oil-resistant finish, inside and out, before final assembly and mounting on the wall.

FOLDING BENCH

Something more substantial than a table is needed for many hobbies, particularly if you need to hammer and saw or plane. Rigidity is necessary, and there must be enough bulk to absorb blows. While the ideal bench is a permanent structure, space problems may be such that there is nowhere for a full-size bench to be put. This design (Fig. 16-12) is for a bench that will fold against the wall. The bench reduces to about 4 inches thick, but it opens to give a working surface extending 28 inches from the wall. There are four legs to the floor, so loads are taken on them and not by the screws to the wall. A long rail holds the legs upright when in use and is used when they are folded to keep them tight against the bench top.

The sizes are for a bench 48 inches long (Fig. 16-13 and Table 16-2). This is the minimum length that will allow the legs to fold conveniently while having lower rails at a convenient height. A shorter top will necessitate bringing the rails higher to allow folding. If you can make your bench top longer than 48 inches, the leg rails can come lower. It will help in getting sizes if you draw a side view (Fig. 16-13A) and the layout when folded (Fig. 16-13B), either full-size or to scale.

Make the top of several boards glued together. Get end grain opposite ways to minimize any tendency to warp. There can be dowels in the joints (Fig. 16-14A), and you can include clamps across

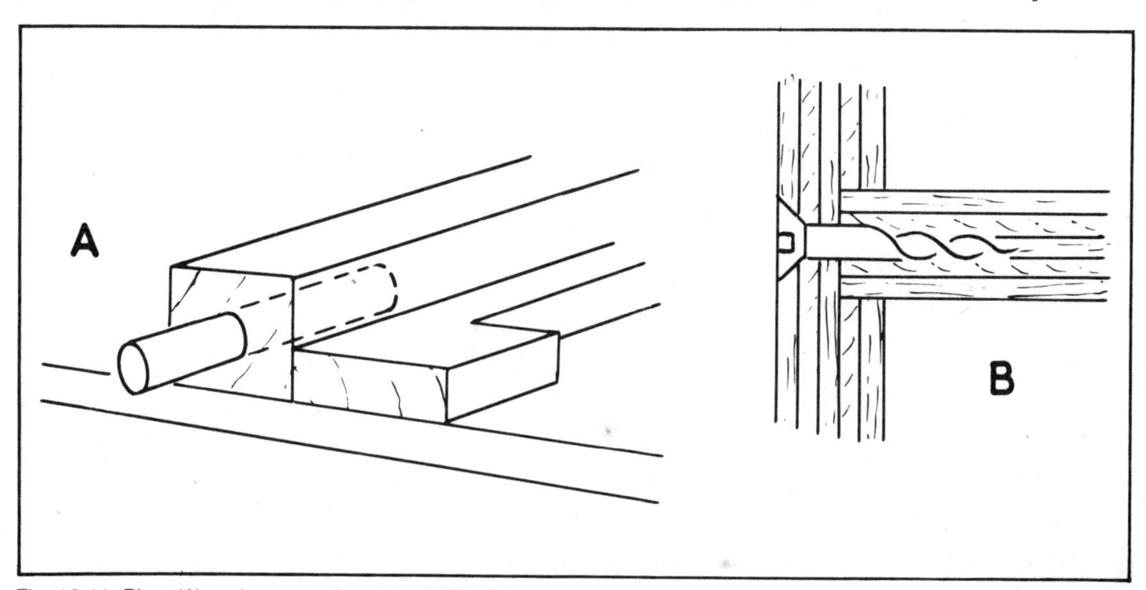

Fig. 16-11. Pivot (A) and constructional detail (B) of the whetstone case.

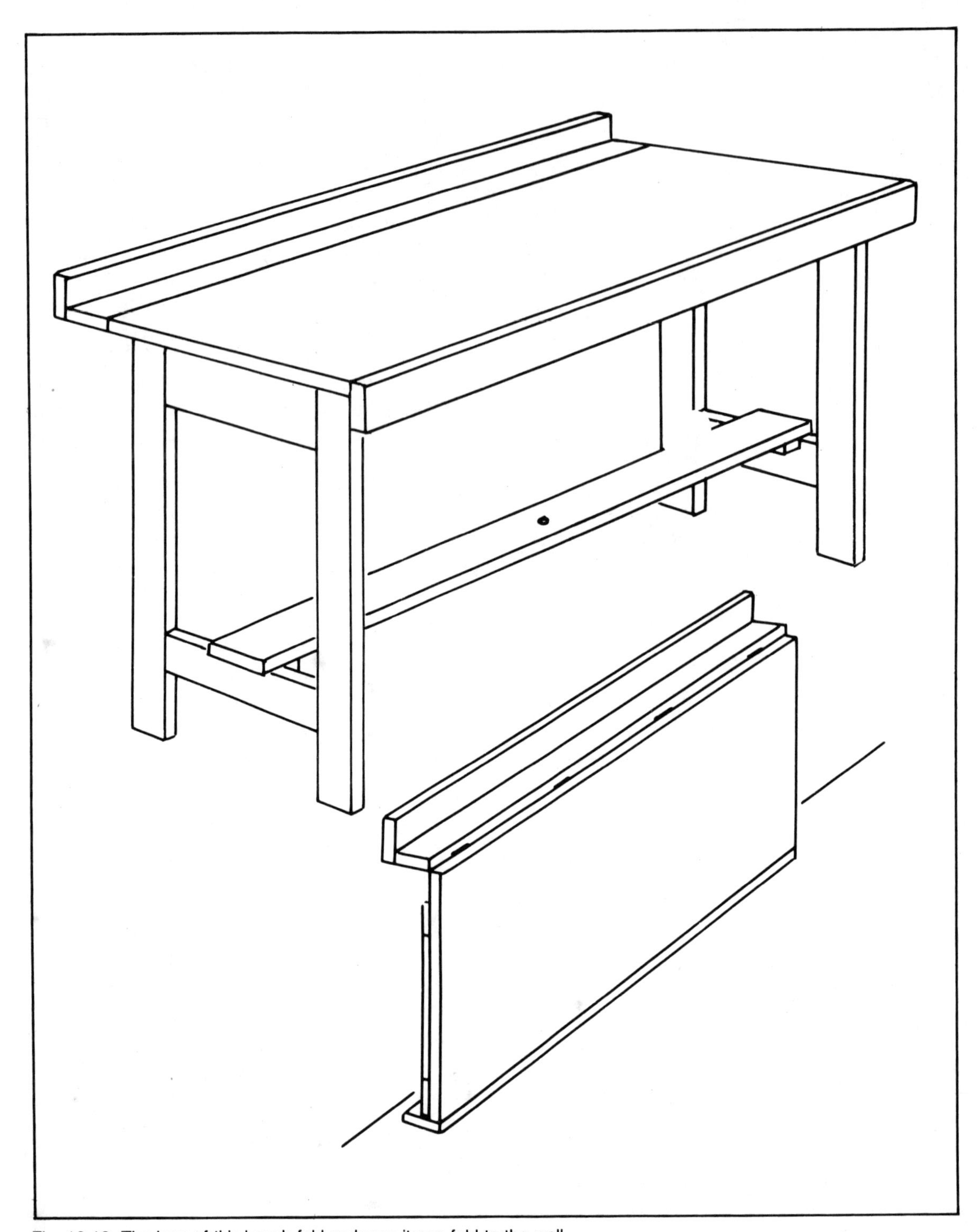

Fig. 16-12. The legs of this bench fold under so it can fold to the wall.

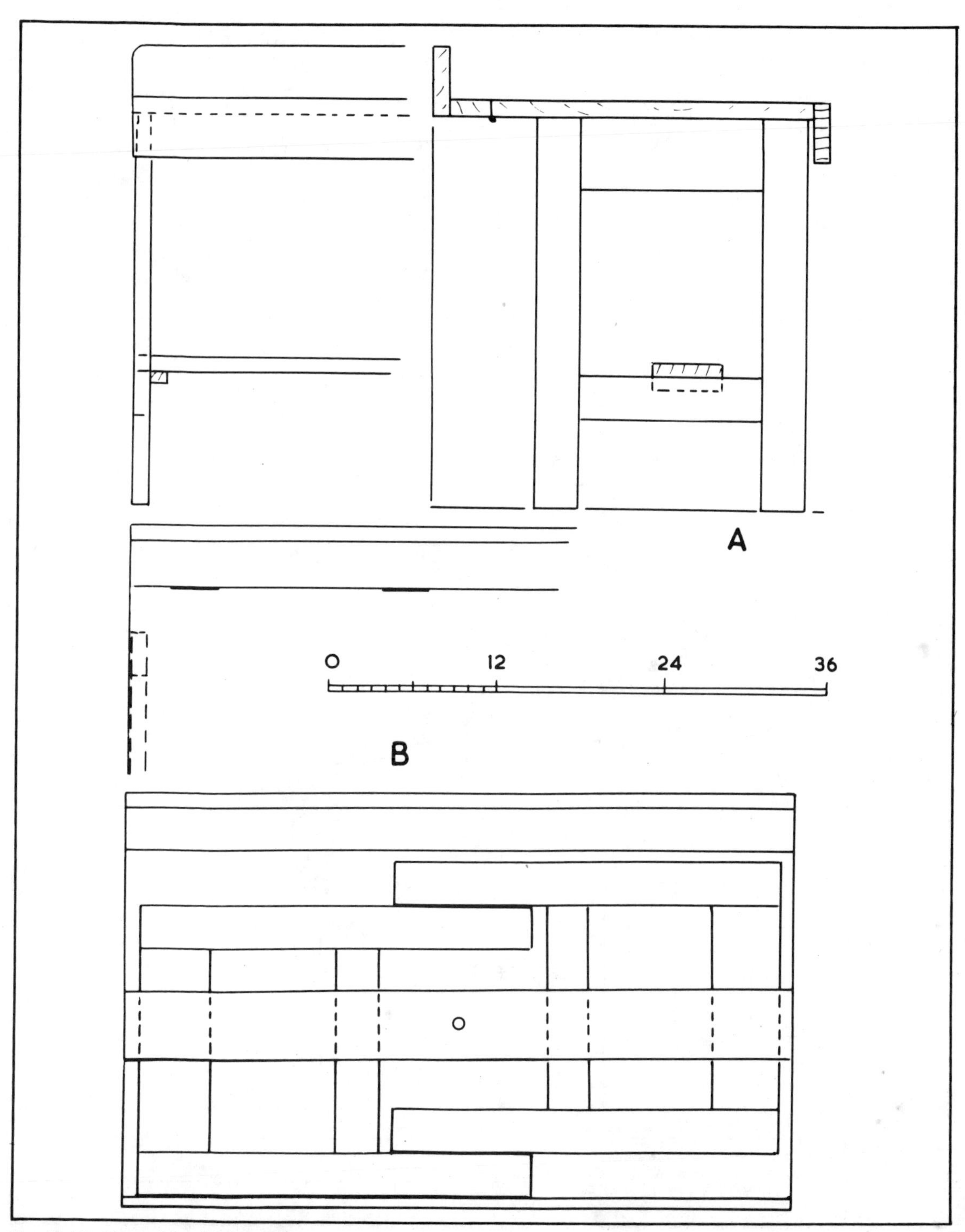

Fig. 16-13. Sizes of the folding bench.

Table 16-2. Materials List for Folding Bench.

1 top	24	×	49	×	1
1 top	4	×	49	×	1
1 back	4	×	49	×	1
1 front	4	×	49	×	1
4 legs	3	×	29	×	1
2 rails	5	×	18	×	1
2 rails	3	×	18	×	1
1 brace	5	×	49	×	1

the ends (Fig. 16-14B). For some craftwork it is useful to have a front apron piece (Fig. 16-14C), held to the top with dowels or counterbored and plugged screws, so no metal is left exposed.

The back assembly has a piece for screwing to the wall. The other part may be glued and screwed to it (Fig. 16-14D), or you can make a tongue and groove joint (Fig. 16-14E). There can be several ordinary hinges underneath, or you can use T hinges with their long arms under the bench top.

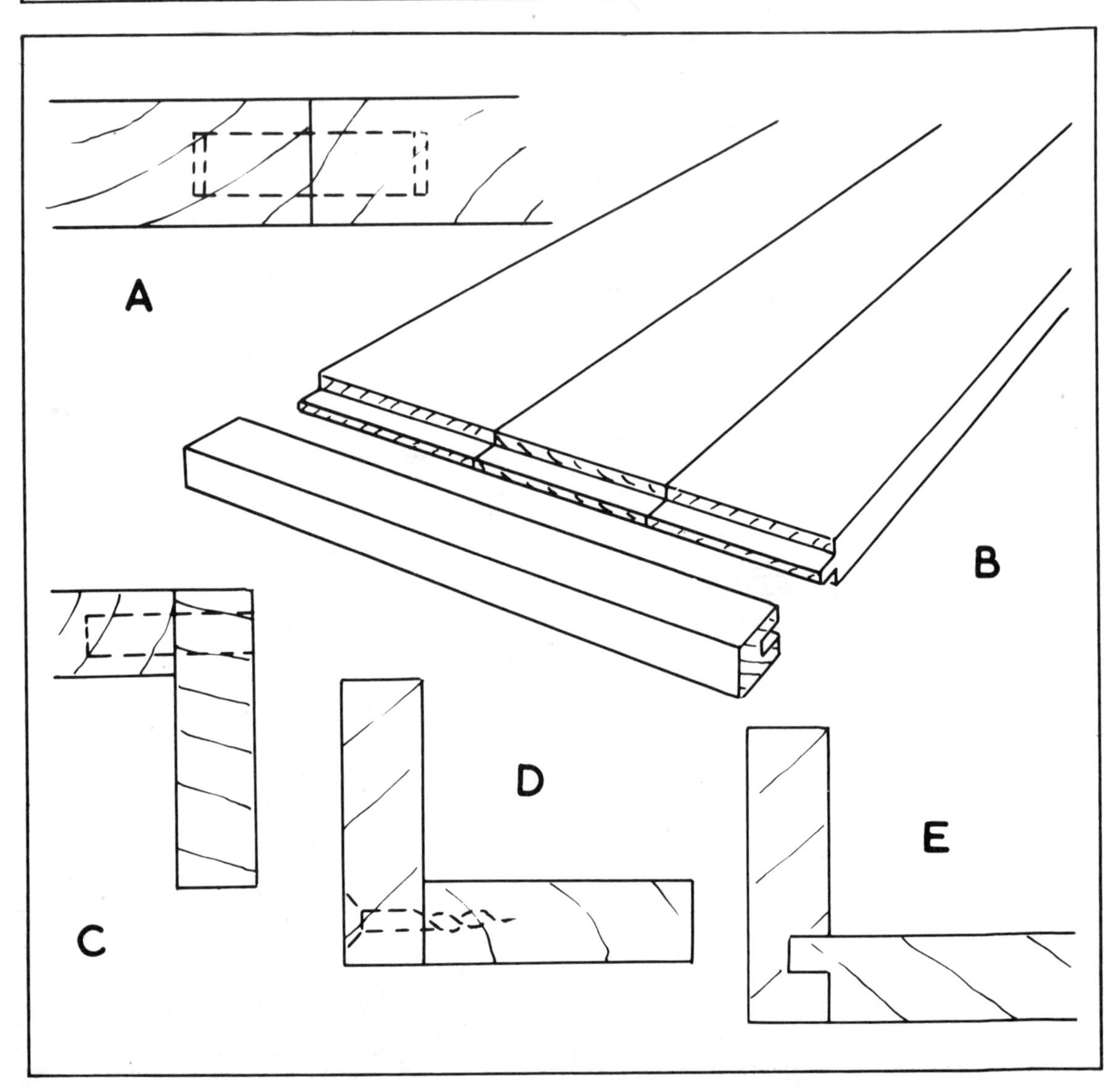

Fig. 16-14. How to make the bench top.

The two leg assemblies are the same, but they are narrow enough to be staggered when they fold (Fig. 16-13B). Keep all the parts in the same plane, so the folded thickness of the bench parts is as small as possible. The rails may be put on the surfaces of the legs, but that will add another 1 inch to the extension from the wall. If the greater projection does not matter, screwing the rails to the legs is simpler.

The rails can be doweled to the legs (Fig. 16-15A). It is better to tenon them (Fig. 16-15B). Clamp while gluing and check squareness and that the assemblies match (Fig. 16-15C).

Hinge the legs under the top, preferably using T or strap hinges, so the legs come under the ends of the top when down. One assembly should swing up with slight clearance inside the front apron. The other assembly should swing up with easy clearance between the bottom of the legs.

Make the brace (Fig. 16-15D) the same length as the top. Put strips across it to press against the leg rails (Fig. 16-15E) and keep them from folding.

At the center of the top and the center of the brace, drill for a coach bolt of ⅜-inch or ½-inch diameter. This is used with a butterfly nut to keep the parts tightly folded when swung down against the wall. Let the bolt head into the top and cover it with a wood plug (Fig. 16-15F). There should be a washer under the nut, but to avoid having a loose one you can let a washer or metal plate into the wood and hold it there with thin nails or screws (Fig. 16-15G).

GARDEN TOOL RACKS

People tend to leave garden tools around, possibly stuck in the ground until the next time they are needed. They suffer from rust, and wood parts may rot or break. Apart from economic considerations, a rusty tool does not work efficiently. Wood that has become rough from exposure is uncomfortable to handle. Then there is the psychological angle; you will work better with tools that are in good condition. If you have racks for the tools, you will know where to find them—assuming you have trained yourself to put tools back in their places after use.

Usually you will have several long-handled tools such as rakes and hoes. There also may be tools such as spades and forks with short handles and some small tools such as trowels and shears. If there is plenty of wall space, you can have racks arranged separately. The short-handled tools can hang in a row for more compact storage, with the small tools above them and the long-handled tools even higher (Fig. 16-16A). Lay out all your tools on the floor and arrange the racks to suit. Allow for some additions and alterations, usually by providing extra slots or divisions.

The racks basically consist of battens attached to the wall (Fig. 16-16B). They should be thick enough to hold off shaped tools, but 1 inch thick by 2 inches or 3 inches should do.

You can arrange pegs in pairs for some tools. Dowel rods sloping up are simple (Fig. 16-16C), or you can turn pegs with knobs (Fig. 16-16D). Large metal hook screws (Fig. 16-16E) have possibilities for some tools. For other tools it is better to notch shelves, either sloped (Fig. 16-16F) or with pieces at the front (Fig. 16-16G) to prevent tools from falling out. In some cases you can use a turn button. If you make it to close downward against a stop (Fig. 16-16H), it is less likely to be left open.

Some small tools may fit through holes in a shelf, but straps are convenient. You can use leather, plastic, or woven strap material in short pieces or a long length. Hold the loops to the wood with screws and washers under their heads (Fig. 16-16J). Some long-handled tools may go through loops with their working ends upward, but you may then want to put another set of loops lower to keep the long handles upright.

Bent hoes and rakes may hang satisfactorily by just being hooked over a rail or shelf. Hold it out with spacers, and an upward-sloping edge is an advantage (Fig. 16-16K).

If there is space to spare above the racks, make a shelf for the many things needed by a gardener that can be stored in boxes and not racks. You can put hooks or even nails in gaps between tools for hanging items. If only a nail is needed to hang something, there is no need to devise something more complicated.

If you have a cultivator or other mechanical

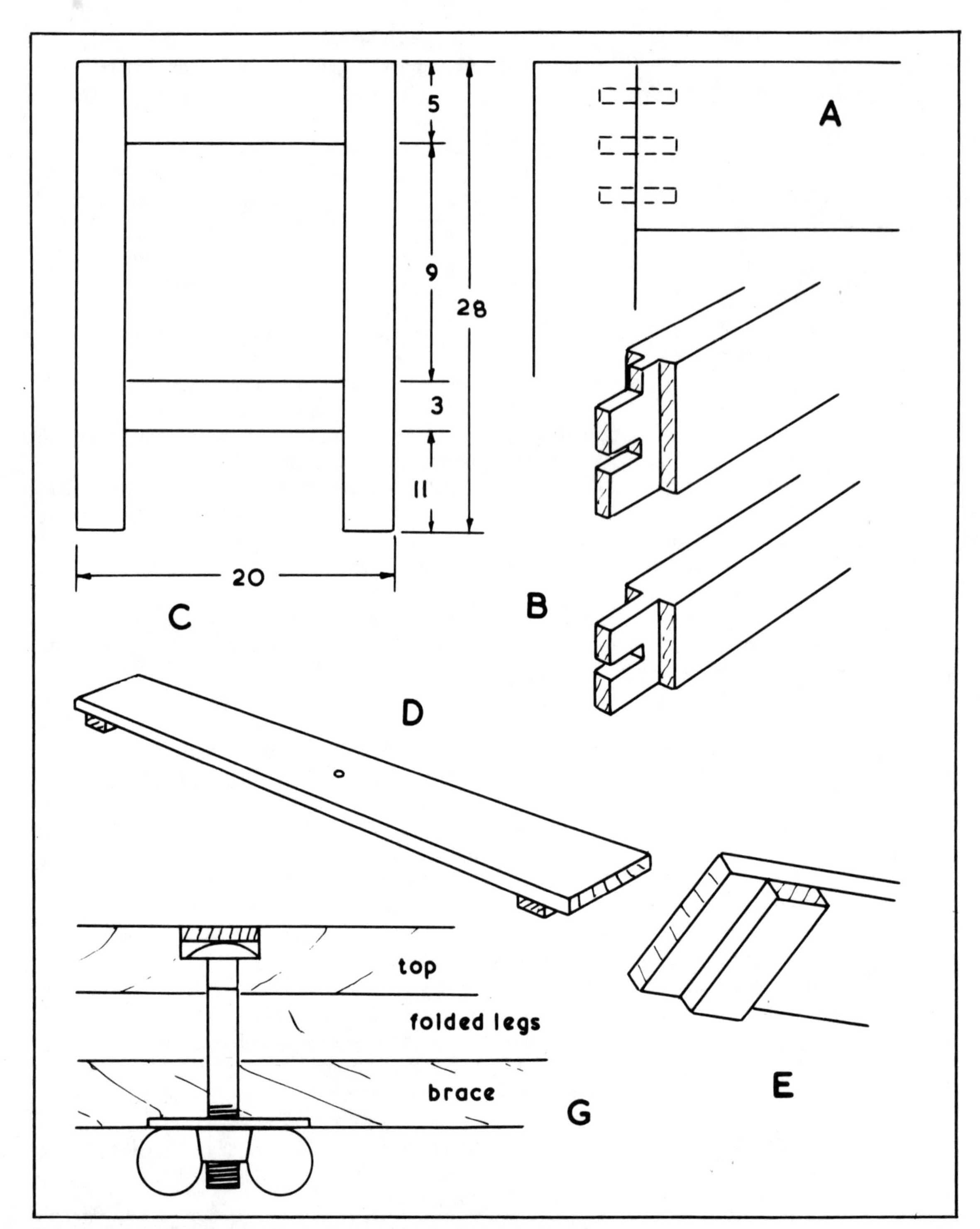

Fig. 16-15. Bench leg construction and how to lock the folded bench parts.

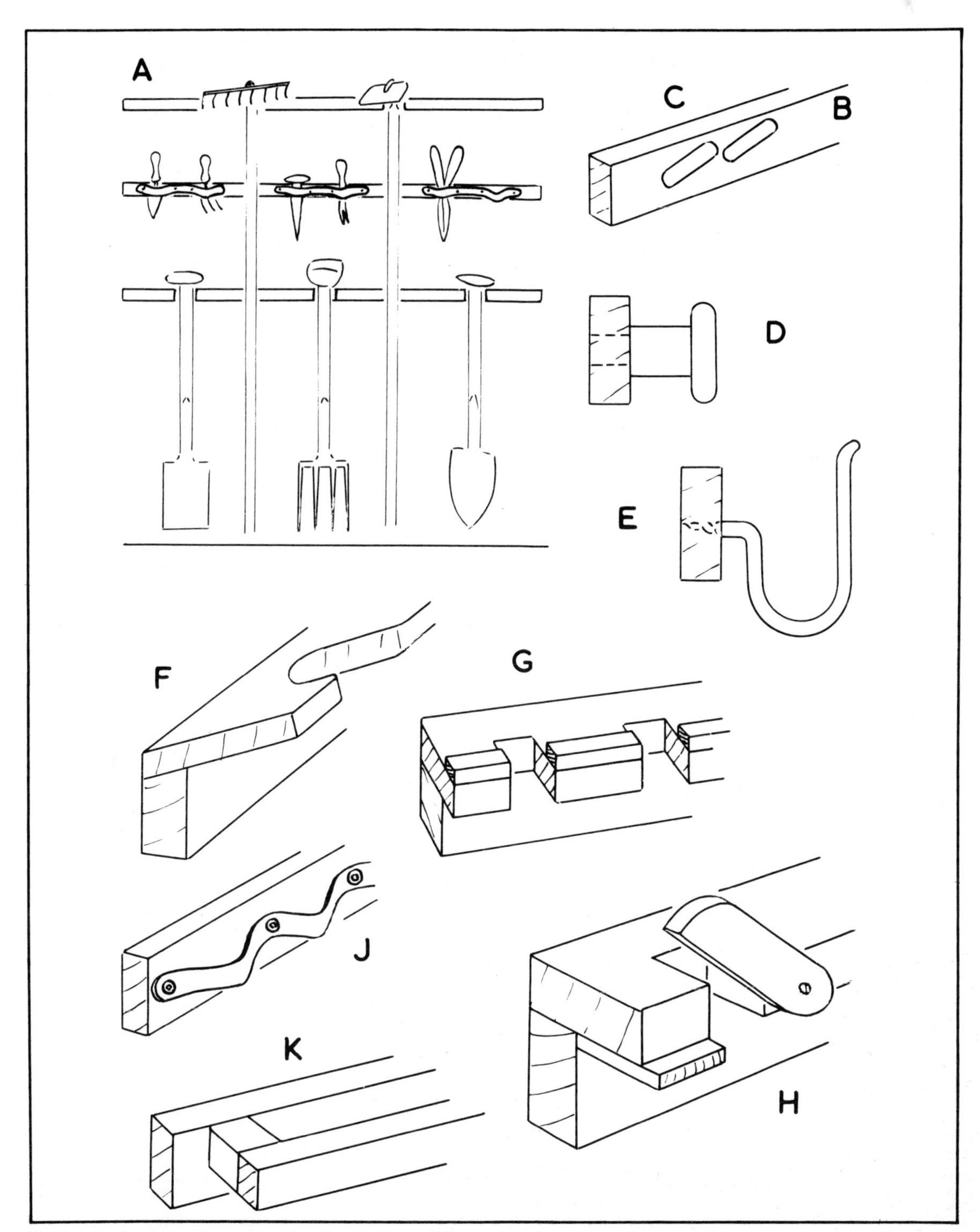

Fig. 16-16. Garden tools need racks of many types if they are to be secure and accessible.

gardening aid, it will almost certainly have spare parts or other things to equip it for different uses. These parts are particularly liable to be mislaid, so racks for them are worth having. It helps to identify a hanging part if you draw its outline on the wall. If it is not in its place, you can immediately see what is missing.

Glossary

Glossary

THE MAKING OF BUILT-IN FURNITURE IS ONLY ONE branch of woodworking. A complete glossary of all the words that might be encountered would be too large for this book. The terms that follow are those likely to be met. Most of the words are in use today, but there are a few obsolescent ones that may be met and not readily understood.

alburnum—The botanical name of sapwood.

annular rings—The concentric rings in the cross section of a tree that form the grain pattern; one ring is added each year.

apron—A piece of wood below a drawer that may have its lower edge decorated by shaping or carving.

arris—The line or sharp edge between two flat or plane surfaces.

astragal—A raised molding or bead on a flat surface.

asymmetrical—A shape that is not symmetrical or of balanced form about a center line.

auger—A long drill with its own handle for deep drilling.

autumn growth—Part of an annual ring in a tree. It is formed as the sap descends.

axis—An imaginary line about which a body can be assumed to revolve. The center line of a solid object.

backboard—The piece of wood closing the back of a cabinet.

backflap hinge—A hinge designed to swing back further than a normal hinge. It is often used under a drop leaf on a table.

bail—A swinging loop handle.

ball peen hammer—A hammer with one side of its head rounded like half a ball.

barefaced tenon—A tenon shouldered on one face only.

base—The foundation of anything or the main bottom portion in an architectural or other assembly.

batten—Any narrow strip of wood. A board fitted

across other boads to join them (also called a cleat), cover a gap, or prevent warping.

batting—A cotton padding material used for upholstery.

bench stop—A wood or metal projection on a bench top. Wood can be pressed against it to prevent movement under a plane or other tool.

bevel—An angle or chamfer planed on an edge. The name of an adjustable tool used for marking and testing angles.

bias—Cloth cut diagonally to the weave.

blind—Not right through, such as a stopped hole.

blind nailing or screwing—Using the fastener in a rabbet or elsewhere that will be covered by another part so that the head is not visible in the finished work.

bow saw—A small frame saw with a narrow blade for cutting curves.

bracket—An angular piece used to strengthen or support a shelf or flap.

bureau—A writing desk with a closable front and storage places inside.

burl—An outgrowth on a tree. It can be cut across to show a very twisted grain that is valued for its decoration when cut into veneers.

burlap—Coarse jute cloth used in upholstery. It is also called hessian.

button—Round or shaped disk used on twine through upholstery for appearance and to retain the stuffing.

buttoning—Securing upholstery with buttons. Deep buttoning is used on indoor furniture only.

cabriole leg—Leg given a flourish so that it curves out from a corner in a stylized form of an animal's leg. It usually finishes in a ball foot.

carcass—The main assembly parts that make up the skeleton of a piece of furniture such as the framework of a table, cabinet, or chest of drawers.

cast—Twisting of a surface that should be flat.

chamfer—An angle or bevel planed on an edge.

check—A lengthwise separation of the grain in a piece of wood.

clamp—A device for drawing things, especially joints, together. Alternative name for a cleat. It is also spelled cramp.

cleat—Any small piece joining other parts together, but particularly a strip across other boards to hold them together and prevent warping.

clench nailing—Using nails long enough to go right through, so the projecting ends can be hammered over.

coniferous—Cone-bearing. Most softwood trees are coniferous.

contact adhesive—An impact adhesive that adheres as soon as parts are brought together. Movement for adjustment is impossible.

conversion—Cutting a log into boards and smaller sections of wood for use.

core—Base wood on which veneer is laid.

cornice—A molding above eye level that projects around the top of a cabinet.

cotton—Natural material woven in many ways for upholstery covering and loosely compounded for stuffing.

cotton batting—Cotton upholstery padding material.

counterbore—Drill a larger hole over a smaller one so the screwhead is drawn below the surface, and it can be covered by a plug.

countersink—Bevel the top of a hole so a flathead screw can be driven level with the surface.

cramp—Usual British name for a clamp.

crossbanding—Decorative veneering that uses narrow strips cut across the joint.

cross-lap joint—Two pieces cut to fit into each other where they cross.

cross peen hammer—Hammer with one face of its head made narrow crosswise.

cup shake—A crack that develops in the growing tree and follows the line of an annual ring.

curly grain—A pattern on the wood surface due to having been cut across an uneven grain.

dado joint—A groove in wood cut across the surface to support a shelf or other part.

dead pin—A wedge and sometimes a dowel.
Deal—Tradename for some softwoods such as pine and fir, but it is now less commonly used. It may also mean a plank or board.
deciduous—A leaf-shedding tree and the source of most hardwoods.
door pull—Door handle.
dovetail—The fan-shaped piece that projects between pins in the other part of a dovetail joint. It is cut to resist pulling out.
dovetail nailing—Driving nails so they slope slightly at opposite angles and resist the boards being pulled apart.
dowel—A cylindrical piece of wood used as a peg when making joints.
draw bore or draw pin—A peg or dowel across a mortise and tenon joint to pull the parts together.

escutcheon—A keyhole or the plate covering and surrounding it.

face marks—Marks put on the first planed side and edge to indicate that further measuring and marking should be made from them.
fall front—A flap that lets down to be supported in a horizontal position. An example is the writing surface of a bureau.
fastenings (fasteners)—Collective name for anything used for joining, such as nails and screws.
featheredge—A wide smooth bevel, taking the edge of a board to a very thin line.
figure—Decorative grain pattern and particularly that shown when the medullary rays are prominent in quartersawed wood. It is especially seen in oak.
fillet—A narrow strip of wood used to fill or support a part.
fillister—A rabbet plane with fences to control depth and width of cut. It is sometimes confused with a plow plane, which is used for cutting grooves.
firmer chisel—A strong general-purpose chisel with square or bevel edges.
folding wedges—Two similar wedges used overlapping each other in opposite directions, so they provide pressure when driven.
foxiness—The signs of the first onset of rot, which may be regarded as decoration.
foxtail wedging—Wedges arranged in the end of a tenon, so it is spread when driven into a blind hole.
frame saw—A narrow saw blade tensioned in a frame.
framed construction—Built of wood strips to form the carcass with the spaces filled by panels.

gateleg table—A table with drop leaves that can be held up by swinging legs like gates.
gauge—A marking tool or means of testing. A definition of size, such as the thickness of sheet metal or the diameters of wire or screws. Numbers are used in recognized systems.
gouge—A type of chisel rounded in cross section.
grain—The striped marking seen in wood due to the annual rings.
groove—Any slot cut in wood such as a dado. It is less commonly a rabbet.
groundwork—The base surface to which veneer is applied.

haft—The handle of a tool, particularly a long one.
half-lap joint—Two crossing pieces notched into each other, usually to bring their surfaces level.
handed—Made as a pair.
hand screw—A clamp usually made entirely of wood.
hanging stile—The stile on which the hinges are attached.
hardwood—Wood from a deciduous tree that is usually but not always harder than softwoods.
haunch—A short cutback part of a tenon that joins another piece near its end.
heartwood—The mature wood near the center of a tree.
hessian—Alternative name for burlap.
housing joint—Alternative name for a dado joint where a shelf fits into a groove in another joint.

impact adhesive—Alternative name for contact adhesive.

inlaying—Setting one piece of wood in another. It can be either solid pieces of wood or veneer.

jigsaw—Fine handsaw in a metal frame. A hand power saw with a projecting reciprocating blade.

jointing—The making of any joint, but particularly planing edges straight to make close glued joints to make up a width.

kerf—The slot made by a saw.

keying—Fitting pieces of veneer into kerfs. It is used particularly to strengthen a miter joint.

knot—A flaw in wood due to where a branch left the trunk. A method of joining cords.

laminate—Construct in layers with several pieces of wood glued together and used particularly to make up curved parts. Plywood is laminated.

lap joint—The general name for joints where one piece of wood is cut to overlap and fit into another.

laying out—Setting out the details of design and construction, usually full-size.

lineal—Length only. It is sometimes used when pricing quantities of wood.

locking stile—The upright against which a door shuts.

mallet—Wood, hide, or plastic hammerlike hitting tool.

marking out—Indicating cuts and positions on wood before cutting, shaping, and drilling.

marquetry—A system of inlaying that uses many woods to produce a pattern or picture using solid wood or veneers.

matched boarding—Joining boards edge to edge with matching tongues and grooves.

medullary rays—Radiating lines from the center of a log, which can be seen in some woods radially cut, but they are invisible in others. The markings are most prominent in oak.

miter—A joint where the meeting angle of the surfaces is divided or bisected, as in the corner of a picture frame.

miter box or board—Guide for the saw when cutting miters.

molding—Decorative edge or border, which may be a simple rounding or an intricate section of curves and quirks.

mortise—The rectangular socket cut to take a tenon.

mortise and tenon joint—A method of joining the end of one piece of wood into the side of another, with the tenon projecting like a tongue on the end to fit into the mortise cut in the other piece.

mullion—Vertical division of a window.

muntin—An internal rail in a framed assembly as between the panels or panes in a window frame.

needle-leaf trees—Alternative name for cone-bearing trees.

nosing—Semicircular molding.

oil slip—A shaped oilstone used on the inside curves of gouges and carving tools.

oil stain—Wood coloring with the pigment dissolved in oil.

oilstone—A sharpening stone for edge tools used with thin oil. It may be called a whetstone.

parquetry—Wood block flooring laid in geometric designs. Not to be confused with marquetry.

patina—Surface texture that is particularly due to old age.

peck marks—Penciled marks used to transfer points on one thing to another.

pedestal—A supporting post. A central support for a table or a support at each of its ends.

pedestal table—A table wih a central support and spreading feet.

peen—A face on a hammerhead.

pegging—Dowels or wooden pegs through joints.

piercing—Decoration made by cutting through the wood. It is similar to fretwork but more robust.

pigeon hole—A storage compartment that is often built into a bureau.
pilot hole—A small hole drilled as a guide for the drill point before making a larger hole.
pinking shears—Scissors that cut a serrated edge on cloth.
plain sawed—Boards cut across a log.
planted—Applied instead of cut in the solid. Molding attached to a surface is planted. If it is cut in the solid wood, it is stuck.
plinth—The base part around the bottom of a piece of furniture.
plow—A plane for cutting grooves with guides to control depth and distance from an edge.
plywood—Board made with veneers glued in laminations with the grain of each layer square to the next.

quartered (quartersawed)—Boards cut radially from a log to minimize warping and shrinking or to show the medullary rays in oak and some other woods.
quirk—A narrow or V-shaped groove beside a bead or the whole bead when worked to form part of a cover or disguise for a joint. A raised part between patterns in turned work.

rabbet (rebate)—Angular cutout section at an edge, as in the back of a picture frame.
rail—A horizontal member in framing.
rake—Incline to the horizontal.
rift sawed—Alternative name for plain sawed.
rive (riven)—Split boards from a log instead of sawing them.
rivet set—Tool to fit over the end of a rivet and drive the parts together. It is often combined with a rivet snap.
rod—Strip of wood with distances of construction details marked on it to use for comparing parts instead of measuring with a rule.
router—Power or hand tool for leveling the bottom of a groove or recessed surface.
rule—Measuring rod. A craftsman does not spell it ruler.
run—In a long length. Lumber quantity can be quoted as so many feet run.

sapwood—The wood nearer the outside of a tree. It is not as strong or durable as the heartwood in most trees.
sash—Molded and rabbeted edge of a window frame. A sash plane cuts the rabbet and molding at the same time.
sawbuck—Crossed sawing trestle. The name may be applied to table legs crossed in a similar way.
scratch molding—Small molding cut with a scratch stock that has a cutter sharpened like a scraper.
seasoning—Drying lumber to a controlled moisture content.
secret dovetail joints—Joint in which the dovetails are hidden by mitered parts outside them.
segments—Curved pieces of wood used to build up table rails and similar things in round work.
selvage—The manufactured edge in a piece of cloth, where the threads turn back and the edge will not fray.
set—To punch a nail below the surface. The tool for doing so. The bending of saw teeth in opposite directions to cut a kerf wider than the thickness of the saw metal.
setting out—Laying out details, usually full-size, of a piece of furniture or other construction.
shake—A defect or crack in the growing tree that may not be apparent until it is cut into boards.
shooting board—A holding device for wood while having its edges planed or molded.
shot joint—Planed edges glued together.
slat—Narrow thin wood.
slip—A shaped small oilstone for sharpening inside the curve of a gouge or similar tool.
softwood—The wood from a coniferous needleleaf tree.
Spanish windlass—A device using rope twisted with a lever to give a tightening effect.
splay—To spread out.
spline—A narrow strip of wood fitting into

grooves, usually to strengthen two meeting surfaces that are glued.

staple—Two-ended nail forming a loop. Two-legged fastener driven by a special tool and used instead of tacks for attaching upholstery cloth.

star shake—A defect in a growing tree, with cracks radiating from the center.

stiff nut—A nut to fit on a bolt that incorporates a means of resisting loosening.

stile—Vertical member in door framing.

stopped tenon—A tenon engaging with a mortise that is not cut through the wood. A stub tenon.

strap hinge—Hinge with long narrow arms.

stretcher—A lengthwise rail between the lower parts of a table or chair.

stub tenon—Alternative name for a stopped tenon.

tabling—The turned-in edge of a piece of cloth to strengthen it or prevent fraying.

tack—Small tapered end of a tool such as a file or chisel to fit into its handle.

template—Shaped pattern to draw around when marking out parts.

tenon—The projecting tongue on the end of one piece of wood to fit into a mortise in another piece of wood.

tote—A tool handle, particularly on a plane.

trunnel (treenail)—Peg or dowel driven through a joint.

tusk tenon—A tenon that goes through its mortise and projects at the other side, where it may be secured with a wedge.

twine—General name for thin string or stout thread used in upholstery.

underbracing—Arrangement of rails and stretchers to provide stiffness between the lower parts of a table or chair legs. It is also called underframing.

varnish—A nearly transparent paintlike finish, once made from natural lacs, but now usually synthetic.

veneer—A thin piece of wood that is usually of a decorative type and intended to be glued to a backing. If very thin and cut from a rotating log, it is cut with a knife. If it is not so thin, it is cut with a saw.

veneer pin—Very fine nail with a small head.

wainscot—This term means the paneling around a room, but it is also applied to quartersawed wood, such as oak, that shows figuring.

waney edge—The edge of a board that still has bark on it or is still showing the pattern of the outside of the tree.

warping—Distortion of a board by twisting or curving because of unequal shrinkage as moisture dries out.

winding—A board or assembly is said to be in winding when it is not flat and a twist can be seen when sighting from one end.

working drawing—A drawing showing sizes, usually in elevations, plan, and sections, from which measurements can be taken to make the furniture. It is not a pictorial view.

Index

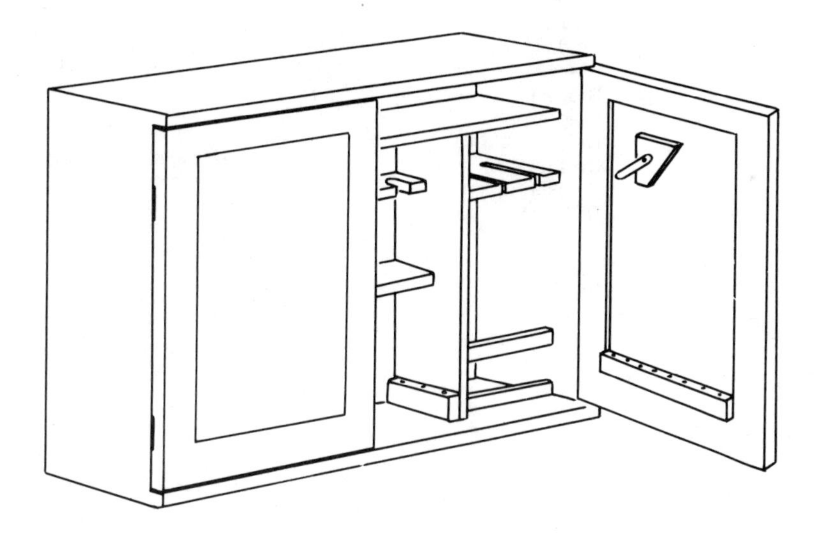

Index

T

U

V

W

Z